Alexander Karmann · Karl Mosler
Martin Schader · Götz Uebe (Eds.)

Operations Research '92

Extended Abstracts of the 17th Symposium
on Operations Research
held at the Universität der Bundeswehr Hamburg
at August 25-28, 1992

With 36 Figures

Springer-Verlag Berlin Heidelberg GmbH

Prof. Dr. Alexander Karmann
Sozialökonomisches Seminar, Universität Hamburg
Von-Melle-Park 5, D-2000 Hamburg 13, FRG

Prof. Dr. Karl Mosler
Institut für Statistik und Quantitative Ökonomik
Universität der Bundeswehr Hamburg,
Holstenhofweg 85, D-2000 Hamburg 70, FRG

Prof. Dr. Martin Schader
Lehrstuhl für Wirtschaftsinformatik III,
Universität Mannheim, Schloß, D-6800 Mannheim, FRG

Prof. Dr. Götz Uebe
Institut für Statistik und Quantitative Ökonomik
Universität der Bundeswehr Hamburg
Holstenhofweg 85, D-2000 Hamburg 70, FRG

Printed with the support of the *„Gesellschaft der Freunde und Förderer der Universität der Bundeswehr Hamburg"*

ISBN 978-3-7908-0679-3 ISBN 978-3-662-12629-5
DOI 10.1007/978-3-662-12629-5

Originally published by Physica-Verlag Heidelberg 1993

Printing: Weihert-Druck, Darmstadt
Bookbinding: T. Gansert GmbH, Weinheim-Sulzbach
7100/7130-543210 - Printed on acid-free paper

Preface

The 17th Symposium on Operations Research was held at Universität der Bundeswehr Hamburg, August 25 - 28, 1992, as the annual meeting of the Gesellschaft für Mathematik, Ökonomie und Operations Research (GMÖOR). It collected some 400 scholars from applied mathematics, economics and computer science to present their research and exchange ideas on problems which are of common interest to their disciplines.

The aim of this book is to provide a timely and comprehensive documentation of the symposium's scientific activities. It contains extended abstracts of most of the papers presented. Long versions of papers are expected to appear elsewhere in refereed periodicals.

The symposium fell into twelve sections and an overlapping cross-section workshop. The sections covered established fields of theory and application: (1) Mathematical Modelling in OR, (2) Stochastic Models of OR, (3) Combinatorial Optimization and Discrete Mathematics, (4) Linear and Non-Linear Optimization, (5) Systems and Control Theory, (6) Decision Support and Information Systems, (7) Applications in Business and Economics, (8) Econometrics and Statistics, (9) Micro-Economics and Game Theory, (10) Macro-Economics and Applied Economics, (11) Decision Theory, Utility and Risk, (12) Banking, Finance and Insurance. As in previous years, the sections on optimization and on stochastic models were the backbone on the mathematics side. In addition, this year's symposium focussed on applications to microeconomics and macroeconomics and to decision, banking and insurance.

As a novelty and an experiment, a cross-section workshop had been included in the program which was devoted to a topic of current political and scientific interest. The purpose of the Workshop on Environmental Systems and Economics was threefold. First, to yield results and solutions to selected environmental problems, second, to serve as a methodological example of research and communication between the disciplines, and third, to address a broader audience beyond the given scientific community. A panel discussion "Political Issues and Scientific Achievements" was held which gathered discussants from science, politics and public administration: Prof. Folmer of Wageningen University and Prof. Karmann of Hamburg University, Dr. Jaeschke of Kernforschungszentrum Karlsruhe, Senator Dr. Vahrenholt and MR Mayer-Föll of the Ministries of Environment in Hamburg and Baden-Württemberg, respectively. The discussion was chaired by Prof. Radermacher of FAW Ulm.

The symposium was highlighted by some 30 invited lectures of prominent scientists. They started with the talks by W.M. Hanemann (Berkeley) on the economics of pollution and H.Th. Jongen (Aachen) on parametric optimization, and they ended with D. Stoyan's (Freiberg) lecture on stochastic geometry and T.C. Hu's (San Diego) lecture on combinatorial and network algorithms.

The symposium was held under the auspices of the First Mayor of Hamburg, Dr. H. Voscherau, who also opened the conference. Further opening addresses were given by Prof. Strunk, President of Universität der Bundeswehr Hamburg, by Prof. Bachem, President of GMÖOR, and by Prof. Mosler on behalf of the organizers. During the opening ceremony, this year's GMÖOR Dissertation Prizes were awarded to four outstanding researchers: K. Sandmann (Bonn), B. von Stengel (München), M. Stoer (Berlin) and G. van Wee (Eindhoven). The extended abstracts of their lectures conclude this volume.

The symposium could not be held without the help of many people and institutions. We would like to thank the authors of papers for presenting their research. In particular, many authors from Eastern Europe have taken enormous efforts to join the conference. We thank the chairmen of sections who helped us in attracting so many distinguished speakers from all over the world. We thank Prof. Bachem and Prof. Radermacher of the GMÖOR for their continuous encouragement and support. Our sincere thanks include Dr. Müller of Physica-Verlag for his once again pleasant cooperation in publishing this proceedings volume and Ms. Marianne Reblin for her diligence in preparing the final version of the papers.

We are deeply indebted to Universität der Bundeswehr Hamburg for hosting the conference and generously supporting it. Among the major sponsors are the European Committee, which especially supported the workshop, the Gesellschaft der Freunde und Förderer der Universität der Bundeswehr Hamburg, and the Freie und Hansestadt Hamburg. A complete list of sponsors is given below. The support of all sponsors was essential for organizing a conference of high scientific standard and international esteem. It is highly appreciated by the organizers.

Finally, yet not least, we would like to thank the members of our organizational staff, who worked beyond and above the call of duty, first of all, Dr. J. Arrenberg who excelled as an assistant to the organizers from the very beginning, two years ago. Thanks to her and all the others.

Hamburg and Mannheim,
December 1992

Alexander Karmann
Karl Mosler
Martin Schader
Götz Uebe

List of Sponsors

Aachener Rückversicherung, Aachen
Axel Springer Verlag, Hamburg/Berlin
J.C. Baltzer Verlag, Basel
BHW, Hameln
Daimler Benz, Stuttgart
Deutsche Bank, Frankfurt
Deutsche Lufthansa, Köln
Deutsche Shell, Hamburg
Europäische Kommission, Brüssel
Freie und Hansestadt Hamburg
Gesellschaft der Freunde und Förderer der
Universität der Bundeswehr Hamburg e. V.
Handelskammer Hamburg
Holsten-Brauerei, Hamburg
IBM Deutschland, Stuttgart
Karlsruher Lebensversicherung
Landeszentralbank Hamburg
Siemens Nixdorf (SNI), Kiel
SGZ-Bank, Frankfurt/Karlsruhe
Springer Verlag, Heidelberg/Berlin
Sun-Microsystems, Hamburg
Systematics, Hamburg
Universität der Bundeswehr Hamburg
Universität Hamburg

List of Sections and Chairpersons

	Workshop on Environmental Systems and Economics F.J. Radermacher
Section 1:	*Mathematical Modeling in OR* W. Krabs, D. Pallaschke
Section 2:	*Stochastic Models of OR* U. Rieder, M. Schäl
Section 3:	*Combinatorial Optimization and Discrete Mathematics* M. Jünger, R.H. Möhring
Section 4:	*Linear and Non-Linear Optimization* K.H. Borgwardt, K.H. Hoffmann
Section 5:	*Systems and Control Theory* G. Feichtinger, H. Knobloch
Section 6:	*Decision Support and Information Systems* W. Gaul, W. Janko
Section 7:	*Applications in Business and Economics* W. Domschke, S. Trautmann
Section 8:	*Econometrics and Statistics* B. Rauhut, F. Schmid
Section 9:	*Micro-Economics and Game Theory* W. Eichhorn, H. Peters
Section 10:	*Macro-Economics and Applied Econometrics* G. Nakhaeizadeh, B. Schips
Section 11:	*Decision Theory, Utility and Risk* G. Bamberg, P. Kischka
Section 12:	*Banking, Finance and Insurance* W.R. Heilmann, K.H. Vollmer

Contents

Workshop on Environmental Systems

Decision Theoretic Analysis of Pollutants Emissions Monitoring Procedures
R. Avenhaus 3

Applied General Equilibrium Modeling for Environmental Policy Analysis
K. Conrad 6

Interconnected Games
H. Folmer, P. v. Mouche 10

Object-Oriented Techniques for the Management of Geographic and Environmental Data
O. Günther, J. Lamberts 13

Problems of Statistical Analysis of Environmental Data
H. Hebbel 17

Planning "Safe" Routes for Transporting Protected Materials through an Alient Area
J. Karkazis 20

Umweltinformationssystem Baden-Württemberg (UIS)
R. Mayer-Föll 23

Some Adaptive Clustering Algorithms
H.-J. Mucha 27

Development of an Energy—Emission Model Using Fuzzy Sets
C. Oder, O. Rentz 32

Efficient Water Management
R. Pethig 36

On Integrity Constraints for a Waste Management Information System
D. Schreiber, M. Grauer 39

Design of a User—Friendly General Purpose Energy Information System
A. Schweiker, H.-M. Groscurth, A. Reuter 42

Interacting Environmental Influences: Concepts of Synergism, Antagonism, and Superposition
F. Stehling, J. Kindorf 45

Multiobjective Decision Making in Forest Management
L. Zadnik Stirn 49

Section 1: Mathematical Modeling in OR

On Some Solution Method of Certain Type of Allocation Problems
Z.M. Farkas 55

Generalized Monotone Maps
S. Schaible 58

Section 2: Stochastic Models of OR

Combinatorial Approach to an r-node Tandem Queue
W. Böhm, S.G. Mohanty, J.L. Lain . . . 63

Individual Blocking Probabilities in the Loss System GI + $M|\vec{M}|N|0$
A. Brandt . . . 67

Artillery Effectiveness Models in Operational Planning
A. Grundt . . . 70

Transmission of Reliability Properties among Record Values from Non-Identically Distributed Random Variables
U. Kamps . . . 74

A New Approach to Compute Performance Sensitivities of Stochastic Discrete Event Dynamic Systems (DEDS)
H. Lucca . . . 78

Probability Maximizing Approach to Optimal Stopping of Random Fields
R. Różański, K. Szajowski . . . 82

Control by Delay of a Service System
H. Schmidbauer, A. Gadjiev . . . 86

Optimal Myopic Policies and Index Policies for Stochastic Scheduling Problems
J. Weishaupt . . . 90

Impulse and Continuous Stochastic Control: A Dynamic Programming Approach
A.A. Yushkevich . . . 94

Section 3: Combinatorial Optimization and Discrete Mathematics

Structure Independent Optimization of Embedding Graphs in Books
T. Bilski . . . 99

An Improved Version of Tabu Search for Irregular Cutting Problems
J. Błażewicz, R. Walkowiak . . . 102

Restrictions of Graph Partition Problems
H.L. Bodlaender, K. Jansen . . . 105

Further Remarks on the Jeep Problem
U. Brauer, W. Brauer . . . 109

A Class of Graphs with good Communicativeness
V.E. Brimkov . . . 112

Resource-Constrained Project Scheduling with Maximum Time Distances
K. Brinkmann . . . 114

Traveling Salesman Problem with Path Dependent Costs—Generalization of One-Dimensional Search with Traveling Costs
B. Cao, K. Rinderle . . . 118

Stochastic Scheduling Flow-Shop No-Wait with Heuristics Using Artificial Intelligence Techniques
U.R. Ferreira . . . 121

Algorithms for Max-Linear and Multi-Criteria Spanning Tree Problems
H.W. Hamacher, G. Ruhe 124

Combinatorial and Network Algorithms
T.C. Hu 128

A Heuristic for the Nesting Problem
R. Lang, T. Milius 130

New Evolutionary Genetic Algorithms for Combinatorial Optimization Problems
D.T. Loan, F.Q. Bac 132

Bicriteria Transportation Problem
P. Neumayer 135

Solving 3-Satisfiability in less than $1,579^n$ Steps
I. Schiermeyer 138

Boltzmann Machine Solution N-Person Games
F. Seredynski 139

Analysis of the Degree of Parallelism for Non-Polynomial, Polynomial, Strongly Polynomial Algorithms for Solving the Minimum Cost Flow Problem
C. Spera, M. Ugolini 142

Decomposition of Multiplace Functions in Operations Research
B. von Stengel 145

Experiences with a Cutting Plane Algorithm in Survivable Network Design
M. Stoer 149

Combinatorial Covering Problems in Coding Theory
G.J.M. van Wee 152

On Benders' Decomposition for the Capacitated Facility Location Problem
P. Wentges 155

Packing Grid Figures
J. Wolffram 159

Section 4: Linear and Non-Linear Optimization

Using Ellipsoids in Weighted Projective Algorithms for Nondifferentiable Optimization
A. Altman 165

About the Method of Minimization of the Function
T.A. Arakelian 168

LPINT: LP Software Based on the Interior Point Method
J. Barle, J. Grad 171

A Convergence Acceleration of the Relaxation Algorithm in Convex Minimization
A. Cegielski 173

On an Algorithm Solving Bilevel Programming Problems
S. Dempe 177

Solving Linear Complementarity Problems by Imbedding
A. Fischer 179

Optimality and Feasibility of Time Schedules in Vehicle Routing and Scheduling Problem with Time Window Constraints
B. Florkiewicz, M. Kulej 182

Discretization of Semicoercive Variational Inequalities
J. Gwinner 185

Methods of Reduced Directions with Differential Cost Function for Nonlinear Programming
V.S. Izhutkin, M.V. Petropavlovskii 188

A Minimization Method for Systems with Singular Value Constraints
C. Jansson, O. Knüppel 190

A Sharper Asymptotic Bound for Average Simplex Complexity
G. Joas 193

Nonlinear Optimization: Stability and Parametric Aspects
H.T. Jongen 196

Circumscribed Spheres via Semi-infinite Optimization
F. Juhnke 197

On the Implicit Function Theorem and Parametric Optimization
G. Kassay 201

On the Variance of the Number of Pivot Steps Required by the Simplex Algorithm
K.-H. Küfer 203

Effective Numerical Methods and Average Errors
E. Novak 207

Optimal Decisions in Multicriteria Problems with Controllable Attributes
A.M.J. Skulimowski 211

Section 5: Systems and Control Theory

The Perturbed Adjoint Operator for Linear Hereditary Differential Systems with Perturbed Delay in Control
L. Bogataj 217

Paths to Constrained Nash Equilibria
S.D. Flåm 220

On a New Finite Perturbation Analysis Algorithm
W. Geiselhart, U. Tüshaus 223

Necessary Properness Conditions in Periodic Control
R.F. Hartl 226

Recent Trends in Mathematical Systems Theory and their Possible Impact on Applications
H.W. Knobloch 230

Difference Methods for Monotone Differential Inclusions
F. Lempio 235

Discrete-Time Markovian Jump Linear Systems
K. Szajowski, W.L. de Koning 237

Change Speeds and Time Scales in Economic Dynamics—
An Insight by Synergetic Economics
W.-B. Zhang 242

Section 6: Decision Support and Information Systems

A Formal Treatment of Relevance Information in Ill-Structured Environments
D. Androutsopoulos, P. Spirakis 245

On Interactive Graphical Application Programs
K. Belling-Seib 249

Embedding OR Techniques in Constraint Logic Programming
A. Bockmayr 252

Cost/Benefit Analysis used in the Feasability Projects
V. Chichernea 255

A Decision Support System for Diet Planning
T. Damij 259

Experimental Results on the Efficiency of Rule-Based Systems
D. Gernert 262

Incorporating 3D-Facilities into Statistical Graphs Using a Description-List-Based Data Presentation
F. Hantelmann 265

Statistical and Machine Learning Approaches in Credit Scoring
F. Jafar-Shaghaghi 270

On Completeness of Rule-Based Systems
A. Ligeza 274

Load Sharing in a Heterogeneous Distributed Object-based System
J. Matulka 278

Machine Learning by Constructing Decision Trees Including Cost Functions
W. Müller, F. Wysotzki 281

MIPS—An Interactive Decision Support System for Hardware Investment Planning
G. Satzger, A. Wirth 285

Expert Systems Applications in Construction Management and Engineering
C.A. Snyder 289

Indices for Characterizing Ordinal Data
U. Tüshaus 292

A Knowledge Based System Managing Sequences of Data Analysis Methods
F. Wartenberg, W. Gaul, D. Baier 295

Section 7: Applications in Business and Economics

Enterprise Input-Output Modelling—Extensions of the Basic Model and its Applications
J. Artenjak 303

The Selection of the Optimum Offers in Crude Oil Market by Linear Programming
G. Barbatu, C.E. Marius, V. Ionescu 306

Scenario Approach to Capacity Planning for the Production of a New Product
M. Bastic 310

Project Scheduling: Models, Methods, and Systems Development
A. Drexl 313

Analysis of Controller Workload Related to Air Traffic Density
S. Gladys, M. Malarski, J. Skorupski 316

Office Automation in the Turkish Establishments
S. Gözlü 320

Method for TWR Simulator Analysis of Chosen Elements of Airport Area Visualisation
S. Jasinski, M. Malarski, J. Skorupski 322

Decision Support in Financial Planning
W. Junginger, A. Kor 326

Section 8: Econometrics and Statistics

Distribution of the Spearman's Rank Correlation Coefficient
A. Baszczyńska, C. Domański 333

Tests for Outliers for Multivariate Normal Distribution
A. Baszczyńska, C. Domański 336

Demographer
D. Čepar, R. Habinc, E. Uršič, R. Založnik 339

Natural Growth Population Models
D. Čepar, E. Uršič 343

Estimated Accuracy of Data and Intervals of Admissible Values for Parameters of Fitting Functions
D. Čepar, M. Marolt, Z. Radalj, M. Ribarič 346

Identification of Multiple Outliers in Time Series
T. Flak, W. Schmid 349

Semiparametric Approaches to Dimension Reduction
W.K. Härdle, B.A. Turlach 352

Maximum Likelihood Estimators in Non Linear Autoregressive Processes
M. Henkouche 370

Bayes Sequential Estimation Procedures
R. Magiera 372

Time-Series Forecasting by Pattern Imitation—further Development
B. Motnikar, D. Čepar, P. Žunko, M. Ribarič 375

Characterizations of the Existence of UMP Tests for Hypotheses Induced by Groups
D. Plachky 379

Statistical Scaling
W. Pölz 384

Full-Information Best Choice Problems with Imperfect Observation
Z. Porosiński 387

A Term Structure Model and Interest Rate Options
K. Sandmann, D. Sondermann 391

Analysis of Dispersion Effects in Fractional Factorial Two-Level Designs
S. Uhlig 394

Section 9: Micro-Economics and Game Theory

Pure Spatial Competition among Firms with more than one Facility
H. Behnke 399

CS-Continuity and Separability
T. Bradtke 402

A Shapley Value for Games with Restricted Coalitions
J. Derks, H. Peters 406

Relationships between Bankruptcy Games and Minimum Cost Spanning Tree Games
T.S.H. Driessen 410

Controlled Communication Networks
V. Feltkamp, A. van den Nouweland 413

Reducing Sequencing Situations
H. Hamers, P. Borm, S. Tijs 416

Coordination Failure and Endogenous Timing
S. Hurkens 419

A Decision Support System for Negotiations on Financing of the
Public Divisible Good
A. Jakubowski 422

The Consumer Budget Set: The Meaning of Mathematical Transformation
T. Junius, K. Nevels 425

Correlated Equilibria in Nonzero-Sum Stochastic Games
A.S. Nowak 428

On the Core of a Set of Coalitions
H. Reijnierse, J. Derks 432

Some Remarks on Simple Games and Matroids
D. Stumpe 436

Risk Averse Utility Functions
G. Uebe 439

A Logic of Rational Play for Games of Perfect Information
A. Vilks 443

Learning Effects in a Heterogeneous and Asymmetric Duopoly
H. Wiese 446

Section 10: Macro-Economics and Applied Econometrics

Chaotic Behaviour in a Simple Macroeconomic Model
D. Chappell 453

A Stochastic Model of Foreign Exchange Dynamics and an Exact Option Pricing Formula
M.T. Cheung, D.W.K. Yeung 455

Transition of Socialist Economies and Redistribution of Wealth
J.A. Čibej 458

Equal Rates of Return and/or Clearing of Factor Markets in Two-Sector OLG-Models with Heterogeneous Capital Goods
K. Farmer 460

Purchasing Power Parity and Cointegration
T. Gerhards 464

On the Modelling of Economic Equilibria by Variational Inequalities
J. Gwinner 469

The Policy of the Deutsche Bundesbank: An Empirical Investigation
M. Hillmer 472

Population Dynamics for the Federal Republic
G. Köpp 477

Testing for a Long Run Relationship between Trend and Difference Stationary Series
P. Kugler, P. Schwendener 481

Deficit Financing Strategies and the Fiscal Multiplier
H. Molana 484

The Disappearing Multiplier: A System Dynamics Approach to Macroeconomics
G. Ossimitz 488

Chaotic Foreign Exchange Rates
B. Reszat 491

Disequilibrium Models and the Use of Business Survey Data
P. Stalder 494

Increasing the Capital Income Tax Leads to Faster Growth
H. Uhlig, N. Yanagawa 499

Section 11: Decision Theory, Utility and Risk

On Solving of a Mulitobjective Nonlinear Programming Problem with General Parameters in the Objective Functions Using the Fuzzy Mathematical Programming
E. Ammar 505

Modeling Attitudes Towards Uncertainty and Risk Through the Use of Monotone Capacities
A. Chateauneuf 509

Case-Based Decision Theory—An Outline
I. Gilboa, D. Schmeidler 512

An Interactive Decision Procedure with Multiple Attributes under Risk
H. Holz, K. Mosler 516

An Insurance Contract for Financial Assets with Experience Rating
W. Jammernegg, P. Kischka 520

Efficiency Improvement in Data Envelopment Analysis
C. Kao 523

Separation in Insurance
I. Meilijson 526

Collective Decisions on Euclidian Spaces
W. Peremans, H. Peters, H. v.d. Stel, T. Storcken 528

The Analytic Hierarchy Process (AHP): Basics and Software
K. Weber 532

Section 12: Banking, Finance and Insurance

ALLFIWIB: Distributed Knowledge Based Systems for Customer Support in Financial Services
H.U. Buhl, H.-J. König, A. Will 537

On the Use of Geometric Brownian Motion in Financial Analysis
M.T. Cheung, D. Yeung, A. Lai 541

Modelling of Catastrophic Events in Insurance and Finance
P. Embrechts 544

Life Insurance Solvency Assessment Using Stochastic Simulation Techniques
M. Hardy 547

Optimal Stop-Loss Limits under Non-Expected Utility Preferences
W. Hürlimann 550

Forecasting Volatility and Option Pricing with GARCH Models
J. Kähler 553

Risk Management in Banks—A Stochastic Approach
U.-C. Kopp 558

Testing Filter-Rule Profits in the Foreign Exchange Market
W. Naggl 561

Bank Branch Computerisation: A Feasible Approach
S.M. Padwal 564

Instalment Credits in a Model of Vertically Differentiated Consumer Durables
U. Schmidt-Mohr 566

The Pricing of Insurance Contracts by Financial Models and Rationality
W. Schott 569

Financial Engineering—A Knowledge Based Buy/Lease Decision Support System
C. Weinhardt 572

The Distribution for Continuous Multiple Life Functions
M. van Wouwe, S. Lorimier 576

Author Index 579

Workshop

Environmental Systems

Decision Theoretic Analysis of Pollutants Emissions Monitoring Procedures

Rudolf Avenhaus
Universität der Bundeswehr München
Werner-Heisenberg-Weg 39, 8014 Neubiberg, Germany

The management of an industrial plant (called the 'inspectee') may be authorized to release some amount of pollutant per unit time into the environment, e.g., air or water. An environmental agency (called the 'inspector') may supervise with the help of randomly sampled measurements whether or not the releases are larger than the permitted ones. The question is what kind of monitoring procedure should be used in order that the inspector meets his responsibility best.

Two different procedures may be considered: The first one is that the inspector uses only his own measurements. The second procedure is that the inspectee has to report all releases regularly, and that the inspector compares his own measurements with the reported ones in order to decide if the reported data are credible, i.e., not falsified. At the same time, the inspector uses the reported data of the inspectee in order to decide if the real releases are below the agreed standards.

Two different sets of 'illegal' strategies correspond to these two procedures, if the inspectee really wants to release more pollutants than permitted which might be economically interesting for him if the disposal of the excess pollutants is expensive. In the former case, the inspectee simply hopes that the test procedure, based on the uncertain measurements and the finite sample of the inspector, will not detect the illegal releases. In the latter case, the inspector falsifies the reported data and hopes that the inspector's comparison of the reported and the independently sampled data will not detect this falsification; in addition, he can also use the afore-mentioned illegal strategy.

In order to find out which of the two procedures is better, we formulate our inspection problem as a non-cooperative two-person game. If the payoff structure of this game does not take into account the internal structure of illegal strategies, then the solution of the game can be decomposed: For a given value of the false alarm probability α only a two-person zero-sum game has to be considered where the probability of detecting illegal behavior is the payoff to the inspector. The value of the 'best' false alarm probability, however, depends on the payoff parameters of the inspectee, and is the solution of a special non-zero-sum game.

Formally, the second monitoring procedure is described as follows: There are n points in time where pollutants can be released. The inspectee measures these pollutants and reports his measurements to the inspector. The inspectee chooses k out of the n time points randomly and measures the emissions independently. Let the reported data of the inspectee be $x_1,\ldots,x_n$, and the independent findings of the inspector $y_1,\ldots,y_k$; we assume that the errors of both sets of measurements are described by independently and identically normally distributed random variables, with variances σ_x^2 resp. σ_y^2 which are known to both 'players'.

The idea for using these two sets of data is that the inspector compares his own data with the corresponding ones of the inspectee in order to find out whether or not the reported data are falsified. Furthermore, he takes the reported data in order to test whether or not excess amounts of pollutants are released. This means that the inspector considers the (transposed) random vector

$$\underline{Z}' = (Z_1,\ldots,Z_{n+k}) = (X_1,\ldots,X_n,Y_1-X_1,\ldots,Y_k-X_k);$$

here, it is assumed that the data are rearranged in such a way that the *first* k reported data are verified.

Without loss of generality we assume that under the null hypothesis - legal behavior - no pollutants are emitted at all, and that no data are falsified. Then $\underline{Z}$ is multivariate normally distributed with zero expectation vector and non-diagonal covariance matrix $\underline{\Sigma}$:

$$f_0(\underline{z}) = (2\pi)^{-\frac{n+k}{2}} \cdot |\underline{\Sigma}|^{-\frac{1}{2}} \cdot \exp(-\frac{1}{2} \cdot \underline{z}' \cdot \underline{\Sigma}^{-1} \cdot \underline{z}).$$

Under the alternative hypothesis H_1 - illegal behavior - we assume that during the i-th interval of time the amount ξ_i of pollutants is released, and that the i-th reported datum is falsified by the amount μ_i with $0 \le \mu_i \le \xi_i$, $i = 1,\dots,n$. Therefore, the density of $\underline{Z}$ under H_1 is

$$f_1(\underline{z}) = (2\pi)^{-\frac{n+k}{2}} \cdot |\underline{\Sigma}|^{-\frac{1}{2}} \cdot \binom{n}{k}^{-1} \cdot \sum_{i=1}^{\binom{n}{k}} \exp(-\frac{1}{2} \cdot (\underline{z}-E_1^i(\underline{z}))' \cdot \underline{\Sigma}^{-1} \cdot$$

$$\cdot (\underline{z}-E_1^i(\underline{z}))),$$

where the transposed expected vector of $\underline{Z}$ under H_1 is

$$E_1^i(\underline{Z})' = (\xi_1-\mu_1,\dots,\xi_n-\mu_n, \xi_{1_i},\dots,\xi_{k_i}), \quad i = 1,\dots,\binom{n}{k},$$

and where $(1_i,\dots,k_i)$ is the i-th sample of k out of n data.

It is surprising now that inspite of the complicated form of the density of $\underline{Z}$ under H_1 one can determine the best test procedure and the optimal falsification strategy: With the help of the Neyman-Pearson Lemma it can be shown that the saddlepoint strategy of the inspectee is to falsify all data by the maximum possible amount, i.e., $\xi_i^* = \mu_i$, for $i = 1,\dots,n$, and that the inspector's saddlepoint strategy is to use exclusively his own data, i.e., to ignore the reported data.

It should be mentioned that in general, i.e., for arbitrary values of μ_i, $i = 1,\dots,n$, the best test procedure of the inspector is complicated and that a a zero-sum game where the inspectee's strategy set is the set $\{\mu_1,\dots,\mu_n\}$ of possible excess releases, the inspector's strategy set is the set of tests for given value of α, and the payoff to the inspector is the probability of detection, cannot be solved analytically.

Applied General Equilibrium Modeling for Environmental Policy Analysis

Klaus Conrad
Lehrstuhl für Volkswirtschaftslehre, Universität Mannheim
6800 Mannheim 1, Schloß, Germany

1. Introduction

Given the challenge to more restrictive environmental regulation by groups in society, it is becoming more and more important to quantify the costs of such a policy. Applied general equilibrium (AGE) modeling is becoming a widely used tool for this purpose. The objective of this paper is to present the conceptual framework for modeling the effects of unilateral environmental control policies on a country's economy. Especially unilateral actions, e.g. a CO_2 control by a small country, will cause a loss of international sector competitiveness in energy intensive industries. AGE models for assessing these effects become more and more sophisticated. From a scientific point of view, research to attenuate some of its unrealistic assumptions is desirable. From a pragmatic point of view, the variety of conceptual approaches makes it more and more difficult to understand, why a certain target for CO_2 emissions, e.g., calls for a tax rate of $ 20 by one model builder and $ 300 by another one. In this paper we will survey some technical details in setting up AGE models. We will also present some results from introducing a cost-effective environmental policy in air pollution or from introducing a CO_2 tax. We will not, however, present a complete survey of the state of art in AGE modeling for environmental policy analysis.

2. Methodological principles

Common methodological features in applied general equilibrium (AGE) models is an activity analysis approach to model the exchange of commodities by agents. Activity analysis is based on the input/output mechanism, both for methodological and data availability reasons. Next, adequate mathematical formulation at the level of the agent has to represent optimal demand for production factors (producers) or for commodities (consumers), through the first order conditions of the optimum. In the case of the producer, the optimizing behavior may be respresented in the form of either the primal problem or the dual problem. Macroeconomic equilibrium models based on the primal approach to production have been used by Shoven and Whalley, whereas the dual (cost-driven) forms have been prefered by Johanson and Jorgenson. Following the primal problem formulation, the agent determines supply quantities as a function of the market prices of commodities, while in the dual problem the supplier is setting the market price of the commodity, he is supplying, by solving the inverse (or dual) supply function, i.e. $p = C_X(x,q)$ where q is a vector of input prices. At the level of the market, the choice of the primal or the dual representation has an important implication on the mathematical form of the market clearing mechanism. Equilibrium models entering within the Johanson-Jorgenson category of the dual problem form have been developed by Jorgenson, Wilcoxen (1990),Burniaux et. al. (GREEN), Bergmann (1990,91) or Conrad/Henseler-Unger (1986) and Conrad/Schröder (1991). These models are built around a flexible (price-driven technical coefficient) input/-output framework and derive equilibrium prices of commodities directly from price (or unit cost) functions. Shephard's lemma is employed for obtaining factor demands (input coefficients). The unit cost pricing of equilibrium is equivalent to the zero-profit condition, which corresponds to one of the two forms of expressing Walras' law. Primary factor prices are, on the other hand, obtained through supply- demand interaction. The models are solved, over a set of periods, as a non-linear system by applying a combination of Gauss-Seidel and Newton algorithms applied respectively to the multi-sectoral and the aggregate primary factors blocs, to which the model is partitioned.

By summarizing, the architecture of the AGE modelling framework is flexible enough to allow for different mathematical formulations and dynamic mechanisms. At the level of the markets either the primal or the dual market forms have to be solved as fixed point problems. If the framework is well specified, one can easily add markets and corresponding agents, in order to augment the generality of the equilibrium computed. The degree of integration between economy, energy and environment is a matter of formulation of the appropriate markets, commodities and agents. In the next sections we will discuss certain aspects of such integrations.

3. Modeling producer and consumer behavior

In the paper we specify restricted cost functions with a quasi-fixed capital stock and with adjustment costs to take into account short-run restrictions in adjusting to price ratios changed by environmental policy instruments. Important aspects in AGE-models are: (1) the adjustment of the quasi-fixed capital stock to its optimal level; (2) the representation of productivity growth as functions of relative prices; (3) the treatment of technical change as (a) autonomous energy efficiency improvements, (b) distinction between "old" and "new" capital vintages, or (c) effective capital stock in the sense of Solow with technical progress embodied in the improving quality of successive vintages of capital investment. For an analysis of the impact of environmental regulation on international competitiveness and on growth, the inclusion of the operating costs of pollution control is of importance. Polluting firms can react to standards and/or emission taxes either by factor substitution or by abatement activities or by both. They have abatement cost functions and determine the level of the abatement activity by equating marginal cost of abatement to the uniform tax rate on emissions. Abatement activities also imply demand for intermediate goods, for capital and for labor. Depending on the objective of the study, several approaches to impose pollution control regulations on the technology can be found in the literature. The easiest way to deal with this problem is to study the economic impact of reducing carbon dioxide emissions. There are no carbon removal technologies available at reasonable economic costs. This explains the popularity of modeling CO_2 policies. The paper surveys the approaches in the literature to incorporate abatement technologies.

In modelling the behavior of consumers it is assumed that the household performs a multistage budgeting procedure in the allocation of labor and leisure, savings and consumption, and the allocation of consumption into several consumption categories.

Since environmental regulation affects the use and purchase of consumer durables, a model of consumer behavior should integrate demand for durables and for non-durables. Furthermore, prices for the durables have to be stated in terms of costs which include all costs of using the durable good.

4. An evaluation of the cost of controlling air pollution

As an example for demonstrating the usefullness of AGE modelling we quantify the welfare gain from cost-effectiveness of market instruments in environmental policy. In a base run we simulate the performance of the economy of a German state (Baden-Württemberg) under the present regulation by standards and commands specified in the air quality acts called "TA-Luft" and GFAVO (Großfeuerungsanlagen-Verordnung from 1983).

The model has been applied to quantify the cost-effectiveness of regulating air pollution under alternative instruments in environmental policy. For that reason the state of the air quality under command and control policy (the base run) will be kept constant for simulating the cost effects under alternative instruments like emission taxes or abatement subsidies. Under a given quality of the environment, the economic impact can be directly compared without having to evaluate the cost and benefit of different states in air pollution.

5. Conclusion and outlook for future research

Future research in the area of environmental AGE modeling will be directed towards a more detailed modeling of the energy sector with its current and future technologies. What is required is a better linkage from changes in relative prices to the installation of now profitable, because more energy-efficient, technologies. Instead of smooth transitions discrete changes might occur. If substitution is the only way to respond to CO_2 taxes because the technology of public utilities is fixed as in Conrad and Schröder, than CO_2 tax rates will turn out to be very high. In reality, however, they will never become so high because in the first place utilities will replace their old processes by those with an improved efficiency.. Therefore cost-benefit calculations have to be part of the model framework for deciding whether a switch to a new input structure is profitable at the prevailing price ratios.

Interconnected Games

Henk Folmer, Pierre v. Mouche
Vakgroep Staathuishoudkunde, Landbouwuniversiteit Wageningen
Postbus 8130, 6700 EW Wageningen, Netherlands

Several real-world problems are characterized by the fact that the same agents are simultaneously involved in several distinct areas of interest. For instance, the Member States of the European Community are simultaneously involved in negotiations about coordinating their economic, foreign and environmental policies. Another example relates to the fact that firms in an oligopolistic setting often simultaneously operate at several distinct markets. The fact that the same agents are simultaneously involved in several areas of interest may put constraints on their strategies in the individual fields but it may also enrich the total of stategies open to them in the sense that there exists greater retaliatory potential. A basic feature of most economic approaches, including game theory, is to model the several areas of interest in isolation. This may seriously limit the applicability and analytic and predictive power of the resulting models, as the consequences of the linkages for the strategy spaces cannot adequately be taken into account. This justifies an interconnected modelling approach. We have learned that this concept has already been discussed in the litterature, but only in the context of very special real world situations and in a not formalized way. This observation inspired the authors of (A) to formalize the notion of interconnected games for two special cases, viz. where each isolated game is a game in strategic form and where each isolated game is a repeated game (with discounting). In this abstract we refer to these types of interconnected games as direct sum games and tensor games, respectively. Properly speaking, only trade-off completely interconnected games were considered in (A).
In the paper (B) underlying this abstract the framework of interconnected games will be extended further by considering also direct sum and tensor games without trade-off and by allowing partial interconnection of the isolated games. The following aspects will be paid attention to:

a. Much more attention than in (A) will be paid to the structure of interconnected games. Direct sum games and tensor games can be interpreted as multiple objective games and as repeated multiple objective games with an additional special structure, respectively. The structure concerned is that of separability. For this reason also some attention will be given to (repeated) multiple objective games. The analogy between the construction of a repeated game out of a sequence of games in strategic form and the construction of a tensor game out of a sequence of repeated games will be considered.

b. It will be shown how the sets of strong (and proper) Nash-equilibria for interconnected games without trade-off are related to the sets of Nash-equilibria of associated trade-off games. Quite general weight functions will be allowed for trade-off games. Concerning partial interconnection it will be shown how the set of strong Nash-equilibria of a partial interconnected game is related to the sets of strong Nash-equilibria of the completely interconnected parts of this game.

c. A central point in the analysis of interconnected games might be to compare how results for topics which have also counterparts in the constituting isolated games relate to each other. In this regard the topics of Nash-equilibria and the set of feasible individually rational payoffs are studied.

In (B) we shall concentrate on the fundamental structure of interconnected games and therefore we shall not endow strategy sets and payoff functions with additional structures. We mention here only the following results obtained in ((A) and) (B):

1. Their exists a canonical bijection between the set of Nash-equilibria of a (strict trade-off) direct sum game and the cartesian product of the Nash-equilibria of its constituting isolated games. These sets are thus idempotent.

2. There exists a canonical injection of the cartesian product of the sets of Nash-equilibria of the constituting isolated games of a tensor game into the intersection of the sets of Nash equilibria of all associated linear trade-off tensor games. In this context we shall define simple and non-simple Nash-equilibria and prove that in general a tensor game has many non-simple Nash-equilibria.

3. For the case of completely additive trade-off tensor games the following result, which is fundamental for Folk theorems, will be proved: The algebraic sum of the sets of feasible individually rational payoffs of the constituting isolated games is contained in the set of feasible individually rational payoffs of the trade-off tensor game. It will be shown that strict inclusion can hold and sufficient conditions for this will be considered.

4. The 'maximal obtainable' total average Nash-equilibrium payoff for a completely additive trade-off tensor game is at least as large as the sum of the corresponding payoffs for its constituting isolated games.

From the above idempotency result it follows that direct sum games are in some sense trivial. However, one reason to nevertheless paying attention to them is that they are fundamental building blocks for tensor games because they serve as their stage games. Contrary to this, tensor games are not trivial constructions at all. The possible argument that a tensor game can be interpreted as a repeated game and therefore is a superfluous concept does not hold. This is already reflected by the lack of an idempotency result for tensor games and can be made also clear by referring to the analogy to the framework of repeated games: A repeated game can be interpreted as a game in strategic form but nobody would claim that the framework of repeated games is therefore superfluous. The point is that in both the case of the repeated and the tensor game construction an additional structure is introduced. A repeated game has a dynamic structure, which a game in strategic form does not have and a tensor game has a multiple objective structure, which a repeated game does not have.
The results obtained in (A) and (B) lead us carefully to the theme "interconnection may sustain more cooperation" for tensor games similar to the theme "repetition enables cooperation" for repeated games. Hence, interconnection may serve as an additional explanation of cooperation.
Especially, the elementary analysis (based to a large extent on results for the games in strategic form, multiple objective games and repeated games) given here for tensor games should be extended to more specific aspects of the interconnected structure. Also more atention should be paid to the interpretation of interconnected games. Topics for further study include inter alia subgame perfection, Pareto optimality and stability. A reconsideration of

the value of the Nash-equilibrium solution concept for interconnected games may also be relevant.
Although (partial interconnected) (trade-off) tensor games already have a rich structure, they still do not have enough structure to adequately model the full complexity of several real world problems. There is therefore some need to extend the framework of interconnected games even further, for example to situations with structural time dependence and to situations where not all players are involved in exactly the same areas of interest.

References:

- (A) Folmer, H., P. v. Mouche and S. Ragland (1992). International environmental problems and interconnected Games. Paper submitted for publication.
- (B) Folmer, H., P. v. Mouche. Interconnected games. Paper in preparation.

Object-Oriented Techniques for the Management of Geographic and Environmental Data

Oliver Günther, Johannes Lamberts
FAW Ulm
P.O. Box 2060, 7900 Ulm, Germany

1 Introduction

Geographic information systems (GIS) are an essential tool for the management and visualization of large amounts of environmental information. The GIS that are available on the market now are the result of an evolutionary application-oriented development based on early research activities by the geoscientific community. Several conceptional deficiencies of these systems have become more obvious recently as research on spatial databases has made some significant progress.

With regard to GIS, many of the problems can be traced back to their original orientation towards file systems, which provided only rudimentary database functionalities and which do not scale up very well to larger amounts of data. Conventional DBMS, on the other hand, usually support data models that are not very well suited for the management of geographic and environmental information. This survey paper briefly describes the properties of object-oriented databases according to the *Object-Oriented Database System Manifesto* and discusses the potential of object-oriented techniques for the management of geographic and environmental information in particular.

2 Object-Oriented Database Systems

So-called object-oriented database systems (OODBS) are a key topic of current database research. The term *object-orientation*, however, has often been used just as a buzzword, without a clear definition of what it entails. In the meantime, database researchers have drawn up check lists of features that should be included if a database system is to be called object-oriented:

Database Management System: An object-oriented database system is a DBMS with an object-oriented data model. It is important to note that it is not sufficient for a system to have just an object-oriented data model if it does not have the full functionality of a DBMS. In particular, this entails persistence, secondary storage management, concurrency control, recovery, and an ad-hoc query facility. Optional features include data distribution and integrity constraints.

Object Identity: In an OODBS the existence of an object is independent of its value. Each object is labeled by some unique identifier that has been created by the system in order to guarantee systemwide uniqueness. The identifier does not change during the lifetime of the object and can not be reused after its deletion.

Structural Object-Orientation: A data model is called ***structurally object-oriented***, if it supports the construction of composite objects (also called complex, structured, or molecular objects). This means in particular that attributes of a tuple may be composite in turn. A system that supports composite objects must provide object-specific operators and so-called type constructors enabling users to build their specific complex object structures on their own.

Behavioral Object-Orientation: A data model is called ***behaviorally object-oriented***, if it supports user-defined types and the definition of operators (in this context usually called *methods*) that are applied to these types. Operators are defined by an interface (name, input parameters, output parameters) and a program to compute it. The OODBS guarantees that operators can not be applied to inappropriate objects.

Classes, Class Hierarchies and Inheritance: In an object-oriented data model similar objects may be grouped together in so-called *classes*. Operators (methods) and attributes are attached to a class, which means that they are valid for all objects belonging to this class. Classes may form a hierarchy, such that objects in any given class are automatically members of all of the superclasses. That also means that they *inherit* all attributes and methods from their superclass(es).

Encapsulation and Overloading: Object-oriented systems support the concept of *encapsulation* in order to hide the internal representation of a data type. Furthermore, an object is only able to access those user-defined or base operators that are defined on its class. Using *overloading*, an OODBS may attach different implementations to a single function name or type specification which is required to use encapsulation in the presence of multiple representations for a single object.

3 The Potential of Object-Oriented Techniques for the Management of Environmental Data

With regard to the efficient management of environmental data, the different aspects of object-orientation are of varying significance. At the *geometry level*, spatial data types and operators can be conveniently integrated using the concept of *behavioral* object-orientation. At the *application level*, one can utilize *structural* object-orientation and *inheritance* to define complex objects and class hierarchies in a flexible manner.

3.1 Behavioral Object-Orientation

Objects in a spatial database are typically associated with a location and a spatial extension. For the geometric representation there exists a large variety of spatial data structures that each support a certain class of spatial operators. Behavioral object-orientation allows the user the utilization of complex data structures and algorithms from computational geometry.

The representation of such complex types and operators also requires a more powerful query language. In particular, it is necessary to provide language constructs for the description and utilization of *user-defined* data types and operators. The details of the implementation are typically not visible to the user. An indirect confrontation of the user with the internal implementation due to performance aspects cannot be avoided, of course. After all, the time for the computation of an operator is closely related to the representation of its operands.

It may sometimes be useful to maintain several representations for the same object class. In that case every object is stored redundantly in several different formats, such that for the computation of different operators one can always choose the representation that is most promising for that case. Note that it is important to propagate updates on one representation to the other representations as quickly as possible to avoid inconsistencies. A good example for the utilization of multiple representations in environmental data management is the simultaneous administration of vector and raster representations of the same geographic area.

3.2 Structural Object-Orientation

Molecular objects can be represented in various ways in the sense of a structural object-orientation. For example, it is possible to embed objects in other objects. This approach can be utilized for geometric modeling purposes, but also for the representation of particular applications. Considering the fact, however, that at the geometric level one requires only very few simple geometric base types, then the advantages at this level seem rather limited.

In the case of environmental application modeling we find a different situation. Many objects in this context have a hierarchical structure and can be modeled nicely using structural object-orientation. A typical example would be the modeling of a *city*, which is made up of *districts*, which contain *streets*, and so on.

3.3 Class Hierarchies and Inheritance

In addition to structural hierarchies, one can also use class hierarchies for the management of geographic data. Once again this type of modeling is mainly useful for application modeling. With regard to the geometry modeling, the efficiency of class hierarchies is not clear at this point. Geometric object hierarchies tend to be rather shallow. Furthermore, the inheritance of algorithms from the general to the special case is usually not very efficient.

3.4 Spatial Database Views

Objects with nested subobjects do not necessarily have a geometric entity associated with it, because in theory their geometric representation can often be inferred from the geometry of their components. In many cases, however, this approach is not a practical solution. On the one hand, generalization algorithms are not advanced enough to generate consistantly nice geometric representations. On the other hand, sometimes one would like to use geometric representations that cannot be derived from the geometries of the components at all (so-called semantic gaps).

We have proposed the notion of ***spatial database views*** as a unified data model that can capture most of the semantics described above. In this concept each simple object is stored separately at the greatest possible detail, together with the spatial location it is associated with. The collection of these atomic objects is stored physically on disk. All molecular objects are then defined as views of this database and mainly exist at the virtual level. Beyond that, however, there is also the possibility of attaching a physical data record to each spatial view. This record may contain, for example, non-spatial attributes. The main advantage of spatial views is the minimization of redundancy in order to avoid contradictions.

Thematic maps of different scales and regions can now also be defined as spatial database views.

4 Conclusions

The utilization of modern database technology for the management of geodata is essential for future geographic and environmental applications. Classical GIS will have major difficulties to manage efficiently the huge amounts of data that are expected for the near future. More recent developments in database research, however, especially work on non-standard and object-oriented databases, seem quite promising in this context. Class hierarchies and the so-called structural object-orientation seem promising for the modeling of complex geo-objects. In addition, behavioral object-orientation allows the modeling of application-specific (especially geometric) data types and operators, which is an essential feature in geographic and environmental applications.

For the integration of GIS and database technologies, there are basically three options:

1. The extension of an existing GIS by database functionalities.
2. The coupling of a GIS with an existing DBMS. Such a coupling is already quite common for holding non-spatial data in commercial GIS.
3. The extension of an existing DBMS by geometric and geographic functionalities. We have recently begun work on a research project which is based on this approach using an OODBS.

Problems of Statistical Analysis of Environmental Data

Hartmut Hebbel
Fachbereich Wirtschafts- und Organisationswissenschaften
Universität der Bundeswehr Hamburg
Holstenhofweg 85, 2000 Hamburg 70, Germany

Relevant environmental problems of many areas are more and more of interest. For all questions it is common that numerous variables were observed in space and time to explain the development and to bring up new results in the effects and mechanisms of the distinct influence variables (control process).

At this analysis the statistician is dependent on the assistance of the special scientist who knows the real dependences and coherences to use these information at the evaluation techniques. At the opposite actions to detect the structures of coherence and dependence only by using statistical methods it cannot be done without the advice of the practitioner. As a rule it needs of a strictly cooperative work together of special scientist (expert) and statistician to complete necessary knowledge of facts and effective statistical methods in an ideal manner.

The most important of the application of statistical methods is *an exact question* and a *precise aim*.

Exploratory graphical data analysis

Hardly all environmental quality variables are continuous in space and time, in other words in principle to determine at every place or position z and every time point t. Only in a few exceptions (i.e. a water-level writer) the data can be noted down continuously. In all other cases the data can only be noted down discretely, observed at some positions $z_1, z_2, \ldots$ and some time points $t_1, t_2, \ldots$. Automatic measuring stations register environmental quality data easy to determine in fixed intervalls (from 5 up to 30 minutes) as arithmetic means for these periods. Consequently there are at least 48 values a day. The result is called a *quasi-continuous observation series*. Difficult evaluating variables (only with an expensive chemical analysis equipment) cannot be observed in this density. In addition the know how of the subject-scientist is asked to find a suitable strategy of sampling (systematic or random) from pre-investigations about the dynamics and with respect to the objectives. It is received a *discrete observation* series.

To represent those discrete data in a curve graph it is to note that rectilinear connections of the points (polygon graph) represent neither an approximation nor an interpolation of the true development but only make plain the local and temporal order of the data. In this situation it is to warn of very different pictures arising from the observations at distinct lattice points.

Often it is not known in which space-time distances a variable is to observe. This problem cannot be solved in general. The solution depends on the individual dynamic of the corresponding variable and the objective of the research.

After the graphical illustration it demands a "*datasnooping*" to detect the behaviour structure. The wide spread proceeding of an analysis of frequencies is not suitable in general because there does not exist global one distribution, but the distribution depends on space and time. The space–time reference is essential to the regarded variable. A static analysis instead of a dynamic view seems to be less effective. It is the spatial and temporal arrangement of the data which is the most important information except for a few applications.

Besides single curves and profils *comparing graphs* are more proper to detect cause–effect relations among the environmental variables possibly changing in space and time. An *association plot* to say a matrix of single scatter plots supports the detection of influence structures as a foundation of later mathematical and statistical modeling. It is advantageous to mark the order in the data by using polygon curves and not only isolated points, but careful interpretations of these patterns are necessary. It is possible that the cause–effect structure is a result of a third variable. Oscillations in two time series with phase angles lead to a "*hysteresis*" in the corresponding scatter plot, see Hebbel (1992). Further tools to bring out characteristic phenomena are elementary operations without loss of space and time order like a *smoothing procedure* or a *Box–Cox–transformation*. A smoothing procedure eleminates random disturbances. The type of mathematical dependence can be found by using a Box–Cox–transformation.

Problems of modeldesign, selection, coherence and estimation

The adequate methods have to be searched in the field of space–time analysis. Starting–point is an environmental quality variable Y (univariate or multivariate) in principle observable at every place z and every time–point t. For this (fictive) value it is written $Y(z,t)$ or short $Y(t)$, where t means both, space and time. In this moment it is not relevant, wether the value $Y(t)$ is in fact exact, with error or non–precise measureable in the practical sence. It is an important problem to describe the behaviour of Y in space and time and this in dependence of further important and observable input variables $X_1, X_2, \ldots, X_k$. According to the principles above it is to design a suitable model, say

$$Y(t) = f_t(X_1(t), X_2(t), \ldots, X_k(t); U(t)),$$

as the *state equation*. All non–important and not measureable influence variables are summarized in the residual variable U which is not observable. For other types of models see e.g. Beck (1987).

To specify the function type a class of models is chosen so that f only depends on a parameter–vector β possibly dependent at t. Favourable with regard to the estimation problem is linearity in constant parameters and furthermore an additive independent and identically distributed innovation process or at least an ARMA–process $U(t)$ (equidistant data).

In addition to the state equation there are the *observed equations* (discrete case)

$$Y(t_i) = f_{ti}(X_1(t_i), X_2(t_i), \ldots, X_k(t_i); U(t_i)), \quad i = 1, \ldots, n,$$

with added errors in variables if needed or other uncertainties like vague information. In the linear and constant parameter case β can be estimated by an iterative linear regression procedure with a special autocorrelation structure. Such a model is used by Hebbel/Heiler

(1988) to create a warning system related to water quality based on half–hour mean values of the quasi–continuous variables air temperature, water temperature, oxygen content, conductivity, pH–value and discharge.

The problem of estimation the function type or prediction of $Y(t)$ cannot be solved generally, it depends on the various types of models.

If the control variables of the output–process $Y(t)$ were unknown groups of the influence variables can be summarized in view of their resulting effects. One gets unobserveable components like trend X_1, saison X_2 and so on:

$$Y(t) = X_1(t) + X_2(t) + U(t),$$

written as an additive model. The evaluation of the components is orientated only at smoothing criteria, due to the real problem, see e.g. Hebbel/Heiler (1987).

The problem to reduce a lot of observed variables $Y_1, \ldots, Y_m$ in space and time to a few numbers of unobserved space time factors F_j as industial pollution, human pollution, pollution by cars and so on is another interesting field. A classical multivariate factormodel with the usual assumptions at the first and second moments where t is regarded as an "object" is not suitable because the Y_i are not independent identical distributed. An extension of the classical model to a space time factor model is given by

$$Y_i(t) = \mu_i(t) + \sum_{j=1}^{l} a_{ij} F_j(t) + U_i(t)$$

with a deterministic linear regression part

$$\mu_i(t) = \sum_{j=1}^{k} X_{ij}(t)\beta_j, \quad i = 1, \ldots, m.$$

Under the assumtion of weak stationarity of $Y_i - \mu_i$, F_j, U_i some classical estimation and rotation procedures can be transfered.

References:

Beck MB (1987) Water Quality Modeling: A Review of the Analysis of Uncertainty. Water Recources Research 23: 1393–1442.

Hebbel H (1992) Probleme bei der statistischen Analyse umweltbezogener Daten. Beiträge zur Umweltstatistik (Ed. Viertl R), Schriftenreihe der TU Wien, Band 29: 141–152.

Hebbel H, Heiler S (1987) Zeitreihenzerlegung über ein Optimalitätskriterium. Allg. Statist. Archiv 71: 305–318.

Hebbel H, Heiler S (1987) Trend and seasonal decomposition in discrete time. Statistische Hefte 28: 133–158.

Hebbel H, Heiler S (1988) Statistische Analyse von Wassergütedaten. Allg. Statist. Archiv 72: 24–39.

Planning "Safe" Routes for Transporting Protected Materials through an Alient Area

John Karkazis
Department of Business Administration, University of the Aegean
8 Michalon str., 82100 Chios, Greece

The problem regards the transportation of goods or materials from a point O (origin) to a point D (destination) on the plane with transportation route having to pass through an unfriendly area. The term "unfriendly" regards a fixed point C on the plane that represents installation or center point of activities that may create damage to these goods or materials. This point will be called thereon "damage source" (abbr. d.s.). Possible applications may involve flights of planes over an alient area where d.s. may represent sites of enemy missile batteries. The problem is to determine a route s along which the expected damage effects D(s) are minimised:

$$F(s)=\int_{P\in S} f(r_P)\,dr_P \qquad (1)$$

where $f(r_P)$ represents the "damage probability density" function with respect to d.s. C, which is a strictly decreasing function of the euclidean distance r_P between P and C, satisfying the following condition:

$$d(f(r)r)/dr<0 \quad \forall\ r>0 \qquad (2)$$

THEORETICAL BACKGROUND

Let $s(\theta)$, $\theta \in [\theta_1,\theta_2]$ be the polar function describing a route s with respect to a d.s. C. Then we define the following two basic types of routes:

<u>Definition 1.</u> If $s(\theta)$=constant $\forall\ \theta \in [\theta_1,\theta_2]$ then s will be called "polar" (or "circular") route with respect to d.s. C whereas if s

is part of a straight line passing through C then s will be called "radial" route with respect to C.

The determination of the optimal route is trivial in the following two cases (described in results 1 and 2):

<u>Result 1.</u> If the origin O and destination D are equidistant from a d.s. C and the damage probability density takes the form f(r)=a/r where a is a constant then the optimal route s* from O to D is the polar route with respect to C confined by points O and D.

<u>Result 2.</u> If the origin O and destination D lie on a straight line passing through d.s. C then the optimal route s* from O to D is the radial (linear) route connecting O and D.

Karkazis (1992) proved that under the broad condition (2) (satisfied among others by the family of functions a/r^k, $k>0$) imposed on f the initial area of search for the problem (1) can be reduced to a polar trapezoid T^0 confined by the radial lines CO and CD and two polar (cyclical) lines centered at C with one of them passing through the origin. He also proved that the optimal route of problem (1) is convex with respect to d.s. C.

The two basic types of routes, the radial and polar lines, play an important role in the theoretical analysis as well as in the construction of a solution process. Using notions associated with these two basic types of routes lower and upper bounds for the damage probability F(s*) along the optimal route s* can be established.

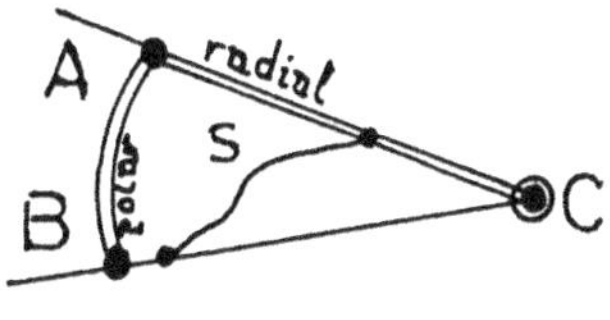

Figure 1. Result 3

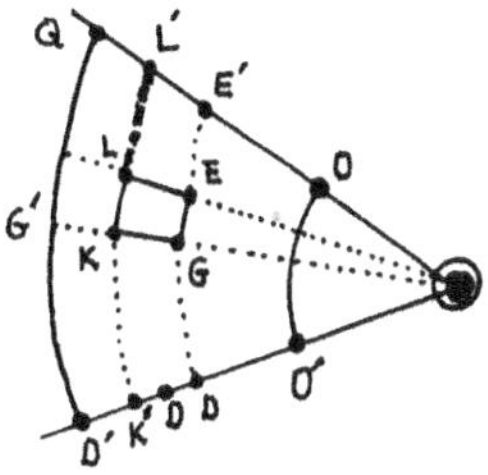

Figure 2. Theorem 1

<u>Result 3.</u> If s is a route enclosed by a polar triangle ACB (see figure 1) then $F(s) \geq \max\{r(C,A), p(A,B)\}$, where $r(C,A)$ is the radial route from C to A and $p(A,B)$ is the polar route from A to B (proof is given by Karkazis (1992)).

METHOD

The solution process for problem (1) takes into account the ideas behind the algorithm proposed by Karkazis and Papadimitriou (1992) for the location of obnoxious facilities on the plane. The polar trapezoid defining the initial area of search is split into smaller equal trapezoids using a grid of polar and radial lines and then a fathoming process is applied which determines if trapezoids possess common points with optimal route s*. The following theorem forms the basis of the proposed method.

<u>Theorem 1 (Bounding relation).</u> Consider a grid G of polar and radial lines dividing the initial area of search $T_0 = OO'D'Q$ and a polar trapezoid T=EGKL (see figure 2) confined by the radial and polar segments of the grid. If s is a route from O to D for which:

$$F(s) < d_1 + d_2 \quad \text{where}$$

$$d_1 = \max\{r(O,E'), p(L,L')\}, \; d_2 = \max\{r(K',D), p(G',D')\} \qquad (3)$$

then the optimal route s* from O to D cannot intersect T.

An immediate consequence of theorem 1 is the following corollary.
<u>Corollary 1 (Fathoming criterion).</u> If F* is the value of the current best solution (route) and T=EGKL is a polar trapezoid for which $F^* < d_1 + d_2$ (d_1, d_2 are defined in (3)) then the optimal route cannot possess common points with it.

References

Karkazis J (1992) Routing of protected materials on the plane: determining routes in an unfriendly environment. to appear: Proceedings, VI Meeting of Euro Working Group on Locational Analysis, University of La Laguna

Karkazis J, Papadimitriou C (1992) A branch-bound algorithm for the location of facilities causing atmospheric pollution. to appear: European Journal of Operations Research

Umweltinformationssystem Baden-Württemberg (UIS)

Roland Mayer-Föll
Ministerialrat im Umweltministerium Baden-Württemberg
Postfach 10 34 39, 7000 Stuttgart 10, Germany

To cope with the requirements of a task requiring preventive and effective environmental conservation, government and administration must have reliable comprehensive, problem-related and up-to-date information at its disposal. The varied data from different sources must be systematically organized and capable of being forwarded to interested parties rapidly and in a userfriendly form. This is the aim of the UIS (German abbreviation for "Environmental Information System") which is to be established as part of Baden-Württemberg's Land System Concept, its purpose being to collate environmental data from all departments, and interlink environmental media and sectors to provide a general overview of problems as a whole.

Kurzfassung:

Eine fortschrittliche, vorsorgende Umweltpolitik ist zwingend auf laufende Meßwerte, auf Umweltbeobachtung und -analyse angewiesen. Aufgaben und Ziele des Umweltinformationssystems sind:

1. Information von Landtag, Regierung und Öffentlichkeit
2. Ermittlung, Analyse und Prognose der Umweltsituation
3. Unterstützung der Bewältigung von Stör- und Vorsorgefällen
4. Einsatz der Informationstechnik zur effektiven Erledigung von Verwaltungsaufgaben mit Umweltbezug
5. Integration der vorhandenen Verfahren zur Umweltinformation.

Die Voraussetzungen wurden 1987 bis 1990 mit der Konzeption des ressortübergreifenden Umweltinformationssystem (UIS) geschaffen. Baden-Württemberg verfügt damit über ein im Ländervergleich beispielhaftes Konzept.

Die zum UIS gehörenden Meßnetze für Boden, Wasser, Luft und Radioaktivität sowie die informations- und kommunikationstechnischen Verfahren in Bereichen wie Wasser- und Abfallwirtschaft, Bodenschutz, Gewerbeaufsicht, Lebensmittelwesen, Naturschutz und Landschaftspflege sind zum Teil aufgebaut. Das Umwelt-Führungs-Informationssystem ist bereits im Einsatz, verschiedene Berichtssysteme und das Räumliche Informations- und Planungssystem entwickelt das Land zusammen mit Externen. Das FAW Ulm und andere Institute führen anwendungsorientierte wissensbasierte Forschungsvorhaben im Auftrage des Landes und mehrerer Firmen durch. Die Feinkonzeption für das UIS-Informationsmanagement wird derzeit erstellt. Im Vordergrund steht nun der weitere Ausbau und die zügige Durchführung der begonnenen Projekte. Damit wird es auch möglich, die Erarbeitung und Ausführung von Umweltgesetzen informationstechnisch zu unterstützen.

Der Datenaustausch mit privaten Einrichtungen, kommunalem Bereich, Bund, anderen Ländern, EG und weiteren Staaten einerseits und der freie Zugang der Bürger zu Umweltdaten andererseits sind zu gestalten. Stellvertretend seien hier die Vorhaben zur Errichtung einer Europäischen Umweltagentur und eines Europäischen Umweltinformations- und Umweltbeobachtungsnetzes sowie zum Aufbau kommunaler Umweltinformationssysteme genannt.

Da das UIS als fach- und ressortübergreifendes Informationssystem angelegt ist, sind Regeln und Standards erforderlich, die die einzelnen Komponenten des UIS verbinden und ein reibungsloses Zusammenspiel zwischen ihnen ermöglichen. Diesem Zusammenwirken wird zum einen durch die Entwicklung eines durchgängigen Berichtswesens, zum anderen durch eine abgestimmte Systemarchitektur für alle UIS-Komponenten Rechnung getragen.

- Ein Leitgedanke der UIS-Berichtsphilosophie ist der Grundsatz der Führungsorientierung: Informationen für Führungskräfte sind situations- und bedarfsgerecht zur Verfügung zu stellen, d.h. es sollen nur diejenigen Informationen bereitgestellt werden, die zur Lösung einer Führungsaufgabe unbedingt notwendig sind. Das Berichtswesen ermöglicht ein zielorientiertes Erkennen von Handlungsbedarf und unterstützt die laufende Erfolgskontrolle von Umweltmaßnahmen. Es erleichtert Rückkopplungen zwischen Legislative und Exekutive sowie zwischen verschiedenen Führungsebenen der Verwaltung. Berichtsinhalte sind alle umweltrelevanten Informationen von der politischen Vorgabe über administrative Maßnahmen und technische Umsetzung bis hin zur Auswirkung auf Schutzgüter und Lebewesen (technologisch-ökologische Wirkungskette).
- Grundlegende Architekturmerkmale des UIS sind die Durchgängigkeit von Daten (der "vertikale Zugriff" auf Daten innerhalb der Verwaltungs- und Systemhierarchie) und ihre Verknüpfbarkeit (die Möglichkeit "horizontaler Verschneidungen" von Daten gleicher Aggregationsstufen) unter einer benutzerfreundlichen Bedieneroberfläche. Verknüpfbarkeit und Durchgängigkeit setzen einen einheitlichen Aufbau von UIS-Komponenten im Hinblick auf Anwendungssoftware, Datenmodell, systemnahe Software und Hardware voraus.

Daneben ermöglicht es die Systemarchitektur, Ergebnisse aus Forschungsarbeiten, wie sie beispielsweise beim Forschungsinstitut für anwendungsorientierte Wissensverarbeitung (FAW) in Ulm in enger Kooperation mit dem Land und den Stifterfirmen vorangetrieben werden, schrittweise in das UIS zu integrieren. Hier finden bereits im Vorfeld der Forschungsarbeiten enge Abstimmungen statt.

Hervorzuheben ist, daß die Systemarchitektur speziell im Hinblick auf die Wahrnehmung von Umweltaufgaben eingerichtet wurde. Damit ist das UIS weitestgehend offen für mögliche organisatorische Veränderungen im Zuge des vom Umweltministerium in Gang gesetzten Projekts "Überprüfung der Organisation der Umweltschutzverwaltung" im Rahmen des Reformvorhabens "Verwaltung 2000".

Das UIS unterscheidet generell drei System-Kategorien:

- Übergreifende UIS-Komponenten,
- UIS-Grundkomponenten und
- Basissysteme.

Mit den folgenden Schaubildern sollen wichtige Punkte der UIS-Rahmenkonzeption verdeutlicht werden.

Das "Ökologie-Modell" dient der Strukturierung von Umweltthemen

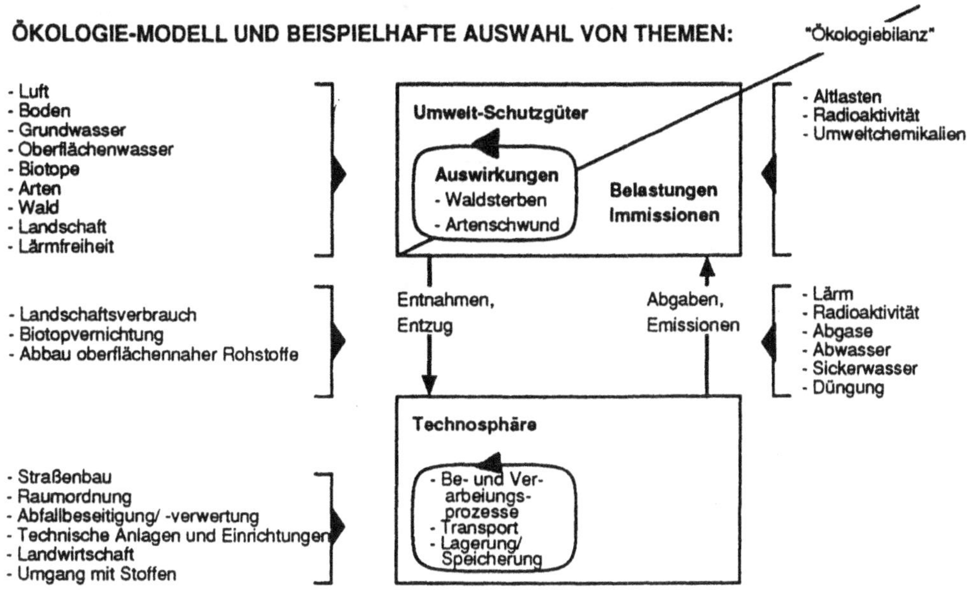

Die UIS-Konzeption verlangt führungsorientierte Aufbereitung der Information und Durchgängigkeit der Daten:

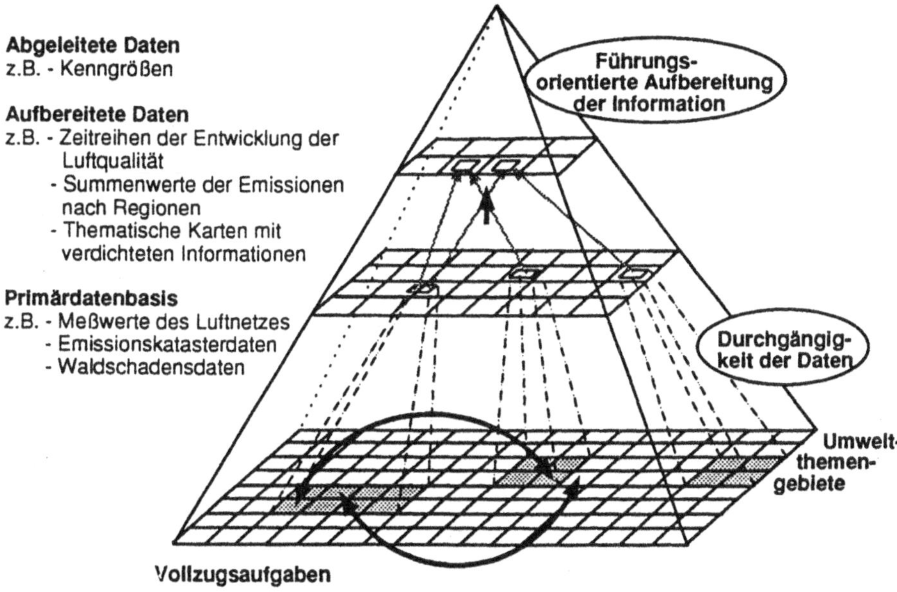

Die UIS-Rahmenkonzeption unterscheidet zwischen drei Systemkategorien, aus denen Schwerpunktprojekte gebildet werden:

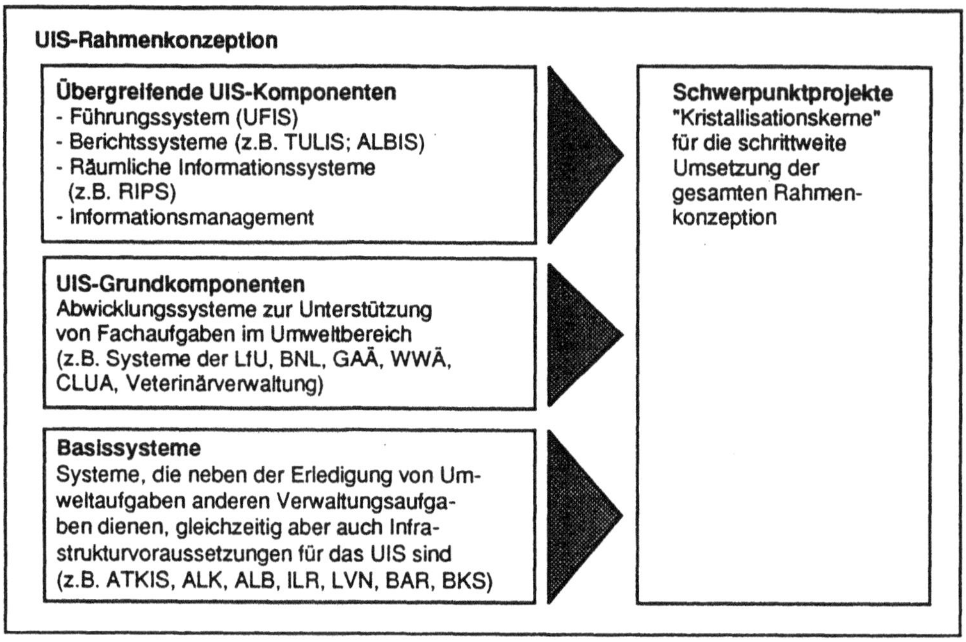

Der Zugang zu Informationssystemen ist daten- und nutzerspezifisch:

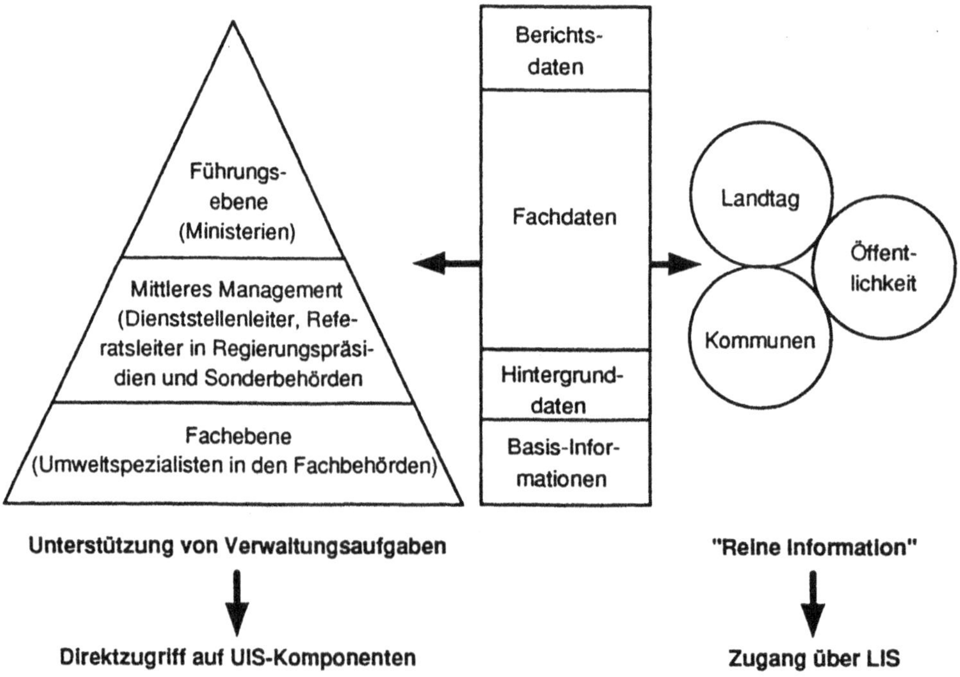

Some Adaptive Clustering Algorithms

Hans-Joachim Mucha
Institute of Applied Analysis and Stochastics
Hausvogteiplatz 5–7, 1086 Berlin, Germany

Cluster analysis attempts to detect structures in the data. Often clustering methods are incorporated into statistical software systems. Some of the most important and widely used methods are the K-means clustering and Ward's hierarchical algorithm. But there is a lack of known successful applications.

Here some adaptive clustering methods (which seem to be a little bit intelligent because of their ability in learning the appropriate distance measures) will be presented. They are based on so-called adaptive distance measures, and they can be carried out using the well-known statistical software SAS, SPSS, S-Plus etc. (in so far as the software contains both data management facilities and the usual K-means clustering, Ward's method etc.).

The stability of results of cluster analysis can be measured using the software *ClusCorr* (Mucha 1992a). The techniques are based on measures for comparing partitions (Hubert and Arabie 1985). Thereby we are able to recommend these adaptive distances, which lead to an improvement of clustering.

Adaptive distances are very important too for multivariate plots obtained by principal components analysis (shortly: PCA). Moreover, clustering some clouds of points by human eyes becomes more and more important. However, the multivariate graphical techniques should support the human eyes in order to avoid delusions. Therefore adaptive dynamic graphics are recommended.

An Adaptive K-means Algorithm

The structure of both row points and column points of a (I×J)-data table $\mathbf{X}=(x_{ij})$, $i=1,2,\dots,I$, $j=1,2,\dots,J$, can be investigated by cluster analysis. I consider the cluster analysis of row points (observations) here only. The basis is the squared weighted Euclidean distance

$$d_Q^2(\mathbf{x}_i,\mathbf{x}_{i'})=(\mathbf{x}_i-\mathbf{x}_{i'})'\mathbf{Q}(\mathbf{x}_i-\mathbf{x}_{i'})=\|\mathbf{x}_i-\mathbf{x}_{i'}\|_Q^2 \qquad (1)$$

between two observations $\mathbf{x}_i$ and $\mathbf{x}_{i'}$. Here $\mathbf{Q}$ is a (J×J) diagonal matrix. The (nonnegative) diagonal elements are called weights. For example, usual weights are $q_{jj}=1/s_j^2$ or $q_{jj}=1$, where s_j^2 is the variance of variable j.

But, which is the best among these so-called weighted Euclidean metrics? A general applicable approach for measuring the stability of clustering was developed by Mucha (1992a). The investigation of the stability of results obtained on the basis of different metrics was presented by Mucha (1992a,c).

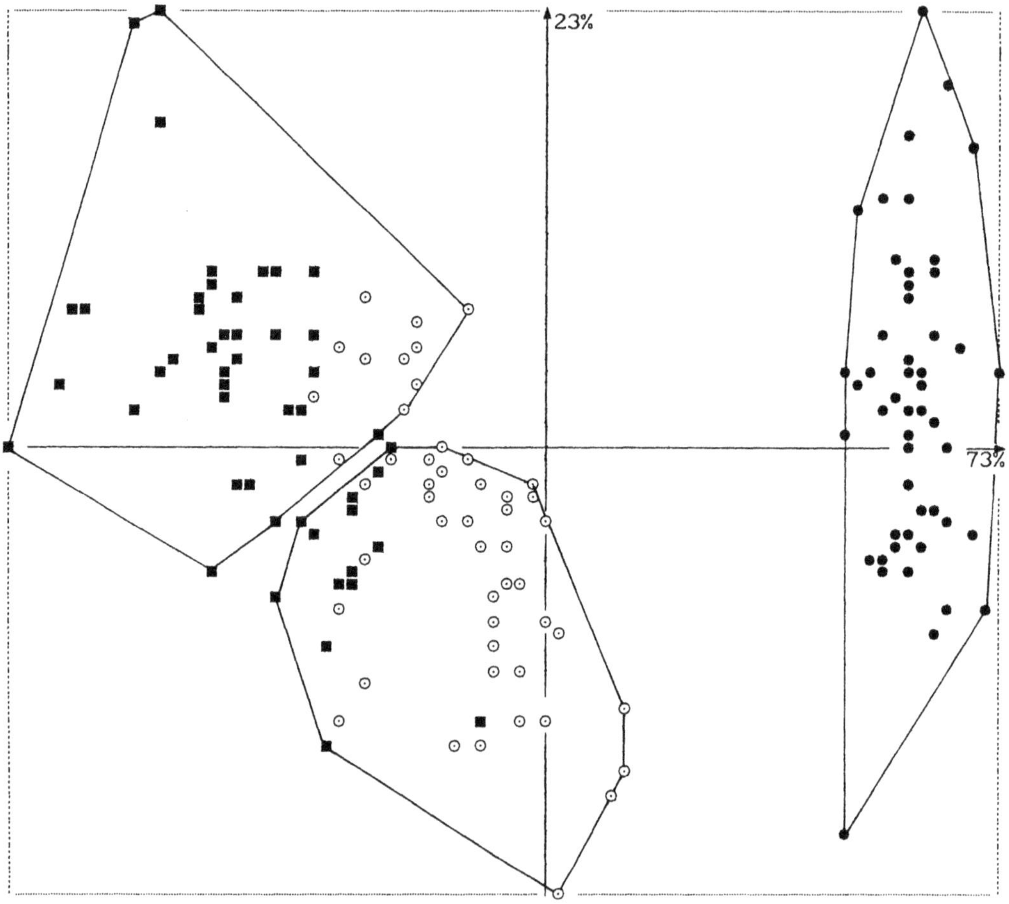

Figure 1. PCA-plot using the weights $q_{jj}=1/s_j^2$. The given clusters are marked by •, ⊙, ▪. The clusters computed by the K-means method are enclosed by lines.

An unusual high stability of a partition P(I,K) of I points into K clusters (K«I) indicates an inherent structure within the data. P(I,K) allocates an integer, the so-called class membership, to every observation i, i=1,2,...,I. Hierarchical cluster analysis computes a nested sequence of partitions.

For increasing the stability in clustering adaptive or specific metrics should be applied instead of "usual" standardizations of data (Mucha 1992c). The K-means clustering (MacQueen 1967) of the Iris-data of Fisher (1936) fails in the case of using the standard weights ($q_{jj}=1/s_j^2$ or $q_{jj}=1$) suggested by SAS, SPSS etc. (figure 1). The Iris-data consists of 3 given classes with 50 observations each. The hierarchical Ward's method fails too: 26 errors were counted. The following adaptive K-means algorithm works very well.

Starting with a random initial partition and the standard weights $q_{jj}=1/s_j^2$ (or other ones like $q_{jj}=1$) the usual K-means method computes an locally optimum partition $P^{(1)}(I,K)$ which minimizes the sum of within clusters variances

$$V_K= V(P(I,K))=\sum_{k=1}^{K}\sum_{i=1}^{I}\delta_{ik}d_Q^2(\mathbf{x}_i,\bar{\mathbf{x}}_k) \tag{2}$$

Here $\bar{\mathbf{x}}_k$ is the mean vector of cluster k, and the indicator function δ_{ik} is 1 if the observation $\mathbf{x}_i$ comes from cluster k, otherwise 0. In a repeated K-means clustering with a new random initial partition the weights

$$q_{jj}^{(1)}=1/\bar{s}_j^2 \qquad \text{with} \qquad \bar{s}_j^2=\frac{1}{I}\sum_{k=1}^{K}\sum_{i=1}^{I}\delta_{ik}^{(1)}(x_{ij}-\bar{x}_{kj}^{(1)})^2 \tag{3}$$

are used. Here $\bar{s}_j>0$, j=1,2,...,J, is the pooled standard deviation of variable j over the K clusters of the partition $P^{(1)}(I,K)$. The new locally optimum partition $P^{(2)}(I,K)$ is used in a next K-means clustering step, and so on.

In our example a stable solution (i.e. $P^{(N)}(I,K)=P^{(N+1)}(I,K)$) is reached after 5 cycles: 6 errors are counted only. The final weights q_{jj} of the variables sepal length, sepal width, pedal length, pedal width are 0.041, 0.093, 0.052, and 0.296. The corresponding standardized weights $w_j=q_{jj}s_j^2$ (see Mucha 1992a) are 2.80, 1.76, 16.2, and 17.1. They allow us to compare the importance of the variables with each other. In consequence these adaptive metrics should be used in PCA too. In that way the PCA-plots give a good support in the interpretation of results of cluster analysis (Mucha 1992b). Instead of (3) other weights like $q_{jj}=s_j^2/\bar{s}_j^2/\bar{s}_j^2$ can be used in the above algorithm.

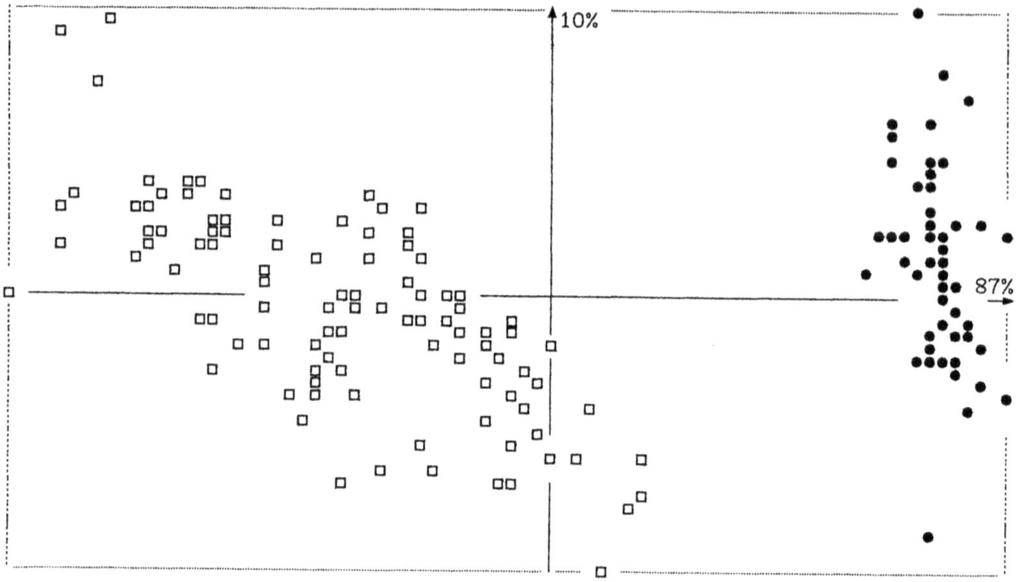

Figure 2. PCA-plot using the adaptive weights $q_{jj}=1/\bar{s}_j^2$, which are computed in the first dividing step of the adaptive hierarchical algorithm.

An Adaptive Hierarchical Divisive Algorithm

This cluster analysis starts with all I observations in one cluster $\mathbb{C}$. Afterwards the cluster $\mathbb{C}$ is divided into 2 subsets (clusters) using the adaptive K-means method described above. Successively, until some stop rules are fulfilled, the new clusters are splitted into 2 clusters each, and so on.

As an addidional result of every dividing step the adaptive weights of the variables are determined. Moreover, the weights are used in PCA after every dividing step too (figures 2 to 3). The PCA-plot of the Iris-data (figure 2) is based on the weights 0.030, 0.083, 0.022, and 0.082. Figure 3 contains the clusters after the second step: Dividing the big cluster (□) of figure 2. At this (as well as in the PCA-plot of figure 3) the observations of the cluster (•) become a supplementary status (Mucha 1992a). In order to compute figure 3 the following weights are used: 0.033, 0.111, 0.037, and 0.221.

A dynamic adaptive graphic is a sequence of pictures like figures 1 to 3, but in 3 dimensions on a color screen with interactive rotation facilities.

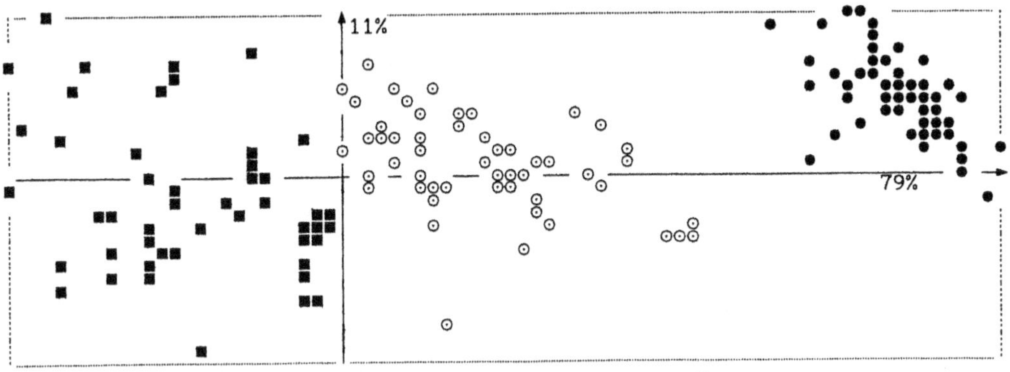

Figure 3. PCA-plot using the adaptive weights $q_{jj}=1/\bar{s}_j^2$, which are computed in the second dividing step. Six errors are counted only.

References

Fisher, R.A. (1936): The use of multiple measurements in taxonomic problems. *Ann. Eugenics 7*, 179-188

Hubert, L.J., Arabie, P. (1985): Comparing partitions. *J.Classif.2*, 193-218

Mac Queen, J.B. (1967): Some methods for classification and analysis of multivariate observations. *Proc. 5th. Berkeley Symp. Statist. and Prob.*, 287-297

Mucha, H.-J. (1992a): Clusteranalyse mit Mikrocomputern. *Akademie Verlag*, Berlin

Mucha, H.-J. (1992b): Specific Metrics for Cluster Analysis and Principal Components Analysis. In: Faulbaum,F.(Ed.): SoftStat'91 Advances in Statistical Software 3. *Gustav Fischer*, Stuttgart, 249-258

Mucha,H.-J. (1992c): Improvement of Stability in Cluster Analysis and PCA by Special Weighting the Variables. In: Gritzmann,P., Hettich,R., Horst,R., Sachs,E.(Eds.): Operations Research '91. *Physica-Verlag*, Heidelberg,351-354

Development of an Energy—Emission Model Using Fuzzy Sets

Carsten Oder, Otto Rentz
Institute for Industrial Production, University of Karlsruhe
Hertzstraße 16, 7500 Karlsruhe 21, Germany

Problem Formulation

Planning tools for the cost–efficient planning of energy supply for a whole country are widely used all over the world. Since the beginning of the 80th, these tools have been modified to allow also for a calculation of emissions related with energy supply. On the basis of these planning systems, strategies for cost–efficient emission reduction have been elaborated for many western countries (see Rentz (1990)). The model structure of those tools usually is a multiperiod linear optimization program, using the minimization of the total discounted costs of energy supply and emission reduction as a cost function. The models are driven by an exogenously given demand of final or useful energy in consecutive periods. The maximum allowed emissions E_i for $i \in \{SO_2, NO_x, CO_2\}$ in one period are also set exogenously as constraints ($e_i \leq E_i$) by the decision maker (DM), who is using the model.

His satisfaction with the solution obtained by the model will therefore be sharp and unsteady: For every e_i below the given level E_i, the DM will be totally satisfied. At the mark E_i his satisfaction jumps from 1 (i.e. totally satisfied) to 0 (i.e. totally discontented). This model behaviour is not suited to reflect the real decision situation. It is well known from empirical investigations (see Zimmermann (1982)) that the satisfaction with the attainment of a given objective declines steady between 1 and 0. There is no real reason for a DM to be absolutely contend with an e just below E but to be totaly discontend with an e only slightly above. This phenomenon of human perception can not be modeled adequately by using standard linear programming technique.

Moreover, data describing the technical details of the present state and the anticipated future developments of the energy system usually are not known in a crisp sense as it is required in traditional models. Technical details like efficiencies, market allocations or fuel input shares as well as their sulphur contents and emission factors contain an intrinsic or informational fuzziness. This is especially true if data has to be aggregated to reduce the size of the models. Special attention has to be paid if these models, which have been developed for market economies, are applied to economies in the transition from a centrally planned to a market economy. The investments to be made and the fix and variable costs to operate a power plant can not be determined like in western countries. This is not a matter of probability but they simply can not be quantified precisely because of the differences of the accounting frameworks. Therefore, a methodology is needed which is able to deal with subjective evaluations of the DM.

METHODOLOGY

The most promising mathematical approach towards a solution of the problems stated above is the theory of *fuzzy sets.* It allows for the weakening of the crisp constraints to model the human sensation appropriately by the concept of graded memberships. An element may not either belong to a set or not but it can belong to set to a certain degree between 0 and 1. For a level $e \geq E$ the DM can assign a value of 0.6 for e belonging to the set of acceptable emisisons. Here, fuzzy sets are used to extend an existing energy emission model (the EFOM–ENV model) to cope with the immanent fuzziness. According to the investigations above, the left hand side of constraints, the technology matrix and the coefficients of the goal function can consist of fuzzy sets.

The underlying crisp **E**nergy **F**low **O**ptimizing **M**odel consists of a network representation of the whole energy conversion chain, starting from the extraction and importation of primary energy, passing through intermediate energy conversion facilities (power plants, distribution grids etc.) to reach different final energy demand sectors (see Voort (1984)). The links of the network represent the flows, the nodes stand for processes of energy treatment. The variables of the model are the flows between and the production level of the processes. The main model equation is the general balance equation, balancing the input and output flows of a node taking into account the yield and losses of a process with regard to different forms of input. Besides different technical equations and restrictions, the abatement level of emissions and the cost function are of special importance. The latter consists of the resource, distribution, demand, process, fixed and investment costs for energy conversion and emisison reduction. They allow for a minimization of the total discounted costs for energy supply and attaining a fixed emmission reduction level.

By observing the different technical parameters describing the network it becomes clear that all parameters, equalities and inequalities contain an immanent fuzziness and must therefore be modeled as fuzzy sets. This especially true because of the lack of statistical data. Otherwise, probability distrubutions could be derived from large amounts of data. Here, the determination of the membership fuctions is achieved by an axiomatic model, which has been derived from the empirical found representation of human perception of vague states. The DM must give only 3 points, where he is totally content ($\mu = 1$), totally discontent ($\mu = 0$) and indifferent ($\mu = 0.5$) concerning his preferences. From these points and the underlying axioms concerning the slope of the membership function, two polynomials of 3rd degree are obtained. To this curve a logistic function ($\mu(x) = \frac{1}{1+e^{-a(x-b)}}$), which can easily be linearized, is approximated via nonlinear regression.

FUZZY LINEAR PROGRAM

The general form of the whole fuzzy linear program is therefore:

$$\begin{aligned} \widetilde{\min} \ \tilde{z}(x) &= \tilde{c}^t x \\ s.t. \ \tilde{A}x &\tilde{\leq} \tilde{b}, \qquad x \in X \end{aligned} \tag{1}$$

Like in most applications of fuzzy linear programming, the problem to be solved is the mathematical representation of the fuzzy unequalities. Therefore, it is distinguished here between technical and emission/budget limitations. Here, the technical unequalities $\tilde{A}_i x \tilde{\leq} \tilde{b}_i, i = 1 \dots r$ are modeled by the concept proposed in Slowinski (1986) using LR–representation of the fuzzy sets:

$$\underline{a}_i(x) - \Delta\underline{a}_i(x) \cdot L^{-1}(\tau) \leq b_i + \Delta\bar{b}_i \cdot L^{-1}(\tau) \qquad (2)$$

$$\bar{a}_i(x) + \Delta\bar{a}_i(x) \cdot R^{-1}(\varepsilon) \leq b_i + \Delta\bar{b}_i \cdot L^{-1}(\varepsilon) \qquad (3)$$

Via ε and τ the DM can interactively prescribe certain levels of possibility and credibility to obtain via an interactive solution procedure a more credible solution. For the restrictions concerning the emission level and the hard currency ($i = r+1 \dots s$), a different objective of the DM applies. Like stated above, he intends to increase his subjective satisfaction with the attainement of the level of total satisfaction. Therefore, they are modeled with regard to the situation proposed in the problem formulation following the concept of Rommelfanger (1988):

$$\bar{a}_i(x) + \Delta\bar{a}_i(x) \cdot R^{-1}(\varepsilon) \leq b_i + \Delta\bar{b}_i \cdot R^{-1}(\varepsilon) \qquad (4)$$

$$\mu_{R_i}(\bar{a}_i(x)) \rightarrow \max \qquad (5)$$

where

$$\mu_{R_i}(\bar{a}_i(x)) = \begin{cases} 1 & for \;\; \bar{a}_i(x) \leq b_i \\ R\left(\frac{\bar{a}_i(x) - b_i}{\Delta\bar{b}_i}\right) & for \;\; \bar{a}_i(x) > b_i \end{cases} \qquad (6)$$

The minimization of the fuzzy goal function is modeled via the concept used in Zimmermann (1978), yielding the additional four goals

$$\mu_{z_1}(\underline{c}(x)),\; \mu_{z_2}(\bar{c}(x)),\; \mu_{z_3}(\underline{c}(x) - \Delta\underline{c}(x) \cdot L^{-1}(\varepsilon)),\; \mu_{z_4}(\bar{c}(x) - \Delta\bar{c}(x) \cdot R^{-1}(\varepsilon)) \longrightarrow \max \qquad (7)$$

To obtain a compromize solution of the fromulated multi–objective decision problem, one must notice the trade–off between emissions and cost reduction. Therefore, only a compensatory aggregator (Min–bounded Sum) for the aggregation of the different membership functions $\mu_{z_1} \dots \mu_{z_4}, \mu_{R_{r+1}} \dots \mu_{R_t}$ and $\mu_{R_{t+1}} \dots \mu_{R_s}$ can be used:

$$\begin{aligned} \max \quad & \delta \cdot \min\left\{\min\left\{\mu_{z_1}, \dots, \mu_{z_4}, \mu_{R_{r+1}}, \dots, \mu_{R_t}\right\}, \min\left\{\mu_{R_{t+1}}, \dots, \mu_{R_s}\right\}\right\} + \\ & (1-\delta) \cdot \min\left\{\min\left\{\mu_{z_1}, \dots, \mu_{z_4}, \mu_{R_{r+1}}, \dots, \mu_{R_t}\right\} + \min\left\{\mu_{R_{t+1}}, \dots, \mu_{R_s}\right\}, 1\right\} \qquad (8) \\ s.t. \quad & x \in X_D \qquad (9) \end{aligned}$$

where the degree of compensation $\delta \in [0,1]$ can be set by the DM. This nonlinear program can be transformed into a standard linear program, which efficiency can be proved. A compromize solution of the problem stated above can be obtained via an interactive procedure.

Implementation

For testing the model, a small part of the whole EFOM–ENV application to Lithuania has been chosen. The model is implemented on a PC 486 using GAMS as the modeling language for linear and nonlinear optimizing problems. Summarizing the first results, one can notice that the *min–bounded sum* operator is well suited to model the underlying decision situation appropriately. If the DM is indifferent concerning the two goals emission reduction and cost minimization, he sets $\delta = 0$. The model solution is presented to the DM, where the sum of the least degrees of accomplishment of the cost and emission goal becomes maximal, i.e. the maximum acceptable exceedance of the emission level is used, if this gives an overproportional improvement of the cost goal. By rising the degree of compensation, the DM achieves a compromize solution that fits better his preferences concerning emissions and costs. A better solution can be obtained in the first step of the interactive process, if the minimum degree of possibility ε is set to $\varepsilon > 0.3$ for instance. This makes the model calculating a solution which is already more credible. By adjusting the parameters and the underlying membership functions, the DM can obtain a more and more credible solution.

References

Rentz, O., et al. (1990) *Optimal Control Strategies for Reducing Emissions from Energy Conversion and Energy Use in all Countries of the European Community*, in: KfK–PEF Schriftenreihe Nr. 72.

Rommelfanger, H. (1988) *Entscheiden bei Unschärfe*, Springer–Verlag, Berlin.

Slowinski, R. (1986) *A Multicriteria Fuzzy Linear Programming Method*, in: Fuzzy Sets and Systems 19, pp. 217–237.

Voort, van der E., et al. (1984) *Energy Supply Modelling Package EFOM–12C Mark I*, Mathematical Description, Cabay, Belgien.

Zimmermann, H.-J. (1978) *Fuzzy Programming*, in: Fuzzy Sets and Systems 1, pp. 3–28.

Zimmermann, H.-J.; Zysno, P. (1982) *Zugehörigkeitsfunktionen unscharfer Mengen*, DFG–Forschungsbericht, Aachen.

Efficient Water Management

Rüdiger Pethig
University of Siegen
Hölderlinstraße 3, 5900 Siegen, Germany

Water resources have to be managed with respect to both their quantity and quality. In its major part this paper deals with water quality management, but it also focuses on an important interface of the management of water quality and water quantity: the provision of drinking water. Throughout the paper a general equilibrium framework is applied in order to capture the main effects and feedbacks of ecological–economic interdependence.

The analysis of water quality management focuses on the basic relationships between the quality of the water resource, industrial sewage, and waste water treatment in two successive steps: intra–industrial waste abatement followed by centralized end–of–pipe purification in (public) purification plants. Purification plants are conventionally viewed as using productive factors to produce 'waste reduction'. Without any substantive change in the basic technological and ecological hypotheses we suggest to consider, instead, purification plants as firms producing water quality with both human inputs and with the water resource's assimilative capacity.

Section 2 studies a two–commodity two–factor general equilibrium model with intra––industrial waste abatement and centralized end–of–pipe purification. The water resource is used both as a waste receptor and as a 'consumption good'. Second–best policy regimes are studied which serve to implement politically predetermined water quality standards. The first strategy under scrutiny is to introduce a competitive market for assimilative services combined with cost–minimizing production of water quality. The second one consists of imposing an industrial sewage charge while the purification plant obeys a self–financing constraint in the sense of matching the plant's operating costs with the revenues from the industrial sewage charge. The allocative implications of these regimes are modeled and compared. Water quality management turns out to become inefficient by requiring to finance purification through the revenue from industrial sewage charges. It is shown, moreover, that industrial waste abatement is too low, and the waste water treatment facility operates at an inefficiently high level.

Section 3 continues to investigate the two–stage purification process. The goal of water management is again to implement a predetermined water quality standard by pricing the use of assimilative services (industrial sewage charge). But in addition an effluent charge is now levied on the purification plant for the residual waste content of the purified water which it releases into the recipient water resource. Such a charge resembles the German waste water charge (Abwasserabgabe).

The model set up in Section 2 is applied to scrutinize the joint impact of sewage and effluent charges under different institutional arrangements: Purification plants are assumed to observe a zero–surplus (or cost–covering) requirement, and/or it may be required by law that the revenues from effluent charges are earmarked in the sense that their proceeds have to be spent for subsidizing waste water treatment processes. For the case of earmarked effluent charges the analysis has to be extended to a two–region model.

If no effluent charge is levied and the regional purification plants are cost minimizers without being required to obey a cost–revenue constraint then the overall allocation of resources turns out to be efficient relative to predetermined water quality standards. An earmarked effluent charge levied on at least one of the regional purification plants does not affect the resource allocation in the absence of cost–revenue constraints, i.e. if an efficient water quality management is pursued based on sewage charges only, then the additional implementation of effluent charges – whether earmarked or not – neither detracts from nor improves upon allocative efficiency.

The results are different and more complex, however, if the regional purification plants are subject to zero–surplus constraints. We know from Section 2 that in the absence of effluent charges purification plants will operate at an inefficiently high level while the associated industrial waste abatement activities will be too low. Implementing non–earmarked effluent charges reduces this type of inefficiency. In fact, there is a tuple of positive regional effluent charges that restore efficiency.

The next step in Section 3 is to assume that the proceeds of the effluent charge are earmarked for purification (like in Germany), e.g. an effluent charge is levied on region 1's purification plant while the effluent charge revenue is redirected as a subsidy to the purification plant of region 2. In this case allocative efficiency increases in region 1 and decreases in region 2. If region 2 was already less efficient than region 1 in the zero–effluent charge situation, any positive effluent charge leads to a global net efficiency loss. Otherwise, the overall efficiency will slightly improve for low rates, but will be impaired if the effluent charge exceeds some positive threshold value.

For many uses of water resources the quantity of water is important along with water quality. A case in point is the provision of drinking water which in many countries has to be generated from polluted raw water. To keep the analysis tractable we assume that water pollution outside of water protection areas is so severe that raw water used for the generation of drinking water must exclusively be taken from these areas. The larger the body of water in that area, the higher its quality resulting from any given pollution spillover. Having in mind European countries like Germany in which water is not scarce if its quantity is considered irrespective of its quality, the central question is whether efficiency requires the price of drinking water to equal its marginal production costs in the water works or whether high quality raw water from water protection areas is a scarce resource.

Section 4 develops a general equilibrium model in which drinking water is produced from raw water with the help of labor whose productivity increases with raw water quality. Raw water quality is assumed to depend on both the size of the water protection area and on that amount of assimilative services of the raw water resource which is not used for waste assimilation.

The first basic but straightforward result is robust to different specifications of the "production technology" of raw water quality: raw water turns out to be always scarce if industrial and/or agricultural pollution does not spill over at all into the water protection area. Since, however, the complete absence of pollution spillovers is of limited empirical relevance, we proceed by assuming that pollution spillovers do occur.

In this case one can show that if the production function of raw water quality is linear homogeneous and the initial situation is a competitive equilibrium with a complete set of – partly fictitious – markets in which raw water is abundant, then raw water becomes less abundant – and possibly eventually scarce – with increasing demand for drinking water, with increasing labor endowment ('economic growth') and with decreasing land endowment. It is possible to identify certain conditions on endowments, technologies and preferences under which the efficient price of raw water is, in fact, positive.

On the other hand, if the production function of raw water quality is homogeneous of degree zero – which appears to be a plausible assumption –, then the efficient allocation cannot be decentralized by (shadow) prices. Suppose that under these conditions raw water quality is managed by a public enterprise that supplies raw water quality efficiently and free of charge. Then the implications with respect to the scarcity of raw water are similar to those under the assumption of linear homogeneous raw water quality production. In particular, conditions are identified under which raw water carries an economic rent or is abundant.

On Integrity Constraints for a Waste Management Information System

Dirk Schreiber, Manfred Grauer
Fac. of Econ., Institute for Inform. & Decision Sciences, University of Siegen
Hölderlinstr. 3, 5900 Siegen, Germany

As an introduction we start with the fact that the ministries of the environment of several states in Germany have enacted laws which force communities and enterprises to develop concepts for waste management. Information about the amount of waste (of several types), their treatment, and disposal are neccessary for generating and controlling these concepts. The project involved was initiated in 1990 to develop a waste management information system for the federal state, Lower Saxony, in Germany [HER92]. The quality of this system essentially depends on the consistency of the underlying relational database system. Many relational database management systems support simple data-type-like integrity constraints, but more complex constraints are realized only through the application programs. Such an implementation of integrity constraints has several drawbacks (e.g. in flexibility, maintenance, etc.) in comparision to coding the rules in the database scheme. The paper focuses on referential and essential semantic integrity constraints in the underlying database scheme and shows the tools applied in the database design process to model and implement these constraints. We refer to the classification of integrity constraints in [ELM89] and follow the main database design process consisting of the four phases information requirement analysis, conceptual modeling, logical design, and implementation.

In the following we will present the problem area. The information requirements are documented by a questionnaire which gathers environmental related data about a given year and a given community. Each community belongs to one of four districts. The aspect of the questionnaire analyzed in this paper gathers data about the question of how much of a particular kind of solid and semisolid wastes has been produced for a given year and a given community.

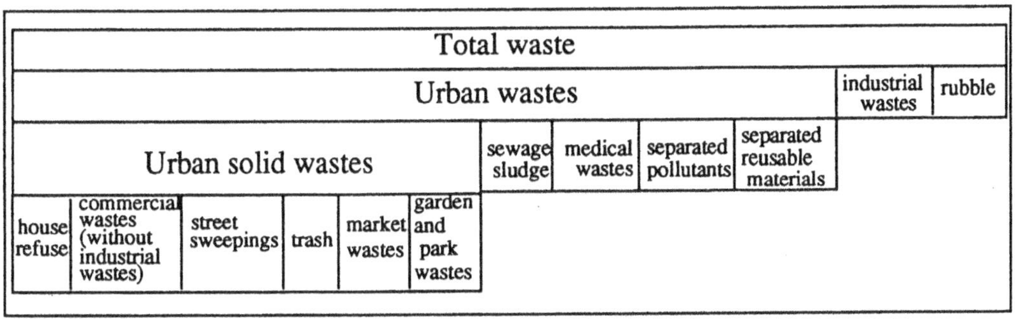

Figure: Wastes (solid and semisolid) classification of the federal state Lower Saxony (Germany)

The wastes classification of the questionnaire used is based on an order of the government of Lower Saxony, which has already classified many types of solid and semisolid wastes in the so-called "Abfallartenkatalog Niedersachsen"[ABF91]. The figure shows the classification and illustrates that some types of waste are, on the one hand, superclass of several subordinated types ,and on the other hand, subclass of another kind of waste. The classification gives a framework for a systematic aggregation of the amounts of waste types. The essential semantic integrity constraint derived from the classification is that the amount of a given kind of waste must be equal to the sum of the amounts of its subordinated waste types. So the wastes types classification includes not only a supertype/subtype, but also a kind of aggregation hierachy.

The solution approach consists of the following steps. On the conceptual level ERDRAW, a graphical X-windows based scheme specification editor to support the design of extended Entity Relationship (ER) diagrams, is used [SZE91]. These diagrams represent ER structures by directed, rather than undirected, graphs. Therefore referential integrity constraints are explicitly specified by the direction of the edges between the objects.

The design of the relational schema and its implementation by the SQL-dialect of the database management system Sybase [SYB90], has been realized by the use of SDT, a database schema design and translation tool developed at Lawrence Berkeley Laboratories [MAR91]. This tool uses an extended ER-schema designed with ERDRWAW as input and generates files containing SQL-statements for table definition, index (key) definition, and creation of triggers enforcing referential integrity constraints. The following tables are presented as an example (key attributes are underlined; references between the tables are shown by arrows):

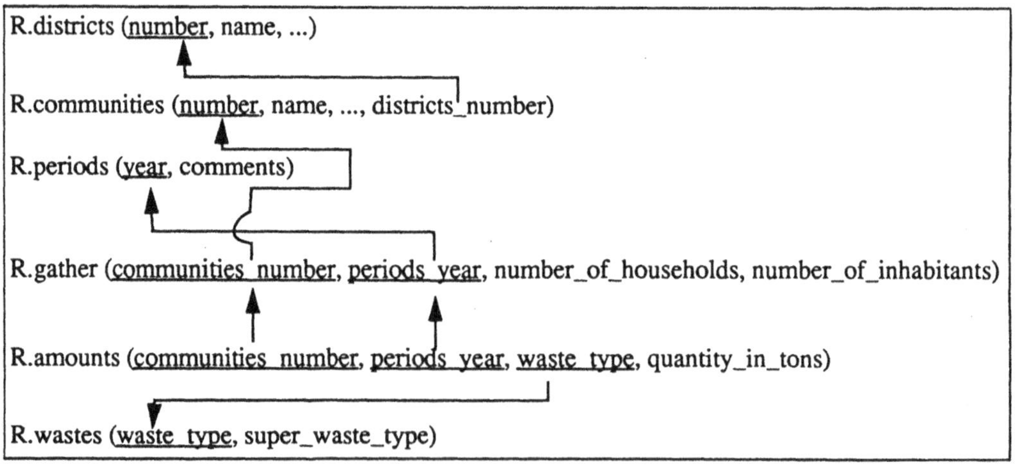

The triggers generated by SDT follow the syntax of Sybase [SYB90]. Each trigger begins with its head containing the table on which the trigger is bound and the operation which fires the trigger. Main part of the trigger is its action which is executed automatically if the operation is applied on its table. The coding of the action can be done by using procedural extensions of SQL. The trigger action normally begins with the declaration of some local variables, then it is checked by a trigger condition whether or not some referential integrity constraints are violated by the intended operation or not. This check is normally an attempt to join the tuple to be deleted, inserted, or updated with tuple in their referenced or referencing table. The number of successfully done joins is assigned to the corresponding variable by a SELECT-statement. If the operation does not violate reference integrity, it is committed, otherwise the user gets a message about the violation, a list of the tuple involved in it and the transaction containing the operation is rolled back.

The triggers of the table *amounts* enforce the aggregation hierarchy constraint by checking the following conditions:

(1) An insert-operation is committed if no subordinated waste types exist, or if the sum of the amounts of the subtypes for the community-year-combination given by the current tuple are equal to the inserted value of column *quantity_in_tons*.

(2) An update-operation is similiar to an insert. It is committed if no subordinated waste types exist, or if the sum of the amounts of the subtypes for the community-year combination given by the current tuple are equal to the inserted value in column *quantity_in_tons*.

(3) A delete-operation is committed if no subordinated waste types exist.

If the current waste type has a superclass, modifications about the amount of the superclass will be executed. If no upper waste type principally exist, the trigger stops.

We would like to add some conclusions. These parts of the trigger which are enforcing referential integrity support operations manipulating several tuples of this table simultaneously. The trigger actions enforcing the constraint of the aggregation hierarchy only work correctly when manipulating each tuple with its own SQL-statement. Therefore applications should not allow operations manipulating several tuples of table *amounts* simultaneously. The triggers work nicely because each subclass belongs to one superclass. If a subclass has multiple superclasses, the cascading modifications are more complex.

The current version of the waste management information which has been used in Lower Saxony since 1991 is implemented by the relational oriented database management system dbaseIV. The next step of the project will be the substitution of the current system by the proposed system to test the effects of the triggers under practical conditions (e.g. concerning performance, data entry facilities).

References:

[ABF91] Ausschuß von Abfällen nach § 3 Absatz 3 AbfG - Abfallartenkatalog Niedersachsen, RdErl. d. MU vom 26.06.1991 in Nds. MBl. Nummer 36/91: 1278 - 1331

[ELM89] Elmasri R, Navathe S (1989): Fundamentals of Database Systems, Benjamin Cummings, Redwood City California

[HER92] Herold H, Schreiber D (1992): DABI - ein Datenbanksystem zur Abfallbilanzierung, Abfallwirtschaftsjournal 1992 Nr. 4: 287-293

[MAR91] Markowitz V, Fang W (1991): SDT A Database Schema Design and Translation Tool, Reference Manual Draft 4.1. Technical Report LBL-27843

[SYB90] Sybase (1990):Transact-SQL User's Guide Release 4.2, Emeryville (California) May 1990

[SZE91] Szeto E, Markowitz V (1991): ERDRAW: A Graphical Schema Specification Tool, Reference Manual Draft 2.2. Technical Report Lawrence Berkeley Laboratory (LBL) PUB-3084

Design of a User—Friendly General Purpose Energy Information System

Alf Schweiker, Helmuth-Michael Groscurth, Albrecht Reuter
Inst. for Energy Econ. & the Rational Use of Energy, Univ. of Stuttgart
Pfaffenwaldring 31, 7000 Stuttgart 80, Germany

Comprehensive interdisciplinary information is needed in order to develop policies in the fields of energy management and environmental protection. A detailed analysis is required for the investigation of possible strategies of the status quo and the historical pathways that led to the present situation. Therefore, the development of a computer-based, user-friendly energy information system is necessary.

Aims

The challenging tasks of the actual environmental- and energy-discussion call for flexible structures of database-design and a guided information retrieval. Hence, the energy information system should support in its main features retrieval, combination and aggregation of data. Energy planners use in many cases PC-based instruments for data storage and evaluation. Therefore, the system should be implemented on low-cost micro- (PC-) computers. It should be easy to use for knowledge-engineers and experts in the energy sector. The system should come with data already collected about topics like energy, economy, and environmental impacts. The system should be expandable by the user.

Database Design Methods

Current paper based energy balances have a 2-dimensional tabular format whereby the rows represent energy sectors and the columns represent energy carriers (see Figure 1). The format of the energy balances is 3-dimensional because all values are time-dependent. To allow insertion into a relational database the row-number, column-number, and the year are used as coordinates for each value.

In the paper based table format there are columns containing aggregated values (=sum of other rows) together with original data. This is in conflict to standard relational theory because values in a single attribute are assigned or interpreted in two different ways. The introduction of an additional row is unavoidable to enable storage and balancing in the database.

Table 1 shows the data structure of the energy balances:

Sector (Row)	Energy-Carrier (Column)	Year	Value
2	1	1990	6030
2	2	1990	156
2	3	1990	31

Tab. 1: Data structure of energy balances

Furthermore, time series are stored in the information system using conventional database design techniques.

Implementation

For ease of programming and presenting rather fast a practical prototype within a short time, we used the commercial relational database Paradox V3.5 and the spreadsheet Quattro/Pro Version 3.0. These tools exchange data automatically and enable the user to generate reports. The excessive use of commercial packages has the additional advantage that exhausting programming of modules that are already commercially available is needless which is expecially in the case of graphics a relief. Furthermore, features of future updates of these software products can increase directly the power of the product.

First Experiences

The first phase of the project indicates that the method of rapid prototyping is useful to increase the developer's knowledge about the specific demands of the users. It reveals the structural inconsistencies in today's paper based energy balance sheets that have to be resolved in order to make them accessible with low redundancy on a PC. Therefore, a different design of balance sheets to enable consistent storage and checks is advisable in the future.

The energy planner requires different graphical ways of presenting results as stacked bar charts or the shares of the energy carriers in a specific sector as pie charts. An overview of the main tasks available and consistent with national, international, or user-defined standards demonstrates the following illustration:

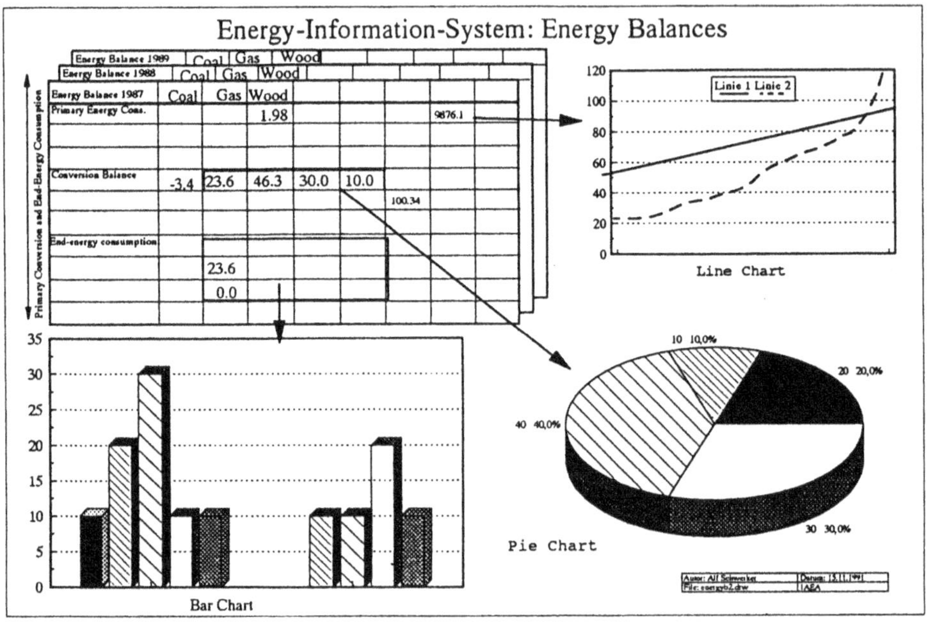

Fig. 1: Graphical representations enabled with the ENIS-System

References

Schweiker, Alf; Reuter, Albrecht; Voß, Alfred 1991: Entwicklung eines Energie informationssystems: 1. Zwischenbericht zum Forschungsbereich II "Energie - Wirtschaft - Umwelt", Institut für Energiewirtschaft u. Rationelle Energieanwendung, Stuttgart 1991

Vetter, Max 1991: Aufbau betrieblicher Informationssysteme mittels objektorientierter, konzeptioneller Datenmodellierung, B.G. Teubner, Stuttgart 1991

Interacting Environmental Influences: Concepts of Synergism, Antagonism, and Superposition

Frank Stehling, Jochen Kindorf
Abt. Wirtschaftswissenschaften, Universität Ulm
Helmholzstraße 18, 7900 Ulm, Germany

Since usually an enormous number of different pollutants is simultaneously present in environmental areas, as in the atmosphere, water, and soil, it must be expected that interactions between at least some of these pollutants may occur. Though some examples of such effects have been observed and reported in the literature not very much is known about the combined impact of several pollutants and the environmental policy ignores these effects in defining pollution standards and limits just for single pollutants. Whereas the terms "synergism" or "synergistic effects" are frequently used in different and vague meanings in the literature, there is a remarkable lack of precise definitions of these terms. Starting from definitions of interactions introduced by Ott [1978] and Stehling [1987] a variety of precise concepts of synergism, antagonism, and superposition for two and more interacting influences will be presented in a deterministic context. Furthermore, it will be analysed which properties a function has to have in order to describe such interactions.

It is assumed that the effect of n variables ("pollutants"), measured in non–negative, real–valued quantities $x_1,...,x_n$ ("concentrations"), can be described by a real–valued deterministic function $D: \mathbb{R}^n_+ \longrightarrow \mathbb{R}$. D may be interpreted as a damage function or as a dose–response function or as an index measuring the quality of an environmental area. For the sake of simplification we choose in what follows the first interpretation. For $\Delta x_i > 0$ let us introduce the following notations:

$$\Delta D_i \ := D(x_1,...,x_i+\Delta x_i,...,x_n) - D(x_1,...,x_i,...,x_n)\ ,$$

$$\Delta D_{ij} \ := D(x_1,...,x_i+\Delta x_i,...,x_j+\Delta x_j,...,x_n) - D(x_1,...,x_i,...,x_j,...,x_n);$$

analogously, ΔD_{ijk} and similar terms are defined; denote by D_{x_i} the partial derivative of D with resp. to x_i, with $D_{x_ix_j}$ the second partial derivative of D with resp. to x_i and x_j and analogously for similar expressions.

If D depends only on two possibly interacting variables there are two simple ways to define interactive effects:

Def. (2–SYN A): Synergism (antagonism, superposition) between x_1 and x_2 prevails if

$$D(x_1,x_2) \underset{(\leqq)}{>} D(x_1,0) + D(0,x_2)\,,$$

where the <–sign holds in the case of an antagonism and the =–sign in the case of superposition.

Def. (2–SYN B): For $x_1>0$, let $x_2>0$ be chosen in such a way that $D(x_1,0) = D(0,x_2)$. Synergism (antag., superpos.) between x_1 and x_2 prevails if for all $\lambda>0$ with $0<\lambda<1$

$$D(x_1,0) = D(0,x_2) \underset{(\leqq)}{>} D(\lambda x_1,(1-\lambda)x_2)\,.$$

Particularly for empirical purposes these definitions are not very useful. It seems much better to define the interactive effects by increments as it is done in the following way which has a clear interpretation:

Def. (2–Syn C): Synergism (antag., superpos.) between x_1 and x_2 if for all (sufficiently small) $\Delta x_1, \Delta x_2>0$

$$\Delta D_{12} \underset{(\leqq)}{>} \Delta D_1 + \Delta D_2\,.$$

The following can be proved:

Theorem 1: Let D be twice continuously partially differentiable with resp. to x_1 and x_2.

a) $D_{x_1x_2} = D_{x_2x_1} \underset{(<)}{>} 0$ implies that D describes synergism (antag.) between x_1 and x_2 in the sense of 2–SYN C. Conversely, if D describes synergism (antag.) between x_1 and x_2 in the sense of 2–SYN C then, $D_{x_1x_2} = D_{x_2x_1} \underset{(\leqq)}{\geqq} 0$.

b) $D_{x_1x_2} = D_{x_2x_1} = 0$ everywhere implies that D describes superposition between x_1 and x_2 in the sense of 2–SYN C.

Whereas 2–SYN A and 2–SYN B can be generalized in an easy and unique way to the case of three and more interacting variables there are different possibilities for a generalization of 2–SYN C. In the case of three interacting variables one possibility is:

<u>Def. (3–SYN C1):</u> Synergism (antag., superpos.) between the first three variables x,y,z prevails if for all (sufficiently small) $\Delta x, \Delta y, \Delta z > 0$

$$\Delta D_{123} \underset{(\leqq)}{>} \Delta D_1 + \Delta D_2 + \Delta D_3 .$$

A consequence for the functional form of D is

<u>Theorem 2:</u> Let D be three times continuously partially differentiable with resp. to the first three variables x,y,z. If synergism (antagonism)) between x,y,z prevails in the sense of 3–SYN C1 then,

$$D_{xy} + D_{yz} + D_{zx} \underset{(\leqq)}{\geqq} 0 .$$

An alternative generalization is

<u>Def. (3–SYN C2):</u> Synergism (antag.,superp.) between the first three variables x,y,z prevails if for all (sufficiently small) $\Delta x, \Delta y, \Delta z > 0$ simultaneously $\Delta D_{123} > \Delta D_{12} + \Delta D_{3},$ $\Delta D_{123} > \Delta D_{23} + \Delta D_{1}$, $\Delta D_{123} > \Delta D_{13} + \Delta D_{2}$.

As a consequence, we have

<u>Theorem 3:</u> Let D be three times continuously partially differentiable with resp. to the first three variables x,y,z. If synergism (antagonism) between x,y,z prevails in the sense of 3–SYN C2 then simultaneously $D_{xz} + D_{yz} \underset{(\leqq)}{\geqq} 0$, $D_{yx} + D_{zx} \underset{(\leqq)}{\geqq} 0$, $D_{xy} + D_{zy} \underset{(\leqq)}{\geqq} 0$.

The difference in the two definitions of a triple synergism is the following: In the first definition the combined effect ΔD_{123} of the whole set {1,2,3} of all three variables is compared with the sum of the additional effects of the special partition P_1={{1},{2},{3}}; in 3–SYN C2, ΔD_{123} is compared with the sums of the additional effects of the partitions P_2={{1,2},{3}}, P_3={{1},{2,3}}, and P_4={{1,3},{2}}. Since it seems to be rather arbitrary to pick out only special partitions for these comparisons it is suggested to consider all partitions which is done in the following general

Def. (m–SYN): Let $P = \{S_1,\ldots,S_{l(P)}\}$ be an arbitrary partition of the set $\{x_1,\ldots,x_m\}$ of $m \leqq n$ variables. Denote by ΔD_{S_i} the additional damage caused by the simultaneous (sufficiently small) increments of the variables in S_i. A proper m–synergism (m–antag., m–superpos.) of $x_1,\ldots,x_m$ prevails if for all partitions $P \neq \{\{x_1,\ldots,x_m\}\}$ of $\{x_1,\ldots,x_m\}$

$$\Delta D_{\{x_1,\ldots,x_m\}} \underset{(\leqq)}{>} \sum_{S_i \in P} \Delta D_{S_i} .$$

The advantage of this definition is that a proper m–synergism cannot be generated already by a synergism of a proper subgroup of variables. The disadvantage is that the number of comparisons which have to be make in order to decide whether an m–synergism actually prevails increases enormously with the number $B^*(m)$ of partitions of a set of m elements.

In the final section, as an application, an empirical example (see Adaros et al. [1991]) is presented which shows that under specific conditions certain plants (wheat and barley) respond sometimes in a synergistic way and sometimes in an antagonistic way if exposed to the pollutants O_3, SO_2, and NO_2.

References:

Adaros G, Weigel HJ, Jäger HJ (1991): Concurrent exposure to SO_2 and/or NO_2 alters growth and yield responses of wheat and barley to low concentrations of O_3. New Phytologist 118: 581–591.

Ott WR (1978): Environmental Indices. Theory and Practice. Ann Arbor.

Stehling F (1987): Environmental Quality Indices: Problems, Concepts, Examples. In: Eichhorn W (1987): Measurement in Economics. Heidelberg. 349–369.

Multiobjective Decision Making in Forest Management

Lidija Zadnik Stirn
Biotechnical Faculty, Dept. of Forestry, University of Ljubljana
Večna pot 83, 61000 Ljubljana, Slovenia

Forest is a renewable natural resource with an extremely large production period and of multiple-use. It is of economic, environmental and social interest as it provides not only forest products but also public benefits. So the decision makers must make forest management decisions which maximize sustained timber production and the net returns to the society at the same time. The forest managers tend to think of sustainability in terms of production levels, i. e. what level of harvest will ensure a sustained yield of timber and will not diminish noncommodity resources such as recreation, water, wildlife, etc.

To assist the search for optimal decision making in forest management and to provide a basis for planning the operations in a forest enterprise a long term discrete dynamic multiobjective model is generated where an interactive multiobjective programming approach is introduced in the N stage dynamic problem in order to select the best decisions in each stage.

THE METHOD

In the model the time horizon of the forest planning process is made discrete, that is, it is divided into stages t of the same length. The number of stages is N, (t=1,2,...,N). The managed forest is presented as a discrete system in time. The state of the system in stage t, signed with $\underline{s}_m(t)$, is defined as a vector with components which present the properties of the elements which compound the forest. Such properties are for example the

growing stock, tree growth capacity, the quality of tree species, etc. The function of each property is finite and discrete and as there is a finite number of properties taken into account, there exists a finite number of possible states $\underline{s}_m(t)$, let us say, M states in each stage t: $(m=1,2,...,M)$, $\underline{s}_m(t) \in S(t)$, $S(t) = (\underline{s}_1(t),...,\underline{s}_M(t))$. The transition from the state $\underline{s}_m(t)$ to the state $\underline{s}_n(t+1)$, $(n=1,2,...,M)$, in stage t determined by a transition function f is described in details by Zadnik (1990):
$\underline{s}_n(t+1) = f(\underline{s}_m(t),\underline{d}_i(\underline{s}_m(t)))$ where $\underline{d}_i(\underline{s}_m(t))$ is the control vector and presents all possible forest management decisions as the quantity of harvesting or thinning, clear cut, exchange of the existing tree species with a new one, etc. which can be undertaken in the forest with the state $\underline{s}_m(t)$. There exists a finite discrete set D of decisions $\underline{d}_i(\underline{s}_m(t)) \in D$ in each stage t and at each state $\underline{s}_m(t)$, let us say, I decisions, $(i=1,2,...,I)$. The decisions are mutually exclusive, what means that in each stage t and at each forest state $\underline{s}_m(t)$ only one decision $\underline{d}_i(\underline{s}_m(t)) \in D$ can be taken. Which decision is going to be chosen depends upon the objective functions $z_k(\underline{s}_m(t), \underline{d}_i(\underline{s}_m(t)))$ such as net revenue from timber harvest and inventory volume, water quality, protection of wildlife, preservation of natural beauty, recreational opportunities, etc., $(k=1,2,...,K)$, which the decision maker is going to maximize in each stage t and at each forest state $\underline{s}_m(t)$.

The general problem of the presented model can be expressed as:

$$\max_{\underline{d}_i(...)} \sum_{t=1}^{N} Z(\underline{s}_m(t),\underline{d}_i(\underline{s}_m(t))) \tag{1}$$

subject to $\underline{s}_n(t+1) = f(\underline{s}_m(t),\underline{d}_i(\underline{s}_m(t)))$,

for $t=1,2,..,N$; $m=1,2,...,M$; $n=1,2,...,M$; $i=1,2,...,I$

where $Z(\underline{s}_m(t),\underline{d}_i(\underline{s}_m(t)))$ is a vector valued function consisting of the objective functions $z_k(\underline{s}_m(t),\underline{d}_i(\underline{s}_m(t)))$, $\underline{d}_i(\underline{s}_m(t))) \in D$ are the decision variables and the constraint set on the decision variables is empirically defined with all possible state transitions.

The problem (1) is a problem of a discrete deterministic dynamic programming in which at each stage the multiple criteria problem should be solved. For this purpose many previous approaches to multiple criteria problems were studied. A survey of a number of such methods is given by Dyer et al.(1992). For the purpose of the problem (1) used in forest decision making we propose the method ICOR (Iterative Compromise Ranking) as presented by Opricović (1989) because we think that it is easily used and workable in practice. Further statements require additional studies. After determining the optimal sequence of decisions by the use of a multicriteria method at each stage of the forest decision process the idea of Bellman's principle of optimality presented by Bellman (1957) can be used on problem (1).

Great attention was paid to the estimation of objective functions. For this purpose the models developed by Bare et al. (1988), Bergen et al.(1992) and Zadnik (1992) were used. The proposed model was because of the great number of empirically defined data and of the comprehension of the variables (M,N,I are large numbers) not yet applied to a real forest process. We did some experiments and results comparison with examples presented in above mentioned papers. This work confirms that the quality of the forest decisions on the base of a proposed model is highly dependent upon the science which produces the input data of the model.

REFERENCES

Bellman R (1957) Dynamic programming. Princeton Univ. Press. Princeton, NJ

Bare B, Mendoza G (1988) Multiple objective forest land management planning. European Journal of Oper. Research 34: 44-55

Bergen V, Brabaender H, Bitter A, Loewenstein W (1992) Monaetere Bewertung landeskultureller Leistungen der Forstwirtschaft. Sauerl. Verlag. Frankfurt

Dyer J, Fishburn P, Steuer R, Wallenius J, Zionts S (1992) Multiple criteria decision making, multiattribute utility theory. Management Science 38/5: 645-654

Opricović S (1989) Kriterijumi odlučivanja u metodama za višekriterialno rangiranje IKOR i PROMETHEE. Zbornik radova. SYMOPIS'89. Naučna knjiga. Beograd: 577-580

Zadnik L (1990) Adaptive dynamic model for optimal forest management. Forest Ecology and Management 31: 167-188

Zadnik L (1992) Combinatorial optimization in a long term forest management process. Mathematical Modelling of Forest Ecosystems, ed.Franke J, Roeder A. Sauerl.Verlag. Frankfurt: 168-174

Section 1

Mathematical Modeling in OR

On Some Solution Method of Certain Type of Allocation Problems

Zoltán M. Farkas
Statistical Institute
Kárpát utca 17, 1133 Budapest, Hungary

Let us assume that a compound production system consists of an n number of production subsystems or equipments and that all of them can be modelled and characterised by certain parameters that determine some development state level of them (such levels may be their productivities, reliabilities, etc.)

Let us further assume that by means of a planned development we want to increase above type original level to a higher one, by using a given amount of resources for it and allocating them among subsystems.

A question arises as follows: how can be allocated resources optimally, if we cannot give explicitly any evaluation (that means: explicit objective function) for it that measures costs needed for this development, only some well-defined properties (based on some assumptions) are known for its characterization.

This paper gives a possible approach of modelling and solution for above type of allocation problems that leads to an optimum-invariant property of synthesis of decisions, made for an optimal allocation of some given amount of resources among subsystems. Results to be presented are some generalizations of the Author's earlier results (see REFERENCES).

A POSSIBLE SOLUTION METHOD FOR THE ABOVE OPTIMIZATION PROBLEM

Let there be given strictly monotonous incresing and continuous function $x = g(s)$ defined on the set $S \subset R^n$ and let there be given values s_i^o, x_i^o further consider variables s_i, x_i as follow:

$g(s_i) = x_i$, $g(s_i^o) = x_i^o$ and $x_i \geqslant x_i^o$ for $i=1,2,\ldots,n$;

We may assume (without loss of generality) order as follows:

$$x_1^o \leq x_2^o \leq \ldots \leq x_{n-1}^o \leq x_n^o$$

Let us examine optimization problem as follows:

$$P(s_1^o, s_2^o, \ldots, s_n^o) = \min_{\{s_i\}_1^n} \left\{ \sum_{i=1}^n p_i f(s_i) \mid \sum_{i=1}^n p_i g(s_i) = b, \text{ where } p_i \geq 0, \sum_1^n p_i = 1, g(s_i^o) \leq g(s_i), i=1,\ldots,n \right\}$$

where s_i is state development level of i-th subsystem further h is an arbitrary (not necessarily explicitly known) strictly monotonous increasing convex function that defines evaluation of costs needed for development of the i-th subsystem in such a way that these costs are equal to the differences

$h(g((s_i)) - h(g(s_i^o))$, where $h(g(s_i)) = f(s_i)$, $i = 1,2,\ldots,n$.

Let us consider recursively given series (k=1,...,n-1):

$$S_1 = \sum_{i=1}^n p_i g(s_i^o), \qquad S_{k+1} = (g(s_{k+1}^o) - g(s_k^o)) \sum_{i=1}^k p_i + S_k$$

and let there be defined an index m such for that $S_m < b \leq S_{m+1}$

Statement: optimization problem P on certain conditions can be solved without explicit knowledge of objective function and solution is as follows:

$$s_i^* = \begin{cases} g^{-1}\left(\dfrac{\sum_{i=1}^m p_i g(s_i^o)}{\sum_{i=1}^m p_i}\right), & \text{if } i \leq m \\ s_i^o & \text{, if } i > m \end{cases} \qquad i=1,2,\ldots,n$$

Consequences: 1. If s_i determine and $g(s_i)$ measures development level of i-th subsystem and f( ) measures development cost needed for a possible development of the whole system subsystems by subsystem, then above method gives a solution of allocation problem defined in the introductory part.

2. This solution is independent from function h (and therefore f), consquently has an optimum-invariant property of synthesis of decisions needed for solution of above mentioned problem.

REFERENCES

Mitten L G (1964) Composition Principles of Synthesis of Optimal Multistage Processes. Operations Research 12: 610-619

Farkas Z (1978) A general application of the method "Optimization with Minimal Information - OMI" to allocation problems (Hungarian with Russian and English resumes). MTA SZTAKI Közlemények (Proc. of Computer and Automation Inst. Hung. Academy of Sciences) 20: 53-69

Farkas Z (1980) Solution of a modified transportation problem with penalty function by the method "OMI". Methods of Operations Research 40: 85-88

Farkas Z (1986) On some Systems Theoretical Aspects of Modelling and Solution of Compound Decision Systems. Methods of Operations Research 53: 399-410

Aczél J, Alsina C (1987) Synthesizing Judgements: A Functional Equation Approach. Math. Modelling 9: 311-320

Farkas Z (1987) An optimal allocation of investment for some development of compound decision systems. Methods of Operations Research 57: 11-12

Farkas Z (1989) On some extension of quasi-arithmetic means and their connection with solution of certain decision problems. Methods of Operations Research 60: 325-326

Farkas Z (1990) On an Optimum-invariance Property of Synthesizing Judgements: a Decision Model Approach. Methods of Operations Research 63: 265-268

Generalized Monotone Maps

Siegfried Schaible
Graduate School of Management, University of California
Riverside, CA 92521, U.S.A.

Generalized convex functions have been introduced, among others, to analyze nonconvex mathematical programming problems. Generalized monotone maps play a role in the study of nonmonotone complementarity problems and variational inequality problems.

In this survey, we present various kinds of generalized monotone maps as introduced recently by S. Karamardian and S. Schaible. Quasimonotone, pseudomonotone, strictly pseudomonotone and strongly pseudomonotone maps are considered. It turns out that in the special case of a gradient map, generalized monotonicity of the gradient corresponds to generalized convexity of the underlying function; i.e., a quasimonotone gradient is equivalent to a quasiconvex function etc. With this, we have extended the theory of generalized convex functions by introducing pure first-order characterizations of generalized convexity.

In case of differentiable maps, necessary as well as sufficient conditions for various kinds of generalized monotonicity have been obtained in collaboration with S. Karamardian and subsequently with J.P. Crouzeix. These extend classical second-order characterizations of generalized convex functions. The analysis is based on the study of the geometrical properties of one-dimensional generalized monotone maps. These have also been the starting-point of related work on generalized monotonicity by E. Castagnoli and P. Mazzoleni. We mention that nondifferentiable generalized monotone maps have recently been characterized by S. Komlosi using directional Dini-derivatives.

The criteria for differentiable generalized monotone maps reduce to simpler and more elegant ones in case of affine maps. These results can be considered as extensions of classical characterizations of generalized convex quadratic functions. In another paper, R. Pini and S. Schaible discuss various invariance properties of generalized monotone maps with an emphasis on the affine case. Among others, generalized monotone matrices are studied.

In a final section, generalized monotone matrices are related to the class of sufficient matrices recently introduced in complementarity theory. These results on the relationship of the two classes of matrices are due to M.S. Gowda.

In summary, we introduce in this paper to generalized monotonicity and demonstrate its relevance to a) the theory of generalized convex functions, b) the analysis of complementarity problems and variational inequality problems, and c) matrix analysis.

Avriel M, Diewert W E, Schaible S, Zang I (1988) Generalized concavity. Plenum Publishing Corporation. New York

Castagnoli E, Mazzoleni P (1989) Order-preserving functions and generalized convexity. Presented at the International Workshop on Generalized Convexity and Fractional Programming. University of California, Riverside

Gowda M S (1990) Affine pseudomonotone mappings and the linear complementarity problem. SIAM Journal of Matrix Analysis and Applications

Karamardian S, Schaible S (1990) Seven kinds of monotone maps. Journal of Optimization Theory and Applications 66:37-46

Karamardian S, Schaible S, Crouzeix J P (1992) Characterizations of generalized monotone maps. Journal of Optimization Theory and Applications. To appear

Komlosi S (1991) Generalized monotonicity of generalized derivatives. Janus Pannonius University, Pécs/Hungary

Section 2

Stochastic Models of OR

Combinatorial Approach to an r-node Tandem Queue

Walter Böhm
Dept. of Math. Statistics, University of Economics
Augasse 2-6, 1090 Wien, Austria
S.G. Mohanty
McMaster University, Hamilton
J.L. Lain
University of New Delhi, New Delhi

Introduction

Consider an r- node tandem queueing model, $r > 1$, subject to the following assumptions:

- customers arrive at the first node according to a Poisson process with rate λ
- the service times at node $i, 0 \leq i \leq r$ are i.i.d. random variables having an exponential distribution with mean $1/\mu_i$
- the service times at various nodes and interarrival times are independent
- initially there are $m_i > 0$ customers waiting at node i

Let $Q_i(t)$ denote the number of customers at node i (including the one being served) at time t and let $T_i = \inf\{t : Q_i(t) = 0\}$. For notational convenience we introduce the vectors $\mathbf{Q}(t) = (Q_1(t), Q_2(t), \ldots, Q_r(t))$, $\mathbf{m} = (m_1, m_2, \ldots, m_r)$,$\mathbf{k} = (k_1, k_2, \ldots, k_r), k_i > 0$ and define $T = \min(T_1, T_2, \ldots, T_r)$.

Massey (1987) published a paper in which he derived by operator analytic methods various expressions of the zero avoiding transition probabilities

$$q_t(\mathbf{m}, \mathbf{k}) = P(\mathbf{Q}(t) = \mathbf{k}, T > t | \mathbf{Q}(0) = \mathbf{m}), \tag{1}$$

in terms of lattice Bessel functions of rank r. Unfortunately it turns out the the representation of $q_t(\mathbf{m}, \mathbf{k})$ in terms of lattice Bessel functions is not very well suited for numerical computation, since the numerical determination of $q_t(\mathbf{m}, \mathbf{k})$ requires the evaluation of $(r+1)!$ lattice Bessel functions, which is a rather time consuming task even for moderate values of r. In this paper we give an alternative derivation of $q_t(\mathbf{m}, \mathbf{k})$ by purely combinatorial arguments which in addition to being conceptually simple, have the appealing property of giving rise to an efficient numerical technique.

Combinatorial approach

Proposition 1 *Let $N(r;\mathbf{a},\mathbf{b})$ denote the number of r-dimensional lattice paths from the point $\mathbf{a} = (a_1, a_2, \ldots, a_r)$ to the point $\mathbf{b} = (b_1, b_2, \ldots, b_r)$ such that every lattice point $(x_1, x_2, \ldots, x_r)$ on the paths satisfies the condition $x_1 \geq x_2 \geq \ldots \geq x_r$. Then*

$$N(r;\mathbf{a},\mathbf{b}) = \left(\sum_{\nu=1}^{r}(b_\nu - a_\nu)\right)! \|c_{ij}\|_{r\times r},$$

where $\|c_{ij}\|_{r\times r}$ is the $r \times r$ determinant with $(i,j)-th$ element given by

$$c_{ij} = \frac{1}{(b_i - a_j - i + j)!} \qquad i,j = 1,2,\ldots,r$$

This proposition can be restated as an $r-$candidate ballot problem and is treated in McMahon's book (1915, p. 133). Other references are Barton and Mallows (1965), Watanabe and Mohanty (1987) and Zeilberger (1983).

Let the point of time where there is either an arrival or a service completion be called an instant. Denote by α_{0j} and $\alpha_{ij}, i = 1,2,\ldots,r$ the number of customers arrived at instant j at the first node and the number of units served at the $i-$th node at instant j, respectively. Since the arrival- and departure processes are Poisson, it follows that $\alpha_{ij} = 0$ or 1 for all $i = 1,2,\ldots,r$ and $\sum_{i=0}^{r}\alpha_{ij} = 1$. Let us assume further that the total number of instants up to time t is equal to N. The event corresponding to $q_t(\mathbf{m},\mathbf{k})$, viz.

$$\{\mathbf{Q}(t) = \mathbf{k}, T > t|\mathbf{Q}(0) = \mathbf{m}\}$$

can occur only if at any node i and for all instants $\nu = 1,2,\ldots,N$ the number of departures is strictly less than the number of arrivals plus the number of customers waiting at time zero. In other words

$$m_i + \sum_{\ell=1}^{\nu}\alpha_{i-1,\ell} > \sum_{\ell=1}^{\nu}\alpha_{i,\ell},$$

or equivalently

$$m_i - 1 + \sum_{\ell=1}^{\nu}\alpha_{i-1,\ell} \;\geq\; \sum_{\ell=1}^{\nu}\alpha_{i,\ell} \qquad \text{for} \quad i = 1,2,\ldots,r; \nu = 1,2,\ldots,N \tag{3}$$

Let us now assume that in $(0,t)$ in total n customers arrive at node 1. Thus

$$\sum_{\ell=1}^{N}\alpha_{0,\ell} = n. \tag{4}$$

Since at time t the number of customers waiting at node i is equal to k_i, we have

$$m_i + \sum_{\ell=1}^{N}\alpha_{i-1,\ell} - \sum_{\ell=1}^{N}\alpha_{i,\ell} = k_i,$$

which together with (4) yields

$$\sum_{\ell=1}^{N} \alpha_{i,\ell} = n + \sum_{j=1}^{i}(m_j - k_j) \qquad \text{for } i = 1,2,\ldots,r. \tag{5}$$

If we set

$$x_{i,\nu} = \sum_{j=i+1}^{r}(m_j - 1) + \sum_{\ell=1}^{\nu} \alpha_{i,\ell} = x_{r,\nu} = \sum_{\ell=1}^{\nu} \alpha_{r,\ell}$$
$$i = 0,1,\ldots,r-1; \quad \nu = 1,2,\ldots,N$$

and

$$\mathbf{x}_0 = (x_{00}, x_{10}, \ldots, x_{r,0}) = \left(\sum_{j=1}^{r}(m_j - 1), \sum_{j=2}^{r}(m_j - 1), \ldots, m_r - 1, 0\right)$$

then relations (3) and (5) become

$$x_{0\nu} \geq x_{1\nu} \geq \ldots \geq x_{r\nu}, \qquad \nu = 0,1,\ldots,N, \tag{6}$$

with $\mathbf{x}_N = (x_{0,N}, x_{1,N}, \ldots, x_{r,N})$ given by

$$x_{i,N} = \sum_{j=i+1}^{r}(m_j - 1) + \sum_{\ell=1}^{N} \alpha_{i,\ell} = n - r + i + \sum_{j=1}^{r} m_j - \sum_{j=1}^{i} k_j, \qquad i = 0,1,\ldots,r$$

where an empty sum has to be interpreted as zero. It follows that the number of sequences $\mathbf{x}_\nu, \nu = 0,1,\ldots,N$, satisfying (6) is $N(r+1;\mathbf{x}_0,\mathbf{x}_N)$.

Consider now the superposition of the arrival process at node 1 and the departure processes at nodes $1,2,\ldots,r$. This process is Poisson with intensity

$$\delta = \lambda + \sum_{i=1}^{r} \mu_i.$$

In $(0,t)$ the process has a total number of jumps equal to

$$N = \sum_{i=0}^{r}\sum_{\ell=1}^{N} \alpha_{i,\ell} = (r+1)n + \sum_{i=1}^{r}(r-i+1)(m_i - k_i) \tag{7}$$

The (conditional) probability that a jump corresponds to an arrival at node 1 equals λ/δ, and that it corresponds to a departure at node i equals $\mu_i/\delta, i = 1,2,\ldots,r$. Thus

$$q_t(\mathbf{m},\mathbf{k}) = e^{-\delta t} \sum_{n \geq 0} \frac{(\delta t)^N}{N!} \left(\frac{\lambda}{\delta}\right)^{\sum \alpha_{0,\ell}} \prod_{i=1}^{r} \left(\frac{\mu_i}{\delta}\right)^{\sum \alpha_{i,\ell}} N(r+1;\mathbf{x}_0,\mathbf{x}_N)$$

If we set

$$\beta_r = \prod_{i=1}^{r} \mu_i^{\sum_{j=1}^{i}(m_j - k_j)}, \quad \gamma_r = \lambda \prod_{i=1}^{r} \mu_i,$$

then using Proposition 1 we find after some simplification finally

Theorem 1

$$q_t(\mathbf{m},\mathbf{k}) \;=\; e^{-\delta t}\beta_r \sum_{n\geq 0} t^N \gamma_r^n C(n,r;\mathbf{m},\mathbf{k}) \tag{8}$$

where $C(n,r;\mathbf{m},\mathbf{k})$ is an $(r+1)\times(r+1)$ determinant, whose entries are given by

$$c_{ij} = \frac{1}{(n+\sum_{\nu=1}^{j} m_\nu - \sum_{\nu=1}^{i} k_\nu)!}, \qquad i,j = 0,1,\ldots,r, \tag{9}$$

where an empty sum has to be interpreted as zero and N is given in (7).

Discussion

Let us now discuss shortly some algorithmic aspects of (7). If we expand the determinant $C(n,r;\mathbf{m},\mathbf{k})$, then it can be shown, that (8) is proportional to the sum of $(r+1)!$ lattice Bessel functions of rank r. Thus there is no substantial difference in the convergence properties of (8) and the representation of $q_t(\mathbf{m},\mathbf{k})$ given by Massey (1987). However, from a computational point of view, formula (8) is preferable, because the number of floating point operations required to evaluate a determinant of order $(r+1)\times(r+1)$ is $O((r+1)^3)$, if we use a Gaussian procedure. This should be seen in contrast to the formulas given by Massey, which require the evaluation of $(r+1)!$ lattice Bessel functions of rank r.

References

[1] Barton D.E., Mallows C.L. (1965) Some Aspects of a random sequence. *Ann. Math. Stat.*, **36**, 236-260.

[2] Massey W.A. (1987) Calculating exit times for series Jackson networks. *J. Appl. Prob.*,**27**, 226-234.

[3] McMahon P.A. (1915) *Combinatory Analysis*, Vol. 1, Cambridge University Press, London.

[4] Watanabe T., Mohanty S.G. (1987) On an inclusion-exclusion formula based on the reflection principle. *Discrete Math.*, **64**, 281-288.

[5] Zeilberger D. (1983) Andre's reflection proof generalized to the many candidate ballot problem. *Discrete Math.*,**44**, 325-326.

Individual Blocking Probabilities in the Loss System $\mathrm{GI} + M|\vec{M}|N|0$

Andreas Brandt
Fachbereich Mathematik, Humboldt-Universität zu Berlin
Postfach 1297, 1086 Berlin, Germany

The traffic offered to service facilities in modern ISDN networks is, in general, a superposition of different traffic streams, where the holding times may depend on the type of traffic. The question of determining the individual blocking probabilities for the different types of traffic is of practical importance, since they may vary considerably. In the first part of the paper we give an analysis of the $GI+M|\vec{M}|N|0$ system. By $GI+M|\vec{M}|N|0$ we denote an N server loss system where the input is a superposition of a renewal process (type 1 customers) with interarrival distribution $A(t)$ and mean $\lambda_1^{-1} = \int_0^\infty (1-A(t))dt$ and a Poisson process (type 2 customers) with intensity λ_2. The type 1 (type 2) customers require an exponentially distributed service time with parameter $\mu_1(\mu_2)$. Let $X_i(t)$ be the number of type i customers at t and $\underline{X}(t) = (X_1(t), X_2(t))$ the vector of type 1 and type 2 customers. The state space $\mathbf{X}$ has the partition $\mathbf{X} = \bigcup_{k=0}^{N} \mathbf{X}_k$, where $\mathbf{X}_k = \{(k,0),\ldots,(k,N-k)\}$. The sequence $\underline{X}_n^1 = \underline{X}(T_n^1 - 0)$ at the arrival instants T_n^1 of type 1 customers is an (embedded) ergodic Markov chain, whose transition probabilities are of the form $r_{\underline{x},\underline{y}} = \sum_{n=0}^{\infty} a_{\underline{x}\underline{y}}^{(n)} \int_0^\infty e^{-qt}\frac{(qt)^n}{n!}dA(t), \underline{x},\underline{y} \in \mathbf{X}$, where q can be chosen appropriately. For the $a_{\underline{x}\underline{y}}(n)$ a numerical algorithm which exploites the decomposition of $\mathbf{X}$ and a block structure property is proposed, Brandt, Fuhge (1992). Thus, the stationary distribution $\varrho_{\underline{x}}, \underline{x} \in \mathbf{X}$ can be computed numerically. In case $N=1$, it can be given explicitely. Using the theory of processes with an embedded marked point process (PEMP) one can construct, by means of the inversion formula for PEMP's, cf. e.g. Franken et al. (1982), a stationary process $\overline{\underline{X}}(t) = (\overline{X}_1(t), \overline{X}_2(t))$. The distribution $q_{\underline{x}} = P(\overline{\underline{X}}(t) = \underline{x})$, $\underline{x} \in \mathbf{X}$, is the steady state distribution of the model in continuous time. Using the intensity conservation principle, cf. e.g. Franken et al. (1982), one can derive, for the vectors $q^{(j)} = (q_{(N-j,0)},\ldots,q_{(N-j,j)})^T$ linear systems of equations:

$$\left.\begin{aligned} A^{(j)}q^{(j)} &= d^{(j)} + (N-j+1)\mu_1\hat{q}^{(j-1)}, j=0,\ldots,N-1 \\ \tilde{A}^{(N)}q^{(N)} &= \tilde{d}^{(N)} + \mu_1\tilde{q}^{(N-1)} \end{aligned}\right\} \tag{1}$$

where $\hat{q}^{(j-1)} = ((q^{(j-1)})^T, 0)^T$, $\hat{q}^{(-1)} := 0$, $\tilde{q}^{(N-1)} = (0, q_{(1,1)}, \ldots, q_{(1,N-1)}, 0)^T$, $d^{(j)} = (d_0^{(j)},\ldots,d_j^{(j)})^T$, $\tilde{d}^{(N)} = (\tilde{d}, d_1^{(N)},\ldots,d_N^{(N)})^T$ and the $(j+1)\times(j+1)$ matrices $A^{(j)} = (a_{k,l}^{(j)})_{k,l=0,\ldots,j}$

and $\tilde{A}^{(N)} = (\tilde{a}_{k,l})_{k,l=0,\dots,N}$ are of the form:

$$a_{kl}^{(j)} = \begin{cases} b_k^{(j)} & \text{for } k = l \\ a^{(j)} & \text{for } l = k-1 \\ c_k^{(j)} & \text{for } l = k+1 \\ 0 & \text{otherwise} \end{cases} \qquad \tilde{a}_{kl}^{(N)} = \begin{cases} 1 & \text{for } k = 0, l = 0, \dots, N \\ b_1^{(N)} & \text{for } 1 \le k = l \\ a^{(N)} & \text{for } l = k-1 \\ c_k^{(N)} & \text{for } l = k+1 \\ 0 & \text{otherwise.} \end{cases}$$

The $a^{(j)}, b_i^{(j)}, c_i^{(j)}, d_i^{(j)}$ and $\tilde{d}$ are given by

$$\begin{aligned} a^{(j)} &= -\lambda_2 \\ b_i^{(j)} &= (N-j)\mu_1 + i\mu_2 + \lambda_2 \mathbb{I}\{i < j\} && ,0 \le i \le j \\ c_i^{(j)} &= -(i+1)\mu_2 && ,0 \le i \le j-1 \\ d_i^{(j)} &= -\varrho_{(N-j,i)}\lambda_1 \cdot \mathbb{I}\{i < j\} + \varrho_{(N-j-1,i)}\lambda_1 && ,0 \le i \le j \\ \tilde{d} &= 1 - \sum_{j=0}^{N-1} \sum_{i=0}^{j} q_{(N-j,i)}. \end{aligned}$$

It can be shown that $A^{(j)}$, $0 \le j \le N-1$, and $\tilde{A}^{(N)}$ are regular. Thus (1) provides a recursive numerical algorithm for computing the $q_{\underline{x}}$ successively for the state stets $\mathbf{X}_N, \dots, \mathbf{X}_0$. The PASTA Theorem and the fact that $\varrho_{\underline{x}}$ is the distribution of the number of customer found by an arriving type 1 customer yield for the individual blocking probability P_{B_i} that an arriving type i customer gets lost:

$$P_{B1} = \sum_{i=0}^{N} \varrho_{(i,N-i)}, \quad P_{B2} = \sum_{i=0}^{N} q_{(i,N-i)} \tag{2}$$

and the general blocking probability is given by $P_B = \frac{\lambda_1}{\lambda_1+\lambda_2} P_{B1} + \frac{\lambda_2}{\lambda_1+\lambda_2} P_{B2}$. Thus the P_{Bi} can be computed in the following way:
Step 1: Compute the stationary distribution $\varrho_{\underline{x}}$.
Step 2: Compute the time stationary probabilities by solving (1).
Step 3: Compute the P_{Bi} by (2).

In case $N = 1$, $\mu = \mu_1 = \mu_2$, i.e. for an $GI + M|M|1|0$ system it can be shown that our results reduce to

$$\left. \begin{aligned} P_{B1} &= 1 - \mu \int_0^\infty e^{-\mu t}(1 - A(t))\lambda_2 \left(\int_t^\infty e^{-\lambda_2 u} du\right) dt \\ P_{B2} &= 1 - \mu \int_0^\infty e^{-\mu t} \lambda_1 \int_t^\infty (1 - A(u)) du e^{-\lambda_2 t} dt. \end{aligned} \right\} \tag{3}$$

The formulas (3) are special case of the loss probabilities given in Willie (1990) for $G_1 + \dots + G_N|M|1|0$.
The results given in our paper generalize those of Kuczura (1973) and Willie (1988).

In the second part we consider the situation when both traffic streams are renewal processes and $N = 1$, i.e. the system $GI + GI|\vec{M}|1|0$. We derive a partial differential system of equations for the system with particular boundary conditions. Although a solution can be given, it is not convenient for numerical computation, cf. Brandt (1992). In case of $\mu_1 = \mu_2$, we can show that the general formulas for the individual blocking probabilities reduce to those given in Willie (1990) for the system $G_1 + \ldots + G_N|M|1|0$.

References

Brandt, A., Fuhge, S. (1992) Individual blocking probabilities in the loss System $GI + M|\vec{M}|N|0$. Unpublished manuscript. FB Mathematik, Humboldt-Universität zu Berlin

Brandt, A. (1992) Individual blocking probabilities in the system $GI + GI|\vec{M}|1|0$. Unpublished manuscript. FB Mathematik, Humboldt-Universität zu Berlin

Franken, P., König, D., Arndt, U., Schmidt, V. (1982) Queues and Point Processes. John Wiley and Sons, New York

Kuczura, A. (1973) Loss systems with mixed renewal and Poisson inputs. Oper. Res. 21, 787-795

Willie, H. (1988) Individual Call Blocking Probabilities in the Loss Systems $SM + M|M|N$ and $G + M|M|N$. EIK 24, 11/12, 601-612

Willie, H. (1990) Individual blocking probabilities in the loss system $G_1 + \ldots + G_N|M|1|0$. Queueing Systems 6, 109-112.

Artillery Effectiveness Models in Operational Planning

Asbjørn Grundt
Norwegian Defence Research Establishment
2007 Kjeller, Norway

1 Introduction.

Modern artillery may have a significant influence on the battlefield due to improved delivery systems and new munition concepts.

In order to assess this influence as realistic as possible, artillery effectiveness models will become necessary tools for operational planning purposes.

This contribution will discuss both stochastic simulation (models) and mathematical expectation models for the artillery and examples of use will be given. The uncertainty caused by systematic errors in evaluating the effect of an artillery engagement and possible methods of reducing this uncertainty will be stressed.

2 Target kill–probability.

The area of vulnerability of a target, A_v, is traditionally modelled as a circular area such that a hit within the circle kills the target and hits outside the circle has no effect. We will instead use a damage function of the form $P = exp\left(-\pi R^2/A_v\right)$, which is radially symmetric, [1]. The kill probability is P when the distance between the target and the point of impact is R. We denote by (X_g, Y_g) the impact point of the grenade, (X_b, Y_b) is the mean point of impact (MPI) and the aiming point is (X_s, Y_s). The target is located in (X_m, Y_m). There are two types of error, precision errors (within series) and systematic (bias) errors (between series). The MPI is normally distributed around the aiming point with standard deviations σ_{Xb}, σ_{Yb} and the impact points are normally distributed around the MPI in the same manner, with standard deviations σ_{Xe}, σ_{Ye}. If we now introduce the notation $\sigma_{X2}^2 = \sigma_{Y2}^2 = A_v/2\pi$, we can express the loss P_e in (X_m, Y_m) given a MPI in (X_b, Y_b) as:

$$P_e = A_v \int\int \frac{1}{2\pi\sigma_{X_e}\sigma_{Y_e}} e^{-\frac{1}{2}\left\{\frac{(X-X_b)^2}{\sigma_{X_e}{}^2}+\frac{(Y-Y_b)^2}{\sigma_{Y_e}{}^2}\right\}} \frac{1}{2\pi\sigma_{X_2}\sigma_{Y_2}} e^{-\frac{1}{2}\left\{\frac{(X-X_m)^2}{\sigma_{X_2}^2}+\frac{(Y-Y_m)^2}{\sigma_{Y_2}{}^2}\right\}} dXdY \tag{2.1}$$

It can be shown that this integral is

$$P_e = \frac{A_v}{2\pi\sigma_X\sigma_Y} e^{-\frac{1}{2}\left\{\frac{(X_b-X_m)^2}{\sigma_X^2}+\frac{(Y_b-Y_m)^2}{\sigma_Y^2}\right\}} = A_v\Phi\left(\frac{X_b-X_m}{\sigma_X}, \frac{Y_b-Y_m}{\sigma_Y}\right) \tag{2.2}$$

where $\sigma_X^2 = \sigma_{Xe}^2 + A_v/2\pi$ and $\sigma_Y^2 = \sigma_{Ye}^2 + A_v/2\pi$.
When a salvo of N rounds is fired, the bias distribution has to be taken into account, and the resulting salvo kill–probability becomes:

$$P_N(X_m,Y_m) = \int\int \Phi(\frac{X_b - X_s}{\sigma_{X_b}}, \frac{Y_b - Y_s}{\sigma_{Y_b}}) \left\{ \sum_{j=1}^{N} (-1)^{j+1} \binom{N}{j} \frac{A_v^j}{j(2\pi\sigma_X\sigma_Y)^{j-1}} \Phi(\frac{X_b - X_m}{\sigma_{X_{2j}}}, \frac{Y_b - Y_m}{\sigma_{Y_{2j}}}) \right\} dX_b dY_b \tag{2.3}$$

Changing the order of integration and evaluating a convolution integral gives:

$$P_N(X_m, Y_m) = \sum_{j=1}^{N} (-1)^{j+1} \binom{N}{j} \frac{A_v^j}{j(2\pi\sigma_X\sigma_Y)^{j-1}} \Phi(\frac{X_m - X_s}{\sigma_{X_{Tj}}}, \frac{Y_m - Y_s}{\sigma_{Y_{Tj}}}) \tag{2.4}$$

where $\sigma^2_{X2j} = \sigma_X{}^2/j$, $\sigma^2_{Y2j} = \sigma_Y{}^2/j$, $\sigma_{X_{Tj}}{}^2 = \sigma_{X_b}{}^2 + \sigma^2_{X2j}$ and $\sigma_{Y_{Tj}}{}^2 = \sigma_{Y_b}{}^2 + \sigma^2_{Y2j}$. This expression can be integrated numerically over an area to get the mean value for the loss of point targets within the area. Similar calculations can be performed for cargo–munitions when the bomblets have a normal distribution. It is also possible to study the effect of adjusted fire as well as several independent *or* dependent firing units.

3 Variance of the kill–probability.

Assessing the effect of an artillery engagement is uncertain at long ranges. In general the bias is very large in this case. When the MPI is given, N is large and the area target is large compared to the precision errors, then the mean loss in the area–target is nearly constant. It is therefore assumed that all the significant variation in kill–probability in this case is caused by the bias error, and hence that the precision errors give very little contribution. We now consider the kill–probability in (X_m, Y_m) after N independent rounds with MPI in $(X_s + X_b, Y_s + Y_b)$:

$$P_N(X_m, Y_m|X_b, Y_b) = \sum_{j=1}^{N} (-1)^{j+1} \binom{N}{j} \frac{A_v{}^j}{j(2\pi\sigma_X\sigma_Y)^{j-1}} \Phi(\frac{X_s + X_b - X_m}{\sigma_{X_{2j}}}, \frac{Y_s + Y_b - Y_m}{\sigma_{Y_{2j}}}) \tag{3.1}$$

Instead of integrating the bias, we would rather like to find the loss in a rectangular area–target normal to the direction of fire. This is given as:

$$P_{ave}(X_b, Y_b) = \frac{1}{A} \int_{Y_1}^{Y_2} \int_{X_1}^{X_2} P_N(X_m, Y_m|X_b, Y_b)\, dX_m\, dY_m \tag{3.2}$$

This can easily be calculated using the Polya–Williams approximation formula [2]. If the area is not normal to the direction of fire one has to use an ordinary numerical integration. The expected value of the loss is then found when we introduce the bias distribution:

$$E(P_{ave}) = \mu = \int_{-\infty}^{\infty} \int_{-\infty}^{\infty} P_{ave}(X_b, Y_b) \Phi(\frac{X_b}{\sigma_{X_b}}, \frac{Y_b}{\sigma_{y_b}})\, dX_b\, dY_b \tag{3.3}$$

The second–order moment of the average loss is evaluated as:

$$E(P^2_{ave}) = \int_{-\infty}^{\infty} \int_{-\infty}^{\infty} P^2_{ave}(X_b, Y_b)\, \Phi(\frac{X_b}{\sigma_{X_b}}, \frac{Y_b}{\sigma_{y_b}})\, dX_b\, dY_b \tag{3.4}$$

This must be done numerically, letting dX_b taking values in the interval $[-3 * \sigma_{Xb}, 3 * \sigma_{Xb}]$ and similarly for dY_b. The variance is then given as:

$$Var(P_{ave}) = \sigma^2 = E(P^2_{ave}) - \mu^2 \tag{3.5}$$

We can also compute $E(P^3{}_{ave})$ and $E(P^4{}_{ave})$ and from them obtaining the skewness (α_3) and the kurtosis(α_4) of the distribution. Using a generalized lambda distribution one can adapt its parameters $(\lambda_1, \lambda_2, \lambda_3, \lambda_4)$ to $(\mu, \sigma^2, \alpha_3, \alpha_4)$ and then find an analytical expression for the probability density function [3]. This is unfortunately only possible for some values of $(\mu, \sigma^2, a_3, a_4)$. Other methods could also be possible, [2].

4 An example.

In order to test the expression 3.1 to 3.5, an example is given that compares a stochastic simulation with the analytical model. The stochastic model draws from the various distributions, and collects mean value, standard deviation statistics and empiric frequency function. In a target–area of 200x200m individual point targets are uniformly distributed with given vulnerability A_v. A gun is firing N rounds at the target center. No adjustment of aimpoint is made. The stochastic simulation is repeated as many as 10 000 times in order to be able to plot a fairly accurate distribution function. Three different bias error distributions $(\sigma_{Xb}, \sigma_{Yb})$ are simulated.

Error distribution	Results Stochastic Simulation	Results Analytic Model
Precision (100,30)	$\mu = 6.09$	$\mu = 6.05$
Bias (170,130)	$\sigma = 6.37$	$\sigma = 6.36$
Precision (100,30)	$\mu = 8.97$	$\mu = 8.88$
Bias (120,100)	$\sigma = 6.50$	$\sigma = 6.48$
Precision (100,30)	$\mu = 16.00$	$\mu = 16.01$
Bias (50,50)	$\sigma = 3.59$	$\sigma = 3.43$

As can be seen from the table, the analytical model is a good approximation, especially for situations where bias is large. The analytical estimate for σ is a lower bound since we have only taken into consideration the variation caused be the systematic error. The correspondance between the simulated and analytical results will generally improve with larger N–values.

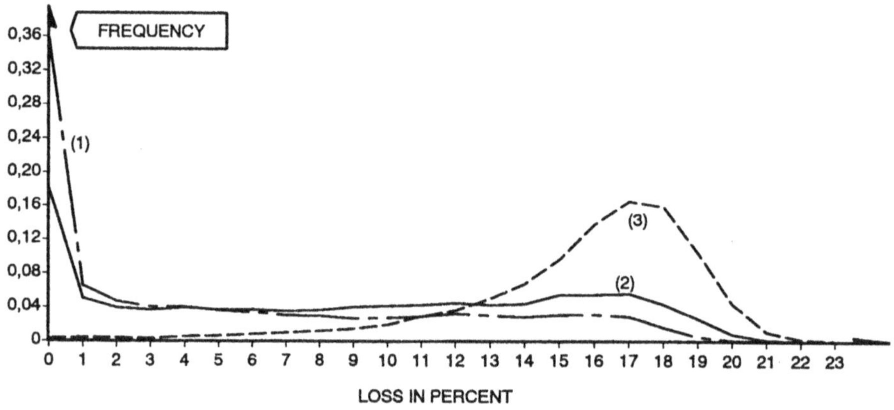

Figure 4.1 Simulation–generated probability density functions for the loss in the area–target for three different bias–distributions.

If one managed to fit a distribution to the moments it is also possible to evaluate the quantiles and find the number of rounds required to achieve for instance 10% loss with 90% confidence. Running the analytic model takes 2–3s on a HP/Apollo 945, while 10000 stochastic simulations takes around 44 hours.

5 Conclusion

An analytical model for artillery fire effectiveness is presented that give a good approximation to stochastic simulation results. The model may be used in operational planning in assessing the effectiveness of accuracy improvement concepts for the artillery. Cost–effectiveness may also be computed as reduction in ammunition costs for given engagement criteria.

References.

1: Frank McNolty: Kill probability when the lethal effect is variable, Operations Research 13, 1965.

2: Abramowitz and Stegun. Handbook of Mathematical Functions, Dover publ., 1965.

3: Ramberg: A probability distribution and its uses in fitting data. Technometrics, Vol 21, Nr 2, May 1979.

Transmission of Reliability Properties among Record Values from Non-Identically Distributed Random Variables

Udo Kamps
Institute of Statistics, Aachen University of Technology
Wüllnerstraße 3, 5100 Aachen, Germany

In reliability theory classes of distributions are considered, which describe the length of life of components or systems. When considering such classes, one is interested in knowing whether we have certain transmission properties at hand. Does the IFR (DFR) property of some distribution imply the IFR (DFR) property of a given statistic?

In this context order statistics are examined (cf. David 1981, Barlow, Proschan 1981, Nagaraja 1990), since the r–th order statistic $X_{r,n}$ from a sample of size n of iid random variables with absolutely continuous distribution function F, $F(0) = 0$, represents the life–length of a (n–r+1)–out–of–n–system (consisting of n components of the same kind with independent life–lengths; $r = 1$: series system, $r = n$: parallel system).

The transmission of the IFR property from some underlying distribution to the order statistics (Barlow, Proschan 1981) is taken up by Takahasi (1988), and generalized to the transmission of the IFR property from the r–th order statistic to the (r+1)–th order statistic. The DFR property of some distribution does not necessarily imply the DFR property of the corresponding order statistics. Takahasi (1988) shows that the DFR property of the r–th order statistic implies the DFR property of the (r–1)–th order statistic; but on the other hand there is no distribution such that all corresponding order statistics possess the DFR property. Nagaraja (1990) generalizes known results with respect to other criteria used in reliability theory, and to other neighbouring order statistics. If the r–th order statistic in a sample of size n possesses the IFR (IFRA, NBU) property, so do $X_{r+1,n}$, $X_{r,n-1}$, $X_{r+1,n+1}$. Analogously, if $X_{r,n}$ possesses the DFR (DFRA, NWU) property, so do $X_{r-1,n}$, $X_{r,n+1}$, $X_{r-1,n-1}$. The above results are described and discussed by Nagaraja (1990) in detail.

As a model for successive extremes in a sequence, record values are defined by Chandler (1952) based on a sequence of iid random variables with a continuous distribution function F. Record values are also used in reliability models. The sequence of record values and the sequence of occurrence times of a nonhomogeneous Poisson process having mean value function M (nondecreasing and continuous on $[0,\infty)$) are identically distributed

iff $1 - F(t) = \exp\{-M(t)\}$, $t > 0$. Gupta, Kirmani (1988) give a survey on the application of nonhomogeneous Poisson processes in the modelling of repairable systems (cf. Ascher, Feingold 1984), and in the context of minimal repair. Moreover, they point out and discuss the connection between record values and the relevation transform.
By analogy with the transmission rules in the case of order statistics it is shown in Gupta, Kirmani (1988) that the IFR property of the r–th record is ensured by the IFR property of the underlying distribution. Kochar (1990) generalizes this result in the sense of Takahasi (1988) using the same argument. Thus, the IFR property of some record is transmitted to the next one, and the DFR property of some record is transmitted to the previous one. Moreover, if we consider an absolutely continuous distribution function, it is not possible that all records possess the DFR property.

Both models, order statistics and record values, are included in Pfeifer's model of records (Pfeifer 1979, 1982a) from non–identically distributed random variables. The distribution of the underlying random variables may change after each record event. So, Pfeifer's model provides a class of structures, which may be used in reliability models; e.g., interventions can be described like modifying the situation after the occurrence of a record.
For our purposes, we consider Pfeifer's model in a restricted version:

Let F be an absolutely continuous distribution function with $F(0) = 0$, and density f.
Let an integer m and positive integers k and n be given satisfying

$$a_r = k + (n-r)(m+1) \geq 1 , \; 1 \leq r \leq n .$$

Let $\{X_{r.j}\}_{1\leq r\leq n, j\in\mathbb{N}}$ be a double sequence of independent random variables on a probability space $(\Omega, \mathcal{A}, P)$ such that $X_{r.j}$, $j \in \mathbb{N}$, are identically distributed according to

$$F_r(x) = 1 - (1-F(x))^{a_r} , \; 1 \leq r \leq n .$$

Then interrecord times are inductively defined by

$$\Delta_1 = 1 , \Delta_{r+1} = \min\{j \in \mathbb{N} ; X_{r+1.j} > X_{r.\Delta_r}\} , \; 1 \leq r \leq n-1 ,$$

and record values by $X_{r.\Delta_r} = X(r,n,m,k)$, say.

The general model is extensively examined in Pfeifer (1979, 1982a,b). E.g., it is shown that, under suitable conditions, the sequence of jump times of an elementary pure birth process and the sequence of record values are identically distributed. As an example for the use of this record model, suppose that the $X_{r.j}$, $j \in \mathbb{N}$, correspond to random shocks attacking a component which works without failure unless a shock greater than

X(r−1,n,m,k) occurs. Then a modified component is used for safety reasons, which endures shocks up to a magnitude of the last record X(r,n,m,k). Now suppose the distribution of the subsequent shocks $X_{r+1,j}$, $j \in \mathbb{N}$, to be given by F_{r+1} different from F_r.
The record values X(r,n,m,k) , $1 \le r \le n$, form a Markov chain with transition probabilities

$$P(\,X(r,n,m,k) > t \mid X(r-1,n,m,k) = s\,) = \left(\frac{1-F(t)}{1-F(s)}\right)^{a_r},\ t \ge s\,,\ F(s) < 1\,,\ 2 \le r \le n\,.$$

Thus, order statistics (m = 0 , k = 1) and ordinary record values (m = −1 , k = 1) are included in Pfeifer's model.
The marginal density function of X(r,n,m,k) , $1 \le r \le n$, is then given by

$$f^{X(r,n,m,k)}(x) = \frac{1}{(r-1)!}\left(\prod_{i=1}^{r} a_i\right)(1-F(x))^{a_r-1} f(x)\, g_m^{r-1}(F(x))\,,\ x < F^{-1}(1)\,,$$

where
$$g_m(y) = \int_0^y (1-t)^m\, dt\,,\ 0 \le y < 1\,,$$

and the corresponding distribution function is given by

$$F^{X(r,n,m,k)}(x) = 1 - \left(\prod_{i=1}^{r} a_i\right)(1-F(x))^{a_r} \sum_{j=0}^{r-1} \left(j!\prod_{i=1}^{r-j} a_i\right)^{-1} g_m^{j}(F(x))\,,\ x < F^{-1}(1)\,.$$

Generalizing results of Takahasi (1988), Nagaraja (1990), Gupta, Kirmani (1988), Kochar (1990) on the transmission of the IFR and DFR property in the case of order statistics and ordinary record values, we give corresponding results concerning the records X(r,n,m,k). For the sake of brevity, 'X(r,n,m,k) IFR' means that the distribution of X(r,n,m,k) possesses the IFR property.

THEOREM

i) If $r \le n-1$, then we find :

$$X(r,n,m,k)\ \text{IFR} \Rightarrow X(r+1,n,m,k)\ \text{IFR}\,,$$
$$X(r,n,m,k)\ \text{DFR} \Leftarrow X(r+1,n,m,k)\ \text{DFR}\,.$$

ii) If $r \le n-1$ and $m \ge -1$, then we have :

$$X(r,n,m,k)\ \text{IFR} \Rightarrow X(r,n-1,m,k)\ \text{IFR}\,,$$
$$X(r,n,m,k)\ \text{DFR} \Leftarrow X(r,n-1,m,k)\ \text{DFR}\,;$$

if $r \le n$ and $m < -1$, then we have :

$$X(r,n,m,k)\ \text{IFR} \Rightarrow X(r,n+1,m,k)\ \text{IFR}\,,$$
$$X(r,n,m,k)\ \text{DFR} \Leftarrow X(r,n+1,m,k)\ \text{DFR}\,.$$

iii) If $r \le n$ and $k \ge m+1$ in the case $r = n$, then we observe :

$$X(r,n,m,k)\ \text{IFR} \Rightarrow X(r+1,n+1,m,k)\ \text{IFR}\,,$$
$$X(r,n,m,k)\ \text{DFR} \Leftarrow X(r+1,n+1,m,k)\ \text{DFR}\,.$$

The following diagram illustrates the transmission properties of the records X(r,n,m,k) , $m \geq -1$, with respect to the IFR property. (If $X(r_0,n_0,m,k)$ possesses the IFR property, then the same property holds for all records belonging to the hatched area.)

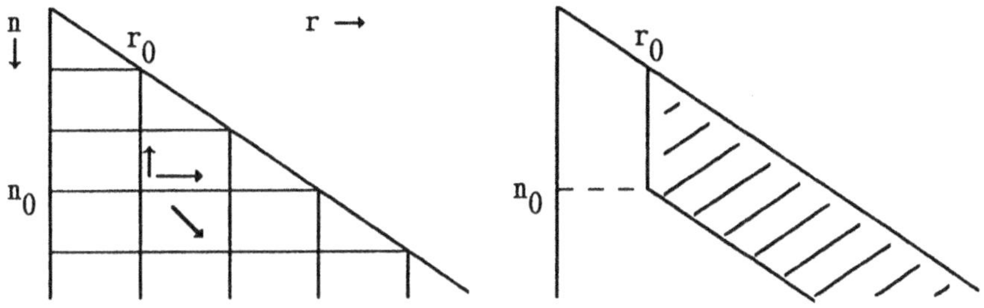

The theorem is stated concerning the IFR and DFR property; however, it may be extended to IFRA and NBU properties or DFRA and NWU properties as pointed out in Nagaraja (1990).

In the literature there are numerous articles investigating partial ordering in the case of order statistics or record values. Gupta, Kirmani (1988) and Kochar (1990) state interesting results for ordinary record values. Analogous properties may also be obtained for records X(r,n,m,k) considered here.

References

Ascher HE, Feingold H (1984) Repairable Systems Reliability. Dekker. New York

Barlow RE, Proschan F (1981) Statistical Theory of Reliability and Life Testing. To Begin With. Silver Spring

Chandler KN (1952) The distribution and frequency of record values. J R Statist Soc B 14: 220–228

David HA (1981) Order Statistics. 2 nd ed Wiley. New York

Gupta RC, Kirmani SNUA (1988) Closure and monotonicity properties of nonhomogeneous Poisson processes and record values. Prob in the Engineering and Inf Sciences 2: 475–484

Kochar SC (1990) Some partial ordering results on record values. Commun Statist–Theory Meth 19: 299–306

Nagaraja HN (1990) Some reliability properties of order statistics. Commun Statist–Theory Meth 19: 307–316

Pfeifer D (1979) Record Values in einem stochastischen Modell mit nicht–identischen Verteilungen. Dissertation. Aachen University of Technology

Pfeifer D (1982a) Characterizations of exponential distributions by independent non–stationary record increments. J Appl Prob 19: 127–135

Pfeifer D (1982b) The structure of elementary pure birth processes. J Appl Prob 19: 664–667

Takahasi K (1988) A note on hazard rates of order statistics. Commun Statist–Theory Meth 17: 4133–4136

A New Approach to Compute Performance Sensitivities of Stochastic Discrete Event Dynamic Systems (DEDS)

Hugo Lucca
Institut für Unternehmensforschung (OR), Hochschule St. Gallen
Bodanstraße 6, 9000 St. Gallen, Switzerland

A. Introduction

To analyse a complex system, e.g. flexible manufacturing systems (FMS), Hospitals, or Airports, viewed as stochastic discrete event systems (DEDS, e.g. [2],[5],[6]), as close to reality as required, there are some alternatives. For the queueing theory, which has obtained a fair amount of success, no analytical (product-form) solution is yet available, as soon as serious restrictions are involved (e.g. blocking only under given additional restrictions, see [1],[5]). Therefore, it is not an appropriate approach for the application to a large category of man-made systems. Thus, one may use, the natural alternative to the exact analysis of an approximated model, which is the approximated analysis of a more exact model, e.g. the Queueing Network Analyser described by Whitt [9]. Finally, experimentation (on a simulation model or the actual system) could be preferred to optimise system performance with respect to given decision parameters. Hence, simulation tools on computers are frequently used, e.g. GASP, SIMULA, or SIMAN, to perform the brute force analysis (e.g. [5],[6]). Simulation, however, is always very time consuming, especially when stochastic components are introduced into the model (Monte Carlo Simulation). Moreover, the computation of performance sensitivities with respect to a discrete parameter θ usually requires two simulation runs (paths), one for the system with the parameter θ (the nominal path) and one for $\theta+\Delta\theta$ (the perturbed path). Thus, one solution to reduce simulation time is to perform the perturbed path analytically. This was proposed by Ho at the beginning of the 1980s (see also [6]) and is known as the Perturbation Analysis (PA) for DEDS. There are two main fields: the Infinitesimal Perturbation Analysis (IPA) and the Finite Perturbation Analysis (FPA). The IPA (e.g. [4],[6],[8]) is a gradient approach, whereas FPA (e.g. [3],[6],[8]) investigates performance estimation perturbing a parameter by a discrete value. The FPA method and also some extensions of the IPA, e.g. the Extended Perturbation Analysis EPA (e.g. [7],[8]), reveal good stability in experiments. In most cases, however, the use of these approaches is difficult because the FPA is a heuristical method and is inadequate to use under the assumption of big parameter changes or even changes in network topology (e.g. buffer capacities or service channel size), which is especially frequent in the analysis of economical models.

B. The New Approach

Consider a closed network of G/G/1/m queueing systems, called units in the following. Simulating this network will supply some time information about arrival and departure time of customers. Assuming independence between the service and routing facilities of the units, no interruption of services, and blocking after service (see [1]), one can define the visit of a customer at a given service facility (server) of unit j as an ordered sequence of:

a no input (NI), followed by a service s, followed by a full output (FO), each of duration ≥ 0,

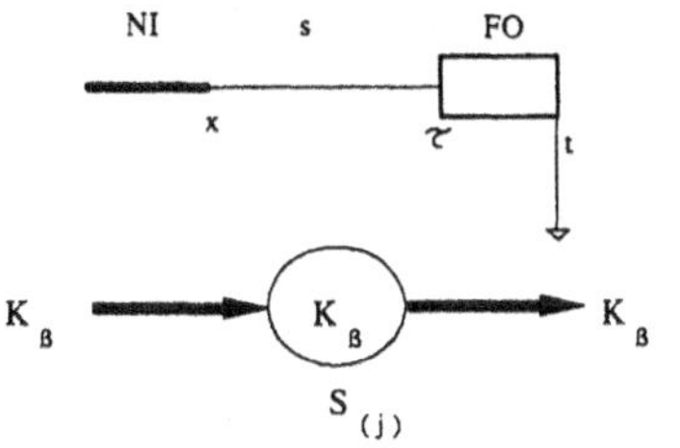

$$x_{(j),\lambda} = t_{(j),\lambda-1} + NI_{(j),\lambda}$$
$$\tau_{(j),\lambda} = x_{(j),\lambda} + s_{(j),\lambda}$$
$$t_{(j),\lambda} = \tau_{(j),\lambda} + FO_{(j),\lambda}$$

called period λ explicitly coupled with a locally served customer K_β. Therefore a period ends each time a customer leaves a server. Hence, the arrival time of a customer at unit j equals the time he leaves the predecessor unit i at $t_{(i),\mu}$, where μ denotes the period of server $S_{(i)}$ at which the arriving customer K_β left. The following holds: $x_{(j),\lambda} = t_{(j),\lambda-1} + \max\{t_{(i),\mu} - t_{(j),\lambda-1}, 0\} = \max\{t_{(i),\mu}, t_{(j),\lambda-1}\}$. An analogous derivation holds for the FO-case: $t_{(j),\lambda} = \max\{t_{(m),\xi}, \tau_{(j),\lambda}\}$ with $t_{(m),\xi}$ the time at which the required place in the successor unit m was freed from a preceding customer K_α leaving server $S_{(m)}$ at period ζ. This gives after transformation the following difference equation, which I call the Discrete Event Simulation (FDES) equation: $t_{(j),\lambda} = \max\{t_{(m),\xi}, t_{(i),\mu} + s_{(j),\lambda}, t_{(j),\lambda-1} + s_{(j),\lambda}\}$. The interpretation of this equation is as follows: the leaving time of a customer is either the end of the FO blockage, his arrival plus service time or the leaving time of the last customer plus service time. Hence, to construct a relation between the periods ζ, μ and, λ at different servers, consider a simple sequential network structure of units (a so-called tandem queueing network (TQN)) with FIFO buffers, where customers cannot overtake one another. That is, <u>the distances λ-μ and λ-ζ are time invariant</u>. Knowing the capacities and the initial state of each queue and assuming $\lambda, \mu, \xi = 0$ at simulationstart those distances are computable as shown in the table below. The important point is that the algorithm will make the use of usual simulation tools for TQN obsolete because the resulting equation is under given conditions quite simple to compute.

periods λ, μ	1	2	3	4	5
customer at $S_{(i)}$	K_1	K_2	K_3	K_4	K_5
$k = 2$; $(k \geq 0)$	↑				
customer at $S_{(j)}$	K_{-2}	K_{-1}	K_1	K_2	K_3

k = customers in unit j at t_0, e.g. $k = 2$

$\mu = \lambda - k$

periods ξ, μ	1	2	3	4	5
customer at $S_{(j)}$	K_1	K_2	K_3	K_4	K_5
$p = 1; (p \geq 0)$	↓				
customer at $S_{(m)}$	K_{-2}	K_{-1}	K_2	K_3	K_4

q = queue capacity of queue of unit m

s = size of service channel (= 1 for G/G/1)

$\xi = \lambda - (q + s - k) = \lambda - p$

e.g. for $q = 3$, $k = 2$, and $s = 1 \rightarrow p = 1$

On this base, the performance sensitivities computation, as one of the application of the FDES, is either computed by the difference of two such equations (the perturbed minus the nominal one) or even more efficient by generating a general propagation rule (GPR) (resulting from the transformation of the basic FDES equation above), when implemented in any usual simulation tool:

$$\Delta\tau_{(j),\lambda} = \Delta t_{(j),\lambda-1} + \max\{t_{(i),\lambda-k'} + \Delta t_{(i),\lambda-k'} - t_{(j),\lambda-1} - \Delta t_{(j),\lambda-1}, 0\} - \max\{t_{(i),\lambda-k} - t_{(j),\lambda-1}, 0\} + \Delta s_{(j),\lambda}$$

$$\Delta t_{(j),\lambda} = \Delta\tau_{(j),\lambda} + \max\{t_{(m),\lambda-p'} + \Delta t_{(m),\lambda-p'} - \tau_{(j),\lambda} - \Delta\tau_{(j),\lambda}, 0\} - \max\{t_{(m),\lambda-p} - \tau_{(j),\lambda}, 0\}$$

with $k' = k$, $p' = p + \Delta q$, where Δq is the queue perturbation. Exact computation may now be done, as long as perturbation generation (the computation of $\Delta s_{(j),\lambda}$, see [6]) is assumed to be correct.

C. Generalisation

The most simple generalisation is to extend the algorithm for structures with arborescent flow, open networks, and some categories of networks with G/G/n/m queueing systems, since one may transform the extended model into a closed unit network (see also [5]). The principal problem remains the dynamic computation of k, p, k' and p', using matrices for those distances. Thus, when a customer transits a splitting node, the distances to all other successors, where the customer K_β does not go, will be increased by one. Unfortunately generalisation of the algorithm implies significant additional effort, summarised in three different problems:

- correct routing: the successor (queue and server) and the predecessor (server) for both paths have to be found at each period;
- accessibility check: k and p may be negative, thus, to solve some inaccessible references some extra checks must be specified, and added to the algorithm;
- efficiency: resolve references efficiently (speed and memory) and solve possible circular references the correct computational order have to be determined.

Thus, the final algorithm could be quite complex and not more efficient than simulation itself. However, more important is the efficiency for sensitivity computation, which can be done even faster, when implemented in simulation tools. Moreover, the new sensitivity method can also be used as a good approximation in general networks, where service order can change after perturbation.

D. Experimental Results

The experimental time for FDES compared to SIMULA 67 was reduced for nominal path computation of TQN by a minimum of a factor 8 and for path estimation of generalised networks by a minimum of a factor 2. This is in fact not so revolutionary. But there is the advantage that the computational speed is independent from time base and that the whole structure information is stored in matrices, which simplifies and increases flexibility in modelling and analysing big DEDS. The presented GPR for simple network structures, shows an impressive stability with little errors when approximating more complex structures but only for their steady state. Particularly stable is the approximation method for big parameter perturbations.

E. Conclusions

The new methodology, which I call the Structured Output Analysis (SOA), offers at least two opportunities. First, a FDES algorithm, without an event list manager is obtained. Secondly, a performance sensitivity method for DEDS, which may be used as an exact method for simple and an approximation method for complex network structures. The results of the GPR are exact when applied to compute sensitivities of dynamically TQN or network structures where customer service order cannot change after perturbation. As demonstrated the queue capacity perturbation is here much easier than in FPA, where computing exact perturbation propagation is still problematic. There will be some speed advantages compared to pure brute force analysis and it will be very simple and flexible for modelling. Hence, simulation of simple DEDS structures can easily be programmed using conventional computer languages like PASCAL or C.

A kind of period concept may also be found for the PA in [2] and [5], but the period starts there at service begins, whereas here the period starts with an NI. The main difference, however, is that in PA all events are treated together, whereas here only those related to unit j are observed by the formula. This extends the similarity assumption concept from the deterministic or statistical to a new service order similarity assumption.

To gerneralise the sensitivity estimation method, the error could be estimated if there exists a correlation to some measurable facts or omitted by a "Cut & Paste" algorithm, which is a similar approach to some extensions of the IPA (e.g. [6],[7],[8]). However, a lot of work in research has to be done to exploit the whole performance of the presented outcomes.

[1] Balsamo, S., and De Nitto-Personé, V.: *Closed Queueing Networks with Finite Capacities: Blocking Types, Product-Form Solution and Performance Indices.* Performance Evaluation, vol. 12, pp. 85-102, 1991.

[2] Cao, X.R. and Ho, Y.C.: *Sensitivity Analysis and Optimization of Throughput in a Production Line with Blocking Models.* IEEE Trans. on Autom. Control, Vol. AC-32, No. 11, Nov. 1987.

[3] Ho, Y.C., Cao, X. and Cassandras, C.: *Infinitesimal and Finite Perturbation Analysis for Queueing Networks.* Automatica, vol. 19, no. 4, pp. 439-445, 1983.

[4] Ho, Y.C., Eyler, M.A. and Chien, T.T.: *A New Approach to Determine Parameter Sensitivities of Transfer Lines.* Management Science, vol. 29, no. 6, pp. 700-714, June 1983.

[5] Ho, Y.C. and Cassandras, C.: *A New Approach to the Analysis of Discrete Event Dynamic Systems.* Automatica, vol. 19, no. 2, pp. 149-167, 1983.

[6] Ho, Y.C. and Cao, X.: *Discrete Event Dynamic Systems: Theory and Applications.* Kluwer Academic Publishers, Boston / Dordrecht / London, 1991.

[7] Jiang, C.Q., Singh, M.G., and Hindi, K.S.: *A New Method of Extended Perturbation Analysis.* Information and Decision Technologies, vol. 17, pp. 215-226, 1991.

[8] Suri, R.: Perturbation Analysis: *The State of the Art and Research Issues Explained via the GI/G/1 Queue.* Proceedings of the IEEE, vol. 77, no. 1, pp. 114-137, 1989.

[9] Whitt, W.: *The Queueing Network Analyzer.* The Bell System Technical Journal, vol. 62, no. 9, pp. 2779-2815, November 1983.

Acknowledgements - This work is generously supported by the "Schweizerischen Nationalfonds zur Förderung der wissenschaftlichen Forschung" (Nr. 20-30302.90) and IBM (Schweiz) AG.

Probability Maximizing Approach to Optimal Stopping of Random Fields

Roman Różański, Krzysztof Szajowski
Institute of Mathematics, Technical University of Wrocław
Wybrzeże Wyspiańskiego 27, 50-370 Wrocław, Poland

The paper deals with a problem of optimal stopping for non-negative random fields. As in Mandelbaum and Vanderbei (1981) we restrict ourselves to the class of predictable stopping points. A necessary and sufficient condition for existence an optimal strategy is given. The result is used to solve the probability maximizing version of the problem of optimal stopping for random fields indexed by a countable partially ordered set. It generalizes the probability maximizing approach to the problem of optimal stopping for stochastic processes formulated by Bojdecki (1978). We specialize our results to the problem of optimal stopping for several Markov chains. Examples concerning the problem of optimal allocation of different treatments and some problems of optimal selection are given.

Optimal stopping of random fields - probability maximizing approach

Let $\mathcal{S}$ be a partially ordered countable set. We assume that there exists a unique element $\leq \in \mathcal{S}$ such that $\leq \preceq \mathsf{s}$ for each $\mathsf{s} \in \mathcal{S}$. By $[\mathsf{r},\mathsf{s}]$ we denote the set of all elements of $\mathsf{u} \in \mathcal{S}$ for which $\mathsf{r} \preceq \mathsf{u} \preceq \mathsf{s}$. We say that a point $\mathsf{s} \in \mathcal{S}$ is a direct successor of r in $\mathcal{S}$ if there exists no point $\mathsf{u} \in \mathcal{S}$ such that $\mathsf{r} \prec \mathsf{u} \prec \mathsf{s}$. In other words - a point s is a direct successor of r if the set $[\mathsf{r},\mathsf{s}]$ consists of only two points r and s. The set of direct successors of a point s will be denoted by $U(\mathsf{s})$. We assume that for each $\mathsf{s} \in \mathcal{S}$ the set $U(\mathsf{s})$ has only finite number of elements. We also assume that for each $\mathsf{r} \preceq \mathsf{s}$ the set $[\mathsf{r},\mathsf{s}]$ is finite. The element of $\mathcal{S}$ which is the successor of each element will be denoted by ∞.

Let $(\Omega, \mathcal{F}, \mathbf{P})$ be a probability space. By $\mathcal{F}_{\mathsf{s}}$ we denote a family of σ-sub-algebras of $\mathcal{F}$ indexed by $\mathsf{s} \in \mathcal{S}$ such that $\mathcal{F}_{\mathsf{r}} \subset \mathcal{F}_{\mathsf{s}}$ for $\mathsf{r} \preceq \mathsf{s}$. A random variable ξ with values in $\mathcal{S}$ is called a stopping point if for each $\mathsf{s} \in \mathcal{S}$ we have $\{\xi \preceq \mathsf{s}\} \in \mathcal{F}_{\mathsf{s}}$ which is equivalent to the condition that for each $\mathsf{s} \in \mathcal{S}$ we have $\{\xi = \mathsf{s}\} \in \mathcal{F}_{\mathsf{s}}$. The class of all stopping points will be denoted by Ξ.

Following Mandelbaum and Vanderbei's (1981) paper we restrict ourselves to the set of predictable stopping points. Let us recall the definition of the set of predictable stopping points.

Let σ_t , $t = 0, 1, 2, \ldots$ be an increasing sequence of stopping points such that

$$\sigma_t \preceq \sigma_{t+1} \qquad \text{for each } t$$

$$\sigma_{t+1} \quad \in \quad \mathcal{F}_{\sigma_t} = \mathcal{G}_t \qquad \text{i.e. } \sigma_{t+1} \text{ is } \mathcal{G}_t \text{ measurable.}$$

The sequence σ_t, $t = 0, 1, 2, \ldots$ will be called a *predictable strategy*. The strategy is continuous if σ_{t+1} is a direct successor of σ_t for each t. A pair $\pi = (\sigma_t, \tau)$ consisting of a continuous strategy σ_t, $t = 0, 1, 2, \ldots$ and a stopping time τ with respect to the family $\{\mathcal{G}_t\}$ is said to be a policy. The set of all policies $\pi = (\sigma_t, \tau)$ for which $\sigma_0 = 0$ will be denoted by Π. Every policy $\pi = (\sigma_t, \tau) \in \Pi$ corresponds to a stopping point $\alpha(\pi) = \sigma_\tau$ with respect to $\{\mathcal{F}_\mathbf{s}\}_{\mathbf{s}\in S}$. Stopping points defined in this way are called predictable. More details about the class of stopping points can be found in Mandelbaum and Vanderbei (1981) and Walsh (1981).

Let $\{Y_\mathbf{s}\}_{\mathbf{s}\in S}$ be a family of non-negative, adapted to $\mathcal{F}_\mathbf{s}$, random variables such that $\mathbf{E}\sup_\mathbf{s} Y_\mathbf{s} < \infty$. In the mentioned paper of Mandelbaum and Vanderbei there was found an optimal policy $\pi^* = (\sigma_t^*, \tau^*)$ in the sense that

$$\mathbf{E}Y_{\alpha(\pi^*)} = \sup_{\pi\in\Pi} \mathbf{E}Y_{\alpha(\pi)}. \tag{1}$$

Other sufficient conditions for the existence of optimal policy are given in Maziotto and Szpirglas (1983).

The theorem which we prove gives a necessary and sufficient condition for the existence of optimal policy.

Theorem 1 *Let us assume that* $\mathbf{E}\sup_\mathbf{s} Y_\mathbf{s} < \infty$ *and* $Y_\infty = 0$*. Then there exists an 'optimal predictable strategy* $\pi^* = (\sigma_t^*, \tau^*)$ *if and only if* $\lim_{t\to\infty} Y_{\sigma_t^*} = 0$ *on the set* $\tau_0 = \infty$.

Corollary 1 *Let* σ_t, $t = 1, 2, \ldots$ *be any predictable strategy. Let us consider the policy* $\pi = (\sigma_t, \tau)$*, where* $\tau = t$ *with probability 1. Then*

$$X_{\sigma_t} = \operatorname*{esssup}_{\pi\in\Pi_{\sigma_t}} \mathbf{E}(Y_{\alpha(\pi)} \mid \mathcal{F}_{\sigma_t}).$$

Corollary 2 *There exists an optimal policy* $\pi^* = (\sigma_t^*, \tau^*)$*, maximizing* $\mathbf{P}(Y_{\alpha(\pi)} \in B, \tau < \infty)$*, if and only if* $\lim_{t\to\infty} Z_{\sigma_t^*} = 0$ *on the set* $\{\tau_0 = \infty\}$ *almost surely, where* $Z_\mathbf{s} = \mathbf{P}(Y_\mathbf{s} \in B \mid \mathcal{F}_\mathbf{s})$*. If the above condition is fulfilled for a continuous predictable strategy* σ_t^0 *then* $\pi_0 = (\sigma_t^0, \tau_0)$ *is optimal.*

Optimal stopping of Markov random fields

Let $Y_\mathbf{z}$ be a random field adapted to a family of σ-algebras $\{\mathcal{F}_\mathbf{z}\}$. The parameter $\mathbf{z} = (s, t)$ is assumed to belong to $N \otimes N$. We assume that the σ-algebras $\{\mathcal{F}_\mathbf{z}\}$ additionally fulfill the $F4$ condition (see Mandelbaum and Vanderbei (1981) and Walsh (1981)). The random field $Y_\mathbf{z}$ may take values from $\Re^n$.

Definition 1 *(Koreziloglu H., Lefort P., Maziotto G. (1981)) A random field Y_z, in $N \otimes N$, adapted to $\{\mathcal{F}_z\}$ is said to have the Markov property if for each $z = (s,t) \in N \otimes N$, $n \in N$, $z_1, z_2, \ldots, z_n \in [0,z]^c$ and any real valued bounded Borel function f the following equality holds*

$$\begin{aligned} \mathbf{E}(f(Y_{z_1}, Y_{z_2}, \ldots, Y_{z_n}) \mid \mathcal{F}_z) &= \mathbf{E}(f(Y_{z_1}, Y_{z_2}, \ldots, Y_{z_n}) \mid Y_{z \wedge z_1}, \ldots, Y_{z \wedge z_n}), \\ z \wedge z_j &= (s,t) \wedge (s_j, t_j) = (s \wedge s_j, t \wedge t_j). \end{aligned}$$

It is worth noting that under the assumption that the σ-algebras $\{\mathcal{F}_z\}$ satisfy the $F4$ condition each random field can be transformed into a Markov random field. Namely, we have the following

Proposition 1 *Let $\tilde{Y}_z = (Y_{(0,0)}, \ldots, Y_u, \ldots, Y_z)$, $u \preceq z$, and $\mathcal{G}_z = \bigvee_{u \preceq z} \mathcal{F}_u$ then under the assumption that the σ-algebras $\{\mathcal{F}_z\}$ satisfy the $F4$ condition, the random field $(\tilde{Y}_z, \mathcal{G}_z)$ is a Markov random field.*

Definition 2 *A Markov random field Y_z is homogeneous if for each z_1, z_2, $h \in N \otimes N$, $h \succeq (0,0)$, $y \in \mathbb{E}$ and $B \in \mathcal{F}$*

$$\mathbf{P}(Y_{z_1+h} \in B | Y_{z_1} = y) = \mathbf{P}(Y_{z_2+h} \in B | Y_{z_2} = y).$$

The random field $U_z = (z, Y_z)$ possesses the homogeneity property with an appropriate transition probability. Thus going along the lines of Neveu's (1975) arguments we can prove

Theorem 2 *Let Y_z be a homogeneous Markov random field with values in a countable state space $\mathbb{E}$. Let*

$$\begin{aligned} P^1(u,t) &= \mathbf{P}(Y_{(i+1,j)} = t | Y_{(i,j)} = u), \\ P^2(u,t) &= \mathbf{P}(Y_{(i,j+1)} = t | Y_{(i,j)} = u). \end{aligned}$$

If $f : \mathbb{E} \to \Re_+$ is a function representing the payoff, we get, deciding to stop after watching Y_z, then there exists such a function v that $v(Y_z)$ is Snell's envelope for the problem of optimal stopping of the random field Y_z (we want to find a predictable strategy maximizing the expectation of the payoff function (cf. Mandelbaum and Vanderbei (1981)). The function v is the limit of the sequence $f_0 = f$, $f_{k+1} = \max\{f, \mathbb{P}^1 f_k, \mathbb{P}^2 f_k\}$, where

$$\begin{aligned} \mathbb{P}^1 f(y) = \mathbf{E}(f(Y_{(i+1,j)}) | Y_{(i,j)} = y), \\ \mathbb{P}^2 f(y) = \mathbf{E}(f(Y_{(i,j+1)}) | Y_{(i,j)} = y). \end{aligned}$$

The function v fulfils the following equality

$$v(y) = \max\{f(y), \mathbb{P}^1 v(y), \mathbb{P}^2 v(y)\} \qquad \text{for each } y \in \mathbb{E}. \tag{2}$$

Examples

Example 1 Let us assume that a physician has two different treatments at his disposal which can be applied sequentially and can be interchanged during a theraphy. We do not observe the presence of an immediate synergistic effect. Mathematically, taking into account the simplest case, the procedure can be described by two independent Markov chains $Y^1_{t_1}$, $Y^2_{t_2}$, $t_1 = 0, 1, \ldots, N$, $t_2 = 0, 1, \ldots, N$ with state space $\mathbb{E} = \{0, 1\}$ and $Y^1_0 = Y^2_0 = 0$ almost surely. $Y^i_{t_i}$, $i = 1, 2$, represents the patient's state of health after t_i-times application of i-th treatment. Thus we have a random field $Y_{(t_1,t_2)} = (Y^1_{t_1}, Y^2_{t_2})$ which describes the patient's therapy. Having observed the random field $Y_{(t_1,t_2)}$ the therapy can be stopped and after some fixed period of time the patient is again examined for his state of health. The result of the examination is described by the random variable Θ taking values 0 or 1. We assume that we know the following conditional distribution of the random variable Θ (the distribution is conditioned by the whole record of a therapy)

$$\mathbf{P}(\Theta = m | Y^1_u = k_u, Y^2_w = l_w, u \leq t_1, w \leq t_2) = Q(m, k_u, l_w, t_1, t_2, u \leq t_1, w \leq t_2).$$

Our aim is to find a predictable policy $\pi^* = (\sigma^*_\tau, \tau^*) = ((\delta_{1,\tau}, \delta_{2,\tau}), \tau^*)$ such that

$$\mathbf{P}(Y^1_{\delta_{1,\tau^*}} = Y^2_{\delta_{2,\tau^*}} = \Theta = 1) = \sup_{(\sigma_\tau,\tau)=((\delta_{1,\tau},\delta_{2,\tau}),\tau)} \mathbf{P}(Y^1_{\delta_{1,\tau}} = Y^2_{\delta_{2,\tau}} = \Theta = 1).$$

□

Example 2 We consider the two parameter generalization of the problem of optimal selection. The optimal strategy is such that maximizies the probability of selection the best object.

□

References

T. BOJDECKI (1978) *On optimal stopping of a sequence of independent random variables - probability maximizing approach*, Stochastic Proc. and their Appl., 6, pp. 153 - 163.

H. KOREZLIOGLU, P. LEFORT, AND G. MAZZIOTTO (1981) *Une propriété Markovienne et diffusione associées*, vol. 863 of Lect. Notes in Math., Springer, Berlin, pp. 243 - 274.

A. MANDELBAUM AND R. VANDERBEI (1981) *Optimal stopping and supermartingales over partially ordered sets*, Zeit. Warscheinlichkeitstheorie verw. Gebiete, 57, pp. 253 - 264.

G. MAZZIOTTO AND J. SZPIRGLAS (1983) *Arrêt optimal sur le plain*, Zeit. Warscheinlichkeitstheorie verw. Gebiete, 62, pp. 215 - 233.

J. NEVEU (1975) *Discrete-Parameter Martingales*, North-Holland, Amsterdam.

J. WALSH (1981) *Optional increasing path*, vol. 863 of Lect. Notes in Math., Springer, Berlin, pp. 172 - 201.

Control by Delay of a Service System

Harald Schmidbauer
Seminar für Angewandte Stochastik, Universität München
Akademiestr. 1/IV, 8000 München 40, Germany
Asaf Gadjiev
Institute of Cybernetics, Academy of Sciences
Agaev Street 9, Baku, 370602, Azerbaijan

1 Introduction

Results concerning waiting times in stochastic systems are sometimes surprising. A simple example in this context is the waiting time from an arbitrary epoch t until the next renewal in a stationary renewal process, that is, the forward recurrence time V_t. It holds that (see [1])

$$\mathrm{E}(V_t) = \frac{\mathrm{E}(X^2)}{2\mathrm{E}(X)} = \frac{\mathrm{var}(X) + (\mathrm{E}X)^2}{2\mathrm{E}(X)} \tag{1}$$

(where X denotes the time that elapses between two successive renewals) so that $\mathrm{E}(V_t) = \mathrm{E}(X)/2$, as might be guessed at first sight, only if $\mathrm{var}(X) = 0$. Obviously, $\mathrm{E}(V_t)$ may be reduced by reducing $\mathrm{var}(X)$, even if $\mathrm{E}(X)$ gets larger at the same time. It is possible to diminish the variance by prolonging very small intervals between successive renewals, i.e. by delaying short intervals. We shall now consider a shuttle (transport) system in which the average waiting time of a passenger until departure of his bus may be reduced by delays, which is analogous to our observation in renewal processes.

2 A Shuttle System that May Be Improved by Delays

Consider the following shuttle system. Passengers arrive at a bus station according to a Poisson process with intensity λ. When a bus arrives, the waiting passengers get on the bus. Each passenger requires one time unit for getting on the bus. Meanwhile, new passengers may arrive at the bus station, each requiring as well one time unit in order to get on the bus. The capacity of the bus is assumed to be infinite. The bus starts as soon as there are no more passengers left at the bus station. As soon as the bus has left, the next bus is called. This bus will arrive at the station in a random amount of η time units. When the bus arrives, the procedure (waiting passengers, who have arrived in the meantime, boarding the bus) starts afresh. The length of the time interval from the instant when the bus was called until the departure of this bus (i.e., the interdeparture time) will be denoted by ξ. This mechanism is illustrated in figure 1a).

We are interested in the total customers' waiting time from their arrival at the bus station until their departure, i.e. until their bus starts. This means that, for our purpose, passengers are considered completely served as soon as their bus has left.

Denote by $W(t)$ and $N(t)$ the expectation of the total waiting time of all customers who arrived in $[0, t]$ from their arrival until the departure of their bus, and the expectation of the number of these customers, respectively. Then

$$W := \lim_{t\to\infty} \frac{W(t)}{N(t)}$$

is the average waiting time of a typical customer. Our aim is to diminish W. This is achieved as follows. At the moment when the bus has picked up the last waiting passenger and thus could leave, his departure is delayed according to the rule

$$\xi^* = \xi + g(\xi), \tag{2}$$

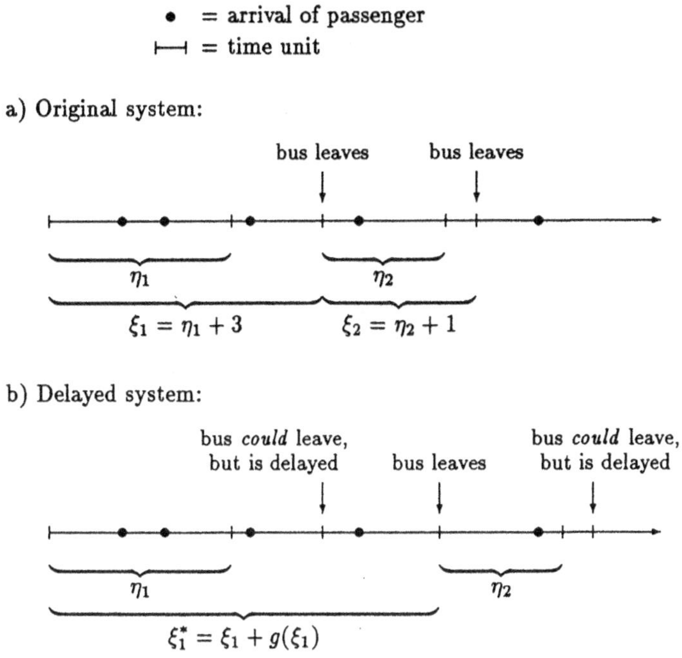

Figure 1: Original and delayed system

where $g \in G$, and G is the class of measurable and nonnegative functions.
Note that the next bus is called immediately after the delayed bus has left, so that the length η of the time interval from order to the arrival of the bus is not affected by the control mechanism. The stream of arriving customers will also remain unaffected.
Define $W(g)$ to be the average waiting time of a customer in the system with control function g. We say that the system can be improved by delay if there exists a function $g \in G$ such that

$$W(g) < W. \tag{3}$$

For the proofs of the following theorems, which essentially use equation (1), see [2].

Theorem 1 *Let $\lambda < 1$, and (η_i) a sequence of i.i.d. random variables such that $E(\eta_i^2) < \infty$. Denote by F_1 the distribution function of the interdeparture times ξ_i. Then the system can be improved by delay in the sense of (3) iff $\exists x_0 < W: \ F_1(x_0) > 0$.*

This condition states intuitively that the probability of small ξ_i's is positive.
Call a function $\hat{g} \in G$ optimal if $W(\hat{g}) = \min_{g \in G} W(g)$.

Theorem 2 *Under the conditions of theorem 1, the optimal delay function is*

$$\hat{g}(x) = \max(c - x, 0)$$

where c is the (unique) solution of the equation

$$c^2 = \int_c^\infty (x-c)^2 \, dF_1(x),$$

and it holds that $c = W(\hat{g})$.

Theorem 2 states that there is a bound, namely c, such that the departure of a bus is delayed only if ξ, the potential interdeparture time, does not exceed c. This strategy has a smoothing effect on the interdeparture times, which become more uniform and less scattered. This ultimately reduces the average waiting time of the passengers.

Example Suppose that η_i has a Poisson distribution with parameter 1. Some results for this case are given in the following table:

λ	W	$W(\hat{g})$	$E(\xi)$	$E(\xi^*)$
3/4	10	6.75	4	7.98
1/2	3	2.37	2	3.23
1/3	1.875	1.55	1.5	2.22
1/4	$1.\bar{5}$	1.31	$1.\bar{3}$	1.90
1/8	1.225	1.05	1.14	1.54

Obviously the average waiting time of the passengers is reduced by the delays although the average interdeparture time increases. The explanation is that the variance of the interdeparture time is reduced, e.g.

$$\begin{aligned} \text{for } \lambda = 3/4: \quad & \text{var}(\xi) = 64, \\ & \text{var}(\xi^*) = 44.03, \\ \text{for } \lambda = 1/4: \quad & \text{var}(\xi) = 2.37, \\ & \text{var}(\xi^*) = 1.36. \end{aligned}$$

3 Another Shuttle System

Suppose passengers arrive at a bus station according to a stationary process with intensity λ. Let the boarding times of the passengers now be zero. The capacity of the buses is again assumed to be infinite. Thus, a bus can leave the station immediately after arrival, so that arrival and departure epochs coincide. Suppose that in the original system the arrival times of the buses form a renewal process, the interarrival times being given by the sequence (η_i). Our aim is once again to diminish the passengers' average waiting time until departure W by means of delay. Now, our strategy is to delay the arrival times of the buses.

The models may be described as follows: The original sequence of interarrival times (which are identical with the interdeparture times) is given by (η_i). The interarrival times in the delayed system are then

$$\begin{aligned} \eta_1^* &= \zeta_1 + g_1(\zeta_1) && \text{with} \quad \zeta_1 \equiv \eta_1, \\ \eta_2^* &= \zeta_2 + g_2(\zeta_2) && \text{with} \quad \zeta_2 = \max(\eta_1 + \eta_2 - \eta_1^*, 0), \\ \eta_3^* &= \zeta_3 + g_3(\zeta_3) && \text{with} \quad \zeta_3 = \max(\eta_1 + \eta_2 + \eta_3 - \eta_1^* - \eta_2^*, 0), \\ & \cdots \\ \eta_n^* &= \zeta_n + g_n(\zeta_n) && \text{with} \quad \zeta_n = \max\left(\textstyle\sum_{i=1}^{n} \eta_i - \sum_{i=1}^{n-1} \eta_i^*, 0\right), \\ & \cdots \end{aligned} \tag{4}$$

where g_i are nonnegative functions (see figure 2). Observe that the structure of this model is much more complicated than the structure of the first model, because each delay depends on all previous interarrival times.

The next step is to compare the waiting time of a passenger from his arrival until departure of his bus in the original and the delayed system. For this purpose, we consider a transport system

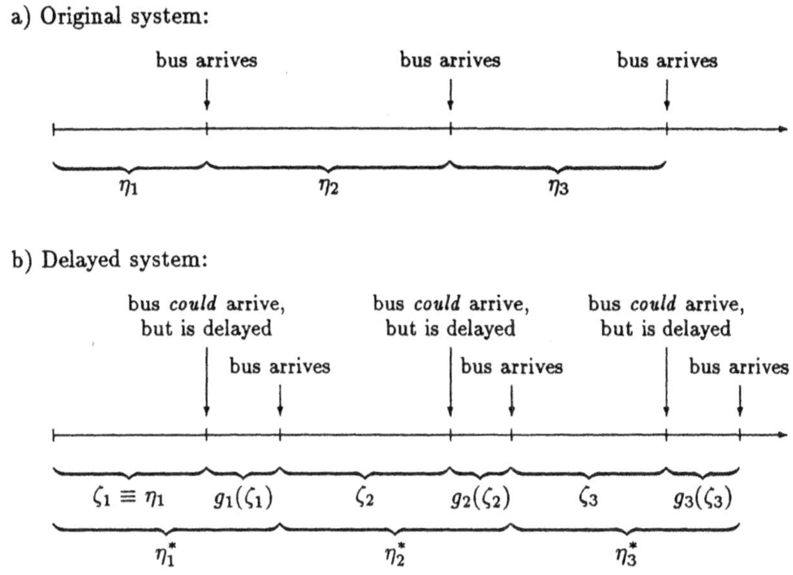

Figure 2: Original and delayed system according to equation (4)

(without delay) where the interarrival times of the buses are given by the sequence (ζ_i). We call this an intermediate system. Denote by W_1 the expectation of the waiting time in this system. Thus, W_1 measures the impact of the delays on the passengers' waiting times: A passenger arriving in the time interval $(\sum_{i=1}^{n-1} \zeta_i, \sum_{i=1}^{n} \zeta_i]$ — that is, he will board the n-th bus in the intermediate system — finds himself in a situation as if all buses *before* his own may have been delayed, but the n-th bus will not be delayed. Denote by W_2 the waiting time of a passenger in the delayed system. The impact of delay may then be studied in terms of the intermediate system and the delayed system, that is, by comparing W_1 and W_2. Thus, we define $M(g) := W_2 - W_1$ where $g = (g_i)$.

Theorem 3 *All the functions g_i must be identical. The optimal delay function is*

$$\hat{g}(x) = \max(\mathrm{E}(\eta) - x, 0).$$

Delay can improve service iff $\mathrm{var}(\eta) > 0$.

References

[1] Cox, D.R.: *Renewal Theory.* Methuen, 1962.

[2] Gadjiev, Asaf / Schmidbauer, Harald: Control by delay of shuttle systems. (To appear.)

[3] Gadjiev, Asaf: Delays reducing the waiting time in queueing systems with cyclic services. *Scand. J. Statist.* 12 (1985), 301–307.

Optimal Myopic Policies and Index Policies for Stochastic Scheduling Problems

Jürgen Weishaupt
Abteilung für Mathematik VII, Universität Ulm
Postfach 40 66, 7900 Ulm, Germany

In this paper we discuss the solution of the following value iteration:

$$V_n(s) = \max_{\{a:s_a>0\}} \{\alpha_n r_a + \beta \sum_x q(x) \sum_{j=0}^{K} p_{aj} V_{n-1}(s+x-e_a+e_j)\},\ s \neq 0, n \in \mathbb{N}$$

$$V_n(0) = \beta \sum_x q(x) V_{n-1}(x),\ n \in \mathbb{N}$$

where e_j denotes the j-th unit vector, $e_0 := 0$ and with $s = (s_1, \ldots, s_K) \in \mathbb{N}_0^K$, the ***system state***, $\alpha_n \geq 0, r_a \in \mathbb{R}$, the ***one-stage rewards***, the ***arrival distribution*** q on $\mathbb{N}_0^K$, $p_{aj} \geq 0, \sum_{j=0}^{K} p_{aj} = 1, a \in \{1, \ldots, K\}$, the ***routing-probabilities*** and $\beta \in \mathbb{R}_+$, the ***discount factor***. We define $V_0 \equiv 0$.

This model describes a discrete-time single-server multi-class queueing system with feedback as follows. A server has to schedule customers at K different queues over a finite number of periods. When he serves a customer at queue a he gets a reward of $\alpha_n r_a$, if there are still n decision-periods remaining. A served customer at queue a will then either leave the system with probability p_{a0} or go to queue j with probability p_{aj}. New customers will arrive in the system according to the probability distribution q independent of the queue lengths and the position of the server. When there are no customers in the system, the server keeps idle without reward. $V_n(s)$ is the maximal expected discounted total reward over n decision periods starting with the system state $s = (s_1, \ldots, s_K)$, where s_a denotes the number of customers present at queue a.

We consider also the case that waiting customers will cause waiting costs. Assuming the waiting costs to be linear in the queue lentghs, we obtain the following value iteration for $K_n(s)$, the minimal expected discounted total waiting costs over n decision periods starting with the system state s (with $K_0 \equiv 0$).

$$K_n(s) = \min_{\{a:s_a>0\}} \{cs + \beta \sum_x q(x) \sum_{j=0}^{K} p_{aj} K_{n-1}(s+x-e_a+e_j)\},\ s \neq 0, n \in \mathbb{N}$$

$$K_n(0) = \beta \sum_x q(x) K_{n-1}(x),\ n \in \mathbb{N}$$

This problem of minimizing expected waiting costs can be transformed in an equivalent maximizing problem with pure rewards.

Lemma 1

Assume $\sum_x xq(x) < \infty$. Then

$$K_n(s) = \alpha_{n+1}cs + \gamma_{n+1} - \beta V_n(s)$$

with $\alpha_n := \sum_{\nu=0}^{n-1} \beta^\nu$, $r_a := c_a - \sum_{j=1}^{K} p_{aj}c_j$, $\gamma_n \in I\!R$.

So we can handle maximizing pure rewards and minimizing waiting costs in one common model.

A quite handsome policy is the so-called ***myopic*** policy, i. e. the sequence of decision rules $(f^*, \ldots, f^*)$, where for $s \neq 0$ $f^*(s)$ is a maximum point of $a \mapsto r_a$, $a \in \{b : s_b > 0\}$. The myopic policy is not necessary an optimal policy for the stochastic scheduling problem. In the following theorem, we give a sufficient condition for the optimality of the myopic policy.

Theorem 2

We make the following assumptions:

i) $\alpha_{n+1} \geq \beta\alpha_n$

ii) $K = 2$ *or*

$K > 2$ and for all $a, j \in \{1, \ldots, K\}$ with $a \neq j$:

$$p_{aj} > 0 \Rightarrow r_j \leq r_a \text{ (\textbf{deteriorating case})}.$$

Then the myopic policy $(f^*, \ldots, f^*)$ is optimal for all finite horizon scheduling problems.

Assumption a) holds, if $\alpha_n \equiv 1$ and $\beta \leq 1$, or $\alpha_n = \sum_{\nu=0}^{n-1} \beta^\nu$ and $\beta \in I\!R_+$. In the special case that a served customer will either leave the system or stay at his queue, i. e. $p_{a0} + p_{aa} = 1 = \mu_a + (1 - \mu_a)$, the deteriorating case in b) holds. For the minimizing waiting costs problem of Lemma 1 we obtain $r_a = \mu_a c_a$ and theorem 2 yields the optimality of the ***μc-rule*** for this model (cf. Buyukkoc/Varaiya/Walrand(1985)).

We consider now the infinite horizon scheduling problem (with $\beta < 1$). The maximal expected discounted total reward over infinite many decision periods is the unique solution of the optimality equation

$$\begin{aligned} V(s) &= \max_{\{a:s_a>0\}} \{r_a + \beta \sum_x q(x) \sum_{j=0}^{K} p_{aj} V(s - e_a + x + e_j)\} \\ V(0) &= \beta \sum_x q(x) V(x) \end{aligned}$$

For the infinite horizon case we obtain the following

Theorem 3

There are $I_1, \ldots, I_K \in I\!R$ so that the stationary policy $(f, f, \ldots)$ is optimal for the infinite horizon scheduling problem, where $f(s)$ is the (greatest) maximum point of $a \mapsto I_a$, $a \in \{b : s_b > 0\}$ $(s \neq 0)$.

We call I_a ***index of a*** and $(f, f, \ldots)$ ***index policy***. The index I_a is a generalization of the well-known Gittins-Index for multi-armed bandit problems (cf. Gittins(1989)). Similar models have been considered by Whittle(1981) and Weiss(1988).

The following theorem gives a representation of the indices and bounds.

Theorem 4

a) $I_a = \inf\{M \in I\!R : V(e_a; M) = M\}$, where $V(\cdot; M)$ is the unique solution of the optimality equation

$$\begin{aligned} V(s; M) &= \max\{M, \max_{\{a:s_a>0\}} \{r_a + \beta \sum_x q(x) \sum_{j=0}^{K} p_{aj} V(s + x - e_a + e_j; M)\}\} \\ V(0; M) &= M \end{aligned}$$

b) $\max\{\frac{r_a}{1-\beta}, h^{-1}(r_a)\} \leq I_a \leq \frac{\max_j r_j}{1-\beta}$, where $h(M) = M - \beta \sum_x q(x) V(x; M)$.

$V(\cdot; M)$ is the value-function of the so-called M-stopping-problem which is obtained from the scheduling problem by adding an action that stops the optimization process with a reward M. From b), one can immediately derive the largest index: For a with $r_a = \max_j r_j$, the index I_a is equal to $\frac{r_a}{1-\beta}$.

Due to a), one can formulate another deteriorating case which is sufficient for the optimality of the myopic policy.

Theorem 5

For all $a, j \in \{1, \ldots, K\}$ with $p_{aj} > 0$ assume $I_j \le I_a$. Then:

$$I_a = h^{-1}(r_a)$$

and the myopic policy $(f^*, f^*, \ldots)$ is optimal for the infinite horizon scheduling problem.

The following theorem gives a sufficient condition for the equivalence of the two assumptions of theorem 2 and theorem 5.

Theorem 6

Let $r_i \neq r_j$ für $i \neq j$. Then the following assertions are equivalent:

a) For all $a, j \in \{1, \ldots, K\}$ with $p_{aj} > 0$ holds $I_j \le I_a$

b) For all $a, j \in \{1, \ldots, K\}$ with $p_{aj} > 0$ holds $r_j \le r_a$

References

Buyukkoc C, Varaiya P, Walrand J (1985) The $c\mu$-rule revisited. Adv. Appl. Probab. 17: 237-238

Gittins J C (1989) Mulit-armed bandit allocation indices. Wiley. Chichester

Weishaupt J (1992) Optimalitätsaussagen für stochastische Schedulingprobleme. Dissertation an der Universität Ulm.

Weiss G (1988) Branching bandit problems. Prob. Eng. Inf. Sci. 2: 269-278

Whittle P (1981) Arm-acquiring bandits. Ann. Probab. 9: 284-292

Impulse and Continuous Stochastic Control: A Dynamic Programming Approach

Alexander A. Yushkevich
Department of Mathematics, Universtiy of North Carolina at Charlotte
Charlotte, NC 28223, U.S.A.

1. A predominant approach to impulse stochastic control is that by functional analysis methods (Bensoussan et Lions (1982)). It originated as a generalization of optimal stopping and an appropriate field of applications of quasivaraitional inequalities (= QVI). One understands here impulse actions as deterministic shifts of the state made at sequentially increasing stopping times, usually without a continuous control between them. As to instantaneous iterations of impulse actions, in most works they are excluded either by definition or informally by a cost structure which makes such iterations certainly unprofitable; in others they are ignored while formally not forbidden. Started with diffusion processes, the study was extended later to other cases, among them to piecewise-deterministic processes (=PDP; Costa and Davis (1989)).

The dynamic programming (=DP) approach to the impulse control is a continuation of the study of finite and countable continuous-time DP models and similar jump-like Borel models. An essential step in this direction was the study of Markov decision drift processes (Schouten (1983)). Under the DP approach, in addition to continuous actions influencing the infinitesimal generator of the process, also impulse actions are allowed that provide immediate jumps of the same random character as others. Policies are treated as functions of histories with values both in the continuous and impulse parts of the action space. Immediate repetitions of the same or different impulse action are permitted, so that it becomes possible to install segments of discrete-time DP in a continuously controlled process. Such a possibility ensures the existence of optimal policies in rather reasonable models in which otherwise such policies do not exist. The DP approach works most consistently in controlled PDP, in which case, because of the open loop character of arbitrary policies, histories reduce to finite collections of time and space coordinates, similar to discrete-time DP models. This analogy with discrete-time DP (in some questions even a reduction to it) allows to exploit the discrete-time ideology and known results, in particular, in utilization of conditional policies and measurability questions.

2. A suitable framework for a rigorous treatment of control problems with allowed immediate iterations of impulse decisions is provided by *processes with time splitting*. In such processes, at some random times $t \geq 0$ there is not a single visited state $x(t)$, but a collection of sequentially visited states $x(t,0)$, $x(t,1)$, ..., $x(t,m_t)$; in a controlled process a decision should be made at each of this states. The number of such t is at most countable. It is convenient to substitute all other t by $(t,0)$, and thus deal all the time with *instants* (t,m). To every instant $T=(t,m)$, $t \geq 0$, $m=0,1,2,...$ corresponds a (non-random) sigma-algebra of events up to T, and basic notions of the general theory of stochastic processes, such as stopping times and related sigma-algebras, progressive measurability, Markov and martingale properties, extend to processes with time splitting (in most definitions one should along with random variables $x(T)$, T=const, consider also variables $x(T_j)$, where T_1, T_2,... are random instants $T=(t,m)$ with $m \geq 1$ enumerated in a measurable way). For PDP it is convenient to split every jump epoch. Then $T_1 < T_2 < ...$ become post-instants of all jumps of the sample path, and the path itself becomes closed on both ends between jumps.

3. Various results on both impulse and continuous control extend to (or find their proper interpretation in terms of) processes with time splitting. For example, consider a version of QVI-type optimality conditions for PDP (cf. Yushkevich (1989)).The model is specified by a state space X in R^d, sets $A^1(x)$ of impulse and $A^2(x)$ of continuous actions admitted at x, a drift coefficient $b(x,a)$, $a \in A^2(x)$ Lipschitzian in x, a bounded jump rate $\mu(x,a)$, $a \in A^2(x)$, a jump distribution $q(x,a,dy)$, $a \in A^1(x) \cup A^2(x)$, a bounded reward rate $r(x,a)$, $a \in A^2(x)$, a bounded impulse reward $R(x,a)$, $a \in A^1(x)$, and a discount parameter $\beta > 0$ (everywhere $x \in X$). We omit measurability etc. conditions and rather complicated definitions of policies. The criterion is

$$v^\pi(x) = E^{x,\pi}\left[\int_0^\infty e^{-\beta t} r(x_t,a_t)dt + \sum_k \exp(-\beta t_k) R(x_k,a_k) \right] \to \max$$

where x is an initial state, π is a policy, x_t and a_t denote the state and action at the instant $T=(t,0)$, and t_k, x_k, a_k are the time, (pre-)state, impulse action of the kth consecutive impulse decision. Let L be a following operator:

$$LF(x,a) = \begin{cases} R(x,a) + \int_X [F(y)-F(x)]q(x,a,dy) - F(x), & a \in A^1(x), \\ r(x,a) + b(x,a)\operatorname{grad} F(x) + \mu(x,a)\int_X [F(y)-F(x)]q(x,a,dy) - \beta F(x), & a \in A^2(x). \end{cases}$$

Then a bounded differentiable, Lipschitzian function $v(x)$ and a stationary policy $a=f(x)$ are the value function $v(x)=\sup_\pi v^\pi(x)$ and an optimal policy, if

$$\sup_{a \in A(x)} Lv(x,a) = Lv(x,a) = 0, \quad x \in X \tag{1}$$

where $A(x)=A^1(x)\cup A^2(x)$. (In the one-dimensional case one may omit differentiability of v, and require (1) only (a.e.) on the set where $f(x)\in A^2$.) The relation (1) is written in a form of Bellman optimality equation together with conserving condition, but indeed it splits into QVI-type conditions.

4. As an application consider a following two-armed bandit problem. An unobserved Poissonian flow of particles of rate 1 should be divided between inputs of two arms of a device in order to maximize the expected total number of particles observed at the outputs of the arms. There are two hypotheses, H_1 and H_2, with known a priori probabilities x and $1-x$. Any particle entering the output of an arm either immediately reaches its output and is observed or vanishes unobserved. According to H_1, probabilities of this two events are p and $q=1-p$ for the first arm, and q and p for the second, $0<p<\frac{1}{2}$. According to H_2, the same is true with a transposition of arms. Continuous actions $a\in[0,1]$ determine probabilities a and $1-a$ that a particle is directed to the first or the second arm. A single impulse action i consists in putting an artificial particle into one of the arms; independent of the outcome, this action yields a negative reward $-c$. The horizon is infinite, and an overtaking or discounted criterion is used (Donchev (1990), Yushkevich (1992)).In terms of a posteriori probabilities x_T and $1-x_T$ of H_1 and H_2, we have here an one-dimensional controlled PDP. Jumps of $\{x_T\}$ correspond to observations of particles and to impulse actions. For $0<c\leq c_0$, an optimal control is given by a stationary policy $a_T=f(x_T)$ where $f(x)=i$ on some closed interval $[x_c,1-x_c]$, $f(x)=1$ on $[0,x_c)$, and $f(x)=0$ on $(1-x_c,1]$. In general, the optimal process undergoes a random unlimited finite number of consecutive instantaneous jumps until it reaches one of the regions where f prescribes actions 0 or 1.

REFERENCES

Bensoussan A, Lions J.L (1982) Contrôle impulsionnel et inéquations quasi variationnelles. Dunod. Paris

Costa O.L.V, Davis M.H.A (1989) Impulse control of piecewise-deterministic processes. Math Control Signal Systems 1:187-208

Donchev D.S (1990) The two-armed bandit problem with continuous time in the presence of gradual and impulsive controls. Russian Math Surveys 45:1:200-202

van der Duyn Schouten F.A (1983) Markov decision processes with continuous time parameter. Math Centrum Tracts. Amsterdam

Yushkevich A.A (1989) Verification theorems for Markov decision processes with controlled deterministic drift and gradual and impulsive controls. Theory Prob 34:474-496

Yushkevich A.A (1992) On a two-armed bandit problem with impulse controls and discounting. Russian Math Surveys (submitted)

Section 3

Combinatorial Optimization and Discrete Mathematics

Structure Independent Optimization of Embedding Graphs in Books

Tomasz Bilski
Dept. of Control, Robotics and Computer Science, Technical University
Piotrowo 3A, 60-965 Poznań, Poland

Generally, in order to embed a graph in a book we have to solve 2 main problems, Chung et al. (1987):

- finding the order of the vertices on the spine,
- assigning the edges to pages.

However, in some applications, the layout of the vertices is fixed, so only the second problem has to be solved.

It has been shown that, the problem of optimum embedding of a graph in a book, with prespecified order of the vertices is NP-complete, Even and Itai (1971) and Garey et al. (1987), so effective algorithm for graph embedding in a book does not exist. For some graph families, structure dependent, effective methods may be used, Bilski (1992). But in a general case, it is necessary to use methods producing nearly optimum results.

The paper deals with heuristic method for graphs with prespecified order of vertices.

FOUNDATIONS

Let us assume, that for graph $G=\{V,E\}$ a 1 to 1 function f indexing the vertices exists, $f: V \rightarrow \{1,2,3,...n\}$, where n is the number of vertices in G (for simplicity assume that n is even).

The vertices of the graph G are ordered on the spine according to values of f(v).

<u>Definition 1:</u> The set $B_{i,j}$ is a set of edges that may not be embedded on the same page with the edge $e_{i,j}$ ($e_{i,j}$ is an edge

connecting vertices i and j).

Definition 2: The set B_p is a set of edges that may not be embedded on page P.

The method presented is based on the following foundation: the probability that the given single edge may be embedded on pages with assigned edges is inversely proportional to:

1) the cardinal numbers of B_p for all pages,
2) the cardinal number of $B_{i,j}$ for given edge.

This foundation leads to the following conclusions:

1) the edges should be sorted decreasingly according to cardinal numbers of $B_{i,j}$ and this should be the order of assigning edges to pages,
2) if the given edge may be assigned to two or more pages, then it should be assigned to the page, for which the increase of the cardinal number of B_p, after the embedding of the new edge, will be minimal.

METHOD

The main steps of the method are presented in two algorithms: the algorithm for graph embedding and the algorithm for single edge embedding.

Graph embedding

1. Embed each edge $e_{i,j}$, such that $j-i=n/2$, on a different page (it may be shown that all such edges must lie separately).
2. For every edge $e_{i,j}$ not assigned to page, find the cardinal number of the set $B_{i,j}$.
3. Sort edges decreasingly according to $\|B_{i,j}\|$.
4. Embed the edges in order computed in step 3 (conclusion 1).

Edge embedding

1. Check, if $e_{i,j}$ may be embedded on currently busy pages.
2. Three cases are possible:

A. If the edge $e_{i,j}$ may not be embedded then
embed the edge on a free page.

B. If the edge $e_{i,j}$ may be embedded on one page P_x only then
embed the edge on this page.

C. If the edge may be embedded on m pages $P_{x1}, P_{x2}, \ldots, P_{xm}$ (m>1) then
for each page P_{xl} (l=1,2,3,...m) find W_{xl},

$W_{xl} = \| B_{Pxl}' \| - \| B_{Pxl} \|$

$\| B_{Pxl} \|$ - the cardinal number of set of edges that may not be embedded on page P_{xl},

$\| B_{Pxl}' \|$ - the cardinal number of set of edges that might not be embedded on page P_{xl} after embedding $e_{i,j}$ on the page,

embed the edge $e_{i,j}$ on page P_{xl}, such that W_{xl}=min (conclusion 2), (if two or more pages P_{xl} have the same W_{xl}=min, embed the edge on page P_{xl}, such that the width of this page will not increase or such that has minimum width).

If in any step of the algorithm the actual number of used pages reaches n/2 then all the edges of the graph may be embedded using the expressions for complete graphs, Bilski (1992), such embedding gives number of pages not greater than n/2.

The computational complexity of the presented method is $O(n^4)$.

REFERENCES

Bilski T. (1992) Embedding graphs in books: a survey, IEE PROCEEDINGS-E, Vol. 139, No. 2, March 1992, pp. 134-138.

Chung F.R.K., Leighton F.T., Rosenberg A.L. (1987) Embedding graphs in books: A layout problem with applications to VLSI design, SIAM J. Alg. Disc. Math., vol. 8, No. 1, January 1987, pp 33-58.

Even S., Itai A. (1971) Queues, stacks and graphs, Z. Kohavi and A. Paz (eds.), in Theory of Machines and Computations, Academic Press, New York, pp. 71-86.

Garey M.R., Johnson D.S., Miller G.L., Papadimitriou C.H. (1980) The complexity of coloring circular arcs and chords, SIAM J. Alg. Disc. Math., vol. 8, No. 1, pp. 216-227.

An Improved Version of Tabu Search for Irregular Cutting Problems

J. Błażewicz, R. Walkowiak
Institute of Computing Science, Technical University of Poznań
Piotrowo 3A, 60-965 Poznań, Poland

Introduction

The two-dimensional cutting problem consists of cutting a set of pieces from a sheet of material in order to minimize a waste. The general problem is NP-hard in strong sense. Thus only approximate polynomial algorithms are useful for standard instances of the problem. For one of the most complex problems in this area - the two-dimensional irregular cutting problem - a few algorithms of this type have been proposed [2, 1, 6]. The problem issue considered in the algorithms is constrained to the sub-class in which the elements of arbitrary shapes are to be placed in or cut from the rectangular area, whose one dimension is fixed and the other is to be minimized. The algorithms contain some idea from the artificial intelligence area, make use of the graph theory and are based on the observation of the manual layout generation process as well. Their scheme is rather rigid and hard to adapt for use with different sets of element's shapes. Also the issue of rectangularity of allocation area is very hard to overcome in those algorithms. Tests made for some algorithms [3] and the results obtained led us through new methods investigation to tabu search approach [5]. The first application of the tabu search for the problem [4] though based on rather simple idea gave very interesting results. Some new elements of the method will be described it this paper.

Method's description

Scheme of the algorithm

The method for automatic generation of elements' layout consists of two stages. At first the initial allocation is found. This phase is to be solved by any method yielding a feasible layout. The algorithm used is based on a simple idea of allocation in holes. A hole is an unused part of allocation area delimited by the allocation area border or allocated elements borders. As the allocation process is carried out new holes are created and possibility of allocation of a next element in holes is tested. The pair hole-element choice is made using the best fit criterion. The areas of the hole and the element are compared.

The second stage of the process use the feasible solution from the first stage and transform it to obtain a better value of the goal function - the minimum length of the area used. At this stage general scheme of tabu search is used. In every iteration at least one final feasible solution is generated.

The geometric phase is used to secure the feasibility of the solution's transformation. The way the second phase operates will be described using the basic notion of tabu search.

A **move** - the way a new solution is obtained - consists in change of allocation of a set of elements. As the element is moved from one hole to another, its allocation is changed. This results in a new solution in the "neighbourhood" of the previous one. The number of elements moved and the way they are moved is to be defined and these parameters specify the neighbourhood. In the new implementation of the algorithm there is no restriction on the number of elements moved simultaneusly.

The **optimum function** is a criterion for evaluating a **move**. It enables us to make an appropriate decision according to removing and reallocation of elements. In each iteration the best move in sense of the optimum function is chosen.

The **tabu** condition defines **moves** which are forbidden at current stage of tabu search procedure. It is usually implemented as a list of moves made in previous iterations or moves reverse to the lately made ones.

Basing on the above given definitions the solution improvement stage can be defined. At first the decision should be made about elements to be taken from the solution. A matching the element and surrounding it allocation area is taken into account. These elements for which the area of surrounding them holes is the biggest are the candidates for a move. At this point the tabu condition is checked. It is implemented as a list of the elements moved during lately made iterations. Any element on the list cannot be removed from the current solution. The minimal number of elements moved during one iteration is specified as a parameter but the final number depends on geometric relations between elements (all elements in solution should have contact with other elements or the borders of an allocation area). The tests showed that the length of the tabu list equal 5 makes the return to the previously obtained solution (cycling of the search process) very unlikely. As the elements are chosen the possibility of their allocation in existing holes is checked. The matching a hole and an element is made according to the best fit rule. The areas of the hole and the element are compared. The allocation of an element inside a hole is determined by the geometrical phase of the algorithm. The stop condition for the iteration process of tabu search is defined by the number of iteration made without solution's improvement. This number was equal 30 for tested instances.

Geometrical phase

The geometrical phase is used to secure the feasibility of solution. The main problem to be solved is finding allocation of an element–polygon within a hole–another polygon. The polygons are "one piece" objects with no holes inside. There is no restriction on convexity of the polygon's shape. Because of the time restriction, simple algorithm for the needs of our method has been used. The procedure [4] is an approximate one in the sense that it can not detect some advantageous allocation places. This is because, while the feasible allocation area are defined, the element moved along a hole border cannot go behind a "bottle neck" of a hole area to the other part of possible allocation area. To overcome this disadvantage hole's parts separated by "bottle necks" have been extracted and the procedure has been repeated for every partial hole. This enables to find additional correct placements of elements.

Results

Comparative tests have been made for the above method and the methods [1, 6]. Average time and quality results are compared in the Figure 1. They show the advantage of the tabu method in respect of solution's quality. Though on average time required for the search process in tabu method is longer than time needed for solution generation by remaining methods, the best solution in tabu method ($TABU^*$) is often found in comparative time.

Remarks

The method implemented under DOS allows solving instances with restricted sizes (maximum about 20 complicated shapes). Computing power of the PC used is insufficient for full use of at

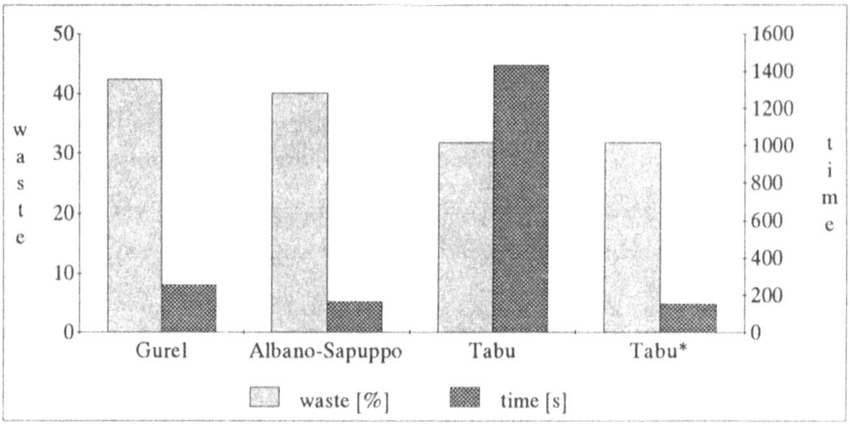

Fig. 1. A comparision of the results obtained by different allocation methods.

least one of the search method advantages - increase in number of solutions compared. The same reason refrained from implementation of optimal polygon placement procedure.

We hope that the use of more powerful computers (multiprocessor parallel machines and more flexible program environments) allows further research resulting in creation of fully professional industry applicable (especially in respect of solution quality) system.

References

[1] A. Albano, G. Sapuppo (1980) Optimal allocation of two-dimensional shapes using heuristic search methods. *IEEE Trans. on Systems, Man and Cybernetics,* Vol. SMC-10, No. 5.

[2] R. C. Jr. Art (1966) An approach to the two-dimensional irregular cutting stock problem. *IBM Report 320-2006,* Cambridge.

[3] J.Błażewicz, M.Drozdowski, B. Soniewicki, R. Walkowiak (1990) Decision support system for cutting irregular shapes - implementation and experimental comparison. *Foundations of Computing and Decision Sciences,* vol. 15, No. 3-4.

[4] J.Błażewicz, P.Hawryluk, R. Walkowiak (1992): Using tabu search approach for solving two-dimensional irregular cutting problem. *Annals of Operations Research on Tabu Search,* to appear.

[5] F.Glover (1989) Tabu search - Part I. *ORSA Journal on Computing* 1/3.

[6] O. Gurel (1969) Circular graph of marker layout. *IBM Data Processing Division, New York Scientific Center Report* No. 320-2965.

Restrictions of Graph Partition Problems

Hans L. Bodlaender
Department of Computer Science, Utrecht Universtiy
P.O. Box 80.089, 3508 TB Utrecht, Netherlands
Klaus Jansen
Fachbereich IV, Mathematik/Informatik, Universität Trier
Postfach 3825, 5500 Trier, Germany

1 Introduction

Let J be a set of n jobs, all with job processing time or job length one, and let M be a set of k machines. Incompatibilities between jobs are described by an undirected graph $G = (J, E)$ with vertex set J. If G contains an edge between two jobs j and j' $(j \neq j')$, we demand that these two jobs can not be executed by the same machine. An assignment of the jobs to the machines, which satisfies the incompatibility relation, is called a schedule. The processing time of a machine is given by the number of assigned jobs, since each job has processing time one.

Given a second constraint, the deadline k', the problem is to find a schedule of the jobs to the k machines such that the processing time of each machine is less or equal to k'.

An important combinatorial problem which is related to the scheduling problem is the coloring problem of an undirected graph $G = (V, E)$. A k-coloring is a mapping $f : V \rightarrow \{1, \ldots, k\}$ with for all edges $(v, w) \in E$, $f(v) \neq f(w)$. A set U is called independent if each pair $v, w \in U$ with $v \neq w$ is not connected by an edge. The k-coloring problem corresponds to the problem of finding a partition of the vertices into k independent sets. It turns out, that the scheduling problem is equal to the problem to find a partition of the incompatibility graph into k independent sets, each of size at most k'. Since a partition into independent sets forms a coloring of the incompatibility graph, the problem is, given a graph G, and two integers k, k', to search for a coloring of G with at most k colors, such that for each color, there are at most k' vertices with that color. We call this problem PARTITION INTO BOUNDED INDEPENDENT SETS and give in the following the complete definition.

Problem: PARTITION INTO BOUNDED INDEPENDENT SETS
Instance: Undirected graph $G = (V, E)$, integers $k, k' \in \mathbb{N}$.
Question: Is there a partition of the vertex set V into independent sets $U_1, \ldots, U_k$ with $|U_i| \leq k'$ for $1 \leq i \leq k$?

Karp [5] has shown that the coloring problem is NP-complete for undirected graphs and up to this time no polynomial-time algorithm is known for this problem. Hence, the problem PARTITION INTO BOUNDED INDEPENDENT SETS is also NP-complete for general undirected graphs.

We consider also the scheduling problem on the complement of G. Then it becomes the following problem:

Problem: PARTITION INTO BOUNDED CLIQUES
Instance: Undirected graph $G = (V, E)$, integers $k, k' \in \mathbb{N}$.
Question: Is there a partition of the vertex set V into cliques $C_1, \ldots, C_k$ with $|C_i| \leq k'$ for $1 \leq i \leq k$?

This problem is NP-complete, because it contains the PARTITION INTO CLIQUES problem [5]. We denote with $\chi(G, k')$ the minimum number of independent sets of size at most k' that cover G and we denote with $\kappa(G, k')$ the minimum number of cliques of size k' that cover G.

However, the coloring problem and the problem partition into cliques become much easier, when we restrict the inputs to certain special graph classes. For example, there are efficient algorithms for interval graphs [4], cographs [8] and bipartite graphs. Therefore we have analysed the PARTITION INTO BOUNDED CLIQUES (INDEPENDENT SETS) problems for these graph classes. For split graphs both problem are solvable in polynomial time, proved by Lonc [6].

But we have also considered the cases that the numbers k or k' are constants. This is related to the case of a constant number of machines or a constant deadline.

2 Cographs

Cographs are graphs without a path of length four as induced subgraph [8]. These graphs can be generated by disjoint union and join operations on graphs starting with single-vertex graphs and can be represented about these operations. For graphs $G_i = (V_i, E_i)$ with $V_1 \cap V_2 = \emptyset$ the union of G_1 and G_2, $\cup(G_1, G_2)$ is given by $(V_1 \cup V_2, E_1 \cup E_2)$. The join of G_1 and G_2, denoted by $+(G_1, G_2)$ is obtained by first taking the union of G_1 and G_2, and then adding all edges $\{v_1, v_2\}$ with $v_i \in V_i$.

Since the complement of a cograph is again a cograph, the same results hold for the complexity of PARTITION INTO BOUNDED CLIQUES and PARTITION INTO BOUNDED INDEPENDENT SETS when restricted to cographs.

Theorem 2.1 *The problems* PARTITION INTO BOUNDED CLIQUES (INDEPENDENT SETS) *remain NP-complete for cographs.*

Since the problems to partition into k cliques or independent sets of size at most k' are NP-complete, we look at instances with constant k or k'. When $k' = 3$ and $k = |V|/3$, we get the problem PARTITION INTO TRIANGLES. For constant k' we can use the recursive structure of the cograph.

Theorem 2.2 *The problems* PARTITION INTO BOUNDED CLIQUES (INDEPENDENT SETS) *of at most a constant size k' can be computed in polynomial time.*

A similar approach we can use for the problems where the number of cliques k is constant. For these problems we describe partitions into cliques $C_1, \ldots, C_k$ by the sizes $|C_1|, \ldots, |C_k|$ and consider sequences of sizes instead of subsets of the vertices V. We call a sequence of sizes *feasible*, if it corresponds to a partition.

Theorem 2.3 *The problems* PARTITION INTO K BOUNDED CLIQUES (INDEPENDENT SETS) *of size at most k' with constant k can be solved in polynomial time for cographs.*

3 Bipartite graphs

A graph $G = (V, E)$ is called bipartite if there is a partition of the vertices V into two disjoint set V_1, V_2 where the set of edges E forms a subset of $\{\{v, w\} | v \in V_1, w \in V_2\}$.

Cliques in a bipartite graph have at most the size two and therefore the problem PARTITION INTO BOUNDED CLIQUES can be solved in polynomial time using a matching algorithm. But for independent sets the situation is more difficult.

Theorem 3.1 *The problem* PARTITION INTO THREE BOUNDED INDEPENDENT SETS *remains NP-complete for bipartite graphs.*

Theorem 3.2 *The problem* PARTITION INTO BOUNDED INDEPENDENT SETS *of size at most k' with constant k' can be solved in polynomial time for bipartite graphs.*

4 Interval graphs

A graph $G = (V, E)$ is an interval graph, iff to each vertex $v \in V$, a closed interval I_v in the real line can be associated, such that for each pair of vertices $u, v \in V$, $u \neq v$, $\{u, v\} \in E$, if and only if $I_u \cap I_v \neq \emptyset$. The complement G^c of an interval graph G can be transitively oriented with $(u, v) \in A$ iff $(x \in I_u, y \in I_v \rightarrow x < y)$. This orientation A induces a partial order $P = (V, A)$, called interval order.

Lemma 4.1 *Let $G = (V, E)$ be an interval graph, let $P = (V, A)$ be the corresponding interval order and let $k, k' \in \mathbb{N}$. Then there is a partition of G into k cliques of size at most k' iff there is a feasible schedule of P with unit-times which needs at most k' machines and k time steps.*

Theorem 4.2 *The problem* PARTITION INTO BOUNDED CLIQUES *can be solved in linear time for interval graphs.*

Theorem 4.3 *The problem* PARTITION INTO BOUNDED INDEPENDENT SETS *remains NP-complete for interval graphs.*

For the problem with constant number k of independent sets we can use the same approach as for the cographs. A partition $U_1, \ldots, U_h$ with $h \leq k$ for an interval graph can be identified with a sequence of sizes $|U_1|, \ldots, |U_h|$ and the last endpoint $x_i = max_{v \in U_i} max(I_v)$ on the real line for each set U_i. Using dynamic programming we can generate all feasible sequences.

Theorem 4.4 *Given a constant k the problem* PARTITION INTO K BOUNDED INDEPENDENT SETS, *each of size at most k' can be solved in polynomial time for interval graphs.*

The complexity of PARTITION INTO BOUNDED INDEPENDENT SETS each of size at most k' is open for $k' = 3$. This problem (for $k' = 3$) contains the problem PARTITION INTO TRIANGLES for the complement of interval graphs (namely when $k = |V|/3$).

Theorem 4.5 *The problem* PARTITION INTO BOUNDED INDEPENDENT SETS *each of size at most four remains NP-complete for interval graphs.*

References

[1] D.G. CORNEIL, Y. PERL, AND L.K. STEWART, A linear recognition algorithm for cographs, SIAM J. Comput. 4 (1985), pp. 926 - 934.

[2] M.R. GAREY AND D.S. JOHNSON, Computers and Intractability: A Guide to the Theory of NP-Completeness, Freeman, San Francisco, 1979.

[3] M.C. GOLUMBIC, Algorithmic Graph Theory and Perfect Graphs, Academic Press, London, 1980.

[4] U.I. Gupta, D.T. Lee and J.Y.-T. Leung, Efficient algorithms for interval graphs and circular arc graphs, Networks **12** (1982), pp. 459 – 467.

[5] R.M. Karp, Reducibility among combinatorial problems, in: Miller and Thatcher: Complexity of Computer Computations, Plenum Press (1972), pp. 85 – 104.

[6] Z. Lonc, On complexity of some chain and antichain partition problems, WG Conference, LNCS **570** (1991), pp. 97 – 104.

[7] C.H. Papadimitriou and M. Yannakakis, Scheduling interval-ordered tasks, SIAM J. Comp. **8** (1979), pp. 405 – 409.

[8] D. Seinsche, On a property of the class of n-colorable graphs, J. Comb. Theory **B 16** (1974), pp. 191 – 193.

Further Remarks on the Jeep Problem

Ute Brauer, Wilfried Brauer
Institut für Informatik, Technische Universität
Arcisstraße 21, 8000 München 2, Germany

Extended Abstract

The classical jeep problem (see [Fin], [Phi], [Gal]) is to compute how far a jeep can go when starting at a dump with n cans of gasoline, provided that it needs 1 canful to drive 1 unit distance and it is allowed to carry 2 canfuls of gasoline (including the contents of its tank). The optimal solution algorithm (see [Gal]) assumes that arbitrary fractions of a canful can be put into the tank. Since this seems to be a bit unrealistic, a discrete variant was considered by D. Wood in [Woo]: It is only allowed to refill the tank, when it is empty and then 1 canful has to be filled in (thus 1 can can be transported). The following solution was proposed in [Woo]: With one canful transport $n-1$ cans to the next dump and go on recursively. This gives the distance function $f_w(n) = 1 + 1 + \frac{1}{3} + \frac{1}{5} + \ldots + 1/(2n-3)$. It seemed to be the natural adaptation of the classical optimal solution.

However in [Bra] we showed that $f_w(n)$ is not optimal for $n \geq 4$ by using a new strategy: With one canful transport only 1 can as far as possible. This means that, for even n, each second can is transported to a dump $\frac{1}{2}$ unit distance away - apart from the last one, which is moved to an auxiliary dump $\frac{3}{4}$ units away, and which is fetched in the next round with the last $\frac{1}{2}$ canful. If $n = 2k+1$ then only $2k$ cans are used for transportation. Let $[x; n]$ denote the situation, that at position x there is a dump containing n cans. We then can describe the procedure by

$$[0; 2\cdot(2k-1)] \rightarrow [\frac{1}{2}; 2k-2]\&[\frac{3}{4}; 1] \rightarrow [1; k] \tag{1}$$

This gives better results than Wood's strategy for $n = 6$ and all $n \geq 12$. The distance function for this procedure is $f_u(n) = f_u(p(t)) = (t+3)/2$ for $p(t) \leq n < p(t+1)$ and $t \geq 1$.

$$\text{where} \quad p(t) = \begin{cases} (2^{t+1}+4)/3 = 2 + 2 + 2^3 + \ldots + 2^{t-1} & \text{for } t \text{ even} \\ (2^{t+1}+2)/3 = 2 + 2^2 + 2^4 + \ldots + 2^{t-1} & \text{for } t \text{ odd} \end{cases}$$

Its asymptotic behaviour is $\frac{1}{2}\lfloor log_2(3n)\rfloor + 1$ while that of $f_w(n)$ is $\frac{1}{2} ln\ n + 1.98$.

But the algorithms given in [Bra] are not always optimal. We still conjecture optimality for $n = p(t)$ where t is odd. For other values of n we have found several other (and better) solutions by slightly weakening the basic strategic idea of moving only 1 can as far as possible with 1 canful - such that it now seems to us that there is perhaps no universally optimal solution, but different procedures for different series of can numbers.

Procedure (1) suggests to consider the following sequences of can numbers $h_s(n)$ where s is a (small) integer and $h_s(1) = s; h_s(n+1) = 4h_s(n) - 2, n \geq 1$. For example $s = 2$ gives the $p(t)$ where t is odd. Obviously $f_u(h_s(n)) = f_u(s) + n - 1$ for $n \geq 2$.

To be able to work efficiently also with can numbers like 3, 4, 5, 6, 7, 8, 9, and also with the $p(t)$ for even t, we allow several auxiliary dumps at varying distances, and we move sometimes two cans forward by using the same tank filling; the resulting modified distance function is denoted by f_{um}

$$[0;3] \to [\frac{1}{3};2] \quad \text{gives} \quad f_{um}(3) = 2\frac{1}{3}$$
$$[0;4] \to [\frac{1}{2}+\frac{1}{6};2] \quad \text{gives} \quad f_{um}(4) = 2\frac{2}{3}$$

Both these values are optimal, since they are the same as in the classical case.

$$[0;5] \to [\frac{1}{4};2]\&[\frac{5}{8};1] \to [\frac{5}{8}+\frac{5}{24};2], \quad \text{i.e. } f_{um}(5) = 2\frac{5}{6}.$$

This seems to be optimal also, since the distance for 5 cans in the classical case is $2\frac{13}{15}$.

More generally we obtain the following procedures:

$$[0;2\cdot 2n] \to [\frac{1}{2};2n-2]\&[\frac{1}{2}+\frac{1}{8};2], n \geq 2 \tag{2}$$

$$\begin{aligned}[x;2j+2]\&[x+a;2] &\to [x+\frac{1}{2};j]\&[x+\frac{1}{2}+\frac{1}{2}a;1], \&[x+a;2] \to \\ &\to [x+\frac{1}{2};j]\&[x+\frac{1}{2}+\frac{1}{8}+\frac{1}{2}a;2], j \geq 2\end{aligned} \tag{3}$$

$$\begin{aligned}[x;4j+4]\&[x+a;2] &\to [x+\frac{1}{2};2j+2]\&[x+\frac{4}{3}a;2] \to \\ &\to [x+\frac{1}{2};2j+2]\&[x+\frac{3}{4}+\frac{2}{3}a;1] \to \\ &\to [x+1;j]\&[x+1+\frac{4}{9}a;2], j \geq 2.\end{aligned} \tag{4}$$

$$[x;4]\&[x+a;2] \to [x+a;2]\&[x+\frac{1}{2}+\frac{1}{4}a;2] \tag{5}$$

Near the end of a jeep's tour we need the following procedure:

$$\begin{aligned}[x;2]\&[x+a;2] &\to [x+\frac{1}{2}+\frac{1}{2}a;1]\&[x+a;2] \to \\ &\to [x+\frac{1}{2}+\frac{1}{2}a+\frac{1}{3}(\frac{1}{2}+\frac{1}{2}a);2] = [x+\frac{2}{3}(1+a);2]\end{aligned} \tag{6}$$

For some odd n we also found a (possibly optimal) starting procedure:

$$\begin{aligned}[0;7] &\to [\frac{1}{4};2]\&[\frac{1}{2}+\frac{1}{16};2] \\ [0;11] &\to [\frac{1}{4};6]\&[\frac{5}{8};1] \to [\frac{3}{4};2]\&[\frac{3}{4}+\frac{1}{16};2] \\ [0;4j+5] &\to [\frac{1}{4};2]\&[\frac{1}{2};2j]\&[\frac{1}{2}+\frac{1}{8};1] \to \\ &\to [\frac{1}{4}+\frac{1}{2};1]\&[\frac{1}{2}+\frac{1}{8}+\frac{1}{8};1]\&[\frac{1}{2};2j] = \\ &[\frac{1}{2};2j]\&[\frac{1}{2}+\frac{1}{4};2], j \geq 1.\end{aligned} \tag{7}$$

Applying these procedures in the appropriate order gives the following values of f_{um}:

$$f_{um}(7) = \frac{3}{18}, f_{um}(11) = 3\frac{1}{3} + \frac{1}{8}$$

$$f_{um}(p(2j)) = f_u(p(2j)) + \frac{1}{16} \cdot (\frac{4}{9})^{j-2} \quad \text{for} \quad j \geq 2$$

$$f_{um}(2^k) = \frac{1}{2}k + \frac{3}{2} + \frac{1}{3}(1 - 2^{1-k}) \quad \text{for} \quad k \geq 1$$

$$f_{um}(2^k + 1) = \frac{1}{2}k + \frac{3}{2} + \frac{1}{3} \quad \text{for} \quad k \geq 1$$

A problem arises when we consider the case $n = 10$. Obviously procedure (1) gives $[0;10] \rightarrow [1;3]$, and the optimal distance for $n = 3$ is $2\frac{1}{3}$. Thus it seems that the optimal distance for $n = 10$ should be $3\frac{1}{3} = f_u(h_3(2))$, since the jeep following procedure (1) always moves forward with a load of one can and never moves back behind a point where its tank was filled. Nevertheless already $f_{um}(9) = f_{um}(2^3 + 1) = 3\frac{1}{3}$. And indeed there is a better procedure for $n = 10$ by using procedures (5) and (6)

$$[0;10] \rightarrow [\frac{1}{4};4]\&[\frac{1}{2} + \frac{1}{16};2] \rightarrow [1\frac{1}{4} + \frac{5}{32};2]$$

That is, the distance reachable with $n = 10$ is $\frac{7}{96}$ units larger than that reached with procedure (1), although the jeep goes back (and forth) more often, and on the other hand the main reason why Wood's strategy is not optimal, seems to be the high number of backward tours.

From this we have to conclude that we cannot assume that the composition of good procedures gives again a good procedure. In particular the values $f_u(h_s(n))$ need not be optimal (although for example $f_u(14) = f_u(h_4(2)) = 3\frac{2}{3}$ looks quite well).

To get a better understanding of the solution possibilities, we may look at some natural constraints on possible solutions. We then see for example, that the constraint to have only one intermediate dump gives Wood's solution, while the constraint to have at most 2 dumps and fixed distances between dumps gives procedure (1).

[Bra] Brauer, U., Brauer, W.: *A new approach to the jeep problem*, EATCS Bulletin **38** (1989) 145-153

[Fin] Fine, N.J.: *The jeep problem*, Amer. Math. Monthly, **54** (1947) 24-31

[Gal] Gale, D.: *The jeep once more or jeeper by the dozen*, Amer. Math. Monthly, **77** (1970) 493-501

[Phi] Phipps, C.G.: *The jeep problem, A more general solution*, Amer Math. Monthly, **54** (1947) 458-462

[Woo] Wood, D.: *Paradigms and Programming with PASCAL*, Computer Science Press, Rockville, 1984.

A Class of Graphs with good Communicativeness

Valentin E. Brimkov
Operations Research Section, Inst. of Mathematics, Bulgarian Academy of Sciences
P.O. Box 373, 1113 Sofia, Bulgaria

We propose online algorithms for solving the well known Path Problem (PP) for searching a path from arbitrary graph vertex to another one in environment of incomplete information. The algorithms work on the introduced below convex graphs. The PP is one of the most intensively explored motion planning problems within the amortized analysis that evaluates the online algorithms with respect to the quality of the solution produced by them (e.g. see Tarjan (1985)).

Very often, depending on the problem nature, some other algorithmic parameters could be of importance. We have developed a general model based on considering of various algorithmic complexity types, measured with respect to one basic complexity - the information one, reflecting the data volume used during the problem solving. Such approach allows to take into account different algorithmic parameters, as well as to consider problems defined on infinite structures (e.g. infinite graphs).

Concerning the PP, here we will suppose that some object $\mathcal{M}$ can move along the graph edges, it is in a position "to see" at any moment an appropriate defined neighbourhood of the graph from its current position, and to perform some operations (calculations, saving information, doing measurings, etc.).

We consider the following variants.

EXECUTION: (a) $\mathcal{M}$ (being at a vertex **s** of graph **G**) must reach another vertex **t** with known co-ordinates;

CONSTRUCTION: (b) $\mathcal{M}$ must construct a path from **s** to **t**, and

(b^*) $\mathcal{M}$ must construct a simple path from **s** to **t**.

CONVEX GRAPHS

Algorithms proposed solve the problem on special space graph structures, called convex graphs.

DEFINITION. Let **V** be a countable subset of R^n without cluster points and **E** be a set of segments with end-points - elements of **V**. We call **G** = (**V**, **E**) n-(dimensional) *convex graph* if there exists a sequence of n-dimensional polytopes with empty intersections of the interiors for every two of them, so that the union of their vertices is **V**, the union of their edges is **E**, and the union of all the polytopes is a polyhedron.

Various properties of the convex graphs can be proven (for example, every n-convex graph is n-connected; every n-polyhedral graph is isomorphous to n-1-convex graph, and others).

ALGORITHMS

The most interesting properties of the convex graphs are the algorithmic ones (which, informally, could be characterized as "good communicativeness"). In Brimkov (1991, 1992) algorithms solving the PP for 2-convex graphs were presented. After some modifications algorithms work in n-dimensional case, too.

The idea of the first algorithm (called SNAKE-Algorithm (SA)) is the following: If at some moment $\mathcal{M}$ is on **st** then move along an edge forming minimal angle with **st**. If $\mathcal{M}$ is on the right of **st** then turn left along the edge forming minimal angle with the previous one. Otherwise, turn right (in analogical manner).

The another algorithm's idea ((right) REFLECT-Algorithm (RA)) is: If $\mathcal{M}$ is on **st** then move along the edge forming minimal angle with **st** and lying on the right of **st**. If $\mathcal{M}$ is on the right of **st** then act as in SA until reaching a new vertex or **st**. If the reaching of **st** happens earlier, come back into the previous vertex and move along the next edge. Repeat this process until getting into new vertex and continue the performance of the algorithm.

By projecting the current visited vertices on some fixed 2- dimensional plane through **st**, the algorithms can be modified for n-convex graphs. It is easy to show that the algorithms solve correctly the problem, as the convexity conditions are essential. The algorithms work also on infinite convex graphs, and (after slight modifications) they solve variants (b) and (b^*). Complexity analysis shows that the algorithms are effective in order with respect to the number of passed edges, calculations, measurings and memory used. Here we will mention that the SA requires only constant memory for the variant EXECUTION.

APPLICATIONS

Various applications of the algorithms presented can be developed. Here we will stop on one of them.

Let us consider the Linear Programming Problem (LPP) supposing known some vertex of the LPP polyhedron which is assumed to be bounded. Many widespread problems can be formulated as LPP under such restrictions.

Beginning from some known vertex **s** and following, for example, the SA with final vertex **t** supposed enough far from **s** and lying on the line through **s** determined by the cost vector, after finite number of steps an optimal target vertex will be obtained.

Such approach seems slightly similar to the Simplex Method which could be considered as a gradient one with respect to the objective function value. Our algorithm is gradient in some geometrical sense. Intuitively, the sequence of vertices projections generated by this algorithm, cannot be too far from one straight line; they have to be relatively near around it. Such non-formal speculations make us to suppose that, in generally, for LP polytopes with very large number of vertices, the number of the passed vertices till reaching the maximum will be relatively small and the algorithms will be effective in practice. We hope, this will be confirmed by experimental work as well as by proving assertion about assimptotical effectiveness on average.

REFERENCES:

Brimkov V (1991) Graph problems with local information. Talk given at the 11th European Congress on OR. Aachen 1991. Abstract booklet: 36-37

Brimkov V (1992) Graph problems under incomplete information. Proc. of the Internat. Symposium on Methodology of Mathematical Modelling. Varna 1992: 253-257

Tarjan R (1985) Amortized computational complexity. SIAM J. Alg. Disc. Meth. 6 No 2: 306-318

Resource-Constrained Project Scheduling with Maximum Time Distances

Klaus Brinkmann
Institut für Wirtschaftstheorie und Operations Research, Universität Karlsruhe
Kaiserstraße 12, 7500 Karlsruhe 1, Germany

The project scheduling problem we are dealing with in this paper forms an extension of the well-known CPM model by additionally allowing maximum time distances between the jobs. This implies that already the determination of a feasible schedule is NP-hard. We have developed some heuristic strategies for this scheduling problem both with respect to the objective of minimizing the project duration and with respect to resource levelling. At the end, the results of an empirical analysis of these methods are given.

I. The Problem

A project P is defined by (cf. Neumann (4))

(1) a set of n jobs which includes two fictitious ones: job 1 stands for the beginning and job n for the termination of the whole project. The job durations D_i (i=1,..,n) are given constants (with $D_1 = D_n = 0$), and job preemption is not allowed;

(2) a set of precedence constraints that contains both minimum and maximum time distance requirements between some jobs;

(3) $K \geq 1$ different resources, each one is renewable and of discrete type with only a limited number of units available (per period). The limit $R_k > 0$ of resource k (per period) is known, likewise is the amount $r_{ik} \geq 0$ that job i needs from resource k.

We agree that P is represented by an activity-on-node network N. (Note that N does contain cycles when maximum time distance requirements occur).

Our objective is to determine a feasible schedule $ZP = (ST_1, \ldots, ST_n)$ of starting times of the jobs that minimizes a given cost function such that all precedence constraints are satisfied and in each period the cumulated resource usage does not exceed the appropriate limit (for every resource).

Bartusch (1) has shown that in this case the construction of one feasible schedule is NP-hard.

For selecting a cost function we distinguish two cases: Firstly, there are cost functions that depend only on the project's makespan $PD = ST_n - ST_1$ and which deliver the problem of minimizing the project duration. Secondly we have functions that describe the absolute level of resource usage respective the variation of the total usage in successive periods. Minimizing a cost function of this second type gives us the problem of resource levelling.

II. The New Heuristic Strategies

The first step is to calculate the maximum slack of subprojects that are defined by cycle structures (i.e., strongly connected components with more than two nodes) in N. Let C be a cycle structure of N, let V^C be the node set of C and E^C_{max} be the set of arcs in C that represent maximum time distances. Let $\hat{I}^C$ ($\hat{J}^C$) denote the set of those nodes in C that are (inside C) negative (positive) incident only with arcs from E^C_{max}. Moreover, suppose that w_{ij} denotes the length of a longest path from node i to node j. It is easy to see that $\hat{I}^C$ and $\hat{J}^C$ are always non-empty and we are able to compute

$$M_C := \max_{i \in \hat{I}^C} \max_{j \in \hat{J}^C} \left(-w_{ji} + D_j\right).$$

We select one pair $(i,j) \in \hat{I}^C \times \hat{J}^C$ for that $M_C = -w_{ji} + D_j$ holds and we force each algorithm to "open" C by scheduling i first (among the jobs in C).

We evaluate $B_{max} = \max\left(0, \max_{i \in V^C}\left(LST_i + D_i - M_C\right)\right)$ where LST_i is the latest starting time of job i (with respect to M_C) to get the following lemma.

Lemma:
The value $uB_C := M_C + B_{max}$ gives the least upper bound for the duration of the subproject C.

Evaluating the lemma for every cycle structure and adding all resulting bounds gives (together with the appropriate values for the other nodes) an upper bound for the duration of the whole project.

The newly developed strategies for the scheduling process can be devided into four categories:

(A) *Direct Methods*
The set of jobs is treated without partition.
(B) *Contraction Methods*
The set of jobs is partitioned into cycle structures; in the first step each cycle structure is scheduled separately, afterwards these separate schedules are put together.
(C) *Rescheduling* (only for minimizing the project duration)
(D) For resource levelling: *Iterating a method for minimizing the project duration.*

RENST - Reduced Enumeration after Stinson et. al. (5) [Direct and Contraction Methods]
Each node in the Branch-and-Bound search-tree represents a feasible partial schedule, the root stands for the "empty schedule". The branching is performed by considering all possible feasible

expansions of the represented partial schedule. In our modification we require that the expansion is maximal and locally optimal with respect to the cost function.

RENTP - Reduced Enumeration after Talbot/Patterson (6) [Direct and Contraction Methods]
The jobs are ordered and successively each job gets the earliest feasible starting time. Once there is a job i so that ST_i cannot be found, the algorithm returns to job i-1 and selects ST_{i-1} newly. We generalize this approach by selecting the best alternative with respect to the cost function and to the current partial schedule as ST_i. Moreover, once a starting time is fixed it will never be deleted. In the class of the direct methods we have made one more modification: Whenever an "opening" node i of some cycle structure is to be scheduled the expected cumulated resource usage in the subsequent periods is estimated and the starting time of i is "suitably" deferred.

RCFN - Reduce to Cycle-Free Network [Contraction Method]
Whenever a cycle structure is planned separately, it will be substituted by a new artificial node in the network N. By that we reduce N to a network without cycles that can be treated by the common methods for CPM-projects.

RELOP -Method with Local Optimization [Contraction Method]
After having scheduled all subprojects separately, we determine for the current period all connected components that can be scheduled (with respect to the precedence constraints). We schedule each of those "temporarily" and the attempt that satisfies a local optimality criterion is fixed.

Rescheduling for minimizing the project duration
We order the jobs according to ascending starting times (with respect to the given feasible schedule ZP). By certain rules this order is permutated which defines a "neighborhood" N(ZP) of ZP; we apply RENTP with the new order of the jobs. If RENTP delivers a "suitable" feasible schedule ZP', we examine the "neighborhood" of ZP' analoguesly. Afterwards we continue with N(ZP).

III. Empirical Analysis

For an empirical analysis we have to guarantee that the set of tested examples forms a representative sample of the underlying population, i.e. the set of "practical" projects. Therefore we classify the networks according to three aspects (for (a) and (b) see also Davis (2)):

(a) General Aspects (structure of the network - without considering cycle structures)
(b) Dependency on the resources
(c) Maximum time distances.

We have applied two methods for statistical inference:

(1) Wilcoxon-Signed-Rank-Test

As nullhypothesis we assume that the assessments of the schedules have the same expected values, and we take α = 0,05 and α = 0,01 as levels of significance.

(2) Estimation of the expected utility (cf. Golden/Assad (3))

We achieve a ranking of the methods by evaluating a risk-averse utility function. The advantages of this approach are the facts that the ranking is not only based on one parameter (e.g. on the mean as in the test) and that all methods can be compared simultaneously.

The analysis of the methods for minimizing the project duration also contains the results of the heuristics by Bartusch (1) and those ones by Zhan's (7) combination of priority rules.

As a result of the analysis we want to point out four features:

(1) There exists a contrary between Zhan's (7) algorithm (good schedules) and the contraction methods (higher number of feasible schedules). Computing the expected utilities, the contraction method dominates all other ones. The Wilcoxon test delivers that Zhan's (7) algorithm is significantly better than the others.

(2) The computational times observed imply that "large" projects can be solved in a justifiable amount of time.

(3) The direct methods are characterized by a quite small number of feasible schedules found. On the other hand they run very fast; the best method is the modification of RENTP.

(4) Bartusch's (1) algorithm needs very much time. In the inference it is inferior to the contraction methods but superior to the direct methods (except RENTP).

The analysis of the algortihms for resource levelling can be summarized by two remarks.

(1) The approaches based on RENTP dominate all other approaches (for every cost function). The "strength" of this dominance depends on the given due date for the project.

(2) The iteration of methods for minimizing the project duration only works well when we aim to minimize the maximum (absolute) resource level. Using other cost functions the results of this technique are quite bad.

References

(1) Bartusch M (1983) Optimierung von Netzplänen mit Anordnungsbeziehungen bei knappen Ressourcen. Dissertation RWTH Aachen

(2) Davis E W (1975) Project Network Summary Measures and Constrained-Resource Scheduling. AIIE Transactions 7, No 2: 132-142

(3) Golden B L, Assad A A (1984) A Decision-Theoretic Framework for Comparing Heuristics. European Journal of OR 18, No 2: 167-171

(4) Neumann K (1975) Operations-Research-Verfahren Band III. Carl Hanser. München/Wien

(5) Stinson J P, Davis E W, Khumawala B M (1978) Multiple Resource-Constrained Scheduling Using Branch and Bound. AIIE Transactions 10: 252-259

(6) Talbot F B, Patterson J. H (1978) An Efficient Integer Programming Algorithm with Network Cuts for Solving Resource-Constrained Scheduling Problems. Management Science 24: 1163-1174

(7) Zhan J (1991) Heuristsiche Ressourcenplanung in MPM-Netzplänen mit beschränkter Kapazität. Dissertation Universität Karlsruhe

Traveling Salesman Problem with Path Dependent Costs —Generalization of One-Dimensional Search with Traveling Costs

Buyang Cao, Klaus Rinderle
Informatik 5, University of the Federal Armed Forces Munich
8014 Neubiberg, Germany

In this paper we propose a generalized model of one-dimensional search problems dicussed in [6,8]. The one-dimensional search problem can be discribed as: given N neighboring cells in a straight line in one of them there is a hidden object to be found. The priori probabilities p_i of the object being in the cells $1, ..., N$ are given. At the beginning of the search the searcher stays at the base, called cell 0. Due to the geographical relationships between the different cells the costs (examination and traveling costs) vary through the search. The search costs consists of two parts:

(i) the distance between the cell i and the previously examined cell j, and

(ii) fixed examination costs t.

The elements c_{ij} of the cost matrix of our problem are defined as

$$c_{ij} \equiv |i - j| + t. \tag{1}$$

Consider now the order of search $(0, i_1, ..., i_N)$, where $i_1,...,i_N$ is some arrangement of $1, ..., N$. The expected cost of the search is then:

$$E(cost) = c_{0i_1} + (1 - p_{i_1})c_{i_1 i_2} + (1 - p_{i_1} - p_{i_2})c_{i_2 i_3} + ...$$
$$+(1 - p_{i_1} - ... - p_{i_{N-1}})c_{i_{N-1} i_N} \tag{2}$$

where 0 is the base.

Let $\bar{c}_{i_k i_{k+1}} \equiv (1 - p_{i_1} - p_{i_2} - ... - p_{i_k})c_{i_k i_{k+1}}$ $(1 \leq k \leq N - 1)$. $\bar{c}_{i_k i_{k+1}}$ can be considered as a "real" expected cost of a search from i_k to i_{k+1}, if a search path from the cell 0 to the cell i_k is once defined. In addition to this we introduce a dummy search from the last examined cell i_N to the cell 0 (the base) and the associated cost $\bar{c}_{i_N 0}$ with the value zero. Each cell is represented by a vertex and each possible search from i_k to i_{k+1} is denoted by an arc in a network. From these considerations we see that the whole search path $(0, i_1, i_2, ...i_N, 0)$ constitutes a Hamiltonian circuit. The optimal search strategy of a one-dimensional search problem selects the Hamiltonian circuit with the shortest length among all possible Hamiltonian circuits in the network.

In our application the cost of any arc (i_k, i_{k+1}) $\bar{c}_{i_k i_{k+1}}$ cannot be determined explicitly until the (search) path from the cell 0 to the cell i_k (a subtour) is defined. This problem is therefore called a **TSP with path dependent costs (TSPPDC)**. We formulate the TSPPDC mathematically with the following model.

$$\text{(TSPPDC)} \qquad \min E(cost) = \min \sum_{p \in P} l(p) x_p \tag{3}$$

$$s.t. \qquad \sum_{p \in P} x_p = 1 \tag{4}$$

$$x_p \in \{0,1\} \qquad \forall\, p \in P \tag{5}$$

where

p: any search path from cell 0 to i_N and returning from i_N to 0 (a tour) ($i_1, ..., i_N$ is an arrangement of $1, ..., N$), it satisfies the conditions of a Hamiltonian circuit;

P: the set of all possible p's;

$l(p)$: the lenght of the tour p, which is determined by (2);

x_p: is a decision variable, which is determined by

$$x_p = \begin{cases} 1, & \text{if the tour } p \in P \text{ is selected} \\ 0, & \text{otherwise.} \end{cases}$$

Because of the distinctive characteristics of the TSPPDC namely it is NP-complete and the cost of an arc in the network is path dependent, a heuristic will be designed for the solution of the practical TSPPDC's. Based on the mathematical model of the TSPPDC (3) - (5) we can explain the basic ideas of our algorithm as following:

At first a tour (a search path) p say $p = (0, 1, 2, ..., N, 0)$ is selected, then another tour p' ($p' \neq p$) will be chosen according to the tour p so that the value of the solution of the TSPPDC may be improved, that means $l(p') < l(p)$, repeat this step until there is no improved solution can be found. In this case the tour with the shortest length at hand is taken as the "optimal" solution of the TSPPDC.

In order to prevent the solution procedure of the TSPPDC from becoming trapped at locally optimal solution, the technique of **tabu search** [4,5] will be employed.

When an initial solution of the TSPPDC is available, we will employ some moves to try to obtain a new solution iteratively and hopefully to reach the optimal solution of the TSPPDC.

In our paper we present the following types of moves:

Turning Move

***k*-Reverse Move**

Insertion Move

The presented algorithm based on tabu search for solving TSPPDC combines all moves mentioned above in order to generate systematically better solutions. Although it cannot be proved to give an exact solution, it provides all optimal solutions of the tested problems proposed in [6,8]. For different structures of search problems, e.g. various priori probabilities, cells are arranged either in a straight line or a plan, our model and algorithm are applicable, what we have to do is the slight modification of the search cost matrix. It is not necessary to design different methods for solving the variety of one-dimensional problems.

References

[1] Cao, B., and Uebe, G., "Solving Transportation Problem with Nonlinear Side Constraints with Tabu Search," Dicussion Paper in Statitics and Quantitative Economics, No. 46, Armed Forces University Hamburg, 1991.

[2] de Werra, D., and Hertz, A., "Tabu Search Techniques: a Tutorial and an Application to Neural Network," *OR Spektrum* **11**, 131 - 141, (1989).

[3] Frieze, A.M., Galbiat G., and Maffioli, F., "On the Worst-Case Performance of Some Algorithm for the Asymmetric Traveling Salesman Problem," *Networks* **12**, 23 - 39, (1982).

[4] Glover, F., "Future Paths for Integer Programming and Links to Artificial Intelligence," *Computer and Operations Research* **13**, No.5, 533 - 549, (1986).

[5] Glover, F., "Tabu Search - Part I," *ORSA Journal on Computing* **1**, No.3, 190 - 206, (1989).

[6] Gluss, B., "Approximately Optimal One-Dimensional Search Policies in Which Search Costs Vary with Through Time," *Naval Research Logistics Quarterly* **8**, 277 - 283, (1961).

[7] Kanellakis, P. and Papadimitriou, C.H., "Local Search for the Asymmetric Traveling Salesman Problem," *Operations Research* **28**, No.5, 1086 - 1099, (1980).

[8] Kikuta, K., "A One-Dimensional Search with Traveling Cost," *Journal of the Operations Research Society of Japan* **33**, No.3, 262 - 276, (1990).

[9] Lawler, E.L., Lanstra, J.K., and Rimooy Kan, A.H.G. (eds.), "The Traveling Salesman," John Wiley & Sons. Ltd, (1985).

[10] Malek, M., Guruswamy, M., Pandy M., and Qwens, H., "Serial and Parallel Simulated Annealing and Tabu Search Algorithms for the Traveling Salesman Problem," *Annals of Operations Research* **21**, 59 - 84, (1989).

[11] Widmer, M., "Job Shop Scheduling with Tooling Constraints: a Tabu Search Approach," *Journal of Operational Research Society* **42**, No.1, 75 - 82, (1991).

Stochastic Scheduling Flow-Shop No-Wait with Heuristics Using Artificial Intelligence Techniques

Ubirajara Rocha Ferreira
Engineering School/Production Dept.
Cx. Postal 205, UNESP/FEG, 12500 Guaratinguetá, SP, Brazil

INTRODUCTION:

This paper treats Scheduling models that can be described by considering in sequence the resources, tasks systems, sequencing constraints and performance measures. The conditions Flow-shop means that the tasks of each job should be processing sequentially, there is one machine for each task, a job is processed using one machine at a time without preemption and a machine process exactly one job at a time. The condition No-wait means that delays between tasks of the same job are not allowed. In this particular case, Flow-shop No-wait, the schedule is determined by a sequence of jobs. The Stochastic hypothesis is that: the processing times of the job i on machine j are random, according to some continuous and independent distribution functions T_{ij} and with the realizations known only during the shop. The Objective is to minimize the expected value of the makespan, where the makespan, c_{max}, is the total amount of time required to completely process all the jobs [Coffman 1976, Ferreira 1990, Frostig 1985]

We start presenting a Start Interval Concept, defining t_{k0}. By using it we can have a TSP formulation for the 3-machine case, also a NP-Complete Problem [Röck 1984]. With this formulation, we discuss AI techniques for these problems. The results permit us to evaluate about the use of the t_{k0}'s and give directions for using Artificial Intelligence Techniques.

START INTERVAL CONCEPT [Ferreira 90]:

Let $t_{k0}(i,j)$ be the interval of time that needs to occur between two sequential jobs at the first machine in a Flow-shop No-wait schedule, by processing job i and j in this order. The Start Interval is the minimum time necessary to prevent a job from catching up with its immediate predecessor on a downstream machine, looking for the Flow-shop No-wait condition and in a stochastic system.

With this concept, we have the Probabilistic Condition for Stochastic Schedules be classified as a Flow-shop No-wait:

Let $U = T_{k-1,2} - T_{k,1}$, $V = T_{k-1,3} - T_{k,2}$, $W = U + V$ be random variables, k=2, ... ,n. Then, the conditions FSNW are satisfied <==> $0 < t_{k0}$, $U < t_{k0}$, $W < t_{k0}$. Therefore, the probability for the conditions FSNW be satisfied is:

$$\alpha = p\,[\,(U < t_{k0}) \cap (W < t_{k0})\,] = p\,[\,U < t_{k0}, W < t_{k0}\,], \quad t_{k0} \geq 0.$$

Hence, by knowing the bidimensional distribution of (U,W), we can obtain the matrix t_{k0} (i,j), for a given α.

As an application for this result, consider $T_{ij} \sim N(\mu_{ij}, \sigma_{ij}^2)$ independent random variables normally distributed, i=1,...,n , j=1,2,3. Then, is possible to show that (U,W) is Normal Bivariate Distributed and by applying numerical methods, we can determine the t_{k0} values in function of α [Ferreira 90].

Because $c_{max} = \sum_{i=1}^{n-1} t_{k0}([i],[i+1]) + \sum_{i=1}^{n-1} t_{[i],1} + \sum_{j=1}^{m} t_{[n],j}$ and since the sum of the processing times at first machine is constant, regardless of sequence, to minimize the makespan is equivalent to minimizing the sum of Start Interval times, that is analogous to the TSP, the Traveling Salesman Problem. Clearly each job in the Scheduling problem correspond to a city; the Start Interval time, $t_{k0}(i,j)$ for a given α, from one job to another corresponds to the costs to travel between cities, and a schedule of the n jobs corresponds to a "tour" for the Salesman.

Many different Operational Research approaches has been applied for TSP, e.g. Branch & Bound and Greedy Algorithms. Also, AI Heuristics, e.g. Simulated Annealing, Genetic Algorithms and Neural Networks.

An AI Technique is a method that exploits knowledge and AI Techniques use Search, Use of Knowledge and Abstraction [Hertz 1991]. In our studies we are applying Genetic Algorithms, a stochastic state-space search techniques modeled on natural evolutionary mechanisms [Holland 1973]. Their strength is in quickly locating the high performance regions of vast and complex search spaces. Because GA's are not well-suited for fine-tuning structures close to optimal solutions, once those regions are located, it is useful to apply local search heuristics (hill-climbing). Local search may be incorporate as a mutation operator in GA's: for a FSNW Scheduling Problem, a mutation operator is reversing a randomly chosen sub-sequence, or just a changing of the position between two jobs. These are Hybrid Systems, by combining OR & AI. From OR, we can use different approaches to generate solutions [Igelmund 1973].

Simulated results were obtained for small problems, where the best solutions were determined by numerical enumeration. The following results about use or not the Start Interval show the trade-off of using it:

(A) without t_{k0}: generate k realizations of the Random Variables, determine the best sequence for each instance, determine c_{max} for each one of them, determine $E(c_{max})[A]$ by considering all instances;

(B) with t_{k0}: by fixing α, determine the matrix $t_{k0}(i,j)$ by numerical integration and add the correspondent value of t_{k0} to the expected value of the processing time at the first job, determine the best sequence for these problems and for sequences generated randomly determine $E(c_{max})[B]$.

The makespan for the 'B' problems presented an increase of about 5% for $\alpha = .05$, 15% for $\alpha = .5$, 20% for $\alpha = .7$, 24% for $\alpha = .8$, 29% for $\alpha = .9$ and 33% for $\alpha = .95$. The validity of the relation between the t_{k0} values and α has been also checked by looking the frequencies of the sequences that satisfies the Flow-shop No-wait condition between all generated.

Genetic Algorithms Heuristics for the 'B' problems has been applied. The results were really impressive and in few generations the best solution is reached for those problems. In order to solve large problems we can measure the performance of the heuristics by using lower bounds [Bruno 86] easly obtained with the t_{k0} values. Next step will be apply parallel GA's.

REFERENCES:

BRUNO, J. L. & DOWNEY, P. J. (1986). Probabilistic bounds on the performance on list scheduling. SIAM J. Comput. 15 (2): 409 - 417.

COFFMAN JR.,E.G. (1976). Computer and Job-Shop Scheduling Theory. New York, John Wiley.

FERREIRA, U. (1990). Stochastic Scheduling Flow-shop No-wait Problems. ITA, São José dos Campos, SP, 1990. Tese de Doutorado.

FROSTIG, E. & ADIRI, I. (1985). Stochastic flow shop no-wait scheduling. J. Appl. Prob. 22: 240 - 246.

GOLDBERG, D. (1989). Genetic Algorithms in Search, Optimization and Machine Learning. Addison-Wesley.

HERTZ J.; KROGH, A. & PALMER, R. G. (1991). Introduction to the Theory of Neural Computation. Addison Wesley.

HOLLAND, J. H. (1973). Genetic algorithms and the optimal allocation of trials. SIAM Journal of Computing 2 (2): 88 - 105.

IGELMUND, G. & RADERMACHER, F. J. (1983). Algorithmic approaches to preselective strategies for stochastic scheduling problems, Network, 13: 29 - 48.

ROCK, H. (1984). The three - machine no - wait flow shop is NP-Complete. Journal of the Association for Computing Machine, 31 (2): 336 - 345.

Algorithms for Max-Linear and Multi-Criteria Spanning Tree Problems

Horst W. Hamacher, Günther Ruhe
Fachbereich Mathematik, Universität Kaiserslautern
Erwin-Schrödinger-Str., Postfach 3049, 6760 Kaiserslautern, Germany

Let $\mathcal{T}$ be the set of all spanning Trees $T = (V,E(T))$ of a given graph $G = (V,E)$. With each edge $e \in E$ is associated a vector of weights $w(e) = (w_1(e),\dots,w_Q(e))$. We consider two related problems.

(1) **Max-linear spanning tree problem ML-ST**

$\min \{ f(T): T \in \mathcal{T}\}$ with

$f(T) := \max \{w_1(T),\dots,w_Q(T)\}$ and $w_q(T) := \sum_{e \in E(T)} w_q(e)$ for $q = 1,\dots,Q$.

(2) **Multi-criteria spanning tree problem MC-ST**

$\min^* \{(w_1(T),\dots,w_Q(T)) : T \in \mathcal{T}\}$

where min* abbreviates the search for trees T such that there is no T':

$(w_1(T'),\dots, w_Q(T')) \leq (w_1(T),\dots, w_Q(T))$

$(w_1(T'),\dots, w_Q(T')) \neq (w_1(T),\dots, w_Q(T))$.

Firstly, we describe a ranking approach for solving (1).

Let $\lambda_1,\dots,\lambda_Q$ be nonnegative real numbers with $\lambda_1 + \dots + \lambda_Q = 1$ and let

$$w(\lambda,e) := \lambda_1 w_1(e) + \dots + \lambda_Q w_Q(e)$$

be a convex combination of the weights on each edge $e \in E$. Correspondingly,

$$w(\lambda,T) = \sum_{e \in E(T)} w(\lambda,e) = \lambda_1 w_1(T) + \dots + \lambda_Q w_Q(T)$$

is a convex combination of the weights $w_q(T)$ of the tree T - *the combined weight of T (with respect to λ).*

Lemma 1:

For all $T \in \mathcal{T}$: $w(\lambda,T) \leq f(T)$.

□

Lemma 2:
Let $T^1 = T^1(\lambda)$ be a minimum spanning tree with respect to combined weight $w(\lambda,T)$. Then $w(\lambda,T^1) \leq f(T^*)$, where T^* denotes an optimal solution of ML-ST.

□

Next, we consider $T^1,\ldots,T^k$, the k best spanning trees with respect to combined weight, i.e.

$$w(\lambda,T^1) \leq w(\lambda,T^2), \leq \ldots \leq w(\lambda,T^k) \leq w(\lambda,T)$$

for all spanning trees T different from $T^1,\ldots,T^k$.

Theorem 3:
Let K be a positive integer such that

$$w(\lambda,T^k) < \min \{ f(T^i) : i=1,\ldots,k\} \text{ for all } k=1,\ldots,K-1$$

but

$$w(\lambda,T^K) \geq \min \{ f(T^i) : i=1,\ldots,K\}.$$

Then

$$T^* := \operatorname{argmin} \{ f(T^i): i=1,\ldots,K\} \text{ is an optimal solution for (1).}$$

□

The above theorem is the foundation of an exact algorithm for the max-linear problem.

Step 1: Choose $\lambda = (\lambda_1,\ldots,\lambda_Q)$ such that λ_q is nonnegative $(q=1,\ldots,Q)$ and $\lambda_1 + \ldots + \lambda_Q = 1$. Compute the combined weights $w(\lambda,e) := \lambda_1 w_1(e) + \ldots + \lambda_Q w_Q(e)$ for all $e \in E$.

Step 2: Apply a ranking algorithm to find the K best spanning trees with respect to weights until

$w(\lambda,T^K) \geq \min \{ f(T^i) : i=1,\ldots,K\}$.

Define $T^* := \operatorname{argmin} \{ f(T^i) : i=1,\ldots,K\}$.

We can stop the procedure when K best spanning trees have been computed, even if the optimality criterion of Theorem 3 is not satisfied. In this situation $w(\lambda,T^K)$ is a lower bound and $\min \{ f(T^i) : i=1,\ldots,K\}$ is an upper bound for $f(T^*)$.

We investigate some relationships between the set of solutions of ML-ST and MC-ST. Let f_{max} be the optimal objective function value of ML-ST and define

$$\mathcal{T}_{max} := \{ T \in \mathcal{T}: f(T) = f_{max} \}.$$

Assume without loss of generality that $f(T) = w_1(T)$. A solution $T' \in \mathcal{T}_{max}$ is said to be dominated by T if

$$(w_2(T'),\ldots, w_Q(T')) \geq (w_2(T),\ldots, w_Q(T)) \text{ and}$$
$$(w_2(T'),\ldots, w_Q(T')) \neq (w_2(T),\ldots, w_Q(T)).$$

Lemma 4:
All non-dominated solutions $T \in \mathcal{T}_{max}$ are efficient spanning trees.
Corollary:
If T is the unique solution of ML-ST then $T \in \mathcal{T}_{eff}$.

□

In what follows, we consider the case Q=2 of two criteria. We present an instance where all existing spanning trees of the K_4 are efficient solutions, i.e., $= \quad _{eff}$.

Lemma 5:
A spanning tree $T \in \mathcal{T}$ obtained from
(3) $\min \{t \cdot w_1(T) + (1-t) \cdot w_2(T) : T \in \mathcal{T}\}$
for a parameter $t \in (0,1)$ is a solution of (2).

□

In general, however, there are efficient spanning trees $T \in \mathcal{T}_{eff}$ which can not be derived from the solution of an appropriate problem (3).

For $i,j \in \{1,2\}$ and $i \neq j$ we define

(4) $l_i := \min \{w_i(T) : T \in \mathcal{T}\}$
(5) $u_i := \min \{w_j(T) : T \in \mathcal{T}_i^*\}$,

where $\mathcal{T}_i^*$ denotes the set of optimal solutions obtained from (4). Additionally, $\mathcal{T}_i^*$ (b) is used for the set of optimal solutions of

(6) $\min \{ w_i(T) : T \in \mathcal{T}, w_j(T) \leq b \}$.

Theorem 6:
$T' \in \mathcal{T}_{eff}$ if and only if there is a bound $b \in [l_1,u_1]$ such that
(7) $T' = \text{argmin} \{w_1(T) : T \in \mathcal{T}_2^*(b)\}$

□

Since the computation of minimum spanning trees subject to an additional (additive) constraint is known to be NP-hard (CAMERINI et al.) we present an approximation algorithm for determining well-distributed solutions.

An ordered set of spanning trees $\{T^1,T^2,\ldots,T^r\}$ is called *well-distributed* if for given $\varepsilon > 0$ and a metric $\rho : \mathcal{T} \times \mathcal{T} \rightarrow \mathbb{R}$ it is
(8) $\rho(T^i,T^{i+1}) \leq \varepsilon$ for all $i = 1,\ldots,r-1$.

The idea of the algorithm is to firstly compute efficient solutions due to (3). Subsequently, local approximation (of order k) is performed whenever two consecutive solutions do not fulfill (8).

References:

Y. AKSOY (1990):
An interactive branch-and-bound algorithm for bicriterion nonconvex/mixed integer programming.
Naval Research Logistics Quarterly 37, 403 - 417.

P.M. CAMERINI; G. GALBIATI; F. MAFFIOLI (1984):
The complexity of weighted multi-constrained spanning tree problems.
Colloquium on the Theory of Algorithms,
Pecs, July 23-27, 1984.

S. CHUNG; H.W. HAMACHER; F. MAFFIOLI; K.G. MURTY (1990):
A note on combinatorial optimization with max-linear objective functions.
Universität Kaiserslautern, Fachbereich Mathematik, Preprint No. 189.
Accepted for Discrete Applied Mathematics.

Z. DREZNER; S.Y. NOF (1984):
On optimizing bin packing and insertion plans for assembly robots.
IEE Transactions 16, 262 - 270.

Combinatorial and Network Algorithms

T.C. Hu
Department of Computer Science and Engineering, University of California, San Diego
La Jolla, CA 92093-0114, USA

We shall discuss three classes of algorithms:

(A) Network algorithms which can be adapted to solve various cost functions.

(B) Auction-type algorithms most suitable for parallel and distributed computations.

(C) Stochastic algorithms such as simulated annealing and its siblings.

(A) Many network algorithms were invented to solve particular problems, e.g., shortest path problems [3, 4, 12], minimum cost binary trees [10], multi-terminal flow problems [6]. Recently, we have begun to realize that the same algorithms can still be used with different types of cost functions [8, 10, 11].

(B) There are three issues in parallel and distributed computing, namely [1, 2]: (i) Assignment of processors to tasks. (ii) Synchronization. (ii) Communication between processors.

In a network environment, we assume that there is a processor at every node, and we do not assume that there is a global clock. For the communication between processors, a processor can proceed on its computation from local data, e.g., the arc flow on adjacent arcs and shadow prices on neighboring nodes. To illustrate the concepts of parallel and distributed computing, we review three auction type algorithms where the bidders are processors and the sellers (or objects) have shadow prices. The three algorithms are

- **(i)** The classical marriage stability algorithm by Gale and Shapley [5, 7].
- **(ii)** The ϵ-auction algorithm by Bertsekas where ϵ-complimentary slackness is used to avoid local optimal solutions [1, 2].
- **(iii)** The symmetrical auction algorithm by Hu where it is advantageous for the buyers and sellers to reveal their true intentions [9].

(C) The simulated annealing algorithms have become standard tools in solving complex problems. The main reasons for its popularity are

(i) Complex problems are hard to formulate but we can often easily identify a good solution when we see it.

(ii) A global optimum solution is not needed and a local optimum solution is acceptable.

(iii) The programming is straight-forward.

(iv) A class of problems have to be solved where the input data are similar.

Theoretically, simulated annealing can be thought of as a person moving on a cost surface to find the global minimum on that surface. In the earlier stages of the algorithm, temperature T is high and the person can move to higher points with positive probability. In the later stages, the temperature is low and as $T \to 0$, the person can only move downhill. The changing temperature T is called the cooling schedule. From the point of view of temperature, the greedy algorithm is equivalent to fixing $T = 0$, a random walk is equivalent to $T = \infty$, and simulated annealing is the hybrid of the random walk and the greedy algorithms. We shall discuss some new variations of simulated annealing such as threshold acceptance.

References

[1] D. P. Bertsekas. *Linear Network Optimization.* MIT Press, Cambridge, MA, 1991.

[2] D. P. Bertsekas and J. N. Tsitsiklis. *Parallel and Distributed Computation.* Prentice Hall, Englewood Cliffs, NJ, 1989.

[3] E. Dijkstra. A note on two problems in connection with graphs. *Numerische Mathematik*, 1:269–271, 1959.

[4] R. W. Floyd. Algorithm 97, shortest path. *Communications of the ACM*, 5:345, 1962.

[5] D. Gale and L. S. Shapley. College admissions and stability of marriage. *American Mathematical Monthly*, 69(1):9–15, 1962.

[6] R. E. Gomory and T. C. Hu. Multi-terminal network flows. *SIAM Journal on Applied Mathematics*, 9(4):551–570, 1961.

[7] D. Gusfield and R. W. Irving. *The Stable Marriage Problem.* MIT Press, Cambridge, MA, 1989.

[8] R. Hassin. Solution basis of multi-terminal cut problems. *Mathematics of Operation Research*, 13(4):535–542, 1988.

[9] T. C. Hu. Beauty contests, college admissions and bargaining. *Journal of Recreational Mathematics*, 14(4):252–261, 1981–82.

[10] T. C. Hu. *Combinatorial Algorithms.* Addison-Wesley, Reading, MA, 1982.

[11] T. C. Hu, D. J. Kleitman, and J. K. Tamaki. Multi-terminal network flows. *SIAM Journal on Applied Mathematics*, 37(2):246–256, 1979.

[12] S. Warshall. A theorem on boolean matrices. *Journal of the ACM*, 9:11–12, 1962.

A Heuristic for the Nesting Problem

Rainer Lang, Thomas Milius
Fachbereich Informatik, Universität Hamburg
Troplowitzstraße 7, 2000 Hamburg 54, Germany

In the sheet metal-processing industry CAD-Systems for the computer-aided production of metal plates are used. Among them there are systems in which the parts made of sheet metal are constructed in the 3D-mode, after them for the production the parts are automatically planished. It arise models for plane metal plates. These parts must be cutted out from larger plates. For the complete automatisation of manufacturing a program for minimizing the total scrap of metal plates is needed.

This problem can be found in the literature under various notations (a survey of the state of art is given in [1]). As introduction into the field the book of J. Terno et al. ([3]) is recommended.

We consider the corresponding geometrical optimization problem called

Nesting-problem:

> Let be given a set M of plane polygons and a rectangle F with given length and breadth. To find is a non-overlapping placement of the polygons of M in F such that the scrap is minimized.

As objective function for this scrap minimization problem the quotient from the sum of the areas of the placed polygons and the area of the used area F_u of F is used. The used area F_u is the area of the smallest axe-parallel rectangle in F containing all placed polygons.

The nesting problem contains the 2-dimensional Bin-Packing Problem as a subproblem and is therefore NP-hard. Thus the existence of an efficient (i.e. polynomial) exact algorithm for the nesting problem is unlikely. It is recommendable to look for good heuristics for the nesting problem.

We have developed a heuristic which differs from other algorithms for the nesting problem in some details.

Our program is an interactive approximation algorithm for the optimal non-overlapping placement of any rectilinear-bounded and multiple-connected planar areas into a planar polygon.

The parts to embed can be non-convex and they can have holes. Our program is able to fill out holes with smaller parts. Moreover, for each part can be determined is it rotatable or not. The program offers the possibilty of correction of solutions automatically found: translation and removing of already embedded parts with following replacement.

In our program the tests for intersection of parts are very time-consuming. Therefore we have installed a modul for controlling of placement which arranges the placement of certain part to the actual borderline and takes on the rotation for rotatable parts. This modul consist of a rough and a fine placement routine.

For the selection of parts essentially the Max-First-Strategy is used. This strategy try at first to place the largest parts as far as possible to the left and than to the top (West-North-Rule). The strategy turned out to be reasonable, since the algorithm can fill in smaller parts into free places arising during the algorithmic process. The selection module always tests several parts before is decided which part is placed ultimately.
After that a subroutine determines the next actual borderline.

The program is implemented on ATARI ST. The placement algorithm is written in ANSI-C, which can be easily integrated via interface into other CAD-Systems. The program works under an users interface, which can also translated to other operating systems.

Experiences:

The tests for non-intersections of polygons need a lot of time. Nevertheless has our algorithm good parameters compared with other methods, which use only more simple patterns, as for instance envelopping retangles.
The strategy to place at first the largest parts and than to attempt to fill into the free places other parts provide satisfactory results.

References:

[1] H.Dyckhoff, G.Wäscher (Eds.): *Cutting und Packing*, European Journal of Operational Research 44, (1990), 133-306.

[2] Milius,T., *Ein heuristisches Verfahren zur optimalen Anordnung geometrischer Objekte in der Ebene*, Diplomarbeit, FB Informatik, Universität Hamburg, 1992.

[3] Terno,J., Lindemann,R., Scheithauer,G., *Zuschnittprobleme und ihre praktische Lösung*, Thun, Frankfurt 1987.

New Evolutionary Genetic Algorithms for Combinatorial Optimization Problems

Do Thi Loan, Fam Quang Bac (Viet-Nam)
Department of Flexible Manufacturing Systems
Mendeleev Institute of Chemical Engineering
ul. Vilisa Lasisa, d. 21/1, 123480 Moscow, Russia

This paper deals with the NP-complete combinatorial optimization problems. A large number of papers has been devoted to them. A traditional approach of Operational Research has been used (Lawler et al. 1985). Kirkpatrick et al. (1983) used Simulated Annealing. Hopfield and Tank (1985) applied a neural networks for finding suboptimal solution for TSP. In recent years interest has raised to apply evolutionary algorithms to combinatorial optimization problems (Holland 1975; Brady 1985).

This paper introduces algorithms, based on the evolutionary approach and new genetic crossover operator. It includes seven sections. In section 2 the generalized formulation of combinatorial optimization problems is defined. Some concrete problems are considered in this section. In section 3 the Goldberg's genetic algorithm (Goldberg and Lingle 1985) is analysed. In section 4 the new crossover-operator based on Non-Abel's group theory is created. In section 5 the evolutionary procedures are proposed. The efficiency of the proposed algorithms is assessed in solving some TSP and scheduling problem in section 6. Finally in section 7 some conclusions are done. Below we present some major results of the work.

New Crossover operator

In this section we suggest the new crossover operator created by Non-Abel's group theory. Consider two permutations A and B. According to the Non-Abel's group theory:

(1) If $A, B \in \Omega$ and $C = A \otimes B$ then $C \in \Omega$
(2) $(A \otimes B) \otimes C = A \otimes (B \otimes C) = A \otimes B \otimes C$
(3) $A \otimes B \neq B \otimes A$
(4) $\exists e : e \otimes A = A \otimes e = A. \quad \forall A, \exists A^{-1} : A \otimes A^{-1} = A^{-1} \otimes A = e$

Take A' and B' as offsprings obtained from A and B: $A' = A \otimes B; \quad B' = B \otimes A$
When creating the crossover operator algorithmically, we use the following formulas:

If $\pi_k = (k(1), k(2), \ldots, k(n)); \quad \pi_j = (j(1), j(2), \ldots, j(n))$
then $\pi_{i^1} = \pi_k \otimes \pi_j = (i^1_{(1)}, i^1_{(2)}, \ldots, i^1_{(n)})$
where $i^1_{(1)} = j(k(1)); \quad i^1_{(2)} = j(k(2)); \ldots; i^1_{(n)} = j(k(n))$
and $\pi_{i^2} = \pi_j \otimes \pi_k = (i^2_{(1)}, i^2_{(2)}, \ldots, i^2_{(n)})$
where $i^2_{(1)} = k(j(1)); \quad i^2_{(2)} = k(j(2)); \ldots; i^2_{(n)} = k(j(n))$

Evolutionary Algorithms

Two evolutionary algorithms were proposed. Below we present algorithm 2 (Local search and crossover):

1. Choose a desired population size $2N$ and randomly generate the starting population $P = \{\pi_j \mid j = 1, 2N\}$. Set $r = 0$.

2. Carry out parallel local search by greedy algorithm starting from individuals of the population P and result in the new population of locally optimal individuals $P^{LS} = \{\pi_j^{LS} \mid j = 1, 2N\}$.

3. Evaluate the objective function for each individual $f(\pi_j^{LS})$, $j = 1, 2N$ and best value $f^{\text{best}} = \min_{j=1,2N} f(\pi_j^{LS})$

4. Crossover N randomly chosen pairs π_j^{LS}, π_k^{LS} from population P^{LS} to receive N pairs of offsprings and to form a new population P' (by Goldberg's operator or Non-Abel's operator).

5. Repeat step 2 for the population P' and receive a population $P'^{LS} = \{\pi_j'^{LS} \mid j = 1, 2N\}$.

6. Compute $f_{\text{min}} = \min_{j=1,2N} f(\pi_j'^{LS})$

7. If $f_{\text{min}} > f^{\text{best}}$ then $r = r + 1$; else $r = 0$.

8. If stopping criteria met $(r > R)$ stop; else set $P^{LS} = P'^{LS}$ and return to step 3.

The computational processes motivated by the proposed algorithms were described as stochastic processes, using population dynamics and interactive Markovian chains.

Experimental results

We present some results of computer simulations of the proposed algorithms for Flow-shop problem and for asymmetric TSP. We denote
algorithm 1;2 with Goldberg's operator — PMX1; PMX2;
algorithm 1;2 with Non-Abel's operator — NAbel1; NAbel2.

So the experimental results show that, in any case NAbel2 and PMX2 perform more superiorly than a standard genetic algorithm (GAØ). Our interpretation is that the population evolved in GAØ fastly is occupied by the individuals of the small number of states. In other words a diversity of the evolved population fastly is reduced and the evolutionary process fastly is finished.

In order to compare NAbel2 and PMX2 in more detail we show how their efficiency depends on population's size $2N$ for Flowshop problem and for asymmetric TSP. In fact, NAbel2 performs better PMX2 in solving Flowshop problem. In solving asymmetric TSP both NAbel2 and PMX2 perform approximately equally.
A new theoretical research and practical applications of evolutionary genetic algorithms will be focused in our further work.

References

Brady, R.M. (1985), *Optimization strategies gleaned from natural evolution.* Nature 317: 804–906.

Goldberg, D.E., Lingle, R. (1985), *Alleles, loci, and the traveling salesman problem.* In Proc. Int. conf. on Genetic Algorithms and their Applications. Carnegie Mellon University, Pittsburgh, pp. 154–159.

Holland, J.H. (1975) *Adaption in nature and artificial systems.* University of Michigan press, ann arbor.

Hopfield, J.J., Tank, D.W. (1985), *"Neural" computation of decisions in optimization problems.* biol cybern 52: 141–152.

Kirkpatrick, S., Gelatt, C.D., Vecchi, M.P. (1983), *Optimization by simulates annealing.* science 220: 671–680.

Lawler, E.L., Lenstra, J.K., Rinnooy, Kan A.H.G. (1985), *The traveling salesman problem.* Wiley, New York.

Bicriteria Transportation Problem

Peter Neumayer
Fachbereich Mathematik, Universität Kaiserslautern
Schrödinger Str., 6750 Kaiserslautern, Germany

INTRODUCTION

In a transportation problem generally only the single criterion of minimizing the total cost is considered. But in certain practical situations two or more objectives are relevant. In the case of continuous variables this problem of finding all efficient points was solved by ANEJA/NAIR [1]. Applying this method to the case of integer variables not all efficient points are found. In this paper we develope a method to find all the efficient points in the criteria space by using a quadratic objective function. Although the method is developed with respect to a bicriteria transportation problem, it is applicable to any bicriteria linear program. In this paper I consider an integer transportation problem with two objective functions and the following representation. Minimize

$$z_1 = \sum_{i=1}^{n} \sum_{j=1}^{m} c_{ij} x_{ij} \qquad \text{and} \qquad z_2 = \sum_{i=1}^{n} \sum_{j=1}^{m} d_{ij} x_{ij}$$

subject to

$$x_{ij} \geq 0 \text{ and integer} \qquad \text{for all i,j} \qquad \text{and}$$

$$a_i = \sum_{j=1}^{m} x_{ij} \qquad \text{for all i =1,... ,n}$$

$$b_j = \sum_{i=1}^{n} x_{ij} \qquad \text{for all j =1,...,m}$$

z_1 and z_2 denote the values of the objective functions in the feasible solution x. Thus, for each feasible solution x we have a pair of values of the objective functions (z_1,z_2) called feasible point $z=z(x)$ and each pair represents an element of $\mathbb{N}^2$ ($\mathbb{N}^2$ is sometimes called objective space or criteria space). $Z \subseteq \mathbb{N}^2$ denotes the set of all feasible points in the objective space. That is, for each feasible point $z \in Z$ there is a feasible solution x corresponding to the feasible point $z=(z_1,z_2)$ in the objective space.

DEFINITION: *Let $Z \subseteq \mathbb{N}^2$ be the set of all feasible points in the objective space. Then $z'=(z'_1,z'_2) \in Z$ is called efficient or nondominated if there is no $z=(z_1,z_2) \in Z$ with $z<z'$, that means $z_1 \leq z'_1$ and $z_2 < z'_2$ or $z_1 < z'_1$ and $z_2 \leq z'_2$.*

THE QUADRATIC FUNCTION

In my approach I use a quadratic function in order to find efficient points. Starting with two efficient points p and q the algorithm determines further efficient points by maximizing the function $f(z_1,z_2)=a*z_1*z_2 + b*z_2 + c*z_1$ $z_1,z_2,a,b,c \in \mathbb{N}$ with:

$$a = (p_1-q_1+1)(q_2-p_2+1) -1$$
$$b = (p_2-q_2-1)(p_1-q_1+1)q_1 + p_1$$
$$c = (q_1-1-p_1)(q_2-p_2+1)p_2 + q_2$$

The parameters a,b and c are changed after each iteration by choosing a new pair of efficient points. The following two propositions characterize the function f and the theorem describes the relation to efficient points.

PROPOSITION 1: *Let p and q be two efficient points in the objective space such that* $p_1<q_1 -1$ *and* $q_2<p_2 -1$. *Let* $G \subseteq Z$ *such that* $G=\{ (z_1,z_2)\in Z \mid p_1\leq z_1\leq q_1$ *and* $q_2\leq z_2\leq p_2$. *Let the function* $f:\mathbb{N}^2 \text{----->} \mathbb{R}$ *with* $f(z_1,z_2)=a*z_1*z_2 +b*z_2+c*z_1$ *be determined by p,q. Then for all* $z,z'\in G$ *follows that* $f(z)>f(z')$ *if* $z< z'$.

PROPOSITION 2: *Let p,q two efficient points and let* $G\subseteq Z$ *such that* $G=\{(z_1,z_2)\in Z \mid p_1\leq z_1\leq q_1$ *and* $q_2\leq z_2\leq p_2\}$. *Let the function* $f:Z\text{----->}\mathbb{N}$ *with* $f(z_1,z_2)=a*z_1*z_2+b*z_1+c*z_2$ *be determined by p,q. Let z' such that* $f(z')= max(f(z) \mid z\in G)$. *Then z' is an efficient point in Z.*

REMARKS: The points p, q are elements of G and therefore G is not empty. The parameters a, b and c are such that the points $p=(p_1,p_2)$, $q=(q_1,q_2)$ and $r=(q_1-1,p_2-1)$ have the same objective function value which may be the maximum value.

THEOREM: *A point* $z\in Z$ *is efficient if and only if z is a solution of* $\max(f(z) \mid z\in G$ *and* $f(z)=f(z_1,z_2)=a*z_1*z_2+b*z_2+c*z_1$) *with a,b and c determined by two efficient points p,q.*

THE ALGORITHM

The algorithm starts with $a=0$ in the quadratic function in order to find the two extreme efficient points, called p,q. Thus, in the first step we consider two transportation problems with only one single linear objective function. With the help of this pair of efficient points the algorithm starts to search for further efficient points in Z. The algorithm determines the parameters a, b and c by choosing a pair (p,q) of known efficient points and then maximizes $f(z)=f(z_1,z_2)=a*z_1*z_2 +b*z_2+c*z_1$ with $z\in G$. Such a maximizing point will always exist and we distinguish two cases. In the first case a new efficient point z is found and the pairs (p,z) and (z,q) are stored. In the second case either p or q is found and we have to check if $(q_1\text{-}1,p_2\text{-}1)\in Z$ since all three points have the same objective function value. If $(q_1\text{-}1,p_2\text{-}1)\in Z$ then we also store two pairs of efficient points. If $(p_1^{(s)}\text{-}1, p_2^{(r)}\text{-}1)\notin Z$ no new efficient point is found. The algorithm labels the used pair of efficient points and continues with another unlabeled pair of efficient points. The algorithm continues until all pairs of efficient points are labeled. In order to solve the maximum-problem a branch-and-bound algorithm or other methods [4] can be used.

Algorithm :

Step 1: Find $p_1^{(1)}$=min(z_1(x)| x∈X) and $p_2^{(1)}$=min(z_2(x)| z_1(x)=$p_1^{(1)}$ and x∈X). Record $p^{(1)}$= $(p_1^{(1)},p_2^{(1)})$. Similarly, find $p^{(2)}=(p_1^{(2)},p_2^{(2)})$ with $p_2^{(2)}$=min(z_2(x)| x∈X) and $p_1^{(2)}$=min(z_1(x)| z_2(x)=$p_2^{(2)}$ and x∈X). If $p^{(1)}=p^{(2)}$ or $p_1^{(2)}$-1= $p_1^{(1)}$ or $p_2^{(1)}$-1=$p_2^{(2)}$ then STOP. Otherwise record $p^{(1)}$ and $p^{(2)}$ and set L={(1,2)}, k=2 and E=∅ . Go to step 2.

Step 2: Choose an element (r,s)∈L, use $p^{(r)}$ and $p^{(s)}$ to determine the quadratic objective function f and find z' with $f(z')$=max($f(z)$ | z∈G). If $p^{(r)}\neq z'\neq p^{(s)}$) then set k=k+1 and $p^{(k)}=z'$. If $p^{(k)}$ = ($p_1^{(s)}$ -1, $p_2^{(r)}$ -1) then L=L\{(r,s)} and E=E∪{(r,k),(k,s)} if $p_1^{(s)}$-1=$p_1^{(k)}$ then L= (L∪{(r,k)})\{(r,s)} and E=E∪{(k,s)} if $p_2^{(r)}$-1=$p_2^{(k)}$ then L= (L∪{(k,s)})\{(r,s)} and E=E∪{(r,k)} else L=L\{(r,s)} and L=L∪{(r,k),(k,s)}. Otherwise if $z'=p^{(r)}$ or $z'=p^{(s)}$ then if ($p_1^{(s)}$ -1, $p_2^{(r)}$ -1)∈Z then set k=k+1, L=L\{(r,s)} and E=E ∪{(r,k),(k,s)} if ($p_1^{(s)}$ -1, $p_2^{(r)}$ -1) ∉Z then L=L\{(r,s)} and E=E∪{(r,s)}.

Step 3: If L=∅ STOP . Otherwise go to step 2.

The complexity depends very much on the number of efficient points. Since for each efficient point we have to solve a QAP exactly, which belongs to the class of NP-hard problems [3], the complexity of this algorithm will not be polynomial in time.

REFERENCES

[1] Aneja,Y.P.;Nair,K.P.K.; Bicriteria Transportation Problem; Management Science, Vol.25 , No.1, 1979

[2] Steuer,R.E.; Multiple Criteria Optimization: Theory, computation and Application; Wiley&Sons, 1986

[3] Burkard,R.E.; Quadratic Assignement Problems, Eur. J. of OR,15, 1984, 283-289

[4] Burkard,R.E.; Methoden der Ganzzahligen Optimierung; Springer-Verlag, Wien New York , 1972

Solving 3—Satisfiability in less than 1,579^n Steps

Ingo Schiermeyer
Lehrstuhl C für Mathematik, Technische Hochschule Aachen
Templergraben 55, 5100 Aachen, Germany

Extended abstract

In this paper we present and analyse an improved algorithm for solving the **k-Satisfiability problem**: Given a family F of r clauses in conjunctive normal form consisting of k literals corresponding to k different variables of a set of n boolean variables. Is F satisfiable?

The best known algorithm with respect to the worst-case complexity of its running-time is due to B. Monien and E. Speckenmeyer [1] from 1985. Especially, it solves the 3-Satisfiability problem in $1,619^n$ steps. Branching at a clause with two literals leads to the constant 1,619.

Inspite of several efforts no one succeeded to improve this 3-Sat algorithm. This gave reason to V. Chvátal and P.L. Hammer at the ARIDAM V to ask whether it is possible to design an algorithm with a better time complexity. The main difficulty is, how to branch more efficiently at a clause with two literals.

Recently, we introduced a new k-Sat algorithm [2]. The basic idea of our k-Sat algorithm may be described as follows: Instead of branching at a single clause C this k-Sat algorithm searches for a set of clauses having some variables in common. It then examines whether there is an autark truth assignment or branches at this set of clauses.

Theorem For the 3-Satisfiability problem this algorithm runs in less than $1,579^n$ steps.

We also analyse the performance of this k-Sat algorithm for hard examples like pigeonhole formulas, Tseitin formulas and Ramsey formulas (related to the computation of classical Ramsey numbers).

References

[1] B. Monien and E. Speckenmeyer, *Solving Satisfiability in less than 2^n Steps*, Discrete Appl. Math. 10 (1985) 287 - 295.

[2] I. Schiermeyer, *Schnelle Algorithmen fúr das k-Satisfiability Problem*, Habilitationsschrift, RWTH Aachen, 1992.

Boltzmann Machine Solution N—Person Games

Franciszek Seredynski
Institute of Computer Science PAS
ul. Ordona 21, 01-237 Warsaw, Poland

Games with limited interaction are considered. A global behaviour of a team of players in the game is observed. The average total payoff received by the team of players is chosen as a criterion of the global behaviour. The game is implemented by a neural network of Boltzmann Machine type. The model is applied to solve an optimal task assignment problem in parallel computers. Results of experimental study of the model are presented.

GAMES WITH LIMITED INTERACTION

A game with limited interaction (GLI) is defined by a set of N *players* $\{P_k\}$, a set $\{f_k\}$ of *actions* for each *player* and a system of payoff functions P^k such a that each function depends only on an *action* f_k of a given *player* and *actions* of his n_k neighbours in the game. GLI can be represented by a graph $G =< V, E >$ called an *interaction graph*. The set V corresponds to the set of *players* and E represents the interaction between *players* in the game. Each *player* in the game selects independently an *action* to maximize his own payoff. A solution of the game is *Nash point*. In GLI we are not interested in a payoff of a *player* in the *Nash point* but in a global measure of the payoff, the average value of payoff functions:

$$\overline{P}(f) = (\sum_{k=1}^{N} P^k(f))/N, \tag{1}$$

where $\overline{P}(f)$ is called a *price* of the *actions'* combination f.

We are interested in behaviour of *players* in the game to find *actions'* combination maximizing $\overline{P}(f)$. Unfortunately, *actions'* combinations with maximal *price* very often do not correspond to *Nash points* and a value of $\overline{P}(f)$ received by the team in the *Nash point* can be very low. For learning automata GLI a solution of the problem is known (Seredynski (1991)) for the class of homogeneous games and was obtained by introducing a local cooperation between *players*. For heterogenous games the problem is a subject of a current study and for this reason we propose here a neural network approach to find a solution of the game.

BOLTZMANN MACHINE IMPLEMENTATION OF THE GAME

We follow here Aarts (1989) approach to optimization problems by a neural network of Boltzmann Machine (BM) type. BM implementing the game consists of a network of $N * d$ logical units having two discrete states "0" and "1", where d—number of *actions* of a *player*.

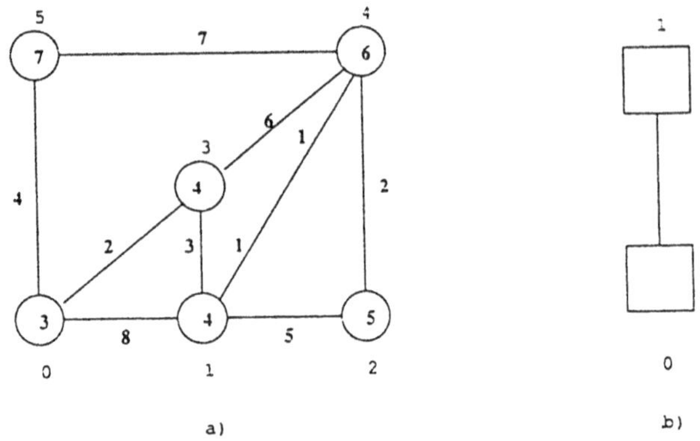

Figure 1: Program (a) and system (b) graphs

The units are connected in some way and with each connection a connection strength is associated. Unit u_{kp} represents an *action* p of a player k; $p = 0, \ldots, d-1; k = 0, \ldots, N-1$.

The set of connections is defined as the union of three sets: payoff connections, inhibitory connection and bias connections. The bias and inhibitory connections are used to implement that each player makes exactly one move. On the payoff connections the payoff system of the game is implemented.

The bias connections are equal to the average value of the sum of the payoff connections:

$$s(u_{kp}, u_{kp}) = -\beta \sum_{q=0}^{d-1} \sum_{l=0, l\neq k}^{N} \sum_{r=0}^{d-1} \frac{s(u_{kq}, u_{k_l r})}{n_k d^2}, \tag{2}$$

where β is a positive number greater than 1. The inhibitory connections are chosen stronger positive than the bias connections are negative, i.e. $s(u_{kp}, u_{kl}) > -s(u_{kp}, u_{kp})$.

Each unit u_{kp} of BM has cooling schedule with a start control parameter c_0^{kp}. The decrement rule from which a subsequent value of the control parameter is calculated is chosen as $c_{t+1}^{kq} = \alpha c_t^{kq}$, where α is a positive number smaller than but close to 1.

TASK ASSIGNMENT PROBLEM

The neural network implementing GLI is applied here to solve an optimal task assignment problem (Indurkhya (1986)) in multiprocessor systems. Let us consider a parallel program represented by a program graph (Fig.1a). For any assignment θ a local cost function $C_{\theta(k)}^k$ is defined for each program node. The function is defined as (Seredynski (1992)):

$$C_{\theta(k)}^k = C_{1\theta(k)}^k + C_{2\theta(k)}^k, \tag{3}$$

where $C_{1\theta(k)}^k$ is a communication cost and $C_{2\theta(k)}^k$ is a computation cost of a given assignment. These functions are defined in the following way:

$$C_{1\theta(k)}^k = 0.5 \sum_{l=1}^{r_k} a_{kl} * d_{min}(\theta(k), \theta(l)), \tag{4}$$

where a_{kl}-data transfer time between neighbour program nodes k and l when they are located in neighbour system nodes; $d_{min}(\theta(k),\theta(l))$- a minimal distance between system nodes $\theta(k)$ and $\theta(l)$; r_k-a number of neighbour program nodes of the node k and

$$C^k_{2\theta(k)} = b_k + \sum_{n=1}^{n_i} b_n, \tag{5}$$

where b_n-running time of the n-th program node located also in the node $\theta(k)$;n_i-number of program nodes in the node $\theta(k)$. The problem of optimal task assignment is formulated as the problem of assigning program nodes into the system graph to minimize the total cost defined as a sum of cost functions (3) taken over all assignments.

The program graph from Fig. 1a can be interpreted in terms GLI as the *interaction graph* of the game with the number of players $N = 6$. Each *player* has a set $\{0,1\}$ of *actions* which correspond to moves to the system node 0 or 1 (Fig. 1b). Local cost functions are implemented in BM by strengths of the payoff connections in the following way:

$$s(u_{kp}, u_{lq}) = \begin{cases} (b_k + b_l) & \text{if after move } p,q \text{ of respectively} \\ & \text{program nodes } k,l, \text{ they} \\ & \text{are in the same system node} \\ a_{kl} d_{min}(\theta(k),\theta(l)) & \text{if after move } p,q \text{ of respectively} \\ & \text{program nodes } k,l, \text{ they} \\ & \text{are in respectively system nodes } \theta(k),\theta(l). \end{cases} \tag{6}$$

The neural network for the presented above task assignment problem was implemented in Occam2 on a 128 Transputer Reconfigurable Machine.

Two solutions for the task assignment problem from Fig. 1 exist. The first one is characterized by a set $(0,0,0,1,1,1)$ of *players' actions*, i.e. *players* 0,1 and 2 choose the *action* 0 and *players* 3,4 and 5 choose the *action* 1. The second solution is a set of *actions* $(1,1,1,0,0,0)$. The total cost of assigning for both solutions is equal to 70. Conducted experiments show that assignment found by BM depend on a value of cooling control parameter. The optimal solution is always found for $\alpha > 0.9$. Suboptimal solutions are found for $0.4 \leq \alpha \leq 0.8$. BM provides suboptimal solutions in comparatively small number of steps, two times faster than the optimal solution.

REFERENCES

Aarts E H L, Korst J H M (1989) Boltzmann machines for travelling salesman problems. Europ. J. of Oper. Research 39: 79-95

Indurkhya B, Stone H S and Xi-Cheng L (1986) Optimal partitioning of randomly generated distributed programs. IEEE Trans. on Software Eng., SE-12(3):483-495

Seredynski F (1991) Self-organization in homogeneous networks of learning automata. Proc. of the 6th Czechoslovak Annual AI Conference, Prague, June 25-27, 1991

Seredynski F (1992) Mapping by migrating Boltzmann Machine. Proc. of Parallel Problem Solving From Nature Conference, Brussels, Sept. 28-30, 1992

Analysis of the Degree of Parallelism for Non-Polynomial, Polynomial, Strongly Polynomial Algorithms for Solving the Minimum Cost Flow Problem

Cosimo Spera, Massimiliano Ugolini
Computer Center, Universita' degli Studi di Siena
Via Bandini 25, S3100 Siena, Italy

0. 1 Introduction

The minimum cost flow problem (**Mcfp**), (or the two equivalent transportation and the minimum cost circulation), plays a crucial role in the network flow optimization mainly because other flow problems can be considered special cases of it. If there are n nodes and m arcs using the matrix notation **Mcfp** can be written as:

$$\min \{c(x) : Ax=b \; l \leq x \leq u \} \qquad (0.1)$$

where c(x) is the objective function, A is the (nxm) arc-node incident matrix, b is the n-array containing the supply or the demand values at node i, x is the arc flow and l and u are respectively the lower and the upper bounds.

Under the assumptions that: **a)** the cost function is linear; **b)** b(1) = (n - 1) and b(i) = -1 i : 2, n **c)** l=0, u=n then the optimal solution for (0.1) sends one unit of flow from 1 to all the other nodes along the **shortest path.**

Under the assumption that: **a)** an extra arc is added (k,r) with cost = -1, and the is capacity equal to infinity; **b)** supply and demand of the other nodes are set to zero; **c)** all the cost arcs are set to zero then the optimal then solution for (0.1) maximizes the **maximum flow** from the source node to the sink node.

Under the assumption that: **a)** the graph can be partitioned in $G(N_1 \cup N_2, E)$ and $\#N_1 = \#N_2$; **b)** the cost function is linear; **c)** b(i)=1 for $i \in N_1$ and b(i) = -1 for $i \in N_2$; d) l=0 u =1 then the optimal solution for (0.1) is the **minimum cost assignment** for the bipartite graph.

The **Mcfp** has also the property to preserve integrality due to the strongly unimodularity of the arc-node incident matrix.

The unimodularity brings the **Mcfp** to be a link between the continues and integer programming.

Some of the first algorithms developed were a specialization of the primal simplex method. These algorithms made use of the property that the basis matrix can be triangularized and therefore can be represented as a tree using the predecessor function.

The function itself is not sufficient to across the tree and to update it after a pivot operation is performed. Therefore a thread and a depth function must be defined.

This basis data structure, or some equivalent, has brought combined with "good" selection rules to very efficient algorithms in practice, in some case they can be classified as pseudo-polynomial.

None of these algorithms, even if their implementation seems to give the best computational results on a very large selection of test cases, run in polynomial time (i.e. the running time is bounded by a low order polynomial function of n , m, log C, log U; where C is the largest cost coefficient and U is the largest capacity on the arcs).

The first (weakly) polynomial algorithm is credited to Edmonds and Karp (1972). It is based on capacity and right-hand-side scaling, Orlin (1988) gave the best known running time strongly polynomial algorithm, (i.e. the running time is bounded by a low order polynomial function of n , m) which is an implementation of the scaling algorithm combined with the idea of *strongly basic variables*.

Another approach credited to M. Klein (1967) is based on the idea to detect negative cycle. Goldberg and Tarjan (1988) have extended this idea finding a rule to discard the minimum average negative cycle. Their algorithm is strongly polynomial.

Bertsekas and Tseng (1988) have proposed a relaxation algorithm; it works on the dual objective function and when its optimal value has determined then the optimal primal solution is obtained.

There are no many attempts to define a highly parallel algorithm for **Mcfp**. Golberg suggested the idea to use a dynamic tree structure, this idea can be used to avoid dependency on the basis data structure, Orlin proved that using n^3 processor then his algorithm can run in $O(n\log^3 m)$. The author has proposed an implementation of the primal simplex method based on the idea of "parallel" pivot. Recent experiments have shown that this problem does not seem to have a particular high degree of parallelization for some random generated test cases.

The aim of this paper is to investigate the possible degree of parallelization for some of the best running time algorithms. This investigation is done both on theoretical and practical base.

The theoretical model used is PRAM (Parallel Random Access Machine) while the practical analysis is carried out looking at the performance on distributed/shared memory and network parallel architectures. The outline of the paper is as following.

In section one the preliminary results are given, in section two both the PRAM and the "real" models are presented. In section three the parallel analysis is carried out, while in section four the possible extension are presented to improve the degree of parallelism. In section five some network problem generator are illustrated; they are designed according to some graph property so that when the problems are tested it will be possible to understand if the parallelism is function of the examples generated. The results are presented in section five, while in section six the conclusion and extensions are given.

0.2. Main results

In this section we try to point briefly out the main goal of the paper. Any parallel model that we are going to consider has n or n^2 processors, therefore the PRAM model will be modified to match this hypothesis. The analysis wants to show how the running time complexity can be effected on a parallel model. In particular we want to analyze if some parallel scheme can effect more the *geometric improvement* than the *scaling* approach or viceversa. On the other hand, once it is defined a class of test cases with some characteristics we want to investigate about the worst case and the average complexity and inferences among the different classes are provided.

keywords : network flow optimization, parallel algorithms, complexity

Main References

Bertsekas, D.P., and P. Tseng. 1987. Relax: A Code for Linear Network Flow Problems. In B. Simeone et al. (eds), FORTRAN *Codes for Network Optimization, Annals of Operation Research*

Bertsekas, D.P., and P. Tseng. 1988. Relaxation Methods for Minimum Cost Ordinary and Generalized Network Flow Problems. *Oper. Res* 36, 93-114

Edmonds, J., and R.M. Karp. 1972. Theoretical Improvements in Algorithmic Efficiency for Network Flow Problems. J. ACM 19, 248-264

Galil, Z., and E. Tardos. 1986. An $O(n^2(m + n \log n) \log n)$ Min-Cost Flow Algorithm. *Proc 27th Annual Symp on the Found. of Comp. Sci.*, 136-146

Goldberg, A.V., and R.E. Tarjan. 1988. Finding Minimum-Cost Circulation by Canceling Negative Cycles. *Proc. 20th ACM Symp. on the Theory of Comp.*, 388-397.

Grigoriadis, M.D. 1986. An Efficient Implementation of the Network Simplex Method. *Math. Prog. Study* 26, 83-111

Klein, M. 1967. A Primal Method for the Minimal Cost Flow. *Man. Sci* 14, 205-220

Orlin, J.B. 1985. On the Simplex Algorithm for Networks and Generalized Networks. *Math. Prog. Study* 24, 166-178

Orlin, J.B. 1988. A Faster Strongly Polynomial Minimum Cost Flow *Proc. 20th ACM Symp. on the Theory of Comp.*, 377-387.

Spera, C. 1989. A Parallel Network Algorithm, *EURO X* 25-30 June 1989, Beograd, Yug.

Spera, C and L. Vettorazzo. 1990. A Parallel Algorithm for Solving Minimum Cost Flow Problems. Working Paper #52 *Istituto di Matematica, Facoltà di Scienze Economiche e Bancarie, Università di Siena*

Decomposition of Multiplace Functions in Operations Research

Bernhard von Stengel
Informatik 5, Armed Forces University Munich
8014 Neubiberg, Germany

This extended abstract summarizes the results of a decomposition theory for multiplace functions that generalizes and unifies theories known from a number of areas in Operations Research. The considered decompositions of a multiplace function are representations as terms of functions of fewer variables where variables may be used only once. This restricted "disjoint" functional superposition or "substitution" has been defined independently in switching circuit design, combinatorial optimization over networks and clutters and ordinal and expected utility theory. There, it has led to interesting results on unique "normal form" representations, like additive utility functions. These results have great similarities that are explained by the proposed theory, where the admitted decompositions are characterized set-theoretically: An n-ary operation f on a given set is decomposed into "conditional" functions obtained from f by fixing variables suitably. The following exposition is fairly technical to state results precisely. Proofs are found in [5] and further references in [4][5].

The ranges for the considered functions and their variables are non-empty sets S_i called *coordinate axes*, indexed by *coordinates* i from some index set I. For a finite set $A \subseteq I$ of coordinates, denote by $\langle A \rangle$ the cartesian product $\prod_{i \in A} S_i$ in its usual set-theoretic definition as the set of functions x defined on A with $x(i) \in S_i$ for $i \in A$ (if $S_i = S$ for all $i \in A$, then $\langle A \rangle = S^A$). This allows to postulate for disjoint sets A, B the equality $\langle A \cup B \rangle = \langle A \rangle \times \langle B \rangle$.

A *multiplace function* f is defined on $\langle N \rangle$ for some finite $N \subseteq I$, where $|N|$ is the *arity* of f. The range F of f is some axis S_j, identified with $\langle \{j\} \rangle$. Only total functions $f: \langle N \rangle \to F$ are considered. With reference to the domain $\langle N \rangle$ of f, call $i \in N$ the coordinates *of* f, indexing the variables of f, and the sets S_i axes *of* f.

The *substitution* of a multiplace function h into a variable of another multiplace function g is defined if $h: \langle A \rangle \to \langle \{i\} \rangle$, $g: \langle \{i\} \cup B \rangle \to F$, where $i \notin B$ and $A \cap B = \emptyset$, resulting into the function $f: \langle A \cup B \rangle \to F$ given by

$$f(x, y) = g(h(x), y) \qquad \text{for } x \in \langle A \rangle,\ y \in \langle B \rangle, \tag{*}$$

which is abbreviated as $f = g[h]$. (This abbreviation is unique since, in particular, the substituted variable of g is stored in the set-theoretic definition of h as the index i of its range, in some sense the "target" of the substitution of h.) Conversely, (*) is a *decomposition* of f for a suitable subset A of f's coordinate set N, where $B = N - A$. Note that A and B are always disjoint, so variables are never repeated; also, f, g, h are always total functions, and g is fully defined by (*) if h is surjective. Decompositions of f are *iterated* by applying them to g or h, and so on.

Applications of this decomposition are obtained by restricting the admitted functions f, g, h. For example, these are *Boolean* functions if all coordinate axes and ranges of the functions are equal to a two-element set $\{0,1\}$, where (*) denotes a "disjoint decomposition" of f, see [1]. If each axis is a real interval and one considers only continuous functions f, g, h strictly *increasing* in each variable, then the decomposition (*) with an interpretation of f as an (ordinal) *utility function* represents a *preference independence* [3] or "separability" [2] of the set A of "decision attributes". Further applications will be sketched at the end of this text.

Decompositions will be considered in a class Σ of multiplace functions that is closed under substitution. Certain axioms for Σ, presented next, shall serve three goals: decompositions in Σ can be done using "conditional functions" (this approach can be nicely developed just regarding a given multiplace function, which is skipped here for brevity); interesting unique representations hold for any $f \in \Sigma$; and a number of applications are obtained as special cases. Throughout, let $f: \langle N \rangle \to F$ be a multiplace function in Σ. Let $A \subseteq N$, $B = N - A$, and y' be any element of $\langle B \rangle$. Then the function $\langle A \rangle \to F$, $x \mapsto f(x, y')$, denoted by $f(\,\cdot\,, y')$, is called an *f-conditional* function, with *reference vector y'*. If this function is unary, with $A = \{i\}$, it is called an *f-translation.* (Thus, an f-conditional function is obtained by fixing the variables indexed by B at $y' \in \langle B \rangle$; each component of this vector y' could be regarded as a constant, defined on $\langle \emptyset \rangle$, substituted into f, but Σ shall *not* contain constants.)

Axiom 1. *$|N| \geq 1$, and for each $i \in N$ there is a bijective f-translation on $\langle \{i\} \rangle$.*

This axiom implies that all coordinate axes S_i, $i \in N$ of the domain of f have the same cardinality as its range F. It holds for Boolean functions f where all variables are *essential* (cannot be dropped) since a nonconstant f-translation $\{0,1\} \to \{0,1\}$ is bijective. By Axiom 1, all unary functions in Σ are bijections.

Axiom 2. *If $|N| = 1$, then the inverse of f belongs to Σ.*

Two multiplace functions $f, g \in \Sigma$ are called *isotopic* if f is obtained from g by composition with unary functions $\phi, \psi_1, \ldots, \psi_n \in \Sigma$ as in $\phi f = g[\psi_1, \ldots, \psi_n]$, where ϕf means $\phi[f]$ and $g[\psi_1, \ldots, \psi_n]$ denotes the "parallel substitution" of all n variables of g by values of the bijections $\psi_1, \ldots, \psi_n$, which can be viewed as transformations of the variables of f ($n = |N|$); if these are all equal to the transformation $\phi: F \to G$ of the value of f, then f and g are (in the usual sense) *isomorphic* operations $F^n \to F$ respectively $G^n \to G$ (a function $F^N \to F$ is hereby regarded as an n-ary operation $F^n \to F$, disregarding names of coordinates). Axioms 1 and 2 show that $f \in \Sigma$ is isotopic to an n-ary operation g on F that has the identity on F as a suitable g-translation on each coordinate axis; for a binary operation g ($n = 2$), this means there is a left- and a right-neutral element for g.

Axiom 3. *With f, all f-conditional functions fulfilling Axiom 1 belong to Σ.*

Axiom 3 is fairly natural. For example, f-conditional functions for Boolean functions f are also Boolean. However, some of them may have inessential variables so Axiom 1 is violated; they are not considered in Axiom 3 since otherwise the axiom would be too restrictive for f.

Axiom 4. *All surjective f-translations are bijective.*

Axiom 4'. *(Alternatively.) All injective f-translations are bijective.*

Axiom 4 (or 4') is only necessary if f is not a discrete function (with finite coordinate axes). Essentially, it guarantees a "compatibility" of reference vectors in decompositions, since if $f = g[h]$, an f-translation ϕ on a coordinate axis of h is composed of a g- and a h-translation, and by Axiom 4 or 4' these translations are bijective if ϕ is bijective.

Let Σ be a collection of functions closed under substitution fulfilling Axioms 1, 2, 3 and 4 or 4', called a *function system*. If $f \in \Sigma$ and there are $g, h \in \Sigma$ with $f = g[h]$ and h is defined on $\langle A \rangle$, then A is called an f-*autonomous* set [4] of coordinates of f. Autonomous sets characterize the decomposition possibilities of f within Σ.

Lemma. *For $f \in \Sigma$, defined on $\langle N \rangle$, a set $A \subseteq N$ is f-autonomous iff $f = g[\phi h]$ for suitable f-conditional functions g, h and a bijection ϕ, with h defined on $\langle A \rangle$. Thereby, the reference vectors for g and h are obtained as parts of z' whenever $f(\,\cdot\,, z')$ is a bijective f-translation on $\langle \{i\} \rangle$ for $i \in A$, $z' \in \langle N - \{i\} \rangle$, and g, h, ϕ belong to Σ.*

This central lemma asserts that decompositions of f can always be represented using f-conditional functions, and their reference vectors are recognized from the bijective f-translations of Axiom 1. The lemma allows to apply decompositions of f to f-conditional functions in other decompositions. This permits simple proofs of the "unique decomposition" theorems presented next.

Iterated decompositions should end whenever the arity of the functions can not be reduced. Call $f \in \Sigma$ *prime* (that is, indecomposable) if f is not unary and $f = g[h]$ implies g or h is unary, for $g, h \in \Sigma$.

Jordan-Hölder-Theorem. *Let $f \in \Sigma$ and $f = ((g_1[g_2])\cdots)[g_k]$. Then if the functions $g_1, \ldots, g_k \in \Sigma$ are prime, they are unique up to their order of substitution and isotopy.*

This theorem is analogous to that for groups. Isotopy is the natural invariance concept here since unary bijections (transformations of variables) followed by their inverses can be interspersed anywhere in the sequence of substitutions. Note that, as for groups, the (isotopy classes of) the prime "factors" $g_1, \ldots, g_k$ usually do not determine f uniquely, so this is weaker than the "decomposition into primes" of natural numbers.

The main representation theorem treats term decompositions that reveal more than iterated substitutions, like $f(x, y, z, t) = g(a(x) \cdot b(y) \cdot c(z), t)$ for functions $f, g, a, b, c \in \Sigma$ with an associative "product" $\cdot$ in Σ showing the autonomy of the coordinate sets A, B, say, that define the variable vectors (x, y) and (y, z). It will be seen that such a product representation can always be found if A and B are autonomous sets that *overlap*, that is, $A - B$, $A \cap B$ and $B - A$ are not empty (note that then these sets, corresponding to the vectors x, y and z, are also autonomous).

Theorem. *Let $f \in \Sigma$, defined on $\langle N \rangle$. Then N and $\{i\}$ are f-autonomous for all $i \in N$. If $A, B \subseteq N$ overlap and are f-autonomous, then so are $A \cup B$, $A \cap B$, $A - B$ and $B - A$. Any collection $\mathcal{C}$ of subsets of N with this property can be represented by a labeled tree $T(\mathcal{C})$ with nodes being those elements of $\mathcal{C}$ not overlapping with any other element of $\mathcal{C}$, root N and leaves $\{i\}$, $i \in N$, where the successors of a node A form a partition $B_1, \ldots, B_m$ of A and the set $\mathcal{C}_A = \{B \in \mathcal{C} \mid B \subseteq A\}$ can be represented as $\mathcal{C}_A = \mathcal{D}_A \cup \mathcal{C}_{B_1} \cup \cdots \cup \mathcal{C}_{B_m}$ with three possibilities for $\mathcal{D}_A$ coded by labels attached to A:*

label "prime": $\mathcal{D}_A = \{A\}$

label "linear": $\mathcal{D}_A = \{\bigcup_{i=l}^{k} B_i \mid 1 \leq l < k \leq m\}, \quad m \geq 3$

label "full": $\mathcal{D}_A = \{\bigcup_{i \in L} B_i \mid L \subseteq \{1, \ldots, m\}, |L| \geq 2\}, \quad m \geq 3.$

In this theorem, $\mathcal{C}$ can be reconstructed from the tree $T(\mathcal{C})$ with the labels, where, if a node A is labeled "linear", the order among its successors matters. With $\mathcal{C}$ as the collection of f-autonomous sets, $T(\mathcal{C})$ is called the *composition tree* for f [2][4]. It corresponds to a unique hierarchical term representation of f.

Theorem. *Let $f \in \Sigma$, defined on $\langle N \rangle$, and $\mathcal{C}$ be the set of f-autonomous sets. Then for each node A of $T(\mathcal{C})$ there is a function h_A defined on $\langle A \rangle$ such that $h_N = f$, and, with successors $B_1, \ldots, B_m$ of A if A is not a leaf, $h_A = g_A[h_{B_1}, \ldots, h_{B_m}]$, where if A is labeled "prime": g_A is prime and unique up to isotopy, "linear": $g_A(y_1, \ldots, y_m) = y_1 \circ \cdots \circ y_m$ with an associative operation $\circ$ in Σ that is unique up to isomorphy and not commutative, "full": then the same holds but with commutative $\circ$.*

Note that this theorem implies that f is a hierarchical term of functions g_A for the non-leaf nodes A of the composition tree $T(\mathcal{C})$ and of unary functions $h_{\{i\}}$; the latter can be omitted by substituting them into the next higher functions if these are prime. These functions can be stored with $T(\mathcal{C})$ to represent f. Any decomposition $f = g[h]$ of f is a subterm of this term since any autonomous set B is coded in $T(\mathcal{C})$, where h, defined on $\langle B \rangle$, may be some "subproduct" taken at some stage if B is the union of successors of a node labeled "linear" or "full".

This theorem has well-known representations as special cases, considering different function systems Σ. For Σ as the class of Boolean functions [1], the associative operation $\circ$ is addition $\oplus$ modulo 2 or conjunction $\wedge$ (via isomorphy, taking complements, also equivalence $\equiv$ or disjunction $\vee$). For monotone Boolean functions, $\wedge$ or $\vee$; their decomposition is the well-known substitution decomposition of *clutters* (antichains in the power set of N), see [4]. "Clutter polynomials" in a semiring like $\mathbb{R}_{\geq}$, max, +, considering $f(x_1, \ldots, x_n)$ as a maximum of sums $\sum_{i \in C} x_i$ for elements C of a given clutter, for example maximal chains C in an order, also form a function system Σ; here $\circ$ is max or +. In this example, the decomposition of f corresponds to a decomposition of the order [4], which is series-parallel iff the prime nodes of the composition tree have only two successors.

Multiaffine are those functions $f: \mathbb{R}^n \to \mathbb{R}$ whose f-translations are of the form $x \mapsto ax + b$. They form a function system Σ, where, interpreting f as an *expected-utility* function, autonomous sets are called *generalized utility independent*. The operation $\circ$ is + or $\cdot$, corresponding to the well-known additive/multiplicative expected-utility function [3]. For the continuous ordinal utility functions mentioned above, strictly increasing in each variable, $\circ$ is (up to isomorphy with a strictly increasing transformation like the logarithm) addition of reals, yielding an additive utility function [2]. For further applications and references see [4][5].

References

[1] Ashenhurst, R.L. (1959). The decomposition of switching functions. Proc. Int. Symp. Theory of Switching (April 1957), Part I. Ann. Comput. Lab. Harvard U. 29, 74–116.

[2] Gorman, W.M. (1968). The structure of utility functions. Rev. Economic Studies 35, 367–390.

[3] Keeney, R.L. (1974). Multiplicative utility functions. Oper. Res. 22, 22–34.

[4] Möhring, R.H. and F.J. Radermacher (1984). Substitution decomposition for discrete structures and connections with combinatorial optimization. Ann. Discr. Math. 19, 257–356.

[5] von Stengel, B. (1991). Eine Dekompositionstheorie für mehrstellige Funktionen. Mathematical Systems in Economics 123, Anton Hain, Frankfurt.

Experiences with a Cutting Plane Algorithm in Survivable Network Design

Mechthild Stoer
Konrad-Zuse-Zentrum für Informationstechnik Berlin
Heilbronner Straße 10, 1000 Berlin 31, Germany

The problem of survivable network design came from an application of telecommunications industry, where network topologies are required to be connected after a failure of a certain number of links or nodes. One way to model survivability, accepted by practitioners at Bell Communications Research, is the following.

Graph-theoretic Formulation

Given a graph $G = (V, E)$, integer node types $r_v \geq 0$ for $v \in V$, two of which are of maximal type k, given also nonnegative costs c_e for all $e \in E$, find a subgraph $N = (V, C)$ of minimum total cost, such that, between all pairs of nodes s, t, there exist $\min\{r_s, r_t\}$ different edge- (or node-) disjoint paths in N.

In most applications of telephone network design, a maximal connectivity of $k = 2$ is required, but we also know of a real-world application with $k = 3$.

ILP-Formulation

First, some notations: With $\delta_G(W)$, or more simply $\delta(W)$, we denote the edgeset of the cut induced by the nodeset W in the graph G. The expression $x(\delta(W))$ stands for the sum $\sum_{e\in\delta(W)} x_e$. The node types can be extended to operate on node sets W by setting $\text{con}(W) := \min_{s\in W, t\notin W} r_s, r_t$. The integer LP-formulation of the survivable network design problem is then, by Menger's theorem:

$$
\begin{array}{lll}
 & \min \sum_{ij\in E} c_{ij}x_{ij} & \\
 & \text{subject to} & \\
\text{(i)} & x(\delta(W)) & \geq \text{con}(W) \\
 & & \quad \text{for all } W \subseteq V, \emptyset \neq W \neq V; \\
\text{(ii)} & x(\delta_{G-Z}(W)) & \geq \text{con}_{G-Z}(W) - |Z| \\
 & & \quad \text{for all } Z \subseteq V,\ \emptyset \neq Z \neq V, \text{ and for all } W \subseteq V \setminus Z, \\
 & & \quad \emptyset \neq W \neq V \setminus Z \text{ with } |Z| < \text{con}_{G-Z}(W); \\
\text{(iii)} & 0 \leq x_e \leq 1 & \quad \text{for all } e \in E; \\
\text{(iv)} & x_e \text{ integral} & \quad \text{for all } e \in E.
\end{array}
\qquad (1)
$$

Inequalities (i) are called **cut inequalities**, inequalities (ii) are called **node cut inequalities**, and inequalities (iii) are the **trivial inequalities**.

The cutting plane method relies on the investigation of the associated polytopes:

$$
\begin{array}{lll}
k\text{NCON}(G; r) & := & \text{conv}\{\, x \in \mathbb{R}^E \mid x \text{ satisfies (i), (ii), (iii), (iv) of (1)} \,\} \\
k\text{ECON}(G; r) & := & \text{conv}\{\, x \in \mathbb{R}^E \mid x \text{ satisfies (i), (iii), (iv) of (1)} \,\}
\end{array}
$$

In [GMS92a], we describe various classes of valid and facet-defining inequalities for $2NCON(G;r)$ and $2ECON(G;r)$ and in [Sto91] for $kNCON(G;r)$ and $kECON(G;r)$.

Partition and r-Cover Inequalities

One class of inequalities are the **partition inequalities** generalizing the cut inequalities. They are induced by a partition $\{W_1, \ldots, W_p\}$ of V into $p \geq 2$ disjoint node sets with $\mathrm{con}(W_i) \geq 1$ for $i = 1, \ldots, p$. Let $[W_1 : \ldots : W_p]$ denote the set of edges having their endnodes in different W_i, and let $I_1 := \{\, i \mid \mathrm{con}(W_i) = 1 \,\}$ and $I_2 := \{\, i \mid \mathrm{con}(W_i) > 1 \,\}$. The partition inequality is then defined as

$$x([W_1 : \ldots : W_p]) \geq \begin{cases} p-1, & \text{if } I_2 = \emptyset, \\ \lceil \frac{1}{2} \sum_{i \in I_2} \mathrm{con}(W_i) \rceil + |I_1|, & \text{otherwise.} \end{cases} \tag{2}$$

Node cut inequalities can be generalized to **node partition inequalities** in much the same way as the cut inequalities by using partitions of $V \setminus Z$.

Finally, we have used the lifted r-cover inequalities. These have been derived from a complete description of the so-called r-cover polytope, which is the convex hull of all integer $x \in \mathbb{R}^E$ satisfying

$$\begin{array}{rl} x(\delta(v)) \geq r_v & \text{for all } v \in V, \text{ and} \\ 0 \leq x \leq 1 & \text{for all } e \in E. \end{array} \tag{3}$$

The so-called r-cover inequalities needed to complete the description of this polytope are

$$x(E(H)) + x(\delta(H) \setminus T) \geq \frac{1}{2}\Big(\sum_{v \in H} r_v - |T| + 1\Big) \tag{4}$$

for all $H \subseteq V$ and all $T \subseteq \delta(H)$ such that $\sum_{v \in H} r_v - |T|$ odd. These inequalities can be lifted to obtain the so-called **lifted r-cover inequalities**. Further generalizations can be found in [GMS92a, Sto91, GMS92c].

Separation Problems

Roughly speaking, one iteration of a cutting plane algorithm solves an LP consisting of valid inequalities, starting from, say, the constraints (3), then finding inequalities violated by the current (nonfeasible) optimal solution, and adding them to the LP. This is done until the solution is feasible and hence optimal, or until no more violated inequalities are found. In the latter case, we have to employ branch and cut. The major algorithmic problem to be solved here is to find inequalities violated by the LP-solution $0 \leq x^* \leq 1$, the so-called separation problem. As shown in [GMS92b, GMS92c, Sto91], the separation problem is polynomially solvable for cut inequalities for the kECON problem, and also for the class containing cut and node cut constraints. The problem is NP-hard for the class of partition inequalities, node partition inequalities and lifted r-cover inequalities. For all these cases, we devised heuristic separation methods.

Computational Results

From Bellcore, we obtained data for seven 2NCON problems, where telephone networks for several North American cities had to be designed. These problems were formulated on extremely sparse graphs, whose sizes ranged from 36 nodes and 65 edges to 116 nodes and 173 edges. With 2NCON-specific reduction (e.g., shrinking paths of nodes of degree 2), the sizes could be reduced even further to graphs of maximally 39 nodes and 86 edges. Most of these problems were solved already in the cutting plane phase without branching. All problems could be solved in less than 30 seconds on a SUN 4/50 IPX. This is described in [GMS92b, Sto91].

We also solved a few random kECON problems for higher connectivities. One test set consisted complete graphs with up to 40 nodes and random cost structure. The node types were uniformly k for all nodes ($k \in \{3,4,5\}$). These problems were mostly already solved in the first iteration with the LP (3)!

Another test set consisted of complete random graphs with forty nodes of type k ($2 \leq k \leq 5$) and with Euclidean cost structure. It turned out that the kECON problems with even k were much easier to solve than the problems with odd k. All problems with even k were solved in the cutting plane phase in a few seconds, whereas for all problems with $k = 3$ and some with $k = 5$, branch and cut had to be employed with running times up to 325 minutes. We concluded from this that the polyhedral description of kECON problems with odd k and also the separation algorithms need to be refined.

Bellcore also provided us with a 3ECON problem that has to do with the design of a communication network on a ship. This problem is defined on a grid graph with a very regular cost structure; it contains 1096 edges and 494 nodes, of which only 33 are of nonzero type and need to be interconnected. We could solve two versions of this problems (where the node types of the 33 nodes were varied) in up to 426 minutes, but for the last interesting version (all 33 nodes of type 3) the gap of 4.64% is still too large to be bridged by branch and cut.

The computational results for the high-connectivity problems are described in more detail in [GMS92c, Sto91].

References

[GMS92a] M. Grötschel, C. L. Monma, and M. Stoer. Facets for polyhedra arising in the design of communication networks with low-connectivity constraints. *SIAM Journal on Optimization*, 2(3), August 1992.

[GMS92b] M. Grötschel, C. L. Monma, and M. Stoer. Computational results with a cutting plane algorithm for designing communication networks with low-connectivity constraints. *Operations Research*, 40(2):309–330, 1992.

[GMS92c] M. Grötschel, C. L. Monma, and M. Stoer. Polyhedral and computational investigations for designing communication networks with high survivability requirements. Konrad-Zuse-Zentrum für Informationstechnik Berlin, Heilbronner Str. 10, Berlin, Germany, 1992.

[Sto91] M. Stoer. Design of survivable networks. PhD thesis, University of Augsburg, 1991. To appear in Lecture Notes in Mathematics, Springer-Verlag.

Combinatorial Covering Problems in Coding Theory

G.J.M. van Wee
Philips Rersearch Laboratories
P.O. Box 80000, 5600 JA Eindhoven, Netherlands

We highlight some of the results in [1].

Consider the following problem. Suppose we have n football matches, which have not been played yet. Each match has three possible outcomes: the home team wins, loses, or the match ends in a draw. So, in total, there are 3^n possible outcomes. By a forecast we mean a list of n predicted outcomes, one outcome for each match. Suppose that people are invited to submit forecasts, as many as they like. For each forecast each participant has to pay a fixed amount of money. In exchange, after the matches have been played, part of the money brought together this way is returned to those participants who had sent in a forecast with only few errors. The amount of money returned for such a forecast depends on the number of errors, and on the total number of forecasts with the same number of errors. We pose the following question: What is the minimal number K such that a collection of K forecasts exists with the property that, whatever the outcomes of the matches turn out to be, there will always be at least one forecast in this collection with at most one error? The problem just described is a famous combinatorial problem. It is known as the *football pool problem*. It is a so-called *covering* problem.

We can state the football pool problem in a more formal and more general way. Let Q be an alphabet consisting of q symbols, where $q \geq 2$. For instance, $Q = \mathbf{Z}_q$, the cyclic group of integers modulo q, or, if q is a prime power, $Q = \mathbf{F}_q$, the finite field with q elements. Let $\mathcal{H} = Q^n$, i.e., the set of n-tuples of elements of Q. The elements of $\mathcal{H}$ are called *words*. Define the metric d on $\mathcal{H}$ as follows: for $\boldsymbol{x} = (x_1, \ldots, x_n) \in \mathcal{H}$, $\boldsymbol{y} = (y_1, \ldots, y_n) \in \mathcal{H}$,

$$d(\boldsymbol{x}, \boldsymbol{y}) = |\{i | x_i \neq y_i\}|.$$

The metric d is known as the *Hamming distance*, while the metric space $\mathcal{H}$ is called a *Hamming space*. A *code* is any nonempty subset C of $\mathcal{H}$, and its elements are called *codewords*. Because $|Q| = q$, we say that C is a q-ary code (*binary* if $q = 2$, *ternary* if $q = 3$, etc.). We call n the *length* of C.

The *covering radius* CR(C) of a code C is defined by

$$\mathrm{CR}(C) = \max\{d(\boldsymbol{x}, C) | \boldsymbol{x} \in \mathcal{H}\},$$

where $d(\boldsymbol{x}, C) = \min\{d(\boldsymbol{x}, \boldsymbol{c}) | \boldsymbol{c} \in C\}$. We define

$$K_q(n, R) := \min\{|C| \mid \text{a } q\text{-ary code } C \text{ of length } n \text{ with } \mathrm{CR}(C) = R \text{ exists}\}.$$

The problem is: Determine $K_q(n, R)$ for all q, n, and R. It is not hard to see that the football pool problem is a restricted case of this problem; namely, when we choose $q = 3$ and $R = 1$.

The determination of $K_q(n, R)$ is a hard combinatorial problem. The state of the art is that, except for the cases in which a perfect code – this notion is explained later – exists, and some other special cases, only rough lower and upper bounds on $K_q(n, R)$ are known. There are very few cases in which the exact value of $K_q(n,R)$ has been determined. In [1] several new lower bounds on $K_q(n,R)$ are obtained. For example, we prove that

$$K_2(n,R) \geq \frac{(n-R+\varepsilon)2^n}{(n-R)\sum_{i=0}^{R}\binom{n}{i} + \varepsilon\sum_{i=0}^{R-1}\binom{n}{i}},$$

where

$$\varepsilon = (R+1)\left\lceil\frac{n+1}{R+1}\right\rceil - n - 1.$$

For $R = 1$ this bound reads

$$K_2(n,1) \geq \begin{cases} 2^n/n, & \text{if } n \text{ is even,} \\ 2^n/(n+1), & \text{if } n \text{ is odd.} \end{cases}$$

This implies

$$K_2(2^r,1) = 2^{(2^r-r)}, \qquad \text{for } r = 1,2,\dots\,,$$

the upper bounds being trivial from coding theory. The only values of r for which this was already known are $1, 2$, and 3.

By excluding one of the three outcomes of each match, binary codes can be useful for football pools. However, usually not *each* match has the property that at least one of the three possible outcomes is very unlikely, but only a few. We are led to the so-called *mixed codes* (more in particular, "*binary/ternary*" mixed codes): For certain matches we exclude one of the three possible outcomes, for others we don't. Suppose there are b matches of the first category, and t of the second. In terms of codes, we are dealing with a new type of Hamming space: A function similar to $K_q(n,R)$ can be defined, but, of course, we have to choose a different notation: $K(t,b,R)$. Lower bounds on $K(t,b,R)$ are discussed in [1].

A code C with covering radius R is called *perfect* if for every $\boldsymbol{x}$ there is not only at least one, but exactly one $\mathbf{c} \in C$ at distance at most R. The covering problem is related to the existence of perfect codes. What about perfect codes in $\mathcal{H} = \mathbf{F}_3^t\mathbf{F}_2^b$? In [1] we show that in $\mathcal{H}$ no other perfect codes exist than the trivial ones, for any covering radius R. This result is a corollary of a more general nonexistence theorem. For the general theorem we do not only consider $\mathbf{F}_3^t\mathbf{F}_2^b$, but we allow $\mathcal{H}$ to be *any* mixed Hamming space. That is to say,

$$\mathcal{H} = Q_1 \times Q_2 \times \cdots \times Q_n,$$

where the Q_i are alphabets consisting of q_i symbols. In the third paper we prove that, for a nontrivial perfect code with covering radius R in $\mathcal{H}$ to exist, it is necessary that

$$q_i - q_j \equiv 0 \pmod{R+1}, \qquad \text{for all } i \text{ and } j.$$

A new method to construct good binary linear covering codes was introduced by Graham and Sloane in 1986. They showed how two binary linear codes A and B, of lengths n_A and n_B, dimensions k_A and k_B, and covering radii R_A and R_B, respectively, can be combined and result in a new code of length n_A+n_B-1, dimension k_A+k_B-1, and, provided A and B both satisfy a certain condition – they called codes satisfying this condition *normal* –, with covering radius at most R_A+R_B. The resulting code was called the *Amalgamated Direct Sum* (ADS) of A and B. The condition mentioned appears to be very weak. Up to the present no abnormal binary linear code has been discovered. The ADS-construction is one of the best general constructions of covering codes known. The ADS and the concept of a normal code were extended to nonlinear binary codes by Cohen, Lobstein, and Sloane. Frankl showed that, in contrast with the linear case, nonlinear abnormal binary codes do exist. Among the good binary covering codes no abnormal codes have been discovered yet. This leads to an interesting conjecture, stated by Cohen, Lobstein, and Sloane:

> For all n and R, among the binary codes of length n with covering radius R and $K_2(n, R)$ codewords, there is a normal code. (1)

In [1] we prove this conjecture for $R = 1$. A further result in [1] is a proof that all binary codes C with $|C| > 1$ and minimum distance $d(C) \geq 2\mathrm{CR}(C)$ are normal.

When generalizing the concept of a normal code to arbitrary q, it turns out that, as opposed to the binary case, normal codes are not at all 'normal' if $q > 2$. That is, for $q > 2$ many good q-ary covering codes are not normal. This is expressed in particular by the following result in [1]:

> A q-ary perfect code is normal if and only if it is binary or trivial,

which immediately disproves the q-ary analogue of (1) for $q > 2$.

For a general Hamming space $\mathcal{H}$, we can reformulate the definition of a perfect code as follows. A code $C \in \mathcal{H}$ is perfect if and only if an $r \in \{0, 1, \ldots, n\}$ exists , such that

$$|B_r(\boldsymbol{x}) \cap C| = 1, \qquad \text{for all } \boldsymbol{x} \in \mathcal{H}.$$

In this case we say that C is a *perfect r-covering* of $\mathcal{H}$. In [1] we consider a generalization: A code C is called a *μ-fold perfect r-covering* of $\mathcal{H}$ if

$$|B_r(\boldsymbol{x}) \cap C| = \mu, \qquad \text{for all } \boldsymbol{x} \in \mathcal{H}.$$

We speak of *perfect multiple coverings* (PMC's). We restrict our attention to q-ary codes. A natural question to ask is:

> For which q, n, r, and μ does a μ-fold perfect r-covering of Q^n exist? (2)

In [1] we give some general constructions of PMC's and we thoroughly analyze (2) in the case $r = 1$. We give a complete solution if q is a prime, and a necessary condition if q is a prime power.

References

[1] G. J. M. van Wee, *Covering Codes, Perfect Codes, and Codes from Algebraic Curves.* PhD thesis, Eindhoven University of Technology, Eindhoven, The Netherlands, June 1991.

On Benders' Decomposition for the Capacitated Facility Location Problem*

Paul Wentges
Institut für Unternehmensforschung, Hochschule St. Gallen
Bodanstraße 6, 9000 St. Gallen, Switzerland

Extended Abstract

Abstract

In [van Roy 1986] an algorithm is presented to strengthen Benders' cuts, if Benders' decomposition is applied to solve the capacitated facility location problem. Referring to this algorithm an idea is presented to construct stronger cuts and first results are discussed. The pareto-optimality of these cuts in the sense of [Magnanti/Wong 1981] is shown under a weak assumption.

1 Introduction

The capacitated facility location problem (CFLP) (see e.g. [van Roy 1986]) consists in choosing a number of sites from a given set of possible locations for facilities (or plants and warehouses, resp.) to supply customers with a certain good. This has to be done in such a way, that the sum of the variable transportation costs to deliver the good and the fixed costs to build/maintain the facility is minimized while the demand of all customers is met and the capacity restriction on each facility is satisfied.
Formally, the problem can be written as follows :

$$(CFLP)\left\{\begin{array}{ll} \min \sum_{j=1}^{n} f_j y_j + \sum_{i=1}^{m}\sum_{j=1}^{n} c_{ij}x_{ij}, & \\ \sum_{j=1}^{n} x_{ij} = d_i \ \forall\, i, & (1) \\ x_{ij} \le d_i y_j \ \forall\, i,j, & (2) \\ \sum_{i=1}^{m} x_{ij} \le s_j y_j \ \forall\, j, & (3) \\ x_{ij} \ge 0,\ y_j \in \{0,1\} \ \forall\, i,j, & (4) \end{array}\right.$$

*This paper was partly supported by "Schweizerischer Nationalfond zur Förderung der wissenschaftlichen Forschung (Grant 12-30140.90)".

where m is the number of customers, n the number of potential facility locations, d_i equals the demand of customer i, and s_j the capacity of facility j. c_{ij} are the costs to transport one unit from facility j to customer i and f_j the fixed costs to maintain/build facility j. The variable y_j indicates, whether facility j is opened ($y_j = 1$) or not, and x_{ij} represents the amount shipped from facility j to customer i.

Applying Benders' decomposition to solve the capacitated facility location problem, we obtain the subproblems (SP_y), which equal problem $(CFLP)$ with fixed variables y, and the following class of master problems (MP_T) :

$$
(MP_T) \begin{cases} \min\limits_{\substack{y\in\{0,1\}^n \\ \rho\in\mathbb{R}}} \rho \\ \sum\limits_{i=1}^{m} d_i\lambda_i^t + \sum\limits_{j=1}^{n} y_j(f_j - \sum\limits_{i=1}^{m} d_i\nu_{ij}^t - s_j\mu_j^t) \le \rho, \quad \forall\, t \in T \subseteq K, & (5) \\ \sum\limits_{j=1}^{n} s_j y_j \ge \sum\limits_{i=1}^{m} d_i, & (6) \end{cases}
$$

where T is an appropriate index set and $\{(\lambda^t, \mu^t, \nu^t) : t \in K\}$ are all extreme points of the dual of (SP_y). The capacity restriction (6) on y is added to ensure feasibility of the corresponding subproblems (SP_y). In the following O shall denote the set of open and C the set of closed facilities in the actual solution $\hat{y}$ of (MP_T). Omitting the restrictions (2), $(SP_{\hat{y}})$ is a normal transportation problem and yields the dual variables $\lambda_i, \mu_j, \nu_{ij}$ for the Benders' cuts (5) by setting $\mu_j = \max_{i=1,\ldots,m}\{0, \lambda_i - c_{ij}\}$ for the closed facilities $j \in C$ and $\nu_{ij} = 0$ for all i, j.

2 An algorithm to strengthen Benders' cuts

In [van Roy 1986] an algorithm is presented to strengthen the "Benders' cuts" (5) for the closed facilities $j \in C$, which means altering the corresponding μ_j and ν_{ij}. In the following it will be shown, how the Benders' cuts can be strengthened for the open facilities $j \in O$, too.
Therefore the dual solution (λ, μ, ν) of the normal transportation problem corresponding to the actual solution $\hat{y}$ with $\nu \equiv 0$ is changed as follows :

Algorithm 1 :

1. FOR $i = 1, \ldots, m$ DO
   α) Determine the smallest (k_i) and second smallest (z_i) value of the set $\{c_{ij} + \mu_j : j \in O\}$.
   It follows : $k_i = c_{ij(i)} + \mu_{j(i)} = \lambda_i$ for some $j(i) \in O$.
   β) IF $w_i := z_i - k_i > 0$ THEN
   $\lambda_i := \lambda_i + w_i$,
   $\nu_{ij(i)} := w_i$.
2. Apply van Roy's algorithm to determine μ_j, ν_{ij} for all $j \in C$.

In general, it is allowed to add every cut (λ, μ, ν) to the master problem (MP_T) as long as (λ, μ, ν) is dual feasible to the problem $(SP_{\hat{y}})$. The new vector (λ, μ, ν) produced by algorithm 1 is dual feasible, since $\lambda_i - \mu_j - \nu_{ij} \leq c_{ij}$ still holds for all i, j. With this procedure those facilities are "rewarded" with an improved, that is a smaller value $(f_j - \sum_{i=1}^{m} d_i\nu_{ij} - s_j\mu_j)$, which can supply certain customers better than all other open facilities.

The algorithm was tested on 15 examples with 19-49 facilities and 65-114 customers on the road network of Switzerland. In these examples, the first two Benders' cuts were always obtained by applying the algorithm 1 to the dual solutions of the transportation problems corresponding to the solutions of the primal heuristics AddHi and DropHi (see e.g. [Domschke/Drexl 1985]).

Performing Benders' decomposition (at most twenty iterations), the alteration of the variables (λ, μ, ν) with the algorithm proved to be advantegeous compared to Benders' decomposition without step 1 of algorithm 1 in all examples : in four cases the optimal solution could now be found, in all other cases the duality gap could be substantially decreased.

The algorithm can be altered with even better results depending on the structure of the problem, if one also considers the closed facilities $j \in C$ in step 1. Therefore one has to perform first van Roy's algorithm (step 2 of the above algorithm) to improve μ_j, ν_{ij} for all $j \in C$ and then the complete algorithm 1 with the following change in step 1 :

Determine, in addition, alternatively the smallest, second smallest or third smallest etc. element e_i of the set $\{c_{ij} + \mu_j \; : \; j \in C\}$ and increase λ_i and $\nu_{ij(i)}$ only by $w_i := \max\{0, \min\{z_i - k_i, e_i - k_i\}\}$.

3 Pareto-Optimality of the strengthened Benders' cuts

The concept of pareto-optimality in this field combined with a linear model to construct pareto-optimal Benders' cuts was introduced by [Magnanti/Wong 1981]. In [Magnanti/Wong 1981] and [Magnanti/Wong 1989] the model is applied to construct pareto-optimal cuts for the p-median-problem.

It is assumed now that $\sum_{j \in O} s_j \geq 1 + \sum_{i=1}^{m} d_i$ holds for the actual solution $\hat{y}$. Let y^0 be an element of $\{y = (y_1, \ldots, y_n) : 0 < y_j < 1 \text{ for } j = 1, \ldots, n; \sum_{j=1}^{n} s_j y_j > \sum_{i=1}^{m} d_i\}$, and $(\hat{\lambda}, \hat{\mu})$ be the dual solution of the transportation problem corresponding to $\hat{y}$.

Applying now Theorem 1 from [Magnanti/Wong 1981], one achieves after some transformations the following linear program to construct pareto-optimal cuts :

$$\begin{cases} \max \sum_{j=1}^{n} (\hat{y}_j - y_j^0) \cdot (s_j\mu_j + \sum_{i=1}^{m} d_i\nu_{ij}), \\ \lambda_i - \nu_{ij} - \mu_j \leq c_{ij} \quad \forall\, i, j, \\ \sum_{i=1}^{m} d_i\lambda_i - \sum_{j \in O} (s_j\mu_j + \sum_{i=1}^{m} d_i\nu_{ij}) = c_0, \\ \lambda_i \in \mathbb{R},\; \mu_j \geq 0,\; \nu_{ij} \geq 0, \quad \forall\, i, j, \end{cases}$$

where $c_0 = \sum_{i=1}^{m} d_i\hat{\lambda}_i - \sum_{j \in O} s_j \hat{\mu}_j$. If one chooses

$$y_j^0 = \begin{cases} 1 - \dfrac{1}{s_j|O|}, & j \in O, \\ \dfrac{1}{2\max_{j \in O}\{s_j\} \cdot |O||C|}, & j \in C, \end{cases}$$

the resulting pareto-optimal cut (λ, μ, ν) is the cut constructed with algorithm 1.

References

[Domschke/Drexl 1985] **Domschke, W. / Drexl, A. :** ADD-heuristics Starting Procedures for Capacitated Plant Location Models. European Journal of Operational Research 21 (1985), p. 47 - 53.

[Magnanti/Wong 1981] **Magnanti, T.L. / Wong, R.T. :** Accelerating Benders Decomposition : Algorithmic Enhancement and Model Selection Criteria. Operations Research 29 (1981), p. 464 - 484.

[Magnanti/Wong 1989] **Magnanti, T.L. / Wong, R.T. :** Decomposition Methods for Facility Location Problems. In : Mirchandani, P.B. / Francis, R.L. (eds.) : Discrete Location Theory, Wiley Interscience, New York 1989, p. 209 - 262.

[van Roy 1986] **van Roy, T. :** A Cross Decompositon Algorithm for Capacitated Facility Location. Operations Research 34 (1986), p. 145 - 163.

Packing Grid Figures

Joachim Wolffram
Lehrstuhl für Anwendungen des Operations Research, Universität Karlsruhe
Kaiserstraße 12, 7500 Karlsruhe, Germany

A not necessarily connected figure consisting of non-overlapping unit squares is called a *grid figure*, e.g., every polyomino is a grid figure. Given a set of grid figures with associated values and a region, which is also represented as a grid figure, we consider the problem of packing grid figures of the given set in a non-overlapping way into the region subject to lower and upper quantity restrictions. The objective is to maximize the total value of the inserted grid figures.

In this extended abstract we will give a brief overview about our work and results on this packing problem we achieved so far. A detailed discussion can be found in [7].

1 Introduction

The grid figure packing problem as stated above is surely of great practical interest. Surprisingly, there is up to our knowledge only one article available (see [1]) which deals with this kind of problem. Only for the special case where all grid figures which have to be packed are restricted to be rectangles, a lot of algorithms have been proposed in the context of cutting stock problems [5].

We will sketch the ingredients of an exact branch and bound algorithm and, as the grid figure packing problem is NP-complete [3], we will briefly describe heuristics which are based on tabu search techniques.

Due to lack of space we avoid the introduction of definitions. We hope that the meaning of the terms we use can be understood intuitively.

2 Enumeration, Domination, and Special Patterns

The branch and bound algorithm relies on a scheme for enumerating candidate solutions and on pruning criterions which allow to reject partial solutions. The idea for the enumeration scheme is to generate successively all feasible patterns for a given problem. This process can be seen as generating a large search tree. The root of the search tree represents the original problem. A son of a node is created by inserting exactly one available grid figure at a fit position into the pattern of the node. Thus every node represents a subproblem.

Properties of optimal patterns are explored which provide methods allowing to delete nodes from the search tree by analyzing the structure of the corresponding patterns.

Further, pruning criterions based on dominance relations of pairs of nodes are investigated.

The special problem types where only copies of one grid figure or only rectangles have to be packed are discussed separately. They allow the introduction of very efficient pruning criterions.

3 Computing Upper Bounds

Upper bounds on a subproblem of the search tree are computed by using a lagrangean relaxation of an IP-formulation of the grid figure packing problem. To approximate the solution of the related lagrangean dual problem we use subgradient optimization and apply the scheme for generating lagrangean multipliers as proposed by Camerini et al. [2].

To strengthen the bounds with respect to given lagrangean multipliers we use a method which implicitly generates surrogate constraints based on a clique partition of an overlap graph corresponding to the actual subproblem.

4 Tabu Search Heuristics

The idea of tabu search was introduced by Glover. In the last years Glover and many other authors reported good results using this technique (see [4] for an overview).

We can roughly describe the main idea of our tabu search heuristics for the grid figure packing problem as follows: Given a region R and grid figures $G_1, \ldots, G_n$. Create a feasible solution by successively inserting a grid figure with a maximal value computed by a valuation function. Find a subregion with minimal value. Declare the subregion as tabu. Delete the grid figures from R which have fields in common with the subregion and declare some of them as tabu. Fill the subregion with grid figures which were not declared tabu. Again, find a non–tabu subregion with minimal value. Iterate until some stopping criterion is satisfied.

This routine is embedded in a frame which collects historical information about generated patterns. Diversification and intensification strategies are integrated which exploit these informations.

Note that this approach explicitly allows the objective value to get worse while cruising through the solution space. Hence there is a possibility to escape local optima. The tabu–states are used to prevent an immediately return to an escaped local optimum.

5 Computational Results

The tabu search heuristics produce very good results in a few minutes even for large problems on a 486 Unix system.

Impressive results were achieved in the case of solving rectangle puzzles, i.e., special problems where a given set of rectangles (of cardinality up to 100) exactly covers a given region (of size up to 25×25). The heuristics were able to solve nearly 99% of hundreds of randomly generated problems.

The branch and bound algorithm is capable to solve medium sized problems. Not surprisingly, the computation time depends strongly on the number, size, values, and quantity restrictions of the involved grid figures.

We solved all instances of packing pentominoes into squares up to a size of 20×20. The smaller problems up to 15×15 were solved in a few minutes, but some of the bigger problems took several hours.

The programs were written in the object oriented programming language *Eiffel* [6] which turned out to be excellent for our purposes.

References

[1] Beasley, J.E.: *An Exact Two–Dimensional Non–Guillotine Cutting Tree Search Procedure*; Operations Research 1985, 49–64

[2] Camerini, P.M.; Fratta, L.; Maffioli, F.: *On Improving Relaxation Methods by Modified Gradient Techniques*; Mathematical Programming Study 3/1975, 26–34

[3] Fowler, R.J.; Paterson, M.S.; Tanimoto, L.: *Optimal Packing and Covering in the Plane are NP–Complete*; Information Processing Letters Vol.12, No.3, 1981, 133–137

[4] Glover, F.: *Tabu Search: A Tutorial*; Interfaces (1990), 20 (4), 74–94

[5] Hinxman, A.I.: *The trim-loss and assortment problems: A Survey*; European Journal of Operational Research 5/1980, 8–18

[6] Meyer, B.: *Object Oriented Software Construction*; Prentice Hall, 1988

[7] Wolffram, J.: *Packing Grid Figures: Exact Algorithms, Heuristics, and Object Oriented Implementation*; Internal Report; Lehrstuhl für Anwendungen des Operations Research, Universität Karlsruhe, Germany

Section 4

Linear and Non-Linear Optimization

Using Ellipsoids in Weighted Projective Algorithms for Nondifferentiable Optimization

Anna Altman
Systems Research Institute, Polish Academy of Sciences
ul. Newelska 6, 01–447 Warszawa, Poland

We show how to modify the method of Goffin et al. (1992) and how to implement it efficiently for nondifferentiable convex minimization (NDCM). It is an application of a variant of an interior point algorithm to a cutting planes method for the minimizing function defined by supporting hyperplanes to its epigraph. In both algorithms new supporting hyperplanes are generated in weighted analytic centers (WAC) of certain polytope containing feasible set. A special ellipsoid centered in WAC is constructed to eliminate inactive supporting hyperplanes.

We consider the generic nondifferentiable convex minimization problem

$$\min_x \{f(x) : l \leq x \leq h\},$$

where $f : \mathcal{R}^n \mapsto \mathcal{R}$ is a convex function, $x, l, h \in \mathcal{R}^n$. We make the general assumption, that at every x we know $f(x)$ and one arbitrary subgradient from the subdifferential $\partial f(x)$.

Every convex function can be treated as an envelope of its supporting hyperplanes

$$f(x) = \max_{i \in I}\{f_i(x)\},$$

where

$$f_i(x) = d_i - \sum_{j=1}^{n} g_{ij} x_j$$

are linear functions and set I can be infinite.

The problem can be approximated by a family of subproblems with finite subsets $K \subset I$. Every subproblem can be formulated as an LP problem in primal form

$$\min b^T x \tag{1}$$

$$\text{s.t. } \tilde{G}_K^T x \geq \tilde{c}_K,$$

where

$$b^T = (1, 0_n^T) \in \mathcal{R}^{n+1}, x \in \mathcal{R}^{n+1},$$

$$\tilde{G}_K = \begin{bmatrix} 0_n^T & 0_n^T & 1_m^T \\ I_n & -I_n & G_K^T \end{bmatrix} \in \mathcal{R}^{(n+1)*p},$$

$$\tilde{c}_K^T = (l^T, -h^T, d_K^T) \in \mathcal{R}^{2*n+m}.$$

Its dual, after adding a homogenizing variable s_1 and normality condition $s_1 = 1$, has the following form:

$$\max \sum_{j=2}^{p+1} c_j s_j \tag{2}$$

$$A_K s = 0,$$

$$s_1 = 1, s \geq 0,$$

where

$$p = 2 * n + m, s^T \in \mathcal{R}^{p+1},$$

$$c_K^T = (-z_U, \tilde{c}_K^T) \in \mathcal{R}^{p+1},$$

$$A_K = \begin{pmatrix} -b & \tilde{G}_K \end{pmatrix} = \begin{pmatrix} -1 & 0_n^T & 0_n^T & 1_m^T \\ 0_n & I_n & -I_n & G_K^T \end{pmatrix} \in \mathcal{R}^{(n+1)*(p+1)},$$

z_U is upper bound for objective function.

For dual (2) we define the weighted potential function of Karmarkar type

$$\phi_K(s) = \nu_0 \ln(-c_K^T s) - \textstyle\sum_{j=1}^{p+1} \nu_j \ln s_j, \tag{3}$$

where ν_j are positive weights and $\nu_0 = \sum_{j=1}^{p+1} \nu_j$.

We define for our relaxed problem (1) the polytope $F_K(z_U)$ called the set of localization or the safeguard polyhedron. It is given by the outer approximation of the epigraph associated with current LP relaxation and limited above by the best objective value - z_U - observed so far. The weighted analytic center of $F_K(z_U)$ belongs to relative interior of the polytope and maximizes weighted product of distances from the hyperplanes defining the safeguard polyhedron. Computing WAC for (1) and minimizing the weighted potential function (3) for (2) are equivalent.

To compute WAC we use algorithm described in Altman (1992a). In every iteration of it for some fixed subset $K \subset I$ a dual pair of points $(x(z_U), s(z_U))$ is computed, where $x(z_U)$ is the approximated WAC for $F_K(z_U)$ and $s(z_U)$ is the minimizer of weighted potential function.

After computing the pair $(x(z_U), s(z_U))$ we generate the supporting hyperplane to the $epi(f)$ in $x(z_U)$ - WAC of $F_K(z_U)$. For the last 30 years the common practice has been to generate cutting planes at a point minimizing the current LP relaxation. The adventage of the technique of generating supporting hyperplanes at WAC stems from the fact that WAC summarizes all the information accumulated about the problem. After generating the new supporting hyperplane our subset K increases. A new variable is added to the dual problem (2) and a new feasible point has to be looked for.

For every set of localization we define two homothetic ellipsoids centered in WAC: E_{int} and E_{out} given by

$$E_{int} = \{x \in \mathcal{R}^{n+1} : \|N^{-\frac{1}{2}} S A^T (x - x(z_U))\|_2 \leq r_{int},$$

$$E_{out} = \{x \in \mathcal{R}^{n+1} : \|N^{-\frac{1}{2}} S A^T (x - x(z_U))\|_2 \leq r_{out},$$

where

$$r_{int} = \frac{(1-\Theta)}{(1+\Theta)} \cdot \frac{(-c_K^T s)}{\nu_0},$$

$$r_{out}^2 = (c_K^T s)^2 - \frac{(z_U - b^T x)^2}{\nu_1},$$

$N^{-\frac{1}{2}}$ is diagonal matrix with entries $\nu_j^{-\frac{1}{2}}$, S is diagonal matrix with entries s_j. The parameter $\Theta \in (0,1)$ is used in the algorithm for computing WAC, cf. Altman (1992a). It can be proved (Goffin et al. (1990)) that

$$E_{int} \subset F_K(z_U) \subset E_{out}.$$

In every iteration the number of supporting hyperplanes grows up. The ellipsoid E_{out} can be used to eliminate inactive supporting hyperplanes. For every supporting hyperplane we construct the homothetic ellipsoid to E_{out} which is tangent to supporting hyperplane in the point nearest to WAC. If the radius of this ellipsoid is greater than r_{out}, the supporting hyperplane can be removed.

After elimination of a supporting hyperplane the subset K becomes smaller, which refers to the variable elimination in the dual problem (2). As after adding supporting hyperplane, we must restore feasibility after deleting inactive hyperplanes. Restoring feasibility is a difficult and time consuming operation. We modified the techniques of Bahn et al. (1991) to keep the objective function as well as possible. Unfortunately, it often happens that after deleting hyperplanes the new objective is worse than the old one.

We detect inactive hyperplanes if the number of generated supporting hyperplanes exceeds twice the number of variables in primal problem (1). We delete inactive hyperplanes if the number of hyperplanes to eliminate is greater than the number of variables in primal problem.

Some standard NDO test problems were solved for different values of weights. A comparison of the old version of algorithm (without elimination) (Altman (1992a)) and the new one is reported in Altman (1992b). Although the number of iterations increases in the new method, the cost of a single iteration is reduced considerably. The total computing time is reduced of about 10%.

References

[1] Anna Altman (1992a). Computer Implementation of Weighted Analytic Centers in Nondifferentiable Convex Minimization, Working Paper of Systems Research Institute, ZTSW-5/A1214/91r.

[2] Anna Altman (1992b). Techniques of Inactive Planes Elimination in Weighted Projective Algorithm for Nondifferentiable Optimization (in preparation).

[3] O. Bahn, J. L. Goffin, J. P. Vial, O. Du Merle (1991). Implementation and Behavior of an Interior Point Cutting Plane Algorithm for Convex Programming: An Application to Geometric Programming, Les cahiers du GERAD G-91-27.

[4] Jean-Louis Goffin, A. Haurie and Jean-Philippe Vial (1992). Decomposition and Nondifferentiable Optimization with the Projective Algorithm. Management Science, vol. 38, No. 2, pp. 284-302.

[5] Jean-Louis Goffin and Jean-Philippe Vial (1990). On the Computation of Weighted Analytic Centers and Dual Ellipsoids with the Projective Algorithm, Manuscript, Départment d'économie commerciale et industrielle, University of Geneva.

About the Method of Minimization of the Function

Tigran A. Arakelian
State University of Yerevan, Faculty of Mathematics
1 Mravian st., 375049, Yerevan, Republic of Armenia

Introduction
Minimization of the function with many variables is a necessary part of optimization tasks. However this task is not simple for the large number of functions. In view of it methods of minimization based on getting the calculating formulas of computing the values of partial derivatives of minimized function are taking a very important place.

1.Minimizing of function without limitations

1.1. The method is used for minimizing of $\tilde{\varphi}(x_1,\ldots,x_n)$, function defined in $\prod_{i=1}^{n}[a_i,b_i]$. The function is rather well approximated by the spline in 4-th degree.
Let we have the systems of nodes:

$$\begin{aligned} a_j = x_{oj} < x_{1j} < \ldots < x_{ij} < \ldots < x_{mj} = b_j \\ u_{1j} < u_{2j} < \ldots < u_{i+1,j} < \ldots < u_{mj}, \end{aligned} \tag{1}$$

with $x_{ij} < u_{i+1,j} < x_{i+1,j} \quad (i = 0,\ldots,m; j = 1,2,\ldots,n)$.
Let $(z-t)_+ = max\{0,(z-t)\}^s$ and $x = (x_1,\ldots,x_n)$.
We define a spline [1]

$$\begin{aligned} \varphi(x) &= \sum_{\substack{k,l=1\\k\neq l}}^{n}\left[\sum_{r,s=0}^{2} a_{rs}^{k,l}(x_k-x_{ik})^r(x_l-x_{il})^s + \sum_{r,s=0}^{2} b_{rs}^{k,l}(x_k-x_{ik})^r(x_l-u_{i+1,l})_+^s\right.\\ &\left.+\sum_{r,s=0}^{2} d_{rs}^{k,l}(x_k-u_{i+1,k})_+^r(x_l-u_{i+1,l})_+^s\right] \end{aligned} \tag{2}$$

with $x_k \in [x_{ik}, x_{i+1,k}], (k = 1,\ldots,n; i = 1,\ldots,m)$ and $x_l \in [x_{il}, x_{i+1,l}], (l = 1,\ldots,n)$.

Definition of partial derivatives of $\varphi(x)$ function:

$$\begin{aligned} \frac{\delta\varphi}{\delta x_k} &= \sum_{\substack{l=1\\l\neq k}}^{n}\left[\sum_{s=0}^{2} a_{1s}^{kl}(x_l-x_{il})^s + 2\sum_{s=0}^{2} a_{2s}^{kl}(x_k-x_{ik})(x_l-x_{il})^s + \sum_{s=0}^{2} b_{1s}^{kl}(x_l-u_{i+1,l})_+\right.\\ &\left.+2\sum_{s=0}^{2} b_{2s}^{kl}(x_k-x_{ik})(x_l-u_{i+1,l})_+ + \psi(x_k,x_l) + \chi(x_k,x_l)\right] \end{aligned} \tag{3}$$

with
$\psi(x_k, x_l) = 2\sum_{s=0}^{2} b_{2s}^{kl}(x_l - x_{il})^s(x_k - u_{i+1,k})$ if $x_k \in (x_{ik}, u_{i+1,k}]$
$\psi(x_k, x_l) = \sum_{s=0}^{2} b_{1s}^{kl}(x_l - u_{i+1,l})_+^s + 2\sum_{s=0}^{2} b_{2s}^{kl}(x_l - u_{i+1,l})_+^s(x_k - x_{ik})$ if $x_k \in (u_{i+1,k}, x_{i+1,k}]$

$$\chi(x_k, x_l) = \begin{cases} 2\sum_{s=0}^{2} d_{2s}^{kl}(x_k - u_{i+1,k})(x_l - u_{i+1,l})_+^s & \text{if } x_k \in (x_{ik}, u_{i+1,k}] \\ \sum_{s=0}^{2} d_{1s}^{kl}(x_l - u_{i+1,l})_+^s + 2\sum_{s=0}^{2} d_{2s}^{kl}(x_k - u_{i+1,k})(x_l - u_{i+1,l})_+ & \\ \qquad\qquad \text{if } x_k \in (u_{i+1,k}, x_{i+1,k}] \end{cases}$$

$(k = 1, \ldots, n; i = 0, \ldots, m-1)$

1.2. Scheme of the method:
Step 1: We define partial derivatives following (3), then compare them to 0.

$$\frac{\delta\varphi}{\delta x_k} = 0, \quad (k = 1, \ldots, n) \tag{4}$$

Further we solve (4) using method [2] and mark solutions of (4) as:
$\tilde{x}_i = (\tilde{x}_{ki}), (k = 1, \ldots, n; i = 0, \ldots, m-1)$.

Step 2: We calculate the values of $|\tilde{\varphi}_{x_k}(z)|$, with

$$z = \{\{\tilde{x}_i\}, (i = 0, \ldots, m-1); a = (a_k); b = (b_k), (k = 1, \ldots, n)\} = L$$
$$|\tilde{\varphi}_{x_k}(\tilde{z})| = \min_{z \in L} |\tilde{\varphi}_{x_k}(z)|.$$

If $|\tilde{\varphi}_{x_k}(\tilde{z})| < \varepsilon_k, (k = 1, \ldots, n)$,then the solution is found. If $\tilde{\varphi}_{x_k}(\tilde{z}) < -\varepsilon_k, (k = j_1, \ldots, j_l)$ then we'll have $a^{j_t} = \tilde{x}_{j_t}, (t = 1, \ldots, l)$, and go to step 1. If $\tilde{\varphi}_{x_k}(\tilde{z}) > \varepsilon_k, (k = q_1, \ldots, q_p)$, then we'll have $b^{q_t} = \tilde{x}_{q_t}, (t = 1, \ldots, p)$, and go to step 1.

1.3. This method is used for minimizing $\tilde{\varphi}(x_1, \ldots, x_n)$ function defined on

$$\Gamma = \{x = (x_1, \ldots, x_n) | \tilde{g}_j(x) \geq 0, (j = 1, \ldots, p)\} \tag{5}$$

set. $\tilde{\varphi}(x_1, \ldots, x_n)$ and $g_j(x)(j = 1, \ldots, p)$ functions are rather well approximated by the 4-th degree spline on (1) set of nodes:

$$\begin{aligned} \varphi(x) &= \sum_{\substack{k,l=1 \\ k \neq l}}^{m} \left[\sum_{r,s=0}^{2} a_{rs}^{kl}(x_k - x_{ik})^r(x_l - x_{il})^s + \sum_{r,s=0}^{2} b_{rs}^{kl}(x_k - x_{ik})^r(x_l - u_{i+1,l})_+^s \right. \\ & \left. + \sum_{r,s=0}^{2} d_{rs}^{kl}(x_k - u_{i+1,k})_+^r(x_l - u_{i+1,l})_+^s \right] \end{aligned} \tag{6}$$

$$\begin{aligned} g_j(x) &= \sum_{k,l=1}^{m} \left[\sum_{r,s=0}^{2} a_{rs}^{jkl}(x_k - x_{ik})^r(x_l - x_{il})^s + \sum_{r,s=0}^{2} b_{rs}^{jkl}(x_k - x_{ik})^r(x_l - u_{i+1,l})_+^s \right. \\ & \left. + \sum_{r,s=0}^{2} d_{rs}^{jkl}(x_k - u_{i+1,k})_+^r(x_l - u_{i+1,l})_+^s \right] \end{aligned} \tag{7}$$

with $x_k \in [x_{ki}, x_{k,i+1}], x_l \in [x_{li}, x_{l,i+1}], (k, l = 1, \dots, n; i = 0, \dots, m-1)$. We define Lagrange's function as

$$L(x, \lambda) = \varphi(x) + \sum_{j=1}^{p} \lambda_j g(x) \tag{8}$$

and look for the solution in the set of stationary points of $L(x, \lambda)$ function, that means:

$$\frac{\delta L}{\delta x_k} = 0 \quad k = 1, \dots, n \tag{9}$$

$$\frac{\delta L}{\delta \lambda_j} = 0 \quad j = 1, \dots, p \tag{10}$$

After placing (6)–(8) into (9), (10) we receive a system of equations.

$$\begin{aligned} \sum_{\substack{l=1\\ l\neq k}}^{n} & \left[\sum_{s=0}^{2} a_{1s}^{kl}(x_k - x_{ik})^s + 2\sum_{s=0}^{2} a_{2s}^{kl}(x_k - x_{ik})(x_l - x_{il})^s + \sum_{s=0}^{2} b_{1s}^{kl}(x_l - u_{i+1,l})^s \right. \\ & \left. +2\sum_{s=0}^{2} b_{2s}^{kl}(x_k - x_{ik})(x_l - u_{i+1,l})^s\right] + \psi(x_k, x_l) + \chi(x_k, x_l) + \sum_{j=1}^{p} \lambda_j \left\{ \sum_{\substack{l=1\\ l\neq k}}^{n} \left[a_{1s}^{jkl}(x_k - x_{ik})^s \right.\right. \\ & \left. +2\sum_{s=0}^{2} a_{2s}^{jkl}(x_k - x_{ik})(x_l - x_{il})^s + \sum_{s=0}^{2} b_{1s}^{jkl}(x_l - u_{i+1,l})^s + 2\sum_{s=0}^{2} b_{2s}^{jkl}(x_k - x_{ik})(x_l - u_{i+1,l})^s \right] \\ & \left. +\psi_j(x_k, x_l) + \chi_j(x_k, x_l) \right\} \end{aligned} \tag{11}$$

$x_k \in [x_{ki}, x_{k,i+1}]; x_l \in [x_{li}, x_{l,i+1}]; (k, l = 1, \dots, n; i = 0, \dots, m-1)$

Then we apply the algorithm of 1.1 method.

References

Hall C.A., *Bicubic interpolation over triangles*, J.Math. Mech. 19, No. 1,(1969), p. 1–11

De Boor C., *On the convergence of odd-degree spline interpolation*, J. Approximation Theory, 1, No. 4, (1968), p. 452–463

Orthega D., Rejnboldt V., *Interpolation Methods of solving of non-linear equations with many variables*, Moscow, 1975

LPINT: LP Software Based on the Interior Point Method

Janez Barle, Janez Grad
Ekonomska fakulteta
Kardeljeva ploscad 17, 61109 Ljubljana, Slovenia

Karmarkar's algorithm (Karmarkar 1984) and other interior point methods are now regarded as a competitive methods for solving linear programming (LP) problems. It is therefore worth-while to undertake development of a professional LP software based on some particular interior point method. We describe design and implementation aspects of LPINT, an LP software package which is based on the primal-dual interior point algorithm. Its main characteristics can be stated as follows:

- high performance is assured by using state of the art algorithms (Lustig et al. 1991) and recent results in sparse matrix research (George, Liu 1981, Duff et al. 1989).
- the overall system design is influenced by proven systems which are based on the simplex method (Suhl 1989). It is also very important to follow the methods and principles of contemporary software engineering. For example, it is desirable to attain a high degree of portability. We also emphasize the need for modularity, ease of use and other software qualities.
- two levels of use are provided: 1. interactive menu driven use, 2. as a library of fortran subroutines which are driven by the user program
- LPINT was extensively tested using the so called NETLIB library of LP test problems (Gay 1985).

At each step of the primal-dual interior point it is necesary to solve the presumably sparse linear least square problem. It is generally accepted that, if problem dimension is not very large, the normal equations approach using sparse Cholesky factorization (George, Liu 1981) is an adequate method. The rows and columns of the normal equations matrix must be preordered in order to exploit sparsity. We have implemented the following methods for doing this: 1. Reverse Cuthill-McKee algorithm, 2. Minimal degree algorithm, 3. Nested dissection method (George, Liu 1981). The corresponding variants of LPINT are called LPENV, LPMDG and LPND, respectively. Our goal was to enable making different comparisons and further testing of the algorithms and LP matrices. Perhaps the most distinguished components of LPINT are different tools for graphical display of LP constraint matrices and corresponding normal equation matrices. A visualization of these matrices could be particularly helpful when one must decide about efficient solution strategy and possible decomposition of the LP model. Our ultimate goal is to create an open software environment for handling and analysing different sparse matrices (Alvarado 1990) which is to be specialized for LP matrices. We believe that these features make LPINT an excellent tool for teaching and research in the field of LP. LPINT is currently implemented only on the PC, but the usage of portable graphical subroutine library makes possible its porting to other software and hardware platforms.

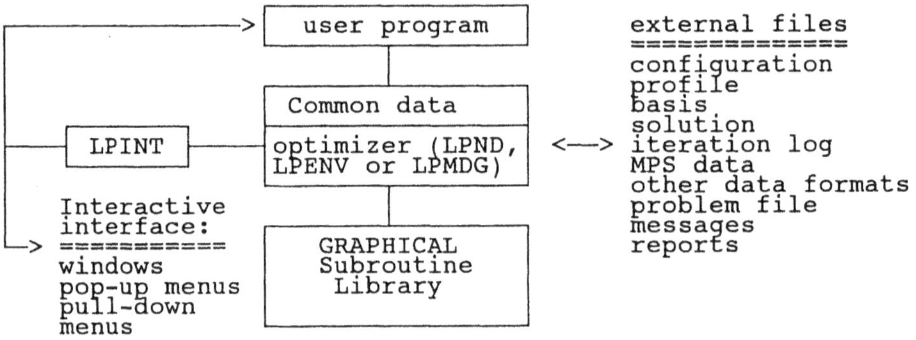

LPINT system architecture

References

Alvarado F.L. (1990) Manipulation and visualization of sparse matrices. ORSA Journal on Computing 2: 187-207

Duff I.S., Erisman A.M., Reid J.K. (1989) Direct Methods for Sparse Matrices. Clarendon Press. Oxford

Gay D.M. (1985) Electronic Mail Distribution of Linear Programming Test Problems. Mathematical Programming Society COAL Newsletter 13: 10-12

George J.A., Liu J.W. (1981) Computer Solution of Large Sparse Positive Definite Systems. Prentice Hall. Englewood Cliffs

Karmarkar N.K. (1984) A New Polynomial-Time Algorithm for Linear Programming. Combinatorica 4: 373-395

Lustig I.J., Marsten R.E., Shanno D.F. (1991) Computational Experience With a Primal-Dual Interior Point Method For Linear Programming. Linear Algebra and its Applications 152: 191-222

Suhl U.H. (1989) Design and Implementation of a Fast and Portable LP-Optimizer. Operations Research Proceedings 1988. Springer Verlag. Berlin Heideberg: 165-173

A Convergence Acceleration of the Relaxation Algorithm in Convex Minimization

Andrzej Cegielski
Institut of Mathematics, Higher College of Engineering
ul. Podgórna 50, 65246 Zielona Góra, Poland

Let $f:\mathbb{R}^n\to\mathbb{R}$ be a convex function such that M = Argmin$\{f(x): x\in\mathbb{R}^n\}\neq\emptyset$. Denote $f^*=f(x^*)$ for $x^*\in M$. Suppose that f^* is known. Consider the following convex unconstrained minimization problem

$$f(x) \to \min\ ,\ x\in\mathbb{R}^n.$$

Some other optimization problems can be reduced to the above problem e.g. convex constrained minimization problem with known minimal value, solution of a system of linear inequalities, convex feasibility problems, or linear programming problems.

Since f^* is known, one can apply the relaxation method of Polyak (1969) to solve the above problem. If the function f is piecewise linear, then one can also apply the relaxation algorithm of Agmon (1954) and Motzkin and Schoenberg (1954), which is in fact a special version of the Polyak algorithm.

A sequence $\{x_k\}$ generated by the Polyak algorithm is Fejer monotone with respect to M. The Polyak algorithm behaves well if the angle between $x_{k+1}-x_k$ and $x_{i+1}-x_i$ for $i<k$ is less than $\pi/2$. However, the angle between $x_{k+1}-x_k$ and x_k-x_{k-1} is often close to π and the angle between $x_{k+1}-x_k$ and x^*-x_k, for $x^*\in M$, is often close to $\pi/2$, and, consequently, the rate of convergence is close to 1. The cause of such behaviour is the Markov character of the Polyak algorithm. The next step depends only on the actual one. We give now a new algorithm which bases on the Polyak relaxation algorithm, but has no more Markov character. To evaluate the next iteration we will use some informations from the previous steps.

Algorithm 1:

$x_0\in\mathbb{R}^n$ - arbitrary, $I_{-1}=\emptyset$. Suppose that we have obtained in the k-th step $x_k\in\mathbb{R}^n$ and $I_{k-1}\subset\{0,1,\dots,k-1\}$. In the $(k+1)$-st step we evaluate:

1° $f(x_k)$; if $f(x_k)=f^*$ then x_k is a minimal point,

2° $g_k=g_f(x_k)\in\partial f(x_k)$ - a subgradient of f in x_k,

3° $b_k=-\|g_k\|^{-2}(f(x_k)-f^*)g_k$ - the Polyak vector,

4° $I_k=\{i\in I_{k-1}:\ \langle b_i,b_k\rangle\le 0\}\cup\{k\}$,

5° $t_k=\sum_{i\in I_k}\alpha_i b_i$ which is a solution of a system of equations:

$$\langle b_i,t\rangle=0 \text{ for } i\in I_k\setminus\{k\} \tag{1}$$

$$\langle b_k,t\rangle=\langle b_k,b_k\rangle, \tag{2}$$

6° $x_{k+1}=x_k+\lambda t_k$, $\lambda\in(0,1]$.

We see that the algorithm has no more Markov character. On each step a family of some previous Polyak vectors is stored and the next step t_k is a linear combination of the stored previous Polyak vectors and of the actual one. More precisely, after the k-th step a family $S_{k-1}=\{b_i:i\in I_{k-1}\}$ is stored which determine an acute cone $C_{k-1}=-(\text{cone}S_{k-1})^*$ such that $M\subset x_k+C_{k-1}$ (C is acute if $\langle x,y\rangle\ge 0$ for all x,y; C is obtuse if C^* is acute). In the $(k+1)$-st step only these vectors b_i from the family S_{k-1} are selected, for which the angle with the actual Polyak vector b_k is greater or equal $\pi/2$. A new family S_k consists of the selected vectors and of the vector b_k. The solution of the system of equations (1)-(2) determines x_{k+1} such that $M\subset x_{k+1}-(\text{cone}S_k)^*$.

Remark. The information from the previous step is stored and used to construct a current step also in some other optimization methods, e.g. in the ellipsoidal method (see Shor (1985)) or in the bundle method (see Zowe (1985) or Kiwiel (1985))

Denote

$$Q_k=\{x:\ \langle b_k,x-x_k\rangle\ge\langle b_k,b_k\rangle\}$$

and

$$M_k=\bigcap_{i\in I_k}Q_i.$$

Furthermore, denote, for $i\in I_{k-1}$,

$$Q_i^k=\{x:\ \langle b_i,x-x_k\rangle\ge 0\}$$

and

$$R_k=\bigcap_{i\in I_k}Q_i^{k+1}$$

Theorem. *The algorithm has the following properties:*

a) $M_k\subset R_k$ *and, for* $\lambda=1$, *there holds the equality in the inclusion,*

b) if x_k *is not a minimal point then then* $S_k=\{b_i:\ i\in I_k\}$ *is a system of linearly independent vectors,*

c) coneS_k is obtuse,

d) the system of equations (1)-(2) has only one solution of the form

$$t_k = \sum_{i \in I_k} \alpha_i b_i ,$$

e) the sequence $\{x_k\}$ is Fejer monotone with respect to M,

f) $x_{k+1} = P_{R_k}(x_k)$, where P_C denotes the metric projection operator onto a convex subset C.

Proof: is based on the following fact. If $S=\{s_1, s_2, \dots, s_r\}$ is a system of linearly independent vectors in an r-dimensional linear space and, for all $s_i, s_j \in S$, $i \neq j$, there holds the inequality $\langle s_i, s_j \rangle \leq 0$ then cone$S$ is obtuse. Details see Cegielski (1992).

Denote $T_k = \bigcap_{i \in J_k} Q_i$, for some $J_k \subset \{0,1,\dots,k\}$. If $I_k \subset J_k$ then we have, for $\lambda=1$,

$$M \subset T_k \subset M_k = R_k \subset Q_k .$$

In the Polyak algorithm we have, for $\lambda=1$,

$$x_{k+1} = P_{Q_k}(x_k).$$

Polyak (1969) has also proposed a modification of his algorithm:

$$x_{k+1} = P_{T_k}(x_k),$$

but in this case on each step a quadratic programming problem has to be solved, connected with the projection onto a convex subset T_k. Observe that, for each $x^* \in M$ and $x \in \mathbb{R}^n$, we have

$$\|P_{T_k}(x) - x^*\| \leq \|P_{R_k}(x) - x^*\| \leq \|P_{Q_k}(x) - x^*\| \leq \|x - x^*\|,$$

i.e. our algorithm converges slower than the modified Polyak algorithm and faster than the original Polyak relaxation algorithm. However, our algorithm requires on each step only the solution of a system of linear equations with the size in most cases significantly smaller than the dimension of the problem. Observe that the system of equations (1)-(2) can easily be solved if one uses the Cholesky decomposition of the Gram matrix of the system of vectors S_k. From the theorem it follows that the system is linearly independent and, consequently, the Gram matrix is positively definite.

The algorithm can be generalized in the following way. Let $J_i \subset \mathbb{N}$ be a sequence of subsets such that $J_0 = \{0\}$, $J_i \subset J_{i-1} \cup \{i\}$ and $i \in J_i$. Let $f_i(x) = \langle g_f(x_i), x - x_i \rangle + f(x_i)$ be a linearization of f in x_i.

Algorithm 2.

1^0-3^0 the same as in algorithm 1,

4^0 $I_k \subset \{i\in J_k : f_i(x_k)\geq f^*\}$ and such that $<b_i, b_j>\leq 0$, for $i\neq j$, $i,j\in I_k$,

5^0 $t_k = \sum_{i\in I_k} \alpha_i b_i$ which is a solution of a system of equations:

$$<b_i, t>=<b_i, x_i - x_k + b_i>, \qquad i\in I_k,$$

6^0 $x_{k+1} = x_k + \lambda t_k$, $\lambda\in(0,2)$.

In fact, for $\lambda=1$, x_{k+1} is a solution of a system of equations $f_i(x)=f^*$, $i\in I_k$. The sequence J_k can be defined sequentially so that J_{k+1} can depend on I_k. If $J_{k+1}=I_k\cup\{k+1\}$ and $\lambda\in(0,1]$ then algorithm 2 is equivalent with algorithm 1. Observe, however, that, in algorithm 2, λ can be taken from the interval $(0,2)$, i.e. an overrelaxation can be made, which is not possible in algorithm 1 (for $\lambda>1$ the algorithm 1 can diverge).

Various variants of the relaxation algorithm have been also studied by Goffin (1980), Maurras, Truemper, Akgül (1981), Schott (1991) and by Butnariu, Censor (1991). Butnariu and Censor (1991) have studied a similar algorithm as given above, applied to convex feasibility problems. On each step of the algorithm a convex combination with positive weights of all projections onto the whole family of convex subsets is evaluated, and this combination, with a relaxation parameter $\lambda\in(0,2)$, is added to a current point x_k.

References.

Agmon S (1954) The relaxation method for linear inequalities. Canad. J. Math. 6: 382-392

Butnariu D, Censor Y (1991) On the behavior of a block iterative projection method for solving convex feasibility problems. Int. J. Comp. Math. 34:

Cegielski A (1992) On a relaxation algorithm in convex optimization problems (submitted)

Goffin J L (1980) The relaxation method for solving system of linear inequalities. Mathematics of Operations Research 5: 388-414

Kiwiel K (1985) Methods of descent for nondifferentiable optimization Springer-Verlag, Berlin, Heidelberg, New York, Tokyo

Maurras J F, Truemper K, Akgül M (1981) Polynomial algorithms for a class of linear programs. Math. Programming 21: 121-136

Motzkin T, Schoenberg I J (1954) The relaxation method for linear inequalities. Canad. J. Math. 6: 393-404

Polyak B T (1969) Minimization of nonsmooth functionals. USSR Comp Math and Math. Phys. 9: 14-29

Schott D (1991) A general iterative scheme with applications to convex optimization and related fields. Optimization 22: 885-902

Shor N Z (1985) Minimization methods for non-differentiable functions. Springer-Verlag. Berlin Heidelberg New York Tokyo

Zowe J (1985) Nondifferentiable optimization - a motivation and a short introduction into the subgradient- and the bundle concept. ASI Proceedings on Computational Mathematical Programming

On an Algorithm Solving Bilevel Programming Problems

Stephan Dempe
Fachbereich Mathematik, Technische Universität Chemnitz
Postfach 964, 9010 Chemnitz, Germany

Consider a situation where two decision makers try to realize best decisions with respect to their own objective functions thereby acting in an hierarchical manner. Assume that the first decision maker's (the leader's) choice y influences the second one's (the follower's) objective function as well as his set of admissible decisions. Thus, the follower's problem can be stated as, say, the following parametric optimization problem:

$$\min_x \{h_0(x,y) \mid h_i(x,y) \leq 0,\ i = 1,\dots,p\}, \tag{1}$$

where $x \in R^n$, $y \in R^m$, and all functions are assumed to be sufficiently smooth. Let the set of optimal solutions of this problem be denoted by $\Psi(y)$. $\Psi(\cdot)$ is, in general, a set-valued function mapping R^m into the power set of R^n. Then, if the leader's objective function is $f_0(x,y)$ depending on both the leader's choice and the follower's response $x = x(y) \in \Psi(y)$, the leader's task of finding the best decision may be stated as the following bilevel optimization problem:

$$\text{“}\min_y\text{”} \{f_0(x,y) \mid f_j(y) \leq 0,\ j = 1,\dots,q,\ x \in \Psi(y)\} \tag{2}$$

(cf. e. g. Dempe(1991a), Marcotte(1986), Petersen(1989)). To avoid certain troublesome difficulties which are due to nonunique optimal solutions in the follower's problem, problem (1) is assumed to be a convex parametric optimization problem for which a regularity and a strong sufficient second-order optimality conditions are satisfied at every

$$y \in \mathcal{B}^0 := \{z \mid f_j(z) \leq 0, j = 1,\dots,q\}. \tag{3}$$

Then, if the function $x : \mathcal{B}^0 \to R^n$ defined by $\{x(y)\} = \Psi(y)$ for all $y \in \mathcal{B}^0$ is substituted into problem (2), the problem

$$\min_y \{f_0(x(y),y) \mid f_j(y) \leq 0, j = 1,\dots,q\} \tag{4}$$

is obtained. This problem may be solved e. g. by means of methods of feasible directions or other descent algorithms if the function $g(y) := f_0(x(y),y)$ is directionally differentiable.

Theorem (Dempe(1991b)): Consider the convex parametric optimization problem (1) at a point $y^0 \in \mathcal{B}^0$ and let Slater's condition, a strong sufficient second-order optimality condition and a constant rank assumption (Janin(1984)) be satisfied. Then, for each direction $r \in R^m$, there exists a vertex $u = u(r)$ of the set of regular Kuhn-Tucker multiplier vectors of problem (1) such that the directional derivative

$$x'(y^0;r) := \lim_{t\to 0+} t^{-1}[x(y^0+tr) - x(y^0)]$$

is equal to the unique optimal solution of the following problem:

$$\frac{1}{2}d^{\mathsf{T}}\nabla^2_{xx}L(x(y^0),y^0,u)d + d^{\mathsf{T}}\nabla^2_{xy}L(x(y^0),y^0,u)r \to \min_d$$

$$\nabla_x h_i(x(y^0),y^0)d + \nabla_y h_i(x(y^0),y^0)r \begin{cases} = 0, & \text{if } u_i > 0, \\ \leq 0, & \text{if } h_i(x(y^0),y^0) = 0, \quad u_i = 0. \end{cases} \qquad (Q(u,r))$$

□

Corollary: Define the sets

$$\mathcal{A}(y^0,r) = \{d \mid \text{there exists a sequence } \{r^k\}_{k=1}^{\infty} \text{ converging to } r \text{ such that } \lim_{k\to\infty} x'(y^0;r^k) = d\}$$

and

$$\mathcal{C}(y^0,r) = \{d \mid \text{there exists a vertex } u \text{ of the set of regular Kuhn-Tucker multiplier vectors such that } d \text{ is equal to the optimal solution of } (Q(u,r))\}.$$

Then, if the gradients $\nabla h_i(x(y^0),y^0)$ of active inequalities with respect to both x and y are linearly independent, then

$$\mathcal{A}(y^0,r) = \mathcal{C}(y^0,r).$$

□

This corollary is an essential tool for proving necessary optimality conditions (Dempe(1991a)) as well as for verifying convergence of a descent algorithm solving sufficiently smooth bilevel optimization problems. This algorithm is essentially simplified if problem (1) is a strongly convex quadratic optimization problem with parameters in the linear part of the objective function and in the right-hand side of the constraints only, function $f_0(\cdot,\cdot)$ is convex and the functions $f_i(\cdot)$ are affine. Then, a descent direction r^0 of problem (4) may be computed by solving a linear optimization problem. A step-size t_0 is obtained by minimizing the convex function $f_0(x(y^0)+tx'(y^0;r^0),y^0+tr^0)$ on a certain interval. After this, the algorithm changes over to the new point $(x(y^0)+t_0x'(y^0;r^0),y^0+t_0r^0)$, and so on.

References

[1] Dempe S. (1991a) A necessary and a sufficient optimality condition for bilevel programming problems. Forthcoming in Optimization.

[2] Dempe S. (1991b) Directional differentiability of optimal solutions under Slater's condition. Forthcoming in Math. Programming.

[3] Janin R. (1984) Directional derivative of the marginal function in nonlinear programming. Math. Programming Stud. No. 21: 110-126.

[4] Marcotte P. (1986) Network design problem with congestion effects: a case of bilevel programming. Math. Programming 34: 142-162.

[5] Petersen T. (1989) Optimale Anreizsysteme: betriebswirtschaftliche Implikationen der Prinzipal-Agenten-Theorie. Betriebswirtschaftlicher Verlag Gabler. Wiesbaden.

Solving Linear Complementarity Problems by Imbedding

Andreas Fischer
Department of Mathematics, University of Technology
Mommsenstr. 13, 8027 Dresden, Germany

Let us consider the linear complementarity problem LCP(M, q)

$$Mx + q = y, \quad y^T x = 0, \quad y \geq 0, \quad x \geq 0, \quad x, y \in R^n$$

with a given positive semidefinite (but not necessarily symmetric) $n \times n$-matrix M and a given vector $q \in R^n$. Different Newton-type methods for solving the linear (and the nonlinear) complementarity problem were developed, see e.g. Mangasarian (1976), Aganagic(1984), Harker/Pang (1990), Harker/Xiao (1990), Pang (1990a), Pang (1991), Grippo/Lucidi (1991), Fischer/Schönefeld (1991), Fischer (1992b).

A general problem concerning the global convergence of such methods is the existence of an accumulation point of the iteration sequence. The paper treats this question for the essential subclass of linear complementarity problems LCP(M, q), which satisfy the strong second order condition:

$$x^T M x > 0 \text{ for all } x \neq 0 \text{ with } x^i = 0 \text{ if } y^{*i} > 0. \tag{1}$$

where (x^*, y^*) denotes one (and consequently the only) solution of LCP(M, q).

In particular, the assumtion (1) is sufficient for proving local superlinear convergence of appropriately constructed Newton-type methods applied to LCP(M, q).

Furthermore, note, that above subclass involves problems for which the matrix M is neither a P-matrix (all principal minors are positive) nor strictly copositive ($x^T M x > 0$ for all $0 \neq x \geq 0$). The first and also the second condition turns out to be sufficient for the boundedness of suitable level sets containing all iterates, such that at least one accumulation point exists, cf. Harker/Pang (1990), Fischer(1992b).

Now, let LCP(M, q) be an arbitrary linear complementarity problem satisfying (only) the assumption (1). Then, in order to generate bounded iterates, a Newton-type method coupled with an imbedding technique is suggested. (Different imbedding approaches can be found e.g. in Leder (1974), Watson (1979), Kojima et al. (1989), Pang (1990).)

For this purpose a mapping $T : R^{2n+1} \to R^{2n+1}$ is defined by:

$$T(w, \rho) := \begin{bmatrix} (M + \rho I)x + q - y \\ \phi(w^1) \\ \vdots \\ \phi(w^n) \\ \rho \end{bmatrix},$$

where $w := (x, y) \in R^n \times R^n$ and $w^i := (x^i, y^i) \in R \times R$ for $i := 1, \ldots, n$. The functional $\phi : R^2 \to R^1$ is given by

$$\phi(\alpha, \beta) := \sqrt{(\alpha)^2 + (\beta)^2} - \alpha - \beta. \qquad (\alpha, \beta \in R)$$

Since $\phi(\alpha, \beta) = 0$ if and only if $\alpha \geq 0$, $\beta \geq 0$, $\alpha\beta = 0$ the problem LCP(M, q) and $T(w, \rho) = 0$ have the same solutions.

Moreover, let $T_\rho : R^{2n} \to R^{2n}$ be defined in the same way as T with the only exception that the last row of T is deleted and the variable ρ becomes a fixed parameter.

For solving $T_\rho(w) = 0$ (with $\rho \geq 0$ fixed) the report Fischer (1992b) presents an inexact damped Newton-type algorithm possessing the following properties:
- all subproblems consist of linear equations only,
- each accumulation point of the generated iterates solves LCP(M, q),
- assumption (1) ensures local quadratic convergence.

Moreover, the following assertion is known.
The equation $T_\rho(w) = 0$ has an unique solution w^*_ρ for $\rho > 0$. If, additionally, the strong second order condition (1) is satisfied, this assertion holds for $\rho \geq 0$. Furthermore, there is a number $D > 0$ such that

$$\|w^*_\rho - w^*_{\rho'}\| \leq D|\rho - \rho'| \qquad (2)$$

for all ρ, $\rho' \in [0,1]$.
(The inequality (2) is a consequence of Theorem 2 of Robinson (1979).)

By these facts it is possible to construct an imbedding method such that the generated iterates follow approximately the solution curve $\{w^*_\rho \,|\, \rho \in [0,1]\}$. For that purpose, the Newton-type algorithm mentioned above could be employed as a subprocedure for the (approximate) solution of $T_{\rho_j}(w) = 0$, where $\rho_j \in [0,1]$, $j = 0,1,2,\ldots$ is a suitably defined finite or infinite sequence of parameters (with $\lim\limits_{j\to\infty} \rho_j = 0$).

In general, the definition of such parameters ρ_j and the question, which accuracy for the approximate solution of $T_{\rho_j}(w) = 0$ is useful, are not simply to answer. In particular, a number $\bar{\rho} > 0$ such that $w^*_{\bar{\rho}}$ lies in the region of local convergence of the Newton-type algorithm for $T_0(w) = 0$ is unknown.

Now, a Newton-type method for solving $T(w, \rho) = 0$ is proposed (with an arbitrary starting vector $(w_0, \rho_0) \in R^{2n} \times (0, \infty)$). As a by-product of this method parameters ρ_j are generated and a simple rule for ensuring a sufficient accuracy is given. In contrast to the pure damped Newton step

S1: Determine $(\hat{w}_k, \hat{\rho}_k) \in R^{2n+1}$ as solution of

$$\nabla T(w_k, \rho_k) \begin{pmatrix} w & - & w_k \\ \rho & - & \rho_k \end{pmatrix} + T(w_k, \rho_k) = 0$$

S2: Find the largest number $t_k \in \{\, (\frac{1}{2})^j \mid j = 0,1,2,\ldots\}$ such that

$$\|T(w_k + t_k(\hat{w}_k - w_k), \rho_k + t_k(\hat{\rho}_k - \rho_k))\| \leq (1 - t_k/2)\|T(w_k, \rho_k)\|.$$

Set $w_{k+1} := w_k + t_k(\hat{w}_k - w_k), \quad \rho_{k+1} := \rho_k + t_k(\hat{\rho}_k - \rho_k)$.

the proposed method uses the subsequent modifications:

1. Since the mapping T is not everywhere differentiable, a generalized Jacobian in the sense of Clarke (1983) is employed, see Fischer/Schönefeld(1991), Fischer(1992b).

2. A step length $t_k = 1$ would immediately lead to $0 = \rho_{k+1} = \rho_{k+2} = \ldots$ and, as prescribed above, it is not clear how to guarantee the boundedness of the iterates. To avoid a step length of 1, t_k is chosen as the largest number in

$$\{1 - \|T(\hat{w}_k, \hat{\rho}_k)\|,\ (\tfrac{1}{2})^j \,|\, j = 1,2,3,\ldots\}$$

such that the condition in step S2 is satisfied.

3. The case that both $\lim\limits_{k\to\infty} \rho_k = 0$ and $\lim\limits_{k\to\infty} \|T(w_k, \rho_k)\| > 0$ is excluded by the following rule (with $0 < \bar{t} < 1$):

If $t_k < \bar{t}$ then determine $\tilde{w}_{k+1}$ as approximate solution of $T_{\rho_{k+1}}(w) = 0$ such that

$$\|T_{\rho_{k+1}}(\tilde{w}_{k+1})\| \leq (1 - t_k/2)\|T_{\rho_{k+1}}(w_{k+1})\|.$$

This rule has to be added at the end of S2. Only if $t_k < \bar{t}$, the next Newton step employs $\tilde{w}_{k+1}$ instead of w_{k+1} as starting vector. In order to compute such an approximate solution $\tilde{w}_{k+1}$ the Newton-type algorithm for solving $T_\rho(w) = 0$ mentioned above with the starting point w_{k+1} can be used. Since $\rho_{k+1} > 0$ the matrix $(M + \rho_{k+1}I)$ is positive definite and finitely many steps suffice for determining $\tilde{w}_{k+1}$.

The following assertions can be shown:

a) The sketched method for solving $T(w, \rho) = 0$ generates iterates (w_k, ρ_k) with $\lim_{k\to\infty} \|T(w_k, \rho_k)\| = 0$.

b) There is a number $\tau > 0$ such that the set $\{w \in R^{2n} \mid \|T(w, \rho)\| \leq \tau\}$ is bounded.

c) Owing to a), b) the iteration sequence is bounded, i.e. possesses an accumulation point.

d) The iterates converge locally superlinearly to the unique solution $(x^*, y^*, 0)$, since (1) is assumed. Note, that the modification 2. concerning the step length t_k does not destroy this property.

References

Aganagic, M. (1984) Newton's method for linear complementarity problems. Math. Programming 28: 349-362.

Clarke, F. H. (1983) Optimization and Nonsmooth Analysis. Wiley, New York.

Fischer, A. (1992a) A special Newton-type optimization method. Optimization 24: 269-284.

Fischer, A: (1992b) A globally and locally Q-quadratically convergent Newton-type method for positive semidefinite linear complementarity problems. Technical Report MATH-NM-04-1992, Department of Mathematics, Dresden University of Technology.

Fischer, A.; K. Schönefeld (1991) Some iterative methods for quadratic programming. Technical Report 07-09-91, Department of Mathematics, Dresden University of Technology.

Grippo, L.; S. Lucidi (1991) A differentiable exact penalty function for bound constrained quadratic programming. Optimization 22: 557-578.

Harker, P. T.; J. S. Pang (1990) A damped Newton method for the linear complementarity problem. *In:* Computational Solution of Nonlinear Systems of Equations. (eds.: Allgower, G.; K. Georg), Lectures in Applied Mathematics, 26: 265-284

Harker, P. T.; B. Xiao (1990) Newton's method for the nonlinear complementarity problem: A B-differentiable equation approach. Mathematical Programming 48: 339-357.

Kojima, M.; Mizuno, S.; Noma, T. (1989) A new continuation method for complementarity problems with uniform P-functions. Mathematical Programming 43: 107-114.

Leder, D. (1974) Automatische Schrittweitensteuerung bei global konvergenten Einbettungsmethoden. ZAMM 54: 319-324.

Mangasarian, O. L. (1976) Equivalence of the complementarity problem to a system of nonlinear equations. SIAM J. Appl. Math. 31: 89-92.

Pang, J. S. (1990a) Newtons's method for B-differentiable equations. Math. of Operations Res. 15: 311-341.

Pang, J. S. (1990b) Solution differentiability and continuation of Newton's method for variational inequality problems over polyhedral sets. JOTA 66: 121-135.

Pang, J. S. (1991) A B-differentiable equation-based, globally and locally quadratically convergent algorithm for nonlinear programs, complementarity and variational inequality problems. Mathematical Programming 51: 101-131.

Robinson, S. M. (1979) Generalized equations and their solution, Part I: Basic theory. Mathematical Programming Study 10: 128-141.

Watson, L. T. (1979) Solving the nonlinear complementarity problem by a homotopy method. SIAM Journal on Control and Optimization 17: 36-46.

Optimality and Feasibility of Time Schedules in Vehicle Routing and Scheduling Problem with Time Window Constraints

Bronisław Florkiewicz, Michał Kulej
Institute of Mathematics, Technical University of Wrocław
Wrocław ul. Wybrzeże Wyspiańskiego 27, Wrocław, Poland

In vehicle routing and scheduling problem with time windows constraints, Golden (1988), specially in construction of heuristics for solving this problem the following problem has occurred. Given a fixed route $T = (0, 1, \ldots, m, 0)$ of the vehicle beginning in the depot 0, visiting the points of localization of clients $1, 2, \ldots, m$ and ending in the depot, find a schedule $X = (x_0, x_1, \ldots, x_{m+1})$ subject to

$$\begin{cases} x_{i+1} \geq x_i + c_i, & i = 0, 1, \ldots, m-1 \\ x_{m+1} = x_m + c_m, & \text{where} \end{cases} \tag{1}$$

x_i – start time of service of client i ($i = 0, 1, \ldots, m+1, x_0$ and x_{m+1} are respectively a start time and end time of T), c_i – service time of client i plus time of driving to the next route client (e.g. the client $i+1$). We dealing with vehicle routing with time windows in this paper, so the service time of each client must start within the time period $[a_i, b_i]$ ($i = 0, 1, \ldots, m$) called "time window". A schedule that fulfills this restriction is called a feasible schedule. Formally we could write them down as follows:

$$\begin{cases} a_0 \leq x_0 \\ a_i \leq x_i \leq b_i, \quad i = 1, \ldots, m \\ x_{m+1} \leq b_0 \end{cases} \tag{2}$$

The problem of existence, for a given route T and fixed "time windows", feasible schedules is given by the following theorem 1.

Theorem 1. The following conditions are equivalent:

(α) There exist feasible schedules of route T.
(β) $e_i \leq l_i$ for $i = 0, 1, \ldots, m+1$.
(γ) $e_i + l_i \leq b_{i+1}$ for $i = 0, 1, \ldots, m$, where $b_{m+1} = b_0$.
(δ) $a_i + c_i \leq l_{i+1}$ for $i = 0, 1, \ldots, m$.

Numbers e_i and $l_i (i = 0, 1, \ldots, m+1)$ are computed as follows:

$$\begin{cases} e_0 = a_0 \\ e_i = \max\{a_i, e_{i-1} + c_{i-1}\}, i = 1, \ldots, m \\ e_{m+1} = e_m + c_m \end{cases} \qquad \begin{cases} l_{m+1} = b_0 \\ l_i = \min\{b_i, l_{i+1} - c_i\}, i = m, \ldots, 1 \\ l_0 = l_1 - c_0 \end{cases}$$

If there exist feasible schedules of T, then $E = (e_0, e_1, \ldots, e_{m+1})$ and $L = (l_0, l_1, \ldots, l_m, l_m + c_m)$ are both feasible schedules, e_i and l_i are respectively the earliest start time of service and the latest start time of service of client i. Solomon (1987) has given the necessary and sufficient conditions for the feasibility of a special type of route which is similar to (γ).

The important problem — if there feasible schedules exist — is finding a minimal schedule e.g. a schedule with the shortest time of realization. Minimal schedules are the solution of the following linear programming problem: Minimize $x_{m+1} - x_0$ subject to (1) and (2).
The optimal solution of this problem could be found directly on the basis of the theorem 2.

Theorem 2. If there exist feasible schedules of route T then each schedule $XE(s)$, where $s \in [l_0 - xe_{m+1}(l_0) + e_{m+1}, l_0]$ is the minimal feasible schedule of T. And if $xe_{m+1}(l_0) = e_{m+1}$ then the schedule $XL(e_{m+1})$ and each schedule $X^* = (x_0^*, \ldots, x_{m+1}^*)$ such that $XE(l_0) \leq X^* \leq XL(e_{m+1})$ is a minimal schedule too. The minimal time of realization of route T equals $xe_{m+1}(l_0) - l_0$.
The schedules $XE(s) = (xe_0(s), \ldots, xe_{m+1}(s))$ and $XL(f) = (xl_0(f), \ldots, xl_{m+1}(f))$ are calculated as follows:

$$\begin{cases} xe_0(s) = s \\ xs_i(s) = \max\{e_i, xe_{i-1}(s) + c_{i-1}\}, i = 1, \ldots, m \\ xe_{m+1}(s) = xe_m(s) + c_m \end{cases}$$

and

$$\begin{cases} xl_{m+1}(f) = f \\ xl_i(f) = \min\{l_i, xl_{i+1}(f) - c_i\}, i = m, m-1, \ldots, 1 \\ xl_0(f) = xl_1(f) + c_0 \end{cases}$$

The proof of this theorem enables also to give immediate formulae for $X^* = (x_0^*, \ldots, x_{m+1}^*)$.
For example if $\sum_{k=1}^{m} p_k \geq l_0 - e_0$ and $u > 1$ and $v < m - 1$ where

$$\begin{aligned} p_i &= \max\{0, a_i - e_{i-1} - c_{i-1}\}, (i = 1, \ldots, m), p_{m+1} = 0 \\ q_1 &= 0, q_i = \max\{0, l_i - c_{i-1} - b_{i-1}\}, i = 2, \ldots, m \\ u &= \min\left\{i : \sum_{k=1}^{i} p_k \geq l_0 - e_0, 1 \leq i \leq m-1\right\} \\ v &= \max\left\{i : \sum_{k=1}^{i} q_k \leq \sum_{k=1}^{m} p_k - (l_0 - e_0), 1 \leq i \leq m-1\right\} \end{aligned}$$

then each schedule $X^* = (x_0^*, \ldots, x_{m+1}^*)$ where

$$\begin{cases} x_0^* = l_0 \\ x_i^* \in \left[\max\{\underline{x}_i, x_{i-1}^* + c_{i-1}\}, \overline{x}_i\right], i = 1, \ldots, m-1 \\ x_i^* = e_i, i = m, m+1 \end{cases}$$

where

$$\begin{aligned} \underline{x}_i &= \begin{cases} l_0 + \sum_{k=1}^{i} c_{k-1}, i = 1, \ldots, u-1 \\ e_i, i = u, \ldots, m-1 \end{cases} \\ \overline{x}_i &= \begin{cases} l_i, i = 1, \ldots, v \\ e_i + \sum_{k=i+1}^{m} p_k, i = v+1, \ldots, m-1 \end{cases} \end{aligned}$$

is a minimal schedule of T.

References

B.L. Golden and A.A. Assad (Editors). 1988. *Vehicle Routing: Methods and Studies*, Elsevier Science Publishers B.V. (North-Holland), 1988.

M.M. Solomon. 1987. *Algorithms for the Vehicle Routing and Scheduling Problems with Time Window Constraints*, Operations Research Vol. 35, No. 2, pp.254–265.

Discretization of Semicoercive Variational Inequalities

Joachim Gwinner
Institut für Angewandte Mathematik, Universität Erlangen-Nürnberg
8520 Erlangen, Germany

In this contribution we report on recent progress towards approximation and discretization theory for semicoercive variational inequalities. We discuss a broad range of applications: approximation and stability results for finite dimensional semidefinite quadratic optimization problems, convergence results for finite element discretizations and for boundary element discretizations of steady–state unilateral problems in mathematical physics, approximation results for elliptic control problems.

Let $(V, \|\cdot\|, <\cdot,\cdot>)$ be a real Hilbert space. Let $\lambda \in V^*$ be a continuous linear form, $K \subset V$ a nonvoid closed, convex subset, and $\beta : V \times V \to \mathbb{R}$ be a continuous bilinear form. With these data given we consider the variational inequality: Find some $\hat{u} \in V$ such that

$$(P) \qquad \hat{u} \in K, \quad \beta(\hat{u}, v - \hat{u}) \geq \lambda(v - \hat{u}) \quad \text{for all} \quad v \in K.$$

We require that β is positive semidefinite, i.e. $\beta(v,v) \geq 0$ for all $v \in V$. We admit a nontrivial kernel of β. But we require that β is semicoercive in the sense that β should satisfy a Gårding inequality

$$(G) \qquad \beta(v,v) + < Cv, v > \; \geq \; c\|v\|^2 \quad \text{for all} \quad v \in V$$

with some real $c > 0$ and a compact linear operator $C : V \to V^*$. In addition we are given a sequence $\{K^{(n)}\}_{n\in\mathbb{N}}$ of closed convex nonvoid subsets of V. This leads to a sequence of variational inequalities: Find $u^{(n)} \in V$ such that

$$(P^{(n)}) \qquad u^{(n)} \in K^{(n)}, \; \beta\left(u^{(n)}, v - u^{(n)}\right) \geq \lambda(v - u^{(n)}) \quad \text{for all} \quad v \in K^{(n)}.$$

We do not require that $K^{(n)} \subseteq K$. Instead we impose Glowinski's realistic assumptions on the approximation of K by $\{K^{(n)}\}_{n\in\mathbb{N}}$ and say that $K^{(n)}$ G–converges to K, if with respect to the weak topology, $w - \limsup_{n\to\infty} K^{(n)} \subset K$ and with respect to the strong topology,

$M \subset s - \limsup_{n\to\infty} K^{(n)}$ for some dense subset M of K holds. Note that if M coincides with K, G–convergence reduces to Mosco–convergence, a much studied concept in optimization theory. With these preliminaries we can formulate the basic approximation theorem of [1] as follows.

Theorem *Let β, λ, K, and $K^{(n)}$ be given as above. Let β satisfy a Gårding inequality. Suppose that $K^{(n)}$ G–converges to K. If the solution $\hat{u}$ of (P) is unique, then $\lim_{n\to\infty} \|u^{(n)} - \hat{u}\| = 0$ holds.*

For applications in finite dimensions we observe that in view of the compactness of the unit ball and the compactness of any linear operator a Gårding inequality trivially holds for any positive semidefinite form β. Hence with $M = K$, stability results in quadratic programming follow immediately. For a stability result for a finite dimensional variational inequality that models constrained equilibria of spatially distributed economic markets we refer to [5]. The latter paper also contains infinite dimensional stability results for Neumann–Signorini boundary value problems.

The full power of the theorem above is needed for the convergence proof of boundary element discretization methods for unilateral boundary value problems from mathematical physics. In particular, based on the ellipticity of the differential operator and exploiting the mapping properties of the boundary integral operators a Gårding inequality can be derived. Moreover piecewise polynomial approximations on the boundary generally lead to nonconform approximation schemas that can be tackled by the theorem above. As a concrete application we refer to [3], where a boundary element procedure is developped for the solution of contact problems in plane linear elastostatics and its convergence is analysed. The analogons convergence result for finite element approximation in the earlier paper [2] is based on a variant of the theorem above that is more confined to the embedding structure of Sobolev spaces. In [4], another variant of the theorem above that deals with nonlinear monotone semicoercive forms β is given and applied to prove convergence of the finite element method for the solution of p–harmonic Signorini problems.

Finally we observe that the maximum principle in distributed optimal control leads to a plentitude of different variational inequalities. For their numerical solution discretization by spline functions, finite elements and boundary elements can be employed. It is expected that the convergence theorem above or variations thereof play an important part also in the numerical analysis of elliptic optimal control problems.

References

1. J. Gwinner, *Discretization of semicoerive variational inequalities.* Aequationes Math. 42 (1991) 72–79.

2. J. Gwinner, *Finite element convergence for contact problems in plane linear elastostatics*, Quarterly of Applied Math. 50 (1992) 11–25.

3. J. Gwinner and E.P. Stephan, *A boundary element procedure for contact problems in plane linear elastostatics*, to appear in Mathematical Modelling and Numerical Analysis.

4. J. Gwinner, *A discretization theory for monotone semicoercive problems and finite element convergence for p–harmonic Signorini problems*, to appear in ZAMM.

5. J. Gwinner, *On stability for semicoercive variational inequalities applied to constrained market equilibria and Neumann–Signorini problems* (submitted).

Methods of Reduced Directions with Differential Cost Function for Nonlinear Programming

Victor S. Izhutkin, Mikchail V. Petropavlovskii
Department of Physics and Mathematics, Mary State University
Lenin sqr. 1, Yoshkar-Ola 424001, Russia

We consider the following nonlinear programming problem

$$\min\{f_0(x) : x \in \Omega\}, \quad \Omega = \{x \in E^n : f_j(x) \leq 0, \quad j \in J = \{1, m\}\}. \tag{1}$$

The sequence of iteration points $x_{k+1} = x_k + t_k s_k, k = 0, 1, \ldots$ is constructed for solving the problem (1). We define directions for moving s by using gradients of the constraints $f_j(x), j \in \hat{J}(x)$ "active" in some sense as

$$s = -P(x)z - R(x)(v + f(x)), \quad z \in E^{n-r}, \quad v \in E^r, \quad f(x) = (f_j(x))_{j \in \hat{J}(x)} \tag{2}$$

where matrices P, R are of full rank n by $n-r$ and n by r, satisfy conditions

$$A^T P = 0, \quad A^T R = I_r, \quad A = (f_j'(x))_{j \in \hat{J}(x)} \tag{3}$$

For example to obtain P and R triangular-orthogonal decompositions may be used

$$A^T = (L; 0)(Q_1; Q_2)^T, \quad P = Q_2^T, \quad R = Q_1^T L^{-1} = A(A^T A)^{-1}.$$

According to (2) the constructing of direction for stepping s may be reduced to choosing the parameters z and v in order to decrease some merit function $\Phi(x)$.
On the frame of this scheme the methods of linearization Izhutkin, Kokurin (1988), and feasible directions methods Izhutkin, Kokurin (1990) has been realized.
Let's consider a differential cost function

$$\Phi_\rho(x) = f_0(x) + \frac{1}{\rho} \sum_{j=1}^{m} \max{}^2\{0, f_j(x)\}, \quad \rho \to 0+ \tag{4}$$

as merit function.
Step size t is chosen by dividing unity until the following inequality (5) is satisfied

$$\Phi_\rho(x + ts) \leq \Phi_\rho(x) + \gamma t \omega_\rho(x, z, v), \quad 0 < \gamma < 0.5, \tag{5}$$

$$\begin{aligned} \omega_\rho(x, z, v) &= < f_0'(x), s > -\frac{2}{\rho} < f^+(x), v + f(x) > \\ &= < g(x), z > + < u(x), v + f(x) > -\frac{2}{\rho} < f^+(x), v + f(x) > \\ &= \omega(x, z, v) - \frac{2}{\rho} < f^+(x), v + f(x) > . \end{aligned}$$

Here $g(x) = -P^T(x) f_0'(x)$, $u(x) = -R^T(x) f_0'(x)$. Parameters z, v and ρ are to be constructed such that $\omega_\rho < 0$. We present three variants of choosing algorithm parameters.

1. Define "active" set by formula

$$\hat{J}(x_0) = J, \quad \hat{J}(x_k) = \{j \in J : f_j(x_k) > 0\} + \{j \in \hat{J}(x_{k-1}) : u_j(x_{k-1}) > 0\}.$$

Suppose $z = -g(x)$,

$$v = \text{Argmin}\left\{< u - \frac{2}{\rho}f^+(x), y + f(x) > + \frac{1}{\rho}\|y + f(x)\|^2\right\} = -\frac{2}{\rho}u(x) + f^+(x) - f(x), \quad (6)$$

and ρ such that $(\rho/2) < f(x), u(x) > -f^{+2}(x) \leq 0$.
Direction s may be also defined by using the linear system

$$s = -f_0' - Aw, \quad (A^T G A)w = -GA^T f_0' + f(x) + v. \quad (7)$$

In this case we get to the method of modified Lagrangian with merit function (4), Biggs (1972).

2. Let $v \in E_+^r$, which gives the most "strict" approximation of the Ω when (2). Suppose $\hat{J}(x) = J(x, \epsilon) = \{j \in J : f_j(x) \geq -\epsilon\}$, $\epsilon \geq 0$. Using formula (5) and $v \geq 0$ we have the following

$$\omega_\rho(x, z, v) = \omega(x, z, v) - \frac{2}{\rho}f^{+2}(x).$$

Analogous to case 1 we get $z = -g(x)$,

$$v = \text{Argmin}\{< u(x), f(x) + y > + \frac{1}{2}\|f(x) + y\|^2\} = (-u(x) - f(x))^+, \quad (8)$$

and $\rho = \alpha\,(2f^{+2}(x)/\omega(x, z, v))$, $\alpha \in (0, 1)$, if $\omega(x, z, v) > 0$.

This algorithm gives the possibility to avoid additional computational expences for the process of minimizing with constant ρ at each iteration.

3. In the case of linearly dependent "active" gradients we construct the direction of moving in the form (7). Choosing $v = -(\rho/2)w$ we obtain for w the following linear system $(A^T G A + \frac{1}{2}I_r)w = -GA^T f_0' + f$. In this case we get to the recursive quadratic programming method, Bartholomew-Biggs (1980).

References

Ижуткин В.С.,Кокурин М.Ю.(1990) Методы приведенных направлений с допустимыми точками для решения задачи нелинейного программи - рования //Ж.вычисл.матем.и матем.физ.-1990-т.30,№2, с.217-230.

Ижуткин В.С.,Кокурин М.Ю(1988) Методы приведенных направлений для решения задачи нелинейного программирования //Ж. вычисл. матем. и матем. физ.-1988-т.28,№12,с.1799-1814.

Biggs, M.C.; (1972), *Constrained Minimization Using Reqursive Equality Quadratic Programming, Numerical Methods for Nonl. Opt.*, ed. by F.A. Lootsma, 1972, Academic Press (London)

Bartholomew-Biggs, M.C.,(1980), *Recursive Quadratic Programming Based on Penalty Functions for Constrained Minimization*, Nonl. Opt. Theory and Alg., ed. by L.C.W. Dixon, Bakhauser Books, 1980.

A Minimization Method for Systems with Singular Value Constraints

Christian Jansson, Olaf Knüppel
Technische Informatik III, TU Hamburg-Harburg
Postfach 90 14 03, 2100 Hamburg 90, Germany

In multivariable control system design and structural engineering the optimization of important structural properties, like robustness, can be expressed as *nondifferentiable* global minimization problems (cf. e.g. [6]).

In [2, 3] a method for calculating approximations of the global minimum value f^* and the set of global minimum points X^* for the problem

$$\min\{\, f(x) \mid x \in X\,\}, \quad f : X \to \mathbb{R}, \quad X := \left\{ x \in \mathbb{R}^n \mid \underline{X} \le x \le \overline{X} \right\} \tag{1}$$

is presented. Besides the calculation of this approximations the method provides a guaranteed lower and upper bound of f^*, i.e.

$$\underline{F}^* \le f^* \le \overline{F}^* \tag{2}$$

The bounds $\underline{F}^*$, $\overline{F}^*$ are always correct despite the presence of rounding errors and the nonlinearity of f. Therefore a computer assisted proof is given.

The method is based on a special branch-and-bound technique in connection with a descent algorithm and uses so-called inclusion functions F of f, i.e. $F(Y)$ always contains the range of f over Y for each box $Y \subseteq X$ (cf. e.g. [1]). Here, we give some ideas how to calculate inclusion functions of the maximal eigenvalue

$$f(x) := \max_{1 \le i \le m} |\lambda_i(x)| \tag{3}$$

of a symmetric $m \times m$-matrix $M(x)$ depending on parameters $x \in X$. $\lambda_i(x)$ denotes the corresponding real eigenvalues of $M(x)$.

One possibility to calculate an inclusion function of (3) is to apply Geschgorin's Theorem to a transformed matrix $V^{-1}MV$. This matrix has the same eigenvalues as M and will have a nearly diagonal form if V contains the eigenvectors of M. More precisely, the following variant of an algorithm described in [4] calculates inclusion functions:

Let $Y \subseteq X$ be a box and $\mathrm{mid}(Y)$ denote the midpoint of Y.

1. Calculate approximations of the eigenvectors of $M(\mathrm{mid}(Y))$. Let V denote the matrix which contains these eigenvectors.

2. Calculate with an inclusion method (cf. [1]) a guaranteed inclusion $[V^{-1}]$ of the inverse of V.

3. With the tools of interval arithmetic calculate guaranteed lower and upper bounds $\underline{m}_{ij}$, $\overline{m}_{ij}$ such that $\{m_{ij}(y) \mid y \in Y\} \subseteq [\underline{m}_{ij}, \overline{m}_{ij}]$ and define $[M] := ([\underline{m}_{ij}, \overline{m}_{ij}])$.

4. Using the interval operations compute $[D] := [\underline{D}, \overline{D}] := [V^{-1}] \cdot [M] \cdot V$.

5. For $i = 1, \ldots, m$ calculate $\underline{\lambda}_i := \underline{d}_{ii} - \sum_{j=1}^{m} |[d_{ij}]|$ and $\overline{\lambda}_i := \overline{d}_{ii} + \sum_{j=1}^{m} |[d_{ij}]|$.

$|[d_{ij}]| := \max\{|\underline{d}_{ij}|, |\overline{d}_{ij}|\}$ denotes the absolute value of an interval. By the Theorem of Gerschgorin all eigenvalues $\lambda_i(x)$ of $M(y)$ are contained in the union of the intervals $[\underline{\lambda}_i, \overline{\lambda}_i]$ for all $y \in Y$, $i = 1, \ldots, m$. Moreover, if $[\underline{\lambda}_{i_0}, \overline{\lambda}_{i_0}]$ is the interval with the maximal absolute value, then

$$F(Y) := \begin{cases} [\underline{\lambda}_{i_0}, \overline{\lambda}_{i_0}] & \text{if } \underline{\lambda}_{i_0} \geq 0 \\ [|\underline{\lambda}_{i_0}|, |\overline{\lambda}_{i_0}|] & \text{if } \overline{\lambda}_{i_0} \leq 0 \\ [0, \max\{|\underline{\lambda}_{i_0}|, |\overline{\lambda}_{i_0}|\}] & \text{otherwise} \end{cases}$$

is an inclusion function of (3). A survey of other methods for the enclosure of eigenvalues and singular values is given in [5, 7].

We present numerical results for a system with a huge number of local minima:

$$M(x_1, x_2) = \begin{pmatrix} d_1(x_1,x_2) & k\sin x_1 & k\sin x_2 & k\cos x_1 & k\cos x_2 \\ k\sin x_1 & d_2(x_1,x_2) & kx_1 & kx_2 & kx_1x_2 \\ k\sin x_2 & kx_1 & 20 - 6\cos 2\pi x_1 & kx_1^2 & kx_2^2 \\ k\cos x_1 & kx_2 & kx_1^2 & d_3(x_1,x_2) & k\sin x_1x_2 \\ k\cos x_2 & kx_1x_2 & kx_2^2 & k\sin x_1x_2 & 20 - 6\cos 2\pi x_2 \end{pmatrix}$$

$$\begin{aligned} \text{with } d_1(x_1,x_2) &= 17.5 - 2e^{-500p(-4,-4)} - (x_1+x_2)/20 \\ d_2(x_1,x_2) &= 20 - (x_1^2+x_2^2)/7 - (x_2+5)\cos\pi\left(x_1^2+x_2^2\right)/2 \\ d_3(x_1,x_2) &= 18 - (x_1^4+x_2^4)/128 - 0.5\cos 6\pi x_1x_2 \\ p(a,b) &= (x_1-a)^2 + (x_2-b)^2 \\ k &= 1.0\cdot 10^{-3}, \qquad -5 \leq x_i \leq 5, \quad i = 1,2 \end{aligned}$$

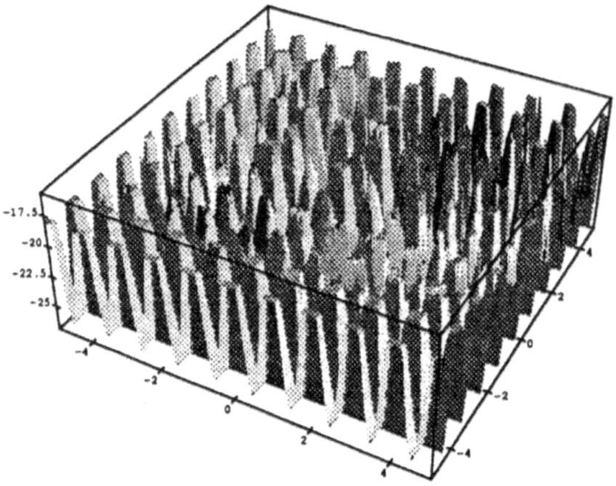

Plot of $-f(x) = -\max_{1 \leq i \leq m} \sigma_i$

Our method calculates the global minimum point x^* and value f^* with a relative accuracy of 10^{-6} giving $x^* = (-3.99997, -3.99997)$, $f^* = \overline{F}^* = -15.9$ and $\underline{F}^* = -15.8978$. 33 calls of $F(Y)$ and 135 calls of $f(x)$ are needed. On a SUN SparcServer 330 the required time is 1.2 seconds. We emphasize that the bounds $\underline{F}^*$, $\overline{F}^*$ are proved to be correct by executing the algorithm.

References

[1] G. Alefeld, J. Herzberger. *Introduction to Interval Computations.* Academic Press, New York, 1983.

[2] C. Jansson. A global optimization method using interval arithmetic. *International Symposium on Computer Arithmetic and Scientific Computation, Oldenburg, Germany, 1.-4. October 1991*, 1992.

[3] C. Jansson, O. Knüppel. A global minimization method: The multi-dimensional case. Technical Report 92.1, TU Hamburg-Harburg, Technische Informatik III, Jan. 1992.

[4] R. Lohner. Enclosing all eigenvalues of symmetric matrices. In *Accurate Numerical Algorithms, A Collection of Research Papers*, volume 1 of *Research Reports ESPRIT, Project 1072, DIAMOND*, pages 87–103. Springer, Berlin, 1989.

[5] G. Mayer. A unified representation of enclosure methods for eigenpairs. *ZAMM*, 1992.

[6] E. Polak, Y. Wardi. Nondifferentiable optimization algorithm for designing control systems having singular value inequalities. *Automatica*, 18(3):267–283, 1982.

[7] S. M. Rump. Zur Außen- und Inneneinschließung von Eigenwerten bei toleranzbehafteten Matrizen. *ZAMM*, 1992.

A Sharper Asymptotic Bound for Average Simplex Complexity

Gabriele Joas
Department of Mathematics, University Augsburg
Universitätsstraße 2, 8900 Augsburg, Germany

PROBLEM

We consider problems of the form

$$\begin{aligned} &\max\ v^T x \\ &\text{s.t.}\quad a_1^T x \leq 1, \ldots, a_m^T x \leq 1 \\ &\text{where}\quad v, x, a_1, \ldots, a_m \in \mathbb{R}^n \quad \text{and} \quad m \geq n. \end{aligned} \tag{1}$$

For all successful probabilistic studies of the simplex algorithm the shadow vertex variant, which comes close to a modification of the Gass-Saaty algorithm (1955), served as the basis. Borgwardt (1987) showed that the average running time of this variant is polynomial, if the input vectors $a_1, \ldots, a_m$ and v are distributed independently, identically and symmetrically under rotations. These studies are on the one hand done for problems with a moderate number of restrictions m, on the other hand for problems, where the number of restrictions tends to infinity, while n remains fixed. In both cases it was possible to give a polynomial upper bound in m and n.

It was our aim to improve the asymptotic upper bound by a factor $\frac{1}{\sqrt{n}}$.

THE ALGORITHM

By $X := \{x \in \mathbb{R}^n \mid a_1^T x \leq 1, \ldots, a_m^T x \leq 1\}$, we denote the feasible region of the problem (1), which is a polyhedron.

The mode of operation of the shadow vertex algorithm is explained at full length in Borgwardt (1987). This algorithm is a parametric one. The complete solution method for (1) works in n–1 stages. Let $\Pi_k : \mathbb{R}^n \to \mathbb{R}^k$ (for $k = 1, \ldots, n$) be the orthogonal projection from $\mathbb{R}^n$ into $\mathbb{R}^k$ such that

$$\Pi_k(x) = \Pi_k \begin{bmatrix} x^1 \\ \vdots \\ x^k \\ \vdots \\ x^n \end{bmatrix} = \begin{bmatrix} x^1 \\ \vdots \\ x^k \end{bmatrix} \quad \text{for all } x \in \mathbb{R}^n. \tag{2}$$

In each single stage $k = 2, \ldots, n$ the shadow vertex algorithm successively solves one of the projected problems I_k:

$$\begin{array}{ll} \max \ \Pi_k(v)^T\Pi_k(x) & \\ \text{s.t.} \ \ \Pi_k(a_1)^T\Pi_k(x) \leq 1, \ldots, \Pi_k(a_m)^T\Pi_k(x) \leq 1 & \\ \text{where} \ \ v, x, a_1, \ldots, a_m \in \mathbb{R}^n \ \ \text{and} \ \ m \geq n. & \end{array} \qquad (3)$$

By X_k we denote the corresponding polyhedron. The reason for the introduction of such a complex dimension-by-dimension algorithm is because of its good analytic properties.

PRIOR RESULTS

Before we start a probabilistic analysis, the probability space has to be specified. Borgwardt (1987) deals with input data $a_1, \ldots, a_m$ and v distributed independently, identically and symmetrically under rotations. For all such distributions with bounded support, he gets the following result.

Theorem 1 *Let $n \geq 2$. Then there is a function $\varepsilon_F(m,n)$, depending on the distribution F, such that $\varepsilon_F(m,n) \to 0$ for $m \to \infty$, n fixed, and the complete solution method for (1) does not take more than*

$$m^{\frac{1}{n-1}} \cdot n^3 \cdot \sqrt{2\pi} \cdot (1 + \varepsilon_F(m,n))$$

pivot steps on the average.

One gets an upper bound by adding the average number of shadow vertices of X_k in the single stages $k = 2, \ldots, n$ of the dimension-by-dimension algorithm.

SHARPENING THE ASYMPTOTIC BOUND

First we should introduce some more notation. Maximizing I_{k-1}, we get an optimal vertex in X_{k-1}, denoted by $\tilde{x}_{k-1}$. $\tilde{x}_{k-1}$ delivers a corresponding vertex in the polyhedron of the next higher dimension X_k named $\hat{x}_k$. This vertex, however, is not necessarily optimal with respect to $\Pi_{k-1}(v)$ in X_k, but it is only the optimum in X_k relative to a certain direction named $\Pi_k(\hat{v})$. For a sharper asymptotic bound we realize that we do not have to count the number of all shadow vertices lying on the shadow border, but only those lying within the path from $\Pi_k(\hat{v})$ to $\Pi_k(v)$. For this purpose we split the path between these two vectors into two subpaths, namely

path 1: from the optimal vertex in X_k with respect to $\Pi_{k-1}(v)$ (named $x_{k'}$) to the $\Pi_k(v)$-optimal vertex in X_k (named $\tilde{x}_k$), and

path 2: from $\hat{x}_k$ to $x_{k'}$.

We could prove that the expected number of shadow vertices lying on the first path is proportional to the angle between $\Pi_{k-1}(v)$ and $\Pi_k(v)$, which is in the average $O(\frac{1}{\sqrt{k}} \cdot \frac{\pi}{2})$.

Lemma 1: *The expected number of pivot steps in stage k for path 1 does not exceed*

$$C_1 \cdot m^{\frac{1}{n-1}} \cdot n \cdot k \cdot \sqrt{n-1}$$

in the moderate case, and

$$C_2 \cdot m^{\frac{1}{n-1}} \cdot \sqrt{n} \cdot k \cdot (1 + \varepsilon_F(m,n))$$

in the asymptotic case.
Here C_1 and C_2 are constants, and ε_F is the same as in theorem 1.

For the second path we get the following lemma.

Lemma 2: *The expected number of pivot steps in stage k for path 2 does not exceed*

$$C_3 \cdot m^{\frac{1}{n-1}} \cdot \sqrt{n} \cdot k \cdot \Delta(m,k)$$

in the asymptotic case, where $\Delta(m,k) \to 0$ for $m \to \infty$, and C_3 is a constant.

Then the following result is at hand.

Theorem 2: *Let $n \geq 2$. Then there is a function $\varepsilon_F(m,n)$, depending on the distribution F, such that $\varepsilon_F(m,n) \to 0$ for $m \to \infty$, n fixed, and the complete solution method for (1) does not take more than*

$$m^{\frac{1}{n-1}} \cdot (1 + \varepsilon_F(m,n)) \cdot O(n^{2.5})$$

pivot steps on the average.

REFERENCES

[1] Borgwardt, K. H.: The Simplex Method, A Probabilistic Analysis, Springer-Verlag, Heidelberg, 1987

[2] Gass, S., Saaty, Th.: The Computational Algorithm for the Parametric Objective Function, Naval Research Logistics Quarterly 2, 1955, 39–45

Nonlinear Optimization: Stability and Parametric Aspects

Hubertus Th. Jongen
Lehrstuhl C für Mathematik, RWTH Aachen
Templergraben 55, 5100 Aachen, Germany

We introduce the concept of structural stability for finite dimensional optimization problems. For differentiable problems with compact feasible set we present a complete characterization of structural stability in terms of partial derivatives of the defining functions up to second order. Here, the Mangasarian-Fromovitz constraint qualification as well as Kojima's strong stability of stationary points play a crucial role. Then, we turn over to continuous deformations of finite dimensional optimization problems. Singularities occur due to the violation of strict complementarity, the violation of constraint qualifications, and the degeneracy of the restricted Hessian of the Lagrange function. The latter singularities will be discussed and, finally, we focus on the pathfollowing of local minima with possible jumps.

References:

1. H.Th.Jongen, P.Jonker and F.Twilt: Critical Sets in Parametric Optimization. Mathematical Programming 34, pp.333-353 (1986).
2. J.Guddat, F.Guerra Vasquez and H.Th.Jongen: Parametric Optimization: Singularities, Pathfollowing and Jumps. J.Wiley (1990).
3. H.Th.Jongen and G.-W.Weber: Characterization of Structural Stability. Journal of Global Optimization 1, pp.47-64 (1991).
4. H.Th.Jongen and G.-W.Weber: Nonconvex Optimization and its Structural Frontiers. In: Modern Methods of Optimization (W.Krabs and J.Zowe, eds.), Lect. Notes in Economical and Mathematical Systems, Vol.378, pp.151-203, Springer Verlag (1992).

Circumscribed Spheres via Semi-infinite Optimization

Friedrich Juhnke
Fakultät für Mathematik, TU Magdeburg
Postfach 4120, 3010 Magdeburg, Germany

Abstract

In the paper the circumsphere of an arbitrarily given compact set K in the n-dimensional euclidean space $\mathbb{R}^n$ will be described as solution of a linear semi-infinite optimization problem using the Minkowski support function. Applying the corresponding linear semi-infinite duality theory, we shall derive characteristic properties of the circumsphere as well as the inequality of Jung between diameter and circumradius. The Jung's upper bound for the ratio of diameter and circumradius can be improved in special cases in which there exists a degenerated optimal dual basic solution.

Let K be a compact set in the n-dimensional euclidean space $\mathbb{R}^n$ with at least two different points. The *circumradius* R of K is defined in the usual way as the smallest radius of a closed sphere $B(x,r)$ containing K, the *circumsphere* $B(x^0,R)$; x denotes the centre and r the radius of $B(x,r)$. Using the corresponding Minkowski support functions

$$k(u) := \sup_{t \in \operatorname{conv} K} u^T t \quad \text{and} \quad h(u) := \sup_{t \in B(x,r)} u^T t = u^T x + r\|u\|,$$

we have the following equivalence

$$\begin{aligned} B(x,r) \supseteq K \quad &\Longleftrightarrow \quad \forall u \in \mathbb{R}^n : h(u) \geq k(u) \\ &\Longleftrightarrow \quad \forall u \in \partial B : u^T x + r \geq k(u). \end{aligned}$$

∂B denotes the boundary of the unit sphere $B := B(0,1)$. In this approach the circumsphere can be obtained as solution of the linear semi-infinite optimization problem

$$\min \left\{ z_P(x,r) = (0^T,1)\begin{pmatrix} x \\ r \end{pmatrix} \;\middle|\; \begin{pmatrix} x \\ r \end{pmatrix} \in M_P \right\} \tag{1}$$

with

$$M_P := \left\{ \begin{pmatrix} x \\ r \end{pmatrix} \in \mathbb{R}^{n+1} \;\middle|\; (u^T,1)\begin{pmatrix} x \\ r \end{pmatrix} \geq k(u), u \in \partial B \right\}. \tag{2}$$

The corresponding dual optimization problem reads as follows

$$\max\{z_D(\sigma,\lambda) \mid (\sigma,\lambda) \in M_D\} \tag{3}$$

where $\sigma := (u^1,\ldots,u^q)$, $\lambda := (\lambda_1,\ldots,\lambda_q)$ and

$$z_D(\sigma,\lambda) \;:=\; \sum_{i=1}^{q} k(u^i)\lambda_i \tag{4}$$

$$M_D \;:=\; \left\{ (\sigma,\lambda) \;\middle|\; \begin{array}{rcl} u^1,\dots,u^q & \in & \partial B \\ \lambda_1,\dots,\lambda_q & \geq & 0 \\ \sum_{i=1}^{q} u^i\lambda_i & = & 0 \\ \sum_{i=1}^{q} \lambda_i & = & 1 \end{array} \right\}. \tag{5}$$

We will show that both the primal problem (1) and the dual problem (3) are solvable and duality proporties of them yield characteristic properties of the circumsphere. -

Each feasible solution (σ, λ) of the dual problem (3) produces a lower bound of the circumradius R, from (2) and (5) we obtain

$$z_D(\sigma,\lambda) = \sum_{i=1}^{q} k(u^i)\lambda_i \leq \sum_{i=1}^{q} \left(u^{iT}x + r\right)\lambda_i = r \tag{6}$$

for any covering sphere $B(x,r) \supseteq K$ (weak duality). Moreover, both problems (1) and (3) turn out to be superconsistent ones. - The primal is said to be superconsistent, if the feasible region M_P contains a *Slater*-point. Such a point is for instance

$$\begin{pmatrix} x \\ r \end{pmatrix} = \begin{pmatrix} 0 \\ 1 + \max\limits_{u\in\partial B} k(u) \end{pmatrix}.$$

The dual is said to be superconsistent, if the gradient $c := \begin{pmatrix} 0 \\ 1 \end{pmatrix}$ of the primal objective function z_P is an interior point of the convex cone ("*moment cone*")

$$W := \operatorname{cone}\left\{ \begin{pmatrix} u \\ 1 \end{pmatrix} \mid u \in \partial B \right\} \in \mathbf{R}^{n+1},$$

generated by the normal vectors of the primal restrictions.- This is fulfilled too: We have at first $W \neq \emptyset$ due to $c = \begin{pmatrix} 0 \\ 1 \end{pmatrix} = \frac{1}{2}\begin{pmatrix} u \\ 1 \end{pmatrix} + \frac{1}{2}\begin{pmatrix} -u \\ 1 \end{pmatrix} \in W$ for an arbitrarily choosen $u \in B$. If c lies at the boundary of W, then there would exist a supporting hyperplane H through c at the cone W, which also contains the vertex 0_{n+1} of W,

$$H := \left\{ \begin{pmatrix} t \\ t_{n+1} \end{pmatrix} \in \mathbf{R}^{n+1} \mid a^T t + a_{n+1}t_{n+1} = 0 \right\} \text{ with } 0_{n+1} \neq \begin{pmatrix} a \\ a_{n+1} \end{pmatrix} \in \mathbf{R}^{n+1}.$$

From $c \in H$ we have $a_{n+1} = 0$ and therefore $\|a\| \neq 0$. The two points $\begin{pmatrix} \frac{a}{\|a\|} \\ 1 \end{pmatrix}, \begin{pmatrix} \frac{-a}{\|a\|} \\ 1 \end{pmatrix} \in \mathbf{R}^{n+1}$ belong to W, but they lie in opposite open halfspaces of H contrary to the supporting property of H. Hence $c \in \operatorname{int} W$ holds.

As a consequence of the superconsistence of (1) and (3), the continuity of the coefficients of the primal restriction hyperplanes (2) and the finite dimension of the parameter set ∂B we obtain the solvability of both the primal and the dual problem and no duality gap ocours, c.f. [1].

Let $\begin{pmatrix} x^0 \\ R \end{pmatrix}$ respectively $(\sigma, \lambda) = (u^1,\dots,u^q, \lambda_1,\dots,\lambda_q)$ be any optimal solutions of (1) respectively (3). This involves

$$z_P(x^0, R) = R = \sum_{i=1}^{q} k(u^i)\lambda_i = z_D(\sigma,\lambda) \tag{7}$$

and the complementarity

$$\lambda_i\left(u^{iT}x^0 + R - k(u^i)\right) = 0, \quad i = 1,\ldots,q \tag{8}$$

holds. In what follows we choose (σ,λ) as a dual optimal solution with a minimal number q of positive components $\lambda_1,\ldots,\lambda_q$. Then (σ,λ) is automatically a feasible basic solution of M_D and $\binom{u^1}{1},\ldots,\binom{u^q}{1}$ are linearly independent, hence $q \le n+1$. According to (8) we have

$$u^{iT}x^0 + R = k(u^i), \quad i = 1,\ldots,q. \tag{9}$$

Let $y^i \in \operatorname{conv} K$ be a supporting point of the hyperplane

$$H_i := \left\{x \in \mathbf{R}^n \;\middle|\; u^{iT}x = k(u^i)\right\}, \tag{10}$$

such that $k(u^i) = u^{iT}y^i$, $i = 1,\ldots,q$. Due to $\operatorname{conv} K \subseteq B(x^0,R)$ and (9) we obtain

$$\begin{aligned} 0 &\ge \|y^i - x^0\|^2 - R^2 \\ &= \|y^i - x^0 - Ru^i\|^2 + 2Ru^{iT}(y^i - x^0 - Ru^i) \\ &= \|y^i - x^0 - Ru^i\|^2. \end{aligned}$$

This shows

$$y^i = x^0 + Ru^i, \quad i = 1,\ldots,q \tag{11}$$

and y^i is unique, moreover it follows that $y^i \in K$, c.f.[3]. Applying (6), we obtain

$$\sum_{i=1}^{q}\lambda_i y^i = \sum_{i=1}^{q}\lambda_i(x^0 + Ru^i) = x^0 \tag{12}$$

and accordingly

$$x^0 \in \operatorname{conv}\{y^1,\ldots,y^q\} \subseteq \operatorname{conv}\left(K \cap \partial B(x^0,R)\right). \tag{13}$$

Conversely let $B(x,r) \supseteq K$ and $x \in \operatorname{conv}\left(K \cap \partial B(x,r)\right)$. Then

$$x = \sum_{i=1}^{m}\mu_i t^i, \quad \sum_{i=1}^{m}\mu_i = 1, \quad \mu_1,\ldots,\mu_m \ge 0, \quad t_i \in (K \cap \partial B(x,r)).$$

Setting

$$u^i := \frac{1}{r}\left(t^i - r\right), \; i = 1,\ldots,m,$$

we obtain the dual feasible solution $(\sigma,\mu) := (u^1,\ldots,u^m,\mu_1,\ldots,\mu_m)$. Each $y \in B(x,r)$ yields to

$$r^2 \ge \|y - x\|^2 = \|y - t^i + ru^i\|^2 = \|y - t^i\|^2 + 2ru^{iT}(y - t^i) + r^2,$$

such that $u^{iT}y \le u^{iT}t^i$ and therefore $k(u^i) = u^{iT}t^i$, $i = 1,\ldots,m$. Consequently

$$z_D(\sigma,\mu) = \sum_{i=1}^{m}k(u^i)\mu_i = \sum_{i=1}^{m}u^{iT}t^i\mu_i = \sum_{i=1}^{m}u^{iT}(ru^i + x)\mu_i = r$$

holds. Therefore B(x,r) is the circumsphere of K according to the weak duality (6) and we have proved the following lemma only using duality properties.

Lemma 1 *$B(x,r)$ is the circumsphere of $K \subset \mathbf{R}^n$ if and only if $B(x,r) \supseteq K$ and $x \in conv\ (K \cap \partial B(x,r))$.*

Similarily the uniqueness of the circumsphere can be deduced from duality properties.

Let $D = D(K) := \sup_{x,y \in K} \|x - y\|$ be the diameter of K. Each pair y^i, y^j of the supporting points (11) yields

$$\|y^i - y^j\|^2 = R^2\|u^i - u^j\|^2 = 2R^2 - 2R^2 u^{iT} u^j, \quad i,j = 1,\ldots,q. \tag{14}$$

Using the description (5) of the dual feasible points we get from (14)

$$\begin{aligned} 2R^2 &= \sum_{i=1}^{q} \lambda_i \|y^i - y^j\|^2 = \sum_{\substack{i,j=1 \\ i \neq j}}^{q} \lambda_i \lambda_j \|y^i - y^j\|^2 \\ &\leq D^2 \sum_{\substack{i,j=1 \\ i \neq j}}^{q} \lambda_i \lambda_j = D^2 \left(1 - \sum_{i=1}^{q} \lambda_i^2\right) \leq D^2 \left(1 - \frac{1}{q}\right), \end{aligned}$$

hence

$$R(K) \leq D(K)\sqrt{\frac{q-1}{2q}} \quad . \tag{15}$$

On account of $q \leq n + 1$ the result (15) implies the *Jung*'s inequality

$$R(K) \leq D(K)\sqrt{\frac{n}{2n+2}} \quad . \tag{16}$$

If there exists a degenerate dual optimal basic solution, i.e. a solution with $q < n + 1$, then (15) includes a better (smaller) upper bound of R/D than the *Jung*'s inequality does. This is the case for instance if K is contained in the boundary of a halfspace, c.f.[2] and [4].

References

[1] Glashoff, K.; S. A. Gustafson: *Linear Optimization and Approximation*, Springer - Verlag New York 1983

[2] John, F.: *Extremum problems with inequalities as subsidiary conditions.* Courant Anniversary Volume, Interscience, New York 1948, pp. 187 - 204.

[3] Juhnke,F.: *Das Umkugelproblem und lineare semiinfinite Optimierung*, Beiträge zur Algebra und Geometrie 28 (1988), 147 - 156.

[4] Santalo, L.A.: *Convex regions on the n - dimensional spherical surface.* Annals of Mathematics, vol. 47 (1946), 448 - 459.

On the Implicit Function Theorem and Parametric Optimization

G. Kassay
Faculty of Mathematics, Babes-Bolyai University Cluj
Str. M. Kogalniceanu 1, 3400 Cluj, Romania

The implicit function theorem plays an important role in the stability and sensitivity analysis of optimization problems. In the last few years many authors obtained results in this sense, by using the implicit function theorem of Robinson (1980) (see e.g. Robinson (1980); Alt (1990), (1991); Ito–Kunish (1989); Malanowski (to appear)).

In a recent paper, Robinson (1991) extended his implicit function theorem for nonsmooth functions, while Alt–Kolumbán (1992) showed that Robinson's result (1991) can be deduced from Kassay–Kolumbán (1989). They also obtained a stability result for quadratic optimization problems (see Alt–Kolumbán (to appear)).

The aim of this note is to obtain a stability result for strongly convex optimization problems which includes in particular Alt–Kolumbán (to appear). In order to obtain our result, we need a slightly modified version of Kassay–Kolumbán (1989) implicit function theorem due to Alt–Kolumbán (to appear).

STABILITY RESULT

Let X and Y be Hilbert spaces and let $L(X,Y)$ be the set of all continuous linear operators from X to Y. For a given topological space W consider the function f: $W \times X \longrightarrow R$ such that $f(w,\cdot)$ are convex and lower–semicontinuous for all $w \in W$. Let $A : W \longrightarrow L(X,Y)$ and $a : W \longrightarrow Y$ be continuous mappings. Further let $C \subset X$ and $K \subset Y$ be closed convex sets. For $w \in W$ consider the following optimization problem:

$(P)_w$ Minimize $f(w,x)$ subject to $x \in C$ and $a(w) + A(w)(x) \in K$.

Let $w_0 \in W$ be a fixed parameter. The problem $(P)_{w_0}$ is considered as the original (unperturbed) problem. Let $x_0 \in X$ be the unique solution of $(P)_{w_0}$. Then $(P)_{w_0}$ is said to be *stable under perturbations* if there exists a neighborhood V of w_0 and a mapping $x : V \longrightarrow X$ continuous at w_0 and such that $x(w_0) = x_0$ and $x(w)$ is the unique solution of $(P)_w$ for all $w \in V$. Denote by $\sum(w)$ the feasible set for $(P)_w$. The definitions of the concepts used below can be found in Alt–Kolumbán (1992), (to appear), Rockafellar (1976) and Kassay (to appear).

THEOREM.
Suppose $\sum(w_0)$ is regular, x_0 is the unique solution of the unperturbed problem $(P)_{w_0}$ and

(i) There exists a neighborhood $W_0 \subset W$ of w_0 such that the functions $f(w,\cdot)$ are uniformly strongly convex on W_0 with respect to $\sum(w)$;
(ii) The mapping $(w,x) \longmapsto \delta f(w,x)$ is continuous at (w_0,x_0) with respect to the Hausdorff metric in $\mathcal{P}(X)$ (the family of all subsets of X).

Then $(P)_{w_0}$ is stable under perturbations.

References

Alt, W. (1990), *The Lagrange-Newton method for infinite-dimensional optimization problems.* Numer Funct Anal and Optimiz 11: 201–224

Alt, W. (1991), *Parametric programming with application to optimal control and sequential quadratic programming.* Bayreuther Math. Schriften 35: 1–37

Alt, W., Kolumbán, I. (1992), *An implicit function theorem for a class of monotone generalized equations.* Proc of Workshop on Nondifferentiable Problems in Optimal Design. Prague

Alt, W., Kolumbán, I. (to appear), *An implicit function theorem for a class of monotone mappings*

Ito, K., Kunish, K. (1989), *Sensitivity analysis of solutions to optimization problems in Hilbert spaces with applications to optimal control and estimation.* Preprint

Kassay, G., Kolumbán, I. (1989), *Implicit function and variational inequalities for monotone mappings.* Babes-Bolyai Univ. Preprint 7: 79–92

Kassay, G. (to appear), *On nonsmooth parametric optimization*

Malanowski, K. (to appear), *Second order conditions and constraint qualifications*, etc. Appl. Math. Optim.

Robinson, S.M. (1980), *Strongly regular generalized equations.* Math. Oper. Res. 5: 43–62

Robinson, S.M. (1991), *An implicit function theorem for a class of nonsmooth functions.* Meth. Oper. Res. 16: 292–309

Rockafellar, R.T. (1976), *Monotone operators and the proximal point algorithm.* SIAM, J., Control and Optimiz. 14: 877–898

On the Variance of the Number of Pivot Steps Required by the Simplex Algorithm

Karl-Heinz Küfer
Department of Mathematics, University of Kaiserslautern
P.O. Box 3049, 6750 Kaiserslautern, Germany

Introduction: Despite their very good empirical performance the known variants of the simplex algorithm require exponentially many pivot steps in terms of the problem dimensions of the given linear programming problem (LPP) in worst-case situtation. The first to explain the large gap between practical experience and the disappointing worst-case was Borgwardt (1982a,b), who could prove polynomiality on the average for a certain variant of the algorithm—the "Schatteneckenalgorithmus (shadow vertex algorithm)"—using a stochastic problem simulation.
He studied LPP of type

(1) $$\max_{x\in X} v^T x;\; X := \{x \in \mathbb{R}^n \mid a_i^T x \le 1;\, i = 1,\dots,m\}$$

with a_i, v, $x \in \mathbb{R}^n$, $m \ge n \ge 2$. The vectors a_i are supposed to be i.i.d.–variables on $\mathbb{R}^n \setminus \{0\}$, whose common distribution is invariant under rotations around the origin. The set X can be considered as a random nonempty polyhedron on $\mathbb{R}^n$. Introducing the notation

(2) $$Y := \{y \in \mathbb{R}^n \mid x^T y \le 1;\, x \in X\} = \mathrm{convhull}(0, a_1, \dots, a_m)$$

for the polar polyhedron Y to X we define corresponding to Borgwardt the random variable $s(X)$ by

(3) $$s(X) := \int_{\omega_n}\int_{\omega_n} s_{u,v}(X)\, d^0_{\omega_n}(u)\, d^0_{\omega_n}(v)$$

where

(3.1) $$s_{u,v}(X) := \begin{cases} \text{number of boundary simplices of } Y \text{ intersected by } cone(u,v) \text{ -1} \\ \quad \text{if } \mathbb{R}^+u \text{ intersects a boundary simplex of } Y \\ \text{number of boundary simplices of } Y \text{ intersected by } cone(u,v) \\ \quad \text{if } \mathbb{R}^+u \text{ doesn't intersect a boundary simplex of } Y \end{cases}$$

$d^0_{\omega_n}(u)$ is the normed differential on the unit sphere ω_n of $\mathbb{R}^n$ in direction of u, i.e. $\int_{\omega_n} d^0_{\omega_n}(u) = 1$.
The above defined number $s_{u,v}(X)$ equals the number of pivot steps, which phase II of the shadow vertex algorithm requires for maximizing the functional $v^T x$ over X when the

iteration starts with a vertex of X, whose polar vertex cone intersects $\mathbb{R}^+u$. So the random variable $s(X)$ is the average number of pivot steps required by phase II of the algorithm to solve an LPP with domain X averaged on the choice of the starting vertex represented by u and the vector v defining the functional to maximize.
The most important tool in Borgwardts above mentioned polynomiality proof is the following estimation of the expectation value $E(s)$ of the random variable s. Independent of the underlying rotationally invariant distribution holds, e.g. Borgwardt (1982a,b):

$$(4) \qquad E(s) \leq \frac{e\pi}{4}\left(\frac{\pi}{2}+\frac{1}{e}\right)n^3 m^{1/(n-1)}.$$

But knowledge about the expectation value alone doesn't allow to quantify the probability of large deviations of the number of pivot steps from its expectation value. So, many researchers,e.g. Shamir (1987), raised the question for higher moments or even for the distribution of the random variable s.
The aim of this paper is to answer this question partially by estimating the quotient $\frac{Var(s)}{E^2(s)}$ asymptotically for a subclass of the rotationally symmetric distributions—the distributions with compact domain.

Main results:

Theorem 1:

For all $a > 0$, all rotationally symmetric distributions on the unit ball Ω_n on $\mathbb{R}^n$, $n \geq 2$:

$$(5) \qquad P\left(\left|\frac{s}{E(s)} - 1\right| > a\right) \leq a^{-2}\frac{Var(s)}{E^2(s)} = o(1),\ m \to \infty.$$

Remarks on theorem 1:

i) The convergence rate on the right depends on the special choice of the distribution and it's no possibility to estimate the quotient with a common algebraic bound as theorem 2 ii) suggests.
ii) As the most important consequence of theorem 1 we state that big relative deviations of s from the expectation value $E(s)$ become rare as m increases.

For a more special class of distributions within the rotationally symmetric distributions on Ω_n we can furthermore provide the convergence rate of the quotient $\frac{Var(s)}{E^2(s)}$ in (5) more exactly.
First of all we need some more notation. Let

$$(6) \qquad F(r) := \begin{cases} P(\|a\|_2 \leq r) & r \in [0,1) \\ 1 & r \geq 1 \end{cases}$$

be the "radial distribution function (RDF)" associated with a rotationally symmetric distribution on Ω_n, then F belongs to the class of "regular varying functions at 1" iff

$$(7) \qquad 1 - F(1-r) \sim r^{\alpha} L\left(\frac{1}{r}\right),\ r \to 0+$$

where $\alpha > 0$ and L is a "slowly varying function at infinity", i.e.

$$L \in \mathcal{L}^1[1,\infty); \lim_{x\to\infty} \frac{L(tx)}{L(x)} = 1 \; \forall t \in (0,\infty). \tag{7.1}$$

We call the class $\mathcal{R}$ of rotationally symmetric distributions on Ω_n with regular varying RDF "distributions with regular varying behaviour near the boundary of Ω_n". Now we are able to state

Theorem 2:

i) *For $n \geq 2$ and a distribution of type $\mathcal{R}$:*

$$\frac{Var(s)}{E^2(s)} = O((1-\tilde{G}(1-\frac{1}{m}))^{\frac{n-1}{2}}),\; m \to \infty \tag{8}$$

where $\tilde{G}$ is the inverse of the function

$$G(t) := P(a^{(n)} \leq t),\; t \in [0,1]. \tag{8.1}$$

ii) *For $n \geq 2$ and a distribution of type $\mathcal{R}$, where the function L of the RDF is a constant function, holds:*

$$\frac{Var(s)}{E^2(s)} = O(m^{-\frac{n-1}{\alpha+n-1}}),\; m \to \infty. \tag{9}$$

Remark on theorem 2:

For the distributions satisfying the propositions of part ii) of the theorem it is possible to evaluate an explicit estimation of the quotient studied with the same techniques the theorem is proved by. This estimation enables us to quantify e.g. the probability of LPP with worst-case complexity of the algorithm's phase II.

In addition to theorem 2 ii) we give two special cases the first having a RDF with $\alpha = 1$ and $L(t) = n$ the latter being a limiting case with $\alpha \to 0$ and appropriately chosen functions L.

Corollary:

i) *For the uniform distribution on Ω_n, $n \geq 2$:*

$$\frac{Var(s)}{E^2(s)} = O(m^{-\frac{n-1}{n+1}}),\; m \to \infty. \tag{10}$$

ii) *For the uniform distribution on ω_n, $n \geq 2$, holds:*

$$\frac{Var(s)}{E^2(s)} = O(\frac{1}{m}),\; m \to \infty. \tag{11}$$

For further details and proofs of the results we refer to Küfer (1992a,b,c).

References:

[1] Borgwardt, K. H. (1982) *Some Distribution-Independent Results About the Asymptotic Order of the Average Number of Pivot Steps of the Simplex Method.* Math. of O. R. 7: 441-462.

[2] Borgwardt, K. H. (1982) *The Average Number of Pivot Steps Required by The Simplex Method is Polynomial.* Z. f. O. R.: 157-177.

[3] Küfer, K. H. (1992) *Asymptotische Varianzanalysen in der stochastischen Polyedertheorie.* Dissertation, Universität Kaiserslautern.

[4] Küfer, K. H. (1992) *A Simple Integral Representation for the Second Moments of Additive Random Variables on Stochastic Polyhedra.* To appear, Preprint Universiät Kaiserslautern.

[5] Küfer, K. H. (1992) *On the Variance of the Number of Pivot Steps Required by the Simplex Algorithm.* To appear, Preprint Universität Kaiserslautern.

[6] Shamir, R. (1987) *The Efficiency of the Simplex Method: A Survey* Management Science 33: 241-262.

Effective Numerical Methods and Average Errors

Erich Novak
Mathematisches Institut, Universität Erlangen
Bismarckstraße 1 1/2, 8520 Erlangen, Germany

1. Summary

The final aim of numerical analysis is the construction and identification of effective numerical methods. Generally spoken, an effective method should be stable in a certain sense and also its error should be small compared to its computational cost. We do not discuss stability here and of course we do not have a definition of an 'effective method' that could always be applied. We only have several notions of the error and the cost of a method on one side and some heuristic ideas acquired by many numerical calculations on the other side.

Up to now, error estimates do not play a major role for the construction of effective numerical algorithms for nonlinear problems. This seems to be closely related to the fact that usually only worst case errors over a class of functions are studied. It can be seen, however, that the investigation of worst case errors does not automatically lead to effective methods in the case of nonlinear problems.

We want to show that the notion of 'average errors' can be useful for finding new efficient numerical methods. We give some results concerning three different problems of numerical analysis: numerical integration, global optimization, and zero finding.

An important practical question is whether we can do better by learning about the function during the process of evaluation some values. The three problems mentioned above behave quite differently with respect to this question. The differences are related to the concept of local errors.

For many problems (integration, global optimization) adaption does not help in the worst case setting because there is a 'worst' function f^* in the class F of admissible functions. Nevertheless adaption helps intuitively and also on the average for some of these problems because we do not have 'many' worst functions. The study of average errors for such problems – and also for other problems such as zero finding – yields new effective methods that could not been found by a pure worst case analysis.

Theoretical results on optimal algorithms did not always yield new algorithms that turned out to be practically effective. We feel that the study of average errors can decrease this gap between a 'theory of optimal algorithms' and our intuitive knowledge on useful algorithms.

2. Some Definitions

On classes F of functions defined on $[0,1]$ or $[0,1]^s$ we consider three problems: numerical integration, global optimization, and zero finding. Since F typically is infinite dimensional, $f \in F$ cannot be involved directly into the computational process. Rather we have to compute some data first that are used during the calculation.

The data about f, the amount of information on f that is used during the calculation, can have the form

$$N_n(f) = (f(x_1), \ldots, f(x_n)).$$

We assume that only the knot x_1 is fixed whereas x_i may depend (for $i > 1$) on the previously computed function values. The selection of the knot in the i-th step is described by a mapping

$$x_i : \mathbf{R}^{i-1} \to [0,1]^s.$$

Of course we can similarly define information operators N_n that also yield values of certain derivatives of f in each x_i and not only the function value. Each method S_n can only use the computed information about $f \in F$, i.e., S_n is of the form

$$S_n(f) = \phi(N_n(f)),$$

where ϕ has values in $\mathbf{R}$, $[0,1]^s$, or $[0,1]$ (for the three problems mentioned above). The individual error of a method S_n, if applied to a function f, is given by

$\Delta(S_n, f) = |\int f dx - S_n(f)|$ for the integration problem, by

$\Delta(S_n, f) = \sup f - f(S_n(f))$ for global optimization, and by

$\Delta(S_n, f) = d(f^{-1}(0), S_n(f)) = \inf\{|S_n(f) - x| \mid f(x) = 0\}$ in the zero finding problem.

The information N_n and the method S_n are called nonadaptive if the x_i are constant functions, otherwise they are called adaptive. It is interesting to know whether adaptive methods are better than nonadaptive methods.

3. The worst case setting

Different methods can be compared by their maximal error, defined by

$$\Delta_{\max}(S_n) = \sup_{f \in F} \Delta(S_n, f).$$

Can adaption help in the worst case setting? For this question the notion of local error is important. For an information operator N_n and function values $y \in \mathbf{R}^n$, the local error of $S_n = \phi \circ N_n$, given y, is

$$\sup\{\Delta(S_n, f) \mid f \in F,\ N_n(f) = y\}.$$

For linear problems and also for some nonlinear problems the following is true: There is a 'worst' element $f^* \in F$ such that the local error, given $N_n(f^*)$, is 'large' for every N_n in the sense that

$$\text{(1)} \qquad \sup\{\Delta(S_n, f) \mid f \in F,\ N_n(f) = N_n(f^*)\} \geq c \cdot \inf_{\widetilde{S}_n} \Delta_{\max}(\widetilde{S}_n)$$

holds with $c = \frac{1}{2}$ or even $c = 1$ and arbitrary S_n. It is enough to consider nonadaptive S_n and $\widetilde{S}_n$ here.

It is not difficult to conclude that adaption cannot help for such a problem. Such a result holds for the problems of numerical integration or global optimization, if F is convex and symmetric, and also in some other cases, for details see [1, 2, 5]. Clearly a similar result does not hold for zero finding. For every $f \in F$ there is a very good information consisting of only one function evaluation, namely $N(f) = f(x^*) = 0$.

But does (1) really mean that adaption does not make sense, for example in the problem of global optimization? Everyone with some numerical experience probably will disagree. We will try to understand the possible advantage of adaption better by studying average errors.

4. Average case setting

The average error $\Delta_{\text{aver}}(S_n)$ is defined by

$$\Delta_{\text{aver}}(S_n) = \int_F \Delta(S_n, f)\, dP(f),$$

where P is a probability measure on F. Using conditional measures we may write

$$\Delta_{\text{aver}}(S_n) = \int_{\mathbf{R}^n} \int_{N_n^{-1}(y)} \Delta(S_n, f)\, dP(f \mid N_n f = y)\, dN_n P(y).$$

The local (average) error at some $y \in \mathbf{R}^n$ is defined by

$$\int_{N_n^{-1}(y)} \Delta(S_n, f)\, dP(f \mid N_n f = y).$$

If S is linear and continuous, $\Delta(S_n, f) = \|S(f) - S_n(f)\|$ with some norm, and P is a Gaussian measure, then the local average error of an optimal approximation $S_n = \phi \circ N_n$ of S is a constant function (of y) for every nonadaptive information N_n. One can conclude that adaption does not help. If $S : F \to \mathbf{R}$ is a linear functional (as in the integration problem) and P is Gaussian, then there is an optimal linear method

$$S_n(f) = \sum_{i=1}^{n} a_i f(x_i) \tag{2}$$

for each N_n and there is a Hilbert space $H \subset F$ such that for every linear method (2) the average error on F is the same as the worst case error on the unit ball of H. In this sense, optimality in the worst case sense and in the average case sense leads to the same methods. Therefore for such problems the study of average errors can not lead to new methods, see [5].

For the proof that adaption does not help on the average we must know that the local error of optimal methods is constant for nonadaptive information, i.e., every $f \in F$ is a 'worst' function. Therefore, roughly spoken, for the result 'adaption does not help' we need much stronger assumptions than in the worst case.

We can often prove that adaptive methods are better (and sometimes even much better) than nonadaptive methods on the average, although adaption does not help in the worst case setting. The study of average case errors can lead to the construction of efficient adaptive methods that could not been found by the study of worst case errors, see [2, 3, 4] for examples and more details.

In nonlinear cases (and also if S is linear but P is not a Gaussian measure) the local average error of optimal nonadaptive methods $S_n = \phi \circ N_n$ usually depends very much on $y \in \mathbf{R}^n$. Sometimes, for example in the problem of zero finding, the local average error even is a discontinuous function of y. This has two important consequences:

- We may get quite different results in average case and in worst case. Quite different methods usually are optimal.

The known results lead to the conjecture that optimal methods (in the average case sense) are often quite efficient and the study of average errors therefore will yield new and powerful algorithms for many nonlinear problems.

– The proof of lower bounds for the average error is much more difficult and only recently such lower bounds could be proved for some problems, see [4].

References

1. E. Novak, Deterministic and stochastic error bounds in numerical analysis. Springer 1988, Lecture Notes in Mathematics 1349.
2. E. Novak, Algorithms and complexity for continuous problems. To appear in: Geometry, Analysis, and Mechanics, J. M. Rassias (ed.), World Scientific Publishing, Singapore, 1992.
3. E. Novak, Quadrature formulas for monotone functions. Proc. of the AMS **115** (1992), 59–68.
4. E. Novak, K. Ritter, Average errors for zero finding: lower bounds. Mathematische Zeitschrift, to appear.
5. J. F. Traub, G. W. Wasilkowski, H. Woźniakowski, Information-based complexity. Academic Press 1988.

Optimal Decisions in Multicriteria Problems with Controllable Attributes

Andrzej M.J. Skulimowski
Institute of Automatic Control, Academy of Mining & Metallurgy
Al. Mickiewicza 30, 30-050 Krakow, Poland

INTRODUCTION

Applying standard static methods of multicriteria decision-making one assumes that the alternatives are characterized by fixed attributes, whereas the main difficulty consists in finding and accepting the nondominated compromise values. In this paper we propose a model for the decision problems with alternatives which change their properties in a direct response to external actions. The changes of attributes may occur spontaneously, as well as they may be systematically influenced by the decision-maker. We assume that the decision-maker's actions resulting in a desired improvement of the criteria values may bear certain cost and may not be immediate, i.e. the lapse of time necessary to realize the desired change may be considered as an auxiliary criterion. Thus we get a bilevel multicriteria optimization problem consisting of the optimal allocation of resources at a lower level, and selecting the related appropriate Pareto-optimal outputs of the original problem in a minimal time at the higher level.

To make the presentation of the above ideas maximally comprehensible, our considerations will be confined to the problems with a finite alternative set Ω, and the performance criterion $F=(F_1,\dots F_N)$ admitting values from a given partially ordered finite set V. Let $V_i:=\{v_{i,1},v_{i,2},\dots v_{i,c(i)}\}$ denote the set of values of the criterion F_i ordered from the least to the most preferred one. Then V is the Cartesian product $V_1\times\dots\times V_N$ with the coordinatewise partial order "$\preceq$". The changes of values of F for a fixed $\omega\in\Omega$ are results of the control actions $u(t)\in U$ considered on a discrete time interval $[t_0,T]$:

$$((F_1(\tau),\dots F_N(\tau)) : \Omega \to V) \to \text{opt}, \quad \text{for a } \tau\in[t_0,T-1],$$

$$F(t+1)(\omega)=\phi(F(t)(\omega),u(t)), \quad \text{for each } \omega\in\Omega,\ t\in[t_0,T-1]. \qquad (1)$$

The optimality principle "opt" in (1) may be formulated e.g. as : "$F(\tau)(\omega)$ is Pareto-optimal and exceeds given $q\in V$ for the minimal $\tau\in[t_0,T]$".

A control u(t) will be identified with a transition $v_i \to v_j$, occurring on the time interval [t,t+1) and resulting from an external action undertaken by the system's supervisor. Besides of controlled transitions we will distinguish the deterministic uncontrolled transitions which may not be influenced, as e.g. passing to the following age classes, random transitions occurring spontaneously, and non-admissible transitions. The classes of controllable and random transitions need not be disjoint. Thus, the evolution of attributes may be modelled in a manner similar to the discrete-event systems described in Skulimowski (1991), whereas the values of F play the role of states. Since the set of alternatives Ω, the values of criteria V, and time are all discrete, such systems will be called *D-D-D-systems*. Their particular relevance consists in the fact that they constitute a natural extension of the discrete choice and outranking methods.

OPTIMIZING THE POPULATION STRUCTURE

The above sketched framework may be used to solve a variety of decision problems. Here, we will formulate the problem of optimizing the structure of a given finite population Ω by assuring that after a fixed time T a maximal number of elements of Ω is characterized by nondominated values of criteria.

We assume that the elements of a finite population Ω are classified according to N ordered classification criteria $F_1,\dots F_N$. Each element ω_α of Ω may pass to another class on the time interval [t,t+1) if, according to (1), a control $u_\alpha(t)\in U(t)$ has been applied to ω_α. All transitions can be described by $M:=\#\Omega$ equations of type (1) sharing the same resources :

$$\sum_{1\le\alpha\le M} b_\alpha J(u_\alpha(t),\omega_\alpha,t) \le u_t, \qquad (2)$$

where $J(u_\alpha(t),\omega_\alpha,t)$ is the cost of applying $u_\alpha(t)$ to ω_α, and $b_\alpha\ge 0$ for all α.

At the macroscopic level the evolution of Ω may be described by the following discrete controlled dynamical system :

$$x_{t+1} = A_t x_t + B_t w_t + \eta_t,$$
$$z_{t+1} = C_t x_t + D_t w_t + \zeta_t, \qquad (3)$$

for $t=t_0,\ldots T-1$, subject to the constraints

$$\sum_{t_0\le t\le T} (u_t + w_t) \le \xi(t_0,T), \qquad (4)$$

where x_t, w_t, and z_t are the state, macroscopic control, and observation vectors, respectively, A_t, B_t, C_t, and D_t are real matrices, and η_t, and ζ_t are random factors perturbing the growth/migration and observation processes. The matrices A_t and B_t may be derived by aggregating the equations (1) for all $\omega_\alpha \in \Omega$. The macroscopic controls w_t allow an "external" migration by attaching to (or removing from) Ω elements independently from "internal" transitions controlled at the lower level (1), and may bear certain additional cost.

The state vectors $x_t=(x_{1t},\ldots x_{nt})^T$ contain the numbers of elements of Ω characterized by the same values of $F_1,\ldots F_N$, for $t=t_0\ldots T$ (cf. Skulimowski and Schmid (1992)). Thus, there is a one-to-one correspondence I between the indices of the state variables and the elements of V, so for each $t\in[t_0,T]$ one may order the state variables $x_{t1},\ldots x_{tn}$ by the partial order generated from V. The values of F corresponding to the state variables are called in the above quoted paper the *interpretation vector* and denoted by $I(F,x_t)$. Assuming that a population Ω is characterized by certain distribution of attributes at an initial moment t_0 represented by the vector $x^0:=x(t_0)$, the aim of control is to achieve an optimal distribution of elements of Ω at time T, using for that a minimal quantity of resources u_t and w_t. Below we propose two of a variety of possible optimization problem statements. According to an initial remark, the first one of them is related to the nondominated values of F.

Let $K:=\{v\in V : \exists\ \omega\in\Omega$ such that $v=F(T)(\omega)\}$, and let $P(K)$ be the set of nondominated values of K. Denote by $\Pi(K)$ the set of nondominated indices of corresponding state variables, i.e. $\Pi(K):=I^{-1}(P(K))$. By definition, the relative population structure will be optimal if

$$\Big(\sum_{j\in\Pi(T)} x_{Tj}\Big) \Big/ \Big(\sum_{1\le k\le n} x_{Tk}\Big) \text{ is maximal,} \qquad (5)$$

$$\sum_{t_0\le t\le T} (q_t u_t + r_t w_t) \text{ is minimal, and } m_0 \le \sum_{1\le k\le n} x_{Tk} \le m_1,$$

where q_t and r_t are positive real coefficients.

For the above problem formulation one may find an ecological motivation, namely, assuming that a population Ω remains stable if under a classification F a maximal number of its members cannot get in touch with other individuals which are better (in the partial order in V) than themselves in all relevant aspects (represented as the criteria $F_1,\dots F_N$). In this setting, it is less important what is the shape of K and where it is situated at time T.

Introducing a *loss function* $\psi: V\times V \to \mathbb{R}_+$, with the property $v_1 \prec v_2$, $v_2 \prec v_3$, and $v_1 \neq v_3 \Rightarrow \psi(v_1, v_2) \leq \psi(v_1, v_3)$, we can evaluate the deviations from the ideal value $v^* := (v_{1,c(1)}, v_{2,c(2)}, \dots v_{N,c(N)})$ at time T for each $\omega \in \Omega$. Consequently, the deviation of the whole set Ω can be characterized by the following criterion σ :

$$\sigma(u(t_0)(\Omega),\dots u(T-1)(\Omega), w_{t0},\dots w_{T-1}) := \sum_{1\leq\alpha\leq M} \psi(v^*, F(T)(\omega_\alpha)) \to \min \qquad (6)$$

which is more suitable for economical applications such as e.g. balancing the portfolio structure than (5). While optimizing σ, we strive to approach the most preferred element of V for a possibly maximal number of elements of Ω. As the result, the alternatives actually characterized by nondominated values of F at the time T need not be numerous, but in average their values are better approximating the ideal value v^* than in case of optimizing the criterion (5).

From a computational point of view a solution to the above problems consists in solving parallelly N discrete optimal control problems coupled by the common resource or expense limitation (2). Thus, this problem requires certain non-standard solution algorithms based on dynamical programming. Since the motivation for introducing the above theory originates from the real-life decision problems, such as personnel choice or portfolio management, one can expect that the new theoretical issues should constitute a basis for a more frequent including the dynamics in the analysis of multicriteria choice problems.

R e f e r e n c e s :

Skulimowski A.M.J. (1991) Optimal Control of a Class of Asynchronous Discrete-Event Systems. *Proceedings of the 11th IFAC World Congress*, Tallinn (Estonia), August 13-17, 1990, Vol.3, pp. 489-495; Pergamon Press, London.

Skulimowski A.M.J., Schmid B.F. (1992) Redundance-free description of partitioned complex systems. *Mathl. Comput. Modelling*, **16**, No.10, 71-92.

Section 5

Systems and Control Theory

The Perturbed Adjoint Operator for Linear Hereditary Differential Systems with Perturbed Delay in Control*

Ludvik Bogataj
Faculty of Economics, University of Ljubljana
P.O. Box 103, 61000 Ljubljana, Slovenia

In the paper we present the new perturbation results for the adjoint operator of the infinitesimal generator of a strongly continuous semigroup of linear operators for linear differential-delay equations (DDE) with delay in the state of the system and in the control. The achieved perturbation results are particularly important because the considered perturbations of the delay in the control can be also of finite magnitude, which is the case frequently encountered in the real-world problems. Our results enable in an easy way to achieve the sensitivity results for the dual problem of linear-quadratic optimal control problem: the so called filtering with delay in observation (see [4]).

Vinter [5] has characterized the adjoint operator for DDE for delays only in the state of the system, which was later upgraded by L.Bogataj [1] to include delays also in the control. To the author's knowledge, the problem of characterizing the perturbed adjoint operator for finite magnitude perturbations of the delay in the control, has been unsolved up to now and the solution of this problem is presented here.

Key words: Hereditary differential systems, delay in the control, perturbation of finite magnitude, adjoint operator

AMS (MOS) subject classifications: 34K,49A10,620,62F, 93C

LINEAR DIFFERENTIAL DELAY EQUATION WITH PERTURBED DELAY IN THE CONTROL

Our model is DDE with time-delay in the state of the system and in the control:

$$\dot{x}(t)=A_0x(t)+A_1x(t-a)+B_0u(t)+B_1u(t-b),\quad 0<t\leq t_1 \qquad (1)$$

with initial data

$x(0)=\phi^0$, $x(s)=\phi^1(s)$ for $-a\leq s<0$, $u(s)=\phi^2(s)$ for $-b\leq s\leq 0$

* This research was supported by Ministry for science and technology of Slovenia under grant P5-0194/584-92.

$u(t)=\phi^2(t)\in L_2([-b,t_1],R^m)$ and $u(t)\equiv 0 \quad (t>t_1)$.

In (1) A_0, A_1 are nxn matrices, B_0, B_1 are nxm matrices, $x\in R^n$, $u\in L_2([-b,t_1],R^m)$ and
$\phi=(\phi^0,\phi^1,\phi^2)\in M^2([-a,0],R^n)xL_2([-b,t_1],R^m)\equiv$
$\equiv R^n x L_2([-a,0],R^n)xL_2([-b,t_1],R^m)$; $a,b\in R$, $a\geq b\geq 0$.

THE PERTURBATION RESULTS FOR THE ADJOINT OPERATOR FOR FINITE MAGNITUDE PERTURBATIONS IN THE DELAY OF THE CONTROL

We consider the perturbed system where the original delay in the control b is replaced by perturbed delay k, $0\leq k\leq b$; $k,b\in R$. Then expressing the model (1) and the perturbed system as abstract evolution equations in product space $Z = R^n x L_2([-a,0],R^n)xL_2([-b,t_1],R^m)$ (for details see [2],[3],[4]), applying the known techniques for DDE in the space Z (for details see [1],[4],[5]) to the case of perturbed operators, we derive our perturbation results. The perturbed abstract evolution equation is:

$$\dot{z}(t)=\tilde{A}z(t)+\Delta\tilde{A}z(t) \quad \text{or} \quad z(t)=\tilde{\tilde{A}}z(t), \quad z(0)=z_0 \tag{1-a}$$

where $\tilde{A}$, $\tilde{\tilde{A}}$ are the infinitesimal generators of a strongly continuous semigroup of the model (1) and the perturbed system, respectively (see [2],[3],[4]), $\Delta\tilde{A}$ is the perturbed part of $\tilde{\tilde{A}}$.

$$\Delta\tilde{A}z=(B_0u(t)+B_1u(t-k),0,0)^T \tag{1-b}$$

THEOREM. The adjoint of perturbed operator $\tilde{\tilde{A}}$ for finite magnitude perturbations in the delay of the control is given by:

$D(\tilde{\tilde{A}}^*)=\{(h^0,h^1,h^2)\in M^2([-a,0],R^n)xL_2([-b,t_1],R^m)|$
$\exists z\in W^{1,2}([-a,0],R^n)xW^{1,2}([-b,t_1],R^m)$ with $z^1(-a)=0$, $z^2(-b)=0$ and

$$h^1(\alpha)= z^1(\alpha)+A_1{}^T h^0 \tag{2}$$

$$h^2(\beta)= z^2(\beta)+\chi(\beta)B_1{}^T h^0 \tag{3}$$

$$\int_{-b}^{t_1} Dz^2(\eta)\,d\eta=-(B_0{}^T+B_1{}^T)h^0\} \tag{4}$$

and the action is

$$[\tilde{\tilde{A}}^*h]^0=(A_0{}^T+A_1{}^T)h^0 + \int_{-a}^{0} Dz^1(\alpha)\,d\alpha \tag{5}$$

$$[\tilde{\tilde{A}}^{*}h]^{1}(\theta)=-Dz^{1}(\theta) \quad (6)$$
$$[\tilde{\tilde{A}}^{*}h]^{2}(\eta)=-Dz^{2}(\eta). \quad (7)$$

In expression (3) $\chi(\beta)$ represents the step function:

$$\chi(\beta)=\begin{cases} 1, & -k\le\beta\le 0 \\ 0, & \text{elsewhere.} \end{cases} \quad (8)$$

COROLLARY. The adjoint of the perturbed part of the operator A ΔA^{*} is given by:

$D\{\Delta\tilde{A}^{*}\}=\{(h^{0},h^{1},h^{2})\in M^{2}([-a,0],R^{n})xL_{2}([-b,t_{1}],R^{m})|$
$\exists z\in W^{1,2}([-a,0],R^{n})xW^{1,2}([-b,t_{1}],R^{m})$ with $z^{1}(-a)=0$, $z^{2}(-b)=0$ and

$$h^{1}(\alpha)=z^{1}(\alpha) \quad (9)$$
$$h^{2}(\beta)=z^{2}(\beta)-B_{1}{}^{T}h^{0}+\chi(\beta)B_{1}{}^{T}h^{0}, \quad (10)$$
$$\int_{-b}^{t_{1}} Dz^{2}(\eta)d\eta=-(B_{0}{}^{T}+B_{1}{}^{T})h^{0}\} \quad (11)$$

and the action is

$$[\Delta\tilde{A}^{*}h]^{0}=\int_{-a}^{0} Dz^{1}(\alpha)d\alpha \quad (12)$$
$$[\Delta\tilde{A}^{*}h]^{1}(\theta)=-Dz^{1}(\alpha) \quad (13)$$
$$[\Delta\tilde{A}^{*}h]^{2}(\eta)=-Dz^{2}(\eta). \quad (14)$$

REFERENCES

[1] L.BOGATAJ, The adjoint operator of the infinitesimal generator for the linear differential-difference equation with delays in the state and in the control, Glasnik Matematicki,24 (1989),pp.349-354.

[2] L.BOGATAJ, Sensitivity of linear-quadratic systems with delay in the state and in the control for perturbation of the system matrices, Glasnik Matematicki, 24 (1989), pp.355-360.

[3] L.BOGATAJ, The estimation of the influence of uncertain delay in the control on the objective function, Matematicki Glasnik, 25 (1990), pp.721-730.

[4] A.ICHIKAWA, Quadratic control of evolution equations with delays in control, SIAM J. Control and Optimization, 20 (1982),pp. 645-668.

[5] R.VINTER, On the evolution of the state of linear differential delay equations in M^{2}; Properties of generator, J.Inst.Math.Appl. 21 (1978), pp. 13-23.

Paths to Constrained Nash Equilibria

Sjur Didrik Flåm
Economics Department, Bergen University
5008 Norway, Norway

Abstract. We report on two gradient-type methods for locating Nash equilibria of constrained, non-cooperative games.

0. Introduction.

This note considers computation of *Nash equilibria* in constrained, *non-cooperative games.* By such a game we understand a finite family $G := (G_i)_{i\in I}$ of *cost functions* G_i , one for every *player* i belonging to a finite set I. Each function G_i maps the entire product $X := \Pi_{\iota\in I}X_\iota$ of individual decision spaces X_ι , $\iota \in I$, into $\mathbb{R}\cup\{+\infty\}$. Here all spaces X_i are real Hilbert, and so is X when endowed with the natural inner product $\langle x,x'\rangle = \Sigma_{i\in I}\langle x_i,x'_i\rangle_i$. The cost figure $+\infty$ is used to reflect implicit constraints. In fact, a joint strategy $x = (x_i)_{i\in I}$ is infeasible, and all $G_i(x) = +\infty$, unless $x \in C$, where C is a closed convex subset of X. An outcome $x^* \in X$ is called a *Nash* (*non-cooperative*) *equilibrium* iff

$$x^*_i \in \operatorname{argmin} G_i(\cdot,x^*_{-i}) \quad \text{for all } i \in I,$$

where $x_{-i} := (x_\iota)_{\iota\in I-i}$ is short notation for actions taken by player i's adversaries. To find at least one equilibrium, assumed to exist, our main object is the correspondence $\partial Gx := (\partial_i G_i x)_{i\in I}$ of *essential marginal costs,* ∂_i denoting here the partial *subdifferential* operator $\partial/\partial x_i$ in the sense of convex analysis. This correspondence ∂G structures our approach because a zero of ∂G and a Nash equilibrium (trivially) is the same thing:

PROPOSITION 0.1. (Equilibria occur where marginal costs are zero)

$$x^* \textit{ is a Nash equilibrium} \quad \textit{iff} \quad \partial G x^* \ni 0. \tag{0.1}$$

The generalized equation (0.1) suggests ways to model out-of-equilibrium mechanisms aimed at driving all variables towards stationary levels. In fact, the two algorithm below are forged precisely in this spirit. For their statement we henceforth write $G_i = F_i + \delta$, where F_i is the real cost of player i, the extended indicator δ being 0 on C and $+\infty$ elsewhere.

1. SUBGRADIENT METODS.

Here we review briefly a projected subgradient procedure (Cavazzuti & Flåm,1990) which needs monotonicity in one form or another.

Definition. (Monotonicity with respect to equilibria).

Henceforth $V := (\partial F + N)^{-1}0$, N being the *normal cone* (correspondence) of C, will be called the set of *variational equilibria*. This name conveys that every $x^* \in V$ satisfies the *variational inequality*

$$<g^*, x - x^*> \geq 0 \quad \textit{for some} \quad g^* \in \partial Fx^* = (\partial_i F_i x^*)_{i \in I} \quad \textit{and all} \quad x \in C.$$

When V *is nonempty closed convex, the correspondence* ∂F *of marginal cost is said to be* <u>*monotone on*</u> C <u>*with modulus*</u> α <u>*with respect to the set*</u> V <u>*of variational equilibria*</u> *(or simply* α*-monotone) if*

$$<x - x^*, g - g^*> \geq \alpha(\| x - x^* \|) \qquad (1.1)$$

for all $x \in C$ *with* $x^* \in V$ closest to x, $g \in \partial Fx$, $g^* \in \partial Fx^*$. Here $\alpha : \mathbb{R}_+ \to \mathbb{R}_+$ is a continuous function vanishing only at 0. The projected subgradient method is now to simulate the continuous time system

$$dx/dt \in P_{Tx}[-\partial Fx] \quad , \quad x(0) \in C \cap \mathrm{dom}\partial F, \qquad (1.2)$$

where, for notational simplicity, mention of time $t \geq 0$, has been ommitted in the state variable x(t), and where P_{Tx} denotes the orthogonal projection onto the *tangent cone* Tx of C at the current point $x \in C$. It turns out that (1.2) furnishes exactly the same solutions as the system

$$dx/dt \in -\partial Fx - Nx \quad , \quad x(0) \in C \cap \mathrm{dom}\partial F, \qquad (1.2')$$

where Nx, as above, is the normal cone of C at $x \in C$.

Theorem1. (Convergence of the projected subgradient method).

Suppose the correspondence ∂F *is maximal monotone, and also* α*-monotone. Then for arbitrary initial* $x(0) \in C \cap \mathrm{dom}\partial F$, (1.2) *and* (1.2') *have the same unique, bounded solution* x(t), $t \geq 0$. *Moreover,* x(t) *remains within* C *and converges monotonically in norm to the set* V *of variational equilibria.. In particular, if* α *in (1.1) is purely quadratic (linear), then convergence is exponential (finite respectively) in time.*

2. A primal-dual method.

To avoid projection, when impractical, we propose the use of a **continuous multiplier method** (2.1) (Flåm,1991). To explain this suppose, without loss of generality, that the constraint set $C \subset X$, can be represented as a lower level set $C := \{x \in X : c(x) \leq 0\}$ of a single continuous convex function $c : X \to \mathbb{R}$. (Extensions to multiple constraint functions are easy). Then, start at arbitrary $x(0) \in \mathrm{dom}\partial F$, $y(0) \in \mathbb{R}_+$, and proceed according to the dynamics

$$dx_i(t)/dt \in -\partial_i[F_i(x(t)) + y(t)c^+(x(t))], \quad \forall i \in I,$$
$$dy(t)/dt = c^+(x(t)) := \max(c(x(t)),0), \tag{2.1}$$

if possible, all the way to a *stationary point* (x^*,y^*). Such points constitutes a set S of *steady states*, all satisfying, by definition, the *generalized equation* system:

$$0 \in \partial_i[F_i(x^*) + y^*c^+(x^*)], \quad \forall i \in I,$$
$$0 = c^+(x^*), \quad \text{with } y^* \geq 0. \tag{2.1*}$$

Assumption. (On subgradient selection) *The subgradients* $g_i \in \partial_i c^+(x)$, $i \in I$, *intervening in* (2.1-1*) *should be chosen so that* $(g_i)_{i \in I} \in \partial c^+(x)$.

Theorem 2. (Convergence of the continuous multiplier method).
(Convergence) *Suppose the correspondence* ∂F *is maximal monotone, and also* α-*monotone. Also supposet that* $\text{dom}\partial F \supset C$. *Then, for arbitrary* $x(0) \in \text{dom}\partial F$, $y(0) \in \mathbb{R}_+$, (2.1) *has a unique, bounded solution* $(x,y)(t)$, $t \geq 0$. *Moreover,* $(x,y)(t)$ *converges monotonically in norm to the set* S *of steady states, assumed non-empty. In particular, we have that* $\text{dist}(x(t),V)$ *tends to* 0, *and* $y(t)$ *converges monotonically upwards to a finite number* $y^* \geq 0$.
(Finite feasibility; phase 1) *Suppose constraints are sharp with modulus* $\sigma > 0$ *in the sense that* $c^+(x) \geq \sigma \text{dist}(x,C)$ *for all* $x \in X$. *Let the initial multiplier* $y(0)$ *be so large that*

$$\sup_{x\in B} \sup_{g\in \partial F(x)} \{\| g \| - \sigma y(0)\} := -\mu < 0,$$

where B *is a closed ball centered at the Nash equilibrium* $x^*(0)$ *with* $(x^*(0),y^*(0)) \in$ S, *(assumed nonempty), closest to* $(x(0),y(0))$ *and with radius majorizing* $\|(x,y)(0) - (x^*,y^*)(0)\|$. *Then* $x(t)$ *is feasible for all* $t \geq \text{dist}(x(0),C)/\mu$.
(Finite convergence; phase 2) *Suppose* $x(t)$, $t \geq 0$, *generated by* (2.1) *is feasible from some time* $\tau \geq 0$ *onwards. Also suppose that the correspondence* ∂F *is sharply monotone with modulus* $\alpha(d) \geq ad$, $a > 0$, *for all* $d \in \mathbb{R}_+$. *Then* $x(t) \in V$, *i.e.,* $x(t)$ *is a variational Nash equilibrium for all* $t \geq \tau + a^{-1}\text{dist}(x(t),V)$.

References.

E. Cavazzuti and S.D. Flåm, "Evolution to selected Nash equilibria", (Economics Dep., Bergen University, Working paper 1990), to appear in the proceedings of the Erice school (1991) on nonsmooth analysis and optimization.

S.D.Flåm, "Paths to constrained Nash equilibria", (Economics Dep., Bergen University, Working paper 1991)to appear in Applied Mathematics and Optimization.

On a New Finite Perturbation Analysis Algorithm*

Wolfgang Geiselhart, Ulrich Tüshaus
Institut für Unternehmensforschung (Operations Research), Hochschule St. Gallen
Bodanstraße 6, 9000 St. Gallen, Switzerland

1 Introduction

Consider a random variable $X_\theta(t,\omega)$ on a countable state space $\mathcal{X}$ which describes the evolution of a discrete event dynamic system (DEDS), e.g., a queueing network. It is assumed that the distribution of $X_\theta(t,\omega)$ depends on, for simplification, one parameter θ with $\theta \in \Theta$. In performance analysis of DEDS the most interesting question is to determine $l_{x_o,T}(\theta) = E(\Psi(X_\theta(T,\omega))|x_o)$ (resp. $l(\theta) = \lim_{T\to\infty} E(\Psi(X_\theta(T,\omega))|x_o)$), where Ψ is the so-called performance-generating function, $x_0 \in \mathcal{X}$ the state of the DEDS for $t = 0$, and $[0,T]$ the observation horizon. Especially in the first step of the optimization of a DEDS it is important to determine the sensitivity of $l_{x_o,T}(\theta)$ with respect to θ, i.e., the derivation $l'_{x_o,T}(\theta) = dl_{x_o,T}(\theta)/d\theta$. Usually, neither for $l_{x_0,T}(\theta)$ nor for $l'_{x_o,T}(\theta)$ analytic solutions are available; only estimates are accessible by an always time consuming simulation experiment (i.e., you have to perform simulation runs under fixed θ to produce trajectories $x_\theta(t,\omega)$ from $X_\theta(t,\omega)$). Methods to reduce total simulation time are needed and important.

In the talk we propose to conduct simulation runs to get estimates for $l_{x_o,T}(\theta)$ and in parallel use the so-called finite perturbation analysis of nth order (FPAn) for DEDS ([8], pp. 185) to approximate $l'_{x_o,T}(\theta)$. Therefore we introduce a new FPAn-algorithm and discuss three of its main features: stochastic similarity (of the trajectories generated by this algorithm), generality, and complexity. The first one provides necessary conditions for unbiased FPAn-estimates. For the second one we show that our algorithm covers well-known perturbation analysis algorithms. Referring to the third one we investigate the question, what is "economically more resonable": to perform a new simulation run or to apply FPA. The whole discussion is based on an important advantage of our algorithm: the specification of the order n as an external variable.

In this extended abstract we shall restrict ourselves to the essence of the new FPAn-algorithm (for further details of the talk, see [3]). Doing so, we give a new proof for general propagation rules. We finish this paper with some hints on recent publications on perturbation analysis.

2 The essence of the new FPAn-algorithm

The main parts of perturbation analysis are perturbation generation and perturbation propagation rules ([8], pp. 21). The essence of the new algorithm are general rules for perturbation

*This paper was supported in part by Schweizerischer Nationalfonds zur Förderung der wissenschaftlichen Forschung (Grant 20-30302.90) and IBM Switzerland.

propagation. We denote these rules as balance-equations of perturbation analysis. An important issue of perturbation analysis is the fact that perturbations are only propagated when idle or blocking periods of a service facility are terminated ([8], p. 32). Periods of the first kind are commonly referred to as *no input* (NI) and the second ones as *full output* (FO) periods. In simplified notation let $[NI]_j$ be the duration of an idle period in the trajectory produced under fixed θ and $[NI]'_j$ the duration of this idle period under fixed $\theta + \Delta\theta$. As general rules for perturbation propagation, we propose the following balance-equations for perturbation analysis:

$$\Delta_{jnew} = \Delta_j + [NI]'_j - [NI]_j, \tag{1}$$

for the termination of an idle period and

$$\Delta_{jnew} = \Delta_j + [FO]'_j - [FO]_j, \tag{2}$$

for the blocked one (here $[FO]_j$ and $[FO]'_j$ is defined for blocked periods as $[NI]_j$ and $[NI]'_j$ for idle periods and Δ_j denotes the perturbation at service facility j, for details, see [8], p. 223).

In an earlier paper [4] we gave an inductive proof of the balance-equations. In this paper we present a new deductive proof. For this purpose, we consider well-known propagation rules and show that they are identical with the balance-equations. For example:

Theorem 1 *The balance-equations hold for the class of systems defined by Cassandras and Strickland [2].*

Proof: To terminate a NI period we have the following propagation rules (see [2]):

$$\Delta_{jnew} = \begin{cases} \max\{\Delta_j - (t_i - t_j), \Delta_k + (t_k - t_j) - (t_i - t_j)\} & : \ (t_i - t_j) > 0 \Leftrightarrow [NI]_j > 0, \\ \max\{\Delta_j, \Delta_k + (t_k - t_j)\} & : \ (t_i - t_j) \leq 0 \Leftrightarrow [NI]_j = 0. \end{cases} \tag{3}$$

Case 1.a.: $[NI]_j > 0$ and $\underbrace{\Delta_j - (t_i - t_j) > \Delta_k + (t_k - t_j) - (t_i - t_j)}_{(*)}$

$$\begin{aligned} (*) & \overset{(t_i - t_j) > 0}{\Leftrightarrow} & \Delta_j > \Delta_k + (t_k - t_j) \\ & \Leftrightarrow & t_j + \Delta_j > t_k + \Delta_k \\ & \Leftrightarrow & [NI]'_j = 0. \end{aligned}$$

For $[NI]'_j = 0$, we get a simplification of (1) as follows: $\Delta_{jnew} = \Delta_j - [NI]_j = \Delta_j - (t_i - t_j)$.

Case 1.b.: $[NI]_j > 0$ and $[NI]'_j > 0$. For this case we have the following propagation rule [2]:

$$\begin{aligned} \Delta_{jnew} &= \Delta_k + (t_k - t_j) - (t_i - t_j) \\ &= \Delta_j + ((t_k + \Delta_k) - (t_j + \Delta_j)) - (t_i - t_j) \\ &= \Delta_j + [NI]'_j - [NI]_j. \end{aligned}$$

Case 2.a.: $[NI]_j = 0$ and $\underbrace{\Delta_j > \Delta_k + (t_k - t_j)}_{(*)}$

$$\begin{aligned} (*) & \Leftrightarrow & t_j + \Delta_j > t_k + \Delta_k \\ & \Leftrightarrow & [NI]'_j = 0. \end{aligned}$$

For $[NI]'_j = 0$ and $[NI]_j = 0$, we get a simplification of (1) as follows: $\Delta_{jnew} = \Delta_j$.

Case 2.b.: $[NI]_j = 0$ and $[NI]'_j > 0$. For this case we have the following propagation rule [2]:

$$\begin{aligned}\Delta_{jnew} &= \Delta_k + (t_k - t_j) \\ &= \Delta_j + (t_k + \Delta_k) - (t_j + \Delta_j) \\ &= \Delta_j + [NI]'_j \\ &\overset{[NI]_j=0}{=} \Delta_j + [NI]'_j - [NI]_j.\end{aligned}$$

Q.E.D.

In the same manner one can show that the balance-equations hold for the system-classes defined in [6], [8], pp. 224, [9].

3 Recent books and papers on perturbation analysis of DEDS

For a quite up-to-date overview on perturbation analysis, see [5] and [8]. Some attractive robustness properties of finite perturbation analysis are discussed in [1]. A reprint of recent papers on DEDS behavior, models for DEDS, qualitative and quantitative performance evaluation of DEDS, and applications in the real world is edited by Ho, see [7].

References

[1] Cassandras, C.G., Gong, W.B., and Lee, J.I.: Robustness of Perturbation Analysis Estimators for Queueing Systems with Unknown Distributions. Journal of Optimization Theory and Applications, vol. 70, no. 3, pp. 491–519, 1991.

[2] Cassandras, C.G. and Strickland, S.G.: Perturbation Analytic Methodologies for Design and Optimization of Communication Networks. IEEE Journal on Selected Areas in Communications, vol. 6, no. 1, pp. 158–171, 1988.

[3] Geiselhart, W.: Finite Perturbationsanalyse zur Sensitivitätsanalyse von Stochastischen Systemen. Thesis, Hochschule St.Gallen, in preparation.

[4] Geiselhart, W., Kischka, P., and Tüshaus, U.: Perturbation Analysis: Basics for Deriving Higher Order Propagation Rules. Proceedings, 16. Symposium on Operations Research, Universität Trier, Germany, 1991.

[5] Glasserman, P.: Gradient Estimation via Perturbation Analysis. Kluwer Academic Publishers, Boston, Dordrecht, London, 1991.

[6] Ho, Y.C., Cao, X., and Cassandras, C.: Infinitesimal and Finite Perturbation Analysis for Queueing Networks. Automatica, vol. 19, no. 4, pp. 439–445, 1983.

[7] Ho, Y.C. (editor): Discrete Event Dynamic Systems: Analyzing Complexity and Performance in the Modern World. A Selected Reprint Volume, IEEE Control Systems Society, IEEE Press, New York, 1992.

[8] Ho, Y.C. and Cao, X.R.: Perturbation Analysis of Discrete Event Dynamic Systems. Kluwer Academic Publishers, Boston, Dordrecht, London, 1991.

[9] Jackman, J. and Johnson, M.E.: Sensitivity Analysis of Serial Transfer Lines Using Finite Perturbation Analysis. International Journal of Systems Science, vol. 20, no. 1, pp. 129–137, 1989.

Necessary Properness Conditions in Periodic Control

Richard F. Hartl
Institute for Econometrics, O.R. and Systems Theory, University of Techn.
Argentinierstraße 8, 1040 Vienna, Austria

This paper deals with optimal periodic control problems and, in particular, with the question of properness. Loosely speaking this means that there is a non-trivial optimal solution which is better than the best constant solution. Two new necessary conditions for properness are presented. First, it is shown, that properness cannot occur in a one-state variable problem if the optimal solution is unique. In other words, a necessary condition for properness is that the dimension of the state space is at least two. The second result is that properness can only occur if the Hamiltonian is non-concave in the state variables.

I. INTRODUCTION

Consider the continuos time time-invariant *optimal periodic control problem:*

$$\max_{u(.)} J(T, u(.), x(.)) = \frac{1}{T}\int_0^T F(x(t), u(t))dt \tag{1}$$

$$\text{s.t.} \quad \dot{x}(t) = f(x(t), u(t)) \tag{2}$$

$$g(x(t), u(t)) \geq 0 \tag{3}$$

$$x(0) = x(T) \tag{4}$$

In words, $x \in R$ is the state variable, $u \in R^m$ is the control; the path constraints (3) with $g \in R^k$ describe the control region $\Omega(x) = \{u | g(x, u) \geq 0\}$ which can depend on the state and may also contain pure state constraints of the type $g(x) \geq 0$.

The corresponding *steady state decision problem* is defined as

$$\max_{\bar{u}, \bar{x}} \bar{J}(\bar{u}, \bar{x}) = F(\bar{x}, \bar{u}) \tag{5}$$

$$\text{s.t.} \quad f(\bar{x}, \bar{u}) = 0 \tag{6}$$

$$g(\bar{x}, \bar{u}) \geq 0 \tag{7}$$

Definition 1.1. Let $(\bar{x},\bar{u})$ be the optimal steady state solution of problem (5)-(7) with corresponding objective value $\bar{J}$. If there exists a period T^* and an admissible pair (u^*,x^*) satisfying (2)-(4) on $[0,T^*]$ such that $J(T^*,x^*,u^*) > \bar{J}$ then the OPC problem (1)-(4) is called *proper.*

In the literature several necessary and sufficient conditions for properness of an OPC problem can be found. The *sufficient conditions* are, e.g., summarised in Colonius (1988). One of them is the so called π-criterion and its use in an economic framework is illustrated, e.g., in Han (1992) and Han, Feichtinger and Hartl (1992).

Necessary conditions are more rarely encountered in the literature. It is the purpose of this presentation to review some recently developed necessary conditions. The first one by Hartl (1992) deals with one-dimensional problems and the second by Han (1992) and Han, Feichtinger and Hartl (1992) points out the role of concavity.

II. ONE-DIMENSIONAL PERIODIC CONTROL PROBLEMS

In some sense the question of properness of OPC-problems is related to the question of whether the optimal solution of an infinite horizon control problem is periodic. In the discounted case Hartl [4] has shown, that a periodic control cannot be optimal in the case of a one-dimensional state variable if the optimal solution is unique. This section deals with a similar result for the zero discounting case.

Consider the autonomous OPC problem (1)-(4) with one dimensional state variable, i.e., n=1.

Theorem 2.1. If OPC problem (1)-(4) with n=1 has a proper optimal periodic solution (T^*,x^*,u^*), then it is not unique. In particular, there is another proper solution with period less than (or equal to) $T^*/2$.

The proof can be found in Hartl (1992). The idea is a dynamic programming argument somewhat similar to Hartl (1987).

Remark 2.2. Theorem 2.1 says that if the optimal solution is unique, then it cannot be proper. Uniqueness can, e.g., be guaranteed by the strict concavity of the maximised Hamiltonian H_0 in the state x.

From the proof of Theorem 2.1. the following result is easily obtained:

Corollary 2.3. If OPC problem (1)-(4) with n=1 has a proper periodic solution (T^*,x^*,u^*), then a sequence of proper periodic solutions (T_i^*,x_i^*,u_i^*) can be constructed such that $T_i^* \rightarrow 0$ and

$$\max_{0\leq t\leq T_i^*} x_i^*(t) - \min_{0\leq t\leq T_i^*} x_i^*(t) \rightarrow 0 \text{ as } i \rightarrow \infty .$$

Remark 2.4. Corollary 2.3 implies, that an optimal "almost constant" state trajectory can be maintained by applying a kind of chattering control. If the problem (i.e. the Hamiltonian) is concave in the control then a constant optimal solution can be constructed which implies that the OPC problem is not proper.

III. NECESSARY CONDITIONS BASED ON NON-CONCAVITY

Another type of necessary conditions is derived in Han (1992) and Han, Feichtinger and Hartl (1992). This approach focuses on the role of concavity for the possibility of having proper solutions:

Theorem 3.1. If the path constraints (3) do not depend on the state and if the maximised Hamiltonian of problem (1)-(4) is concave in x for λ equals the Lagrange multiplier of (6) in the Kuhn-Tucker conditions corresponding to (5)-(7), then the OPC problem (1)-(4) has no proper optimal periodic solution.

In other words, a necessary condition for properness is the non-concavity of the maximised Hamiltonian w.r.t. the state.

The proof of Theorem 3.1 is carried out by contradiction and the essential steps are similar to the derivation of sufficient optimality conditions; see e.g. Feichtinger and Hartl (1986). Another result which is used in the proof is that the value of the objective functional equals the maximised Hamiltonian which is constant in the autonomous case.

Theorem 3.1 deals with the free period problem. However, this result can also be extended to the fixed period problem:

Corollary 3.2. Under the assumptions of Theorem 3.1, if an optimal solution for the free period problem exists, then also the fixed period problem is not proper.

This result is immediately clear from the fact, that the value of the objective function for the fixed period problem is at most as good as that of the free period problem.

IV. REFERENCES

Colonius F (1988) *Optimal Periodic Control.* Lecture Notes in Mathematics 1313. Springer Verlag. Berlin.

Han M (1992) *Optimal Periodic Control Models and their Economic Application.* PhD-thesis. Institute for Econometrics, O.R. and Systems Theory. Vienna University of Technology.

Han M, Feichtinger G, Hartl R (1992) Non concavities and properness in optimal periodic control models. Working paper. Institute for Econometrics, O.R. and Systems Theory. Vienna University of Technology.

Hartl R (1987) A simple proof of the monotonicity of the state trajectories in autonomous control problems. *Journal of Economic Theory* **40**: 211-215.

Hartl R (1992) On the properness of one-dimensional periodic control problems. Working paper. Institute for Econometrics, O.R. and Systems Theory. Vienna University of Technology.

Recent Trends in Mathematical Systems Theory and their Possible Impact on Applications

Hans W. Knobloch
Mathematisches Institut
Am Hubland, 8700 Würzburg, Germany

The traditional view of control theory in applied sciences - outside engineering - reflects the state of art twenty years ago when control theory was considered as being identical with optimal control. This attitude has in part prevented the inflow of new ideas from system theory into bio- and social sciences. The range of optimal control methods is limited by the requirements that precise mathematical models are available. Modern geometric control theory has found various ways to overcome this obstacle by generalizing concepts from linear to nonlinear situations.

1 MODELLING.

econometrics was the first area outside the engineering sciences which developed some interest in control theory. The reason was obvious: Control theory is a mathematical discipline which is devoted to a systematic study of intertemporal decision making. In the jargon of specialists these decision policies are called control laws. A control law is a rule for specializing the input u of a control system given a time instant t and the measured value of the output until this time. Before we enter into a discussion of these notions we would like to stress the fact that control theory is concerned with *mathematical models* of real world systems. Hence the relevance of a control law for the needs of applications depends upon how realistic is the underlying mathematical model.
In the context of this exposition a control system is defined by writing down two relations: A dynamic input/state relation and a static state/output relation:

$$\dot{x} = f(x, u), \quad y = c(x). \tag{1.1}$$

The input u describes the way in which the environment interferes with the system, the output y describes the action of the system on its environment. A further explanation: y is the information which is available to the environment about the internal state x of the system. This definition comes close to the standard practice in setting up a mathematical model of type (1.1) for a concrete control system. One starts with input and output and then adds to the output as many variables as are necessary in order to write down a dynamical law say as a balance equation. In control system models the state plays the role of an auxiliary variable and one has freedom to decide what to include into the state and what not. One can go a step further and admit fictitous quantities - which even in principle are not accessible to measurement - as state variables. Using e.g. a variable with the label 'sympathy' does not mean that one has to explain how sympathy is measured. What is necessary is to

demonstrate that this variable reflects the *effect* of sympathy in the balance equation. There is a prize which one has to pay for the freedom in building up the state of a system starting from the output: The dynamics will contain 'uncertainties'. There are attempts to treat 'uncertain dynamics' within the frame of classical (optimal) control theory by adapting the precision of mathematical analysis to the precision of the mathematical model, i.e. passing from differential equations to differential inclusions. Contributions to this 'set valued analysis' of control systems can be found elsewhere in this volume, cf. e.g. [5].
The purpose of this presentation is to report on some developments within the controltheoretic community which allow to view the problem of dealing with uncertain dynamics under a different angle. This can be best demonstrated by means of a stock example for design of harvesting policies of renewable ressources. Similar examples have been treated elsewhere in this volume via the classical optimal control approach, cf. [6].
Let $y = y(t)$ be the biomass of a fish population at time t and u the (annual) harvesting rate. The time evolution of y is assumed to obey the dynamical law

$$\dot{y} = y\lambda(y) - uy. \tag{1.2}$$

The growth factor $\lambda(y)$ in general should be such that in case $u = 0$ one arrives at the typical population-dynamical law for the growth of one species with bounded supply of food: $\lambda(y) > 0$ for $y < y^*, \lambda(y) < 0$ for $y > y^*, y^*$ some positive number. A true realistic model would contain no information beyond that point. We however will assume here that we have logistic growth in $(1.2) : \lambda(y) = y^* - y$. This reduces the model uncertainty to the case of a single hidden parameter, namely the threshold value y^*. We will deal here with the problem of determining y^* (at least approximately) from repeated measurements of y. A possible approach to the more general problem of identifying the whole coefficient $\lambda(y)$ - without any a-priori information beyond that what we have stated above - has been outlined in the introduction of [4].
Following our previous suggestion we update the unknown parameter y^* formally to a component of the state variable. Thereby we are arrived at the complete model: the state x is a pair $(y, p), y$ is the output and the dynamics is given as

$$\dot{y} = y(p - y) - uy, \quad \dot{p} = 0. \tag{1.3}$$

This formal way of treating parameter uncertainty allows to subsume the identification problem under the more general problem of reconstructing the state at time t from incomplete and inaccurate measurements up to time t. Incomplete means: The available information consists of the values $y(\tau), (\tau \leq t)$. Inaccurate means: What is actually known is a time series $y_m(t)$ and a bound δ such that

$$||y(t) - y_m(t)|| \leq \delta \text{ for all } t. \tag{1.4}$$

2 STATE ESTIMATION.

We consider the problem

$$\text{Given } y_m(\tau) \text{ for } \tau \leq t \text{ (cf.((1.4) find an estimate } \hat{x}(t) \text{ for } x(t). \tag{2.1}$$

The method which we propose is dynamic estimation. It requires - in contrast to statistical methods - the full infinite time interval $[0, \infty[$ for arriving at its objective. In return it offers two advantages.

(i) A guaranteed accuracy of the prognosis for each individual sample path despite the fact that a measurement error (bounded by δ) may persist, i.e. occur at each time instant t. More precisely the dynamic estimate is asymptotically correct in the following precise sense

$$||x(t) - \hat{x}(t)|| \text{ decays exponentially as } t \rightarrow \infty \text{ to a bound which is proportional to } \delta. \tag{2.2}$$

(ii) It can be performed on line without employing the control variable for identification experiments. This is important in technical applications where u is used say to keep the system in an equilibrium. But it is also important for applications in bio- and social science where experimental use of the steering policies is out of discussion.

State estimation is well understood within the context of linear control theory. One can characterize completely the linear systems where the state is 'observable', i.e x is accessible to dynamic estimation given the output y. One also knows how the actual process of estimation can be carried out in practice via the so called 'dynamical observer'. As far as the nonlinear observer is concerned both the theoretical background as well as the practical implementation are far from being developed as well as in the linear scene. A recent proposal which will be presented in [3] follows the prediction-correction scheme of the linear theory. The estimate $\hat{x}(t)$ for $x(t)$ is provided by the state of a dynamical system

$$\dot{\hat{x}} = \hat{f}(t, \hat{x}, u, y)$$

whose input consists of input and output of the given system. There is a simple geometric idea behind the construction of $\hat{f}$. Whether it will actually lead to a dynamic estimation having the property (2.2) has been cleared so far only in special cases where the components of the state which are not part of the output have the meaning of parameters, cf. [3]. A typical example has been discussed at the end of the previous section. The problem there is to estimate the (constant) value of p given a time series

$$\{y(t_1), y(t_2), \ldots\} \tag{2.3}$$

of consecutive measurements of y. The first step in the identification procedure is then to pass from the sequence (2.3) to a continuous function $t \longrightarrow y_m(t)$ say by interpolation. This gives rise to a measurement error δ cf. (1.4). The next step is then the set up of the dynamical equations for the observer. Due to the simplicity of the given system they are particularly simple in case $u = 0$, i.e. when there is no harvesting and the identification of y^* from a given time series (2.3) is treated as problem in its own right. Let $\hat{x} := (\eta, \pi)$, then the observer equation contains two positive real numbers χ_i- which have to be chosen appropriately - and looks as follows

$$\dot{\eta} = \eta(\pi - \eta) + \chi_1(\eta - y_m(t)), \dot{\pi} = -\chi_2(\eta - y_m(t)).$$

Let us repeat for this particular example how dynamic state estimation works: Regardless of the initial guess for η, π and as time increases to infinity the difference $\pi(t) - y^*$ will tend exponentially to a quantity which is proportional to the measurement error δ.

The construction of the nonlinear observer is an outgrowth of the geometric approach to control problems which has dominated the field within the last decade. A further application of nonlinear geometric control theory will be discussed in the next section.

3 COMPENSATION OF EXOGENOUS DISTURBANCES.

Given a control system influenced by two inputs u, v

$$\dot{x} = f(u, x, u, v), \qquad y = c(x). \tag{3.1}$$

u is the control which we have at our disposal at each time instant, v is an exogenous disturbance which we cannot eliminate directly and even sometimes cannot measure.
The problem is then to find a control law which reduces the influence of the disturbance upon the output, e.g. brings y close to 0 (= the value it would assume in case of the input 0).
There is an optimal control approach to this problem assuming the 'worst case' as far as the disturbance is concerned. In other words: (3.1) is treated as a two-person-zero-sum differential game and one is looking for a minimax-strategy for the player who chooses u. This interpretation avoids any assumptions concerning the nature of the disturbance. It is however not an economical solution. The best one can hope for is to arrive at a small bound for the ratio

$$\int_0^\infty ||y(t)||^2 dt \Big/ \int_0^\infty ||v(t)||^2 dt.$$

This is the ultimate goal of the so called H_∞-approach to the problem of disturbance attenuation. Note however that H_∞-theory works for disturbances with bounded total energy (i.e. $\int_0^\infty ||v(t)||^2 dt < \infty$) only. There are on the other hand practical situations where the system is under the influence of a persistent disturbance which has unbounded total energy. The approach which geometric control theory offers for the problem of disturbance attenuation is tailord to the situation. A control law which is constructed according to the geometric 'principle of internal modelling' is called a compensator. Compensation means: The deviation $y(t)$ of the output decays exponentially to its nominal value 0 even if the disturbance is persistent on $[0, \infty[$. 'Internal modelling' means that one assumes for the disturbance signal a dynamic model which then enters into the construction of the control law. One way of setting up a dynamic model is to write $v(\cdot)$ as a deterministic time signal depending upon 'hidden parameters'. Example (in case of a scalar v):

$$v(t) = \sum_i a_i \cos(\omega_i t + \varphi_i), \tag{3.2}$$

$\alpha_i, \omega_i, \varphi_i$ unknown. This 'Ansatz' covers a wide range of recurrent time signals. Working with it offers two advantages compared with the traditional stochastic approach. (i) There is no need to enter into discussion beyond (3.2), e.g. make assumptions concerning distribution of the paramters. (ii) The compensator does his job - bringing $y(t)$ asymptotically to 0 - in any individual case, not only in the statistical sense. He can do so because he has a learning capacity, i.e. he learns in the course of the time as much about the parameters as is necessary in order to outmanoeuvre the disturbance.
A comprehensive account of the construction of compensators - both for linear and nonlinear models - will be given in [3].

References

[1] N.Fenichel, Persistence and smoothness of invariant manifolds for flows. Indiana Univ. Math. J. vol 21 (1977) pp. 193-226.

[2] H.W.Knobloch, Foundations of invariant manifold theory for ordinary differential equations. In 'Recent Trends in Differential Equations', R.G. Agarwal ed., World Scientific Series in Applicable Analysis, vol. 1. World Scientific, Singapore etc., 1992 . pp. 365-392.

[3] A.Isidori, H.W.Knobloch and D. Flockerzi, Topics in Control Theory. To appear 1993, Birkhäuser Verlag, Basel

[4] H.W.Knobloch, Control under uncertain dynamics. To appear in 'Nonlinear Methods in Economic Dynamics and Optimal Control', G. Feichtinger and R.F. Hartl eds., Annals of Operations Research vol. 37 (1992).

[5] F.Lempio, Difference Methods for Monotone Differential Inclusions, see this volume.

[6] M.Schäfer, Exploitation of natural Ressources and Pollution, see this volume.

Remark. [1] and [2] are devoted exclusively to the mathematical foundation of the notion of an invariant manifold, a summary of it is given in [3] together with applications in control theory.

Difference Methods for Monotone Differential Inclusions

Frank Lempio
Lehrstuhl für Angewandte Mathematik, Universität Bayreuth
Postfach 10 12 51, 8580 Bayreuth, Germany

Differential equations, which are discontinuous with respect to the state variables, and differential inclusions model a whole variety of applications, e.g. mechanical systems with dry and viscous damping, electrical networks with switches, oscillations in visco-elasticity, optimization problems with nonsmooth data, dynamical systems with nondifferentiable potential, optimal control problems.

In the first part of our talk we give a short introduction into these applications, primarily by a series of test examples and model problems. Then the talk focusses on difference methods for initial value problems, especially on order of convergence results for the discrete approximation of the exact solution (in the uniquely solvable case) respectively the reachable set (in the non-uniquely solvable case). For a general introduction into these topics compare the survey paper [4] and the literature cited therein.

In the second part of our talk, as a model for an order of convergence analysis based on non-standard assumptions, order of convergence of Euler's method is investigated. Numerical tests with the classical explicit Euler method for special classes of problems suggest first order of convergence, although the classical Lipschitz condition does not hold, and although the exact solutions may stick to manifolds of discontinuities of their derivatives. The mathematical proof of this suggestion is sketched, exploiting a so-called strengthened one-sided Lipschitz condition, which is weaker than the classical Lipschitz condition, but stronger than the one-sided Lipschitz condition familiar from the numerical analysis of stiff differential equations. This strengthened one-sided Lipschitz condition is closely related to monotonicity properties of the underlying differential inclusion. For more details compare [6], for complete proofs [7]. First order convergence of explicit Euler method is illustrated by several numerical test examples. Moreover, it is demonstrated numerically that, even for more general explicit methods, higher order of convergence cannot be expected without additional transformation or localization techniques.

It is much more difficult to derive order of convergence results for difference methods approximating the whole solution funnel of general differential inclusions. For results concerning Euler's method and special classes of Runge-Kutta methods compare [4]. In the last part of our talk, we concentrate on a special approach for the numerical approximation of the reachable set of linear differential inclusions. This approach is based on the computation of Aumann's integral for set-valued mappings. It consists in exploiting ordinary quadrature formulae with nonnegative weights (e.g. certain closed or open Newton-Cotes formulae, Gauß quadrature, Romberg integration) for the numerical approximation of the dual representation of Aumann's integral via its support functional. This approach was outlined in the joint paper [2]. For problems which are smooth in an appropriate set-valued sense, this approach yields numerical methods of arbitrarily high order, e.g. extrapolation methods based on Romberg integration. For problems which are not smooth enough in that sense, this approach yields further insight into the order reduction phenomena encountered in the papers [8] and [9]. An indirect approach to numerical integration of set-valued mappings, based on embedding theorems for spaces of convex sets, is indicated in [5]. The talk finishes with visualizations of discrete approximations of reachable sets for linear differential inclusions by a series of computer plots.

References

[1] R. J. Aumann (1965) Integrals of Set-Valued Functions. *Journal of Mathematical Analysis and Applications*, **12**, no. 1, pp. 1–12.

[2] R. Baier and F. Lempio (1992) Computing Aumann's Integral. To appear in *Proceedings of the Workshop on Modelling Techniques for Uncertain Systems, July 6–10, 1992, Sopron (Hungary).*

[3] B. D. Doitchinov and V. M. Veliov (1991) Parametrizations of Integrals of Set-Valued Mappings and Applications, to appear in *Journal of Mathematical Analysis and Applications.*

[4] A. Dontchev and F. Lempio (1992) Difference Methods for Differential Inclusions: A Survey. *SIAM Review*, **34**, no. 2, pp. 263–294.

[5] T. D. Donchev and E. M. Farkhi (1990) Moduli of Smoothness of Vector Valued Functions of a Real Variable and Applications. *Numerical Functional Analysis and Optimization*, **11**, no. 5&6, pp. 497–509.

[6] F. Lempio (1990) Modified Euler Methods for Differential Inclusions. To appear in *Proceedings of the Workshop on Set-Valued Analysis and Differential Inclusions, September 17–21, 1990, Pamporovo (Bulgaria).*

[7] F. Lempio (1992) Euler's Method Revisited. Preprint.

[8] V. M. Veliov (1989) Discrete Approximations of Integrals of Multivalued Mappings, *Comptes rendus de l'Académie bulgare des Sciences*, **42**, no. 12, pp. 51–54.

[9] V. M. Veliov (1992) Second Order Discrete Approximation to Linear Differential Inclusions, *SIAM Journal on Numerical Analysis*, **29**, no. 2, pp. 439–451.

Discrete-Time Markovian Jump Linear Systems

K. Szajowski
Institute of Mathematics, Technical University of Wrocław
Wybrzeże Wyspiańskiego 27, 50-370 Wrocław, Poland
W.L. de Koning
Faculty of Technical Mathematics and Informatics, Delft University of Technology
Mekelweg 4, 2628 CD Delft, Netherlands

The research is oriented to the control of discrete - time linear systems with randomly changing parameters which can be described by a finite - state Markov chain. The cost critrion is a quadratic form of the controls and states of the system. The criterion parameters also depend on the states of the Markov chain. Two models of observation of the Markov chain are adopted – delay for one step and undelay. It is shown that under appropriate mean square detectability and stability conditions the infinite horizon optimal control problem for the general case of Markovian jump linear quadratic systems has a unique solution when the control system is mean square stable. Necessary and sufficient conditions are given to determine if a system is mean square stable.

This model can be use to formulate systems that are subject to abrupt changes in their structure and components due to failure, repairs, changing subsystem interconnections or system environment. This type of systems is sometimes called a "hybrid system". The stability and detectability properties for these systems are investigated.

Such systems were studied by Ji and Chizeck (1990). The case of i.i.d. parameters was considered by many authors. For references see Ji and Chizeck (1990) and de Koning (1982). Related results concerning the stability of such systems were obtained by Costa and Fragoso (1991). The control of such systems were considered recently by Blom (1991) and Yang and Bar-Shalom (1991). However, these results were based on other assumptions about the parameters or knowledge taken into account in the construction of the control.

Formulation of the problem

The paper deals with a discrete time linear system with Markovian jumps, modeled by

$$x_{k+1} = A(r_k)x_k + B(r_k)u_k, \tag{1}$$

where $k = 0, 1, \cdots, N$, $x_k \in \Re^n$, $u_k \in \Re^m$, $A \in \mathcal{M}^n_{\mathbb{E}}$, $B \in \mathcal{M}^{nm}$. $\mathcal{M}^{mn}$ denotes the space of all real $m \times n$ matrices with norm $\|A\| = \sup_{|x|=1} |Ax|$, where $A \in \mathcal{M}^{mn}$ and $x \in \Re^n$. We denote $\mathcal{M}^{nn}$ by $\mathcal{M}^n$ and let $\mathcal{S}^n \subset \mathcal{M}^n$ be a space of the real symmetric matrices. The zero and identity element in $\mathcal{M}^n$ are $\boldsymbol{O}$ and $\boldsymbol{I}$, respectively. The set of all non-negative definite matrices of $\mathcal{S}^n$ is denoted by $\mathcal{K}^n$. Put $\mathbb{E} = \{1, 2, \cdots, s\}$. We will denote by $\mathcal{M}^{mn}_{\mathbb{E}}$

the set of functions defined on $\mathbb{E}$ with values in $\mathcal{M}^{mn}$. Denote $\mathbb{I}$ the element of $\mathcal{M}^n_{\boldsymbol{E}}$ such that $\mathbb{I}(i) = \boldsymbol{I}$ and let $\Theta \in \mathcal{M}^n_{\boldsymbol{E}}$ be such that $\Theta(i) = \boldsymbol{O}$. For $f \in \mathcal{M}^{mn}_{\boldsymbol{E}}$ we define norm $\|f\|_* = \max_{r\in \boldsymbol{E}}\{\|f(r)\|\}$. N can be finite or infinite. It is assumed that x_0 is given and $\{r_k\}_{k=0}^N$ is a homogenous Markov chain defined on a fixed probability space $(\Omega, \mathcal{F}, P)$ with values in $\mathbb{E}$. Let $(p_i)_{i\in \boldsymbol{E}}$ and $(p_{ij})_{i,j\in \boldsymbol{E}}$ denote the initial and transition probabilities for this Markov chain, respectively. Let $\vec{u} = (u_0, u_1, \ldots, u_{N-1})$. In the finite horizon case, system (1) is considered with the cost criterion

$$J_N(\vec{u}, x_0) = \mathbf{E}\{\sum_{i=0}^{N-1}[x_i^T Q(r_i)x_i + u_i^T R(r_i)u_i] + x_N^T H(r_N)x_N|x_0\} \tag{2}$$

and in the infinite horizon case with the cost criterion

$$J(\vec{u}, x_0) = \mathbf{E}[\sum_{i=0}^{\infty} x_i^T Q(r_i)x_i + u_i^T R(r_i)u_i|x_0] \tag{3}$$

where $Q, H \in \mathcal{K}^n_{\boldsymbol{E}}$, $R \in \mathcal{K}^m_{\boldsymbol{E}}$.

Denote $r^k = (r_0, r_1, \ldots, r_k)$ and $z^k = (x_0, u_0, \ldots, x_{k-1}, u_{k-1}, x_k)$. The different classes of admissible controls can be considered for system (1) with criterion (2) or (3). We focus our attention on two different classes of strategies:

(D0) $u_i = g_i(z^i, r^i)$ - the control at moment i is based on information about the states, controls and states of the Markov chain up to moment i;

(D1) $u_i = g_i(z^i, r^{i-1})$ -uses the same information about the states and controls of the system as in (D0) but there is a one step delay in the observation of the state of the Markov chain.

We consider the optimal control problem for the classes of strategies (D0) and (D1). For i.i.d. random variables $\{r_n\}_{n=0}^N$, the knowledge of $r_0, \ldots, r_{k-1}$ has no influence for the *posterior* distribution of r_k. Taking this into account, the results of the paper for the class of control policies (D1) are a generalization of the considerations in De Koning (1982).

Finite horizon optimal control

Let us consider the case of controls (D1) i.e. based on the observation of states and for-one-step-delayed observations of the Markov chain. We assume $\mathbf{P}(r_{-1} = 1) = 1$ and $\mathbf{P}(r_0 = i|r_{-1} = j) = p_i$, $i, j \in \mathbb{E}$. For $A \in \mathcal{M}^{mn}_{\boldsymbol{E}}, B \in \mathcal{M}^n_{\boldsymbol{E}}$ adopt the following convention: $A(r)B(r) = [AB](r)$. The point of the following lemma is in the preliminary calculation of criterion (2) for the given controls. Denote $\bar{X}(r) = \mathbf{E}[X(r_1)|r_0 = r]$ for $X \in \mathcal{S}^n_{\boldsymbol{E}}$.

The cost criterion can be retyped in the equivalent form

$$\underline{J}_N(\vec{u}, x_0) = \mathbf{E}\{\sum_{i=0}^{N-1}[x_i^T \bar{Q}(r_{i-1})x_i + u_i^T \bar{R}(r_{i-1})u_i] + x_N^T \bar{H}(r_{N-1})x_N|x_0\} \tag{4}$$

and

$$\underline{J}_{n,N}(\vec{u}, x^n, r^{n-1}) = \mathbf{E}\{\sum_{i=n}^{N-1}[x_i^T \bar{Q}(r_{i-1})x_i + u_i^T \bar{R}(r_{i-1})u_i] + x_N^T \bar{H}(r_{N-1})x_N | x^n, r^{n-1}\}.$$

Let $\Psi \in \mathcal{M}^n_{\boldsymbol{E}\times\boldsymbol{E}}$ and $X \in \mathcal{M}^n_{\boldsymbol{E}}$. Denote $\overline{\Psi^T X \Psi}(r) = \mathbf{E}[\Psi^T(r_0, r_1)X(r_1)\Psi(r_0, r_1)|r_0 = r]$.

Lemma 1 *Let us consider system (1) with cost criterion (4). Suppose*

$$u_i = -L(r_{i-1})x_i \,, \tag{5}$$

where: $L \in \mathcal{M}^{mn}_{\boldsymbol{E}}$, then for every x_0

$$\underline{J}_N(\vec{u}, x_0) = x_0^T \mathcal{G}_L^N \bar{H}(r_{-1})x_0, \tag{6}$$

where: $\mathcal{G}_L : S^n_{\boldsymbol{E}} \to S^n_{\boldsymbol{E}}$ is defined by

$$\mathcal{G}_L X(r) = \mathcal{H}_L X(r) + \tilde{Q}_L(r)$$

where

$$\mathcal{H}_L X(r) = \overline{\Psi_L^T X \Psi_L}(r),$$

$\tilde{Q}_L(r) = \bar{Q}(r) + [L^T \bar{R} L](r)$ and $\Psi_L(r, s) = A(r) - B(r)L(s)$.

By the dynamic programming principle for the systems with the Markovian parameters (see Szajowski & de Koning (1992)) we get

Proposition 1 *Let the system be described by (1) with the cost criterion given by (2). The solution of the finite horizon optimal control problem with a delay in the observation of Markov parameter r_n for one step is given by*

$$\begin{aligned} u_N^* &= 0 \\ u_n^* &= -\bar{\mathcal{L}}\mathcal{G}^{N-n-1}\bar{H}(r_{n-1})x_n \end{aligned}$$

for $n = 0, 1, \ldots, N-1$ and

$$\underline{J}_N(\vec{u}^*) = x_0^T \mathcal{G}_*^N \bar{H}(r_{-1})x_0,$$

where $\mathcal{G}_* X(r) = \mathcal{G}_{\bar{\mathcal{L}}X} X(r)$,

$$\bar{\mathcal{L}}X(r) = [(\overline{B^T X B} + \bar{R})^+ \overline{B^T X A}](r).$$

The open form of operator $\mathcal{G}_*$ is as follows

$$\begin{aligned} \mathcal{G}_* X(r) &= \bar{Q}(r) + \overline{A^T X A}(r) \\ &\quad - [\overline{A^T X B}(\overline{B^T X B} + \bar{R})^+ \overline{B^T X B}](r) \end{aligned}$$

Infinite horizon optimal control

The properties of operator $\mathcal{G}_*$ and $\mathcal{G}_L$ show that the finite horizon optimal control problem is an approximation for the infinite horizon control problem (see de Koning (1982)). We get

Theorem 1 *If system (1) is ms-stabilizable by a control dependent on the delayed observation of the Markov chain, then* $S(r) = \lim_{N\to\infty} \mathcal{G}_*^N \Theta$ *exists and* S *is the minimal solution in* $\mathcal{K}_{\mathbb{E}}^n$ *of the equation* $S = \mathcal{G}_* S$.

and

Theorem 2 *Let* $S = \lim_{N\to\infty} \mathcal{G}_*^N \Theta$ *exist and* $u_i = -\mathcal{L}S(r_{i-1})x_i$ *for every* $i \in \mathbb{N}$. *We have*

$$J(\vec{u}) = x_0^T S x_0.$$

We can also obtain the stability condition for the optimal control.

Theorem 3 *Let* $S = \lim_{N\to\infty} \mathcal{G}_*^N \Theta$ *exist. If* $\bar{R}(r)$ *is positive definite for every* r, (A, C) *is ms-detectable or* $\bar{Q}(r)$ *is positive definite then system (7) with* $\Psi(r,s) = \Psi_{\mathcal{L}S}(r,s)$ *is stable and* $S(r)$ *it is the unique non-negative definite solution of the equation* $S = \mathcal{G}_* S$.

The equivalent conditions and theorem can be stated for the system without a delay of the observation of the Markov chain. To this end, operator $\mathcal{G}_*$ should be replaced by $\mathcal{D}_*$ and $\bar{R}, \bar{Q}$ by R, Q, respectively.

On the basis of the solution of the infinite horizon optimal control problem one can state the criterion of stabilizability. Let us consider the stability of the close loop control system

$$x_{k+1} = \Psi(r_{k-1}, r_k)x_k \tag{7}$$

for $k = 0, 1, 2, \ldots, N-1$. System (7) can be obtained from (1) when we assume controls (5).

Theorem 4 *System (1) is ms-stabilizable by controls based on the delayed observation of the Markov chain if and only if sequence* $\{K_n(r)\}$, *obtained from the following recursive equation*

$$\begin{aligned} K_n &= I + \overline{A^T \bar{K}_{n-1} A}(r) \\ &- \overline{A^T \bar{K}_{n-1} B}(I + \overline{B^T \bar{K}_{n-1} B})^+ \overline{B^T \bar{K}_{n-1} A}(r) \end{aligned} \tag{8}$$

with initial condition $K_0(r) = 0$ *for every* $r \in \mathbb{E}$, *converges to a set of symmetric, non-negative definite matrices as* n *tends to infinity.*

References

H. A. BLOM (1991) *Hybrid state estimation for systems with semi-markov switching coefficients*, in Trans. of European Control Conference '91 Grenoble, France, pp. 1132 - 1137.

L. V. COSTA AND M. D. FRAGOSO (1991) *Stability results for discrete-time linear systems with markovian jumping parameters*, Relatiórios de pesquisa e desenvolvimento 021/91, LNCC/CNPq Rio de Janerio, Nov. 1991.

W. L. DE KONING (1982) *Infinite horizon optimal control of linear discrete time systems with stochastic parameters*, Automatica, 18, pp. 443–453.

Y. JI AND H. CHIZECK (1990) *Jump linear quadratic gaussian control: stady-state solution and testable conditions*, Control-Theory and Advanced Technology, 6, pp. 289 - 319.

K. SZAJOWSKI AND W. DE KONING (1992) *Discrete-time markovian jump linear systems*, Tech. Rep. 92-37, Fac. Mathematics and Informatics, Delft Univ. of Technology.

C. YANG AND Y. BAR-SHALOM (1991) *Stabilizing control of partially observed hybrid systems*, in Trans. of European Control Conference '91 Grenoble, France pp. 1152 - 1157.

Change Speeds and Time Scales in Economic Dynamics —An Insight by Synergetic Economics

Wei-Bin Zhang
Institute for Futures Studies
Hagagatan 23B, Box 6799, 113 85 Stockholm, Sweden

The purpose of this study is to discuss the relationship between change speeds of economic variables and time scales in economic dynamics in the light of synergetic economics. First, we theoretically discuss the issue. Second, we argue that economic variables have different change speeds in different societies. The following table provides, in rough sense, some examples about the relationship between "types", such as agriculturial, industrial and knowledge-based, of societies and change speeds of the three important - population, capital and knowledge - variables.

Change Speeds of the Economic Variables

	agriculture	industry	knowledge
population	fast	fast/slow	slow
capital	slow	slow/fast	fast
knowledge	slow	slow/fast	fast

Third, we show that it is possible to classify the classical economic theories by, e.g., Adam Amith, Ricardo, Malthus, Marx and neoclassical growth economists, according to the relationship between change speeds and time scales. Fourth, we provide a dynamic economic development model with endogenous population, capital, knowledge and economic structure. Finally, we conclude the study. In the appendix we provide a theorem by Pliss and Sell, which shows a dynamic structure with fast and slow process.

Section 6

Decision Support and Information Systems

A Formal Treatment of Relevance Information in Ill-Structured Environments

D. Androutsopoulos
Dept. of Information Technology, Lappeennranta Univ. of Technology
PL 2O, 53851 Lappeenranta Finland
P. Spirakis
Computer Technology Institute, Patras University
P.O. Box 1122, 26 110 Patras, Greece

Information pertaining to real-life problems is rarely known with complete confidence. It is usually uncertain. In such an environment of uncertainty and imprecision, rational decision making depends not only on the facts and rules explicitly connected to a problem, but also on knowledge pieces not very clearly connected to the considered case. The problem of processing the evidence in a knowledge-based system requires, for its solution, to articulate the conditions under which an item of information is <u>relevant</u> to another.

The notion of relevance is especially useful in some ill-structured application domains. Such a domain is the <u>management of risks</u> in software projects concerning large information systems. In such projects, the strategy of the manager is based upon her/his (maybe only intuitive) knowledge of the degree of relative importance among knowledge pieces. A formal support of the notion of relevance might be useful in enhancing the abilities of existing decision-making tools to capture the human experts intuition. At least, the information pieces of critical importance to the success of a project should be highlighted by a succesful tool.

The method of <u>factors of relative importance</u> (FRI's) has been proposed in [Androutsopoulos, 90] in order to characterize the relation of knowledge pieces not directly connected to a particular problem:

<u>Definition 1</u> : Given two knowledge pieces k and i (where i maybe an item of some domain) the factor of relative importance (FRI) of k for i (denoted by FRI (k,i)) is the belief of the importance of k for i. FRI (k,i) is a number in [0,1]. (see also [Androutsopoulos, 90]).

---

*

This work was partially supported by the EEC ESPRIT Basic Research Actions Project ALCOM (3075)

Note that relative importance is not a symmetric notion ("Mary is pregnant" can be extremely important for "the project will fail" but not vise-versa).

In this work, we have chosen the probabilistic approach to formally support the FRI's. As many researchers have noticed, the notions of the relevance and dependence are similar and can be expressed qualitatively through the probabilistic approach ([Rich, 83], [Mc Carthy, 86], [Pearl, 88]).

Hypothesis I for FRI's For any set of consistent FRI's in a knowledge base, there exists a probability distribution over elementary knowledge pieces so that, for each k and i, FRI (k,i) = Prob {i given k}.

In the sequel, we shall represent knowledge pieces by propositional variables or propositional formulas. It is interesting to note that a similar approach to that of conditional probabilities can be followed when using other uncertainly calculi to model FRI's (e.g. Dempster-Shafer, fuzzy sets or MYCIN/EMYCIN calculi). However serious semantic and computational complexity differences appear, (see [Henkind, Harrison, 88,[Buxton,89]) whose investigation is an interesting, open, research question.

Definition 2: A knowledge piece b is of no importance to another knowledge piece a given the knowledge piece k if $FRI(b \wedge k, a) = FRI(k,a)$ when this holds $\forall K$ other than b and a, then b is called irrelevant to a.

Clearly, FRI's can be represented by Bayesian Networks i.e. directed acyclic graphs in which the nodes are knowledge pieces and the arcs signify the relative importance of the tail for the head by weight (strength) number. Following our formalism, FRI's can be updated by the Bayesian law ie

$$FRI\_(e,a) = FRI(b \wedge e,a) * FRI(e,b) + FRI(\bar{b} \wedge e,a) * FRI(e,\bar{b})$$

where $\bar{b}$ is the negation of b.

The inference problem for FRI's is a central problem (as in any uncertainty calculi intented to be used by knowledge-based systems). The problem is the following:

Definition 3 Given a set of FRI's for knowledge pieces of a knowledge base and two such pieces x and y, **the inference problem for FRI's** is the problem:
"Is the statement $FRI \geq (x,y)$ v (where v E [0,1]) consistent with the given set of FRI's?"

The above problem asks to find whether there exists an underlying joint probability distribution on elementary knowledge pieces to support the augmented set of FRI equalities or inequalities. Unfortunately:

Theorem 1 The inference problem for FRI's is NP-complete, even when the related information pieces are elementary.

Proof We reduce the problem of coloring the vertices of a graph with 3 colours to it (see full paper for details).

To overcome the inherent difficulty of inference for FRI's we have either to use approximations (linear programming over the set of variables satisfying the FRI constraints (see full paper) or to employ restricted sets of FRI's (e.g. in Bayesian networks with disjoint or independent evidence assumptions an inference can be judged in time proportional to the number of network links).

FRI's can be used as importance constraints (ie a special form of integrity constraints) in order to give semantics to database relations.

Definition 4 In a relational database, let each relation R $(A_1, \ldots, A_n)$ be accompanied by a set of FRI's of the form FRI $(S_\lambda, A_k) = v$
where S_λ is the conjuction of some A_j's and $0 \leq f \geq 1$. These FRI's are called importance constraints E.g. a rule $A_i \Longrightarrow A_j$ is represented by FRI $(A_i, A_j) = 1$.

Which are the knowledge pieces of almost critical importance to all the knowledge-base?
We capture this by the notion of ε-keys:

Definition 5 Let $\varepsilon > 0$ a small real number. The ε-keys of R $(A_1, \ldots, A_n)$ are the minimal subsets S of $\{A_1, \ldots, A_n\}$ for which, for all i, FRI $(\Lambda S, A_i) \geq 1 - \varepsilon$ (Λ S means the conjuction of all attributes in S).

The handling of ε-keys resembles ε-semantics and ε-entailment (see e.g. [Adams, 75]). The notion of ε-keys (and ε-implication) is axiomatized in the full paper. By working through an iteration process we can show that

Theorem 2 Let R $(A_1, \ldots, A_n)$ a relation and F the set of associated FRI's. If the diameter of the Bayesian network representing F is small compared to $1/\varepsilon$ then an ε-key can be found in time $O(n^* |F|^* \lambda)$ where λ = length of longest FRI in F.

REFERENCES

[Adams,75] Adams E., "The logic of conditionals", Dordrecht, Netherlands, D. Reidel.

[Androutsopoulos,90] Androutsopoulos D., "Relating Domain Knowledge in an ill-structured software environment", COGNITIVA, 90.

[Buxton,89], Buxton R. "Modelling Uncertainly in Expert Systems", Int. J. Man-Machine Studies, (1989) 31, 415-476

[Dempster,68] Dempster A.P., 68, "A generalization of Bayesian inference" J. Royal Statist.Soc.Ser. B 30: 205-247

[Geiger, Pearl,88] Geiger D., Pearl J., "On the logic of influence diagrams", Proc. 4th Workshop on Uncertainty in AI, Proceedings.

[Henkind, Harrison,88] Henkind S., Harrison M. "An Analysis of Four Uncertainty Calculi", IEEE Trans on Systems, Man and Cybernetics, 18,(5), 700-713.

[Kim, Pearl,87] "CONVINCE: A conversational inference consolidation engine", IEEE Trans. on Systems, Man and Cybernetics, 17 (no.2), 120-132.

[Mc Carthy,86] Mc Carthy J., "Applications of circumscription to formalizing common-sense knowledge", Artificial Intelligence, 28 (no.1), 89-116.

[Pearl,82] Pearl J., "Reverend Bayes on inference engines: A distributed hierarchical approach", Proc.Nat.Conf. on AI (Pittsburgh), 133-136.

[Pearl,88] Pearl J., "Probabilistic Reasoning in Intelligent Systems", Morgan-Kaufmann ed.

[Schmalhofer,92] Schmalhofer F., Thoben J., "The model-Based Construction of a Case-Oriented Expert System", AICOM 5(1), March 1992., 3-18.

[Shafer,76] Shafer G., "A mathematical theory of evidence", Princeton Univ.Press.

[Verma,86] Verma T.S., "Causal Networks: Semantics and expressiveness" TR R-65, CS Lab, UCLA.

On Interactive Graphical Application Programs

Katharina Belling-Seib
Almanca Isletme ve Enformatik Bölümü, Marmara Üniversitesi
Anadoluhisari Kampüsü, Istanbul, Turkey

Today there is an increasing interest in *interactive graphical application programs*, that is in software that allows to run applications interactively using graphical interfaces. These applications may be OR applications from the mathematical programming field: modelling or solving a LP/IP based decision problem or from application fields like production planning or scheduling.

The following example will stress the characteristics of an interactive graphical application program. It deals with a simple linear programming problem with 2 variables: Fig.1 presents the problem. Two ways of representing an LP-problems with two variables have been chosen for presentation: the tableau format and a graphical format.

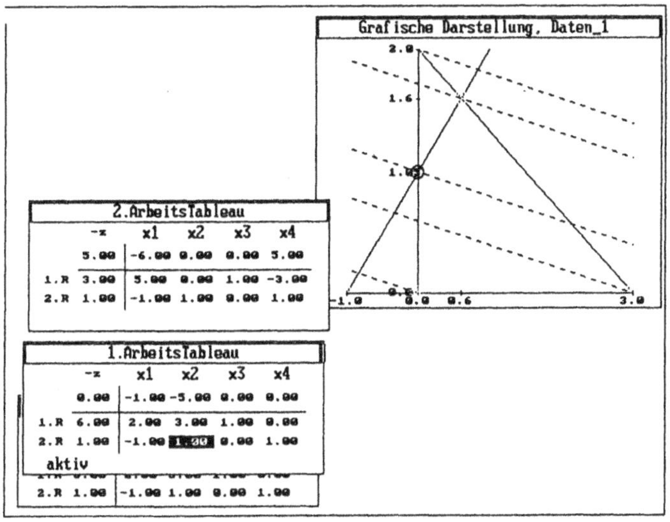

Fig.1: '1.ArbeitsTableau' contains the problem data; '2.ArbeitsTableau' shows the data after pivoting on the item marked in the active tableau. In the graphical representation the corner point that corresponds to the current solution is marked.

The interactive application program supports among others the following interactions between the (end-)user and the computer system with respect to the application:

- The user chooses a pivot element from the active tableau via some select mechanism. System reaction: If the element is nonzero, the selected element is highlighted and the pivot step executed. The solution that corresponds to the active tableau is also marked in the geometrical representation of the tableau (fig.1).

The user modifies the problem data by selecting the element whose value will be changed from the tableau with the problem data (AusgangsTableau, which is hidden in fig.1).
System reaction: A box is displayed where the new value is typed in. The new value is written to the tableau and on request all information presented to the user is adjusted to the modified problem (not shown here).

According to this example an interactive graphical application program is characterized as a software program that allows the user to run an application interactively on a graphical interface. In most cases the user is in charge of the interactions, i.e. the user is free to choose among a number of currently valid options, he thus takes the iniatives in the dialogue. The application need not be graphical by nature; i.e. the graphical presentation usually is a visualisation of the application, not the application itself.

Today, most of the interactive application programs exist in non-OR disciplines like the CAx applications and in an increasing number and variety of information systems.

For the design and the implementation of an interactive graphical application program some decisions have to made, decisions on

- what precisely is the application
- what should be presented to the user and in what way
- what interactions between the user and the system should be allowed.

There are three ways of how a user can get an interactive graphical application program. The first way is buying a program that is basically ready for use. These programs have the advantage that no or almost no preprocessing is required, but this for the prize of only minimal customization. The second way is doing most of the development oneself including all programming (but possibly excluding subtasks which can be handed over to application independend tools) - or asking someone to do that task; this method renders a broad scope for the design of the final product. It, however, is very expensive and may restrict or even prevent later changes of the final product. The third way is using a development environment (toolset) that allows an *application programmer* to develop an interactive graphical application program from prespecified components. This environment will be tailored to the respective application. Apart from that, it should render free scope for modelling the final program.
The paper concentrates on this type of development systems, which is expected to framework future interactive application systems: These development systems are able to provide a maximum of flexibility w.r.t. the field of applications as well as to the end-users' needs. A system that allows an application programmer to specify the application and the grafical representation and hence to model the activity space for the end-user is comparable to an authoring system in that an author specifies which information to present and which user-system-interactions to permit; it also compares to an user-interface management system in that screen layout, interactions and system reactions have to be specified. Development systems considered here, however, put more emphasis on the application side than user-interface management systems today do. Since such development systems combine features of the aforementioned systems they are more complex.

In order to provide to the application programmer an effective environment we need to have

- a carefully designed architecture of the final software product, the graphical application program, which serves as basis for
- a carefully designed architecture of the development systems that will be used by the application programmer to develop the application program.

Since the application programmer is rather on the user's side than on a programmer's side the applicability of the development systems depends heavily on the language the application programmer will use to specify the graphical application program. The specification language will be the essential part of the application programmer's interface.

An interactive graphical application program typically consists of subsystems that accomplish specific tasks. The graphical, the application and the control subsystems are the main subsystems; they in turn are built from subsystems. The graphical subsystem provides and controls the display objects and their functionality; it transforms user input into actions and vice versa transforms behavior of system components into output; it also controls the purely graphical actions (like changing size or position of windows, zooming or scrolling the contents of a window). The application subsystem provides and controls the application objects and their functionality; it also controls application oriented operations. The control subsystem is in charge of the interaction between the end-user and the graphical subsystems as well as of the interaction between the graphical subsystem and the application subsystem. It is responsible for the overall stability.

This structure of an interactive graphical application program is mirrored by the development system. It supplies 'bricks' to the application programmer. According to the above scheme the bricks partition into graphical components, application components, and into agents for the interactions tasks. The agents are in charge for the event handling which is the most complicated part within the dialog control system.

The application programmer's interface (API) is part of the development system; it mediates between the user of the system, hence the application programmer, and the computer system. The API is characterized by the language the application programmer uses to specify the application program. Current software technology and lack of experience in the field of interactive application programs limit the collection of specification languages that can be translated automatically into the interactive application program [Pomberger, 1990], [Brass/Coutaz, 1991]. The type of language mostly used is the generation of interactive application programs from specifications formulated in a graphical or high-level textual language.

The software system that served to produce the above example is currently being redesigned. The component culture of the object-oriented design principles will serve as basis for the architecture of the final application programs as well as for the development system which will allow a user-oriented specification of the application program. Consequently, the process of generating the application program and running the application will be strictly separated. The field of application will be taken from the vehicle scheduling realm because the basic problem is easy to survey. Tackling the problem, however, requires the flexibility to shift between several solution methods, most of them heuristics including some operations 'by hand'.

References

Bass,L. and Coutaz,J. (1991) Developing Software for the User Interface, Addison-Wesley, Reading MA.

Pomberger, G (1990) Methodik der Softwareentwicklung, in K.Kurbel and H.Strunz (eds), Handbuch der Wirtschaftsinformatik, Stuttgart 1990.

Embedding OR Techniques in Constraint Logic Programming

Alexander Bockmayr
Max-Planck-Institut für Informatik
Im Stadtwald, 6600 Saarbrücken, Germany

1 Constraint Logic Programming

Constraint logic programming has been one of the major developments in the area of declarative programming during the last five years [Col87, JL87, DvHS+88, ASS+88]. The main idea is to combine the expressive power of a logic programming language similar to PROLOG with the efficiency of a constraint solver for a specific domain of computation. The most important constraint domains that have been considered so far are linear arithmetic over real or rational numbers, Boolean algebra, finite domains, and lists.

A *constraint logic program* over an algebra $\mathcal{A}$ [JL87] consists of a finite set of *rules* of the form

$$p_0(\vec{t_0}) :- c_1(\vec{u_1}), \ldots, c_m(\vec{u_m}) \parallel p_1(\vec{t_1}), \ldots, p_n(\vec{t_n})$$

where p_i, $0 \leq i \leq n$, are predicate symbols different from the relation symbols in $\mathcal{A}$, c_j, $0 \leq j \leq m$, are symbols denoting relations in $\mathcal{A}$, and $\vec{t_i}, \vec{u_j}$ are tuples of terms of $\mathcal{A}$ with additional free function symbols. The *declarative semantics* of such a rule is that the *head* $p_0(\vec{t_0})$ is logically implied by the conjunction $c_1(\vec{u_1}) \wedge \ldots \wedge c_m(\vec{u_m}) \wedge p_1(\vec{t_1}) \wedge \ldots \wedge p_n(\vec{t_n})$ of all *constraints* $c_j(\vec{u_j})$ and *atoms* $p_i(\vec{t_i})$ in the *body*.

Given a constraint logic program one has to choose a *goal*, which has exactly the same form as the body of a rule. The *operational semantics* is based on two components: a constraint solver for $\mathcal{A}$-relations and an adaptation of the goal reduction technique in classical logic programming. For example, from the goal

$$?- \ c(t_1) \parallel p(t_2)$$

and the rule

$$p(t_3) :- d(t_4) \parallel q(t_5)$$

we may derive the new goal

$$?- \ [c(t_1), t_2 \doteq t_3, d(t_4)]' \parallel q(t_5)$$

provided that the constraint $c(t_1), t_2 \doteq t_3, d(t_4)$ is solvable in $\mathcal{A}$ and $[c(t_1), t_2 \doteq t_3, d(t_4)]'$ is its *solved form*. A *derivation sequence* consists of goals with solvable constraints. It is *successful* when the last goal contains only constraints. These are called *answer constraints* and constitute the output of the program. A derivation sequence is *finitely failed* if the last goal cannot be expanded.

It has turned out that for the design of constraint solvers, mathematical programming techniques are extremely useful. For example, the constraint solvers for linear arithmetic are based on modified versions of the simplex algorithm. More generally, the combination of logic programming and constraint solving has the following benefits. From the viewpoint of logic programming, constraint solving techniques enhance the efficiency of logic programs. From the viewpoint of operations research, a high-level declarative programming language is available in addition to a mathematical programming tool. This means that the problem to be solved can be represented in a natural and declarative way. Moreover, one can express even those problem features that do not fit into the mathematical programming formalism. Finally, the use of symbolic constraints may help to reduce the search space [vH89].

2 Logic Programming with Pseudo-Boolean Constraints

In [JL87] a general scheme CLP($\mathcal{X}$) for constraint logic programming languages has been developed. We now focus on a specific instance of this scheme, the language CLP($\mathcal{PB}$) for logic programming with pseudo-Boolean constraints which was introduced in [Boc92].

A *pseudo-Boolean function* is an integer-valued function $f : \{0,1\}^n \rightarrow \mathcal{Z}$ of 0-1 variables [HR68]. Any such function can be represented as a multilinear polynomial in its variables. A *pseudo-Boolean constraint* is an equation or inequality between pseudo-Boolean functions. One of the most interesting aspects of pseudo-Boolean constraints is that they make it possible to combine two of the most important domains in constraint logic programming: arithmetic and Boolean algebra.

A very simple example for the language is the following knapsack problem. Suppose there is a vessel with capacity w and goods g_i with weight w_i and value v_i for $i = 1, \ldots, n$. We introduce a Boolean variable $X_i, i = 1, \ldots, n$, which indicates whether or not g_i is loaded on the vessel. The possible cargos not exceeding the capacity of the vessel can be determined by the following rule involving a pseudo-Boolean constraint

$$\texttt{cargo}(X_1, \ldots, X_n) \texttt{ :- } \\ w_1 * X_1 + \ldots + w_n * X_n \leq w \, .$$

If we want to find the most valuable cargo, this can be done using a two-place metapredicate *max* that maximizes a pseudo-Boolean function subject to some pseudo-Boolean constraint.

$$\texttt{most-valuable-cargo}(X_1, \ldots, X_n) \texttt{ :- } \\ \texttt{max}(v_1 * X_1 + \ldots + v_n * X_n, \ \texttt{cargo}(X_1, \ldots, X_n)) \, .$$

From the general results of [JL87] we can derive for the language CLP($\mathcal{PB}$):

- the existence of a canonical domain of computation
- the existence of a least and greatest model semantics
- the existence of a least and greatest fixpoint semantics

- soundness and completeness results for successful derivations of the underlying implementation model
- soundness and completeness results for finitely failed derivations of the underlying implementation model
- soundness and completeness results for negation as failure

For the moment, only a prototype implementation of CLP($\mathcal{PB}$) is available [Bar92]. It is based on a meta-interpreter written in CLP($\mathcal{R}$), a constraint logic programming language for linear arithmetic over real numbers [JMSY90]. The meta-interpreter consists of only 300 lines of source code and should be seen as a platform for testing various methods for constrained nonlinear 0-1 programming [HJM89].

References

[ASS+88] A. Aiba, K. Sakai, Y. Sato, D.J. Kawley, and R. Hasegawa. Constraint logic programming language CAL. In *Fifth Generation Computer Systems, Tokyo, 1988.* Springer, 1988.

[Bar92] P. Barth. CLP(PB): A Meta-Interpreter in CLP(R). Technical report, Max-Planck-Institut für Informatik, Saarbrücken, 1992.

[Boc92] A. Bockmayr. Logic programming with pseudo-Boolean constraints. In A. Colmerauer and F. Benhamou, editors, *Constraint Logic Programming - Selected Research.* MIT Press, 1992. (to appear).

[Col87] A. Colmerauer. Introduction to PROLOG III. In *4th Annual ESPRIT Conference, Bruxelles.* North Holland, 1987.

[DvHS+88] M. Dincbas, P. van Hentenryck, H. Simonis, A. Aggoun, and T. Graf. The constraint logic programming language CHIP. In *Fifth Generation Computer Systems, Tokyo, 1988.* Springer, 1988.

[HJM89] P. Hansen, B. Jaumard, and V. Mathon. Constrained nonlinear 0-1 programming. Technical Report RRR 47-89, Rutgers Center for Operations Research, 1989.

[HR68] P.L. Hammer and S. Rudeanu. *Boolean Methods in Operations Research and Related Areas.* Springer, 1968.

[JL87] J. Jaffar and J.-L. Lassez. Constraint logic programming. In *Proc. 14th ACM Symp. Principles of Programming Languages*, Munich, 1987.

[JMSY90] Joxan Jaffar, Spiro Michaylov, Peter Stuckey, and Roland Yap. The CLP($\mathcal{R}$) language and system. Technical Report RC 16292 (#72336) 11/15/90, IBM Research Division, November 1990.

[vH89] P. van Hentenryck. A logic language for combinatorial optimization. *Annals of Operations Research*, 21:247–274, 1989.

Cost/Benefit Analysis used in the Feasability Projects

Virgil Chichernea
Informatics Division, Ministry of Education and Science
70738 Bucharest, Romania

The purpose of any cost/benefit analysis is to balance the cost against the benefits associated with an activity. The fesability projects, like other economic projects, should be measured by its ability to provide sufficient benefits to justify its cost. The objective of cost/benefit analysis, method developed by the International Bank for Reconstruction and Development, is to use objective economic criteria in all our judgements to select efieciently fesability studies.

I. "THE DIESEL ENGINE" - CASE STUDY

1. The Project's Background.

The project includes the construction of new DIESEL ENGINE for cut down the operation expenses and mentenance. The cost of this project (research and design activities) is about of 1300 monetary units (m.u.) and working time for do it is 1 year. The actual operation expenses are 1270 m.u./year and new operation expenses (when this project will be working) will be roughly 1060 m.u./year.

Knowing that lifetime of this project is 10 years, and last stage of rate of return is 12%, we need to decide if this project is acceptable. We observe that the difference between old operation expenses and the new ones represents the net profit of this project and its achievement is simultaneously with actual DIESEL ENGINE using. Consequently the cost in the first year of lifetime of this project is: 1270 +1300 = 2570 m.u. The data of this project are presented in table 1 (discount rate: i = 12% and i = 10%).

TABLE No. 1

YEAR	THE COST STREAMS ACTUAL	NEW PROJECT	NET BENEFIT	i=12%	PRESENT VALUE	i=10%	PRESENT VALUE
1	-1270	-2570	-1300	0.893	-1161	0.909	-1055
2	-1270	-1060	+ 210	0.797	167	0.826	173
3	-1270	-1060	+ 210	0.712	150	0.751	158
4	-1270	-1060	+ 210	0.636	134	0.683	143
5	-1270	-1060	+ 210	0.567	119	0.621	130
6	-1270	-1060	+ 210	0.507	106	0.564	118
7	-1270	-1060	+ 210	0.452	95	0.513	108
8	-1270	-1060	+ 210	0.404	85	0.467	98
9	-1270	-1060	+ 210	0.361	76	0.424	89
10	-1270	-1060	+ 210	0.322	68	0.386	81
11	-1270	-1060	+ 210	0.287	60	0.350	74
TOTAL	-13970	-13170	+ 800		-101		+117

The net profit of this project (from table 1) is 210 m.u./year and though total cost of project (investment is 1300) is recover in 7 years, nevertheless this project is rejected because:

Benefit/Cost Ratio = 0.91 < 1; Rate of Return = 11.07 < 12%.

In this context the management team of this project obtain 2 new technical solution :

TABLE No. 2

COST STREAMS	TECHNICAL SOLUTION A	B
Total project cost	2200 m.u.	2630 m.u.
Operation expenses/year	860 m.u./year	804 m.u./year

The lifetime of both solution of this project is 10 years, the lost stage of rate of return is 12% and operation expenses and maintenance for actual DIESEL ENGINE is 1270 m.u./year. The work time for achieve this project in each version is 1 year and the achievement of these activities is simultaneously with actual DIESEL ENGINE using. We need to choise one of these technical solution. To select one of the two fesability study (technical solution) we use teh cost/benefit analysis: TABLE 3

COST/BENEFIT INDICATORS	FESABILITY STUDIES (technical solution)	
	A	B
Benefit Cost Ratio	1.05	1.00
Present Value	+103	+ 2
Rate of Return	12,3%	12.0%

The version A is selected. Cost Parametric Analysis and Risk Analysis will be offere new information about this project.

II. COST BENEFIT PACKAGE (ACB/PC)

The cost/benefit analysis includes computational procedure to obtain the following:

1. **Rate of Return (RR)** is the discount rate that makes the net present value of a project equal to zero. This implies solving for the discount rate R the polynomial equation:

$$\sum_{i=1}^{N} \left(\left(\sum_{j=1}^{N1} Bij - \sum_{j=1}^{N2} Cij \right) / \left(1 + 0.01R \right)^{i-1} \right) = 0 \quad (1).$$

where: N1 is the number of benefit streams;
N2 is the number of cost streams;
R is the discount rate expressed as a percentage;
N is the lifetime of the project in years;
Cij is the i item, in the j cost stream;
Bij is the i item, in the j benefit stream.

Equation (1) is solved by succesive approximations for range -20% to 100%.

2. **The Present Value (PV)** is the discounting procedure which is performed over the set of curent streams. The procedure is performed as many times as discount rates (R) are given by the user.

$$PV = \sum_{i=1}^{N} \left(\left(\sum_{j=1}^{N1} Bij - \sum_{j=1}^{N2} Cij \right) / \left(1 + 0.01R \right)^{i-1} \right) \quad (2).$$

Where all symbols have the same meaning as in (1).

3. **Cost Parametric Analysis (CPA)** explores the effect of changes in constuction costs on the internal rate of return and timing of a project. The analysis is performed simultaneously for total benefit as defined (base benefits) and for changes between -15% and +15%. The names of the streams containing the construction costs are given by the user.

The procedure assumes that:

- the number of construction years remains unchanged;
- the yearly percentwise distribution of construction costs remains unchanged unless a new set of percentages is given.

4. **Benefit/Cost Ratio (BCR)** is defined as the ratio, expressed as a decimal fraction between the present value of total benefits and the present value of total costs of a project:

$$BCR = \left(\sum_{i=1}^{N} \left(\sum_{j=1}^{N2} Bij \,/\, (1+0.01R)^{i-1} \right) \right) \Big/ \left(\sum_{i=1}^{N} \left(\sum_{j=1}^{N1} Cij \,/\, (1+0.01R)^{i-1} \right) \right)$$

The benefit cost ratio is computed for a many discount rates as given by the user.

5. **A Risk Analysis** can be performed over any cost/benefit parameter accepted by ACB/PC package. It amounts to repeated computations of the same parameter, using in each case cost/benefit data that is modified by random variation expressed as a percentage of original values prior to each computation. The sample being analysed is an artificial sample made on the basis of random patterns of variations (probability distributions accepted are: uniform; normal; beta; discrete; step rectangular; triangular; trapezoidal distribution) which, in the analyst's judgement, reflect the real uncertainty of his cost and benefit estimates. The streams affected by uncertainty are designated by the user upon request by ACB/PC, DOS package.

REFERENCES

1. Louis Y. Poliquen. Risk Analysis in project appraisal. The World Bank Group (1983).

2. Cost Benefit Package (CBPACK). Users Manual - The World Bank Group

A Decision Support System for Diet Planning

Talib Damij
Faculty of Economics, University of Ljubljana
Kardeljeva pl. 17, 61000 Ljubljana, Slovenia

Introduction

Dietary experts have to deal with very different requirements, specific situations and many cases of decision making in both their daily work and their research. That is why they need efficient and specialized software to support their efforts to find a satisfactory number of convenient meals to generate different nutrition plans for any specified diet.

The general objectives of diet planning are recognized as achieving palatable, nutritionally balanced and economical diets, that satisfy a certain set of requirements. The objectives of palatability in diet planning are carried through by imposing formal requirements on the structure of menu components and also on the variety of menu items within the components.

The nutrition planning problem is concerned with finding the optimal solutions (combinations of menu items) which satisfy specified nutritional, structural and variety requirements for a sequence of days. The nutritional requirements are determined by physicians. The structural requirements are determined by diet experts and defined by partitioning the menu items into specified classes. This specification enables the system to obtain such a solution which has mostly one menu item from each class. So, food classes make up the structure of meals depending upon the habits and standards of institutions. The variety requirements are defined by dietary experts by determining a number of days for every menu item. These requirements are satisfied by restricting the repetition of menu items for a predetermined number of days.

The Methodology

The best solution for this problem can be obtained with the use of mathematical programming methods such as linear and goal programming approaches. The most popular technique is linear programming. Linear programming is used to find the minimum cost combination of menu items which satisfies nutritional and other requirements. The goal programming method is a modification and extension of linear programming which can be used to optimize the nutritional balance which is achieved through replacement of cost minimization in the objective function with the total deviation of the nutrients from specified levels required for optimum balance (Anderson 1983).

After many experiments an efficient algorithm was developed, which finds the optimal solution and helps to create an interactive dialogue between the system and the dietary expert. The dietary expert may define his judgement to accept, modify or refuse the solution.

The System

DOPTIS (Diet Optimization System) is a Decision Support System specialized for the field of nutritional planning. This system consists of three parts or subsystems.

DOPTIS (Diet Optimization System)

- DOPTIS
  - Data
    - Foods
    - Menu Items
    - Meals
    - Diets
    - Plans
    - Conditions
  - Methodology
    - Cost Optimization
    - Nutritional Balance Optimization
    - Manual Meal Creation
  - Reports
    - Foods
    - Plans
    - Diets

The first subsystem deals with the creation of the system's data base by assembling and updating the needed data. This data base maintains data about foods, menu items, meals, diets, plans and other information and requirements essential to the system.

The second subsystem defines the methodology used to develop different diet plans successfully. This subsystem offers three approaches to diet planning in order to satisfy any special demands. These approaches are:

- Find the cheapest meal which satisfies nutritional and other requirements by using the linear programming method.

- Find the most nutritionaly balanced meal by using the goal programming method.
- Give the dietary experts the possibility to create meals themselves.

The third subsystem creates different reports about plans, meals, diets and also calculates and reports the amount of raw foods needed to realize any diet plan.

The main reason for using different methods in this system is to give dietary experts an opportunity to choose the most convenient method and to find the optimum solution for any specific situation. Generating a lot of solutions will enable the system to create a file called the Meals-Container. This Container will grow in time and will make the system capable of offering different as well as acceptable nutrition plans for any diet. When the Container is rich enough with diet specialized meals, it will help in covering the whole area and transforming this system into an indispensable Decision Support System for diet planning.

Conclusion

DOPTIS is specialized decision support system which covers the whole area of nutritional planning. It enables dietary experts to use some very efficient mathematical programming methods in the process of generating diet plans by developing an interactive dialogue between the system and the expert. So, dietary experts may integrate their knowledge in the process and define their judgement about the solutions obtained.

References

Anderson A. M., Earle M. D. (1983) Diet Planning in the Third Word by Linear and Goal Programming. Journal Operational Research Society 34: 9-16.

Balas E. (1965) An Additive Algorithm for Solving Linear Programs with Zero-One Variables. Operations Research 13: 517-546.

Balintfy L. J. (1964) Menu Planning by Computer. Communications of the ACM 7: 255-259

Balintfy L. J. (1967) Computer Applications in Diet Therapy. Symposium on Therapeutic Nutrition, Freeborn Hall, University of California, Davis: 1-15.

Balintfy L. J. (1975) A Mathematical Programming System for Food Management Applications. Interfaces 6: 13-31.

Damij T., Grad J. (1988) An Algorithm to balance the Solution of the Nutrition Problem LP. SYM-O-PIS, Brioni, Yu: 205-208.

Experimental Results on the Efficiency of Rule-Based Systems

Dieter Gernert
Technische Universität München
Arcisstraße 21, 8000 München 2, Germany

Abstract: In rule-based systems several strategies can be developed which permit to speed up the inference process, always leaving the quality of the results unchanged. For this purpose, the set of all rules is partitioned into subsets according to one or another heuristic principle; in the beginning, the inference process is run on a small subset only, whereas later on further subsets of rules are activated step by step, until finally the total set of rules is included. Experimental results on the speed-up, which depends on the way of partitioning the set of rules, will be presented, together with some further data on the parameter-dependency of the time required for inference processes.

1. HOW TO SPEED UP THE INFERENCE PROCESS

In a typical rule-based system a problem description supplied by the user will be confronted with a comprehensive list of stored rules in order to derive new conclusions. Generally, such a process of "knowledge expansion" consists of several runs.

The total time required for an inference process can be significantly reduced by partitioning the rule base into subsets, which may be called e.g. "very important rules", "rather important rules", and "less important rules". In the beginning of an inference process only a small proportion of the existing rules (e.g. the "very important" ones) are considered, whereas in subsequent runs further subsets of rules will be activated, step by step, according to their predefined rank, until finally the total rule base will be incorporated.

The experimental results reported here are all based on experience with a real system. Nevertheless, the present paper is written in such a way that no knowledge about the underlying system is needed (so that Sect. 2 can be skipped). It seems that - aside from exotic special cases - the basic strategies can be transferred to other rule-based systems with a great number of rules.

2. A SKETCH OF THE UNDERLYING SYSTEM

At present, the rule-based system KBGRAPH is centered around a collection of about 1500 "formulas" from graph theory. These are conditional or unconditional relations (equations or inequalities) between graph invariants (including Boolean invariants). The main purpose of KBGRAPH is to obtain new information about a given class of graphs (e.g. the class of all possible counterexamples to a certain conjecture). This is achieved by confronting all restrictions given by the user with all entries of the knowledge base. For details about relations between graph invariants see Brigham and Dutton (1991), and for an outline of KBGRAPH see Gernert (1989).

3. DIFFERENT CONTROL STRATEGIES AND THEIR INFLUENCE UPON EFFICIENCY

In the sequel only systems with a great number of rules are regarded. Subsets S_1, S_2, ... S_N of the rule base are defined such that always S_i is a proper subset of S_{i+1}, and S_N is the complete rule base. The influence of that number N, as well as different strategies for defining the subsets S_i were tested experimentally (Thomas (1989)).

Four criteria were set up for assigning a formula to one of the subsets S_i:

C1: complexity of the if-part,

C2: length of the formula,

C3: connection with the problem description,

C4: ranks of the invariants in the formula.

The criterion C1 is based on the fact that shorter if-parts are more likely to come true rather soon. It is clear that short formulas should be used already in early phases of the inference process in order to get partial results quickly, whilst extremely long formulas should be used only for tiny improvements in later phases, so that C2 becomes plausible. A formula which contains some variable also occurring in the problem description (criterion C3) may promise a quick contribution to the problem. Finally, the same is true for formulas in which variables with a "high rank" - in the sense of the user's previous settings - are contained (criterion C4).

It was found that in almost all cases any of these four criteria for partitioning the rule base leads to a reduction of computing time. Very often C1 (complexity of the if-part) gives the best result, closely followed by C2. The time saved is about 25 to 30%, in favourable cases about 32%. C1 is taken as a "standard proposal" when the user does not make a choice. Comparing N = 5 and N = 3, the latter value turned out to be better.

The number of inference runs ranges from 5 to 9; the lower value is likely to be assumed if the problem description includes many equations, whereas many inequalities tend to raise the number of required inference runs.

REFERENCES

Brigham RC, Dutton RD (1991) A compilation of relations between graph invariants - Supplement I. Networks 21: 421-455

Gernert D (1989) A knowledge-based system for graph theory. Methods of Operations Research 63: 457-464

Thomas C (1989) Interaktive Beeinflussung von Inferenzprozessen in einem wissensbasierten System. Unpublished diploma thesis, TU München.

Incorporating 3D-Facilities into Statistical Graphs Using a Description-List-Based Data Presentation[1]

Fred Hantelmann
Fachbereich Wirtschafts- und Organisationswissenschaften
Universität der Bundeswehr Hamburg
Holstenhofweg 85, 2000 Hamburg 70, Germany

Introduction

Statistical graphs are powerful tools that help an analyst by offering him/her a quick impression on statistical properties on one or more sets of data. With increasing power of computers and graphical displays presentation of static 2D-images is only one goal of statistical graphs. Three-dimensional scenes with interactive manipulation of the view point as well as animated movies can now be computed in real time so that smooth variation of parameters from the underlying statistical model may be observed and analyzed.

With respect to computer displays three-dimensional graphical scenes normally are projected onto a two-dimensional surface. Three-dimensional perception often is enforced using graphical techniques like perspective, depth-cueing or stereo pictures. To change the view onto a graphical 3D-scene the analyst therefore needs a special interface for controlling the scene. If sequences of scenes that differ from each other are composed to a movie a mechanism is needed for forward and backward control of the time-based sequence.

In recent years many of the most popular statistical software packages have added graphical facilities to help with interpretation of numerical results. Within packages like, i.e. SAS, SPSS-X or S-Plus, the user is given control of several aspects that enforce perception of statistical properties from the data to be shown graphically. Using such a package interaction with graphics is only possible on a subset of those techniques defined within computer graphics and data visualization. Discussion on basic techniques of computer graphics and scientific visualization with many references may be found in [1] and [4].

As a part of the WIMDAS-Project (WIssensbasiertes MarketingDaten AnalyseSystem, see [5]) a concept has been developed that offers full control of the graphical characteristics a statistical graph is built from. Guided to help on interpretation and learning from a session with the knowledge-based decision supporting analysis system WIMDAS the graphical component of WIMDAS has been realized as a standalone package called the Data Display Subsystem DDS [6]. Statistical graphs are built from description lists containing both statistical data and additional information on graphical aspects that control the appeareance of the statistical information to be visualized.

The Data Display Subsystem DDS is written in WEB [10] and coded for portable C following the syntax defined by Kernighan and Ritchey [9]. The graphics part of DDS is an application programmer's interface to the Programmer's Hierarchical Interactive Graphics System (PHIGS) using the C language binding of the ISO specification 9593-4 [8]. DDS is designed to run on a Unix-based Workstation or inside a Unix-based computer network upon

[1]Research has been supported by the Deutsche Forschungsgemeinschaft

the X11 window system. Communication between DDS and other components of WIMDAS follows the client/server concept using socket-based interprocess communication [3], [7]. The user is given control of the graphic display by a user interface designed conforming to the OpenLook graphical user interface specifications [11].

Statistical Graphs and Computer Graphics

Though most software packages designed to graphically present statistical information offer powerful environments in order to support the user during construction of a highly fashioned picture, most commercial all-in-one products are not based on graphical standards like GKS or PHIGS which have been designed by computer graphics experts. Computer graphics standards describe graphical primitives and attributes specifying the appeareance of primitives as well as concepts for grouping primitives with related attributes to objects (GKS: segments; PHIGS: structures), adding information on geometric transformation of objects (shift, rotate, scale) and define capabilities of a graphical workstation for graphical input and output. The goal of computer graphics standards is to provide basic elements and basic functions that ensure graphical presentation of geometric information independent of the area of research that needs graphics.

Statistical graphs in contrast are complex graphical scenes that need to be constructed from high level objects which may be composed of elements given by a computer graphics standard. Besides this, research on graphical presentation of statistical data has given many types of statistical graphs long before any graphical standard had been accepted by the international standards organization ISO. Concurrently, the software industry developed some industry standards like Calcomp, Disspla (Computer Associates), PLOT10 (Tektronix) or DGL (Silicon Graphics) to provide graphics programming environments or toolkits for several applications, including some basic statistical graphs.

So far, the role of graphics in statistics significantly has increased and statisticians now need the power of graphical standards to ensure perception of that information the analyst wants to emphasize. During the last years, the software industry developed some programming libraries based on graphical standards (GKS: Simpleplot, PHIGS: PHIGSt) providing a couple of functions that solve some commonly needed tasks to support application developers. Since statisticians in general neither are computer graphics experts nor like spending most time of analysis for application programming, a black-box engine is needed that provides an easy to use interface and meets the expectations of both statisticians and computer graphics experts. The DDS is an attempt to fill this hole.

Statistical Graphs and Description Lists

Depending on taxonometric characteristics of the statistical data to be visualized several types of statistical graphs have been developed (a structured overview may be found in [2]). On a given set of data the knowledge of an expert is needed to decide which type of statistical graph should be chosen to represent the statistical properties contained in the data. Additionally, the data should be formatted with respect to the syntax required by the visualization system used. So far every software package defines its own internal and external data representation. For practical purposes a common data representation is needed. An attempt to solve this problem has been developed as a part of the DDS.

The basic idea of the DDS data representation format is that statistical objects as well as graphical properties can be coded in description items and a properly arranged list of description items contains the complete statistical and graphical information on a statistical graph. Definition of a suitable syntax for description lists representing statistical graphs first seemed to be a straight forward task, but experiments with a sample implementation has shown that many side effects occur and attention is to be paid on management of statistical and graphical data inside the software system. Also, every statistical object must be connected to a record representing all possible graphical attributes a statistical object can be decorated with.

DDS description items are coded in a keyword/data syntax. Keywords for statistical objects are:

`Objects:`	<number>	the number of statistical objects;
`Groups:`	<number>	the number of groups to build from the objects;
`Data:`	<data information>	the statistical data;
`Label:`	<string>	text information on objects;
`Legend:`	<string>	text information on groups;
`Key:`	<string>	optional information on objects.

The `Key:` item is used for interaction with the calling process and deferred to it if the user intends to submit the graphical pick detection of a statistical object. Additional description items that may be omitted refer to heading (`Header: <string>`) and coordinate axis labels (`Xaxis: <string>`, `Yaxis: <string>`, `Zaxis: <string>`). A description list for a pyramid and the picture DDS creates from it is shown below.

The general syntax of a DDS description list has been defined as follows:

- A heading keyword denotes the type of statistical graph to be constructed from the description list. Possible heading keywords are `#BarChart:`, `#Boxplot:`, `#CloudChart:`, `#Dendrogram:`, `#LineChart:`, `#Pyramid:`, `#PieChart:`, `#Text:` and `#ScatterPlot:` for two-dimensional statistical graphs. `#CloudChart3:` and `#LineChart3:` invoke the drawing of threedimensional statistical graphs.

- A description list consists of description items containing either statistical data or graphical information. The list itself is surrounded by curly braces.

- A description list is of correct syntax if all description items are correct and if it contains that number of `Data:` items required by the number of objects demanded by the `Object:` item which must preceed any `Data:` item.

```
#Pyramid:
{
Objects: 5
Data:
4
4 2
6 6 2
6 6 3 3
Order: 4 5 2 1 3
}
```

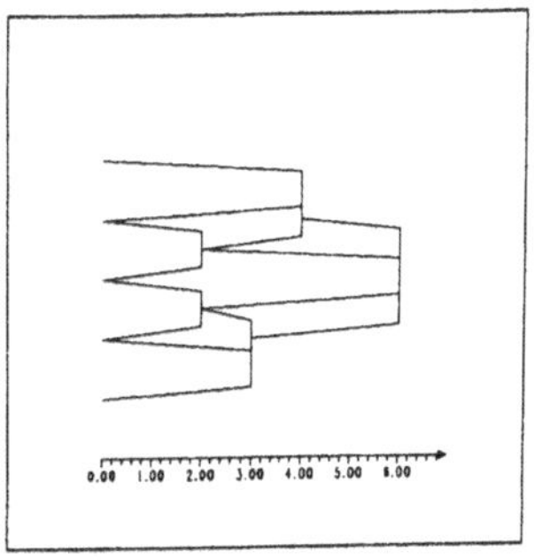

Fig. 1: Example description list and resulting statistical graph

3D-Extensions to DDS

As shown in the previous section CloudChart3 and LineChart3 are the only two three-dimensional statistical graphs implemented in DDS so far. Animating piecharts or barcharts as three-dimensional graphs offers better looking pictures but, compared to a 2D-representation of the same data there are no additional statistical informations visible. Dendrogram, pyramid and boxplot also may provide higher fashioned charts with statistical data as a minor part of information perceptable from such a graph. Scatterplots in three dimensions could be thought of as a special cloudchart having no labels added to each point.

Using the 3D-capabilities of DDS two-dimensional statistical graphs are treated like flat surfaces that may be shifted, rotated and scaled. These features seem to be not important to graphical data analysis, but there are examples that show usefulness of this properties. A scatterplot matrix built from a set of data with three variables may be arranged as three connected surfaces on a cube. Compared with a three-dimensional cloudchart on the same data the cubes surface shows scatterplots on every pair of variables and the cloudchart represents a projection of arbitrary combined variables. An example is shown on the picture below.

Controlling of the three-dimensional geometric operations rotate, shift and scale is done either interactive using the user interface of the front end DDScontrol (for details on DDS-architecture and DDScontrol refer to [6]) or by description items that have been defined as 3D description items extending the DDS protocol. The 3D-extension description item are named

Rotate:	**<rotate_x rotate_y rotate_z>**	rotate angles;
Shift:	**<shift_x shift_y shift_z>**	shift vector;
Scale:	**<scale_x scale_y scale_z>**	scale factors.

Given values are taken absolute, incremental operation currently is not supported. Each item may occur inside or outside of a description list. If a 3D-extension item is given outside a description list, operatation is performed by a **Transform** item. This way geometric 3D-transformations may be invoked by a remote process.

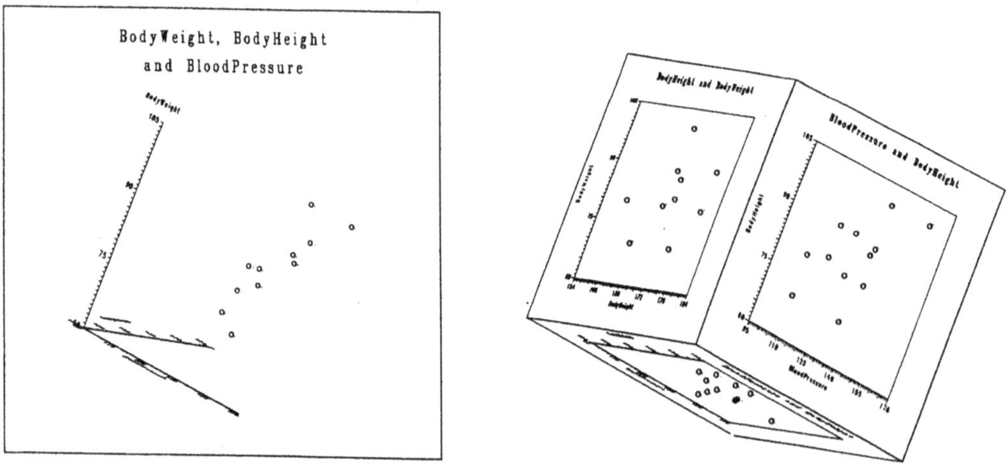

Fig. 2: CloudChart3 on bloodpressure, bodyheight and bodyweight with scatterplots on a cubes surface

Outlook

The display server concept as implemented within the DDS is a technique that originally has been designed within the Athena project at MIT during developement of the X window system. The binary protocol transferred between X-clients and X-server is generated internally and not visible by the user of the X window system. By the way, the X-protocol is intended to support general bitmap-based window system requirements.

The DDS-protocol has been defined as a readable data stream dedicated to presentation of statistical graphs that can easily be realized with few modifications of the output part of numerical algorithms and that also can be written using any text editor program. The 3D-extensions of DDS offer control of three-dimensional statistical graphs by the application driving DDS. So far, controlling the graph derived from a description list is highly menu supported by DDScontrol. An additional package managing sequences of description lists and providing movie visualization is under developement.

References

[1] BRODLIE, K. U. ET AL.: *Scientific Visualization.* Springer-Verlag, 1992.

[2] CHAMBERS, J. M., CLEVELAND, W. S., KLEINER,B., TUKEY, P. A.: *Graphical Methods for Data Analysis.* Wadsworth & Brooks, Pacific Groove CA, 1983.

[3] CORBIN, J. R.: *The Art of Distributed Applications – Programming Techniques for Remote Procedure Calls.* Springer-Verlag, 1991.

[4] ENCARNACAO, J., STRASSER, W.: *Computer Graphics.* Oldenbourg Verlag, 1988.

[5] GAUL, W., SCHADER, M., BOTH, M.: *Knowledge-Oriented Support for Data Analysis Applications to Marketing.* In: Gaul, W., Schader, M. (eds.): Knowledge, Data and Computer-Assisted Decisions. Springer-Verlag, Heidelberg, p. 259–271, 1990.

[6] HANTELMANN, F.: *Graphical Data Analysis in a Distributed System.* In: Diday, E., Lechevallier, Y. (eds.): Symbolic-Numeric Data Analysis and Learning. Nova Science Publishers, New York, 1991.

[7] HANTELMANN, F.: *Application-Interfaces for AI-Environments in Example of the* WIMDAS-*Project.* In: Gaul, W. et al (eds): Operations Research Proceedings 1991. Springer-Verlag, Heidelberg, 1992.

[8] INTERNATIONAL STANDARD ISO/IEC 9593-4: *Programmer's Hierarchical Interactive Graphics System (PHIGS) language bindings Part 4: C.* ISO/IEC Copyright Office, Genève, Switzerland, 1991.

[9] KERNIGHAN, B., RITCHIE, D.: *The C programming language.* Prentice-Hall, Englewood Cliffs, NJ, 1978.

[10] KNUTH, D. E.: *Literate Programming — The original introduction of WEB.* Computer Journal 27:2, p. 97–111, 1984.

[11] SUN MICROSYSTEMS, INC.: *OpenLook™ Graphical User Interface Functional Specification.* Addison Wesley, Reading MA, 1989.

Statistical and Machine Learning Approaches in Credit Scoring

Fariba Jafar-Shaghaghi
Institut für Statistik und math. Wirtschaftstheorie, Universität Karlsruhe
Postfach 6980, 7500 Karlsruhe 1, Germany

1. Introduction

This paper and another related to it (Jafar-Shaghaghi (1992)) are intended to compare two classification methods, namely discriminant analysis in statistics with classification in machine learning through their application in the area of economics. This paper uses credit assessment as an area for applying and analysing these two methods. In section two the theoretical background of this topic will be described. Section 3 is devoted to credit assessment methods. Empirical and theoretical evaluation will be discussed in section 4.

2 Theoretical background

- Discriminant analysis is a statistical multivariate analysis for classification and prediction (Lachenbruch (1975)). It refers to classifying observations into two or more known classes depending on one or more quantitative variables through building the polynomial function. According to assumptions about the normality of attribute distribution and equality of covariance matrices different discriminant functions have been developed.

- Machine learning is a subarea of artifitial intelligent. One of the central topics in machine learning is inductive learning. Quinlan's ID3 algorithm (Quinlan (1986)) is an efficient induction of classification procedure (decision tree) from large collection of positive and negative examples of a concept. ID3 is one of the TDIDT family (Top Down Induction of Decision Tree) of algorithms. The purpose of ID3 is to take instances whose classes are predefined through a fixed amount of properties. Then to draw a decision tree over these properties, such that, all instances can be correctly classified.

3. Credit assessment methods

Two well konwn methods are 1) traditional method
2) numerical scoring

- Traditional method is being practiced for many decades by credit officers, using their own experience and considering the famous 3 "C's" of credit: character, capacity and capital, combining these with some other credit history indicators.

- Numerical scoring system : since 1960 computer based system called credit scoring system are in practice. It is based on using some positive and negative examples from the consumers's file. Discriminant analysis is the most accepted multivariate statistical technique employed. The evaluation procedure is due to summation of the score given to credit history indicators. If the credit scoring system is based on single cut-off point method, then the applicant total score will be compared with the given threshold. By exceeding this point the applicant is granted credit, otherwise there is no credit granting. By two thresholds systems, if the total score is less than the lower threshold, there is no credit; if greater than the upper threshold, credit will be granted. Is the total score between two thresholds, credit history information ought to be investigated (Capon (1983)).

4) Empirical evaluation and comparison

A sample of 1000 credit applicant of a bank in Germany has been used to analyse the performance of two above mentioned classification methods (see table 1). The program packets which have been used are: SAS for discriminant analysis, Assistant Professional for ID3 and IXL for rule induction (see table 2).

Table 1. data set characteristics

number of total examples	1000
number of attributes	20
number of classes	2
number of training examples	665
number of test example	335

Table 2. Result of data analysis

classification techniques	program packet	classification accuracy
discriminant function	SAS	% 72.3
ID3	Assist. Prof.	% 71.4

Furthermore I have used the IXL tool to induce production rules. 28 rules have been induced.
Although the result of the empirical tests are almost the same, I would like to discuss some properties of different methods.

- Disadvantages of credit scoring method:
It is based on discriminant analysis which has the following shortcomings for credit assessment task:
1) Attributes which are not numerical have to be converted to numerical values.
2) The assumption about normal distribution and common covariance matrix is not valid alwayes for credit assessment files.
3) Adding applicant scores is not an exhaustive criteria for credit worthiness judgment .
4) The output of the classification system is not an explanatory model.

- Advantage of machine (inductive) learning methods:
1) ID3 builds decision tree, using discrete as well as numeric values to classify all examples in the training set.
2) Decision trees are easier to understand and to handle than mathematical equations.
3) Decision trees can be converted into a set of production rules, which are a popular knowledge representation for expert systems.
4) Rule induction techniques transform data set into a set of accurate rules which are understandable by human experts.
5) Rule induction techniques discover "logical relationship", which are expressed in terms of rules rather than mathematical equations.

References:

Bertzger, T.M. (1991), "*Die Anwendung statistischer Verfahren zur Risikofrüherkennung bei Dispositionskredit*" Studienreihe der Stiftung Kreditwirtschaft an der Universität Hohenheim, Bd. 9.

Capon,N. (1982), "*Credit Scoring System: A Critical Analysis*", Journal of Marketing, Spring 1982, Vol.46, 82-91.

Carter, C. and Catlett, J. (1987), "*Assessing Credit Card Application Using Machine Learning*", in: IEEE Expert, Fall 1987, 71-79.

Jafar-Shaghaghi,F. (1992), "*Theoretical and Empirical Evaluation of some Inductive Based Methods in Artificial Intelligence and Statistics*",in Operations Research 91, Gritzmann, P. et al (eds) Phisica-Verlag, Heidelberg, pp 519-522.

Lachenbruch, P.A. (1975), "*Disriminant Analysis*", Hafner, New York.

Quinlan, J.R. (1986), "*Induction of Decision Trees*", Machine Learning, Vol. 1, Nr. 1.

Qiunlan, J.R. (1987), "*Decision Trees and Multivariate Attributes*", in Machine Intelligence 11, J.E. Hays and D. Michie (eds), Oxford University Press.

Assistant Profesional is a machine learning tool (developed at the Josef Stefan Institute of Ljubljana university).

IXL is a machine learning tool (IntelligenceWare,Inc. 5933 West Century Blv. Los Angeles, CA, 90045).

On Completeness of Rule-Based Systems

Antoni Ligeza
Institute of Automatics AGH
al. Mickiewicza 30, 30–059 Kraków, Poland

INTRODUCTION

Rule-based systems are the most popular means for modeling, analysis, control and diagnosis of numerous complex systems, especially those having no classical mathematical models in the form of differential or difference equations. The behaviour and properties of such systems are described with use of relations and therefore logic-based formalisms are best suited for knowledge representation and reasoning. The development of non-trivial systems is a tedious task, since knowledge acquisition and encoding must be mostly done by hand. Moreover, putting together many separately created rules must take into account the interrelationship among them. Testing and debugging a knowledge-base is always a hard, time-consuming task. Moreover, in order to assure satisfactory work of such systems some theoretical properties of them should be verified (see Andert, 1992).

In this paper, we present the application of a simple method of theorem proving, so-called *backward dual resolution* (for details see Ligeza, 1992a, 1992b) to proving *completeness* of rule-based systems. The presented method is a logical one and in fact is dual to resolution method (Chang, 1973). The method was initially introduced as a basic reasoning paradigm for knowledge-based control systems (Ligeza, 1992a,1992b). The idea of the method consists in proving *validity* of a given formula in disjunctive normal form. Thus, the initial form is in fact *dual* to the one in resolution method. Further, the proposed method works in fact *backwards*. This means that during the process of derivation one generates new formulae from parent formulae starting from the initial formula to be proved – but with regard to logical inference, the alternative of parent formulae is a logical consequence of the derived formula! Thus, at any step of reasoning the derivation process is reversed with regard to finding logical consequences. The process of derivation is successful if it eventually ends up with an empty tautology formula which (here) is always true – in this case, the initial formula, as a logical consequence of it, is proved.

Practical definitions of completeness of rule-based systems are presented and a formal method based on backward dual resolution for verification of logical completeness of such systems is outlined. The proposed approach takes into account the fact that a strictly logical definition of completeness, although possible to analyze, can be in most cases too strong for practical systems. The concept of a weak (relative) completeness is proposed and an approach to testing completeness is outlined.

[1]This research was supported by State Committee on Scientific Research within the Project *Computer Systems of Control and Decision Making - Elements of Theory, Formal Tools and Computer Aided Design*, Grant No. 8-8528-9102

BD-RESOLUTION

In this section we shall briefly recapitulate the idea of backward dual resolution (for details concerning logical bases and classical resolution see Chang, 1973). More detailed presentation, proofs and examples can be found in (Ligeza, 1992b).

Let us start with an observation, that instead of converting a formula to its clausal form one can transform the initial formula to a dual form, consisting of an alternative of conjunctions of literals. Now, the following definition will be helpful.

Definition 1 *Let $q_1, q_2, \ldots, q_k$ be literals (atomic formulae or their negations). A formula $\phi = q_1 \wedge q_2 \wedge \ldots \wedge q_k$ will be called a* simple formula. *Further, let $\phi_1, \phi_2, \ldots, \phi_n$ be some simple formulae. Any formula $\Phi = \phi_1 \vee \phi_2 \vee \ldots \vee \phi_n$ will be called a* normal formula.

A normal formula is also called in literature a formula in *disjunctive normal form (DNF)*. Now the basic definition of *backward dual resolvent* can be stated.

Definition 2 (Backward dual resolvent) *Let $\psi^1 = \psi^{<1>} \wedge q^1$ and $\psi^2 = \psi^{<2>} \wedge \neg q^2$ are simple formulae, and let there exist a most general unifier (mgu) σ for q^1 and q^2. Then, a formula ψ*

$$\psi = \psi^{<1>}\sigma \wedge \psi^{<2>}\sigma \tag{1}$$

will be called a backward dual resolvent *(*bd-resolvent*) of ψ^1 and ψ^2.*

For backward dual resolution (bd-resolution, for short) the following theorem holds.

Theorem 1 (Soundness of bd-resolution) *Let ψ be the bd-resolvent defined as above (1). Then $\psi^1 \vee \psi^2$ is the logical consequence of ψ.*

In order to pass to completeness verification with bd-resolution let us define an idea of *derivation* with use of bd-resolution. Below, by a *factor* of a formula we shall understand the result of applying some substitution to the formula in order to replace certain variables with terms. Note that the initial formula is a logical consequence of any of its factors.

Definition 3 (bd-derivation) *A* bd-derivation *(or derivation, for short) of a simple formula ψ from a normal formula Ψ is any sequence of simple formulae $\psi^1, \psi^2, \ldots, \psi^k$, such that: (i) for any $i \in \{1, 2, \ldots, k\}$, ψ^i is a bd-resolvent or a factor of simple formulae either belonging to Ψ or generated earlier bd-resolvents, and (ii): $\psi = \psi^k$. Formula ψ is said to be* derived *from Ψ.*

For convenience, if $k = 1$ ($\psi \in \Psi$) we shall also say that ψ is derived from Ψ.

Theorem 2 (Soundness of bd-derivation) *Let Ψ be a normal formula. If an empty tautology formula (always true, denoted with $\top$) can be derived from Ψ, then Ψ is valid (is a tautology).*

PROVING COMPLETENESS

From logical point of view, a complete system of rules is one having the capability of dealing with any potentially occurring formula. Thus, the alternative of the rule precondition formulae should constitute an empty tautology formula ($\top$). In such a case, for any potentially possible formula describing some state (state formula) ϕ, some of the precondition formulae must "cover" ϕ. Logically, the condition can be written as $\phi \vdash \Psi_i$, where Ψ_i is a normal formula defining preconditions of some i-th rule. However, the strictly logical completeness will in most cases be too strong for practical applications. This is so, because most of the systems are incomplete with regard to possible state representation and thus, there is no need to "cover" all the possibly existing states but only the really existing ones. Thus the following definitions of completeness are proposed.

Definition 4 (Completeness) *Let us consider knowledge-based system consisting of a set* **T** *of k production rules, each of them having its precondition formula* Ψ_i, $i = 1, 2, \ldots, k$. *The system is:*

- *logically complete, if and only if the alternative of the preconditions formulae satisfies the following condition:*
$$\vdash \Psi_1 \vee \Psi_2 \vee \ldots \vee \Psi_k,$$
(in other words, $\Psi_1 \vee \Psi_2 \vee \ldots \vee \Psi_k$ *is a tautology),*

- *physically complete, if and only if for any state s described with formula* ϕ *there exists at least one rule in* **T** *applicable to s, i.e. there is*
$$\phi \vdash \Phi_i$$
for some $i \in \{1, 2, \ldots, k\}$

Definition 5 (Specific completeness) *Consider a knowledge-based system as above. The system is:*

- *specifically logically complete with regard to formula* Ψ, *if and only if the following condition holds*
$$\Psi \vdash \Psi_1 \vee \Psi_2 \vee \ldots \vee \Psi_k$$

- *specifically physically complete with regard to a situation (set of states) S described with formula* Ψ, *if and only if for any state s described with formula* ϕ *and such that* $s \in S$ ($\phi \vdash \Psi$) *there exists at least one rule in* **T** *applicable to s, i.e. the following condition holds for some i*
$$\phi \vdash \Psi_i.$$

Thus, a set of rules can be complete in a strictly logical sense (logical completeness) or complete with reference to the particular universe of discourse (physical completeness). Of course, the logical completeness constitutes a stronger requirement.

On the base of the presented logical approach, the following algorithm can be suggested for checking specific completeness with regard to a given formula Ψ (for logical completeness it is enough to replace Ψ with $\top$).

Algorithm for checking completeness

1. Build a formula describing the sum of all the appropriate precondition formulae (the normal formula of the form $\Psi_1 \vee \Psi_2 \vee \ldots \vee \Psi_k$).
2. Perform any possible derivation of bd-resolvent, *e.g.* by applying the level-saturation method (see Chang, 1973), or any other complete strategy so as to prove that $\Psi \vdash \Psi_1 \vee \Psi_2 \vee \ldots \vee \Psi_k$.
3. If the above generalization is eventually proved, then the system is complete with regard to Ψ.
4. In other case (due to the completeness of the bd-resolution) the system is incomplete. The derived formulae describe the situations which are "served" (i.e. the system is complete with regard to at least the obtained formulae).

CONCLUSIONS

The proposed approach based on first order logic and theorem proving dual to resolution method provides theoretical bases for improving the design of knowledge based systems. It suggests a possibility of checking the system for completeness based on first-order logic rather than simple exhaustive inspection of possible parameters/conditions combinations (see Suwa, 1984; Andert, 1992).

The approach can be applied to rule-based systems, where precondition formulae are in the form of normal formulae. Logical explicit negation should be used rather than the implicit one. For practical reasons, in another paper (Ligeza, 1992b) a generalized bd-resolution taking the advantage of knowing the intended interpretation is proposed; its application can improve efficiency of the proposed paradigm.

REFERENCES

Andert E.P. (1992) Integrated knowledge-based system design and validation for solving problems in uncertain environments. *International Journal of Man-Machine Studies*, **36**, pp. 357-373.

Chang C. L., Lee R. C. T. (1973) *Symbolic Logic and Mechanical Theorem Proving.* Academic Press, New York and London.

Ligeza A. (1992a) A logical formalism for dynamic systems. In R. Trappl (Ed.) *Cybernetics and Systems Research'92. Proceedings of the Eleventh European Meeting on Cybernetics and Systems Research*, Vienna. World Scientific, Singapore, New Yersey, London, Hong-Kong, pp. 1545-1552.

Ligeza A. (1992b) Logical foundations for knowledge-based control systems. Knowledge representation, reasoning and theoretical properties. Report of Laboratoire d'Automatique et d'Analyse des Systemes, Toulouse, France, No. 92269.

Suwa M., Scott A.C., Shortliffe, E.H. (1984) Completeness and consistency in a rule-based system. In B.G. Buchanan and E.H. Shortliffe (Eds.) *Rule-Based Expert Systems*, Chapter 8, pp. 159-170. Addison-Wesley, London.

Load Sharing in a Heterogeneous Distributed Object-based System

Josef Matulka
Dept. of Applied Computer Science, University of Economics and Business Adm.
Augasse 2–6, 1090 Vienna, Austria

Networks are quite commonplace nowadays; physically combining heterogeneous computers in a local area network is not a problem any longer. Distributed software that makes efficient use of this hardware, on the contrary, is much more difficult to design. The object based approach is a promising paradigm for designing and implementing distributed software; unfortunately it is notorious for its performance problems.

Given an efficient network communication mechanism, one can use load sharing algorithms to increase performance. A huge number of such algorithms have been developed in the last decade (see Casavant and Kuhl (1988) for a survey) which can be broadly classified in performance-oriented and cost-oriented approaches. The former use a queueing system to model the computer hardware, typically only consider jobs that do not communicate with each other and focus on obtaining performance improvements rather than determining an optimal solution. The latter allow for interaction between different jobs but lack a realistic hardware model; integer programming is used to derive an exact solution of the load balancing problem.

Both approaches have their merits, but are inadequate for object based systems. In this paper we derive an algorithm that integrates these approaches by using several phases that build upon each other. In principle, we answer the following question: Given a set of heterogeneous objects with known workload characteristics and a set of hosts consisting of ressources (CPU, disks, etc.) with known performance, what is the optimal allocation of objects to hosts?

In the first phase (*structural analysis*) we analyse the structure of a distributed object based system. The *performance analysis* is an application of the theory of separable queueing networks. We determine the input parameters needed to compute different performance metrics (utilization, response time) for each fixed assignment of objects to hosts. During *optimization analysis* we specify a cost function as a combination of performance metrics and formulate an assignment problem. In the last phase (*coordination analysis*), the assignment problem is interpreted as coordination problem between hosts for which a team-theoretically inspired solution algorithm is given.

In the following we only sum up the model and the algorithm; a more detailed derivation together with some examples can be found in Matulka (1992); an application to client-server systems is described in Matulka (1991).

Structural Analysis

A distributed object-based system consists of a set of interacting objects running on a set of hosts connected by a (local area) network. Each host h consists of a number of ressources k (such as CPU, disk, and network interface). Each object o consists of a number of methods m. The object is the unit of allocation (all methods of one object have to be allocated to the same host) whereas the method is the unit of computation (all workload of the system is generated by some method).

The allocation U is a matrix that links the software (objects) to the hardware (hosts) by specifying which host each object is allocated to. Finding the optimal allocation U^* is the goal of our algorithm.

Performance Analysis

In order to be able to compute performance indices, we specify a queueing network model of the distributed object based system. Each ressource is modeled as a service center, for each method the services required are specified. The ressources of the hosts provide the services demanded by the methods. In our view, two activities are characteristic of hosts as well as methods: computation and communication. We assume that only remote communication requires service, thus neglecting the comparatively small amount of service required by local communication.

For each method m we have to know:

- $d_{m,k}^{comp}$, the mean service required by one invocation of method m at ressource k.
- The mean number d_m^{comm} of bytes transmitted in case of a remote invocation of method m.

The interaction between methods is specified by the interaction matrix Λ

$$\Lambda = \begin{pmatrix} \lambda_{m_1,m_1} & \cdots & \lambda_{m_1,m_{|M|}} \\ \vdots & \lambda_{m_i,m_j} & \vdots \\ \lambda_{m_{|M|},m_1} & \cdots & \lambda_{m_{|M|},m_{|M|}} \end{pmatrix} \tag{1}$$

where λ_{m_i,m_j} denotes the rate of invocations of method m_j by method m_i and $|M|$ denotes the number of methods.

While this *workload model* has extended the description of the object based system, we also need some additional parameters to get the *configuration model* of the distributed system:

- A factor of proportionality $\beta_{k,h}^{comp}$ for each ressource k of each host h that defines the performance of this ressource relative to some defined standard ressource. A factor $0 < \beta_{k,h}^{comp} < 1$ means that the ressource k of host h is faster than the defined standard ressource. $\beta_{k,h}^{comp}$ is set to ∞ if the ressource k does not exist at host h.
- The service needed at each ressource k of each host h to transmit (send and receive) a message of known length.

Given the workload and the configuration model *and* assuming a fixed and known allocation U the BCMP-algorithm (cf. Basket *et al.* (1975)) can be used to compute performance indices such as

- the mean number $Q_{m,h}^{comp}$ of concurrently active invocations of each method m at host h, and
- the mean number $Q_{m,h}^{comm}$ of concurrently active protocol conversion processes caused by remote invocations of method m at host h.

Optimization Analysis

In order to compute an optimal allocation, we have to specify a cost function $\gamma(U)$. The following function to be minimized (see Matulka (1992) for alternative specifications) denotes the sum of active method invocations and protocol conversions (using the Law of Little this can be shown to be equivalent to a weighted sum of response times):

$$\gamma(U) = \sum_h \sum_m \left(Q_{m,h}^{comp} + Q_{m,h}^{comm} \right) \tag{2}$$

Coordination Analysis

In order to compute the optimal allocation we can group the set of hosts in a hierarchical way, thus obtaining a coordination tree. The leafs of this tree are called *ordinary hosts*. All other hosts are called *coordinators*, with the root of the tree being the *chief coordinator*. The optimal allocation can then be computed by a team-theoretically inspired algorithm which we sketch in the following:

Step-0: Each host h computes its *local cost function* which specifies the costs for each possible allocation of objects to this host.

Step-1: Each host forms an optimal team cost function by combining its own local cost function and the cost functions reported to it and sends this new function to its coordinator. The optimal team cost function denotes the minimal costs incurred for each allocation of objects to the team coordinated by the host.

Step-2: Starting with the chief coordinator, each coordinator uses the optimal team cost function to compute the optimal allocation of the objects to the teams coordinated by it.

During phase 1 information is passed up the coordination tree to recursively determine the minimal costs for each allocation. During phase 2 information is passed down the coordination tree to recursively determine the optimal allocation of objects to hosts.

References

Baskett *et al.* (1975) Open, closed, and mixed networks of queues with different classes of customers. Journal of the ACM 22(2): 248–260

Casavant T, Kuhl J (1988) A taxonomy of scheduling in general-purpose distributed computing systems. IEEE Transactions on Software Engineering SE-14(2): 141–154

Matulka J (1991) Lastverteilung in einem Klienten-Server-Modell als teamtheoretisches Problem. In: Busch (1991) ed. Operations Research und wissensbasierte Systeme: Modelle, Konzepte und Perspektiven für betriebliche Anwendungen. Springer-Verlag. Berlin Heidelberg New York

Matulka J (1992) Lastverteilung in einem heterogenen verteilten objektorientierten System. Servicebetriebe der Wirtschaftsuniversität Wien (forthcoming)

Machine Learning by Constructing Decision Trees Including Cost Functions

Wolfgang Müller, Fritz Wysotzki
Fraunhofer Ges. Institut für Informations- u. Datenverarbeitung Karlsruhe
Kurstraße 33, 1086 Berlin, Germany

Machine Learning is now in a state to get major industrial applications. The most important application fields are diagnosis and prediction being special forms of classification. One approach to classification learning is the construction of decision trees from examples. In this case the learning algorithm constructs a decision tree from a training data set. Let the assumed training data set include n samples, each defined by a vector m_j, containing the attributes $p_1,...,p_r$ and an attached class label c_j ($j = 1,...,k.$). This data set can be interpreted as a set of n points in an r-dimensional feature space , defined by the dimensions $p_1, .. , p_r$ and partitioned into class regions characterised by a class label. Applications of classification learning of more static character are medical diagnosis, forecasting in banking and economy, satellite image interpretation, etc., but there is an increasing interest in application in process diagnosis and control. The classes may reflect either discretisized objective functions (e.g. intervals of high water levels as shown in the example below) or qualitative statements (e.g. the amount of the dust emitted at a power station).The below described classification algorithm CAL5 tries to discretisize automatically the feature space into areas with unique class labels. Its output is a decision tree (see figure) reflecting the resulting discretization with a high transparency. This algorithm is especially suitable for continuous and ordered discrete valued attributes p_i, respectively.

Description of the algorithm

In addition to the set of learning samples a decision threshold $S <= 1$ is assumed. The goal is to separate the feature space into areas represented by subsets of samples, where the class c_i, $i = 1,...,k$ is decided with a probability

$$p (c_i) >= S \, , \qquad (1)$$

That is each area for which (1) holds generalises class c_i. By decision tree methods only class areas bounded by hyperplanes parallel to the axes of the feature space are possible. By the learning algorithm described below a tree will be constructed sequentially starting with one attribute and branching with other attributes recursively, if no sufficient discrimination of classes can be achieved. The algorithm can be divided into 4 steps:

step1: Choice of the best attribute

Let be x a certain intermediate node in the tree construction process. At first the attribute with the best local discrimination measure at this node has to be determined. For this a method described in /1/ is used. At each current node x all available attributes $p_1,...,p_r$ are considered anew. If the selected attribute occurs already on the path to x, than the discretization procedure (see below) leads to a refinement of an already constructed area corresponding to that path.

step 2: Discretization (interval formation)

All samples reaching the current terminal node x are ordered along the axis of the selected new attribute p_t according to increasing values. After that intervals are formed recursively on the p_t-axis by collecting samples from left to right until a class decision can be made on a given level of confidence.

Let be I a current interval containing n samples of different classes and n_{ci} the number of samples belonging to class c_i. Then $q_{ci} = n_{ci} / n$ is an estimate of the probability $p(c_i/x)$ on the current node x. The hypothesis

H1:"There exists a class c_i occurring in I with $p (c_i/x) >= S$ " will be compared with the alternative hypothesis

H2: "For all classes c_j occurring in I the inequation $p (c_j/x) < S$ holds" on a given level of confidence 1 - a .

Now the following "meta decision" on the dominance of a class in I will be made by CAL5:

(a) If there exist a class c_j, where **H1** is true on the level of confidence 1 - a then c_j dominates in I. The interval I is closed. The corresponding path of the tree is terminated with the decision for the class c_j.

(b) If for all classes appearing in I the hypothesis **H2** is true, then no class dominates in I . The interval will be closed, too. A new test with an other attribute is necessary.

(c) If neither **(a)** nor **(b)** can be decided on 1 - a (due to the lack of statistics), the interval I has to be extended by the next sample of the order of the values of the current attribute. A majority decision will be made, if there are no more samples for a further extension of I.

step3: Merging

Adjacent intervals I_l , I_{l+1} with identical unique class labels will be merged. These class labels of the resulting intervals yield the **terminal nodes** of the decision tree. The same rule is applied for adjacent intervals where no class dominates and which contain identical unions of classes. Intervals containing unions of classes yield the **intermediate nodes** in the construction of the decision tree, for which further branching will be performed.

step4 :Iteration

Every intermediate node becomes the start node for a further iteration step repeating the steps from 1 to 3. The algorithm stops if all intermediate nodes disappeared.

Inclusion of costs into CAL5

As can be seen from the above the parameters S (predefined threshold) and 1 - a (predefined confidence level) affect the tree construction process. If the conditional probability of a class exceeds the threshold S the tree is pruned at that node. The choice of S determines the accuracy of the approximation of the class regions, i. e. the admissible error rate. Therefore by selecting the value of S the accuracy of the approximation and simultaneously the complexity of the resulting tree can be controlled by the user. In addition to a constant S the algorithm allows to choose the threshold S in a class dependent manner. Let be S_{ci} a threshold depending on the class c_i. If for instance the interval I contains approximately the same numbers of samples of classes c_i and c_j and $S_{ci} < S_{cj}$, the algorithm will decide for c_i,i.e is more sensitive to c_i then c_j.

The influence of a given cost matrix can be taken into account during the learning phase, if the different costs for misclassification can be reflected by a class dependent threshold vector. The costs are given in form of the (r,r)- matrix K. The entry $k_{i,j}$ is the cost factor of misclassifiction of class c_i into c_j. One approach to solve this problem we have used was to choose the values of the class dependent thresholds proportional to the corresponding column sums of the cost matrix, which can be interpreted as a penalty measure for misclassification into those classes .

Applications

CAL5 is implemented on a SUN SPARC-station and is written in C++. The resulting decision trees can be in principle decomposed into a set of production rules, this way providing a knowledge base for Expert Systems. But a better real time behaviour will be obtained by using the tree directly as a classifier. CAL5 was successfully used in different classification and prediction tasks within the EC -Project Statlog ranging from medical diagnosis and satellite data interpretation to economical and financial forecasting.

An example of a decision tree built by CAL5 is shown in the figure. In the frame of the National Project WISCON supported by the Ministry of Science and Technology CAL5 is used for high water forecasting in the Werra Valley in Thuringia. The high water level has to be predicted at the town Meiningen. The learning data set contains 10 attributes, representing the water levels and water flows, measured at Meiningen and at several locations upstream at appropriate time steps before. Therefore the prediction problem was transformed into a classification problem by dividing the to predicted water level in 5 discrete intervals (classes). The accuracy of the results of CAL5 was in the order of magnitude of predictions using hydrological models (the models were obtained by the TH Ilmenau). The effort for the development of that mathematical model however was very high, while the decision tree model requires only a learning data set and some qualitative knowledge how to define the classes and to choose the most efficient attributes.

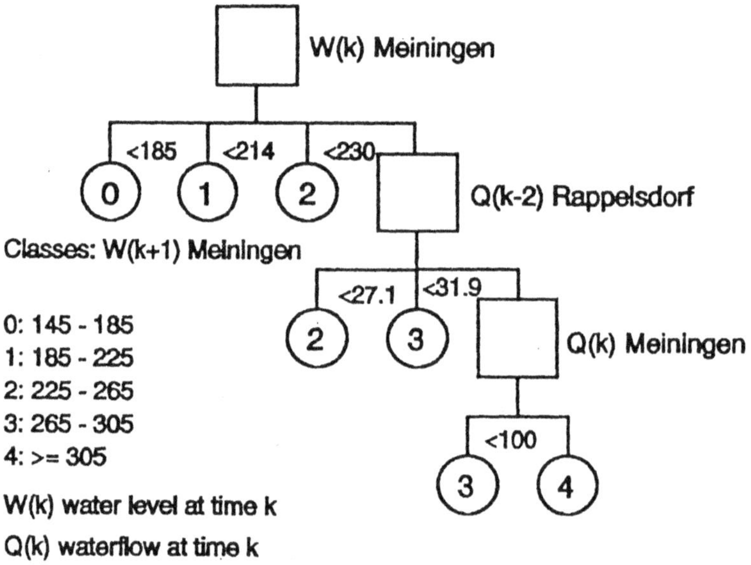

Prediction of High Water

References

/ 1 / Meyer - Brötz,G., Schürmann,J., Methoden der automatischen Zeichenerkennung, Akademie Verlag Berlin, 1970.

/ 2 / Unger,S., Wysotzki,F., Lernfähige Klassifierungssysteme, Akademie Verlag Berlin, 1981.

/3/ Wehenkel, L. et al.: Artificial Intelligence Applied to On-line Transient Stability Assessment of Electric Power Systems, Proc. 10.th World Congress on Automatic Control, Vol. 6, Munich, 1987 , pp 308 - 313.

/4/ Müller, W.: Algorithm description CAL5, STATLOG (ESPRIT Project no. 5170), Deliverable D.2.2. Learning Algorithms and Datasets used in Statlog, 1991.

/5/ Wysotzki,F., Müller,W.: Anwendung von Lernverfahren in der Prozeßdiagnose, Fachtagung Automatisierung der TU Dresden, Vol. 5 Dresden, February 1992, pp 144 - 154.

MIPS—An Interactive Decision Support System for Hardware Investment Planning

Gerhard Satzger, Andrea Wirth
IBM Deutschland GmbH
Pascalstraße 100, 7000 Stuttgart 80, Germany

1. Introduction

With information technology gaining more and more strategic importance in today's business world, enterprises have more than ever to be aware of supplying the computing services the company needs. On the other hand, IS resources are a major cost issue. Therefore, capacity planning can no longer be defined as just projecting system growth and hardware requirements. Instead its ".. ultimate purpose must be to project capital expenditures into the future as part of an organizational plan" (Thewlis (1990), p. 47). If capacity planning is, therefore, understood as a process that must be performed by both technical *and* financial experts, it is evident that there is a need to simultaneously consider the implications of investment decisions in both areas.

In this note we give a short overview, how an interdisciplinary approach can be taken to provide decision support for hardware investment planning. For that purpose we utilize and combine methods from investment theory, operations research and artificial intelligence to develop a PC-based system that can interactively be used by the planners to derive and evaluate investment proposals. The MIPS[2] system was developed in a joint project of the University of Giessen and IBM Germany, and has been implemented under OS/2 1.3 using the OS/2 Database Manager, C/2, the TIRS expert system shell and the 4GL-tool ENFIN/2.

2. Concept

As a tool to reduce the complexity of decisions when planning the hardware for large computing facilities, MIPS is focussing on CPU investments accounting for a large percentage of total hardware costs. In very general terms, its main purpose is to identify the "efficieny curve" in the space of possible investment programs shown in figure 1. As a consequence, the technically best investment program should be found for any given financial level or the financially best solution

---

[1] Dipl.-Wi.ing. Gerhard Satzger, IBM Deutschland GmbH, Pascalstr. 100, W-7000 Stuttgart 80
Dipl.-Math.-oec. Andrea Wirth, Fachbereich Wirtschaftswissenschaften, Universität Gießen, Licherstr. 60, W-6300 Gießen

[2] MIPES is short for: Mainframe Investment Planning System

for any desired technical level. With these curves at hand for different capacity levels, planners could easily judge the financial impacts of new capacity demands and/or technical requirements. Changing the capacity means "moving the curve itself", whereas changing the technical level means "moving along the curve".

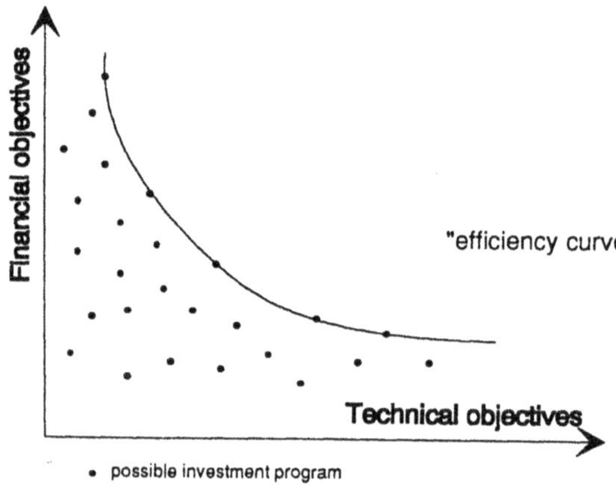

Figure 1: "Efficient" investment programs

3. Steps in the decision support process

Four steps constitute the decision support process: generation of investment alternatives, financial analysis, technical evaluation and creation of optimal investment programs. These steps are shown in figure 2 and will briefly be discussed:

Generating investment alternatives: The first task to be accomplished is to create all (partial) investment alternatives that can be included into an investment program. In general, capacity can be made available in several ways[3]: using existing machines (and, therefore, forego the opportunity to sell them), purchasing new machines, purchasing used machines as well as upgrading existing, new, and/or used ones. MIPS extracts the relevant data from a relational database and configures the machines by adding features and additional equipment needed to operate them.

Financial analysis: According to the specified financial objectives (i.e. generally the after-tax net present value), all investment alternatives are analyzed and evaluated from a financial point of view. The analysis includes the cash flows for investments as well as for maintenance and operating costs, depreciation schedules and tax treatment, the decrease of market values, and future replacement possibilities.

[3] The possibility to rent or lease machines is not included in the current system, but could be added if necessary.

Technical evaluation: With respect to a technical profile of the planning situation being provided by the user, a knowledge based component evaluates the suitability of each alternative on a scale from 0 to 1000. In particular, this component utilizes the capabilities of knowledge based systems to handle judgements and uncertain data .

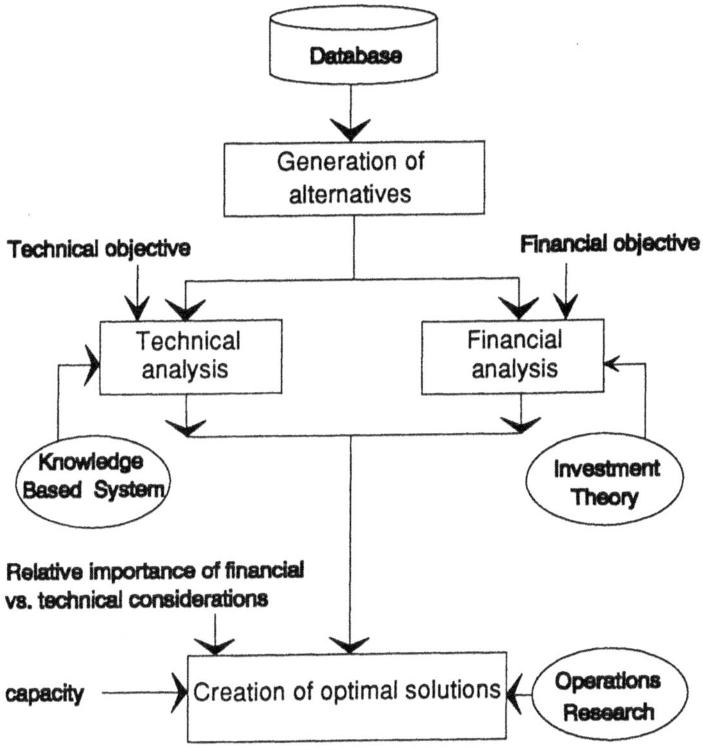

Figure 2: The steps in the decision process (e.g. financial analysis), the methods used in this process (e.g. investment theory), and the control variables supplied by the user (e.g. the financial objective)

Creating optimal investment programs: Based on both financial and technical evaluations of the alternatives, a set of optimization problems to find adequate tradeoffs can be defined with $\lambda \in [0,1]$ denoting the weight of the financial point of view.

With the following notation

$f_i \in [-1,0]$	:	normalized financial evaluation of the alternatives i=1,...,n
$t_i \in [0,1]$	:	normalized technical evaluation of the alternatives i=1,...,n
$c_i > 0$	:	capacities of the alternatives i = 1,...,n
$x_i \in \{0,1\}$	:	decision variable for alternative i = 1,...,n
C	:	needed overall capacity,

the set of problems is given[4] by

$$\text{Maximize:} \quad \sum_{i=1}^{n} [\lambda * f_i + (1-\lambda) * t_i] * x_i$$

$$\text{subject to:} \quad \sum_{i=1}^{n} c_i * x_i >= C$$

To provide the planner with a range of solutions (i.e. investment programs) to start with, initially some optimal[5] solutions are generated for $\lambda = 0, 0.2, 0.4, \ldots, 1$, where the optimization with $\lambda = 0$ represents a purely technical, the optimization with $\lambda = 1$ a purely financial point of view. The user can simply select any of the solutions generated to obtain all its components. He may now wish to refine the list of solutions by selecting a λ-intervall, e.g. [0.4,0.6] which is then used for creating further solutions (e.g. for λ=0.45,0.50,0.55). Alternatively, the user can specify λ directly, and he can manually develop solutions and compare them to the investment programs suggested by MIPS. This approach enables the user to work with the efficieny curve in the space of optimal investment programs that was depicted in figure 1.

4. Conclusion

The approach taken in MIPS showed that investment planning involving a high degree of technical expertise can significantly be improved by a Decision Support System combining algorithmic and knowledge based components - a *tandem expert system* in the terminology of Kusiak/Heragu (1989)). It could be expected that this approach would work also in any technically complex area other than IS hardware planning.

5. References

Kusiak, A. / Heragu, S. (1989): Expert Systems and Optimization. In: IEEE Transactions on Software Engineering, 8/1989, p. 1017-1020

Thewlis, D. (1990): DP to Finance: We Have to Talk. In: Software Magazin, 1/1990, p. 47-56

---

[4] Additional restrictions to include upgrade dependencies are omitted for simplification purposes.

[5] MIPS offers both an exact optimization routine suited to solve "small" problems as well as a heuristic approach to efficiently handle larger problems.

Expert Systems Applications in Construction Management and Engineering

Charles A. Snyder
Department of Management, Auburn University
Auburn, AL 36849, U.S.A.

Expert System (ES) technology can improve construction quality and productivity. Although commercial interest began in 1980 and there has been a clearly felt need, the development of ES for construction has been rather slow. One of the reasons could be the non-realization of the promise of these systems by the industry which resulted in relatively poor funding of such developments. This paper summarizes the concepts of ES for construction management, hardware/software requirements, and lists potential areas for development of ES in the industry. The ES availability in the industry is summarized.

1.0 NEED FOR EXPERT SYSTEMS IN CONSTRUCTION MANAGEMENT AND ENGINEERING

Expert Systems should have a special appeal to the construction professions because they can combine factual knowledge with judgement, handle incomplete and uncertain data and can communicate with their users in natural language. The following features of the construction environment make it an ideal candidate for development and application of ES. (See e.g., Adeli,1988; Kostem & Maher 1986).

a) Construction is nonrepetitive. Ready algorithmic solutions are not applicable to day-to-day construction problems since each project is different in design, layout, materials used, construction methods, time, crew, weather, management, etc.

b) Construction environments are full of uncertainties with respect to labor and equipment productivity, market forces, material availability and changes, variation in regulations, influence and variation in weather. Algorithmic computer programs cannot properly handle such uncertainties.

c) Knowledge of Construction engineering and management has not yet been adequately formalized and encoded. The industry runs on conventional knowledge and experience-based judgement.

d) In many construction situations there is not enough time to make a detailed analysis of all relevant factors, therefore decisions must often be made so that the construction process is not interrupted.

e) Many construction decisions; e.g., safety management, labor relations, amount to bid, bid evaluation, and risk management are qualitative and subjective, thus needing heuristics.

f) All of the necessary information on a construction project decision area is never completely known and decisions have to be made on the basis of incomplete information.

g) Many construction professionals and managers do not have enough knowledge or training to be able to use and update algorithmic computer programs.

e) Expert system building requires domain experts, and there are highly knowledgeable experts in the construction industry who have successfully completed several projects.

The development of ES in construction is in its early stages (Babcock, 1991) and few operational systems exist. Two of the factors for the slow development of ES in the field could be:

a) lack of awareness of the industry about the capabilities of ES and about the people who could develop them.

b) The nature of the industry which is very competitive and risk averse and where specialized problem-solving knowledge is considered proprietary.

2.0 POTENTIAL EXPERT SYSTEM APPLICATION AREAS IN CONSTRUCTION MANAGEMENT AND ENGINEERING.

Several areas in construction engineering and management, apart from strategic bidding, planning and financial management, are potential candidates for ES. Some of them are:

a) Design of construction methods.
b) Concrete mixing and placement.
c) Constructability evaluation.
d) Temporary facilities layout.
e) Project planning, scheduling, and control.
f) Project management.
g) Construction quality control.
h) Construction company management.
i) Equipment selection ,diagnosis, and repair.
j) Human resource management.
k) Operational problems in constructed facilities.
l) Materials management and Bill of Material pricing.
m) Legal and regulartory issues.
n) Facility maintenance.
o) Design change accounting.

Some of these areas have been the subject of recent research into subjective decision support systems that incorporate the ES to provide total recall of previous decisions that had similar characteristics. Thus, the ES assists the user to continuously enhance the heuristics incorporated in the mental model and the ES itself. Other recent ES development combines architectual graphics, bills of materials, pricing, and scheduling to present all major impacts of a design or specification change at the time the visual model is modified.

3.0 CHARACTERISTICS OF EXISTING EXPERT SYSTEMS IN CONSTRUCTION

Mohan (1990) summarized the state-of-the-art ES in construction, their input-data requirements, system output, knowledge structure, control strategy, and the type of hardware/software used. According to his survey, there are 37 ES in various stages of development.

4.0 CONCLUSION

Knowledge Based Expert Systems Technology of today parallels that of the FORTRAN language of the 1950s, the problem-oriented languages of the 1960s and the CAD of the 1970s. The contribution of Expert Systems to the extension of human capability and their effectiveness as managers should be profound in the coming years.

Expert Systems in construction management and engineering have a natural fit. ES should cover most of the construction management aspects that present the greatest problems and help the industry to become more efficient.

5.0 REFERENCES

Adeli, H., ed.(1988). Expert systems in construction and structural engineering: Chapman and Hall.

Babcock, Daniel L. (1991). Managing Engineering and Technology: Englewood Cliffs, NJ Prentice Hall.

Kostem, Celal & Maher, Mary (1986). Expert systems in civil engineering: ASCE.

Mohan, Satish (1990). Expert systems applications in construction management and engineering. Journal of Construction Engineering & Management, vol. 116 no. 1, Mar.1990, 87-99.

Indices for Characterizing Ordinal Data

Ulrich Tüshaus
Institut für Unternehmensforschung, Hochschule St. Gallen
Bodanstraße 6, 9000 St. Gallen, Switzerland

Introduction

In a well-known approach for the analysis of qualitative data, the information on the objects contained in each (qualitative) variable is represented by a corresponding binary relation on the set of objects. The aim is then to find, for example, a single relation—a *median relation*—approximating best the input data. Barthélemy and Monjardet (1980/81, 1987) give an excellent overview of the underlying concept, suitable objective functions and solution methods.

The median complete order relation

We denote $I = \{1, \ldots, n\}$ the set of objects, $M = \{1, \ldots, p\}$ the set of variables and α_{im} the value of variable m for object i. Thus, the set $A_m := \{\alpha_{im} : i \in I\}$ contains all observed values for m.

In the ordinal case (i.e. A_m is completely ordered), we can determine for $\alpha_{im}, \alpha_{jm} \in A_m$ if $\alpha_{im} \leq \alpha_{jm}$ or $\alpha_{im} \geq \alpha_{jm}$ (or both) holds. Therefore, the complete information on the objects given by the variables and their values can be represented by a family $(R_m)_{m \in M}$ of binary relations on I with $iR_mj :\Leftrightarrow \alpha_{im} \leq \alpha_{jm} \quad (i, j \in I,\ m \text{ ordinal})$

Using the classic *symmetric difference distance*, i.e.

$$|R_m \bigtriangleup R| = |R_m \cup R| - |R_m \cap R| = |R_m - R| + |R - R_m|$$

the search for the median (complete order) relation R^* can be formulated, for example, as follows:

$$\sum_{m \in M} |R_m \bigtriangleup R| \longrightarrow \min_{R \text{ is complete order relation}}$$

With $r_{ij} = 1$ if and only if iRj and $r_{ij} = 0$ otherwise, $|R_m \bigtriangleup R|$ can be rewritten as

$$\begin{aligned} |R_m \bigtriangleup R| &= \sum_{(i,j) \in I \times I} (r_{mij} - r_{ij})^2 = \sum_{(i,j) \in I \times I} r_{mij} + r_{ij} - 2r_{mij}r_{ij} \\ &= \sum_{(i,j) \in I \times I} r_{mij} + \sum_{(i,j) \in I \times I} (1 - 2r_{mij})r_{ij} \end{aligned}$$

Thus,

$$\sum_{m \in M} |R_m \bigtriangleup R| = \sum_{m \in M} \sum_{(i,j) \in I \times I} r_{mij} + \sum_{(i,j) \in I \times I} (p - 2 \sum_{m \in M} r_{mij}) r_{ij}.$$

As it is easy to express the restriction "*R is complete order relation*" by equality and inequality constraints on the r_{ij}, it is possible to define this problem as a binary linear program; a suitable solution method is discussed, for example, in Schader and Tüshaus (1986).

Consensus, concordance and coherence

While the concept of *consensus*—as general agreement in matters of opinion—has always been central within the political and social sciences, its use in data analysis is more recent (see Day (1987) for an overview). For example, the problem described above can been seen as a „consensus problem“ on a class of binary relations (on a given finite set I) where several relations have to be mapped into one of the same class: a „consensus method“ then returns a „consensus object“ (here, the median relation) representing (or aggregating) the information shared among the data relations, while a „consensus index“ returns a quantitative measure of agreement among data relations (Day and McMorris, 1985). Within the data analysis the term consensus is aimed at the description of the aggregation process (i.e., objectives and methods).

A different aspect of the problem is characterized as the *concordance* (or cohesiveness) of the data relations. Being independent of the solution, it can be used to describe the quality of the data (i.e., the overall agreement among the data relations).

For this purpose, several concordance indices have been developed (see Marcotorchino (1981) for some examples and Monjardet (1985) for a general study of indices for complete orders). These are mostly based on Kendall's τ and generalized for the case with more than two orders. Monjardet (1985), for example, derives from τ a coefficient K,

$$K = 1 - \frac{2\sum_{k,l\in M}|R_k \triangle R_l|}{p^2 n(n-1)} \quad \text{with} \quad \begin{array}{cc} 0 \leq K \leq 1 & p \text{ even} \\ 1/p^2 \leq K \leq 1 & p \text{ odd} \end{array}$$

This coefficient takes its maximal value for $R_k = R$ (all relations being equal (unanimity)). The minimal value depends on the parity of p. For p being even, $K = 0$; as an example, consider $p/2$ identical complete orders and $p/2$ identical complete orders with the order of the objects completely reversed (maximal contradiction). The generalization of coefficient K into a concordance index is straightforward.

In contrast to concordance, the notion of *coherence* is used to describe the quality of the solution of a consensus method. In our case, the median relation being a complete order relation, the underlying concept is the following.

For the aggregation of several complete orders by a "simple majority rule", it is well-known that the resulting relation must not necessarily be a complete order again. Let $\mathcal{R}_{RAC}$ be the set of all tournaments (reflexive, antisymmetric and complete relations) on $I \times I$, then the values $\max_{R\in\mathcal{R}_{RAC}}\{\sum_m |R_m \triangle R|\}$ and $\min_{R\in\mathcal{R}_{RAC}}\{\sum_m |R_m \triangle R|\}$ are easily determined because $\sum_{m\in M}|R_m \triangle R|$ is linear in r_{ij}. These are extremal or boundary values of the objective function when neglecting the transitivity restriction (which, however, the median complete order R^* must fulfill).

A suitable coherence index has been proposed by Marcotorchino (1981):

$$\frac{\max_{R\in\mathcal{R}_{RAC}}\{\sum_m |R_m \triangle R|\} - \sum_{m\in M}|R_m \triangle R^*|}{\max_{R\in\mathcal{R}_{RAC}}\{\sum_m |R_m \triangle R|\} - \min_{R\in\mathcal{R}_{AC}}\{\sum_m |R_m \triangle R|\}}$$

This index takes into account, how 'intransitive' the simple majority result is and how 'far' the median relation had to depart from it to achieve transitivity.

Here, in the context of median relations, the notions of concordance and (respectively, coherence) have been used for characterizing the data (respectively, the solution). In other areas, e.g. when comparing trees representing hierarchical classifications, different definitions (and opinions) exist (see Day and McMorris (1985) for a discussion of consensus indices and „consensus object invariants“ (measuring the information content of a consensus object)).

Concluding remarks

Whereas the classical concept of concordance has originally been defined for other structures, this concept can be transformed and adapted to the problem of finding a median order relation.

The notion of coherence is also meaningful for this type of problem; however, an investigation from a more theoretical point of view has still to be made. Besides, the different terms of the corresponding index can be used during the search for the optimal median relation: the choice of the parameters, e.g. the step size, of the subgradient method (see Schader and Tüshaus (1986)) can be based on them.

Moreover, the indices (of concordance as well as of coherence) are very useful in the interpretation step of an analysis of qualitative data: lacking an easy visual (or geometrical) representation, the investigation of the structural information contained in the relations can be supported.

References

[Barthélemy and Monjardet, 1980/81] Barthélemy, J. P. and Monjardet, B. (1980/81). The median procedure in cluster analysis and social choice theory. *Mathematical Social Sciences*, 1(3):235–267.

[Barthélemy and Monjardet, 1987] Barthélemy, J. P. and Monjardet, B. (1987). The median procedure in data analysis: New results and open problems. In [Bock, 1987], pages 309–316.

[Bock, 1987] Bock, H. H., editor (1987). *Classification and Related Methods of Data Analysis*, Proceedings of the First Conference of the International Federation of Classification Societies (IFCS), Technical University of Aachen, F.R.G. North-Holland, Amsterdam, 1988.

[Day, 1987] Day, W. H. E. (1987). Consensus methods as tools for data analysis. In [Bock, 1987], pages 317–324.

[Day and McMorris, 1985] Day, W. H. E. and McMorris, F. R. (1985). A formalization of consensus index methods. *Bulletin of Mathematical Biology*, 47(2):215–229.

[Marcotorchino, 1981] Marcotorchino, F. (1981). *Agrégation des similarités en classification automatique*. Thèse de Doctorat d'État ès Sciences Mathématiques, Université Pierre et Marie Curie—Paris VI.

[Monjardet, 1985] Monjardet, B. (1985). Concordance et consensus d'ordres totaux: les coefficients K et W. *Revue de Statistique Appliquée*, 33(2):55–85.

[Schader and Tüshaus, 1986] Schader, M. and Tüshaus, U. (1986). Subgradient methods for analyzing qualitative data. In Gaul, W. and Schader, M., editors, *Classification as a Tool of Research*, Karlsruhe, pages 397–403. North-Holland, Amsterdam.

A Knowledge Based System Managing Sequences of Data Analysis Methods

F. Wartenberg, W. Gaul, D. Baier
Institute of Decision Theory & Operations Research, University of Karlsruhe
7500 Karlsruhe 1, Germany

1. Introduction

WIMDAS-PS (WIssensbasiertesMarketingDatenAnalyseSystem-Positionierung/Segmentierung) is a knowledge-based system which aims at supporting users who are not familiar with the analysis of marketing data. Questions and problems from the area of (marketing) data analysis can require proper application of *alternating sequences of data analysis methods and input/output data arrays* (abbreviated as: sequences of data analysis methods) where the output of one method can be used as input to another method. Appropriate interconnections between user wishes, (data analysis) objectives, methods, and data are modeled in order to provide substantial support concerning the management, e.g., the generation, selection and execution, of adequate sequences of data analysis methods.

Sequences of data analysis methods that are generated by the system's inference engine are called *proposals*. If more than one proposal is suggested by WIMDAS-PS a possible user must decide which proposals in which order he wants to select for execution.

In this paper, special attention is given to the concept of knowledge-based comparisons of proposals by WIMDAS-PS where confidence factors are used for the calculations. Moreover, the creation of graphical representations of proposals is demonstrated which provides additional support for the understanding of the underlying possibilities within WIMDAS-PS and for the distinction of different sequences of data analysis methods. The reliability of this concept is tested by means of a simulation study.

2. WIMDAS-PS: System description

The development of the knowledge based system WIMDAS-PS is part of the joint research project WIMDAS (Wissensbasiertes Marketing Daten Analyse System) which is tackled together with a research group in Hamburg and Mannheim (see, e.g., Baier, Gaul (1990a,b), Gaul, Schader, Both (1990) for recent reports). At the moment WIMDAS-PS covers the problem domains "positioning analysis" and "segmentation analysis". The analyses are

---

1 Research has been supported by the Deutsche Forschungsgemeinschaft

performed on basis of market research and marketing data which can be acquired - for example - from market research companies. These survey data are stored as data arrays in the system's database, together with corresponding data array characterizations.

Data analysis methods are incorporated into the system by integration as rules of applications of data analysis methods on data arrays into the system's knowledgebase and by implementation of corresponding methods into the system's method base.

User access to the system is provided by the user interface which allows selection of a survey, selection of relevant data which should be included in the analysis, and selection of goals, which - altogether - allow the activation of the inference engine and the generation of proposals. Of course, a selection and execution of the proposals generated is possible and leads to the presentation of results (see, e.g., Baier, Gaul, Wartenberg (1991) for more information about the current implementation of WIMDAS-PS).

For an inquiry to the inference engine the following information is needed: the data array characterizations of those data arrays which are available in the system's database, the survey selected and the goal which describes results desired by means of data array characterizations. A successful search of the inference engine leads to the generation of one or more proposals. Depending on the data selected and the goal specified there could be many proposals at the same time, which might differ by the application of methods and the input/output data arrays used. Therefore the user faces a decision problem of combinatorial complexity where assistance by the system must be given. This is achieved by an ordering and a generation of a graphical representation of the proposals.

3. Rating and selecting (alternating) sequences of data analysis methods (and input/output data arrays)

To obtain such an ordering of proposals we need some kind of assignment of "quality" values to proposals, where the quality of a proposal is influenced by the rules needed for the generation of the proposal, i.e. by the quality of the methods applied, and by the quality of the data used. Therefore the quality values of proposals may be uncertain, which leads to considerations concerning the representation of uncertain information in expert systems (see, e.g., Spiegelhalter (1986) or Ng, Abramson (1990) for a general view of uncertainty management in expert systems).

For our purpose we used confidence factors in the following way: a rule describes the application of a method m_i on some input data arrays I_k ($k=1,\ldots,n_i$) leading to an output data array O_i.

The rating of a method m_i (or the rating of the corresponding rule) is expressed by a confidence value $CF(m_i)$.

The rating $CF(I_k) \in [0,100]$ of an input data array I_k is set according to the following scheme:

- If an input data array I_k consists of raw data, I_k can be assigned a CF-value of 100 (Smaller values can be used, for instance, to account for missing values.).

- If input data arrays consist of already derived data, they are output data derived by previous application of methods on some other data. In this case the *CF*-value would be set according to the formula which belongs to an output data array.

The *CF*-value of the output data array O_i is obtained by the following formula:

$$CF(\mathrm{O}_i) := CF(\mathrm{m}_i)\frac{\min\{CF(\mathrm{I}_1),\ldots,CF(\mathrm{I}_{n_i})\}}{100}.$$

By applying these formulae to the generated proposals an ordering can be established. Figure 1 shows a typical situation during the selection of proposals. The inference engine has generated proposals which are partly visible in the "Proposal Selection" window on the lower left of the screen (In this case abstract proposals have been used.). As can be seen they are ordered in decreasing order of *CF*-values. For more information the user has activated the graphical representation of the proposal selected which is displayed in a pop-up window on the right.

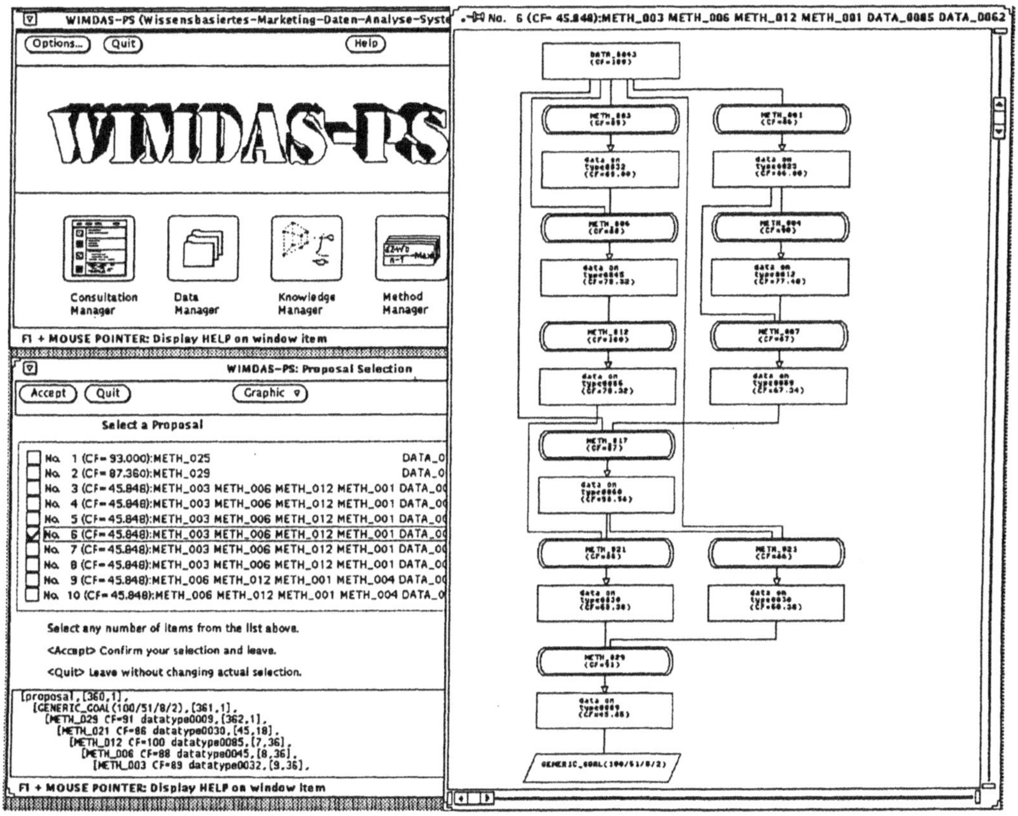

Figure 1: A typical WIMDAS-PS screen during the proposal selection process

4. Simulation study

As we did not know whether the order of the proposals resulting from our application of confidence factors would be suitable for our selection problem, (e.g., whether the proposal with the "highest quality" would be on top of the list) we conducted a simulation study. With a set of proposals P, sets of rating functions for methods ($f_M \in F_M$), data arrays ($f_D \in F_D$), and proposals ($f_P \in F_P$), the values of which could be interpreted as *CF*-values, we formulated general criteria which should be met by the rating of proposals.

First criterion: *Proposals consisting of short sequences of data analysis methods should be preferred to proposals with longer sequences.*

Using a function $L(p_i)$ to describe the length of the longest sequence in proposal $p_i \in P$, we can express this criterion in the following way: If $L(p_i) \leq L(p_j)$ then it should follow $f_P(p_i) \geq f_P(p_j)$.

Second criterion: *Proposals using data analysis methods which are considered to be better in terms of ratings or "quality" values than those used in other proposals should be preferred.*

Using $MQM(p_i, f_M)$ to describe the mean quality of methods used in proposal p_i, this criterion is expressed as: If $MQM(p_i, f_M) \geq MQM(p_j, f_M)$ then it should follow $f_P(p_i) \geq f_P(p_j)$.

Third criterion: *Proposals using data arrays which are considered to be better in terms of ratings or "quality" values than those used in other proposals should be preferred.*

With $MQD(p_i, f_D)$ representing the mean quality of data arrays used in proposal p_i we can express this criterion in the following way: If $MQD(p_i, f_D) \geq MQD(p_j, f_D)$ then it should follow $f_P(p_i) \geq f_P(p_j)$.

Examples, which show that these criteria must not be fulfilled in general can be easily constructed. However, they seem to be reasonable and - therefore - should be fulfilled to a satisfying degree in the simulation study in which we tried to check whether our application of confidence factors was useful.

In the simulation study we used randomly constructed graphs which have the same structure as proposals and take into account the same characteristics as our rulebase from which proposals - in the simulation called *proposal structures* - could be generated. With nodes representing data arrays and methods we varied the number δ of different data types, the number ρ of rules (respectively nodes representing methods), the number γ of given data and the maximal number λ of input data arrays for a method (respectively the maximal number of direct predecessors of a method node).

The generation of *proposal structure sets* was performed according to the following scheme:

- First, a random inquiry to the inference engine was generated, consisting of rules, given data, and a goal.
- Second, the inference engine was activated and if more than one proposal structure was found the whole set was stored for later evaluation.
- Then, the configuration (δ, ρ, γ, λ) was randomly changed and the previous steps were repeated.

For the evaluation of the results all generated proposal structure sets have been taken, the single proposal structures have been rated with *CF*-values, furthermore length, mean quality of the sequences of input/output combinations and mean quality of the data have been calculated and checked against the rating of the input/output combinations. Additionally, coefficients as, e.g., Pearsons correlation coefficient and Spearmans rank order correlation coefficient were calculated for further information.

The results have been favourable to our concept of confidence values, as, e.g., the ratio of the number of successful comparisons to the total number of comparisons has been 87.6% for criterion 1 (respectively 64% and 52% for criterion 2 and 3). The additional coefficients computed showed that the criteria were unrelated.

5. Conclusions

From the results presented one can conclude that usage of confidence factors is a suitable way to represent uncertain information in our problem domain and can be used to provide an ordering for generated alternating sequences of data analysis methods and input/output data arrays. This ordering, together with a graphical representation of proposals allows an easier comparison and selection of proposals and substantially supports the user of WIMDAS-PS.

6. References

Baier,D., Gaul,W. (1990a):
Entscheidungsunterstützung bei der Auswertung von Primärforschungsdaten — Ein Konzept zur Verbindung von Wissensbasis, Datenbank und Methoden,
in: Operations Research Proceedings 1989, Springer, Berlin Heidelberg New York, 406-413.

Baier,D., Gaul,W. (1990b):
Computer-Assisted Market Research and Marketing Enriched by Capabilities of Knowledge-Based Systems,
in: New Ways in Marketing and Market Research, EMAC/ESOMAR Symposium, Athens, Greece, 139-160.

Baier,D. Gaul,W., Wartenberg,F.(1991):
Positioning Analysis using Knowledge-based Support, to appear.

Gaul,W., Schader,M., Both,M. (1990):
Knowledge-Oriented Support for Data Analysis Applications to Marketing,
in: Knowledge, Data and Computer-Assisted Decisions, M.Schader and W.Gaul (eds.), Springer, Berlin Heidelberg New York, 42-53.

Ng,K.-C., Abramson,B. (1990):
Uncertainty Management in Expert Systems, in: IEEE Expert, April, 29-47.

Spiegelhalter,D.J. (1986):
A Statistical View of Uncertainty in Expert Systems, in: Artificial Intelligence&Statistics, W.A.Gale(ed.), Addison-Wesley, Reading, 17-55.

Section 7

Applications in Business and Economics

Enterprise Input-Output Modelling—Extensions of the Basic Model and its Applications

Janez Artenjak
Faculty of Business Economics Maribor
Razlagova 14, Maribor, Slovenia

Enterprise models discussed by Pichler (1961), Mueller-Mehrbach (1964), Teusch-Schluetter (1985), and Mesko (1986) depend on the characteristics of the production process and on the operative purposes but they represent only a specific form of the input/output modelling (Kloock, 1969). The assumptions that each product is produced in the same technological way and at the same production centre can sometimes limit the applicability of input/output modelling.

Therefore, the model approach to overcome the problems arising, firstly from producing more products at the same production centre, and secondly from producing the same product by different technological way is considered. The emphasis is given to the cost-oriented price model enabling the marketing management to improve decision making associated with pricing policy.

METHODOLOGY AND EXTENSION OF THE MODEL

In the production process, decomposed on basis of structural analysis to n production centres, physical flows between production centres in reproduction process and markets can be expressed in form

$$x=A.x+q, \tag{1}$$

where components of $x \in R^n$ represent the size of products measured in quantitative units (q.u.); A is a n x n matrix whose elements define the direct consumption of the intermediate products in reproduction process; components of $q \in R^n$ denote the sizes of sale.

The solution of (1) for x,

$$x=(I-A)^{-1}.q, \tag{2}$$

is possible to use for analyzing the impact of different sales alternatives on the level of production. Matrix $(I-A)^{-1}$, with matrix I as identity matrix, represents inversion of the matrix (I-A). The elements r_{ij} $(i,j=1,2,...,n)$ of the inversion matrix are production multipliers which reflect the elasticity of production to changes of demand. These parameters are very important not only in input/output modelling but also for the construction of the other business models (Artenjak 1992).In a reproduction process there are needed costs inputs which structure and size are defined by relation

$$x^d=A^d.x, \tag{3}$$

where components of $x^d \in R^m$ denote the size of inputs, and where A^d is a m x n matrix whose elements represent the coefficients defining direct consumption of the inputs. Matrix A^d and vector x^d can be partitioned to distinguish, for instance, the inputs of raw material from direct labour inputs.

If some products can be produced in different technological ways it is possible to analyze the impact of natural and/or financial flows of these production centres on others by introducing fictitious centres. Relations between the production centres representing different technological ways and the relating of fictitious production centres are expressed by input coefficients whose values denote the share of each technology in the production of 1q.u. of fictitious products, and they are obtained by experience or by optimization. All other input coefficients of the considered fictitious production centre have a value equal to zero.

The problem of producing more products at the same production centre can be solved by introducing the matrix A^+ whose elements a^+_{ij} denote the quantity of the i-th by-product which is obtained by the production of the j-th output unity. In price models, the by-products are treated as final products which should strengthen the competitive position of the main products. For this reason, the coefficients of the matrix A^+ in the price models appear with the negative sign.

To construct a suitable price model (Artenjak, 1991) it is necessary to define the total costs consisting of direct costs, derivative costs and added costs what can be expressed in matrix form as

$$X=\check{x}(-A^{+T}p^{+}+A^{d}p^{d})+B^{T}X+d, \qquad (4)$$

where components of $X \in R^{n}$ denote the amount of total costs, $\check{x}$ is a n x n diagonal matrix whose elements are equal to sizes of production, components of $p \in R^{r}$ define the selling prices of the products obtained in the production process, components of $p^{d} \in R^{m}$ denote the purchasing prices of the costs inputs, B is a n x n matrix whose elements define consumption shares of the i-th product in the production of the j-th product, and components of $d \in R^{n}$ represent the amount of fixed costs with the required profit. Considering relation $B=\check{x}^{-1}.A\check{x}$ and price equation $p=\check{x}^{-1}.X$ in (4), the following price models can be obtained:

$$p^{v}=(I-A^{T})^{-1}(-A^{+T}p^{+}+A^{dT}p^{d}) \qquad (5)$$

and

$$p^{c}=p^{v}+(I-A^{T})^{-1}\check{x}^{-1}d \qquad (6)$$

Price model (5) indicates the lower bound under which it is, from the economical point of view, not any more reasonable to produce and to sell the product. Price model (6) is the model which can be very usefully applied for analyzing the effects of the changing operating production level and changed prices of costs inputs, technological and institutional conditions on full cost pricing.

REFERENCES:

Artenjak J (1991) Enterprise Pricing of Multiphase Production by using Input-Output Modelling. Economic Analysis, Beograd, No. 2, 171-177.

Artenjak J (1992) Optimization of Industrial Advertising Expenditures on Market Segments. Proceedings of the 21th Annual Conference of the European Marketing Academy, Vol I, 37-46.

Kloock J (1969) Betriebswirtschaftliche Input-Output Modelle, Verlag Dr. Th. Gabier-Wiesbaden.

Mesko I (1986) Analysis of Business Process by Opportunity Costs, Economic Analysis, Beograd, No. 3, 307-310.

Mueller-Mehrbach H (1964) Die Berechnung des Nettoteilbedarfs aus dem Gozinto-Graph. Ablauf- und Planungsforschung, 5, 191-198.

Pichler O Kostenrechnung und Martizenkalkuel. Ablauf - und Planungs forschung, No 2, 29-46.

Teusch W and Schluetter J Kostenplannung und Dualitaet bei Pichler-Modellen. Zeitschrift fuer Betriebswirtschaft, 924-936.

The Selection of the Optimum Offers in Crude Oil Market by Linear Programming

Gheorghe Barbatu, C.E. Marius, V. Ionescu
Str Mircea 150A Bloc MD10SC-A AP18, Romania

As it is known, the selection of the optimum offers on the international crude oil market is a very important problem. In this paper we present a mathematical, technological model discovered by us for the scientific motivation of the selection and elaboration of the best crude oil importation programme. The best quality of crude oil at the lowest possible cost price is assured.
In case of spot lot appearance, the linear programming model, solved on a computer, shows if it is competitive or not.
One real example regarding the importation of crude oil by Romania is considered. It was necessary to import 11,889,000 tons of crude oil after selection of the best offers from 21 available partners, as it is shown in table 1.

TABLE 1

Type of crude oil	Available quantity tons	Price $/ton	Light fractions content	Freezing point ^{0}C M.I.		Viscosity S cst M.I. at 20^0 C		%	Optim. solution
0	1	2	3	4	5	6	7	8	9
SARIR	500,000	219.22	45.6	+17	68.2	10.0	23.58	0.5	x_1
ESSIDER	600,000	220.41	50.8	+3	40.9	6.9	20.43	0.5	x_2
MANDJI	100,000	203.83	41.2	+15	62.8	18.5	26.74	1.5	x_3
SIRIAN	5,000,000	177.72	40.0	-20	21.8	27.0	28.35	4.0	x_4
ROMASKIN	150,000	210.34	49.7	-3	34.0	7.5	22.00	1.8	x_5
SUEZ BL	1,200,000	218.99	43.8	+10	52.0	13.0	24.98	1.4	x_6
ARABIAN	200,000	239.33	56.8	-25	19.4	4.5	18.34	1.3	x_7
URAL	1,200,000	211.09	49.5	-5	31.8	9.0	22.97	2.0	x_8
TACHING	300,000	209.42	28.2	+30	120.7	24.0	29.81	1.1	x_9
AAMNA	1,500,000	212.11	42.3	+25	97.6	16.0	26.05	0.5	x_{10}
BELAYM	200,000	196.98	36.0	+5	43.8	31.0	28.90	2.3	x_{11}
IRAN H.	2,000,000	207.65	41.9	-15	24.5	13.0	4.98	1.9	x_{12}
IRAN L.	1,000,000	216.53	49.0	-15	24.5	8.0	22.27	1.6	x_{13}
SALMAN	100,000	218.86	60.1	-12	26.2	6.0	20.43	1.8	x_{14}
KIRKUK	200,000	225.78	51.7	-20	21.8	8.0	22.27	2.2	x_{15}
SHENGLY	1 200,000	165.88	28.2	+27	105.8	24.0	29.81	1.6	x_{16}
ASHTART	200,000	193.81	44.7	-7	29.8	4.2	17.68	1.2	x_{17}
ARABIAN H.	1,500,000	214.34	51.0	-20	21.8	5.1	19.20	1.4	x_{18}
KHAFJI	350,000	199.92	40.1	-30	17.6	20.0	27.11	3.0	x_{19}
ARABIAN M.	500,000	220.20	55.0	-23	20.3	5.1	19.20	1.3	x_{20}
RAS GARIB	100,000	188.25	26.5	+12	56.3	85.0	32.65	4.0	x_{21}

It is request:
The optimum importation programme, taking in consideration the following restrictions:

- light fractions content to be not less than 42.55%
- the maximum freezing point allowed to be with 7°C under earth temperature
- the medium viscosity not to overpass 18 cst, that is 25.64 in linear units
- S(sulphur content) not to overpass 2.26 %

Taking in consideration the above data we have developed the following mathematical model:

$$\begin{aligned}\min F \;=\; & 219.22x_1 + 220.41x_2 + 203.83x_3 + 177.72x_4 + 210.34x_5 + 218.39x_6 \\ & +239.33x_7 + 211.09x_8 + 209.42x_9 + 212.11x_{10} + 196.98x_{11} + 207.65x_{12} \\ & +216.53x_{13} + 218.86x_{14} + 225.78x_{15} + 165.88x_{16} + 193.81x_{17} + 214.34x_{18} \\ & +199.92x_{19} + 220.22x_{20} + 188.25x_{21}\end{aligned}$$

with the following restrictions:

$$\sum_{i=1}^{21} x_i = 11,889,000$$

$$\begin{aligned} & 45.6x_1 + 50.8x_2 + 41.2x_3 + 40.0x_4 + 49.7x_5 + 43.8x_6 + 56.8x_7 \\ & +49.5x_8 + 28.2x_9 + 42.3x_{10} + 36x_{11} + 49.11x_{12} + 49x_{13} + 60.1x_{14} \\ & +51.7x_{15} + 28.2x_{16} + 44.17x_{17} + 51x_{18} + 40.1x_{19} + 55x_{20} + 26.5x_{21} \;\geq\; 42.55 * 11,889,000\end{aligned}$$

$$\begin{aligned} & 68.2x_1 + 40.9x_2 + 62.8x_3 + 21.8x_4 + 34x_5 + 52x_6 \\ & +19.4x_7 + 31.8x_8 + 120.7x_9 + 97.6x_{10} + 43.8x_{11} + 24.5x_{12} \\ & +24.5x_{13} + 26.2x_{14} + 21.8x_{15} + 105.8x_{16} + 29.8x_{17} + 21.8x_{18} \\ & +17.6x_{19} + 20.3x_{20} + 56.3x_{21} \;\leq\; 41.41 * 11,889,000\end{aligned}$$

(freezing point restriction)

$$\begin{aligned} & 23.58x_1 + 20.43x_2 + 26.74x_3 + 28.35x_4 + 22x_5 + 24.98x_6 \\ & +18.34x_7 + 22.97x_8 + 29.81x_9 + 26.05x_{10} + 28.91x_{11} + 24.98x_{12} \\ & +22.37x_{13} + 20.43x_{14} + 22.27x_{15} + 29.81x_{16} + 17.68x_{17} + 19.20x_{18} \\ & +27.11x_{19} + 19.20x_{20} + 32.65x_{21} \;\leq\; 25.64 * 11,889,000\end{aligned}$$

(viscosity condition)

$$\begin{aligned} & 0.5x_1 + 0.5x_2 + 1.5x_3 + 4x_4 + 1.8x_5 + 1.4x_6 + 1.3x_7 \\ & +2x_8 + 1.1x_9 + 0.5x_{10} + 2.3x_{11} + 1.9x_{12} + 1.6x_{13} + 1.8x_{14} \\ & +2.2x_{15} + 1.6x_{16} + 1.2x_{17} + 1.4x_{18} + 3x_{19} + 1.3x_{20} + 4x_{21} \;\leq\; 2.6 * 11,889,000\end{aligned}$$

(sulphur content quantity)

Restrictions regarding available quantity:

$x_1 \leq 500,000$	$x_8 \leq 1,200,000$	$x_{15} \leq 200,000$
$x_2 \leq 600,000$	$x_9 \leq 300,000$	$x_{16} \leq 1,200,000$
$x_3 \leq 100,000$	$x_{10} \leq 1,500,000$	$x_{17} \leq 200,000$
$x_4 \leq 5,000,000$	$x_{11} \leq 200,000$	$x_{18} \leq 1,500,000$
$x_5 \leq 150,000$	$x_{12} \leq 4,000,000$	$x_{19} \leq 350,000$
$x_6 \leq 1,200,000$	$x_{13} \leq 2,000,000$	$x_{20} \leq 500,000$
$x_7 \leq 200,000$	$x_{14} \leq 200,000$	$x_{21} \leq 100,000$

$$x_i \geq 0$$

The mathematical model solved on the computer, with PROGEN programme, offered the optimum solution. It is compared in table 2 with the manual solution, used by ROMANIA in the first 10 months of 1983.

TABLE 2:

Crude oil from partner P_i	Quantity imported (hand made)	$\frac{\$}{ton}$	Manual programme $	Optimum solution obtained by linear programming (computer) tons	$
P-1	328,000	219.20	71,897,600	500,000	109,600,000
P-2	440,000	220.41	96,980,000	600,000	132,246,000
P-3	75,000	203.83	15,287,000	100,000	20,383,000
P-4	3,680,000	177.72	654,009,600	2,299,854	764,170,053
P-5	90,000	210.34	18,930,000	150,000	351,551,000
P-6	960,000	218.99	210,230,400	0	0
P-7	75,000	239.33	17,949,750	0	0
P-8	815,000	211.09	172,038,350	0	0
P-9	170,000	209.42	35,601,400	0	0
P-10	1,007,000	212.11	213,594,770	1,135,061	240,757,789
P-11	155,000	196.98	30,531,900	0	0
P-12	1,337,000	207.65	277,628,050	1,548,396	321,524,429
P-13	617,000	216.59	133,599,010	0	0
P-14	85,000	218.86	18,603,100	155,689	34,074,094
P-15	140,000	225.78	31,609,200	0	0
P-16	775,000	165.88	128,557,000	1,200,000	199,056,000
P-17	65,000	193.81	12,597,650	200,000	38,762,000
P-18	575,000	214.34	123,245,500	1,500,000	321,510,000
P-19	290,000	199.92	57,976,800	0	0
P-20	150,000	220.20	33,030,000	500,000	0
P-21	100,000	188.25	11,295,000	0	0
	11,889,000		2,365,192,080 $		2,323,734,365 $

The efficiency of the model is: 2,365,192,080 $ – 2,323,734,365 $ = 41,457,715 $

Let us suppose that on the international oil market it is appeared a spot of 71,000 tons of crude oil, with 210 $/ton, 45% light fractions content, 68.2 freezing point, viscosity 30 and sulphur content 2.26%.

It is necessary to answer if this "spot lot" is competitive or not. For this reason we have completed our model with x_{22} corresponding to "spot lot". Solved on a computer, the new optimum solution is:

$$
\begin{array}{lcrlcrlcr}
x_1 & = & 500,000 & x_6 & = & 0 & x_{11} & = & 0 \\
x_2 & = & 600,000 & x_7 & = & 0 & x_{19} & = & 0 \\
x_3 & = & 1,000,000 & x_8 & = & 0 & x_{20} & = & 500,000 \\
x_4 & = & 255,973 & x_9 & = & 0 & x_{21} & = & 0 \\
x_5 & = & 150,000 & x_{10} & = & 1,107,734 & x_{22} & = & 71,000
\end{array}
$$

CONCLUSION: The "spot lot" is competitive.

Scenario Approach to Capacity Planning for the Production of a New Product

Majda Bastic
Faculty of Business Economics Maribor
Razlagova 14, Maribor, Slovenia

The decision about the production of a new product is an important strategic decision which affects the future production scheduling decisions and it requires large amounts of capital for the new equipment as well as for the development and promotion of the new product. The scenario approach is used so that the actions of competition, which affect the part of demand to be satisfied with the new product, can be taken into account too (Dembro). In this problem, where large amounts of capital are involved, the expected profit as well as the risk is the greatest management's concern. Considering all that the simple recourse model with stochastic risk constraints, in which the decision maker's attitude toward risk is considered, can be used.

Let deviations in stochastic constraints be defined by

$$u_i - v_i = r_{io} - r_{i1}x_1 - r_{i2}x_2 - \ldots - r_{in}x_n \qquad i \in S \qquad (1)$$

where $r_{ij}(j=0,1,\ldots,n)$ are random variables with mean $\bar{r}_{ij}$ and variance s_{ij}. The penalty caused by the deviations must be proportional with the deviations and $p_i+q_i \geq 0$ (Kall).

Let

a_{ij} = the quantity of the i-th element consumed for the production of one unit of the j-th product

b_i = the upper limit of the capacity of new equipment $i(i=m+1,\ldots,M)$

b_{ik} = available quantity of the i-th element under scenario k

d_{hjk} = the upper limit for the quantity of the j-th product sold under scenario k at the net price c_{hjk}

f'_i = the purchasing price of the equipment $i(i=m+1,\ldots,M)$

f_i = fixed cost per year caused by the purchase of the equipment $i(i=m+1,\ldots,M)$

f_{hkj} = the unit cost of promotion and advertising needed so that the quantity of the j-th product sold is in interval $[d'_{h-1,jk}, d'_{hjk}]$ and $d'_{hjk} = d'_{h-1,jk}+d_{hjk}$

z_{ok} = minimal amount of contribution acceptable for the decision maker under scenario k

f_0 = capital available for investment and advertising

c_{hjk} = the price of the j-th product under scenario k, reduced for the cost of advertising and promotion

c_{ik} = the purchasing price of the i-th element or unit operating cost under scenario k

100r = interest rate

The following decision variables are used

b'_{ik} = the unexhausted capacity of the element i(i=m+1,...,M) under scenario k

x_{jk} = the quantity of the j-th product produced under scenario k

y_{ik} = the quantity of the i-th element needed for the production process under scenario k

z_i = 1 if i-th equipment is purchased and 0 otherwise

z_{hjk} = the quantity of the j-th product sold at the net price c_{hjk} under scenario k

To simplify the notation of the model the constraints are written only for one year. The problem described can be solved by the model, where objective is defined by

$$minE(\sum_{i\in S}\sum_{k=1}^{K}(p_{ik}u_{ik}+q_{ik}v_{ik})+\sum_{i=m+1}^{M}\sum_{k=1}^{K}rb'_{ik}) \qquad (2)$$

subject to nonnegative variables and

$$y_{ik}-\sum_{j=1}^{N}a_{ij}x_{jk}\geq 0 \qquad i=1,...,M \quad k=1,...,K \qquad (3)$$

$$y_{ik}\leq b_{ik} \qquad i=1,...,M \quad k=1,...,K \qquad (4)$$

$$y_{ik}-b_i z_i+b'_{ik}=0 \qquad i=m+1,...,M \quad k=1,...,K \qquad (5)$$

$$x_{jk}-\sum_{h=1}^{H_j}z_{hjk}\geq 0 \qquad j=1,...,N \quad k=1,...,K \qquad (6)$$

$$\sum_{i=m+1}^{M}f'_i z_i+\sum_{k=1}^{K}\sum_{j=1}^{N}\sum_{k=1}^{H_j}f_{hjk}z_{hjk}\leq f_o \qquad (7)$$

$$z_{hjk}\leq d_{hjk} \qquad j=1,...,N \quad k=1,...,K \quad h=1,...,H_{j-1} \qquad (8)$$

$$z_{hjk}\leq d_{hjk} \qquad j=1,...,N \quad k=1,...,K \quad h=H_j \qquad (9)$$

Risk constraints are defined by

$$\sum_{j=1}^{N}\sum_{k=1}^{H_j} c_{hjk}z_{hjk}-\sum_{i=1}^{M} c_{ik}y_{ik}-\sum_{i=m+1}^{M} f_i z_i = z_{ok} \qquad K=1,\dots,K \qquad (10)$$

where (9) and (10) are stochastic constraints. Let K be the number of constraints (10) and S=K+s be the number of constraints (10) and (9). For i=K+1,...,S variables u_i mean the quantity of the unsatisfied demand of the new product and the cost associated with the acquiring of the new buyers can be expressed by p_i. Variables v_i mean the quantity of the new product which will not be sold and the lost unit contribution can be expressed by q_i. For i=1,...,K variables u_i mean that the total expected contribution of scenario i is less than the minimal contribution acceptable for the decision maker and p_i must be a large number. And variables v_i mean that the total expected contribution of scenario i exceeds the minimal contribution therefore q_i equal the probability that scenario i occurs and have in (2) negative values.
Denote with S_1 the scenario which occurs when neither our firm nor our competition invest in the production of the new product and with S_2 the scenario which occurs if only our competition invest. Let α_k be the probalibity that scenario k occurs. The yearly investment contribution of one monetary unit invested
is then defined by

$$CI=(z_2^*-z_1^*)/f_i$$

where z_2^* is the optimal expected value of the function

$$z=\sum_{k=1}^{K}\alpha_k\Big(\sum_{j=1}^{N}\sum_{h=1}^{H_j} c_{hjk}z_{hjk}-\sum_{i=1}^{M} c_{ik}y_{ik}\Big)-\sum_{i=m+1}^{M} f_i z_i$$

subject to (3)-(10) and z_1^* is the optimal expected contribution in the case that S_1 or S_2 occur, where also the interest of kapital needed for the investment are considered (Bastic).

REFERENCES

Bastic M (1986) Optimalizacija proizvodnog programa i odlucivanje o investicijama pomocu stohastickog programiranja. Doktorska disertacija, Ekonomski fakultet Zagreb, Maribor, 1986.

Dembro R (1991) Scenario optimization. Annals of Operations Research, vol.30: 63-80.

Kall P (1976) Stochastic linear programming. Springer-Verlag, Berlin Heidelberg New York.

Project Scheduling: Models, Methods, and Systems Development

Andreas Drexl
Institut für Betriebswirtschaftslehre, Christian-Albrechts-Universität zu Kiel
2300 Kiel 1, Germany

Introduction

Project scheduling is one of the most important disciplines of Operations Research with respect to applications. Especially the simple methods associated with CPM or MPM are applied rather oftenly in practice. However, cost and especially resource–oriented project scheduling methods are in practical use only rarely – despite a lot of new and promising concepts. We survey recent advances in modeling and solving deterministic resource–constrained project scheduling problems suitable for project planning and control.

The main topics are nonpreemptive time/cost/resource–tradeoff models with renewable, nonrenewable and doubly–constrained resources.

In addition, we describe the features of two project scheduling software packages: The LEINET–system (Leipziger Programmpaket Netzplantechnik), which has been developed in the former DDR over several decades. The PRISMA–system (Production Improvement of Small Batch Machine Tool Assembly), which has been developed recently for production scheduling in small batch machine tool assembly, where several make–to–order products have to be manufactured in a multi–stage production system.

Models and Methods

Traditional multiple resource–constrained project scheduling problems of either the preemptive [3] or the nonpreemptive type have been restricted to the *single–mode case* i.e. each job has to be performed in exactly one predefined way. In this case each job may be characterized by a unique duration and a singular collection of resource requirements that have to be met each time period the job is being processed [1, 4].

Recently efforts have been made to formulate and to solve the more general *multi–mode* project scheduling problems where job durations are functions of consumed resources [3, 5, 7, 11]. Regarding the formulation and solution of *nonpreemptive* project scheduling problems where job durations are discrete functions of job performance modes in the last decade efforts have been documented in literature [5, 13].

We consider the problem of nonpreemptively *minimizing project makespan* subject to job completion constraints, precedence relations as well as resource restrictions, where the resources are distinguished to be renewable or nonrenewable. The fundamental assumptions may be given as follows: Without loss of generality we assume a project with one unique source and one unique sink being depicted by an acyclic activity-on-node graph where jobs are numerically labeled such that successor jobs always have higher numbers (labels) than all their predecessors. Specifically the following may hold:

The project consists out of jobs $j = 1,...,J$. $j = 1$ ($j = J$) is the unique source (unique sink). $\mathcal{V}_j$ is the set of all immediate predecessors of job j. Job j may be performed in one of the modes $m = 1,...,M_j$. Each job, once initiated in a specific mode, must be finished without changing mode. Scheduling job j in mode m takes d_{jm} time units (duration). There exists a set of $\mathcal{R}$ renewable resources (=machines), where machine $r \in \mathcal{R}$ has a capacity of κ_r units per period; scheduling job j in mode m *uses* k_{jmr} units per period from resource r. Additionally we have a set of $\mathcal{N}$ nonrenewable resources (=budgets), where resource $r \in \mathcal{N}$ is available with K_r resource units in total; scheduling job j in mode m *consumes* $k_{jmr} \cdot d_{jm}$ units from resource r.

Assuming an upper bound $\bar{T}$ for project makespan to be known in advance (heuristically determined), we may calculate earliest and latest start times ES_j and LS_j as well as finish times EF_j and LF_j of job j by traditional forward and backward recursion using shortest durations $dmin_j := \min \{d_{jm} \mid m = 1,...,M_j\}$ for all jobs j. Thus $[EF_J , LF_J]$ represents a bound on the maximum time interval the project may be finished in without violating resource constraints.

Based on these assumptions we may fomulate a binary model establishing the optimization problem under consideration appropriately.

The model may be solved to optimality by the branch-and-bound method of [11], which simultaneously decides about job-mode assignment and job sequencing. Due to the lack of tight bounds with this method problem instances with (depending on the problem structure) only 15 to 30 jobs may be solved to optimality within a reasonable amount of time. Otherwise approximate solutions may be obtained by the use of deterministic [9] or stochastic scheduling rules [7], where the latter are based on the concept of randomized regrets introduced in [6].

Systems Development

In the following we describe the basic features of two project-scheduling software packages (other systems are described in, e.g., [2, 12]).

The **LEINET–system** [10] is based on a general network model which includes classical CPM and MPM models, on a functional (linear) relation between job duration and allotted amount of renewable resources as well as on a project performance cost minimization objective function. LEINET uses network flow optimization algorithms as well as several heuristic strategies.

The **PRISMA–system** and its applications may be characterized as follows: In machine tool assembly several make–to–order products have to be manufactured simultaneously in a multi–stage production system. Due to customer requirements batches are very small. A process plan (=mode) specifies the requirements for machines, tools, auxiliary devices as well as operations to be performed. This problem basically relates to nonpreemptive multi–project multi–mode resource–constrained project scheduling. The assembly structure of each of the products may be represented as a single project being depicted by an acyclic activity–on–node graph. The scheduling models and methods sketched out in [8] have been implemented in a prototype DSS–leitstand within an EUREKA–project. PRISMA has been initiated by the WZL–Laboratory, RWTH Aachen, in cooperation with several european machine tool manufacturers, software companies as well as research institutes. The *main features* of the PRISMA–leitstand are: Schedule generation components, layout and ordering component, simulation capabilities, hierarchical scheme of working, C implementation on Sun Sparcstations under UNIX; INGRES relational database system, etc.

References

[1] Bartusch M, Möhring RH, Radermacher FJ (1988) Scheduling project networks with resource constraints and time windows. Annals of Operations Research 16: 201–240

[2] Bartusch M, Möhring RH, Radermacher FJ (1989) Design aspects of an advanced model–oriented DSS for scheduling problems in civil engineering. Decision Support Systems 5: 321–344

[3] Błażewicz J, Cellary W, Słowiński R, Węglarz J (1986) Scheduling under resource constraints - deterministic models, Basel 1986 (Annals of Operations Research 7)

[4] Demeulemeester E, Herroelen W (1991) A branch–and–bound procedure for the multiple resource–constrained project scheduling problem. Research Report, Leuven

[5] Domschke W, Drexl A (1991) Kapazitätsplanung in Netzwerken - Ein Überblick über neuere Modelle und Verfahren. OR Spektrum 13: 63–76

[6] Drexl A (1991) Scheduling of project networks by job assignment. Management Science 37: 1590–1602

[7] Drexl A, Grünewald J (1992) Nonpreemptive multi–mode resource–constrained project scheduling, to appear in IIE Transactions

[8] Drexl A, Kolisch R (1992) Production scheduling in small batch machine tool assembly. Paper presented at the 2nd ISDSS Conference, FAW (Ulm)

[9] Kurtulus IS, Narula SC (1985) Multi–project scheduling: analysis of project performance. IIE Transactions 17: 58–66

[10] Nägler G, Schönherr S (1989) Resource allocation in a network model - the LEINET system, in: Słowiński R, Węglarz J (eds.) Advances in project scheduling, Amsterdam, 327–354

[11] Patterson J, Słowiński R, Talbot B, Węglarz J, (1990) Computational experience with a backtracking algorithm for solving a general class of resource constrained scheduling problems. European J of Operational Research 49: 68–79

[12] Słowiński R, Soniewicki B, Węglarz J (1991) DSS for multiobjective project scheduling subject to multiple–category resource constraints. Research Report, Poznań

[13] Talbot FB (1982) Resource–constrained project scheduling with time–resource tradeoffs: the nonpreemptive case. Management Science 28: 1197–1210

Analysis of Controller Workload Related to Air Traffic Density

Sylwester Gladys, Marek Malarski, Jacek Skorupski
Institute of Transport, Warsaw University of Technology
75 Koszykowa Str., 00662 Warsaw, Poland

Abstract

In this paper analysis of controller workload - T related to air traffic density X is presented. This relation may be analysed using appropriate edge distributions. This leads to definition of air traffic sector capacity as a quantile of edge distribution of two-dimensional random variable.

Another approach is to treat random variables X and T jointly. It was proved that two-dimensional random variable (X,T) has normal distribution.

1. Introduction

Civil air traffic in suitably organised airspace (FIR) is in keeping with precise rules and subject to air traffic control (ATC). Air traffic in FIR is initially planned and coordinated, however its realization undergoes many random disturbances. The ATC services watch the real realization of this traffic and take measures to eliminate collision hazards. The air traffic controller is the principal person of the air traffic control system (ATCS). He must be in constant contact with many planes, be able to foresee the development of the operational-traffic situation and execute many other time consuming operations. If the density of these operations begins to exceed the limits of the capacity of human memory and divisibility of attention, the probability increases that decisions taken by controller under certain circumstances will not ensure full security of flights.

The air traffic flow management (ATFM) minds that the flow capacity (limited by the control load), called the sector capacity, not be exceeded in any of the ATC sectors. In practice, the capacity of ATC sector is understood as the number of planes that are in the sector in a given period of time [2], for which it is possible to provide service according to the ICAO rules[3].

2. Definitions of controller workload, air traffic density and ATC sector capacity

Traffic density is a quantity characterizing the air traffic in the ATC sector. It is defined as a number of planes residing in the ATC sector for one hour. Meteorological factors and other traffic limitations make the air traffic process a random process and the traffic density (X) charakterizing it a random variable of step character. The flight of plane initiating a series of entries submittet to the ATC sector controller is the elementary realization of the air traffic process. The total time of servicing all the entries taking placed in one hour is the quantity characterizing the control load. The control load (T) in the ATC sector is a random variable depending on air traffic density. Air traffic density and control load can be treated as interdependent random variables with an appriopriate joint probability distribution.

It is possible to determine certain boundary values of density xp_x and load tp_T, for witch the probability of realization of a two-dimensional random variable (X,T) beyound the area defined by (xp_x, tp_T) will be smaller than the set value p_{XT}:

$$p_{XT} = F_{XT}(xp_x, tp_T)$$

where: F_{XT} is the distribution function of two-dimentional random variable (X,T).

There may be many pairs (x_{p_x}, t_{p_T}) which fulfil the above condition, so the determination of (x_{p_x}, t_{p_T}) is equivocal. In practice it occurs therefore that it is more adventageous to define x_{p_x} and t_{p_T} as the position parameters of suitable edge distribution of the random variable X and the random variable T in the distribution of the two dimentional random variable (X,T).

Let x_{p_x} be a quantile of the order p_X , and t_{p_T} a quantile of the order p_T than:

$$\{x_{p_x}: [P(X \le x_p) \ge p] \wedge [P(X \ge x_P) \ge 1-p]\}$$

$$\{t_{p_T}: F_T(t_{p_T}) = p_T\}$$

The determined value of the quantil x_{p_x} gives the capacity of the ATC sector. This capacitycan thus be defined as follows: *the capacity of the ATC sector with a given organization is the quantil x_{p_x} of the order p_X of the distribution of the number of planes residing in the ATC sector for one hour (traffic density) which can be serviced by ATC at a given admissible control load measured by the quantil t_{p_T} of the order p_T on the load distribution* [2].

3. Method of determining the ATC sector capacity

The method makes use of the stochastic relatioship between the random variables X (traffic density) and T (control load). The method was implemented by building a simulation model of the air traffic system and its control (ATCS) [1]. This model allows to estimate the level of control load in given time intervals for various organizations of the ATCS system.

The method of determining the capacity of the sector of air traffic control has been split into two steps. In step 1 the suitable parameters of edge distributions of the variable (X,T) are determined for real traffic. Estimation of the capacity of sectors in designed ATCS systems (step 2) consists in carrying out simulation experiments of operation of the designed system (algorithm - fig. 1).

4. Approximate analysis of controller workload and traffic density

During approximate analysis, air traffic density can be treated as a continuous random variable. Real air traffic observations and numerical experiments on the model proved that two-dimensional random variable (X,T) with given joint probability distribution has linear regressive function. Edge distributions of both random variables can be very well approximated by normal distribution. So we may assume, that obtained random variable has two-dimensional normal distribution. Density function of these two-dimensional random variable (X,T) is:

$$f(x,t) = \frac{1}{2\pi\delta_x\delta_t\sqrt{1-\rho^2}}\, e^{-\frac{1}{2(1-\rho^2)}\left\{\frac{(x-m_X)^2}{\delta_X^2} - 2\frac{\rho(x-m_X)(t-m_t)}{\delta_X\delta_t} + \frac{(t-m_t)^2}{\delta_t^2}\right\}}$$

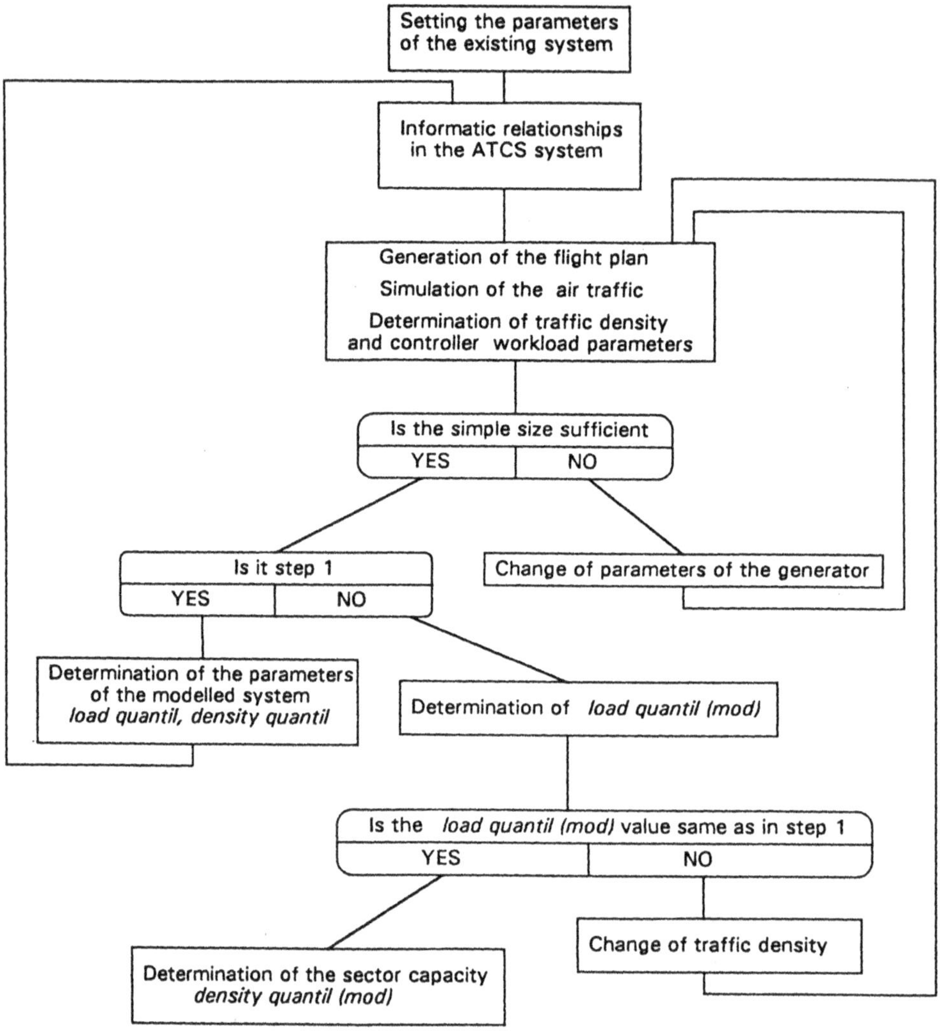

Fig. 1. General scheme of the algorithm for determining the capacity of the sector

where: m_x , m_t - mean values of suitable edge distribution (traffic density, control load),

δ_x , δ_t - variances of these edge distribution,

ρ - correlation coefficient of random variables: traffic density and control load.

So, conditional density of random variable of controller workload on condition that random variable of traffic density X = x is:

$$f(t|_{X=x}) = \frac{1}{\delta_t\sqrt{2\pi(1-\rho^2)}}\, e^{-\frac{1}{2\delta_t^2(1-\rho^2)}\left\{t-\left(m_t+\frac{\rho\delta_t}{\delta_x}(x-m_x)\right)\right\}^2}$$

This is mean value of controller workload in function of traffic density. So, the conditional mean value of control load (random variable T) with a given air traffic realisation (condition X = x)

$$\text{is: } m(x) = m_t + \frac{\rho\,\delta_t}{\delta_x}(x - m_x)$$

This is regression curve type 1 equation of controller workload in relation to traffic density.
Similarly, the conditional variance of random variable T with condition X = x is:

$$\delta(x) = \delta_t\sqrt{(1 - \rho^2)}$$

It means that we can directly sector capacity defined from admissible control load (determined from investigations in agreement with ATC controllers t_p = 80%).

Reference

[1] Gladys S., Malarski M., Urbanik A. (1988) Model Analysis of Air Traffic Control Systems in FIR Warsaw Performed in View of Its Modernisation. Transportation Forum, Toronto. Canada

[2] Gladys S., Malarski M. (1990): Model Estimation of Air Traffic Control (ATC) Sectors Capacity for Solving the Air Traffic Flow Management Task. Archives of Transport, v.2, N 1, p.7-19.

[3] -.: A Method of Estimating the Capacity of Air Traffic Sectors - An Interim Report. CAA(UK) DORA Research Paper 7301, 7402.

[4] -.: Re - assessment of the capacity of the control sectors of Maastricht UAC. Eurocontrol, Ref. OPS/131/4, 1984.

[5] -.: The Air Traffic Controller's Contribution to ATC System Capacity in Manual and Automated Environments. Stanford Research Institute Report No. FAA-RD 72-63.

Office Automation in the Turkish Establishments

Sitki Gözlü
Faculty of Management, Istanbul Technical University
Maçka 80680 Istanbul, Turkey

Computerized and automatic information systems enable the business and industrial managers to cope with the information explosion that has been taking place during the last three decades. The adoption of office automation renders a better communication and information flow.

THE SCOPE AND METHOD

In this research study, a questionnaire survey was conducted encompassing 200 establishments in Turkey. 50,0 % of the establishments are from the industrial sector and the other 50,0 % from the commercial and services sectors. Since office automation is adopted in many different types of establishments, it is difficult to determine the population. For this reason, 200 samples were selected randomly from the indefinite population and analyzed. The Statistical Language for Microcomputers (SLM) program was employed for the evaluation of the questionnaires.

RESULTS

The most extensively employed office automation machinery and equipments are word processing systems, central computer, personal computer, communication systems like telex, photocopier, facsimile, digital telephones, and voice message systems. Other types of equipments such as optical bar code reader, optical character scanner, public area network, and local area network are in medium use; while equipments such as microfilm system, microfiche system, dictation equipment, offset printing equipment, and optical disc (laser) storage are little used. Central and as well as personal computers are sometimes used to perform the functions of word processing systems, optical character scanner, optical bar code reader, voice message system, and communication systems like telex.

The office automation machinery and equipments are acquired by purchasing except telex appliances, which are also hired. Very little of central and personal computers ar also, hired.

Among the channels influencing the choice and purchase of office automation machinery and equipments; "expositions of the sale company" is the most important. "Fairs" and "publications" are other important channels influencing the choice and purchase of equipments. On the other hand, it is reported that advertisements and exhibitions play little role in influencing firms' decisions. However, 41,5 % of the establishments have reported the channels, influencing the choice and purchase of office automation machinery and equipments, as a combination of advertisements, exhibitions, fairs, exposition of the sale company and/or publications.

The office automation machinery and equipments are mostly employed in financial transactions, budgeting, personnel business, sales and orders, and inventory control operations. Production, general management, banking and insurance, and technical calculations are other fields of application, in where the office automation appliances are in medium use. According to this research study, the office automation machinery and equipments are little used in transportation and communication, education, and research and development activities. However, it must be taken into account here that banks constitute only 11,0 % of the total establishments involved in the questionnaire survey.

The personnel employed for office automation, are mostly university graduates for the positions such as manager, system analyst, system programmer, program practioner, and office automation user. For the positions such as repair and maintenance personnel, office automation user, operator, and data processing operator; they are mostly secondary school graduates. There are also a few primmary school graduates among the personnel employed for office automation.

Method for TWR Simulator Analysis of Chosen Elements of Airport Area Visualisation

Slawomir Jasinski, Marek Malarski, Jacek Skorupski
Institute of Transport, Warsaw University of Technology
75 Koszykowa Str., 00 662 Warsaw, Poland

Abstract

This paper presents results of preliminary research under construction of airport simulator, that is necessary for air traffic control purposes. A method of describing complex objects (such as airplane) used for their computer animation is presented. A computer program for data input (describing parts of airplanes and airport facilities according to given structure) was elaborated. Main objective of presented research work is minimization of complexity of object description, given level of prototype similarity.

1.Introduction

While solving problems connected with designing and utilization of systems that building costs are very high, and that are responsible for peoples safety, simulating techniques are used more often nowadays. In these cases one can use simulators that can be divided into two groups:
- research simulators - they simplify collecting information about existing or planned system,
- training simulator - they are used for teaching purposes.

Air traffic controller is expected to provide safe and accurate flight of aircraft. Correct realization of these objectives depends on such factors as: professional qualifications, practice, health and many others. Correct controller teaching and preparing him to work needs training with use of a simulator, that gives him possibility to learn activities, procedures and rules of behavior in all situations that he may face during his work. Simulator is to help him to become familiar with procedures used in different situations and also to possess certain necessary habits.

2.Requirements for visualization.

Research under collecting information proves that almost 80% of it reaches a man in visual form. A main objective of picture generation is conforming the rules of its forming, but also introducing special illusions. Adequate graphic means of expression should make possible for man's brain to recover such environment that he got used to. Those requirements may be related to different features of generated picture. Some of them relate to its quality, that can be expressed according to:
- realism of situation reproduction,
- efficiency of reproduction of images.

Other requirements relate to possibility of image control, it depends on:
- numbers of observer's degrees of freedom,
- range of observers movements,
- dynamics of images changes,
- repeatability of generated picture.

In digital image generation systems only mathematical description of space is used. Lack of any physical equivalents (models) of terrain, results in flexibility of such systems. Changes of any kind may be done by exchange of information in memory. Details of processes that take place in digital image generation systems depend on model destination, its possibilities, characteristics of generated picture, data structure and kind of peripheral device.

3.Geometry in space

Points in space can be described by their coordinates in given coordinate system. Usually cartesian coordinates are used. But sometimes other systems (such as polar) are more convenient. In computer graphics it is essential not only to transform objects but also to describe it in different coordinate systems. Transformations of objects in space consist of: translation, scaling, rotation, projection and transformation of coordinate systems.

4.Data structure

This paper presents preliminary research work that is going to result in obtaining data structure suitable for description of complex objects (such as aircraft, radar etc.) for their computer animation. On the basis of performed analysis, computer program for data input was elaborated. Program enables description of parts of airplanes and airport facilities according to given structure, and then data processing to obtain orthographic projections along x,y,z axis. They allow more convenient edition than perspective projection.

Main feature that influenced data structure was the necessity of giving possibilities to define any complex objects. Those objects may exist in relation to any other complex objects. As a result of such assumptions hierarchical structure of data was accepted. It allows to generate complex objects by using simple ones. Thanks to this data structure it is possible to define small fragments, then join them, and as a result obtain complex object.

Numerous procedures and functions for that purpose were elaborated and tested. To represent such data structure in memory dynamic variables were used. Those variables create lists that are very flexible in use. Lists are not constrained as to the number of elements.

5.Data description model.

Data describing objects or scenes in the airport have hierarchical structure. It means that higher level objects are defined by basic elements of lower level. We can distinguish a set of basic elements E_p, that consists of three subsets:

$$E_p = \Pi \cup \Omega \cup \Sigma$$

where

Π - set of elements π_i of type *section*,

Ω- set of elements ω_i of type *polygon*,

Σ - set of elements σ_i of type *wall.*

We can also define a set of descriptive elements E_o, that consists of two subsets:

$$E_o = B \cup M$$

where

B - set of elements β_i of type *BigBOX*

M - set of elements μ_i of type *SmallBOX*

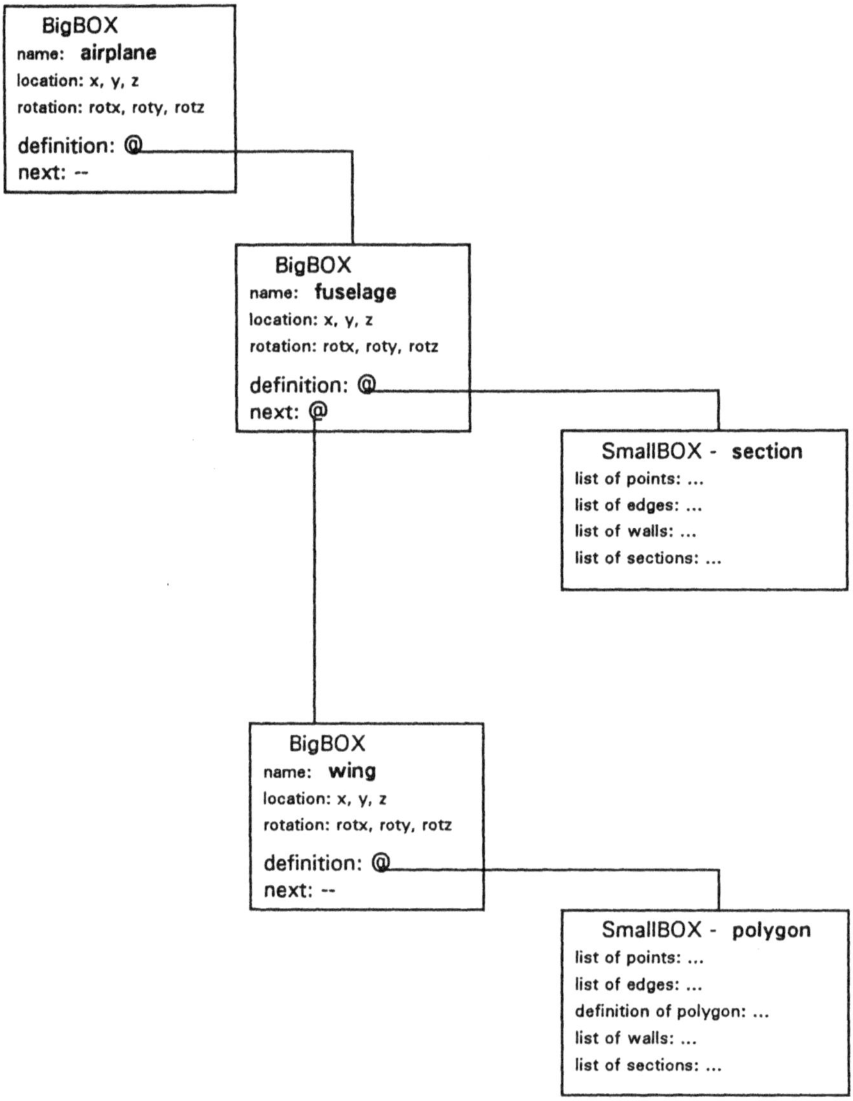

Fig.1. Schematic diagram of describing complex element "airplane".

On sets of basic elements E_p we can define operation *description*, that transforms set E_p to set M of descriptive elements.

$$\Pi \xrightarrow{description} M$$
$$\Omega \xrightarrow{description} M$$
$$\Sigma \xrightarrow{description} M$$

On sets of descriptive elements E_o we can define operation *joining* that transforms it to the set of descriptive elements B.

$$B \xrightarrow{joining} B$$
$$M \xrightarrow{joining} B$$

As an effect of those operations we obtain one complex element of descriptive type B, that defines all scene. Example schema of description of complex object *airplane* is presented on fig.1.

We can introduce a problem of finding such way of graphical scene description to minimize complexity of description, given the level of prototype similarity. This problem reduces to choosing proper basic elements π, ω, σ and descriptive ones: β and μ, and also to define which of those elements should be exposed to the action of operators *description* and *joining*.

It is not possible to find optimal solution of this problem, because of its complexity and also troubles in its formulation. Method of graphic screen description presented in this paper is a try to find suboptimal solution of this problem.

References

Knowlton K. (1981): Computer-aided definition, manipulation and description of objects composed of spheres. ACM Computer Graphics, No.15 s.48-71.

Lane J. M., Riesefeld R.F.(1980) A theoretical development for the computer generation and display of piecewise polynomial surfaces. IEEE Trans. on Pattern Analysis and Machine Inteligence, No.2, , s.35-46.

Pavlidis P (1982) Algorithms for Graphics and Image Processing. Computer Science. Press Inc. Maryland USA

- (1986) Flight Simulator Design and Performance Data Requirements, IATA.

Decision Support in Financial Planning

W. Junginger, A. Kor
Institut für Informatik, Universität der Bundeswehr
Holstenhofweg 85, 2000 Hamburg 70, Germany

1 Introductory Remarks

Talking about financial management, about financial consulting, or even about capital consulting, often causes an association of all kinds of speculations at the stock-exchange and future markets. But, of course, the main objective and the key for the success of a company is a cost-minimizing production management and a profit-maximizing marketing policy. Within this range of action, financial management and financial planning, respectively, has to select optimal financial activities. This can be achieved by aid of a multi-step optimization model for decision support, as it is outlined in this paper.

2 A Model for Financial Planning

In this model, at first a cash plan is determined for the planning period (e.g. 6 months divided into 26 periods) without taking into account any financial activities. In a next step, called planning step A, suitable short-run financial activities will be included into a LP-model. The optimal values gained by this model are then transferred as relevant data into the following step. In this step, called planning step B, long-run financial activities and activities in the company's production sector are used as decision variables. However, these variables need to be defined for critical periods only. They are incorporated into an Integer Programming model, whose optimal solution yields the optimal activities.

2.1 Determining a Cash Plan

A cash plan consists of a highly-aggregated report of receipts and expenditures. Usually, *extrapolating* and *causal prognosis techniques* [Hauschildt (1981), p. 112] are used for generating such a plan. However, these techniques are disadvantageous because they process data at an already aggregated level and they don't start at the cash-causing objects. Such an object might be the orders themselves, or groups of orders, or projects, or even well-defined parts of a whole profit-centre. Therefore, a cause-based financial forecast should plan any payment at the level of these cash-causing objects. As an example, consider the table on the following page: In the *20th* week, there are expected material payments of *10.000 DM* for project *1-0391-012*.

2.2 Planning Step A

In planning step A the decision maker has to look for financial alternatives and investments and to evaluate their cost and terms. The optimization of these alternatives is an interdependency problem of factual and time; it can be solved satisfactorily by linear programming. The appropriate LP-model is outlined in [Junginger (1992)]. Its structure will be demonstrated here using **discounts** as an example. Let w_{ts} be the par value of all bills of exchange with maturity s which are handed in prematurely in the period $t \leq s$ and let δ_{ts} be the correspondent discount rate. Then we can write the effect on the cash balance as:

$$\sum_{s=t}^{S}(1-\delta_{ts})w_{ts} \qquad \forall t \tag{1}$$

Expressions just as (1) are part of the **liquidity constraints**, as well as the decision-independent receipts E_t and expenditures A_t. Thus, we have

$$(1) + \quad \ldots \quad + E_t - A_t \quad = \quad l_t^+ - l_t^- \qquad \forall t \tag{2}$$

as constraints. Here, l_t^+ denotes the surplusses and l_t^- the deficits. Multiplying l_t^+ and l_t^- by adequate opportunity cost c^+ and c^- in the objective function, this model will guarantee low variations of liquidity. Furthermore, the effect of the financial activities on the profit must be concidered in the objective function. We demonstrate this by the aid of interest cost for the discounts, as an example. Then, we have as an objective function:

$$Z \;=\; +\sum_t l_t^+c^+ + \sum_t l_t^-c^- + \sum_{t=1}^{T}\sum_{s=t}^{S}\delta_{ts}w_{ts} + \ldots \;\longrightarrow\; \min \tag{3}$$

2.3 Planning Step B

The optimal solution of this LP-model constitutes an excellent indicator for impending structural liquidity unbalancements: If there are periods, in which the optimal financial activities cannot compensate for the deficits (that is, there are high values of l_t^+ or l_t^-) then the financial sector will be the company's bottleneck. In this case it would be fatal to try to meet such structural unbalancements by short-run financial activities. [Perridon (1988), p.396]. It would rather be appropriate to revise those plans that have supplied the data for the financial planning: The production plans would have to be reduced to the level of the bottleneck. This is the objective of planning step B.

For this, the decision maker has to look for possibilities of delaying or advancing cash-causing production activities (e.g. projects) [Hinzen (1975), p. 49]. Delaying expenses may be done by protracting material orders or investments or maintenance. On the other hand, receipts could be advanced by advancing the dates of delivery, or project phases, or by doing emergency sales. Such alternatives and their effects on payments need to be planned for critical periods and projects only. In the figure below, as an example, the project *1-0391-012* may be critical: *35%* of the material payments planned for the *26th* week can be delayed by *3* weeks. Each delayed week causes cost of *300.- DM*.

	material	week	variable	Δ weeks	DM/week
Projekt-No.: 1-0391-012	10.000	20/91			
	40.000	26/91	35%	+3	300
	44.000	29/91	25%	+2	400
	94.000				

These data are used to build the optimization model B. This model has to determine until which period k an expense i that is planned for period t (a_{it}) should be delayed; and into which period k a receipt j that is planned for period t (e_{jt}) has to be advanced. For this, we define binary variables g_{itk} and g_{jtk} which values are 1 iff i and j, resp., are moved from t to k. Using these variables, we get as constraints:

$$\sum_{k=t}^{T_{it}} g_{itk} = 1 \quad \forall\, i,t \qquad\qquad \sum_{k=T_{jt}}^{t} g_{jtk} = 1 \quad \forall\, j,t \tag{4}$$

Here, T_{it} (resp., T_{jt}) denote that periods into which a_{it} (resp., e_{jt}) can be moved at most. Now we can state the (sharp) liquidity constraints: Firstly, we consider the optimal values l_k^+ and l_k^- gained by step A. This has to be reduced by those expenses a_{it} which were initially planned for period t and which are now to be moved to k. Additionally, any receipt e_{it} which was planned for period t but which is to be advanced to k must be added. Finally, the payments a_{ik} and e_{jk} have to be eliminated in those periods for which they had been planned initially:

$$l_k^+ - l_k^- - \sum_i \sum_t g_{itk} a_{it} + \sum_j \sum_t g_{jtk} e_{jt} + \sum_i a_{ik} - \sum_j e_{jk} \geq 0 \qquad \forall\, k \tag{5}$$

Of course, the movements of payments will cause additional cost, which is denoted by c_{it} and c_{jt}. These cost are minimized by the following objective function:

$$Z = \sum_i \sum_t \sum_k (k-t) c_{it} g_{itk} + \sum_j \sum_t \sum_k (t-k) c_{jt} g_{jtk} \rightarrow \min \tag{6}$$

Thus, (6), (5) and (4) describe the binary integer programming model. Its optimal solution yields a package of activities that minimizes the movement cost while ensuring the liquidity balance. The profit and the financial aspect are considered simultaneously.

3 Concluding Remarks

In this paper we have presented a multi-step decision model. It ensures that the decision-maker is highly involved in the problem solving process. Our model is intentionally kept as simple as possible in order to increase practical acceptance. Of course, this planning process has to be supported by an integrated software system. Important features of such a system should be the optimal adjustment of its data interfaces to the company's information system and an efficient graphic tool to present its optimal proposals in an obvious and comprehensive way.

References

[Hauschildt (1981)] Hauschildt J, Sachs G, Witte E: Finanzplanung und Finanzkontrolle. München.

[Hinzen (1975)] Hinzen E: Partialmodelle zur kurzfristigen Finanzplanung. Meisenheim aG

[Junginger (1992)] Junginger W, Kor A: LP-orientierte Finanzplanung mit dem PC. in: Uniforum 2/1992

[Mao (1980)] Mao JCT: Application of Linear Programming to Short-Term Financing. in: Seelbach (eds.). Finanzierung. München: 146-162

[Perridon (1988)] Perridon L, Steiner M: Finanzwirtschaft der Unternehmung. 5th ed. München

[Preßmar (1986)] Preßmar DB: Computergestützte Planung und mathematische Programmierung. in: Operations Research Proceedings

[Witte (1981)] Witte E: Die Finanzwirtschaft der Unternehmung. in: Jacob H (eds.). Allgemeine Betriebswirtschaftslehre. 4th ed. Wiesbaden: 515-608

Section 8

Econometrics and Statistics

Distribution of the Spearman's Rank Correlation Coefficient

Aleksandra Baszczyńska, Czesław Domański
Department of Statistical Methods, University of Łódź
Rewolucji 1905 Nr 41, Łódź 90–214, Poland

1. Introduction

Methods based not on observed values of random variables but on ranks corresponding to these values are more and more used in statistical research. On the ground of research in the rank application theory we can formulate the thesis that statistical methods based on ranks allow to solve majority of problems of statistical practice. The object of our consideration is the Spearman's rank correlation coefficient which is often applied to empirical research. The aim of this work ist to show recurrent formula of the distribution of the Spearman's rank correlation coefficient which allows to construct the tables of its basic quantiles. Exact distribution of the Spearman's rank correlation coefficient was tabled first by Owen (1962), and next for $n = 12(1)16$ by Otten (1973). Zar (1972) used approximation based on the Pearson's distribution of the 2nd type and showed critical values for $n = 4(1)50(2)100$ and $\alpha = 0.50, 0.20, 0.10, 0.05, 0.02, 0.01, 0.005, 0.002, 0.001$. It can be noticed that 16 values (given by Zar (1972)) out of 45, differ from the values given by Otten (1973). Apart from the methods of the Spearman's rank correlation coefficient approximation, it is worth considering the possibility of finding the numerical effective algorithm for calculation the direct distribution. To construct tables published so far (compare Otten (1973)), an algorithm generating all or a half of permutations of n-element set was used. In spite of the development of computer calculations techniques this method seems to be useless in case of n much greater than 20.

In this work we present the method mentioned above. Nevertheless, the possibilities of computer calculations using this method are limited. The algorithm needs keeping in the computer memory a great amount of partial results — so it needs having much larger memory units than those which the authors have at their disposal.

2. The W Statistics

Let

$$(X_1, Y_1), (X_2, Y_2), \ldots, (X_n, Y_n)$$

be a simple sample of 2-dimensional continuous random variable (X,Y) realizations. Let

$$r_1, r_2, \ldots, r_n \tag{1}$$

be ranks of observations of variable X, that is

$$X_{r_1} < X_{r_2} < \cdots < X_{r_n}$$

and let

$$s_1, s_2, \ldots, s_n \tag{2}$$

be ranks of observations of Y

$$Y_{s_1} < Y_{s_2} < \cdots < Y_{s_n}.$$

The formula of the Spearman's rank correlations coefficient is

$$R = \frac{12}{n(n^2-1)} \sum_{i=1}^{n} r_i s_i - \frac{3(n+1)}{n-1}.$$

The subject of our considerations is R distribution under the condition, that variable X and Y are independent, that is, when permutations (1) and (2) have equal probabilities. The Spearman's rank correlation coefficient is a linear function of variable

$$W = \sum_{i=1}^{n} r_i s_i.$$

Let us denote $i_r = i \Longleftrightarrow r_i = r$ for $r = 1, \ldots, n$, then

$$W = \sum_{r=1}^{n} r_i s_{i_r} \quad \text{or} \quad W = \sum_{r=1}^{n} r s(r), \tag{3}$$

where $s(r) = s_{i_r}$. To define the Spearman's rank correlation coefficient distribution it will be enough to study the distribution of (3) statistics on set of all n-element permutations s.

3. The Recurrent Formula

The following formula

$$\phi(L(K,h,j),x) = \sum_{l \in N \setminus K \setminus \{j\}} \phi(L(K \cup \{j\}, h, l), x + (h-j)(j-l)) \tag{4}$$

for $x \in N_1^{n!}, K \subset N, h, j \in N \setminus K$ shows the basic recurrent relation between distributions of W statistics on subsets of k-element and $(k+1)$-element and $(k+2)$-element sets of K constant points. This formula allows us to start with permutations of $K = N$ set of constant points: $s(h) = h$ dla $h \in N$, and to calculate function ϕ on all sets $L(K,h,j)$, where

$$\phi : 2^P \times N_d^g \longrightarrow N_1^{n!}$$

$$\phi(Q,x) \stackrel{def}{=} \text{card}\{s \in Q : w(s) = x\}.$$

and

$$L : 2^N \times N \times N \longrightarrow P$$

$$L(K,h,j) \stackrel{def}{=} \begin{cases} \{s \in Q(K) : s(h) = j\} & for \quad h \neq j \\ Q(K \cup \{h\}) & for \quad h = j \end{cases}$$

On the basis of the recurrent formula (4) we can construct an algorithm of calculating the Spearman's rank correlation coefficient. This procedure demands many calculations, but their number is much lower, particulary for big n, than in the case of performing the classical algorithms generating permutations.

References

Gibson, J. (1987), *Nonparametric Statistical Inference*, McGraw-Hill Book Company, New York.

Otten, A. (1973), *The Null Distribution of Spearman's S when* n = 13 *(1) 16*, Statistica Nearlandica 27, 19–20

Otten, A. (1973), *Note on Spearman Rank Correlation Coefficient*, JASA 585

Owen, D.B. (1962), *Handbook of Statistical Tables*, Addition-Wesley Publishing Company, In e., 400–406

Spearman, C. (1904), *The Proof and Measurement of Association Between Two Things*, American Journal of Psychology 15, 1904, 72–101

Zar, J.H. (1972), *Significance Testing of the Spearman Rank Correlation Coefficient*, JASA 67, 578–580

Tests for Outliers for Multivariate Normal Distribution

Aleksandra Baszczyńska, Czesław Domański
Department of Statistical Methods, University of Łódź
Łódź 90–214, Rewolucji 1905 Nr 41, Poland

1. Introduction

In this paper we present tests veryfing hypothesis about existing any outliers in a sample, which comes from a population with normal distribution and tests veryfing the same hypothesis in the case of multivariate normal distribution. Possibly existence of one and two outliers is disscused.
Up to now statisticians have used tables with critical values only for some sample sizes and only for $p = 1, \ldots, 5$. The authors extend the tables for $p = 1, \ldots, 20$.

2. Methods

Let $X_1, \ldots, X_n$ denote a sample coming from a population with p-dimensional normal distribution $N_0(\mu, \Sigma)$, where μ is a vector of expected values, and Σ is a covariance matrix. We assume that μ and Σ are unknown.
On the basis of the sample's results $X_1, \ldots, X_n$ we account p-dimensional vector of means $\overline{X}$ and $(p \times p)$-dimensional matrix A

$$A = \frac{1}{n-1} \sum_{j=1}^{n} (X_j - \overline{X})(X_j - \overline{X})'$$

We assume that $n > p + 3$ and that matrix A is nonsingular with probability 1.

2a. Test for one outlier

One vector in the sample $X_1, \ldots, X_n$ is excluded and we compute determinant from the remaining $(n-1)$-element-sample. We do that for every vector from the sample and we got n determinants. $|A(1)|, \ldots, |A(n)|$, and then we compute quotients

$$W_j = \frac{|A(j)|}{|A|}, \quad \text{for } j = 1, \ldots, n.$$

These quotients are a measure of dispersion for one outlier. Let $W_{(1)} \leq \ldots \leq W_{(n)}$ denote the ordered values of the quotients. In this way we can get the number of the vector $j_{(1)}$ corresponding to the quotient $W_{(1)}$ and the vector corresponding to this number can be regarded as outlier.
If $W_{j1} < W_1(\alpha; p, n)$ then vector X_{j1} is regarded as an outlier in the sample $X_1, \ldots, X_n$ for assumed level of significance α. The critical values $W_1(\alpha; p, n)$ for $\alpha = 0.05$ we show in table 1.

2b. Test for two outliers

We exclude two vectors X_k and X_l from the sample $X_1, \ldots, X_n$ $(1 \leq k < l)$. For $(n-2)$-element-sample we compute determinants:
$|A(k,l)|$, and then quotients of every of the following form:

$$W(k,l) = \frac{|A(k,l)|}{|A|},$$

which describe a measure of dispersion for two outliers. After arranging them in non-increasing order we compute:

$$W(j_1, j_2) = \min\{W(k,l)\}, \quad \text{for } 1 \leq k < l \leq n.$$

The pair (j_1, j_2) indicates the number of the vectors in the sample which can be regarded as outliers.
If $W(j_1, j_2) < W_2(\alpha; p, n)$ then vectors X_{j1} and X_{j2} are regarded as outliers in sample $X_1, \ldots, X_n$ for assumed level of significance α. The critical values $W_2(\alpha; p, n)$ for $\alpha = 0.05$ we show in table 2.

Table 1. Critical values for investigating one outlier in samples coming from a population of multivariate normal distribution.
Level of significance 0.05 .

N	p=2	p=4	p=6	p=8	p=10	p=12	p=14	p=16	p=18	p=20
10	0.22007	0.07438	0.01103	0.00000						
11	0.25965	0.10731	0.02805	0.00114						
12	0.29584	0.14050	0.05036	0.00745	0.00000					
13	0.32886	0.17285	0.07560	0.02001	0.00077					
14	0.35897	0.20383	0.10213	0.03727	0.00544	0.00000				
15	0.38650	0.23319	0.12891	0.05750	0.01521	0.00056				
16	0.41171	0.26086	0.15530	0.07939	0.02913	0.00417	0.00000			
17	0.43487	0.28686	0.18096	0.10203	0.04589	0.01208	0.00042			
18	0.45620	0.31124	0.20566	0.12482	0.06441	0.02364	0.00332	0.00000		
19	0.47591	0.33412	0.22932	0.14737	0.08391	0.03785	0.00989	0.00033		
20	0.49417	0.35558	0.25188	0.16943	0.10385	0.05383	0.01972	0.00272	0.00000	
25	0.56838	0.44513	0.34918	0.26899	0.20057	0.14217	0.09313	0.05354	0.02411	0.00614
30	0.62260	0.51248	0.42488	0.34989	0.28395	0.22540	0.17338	0.12752	0.08781	0.05451
35	0.66402	0.56478	0.48477	0.41530	0.35322	0.29700	0.24579	0.19913	0.15679	0.11872
40	0.69675	0.60654	0.53315	0.46883	0.41076	0.35757	0.30845	0.26293	0.22074	0.18172
45	0.72331	0.64067	0.57298	0.51328	0.45901	0.40891	0.36226	0.31859	0.27762	0.23917
50	0.74532	0.66909	0.60634	0.55072	0.49992	0.45277	0.40860	0.36698	0.32765	0.29039
60	0.77976	0.71377	0.65906	0.61026	0.56537	0.52343	0.48384	0.44624	0.41037	0.37606
70	0.80554	0.74735	0.69889	0.65546	0.61535	0.57770	0.54202	0.50796	0.47531	0.44390
80	0.82561	0.77356	0.73006	0.69096	0.65474	0.62065	0.58823	0.55720	0.52735	0.49854
90	0.84172	0.79462	0.75515	0.71960	0.68660	0.65547	0.62580	0.59735	0.56991	0.54337
100	0.85494	0.81192	0.77580	0.74320	0.71290	0.68427	0.65694	0.63068	0.60533	0.58076
110	0.86601	0.82641	0.79310	0.76301	0.73500	0.70849	0.68317	0.65881	0.63525	0.61239
120	0.87542	0.83872	0.80782	0.77987	0.75383	0.72916	0.70557	0.68285	0.66086	0.63951
130	0.88353	0.84933	0.82051	0.79441	0.77007	0.74701	0.72493	0.70365	0.68304	0.66300
140	0.89059	0.85857	0.83155	0.80708	0.78424	0.76258	0.74183	0.72181	0.70242	0.68356
150	0.89679	0.86668	0.84127	0.81822	0.79670	0.77628	0.75671	0.73782	0.71951	0.70169

Table 2. Critical values for investigating two outliers in samples coming from a population of multivariate normal distribution. Level of significance 0.05 .

N	p=2	p=4	p=6	p=8	p=10	p=12	p=14	p=16	p=18	p=20
10	0.24188	0.07881	0.00736	0.00000						
11	0.28462	0.11716	0.02617	0.00011						
12	0.32286	0.15489	0.05222	0.00464	0.00000					
13	0.35711	0.19085	0.08157	0.01804	0.00006					
14	0.38792	0.22462	0.11191	0.03790	0.00319	0.00000				
15	0.41573	0.25609	0.14199	0.06131	0.01333	0.00004				
16	0.44096	0.28532	0.17114	0.08636	0.02913	0.00233	0.00000			
17	0.46394	0.31244	0.19904	0.11188	0.04840	0.01032	0.00003			
18	0.48496	0.33763	0.22556	0.13720	0.06955	0.02329	0.00178	0.00000		
19	0.50426	0.36103	0.25065	0.16191	0.09156	0.03954	0.00827	0.00002		
20	0.52205	0.38281	0.27435	0.18580	0.11378	0.05774	0.01917	0.00140	0.00000	
25	0.59354	0.47215	0.37427	0.29072	0.21817	0.15527	0.10163	0.05764	0.02459	0.00488
30	0.64513	0.53799	0.45001	0.37328	0.30487	0.24336	0.18807	0.13875	0.09550	0.05878
35	0.68424	0.58850	0.50896	0.43875	0.37524	0.31713	0.26370	0.21458	0.16959	0.12875
40	0.71502	0.62850	0.55607	0.49163	0.43281	0.37844	0.32784	0.28061	0.23650	0.19540
45	0.73992	0.66101	0.59458	0.53514	0.48057	0.42978	0.38216	0.33730	0.29496	0.25498
50	0.76052	0.68798	0.62665	0.57155	0.52074	0.47324	0.42847	0.38605	0.34573	0.30736
60	0.79271	0.73021	0.67707	0.62904	0.58451	0.54262	0.50288	0.46495	0.42862	0.39372
70	0.81678	0.76185	0.71495	0.67242	0.63284	0.59546	0.55986	0.52575	0.49292	0.46123
80	0.83553	0.78650	0.74452	0.70636	0.67074	0.63704	0.60484	0.57391	0.54406	0.51516
90	0.85057	0.80627	0.76827	0.73365	0.70129	0.67061	0.64125	0.61298	0.58565	0.55913
100	0.86292	0.82251	0.78779	0.75611	0.72646	0.69830	0.67132	0.64531	0.62012	0.59565
110	0.87327	0.83611	0.80413	0.77493	0.74756	0.72155	0.69659	0.67251	0.64917	0.62646
120	0.88207	0.84766	0.81802	0.79093	0.76552	0.74134	0.71814	0.69572	0.67397	0.65279
130	0.88966	0.85761	0.82999	0.80472	0.78100	0.75842	0.73672	0.71576	0.69540	0.67557
140	0.89627	0.86628	0.84040	0.81672	0.79448	0.77330	0.75293	0.73324	0.71411	0.69546
150	0.90209	0.87389	0.84956	0.82728	0.80634	0.78639	0.76720	0.74863	0.73058	0.71299

Demographer

Drago Čepar, Rok Habinc, Erika Uršič, Rok Založnik
Jožef Stefan Institute, University of Ljubljana
Jamova 39, 61111 Ljubljana, Slovenia

1 Introduction

The Demographer is a menu-driven user-friendly software package for population projections. They are based on a mathematical model assuming that some crucial demographic variables such as age-specific fertility and survival ratios remain unchanged. They can serve as predictions of future population changes or/and as indications or warnings about future population trends if the existing population parameters remain unchanged. The underlying mathematical model is briefly described in section 2 and the programme itself in section 3.

2 Annual model for natural population growth

It is described by the following equations:

$$\begin{gathered} N_{s,i+1}^{t+1} = N_{s,i}^{t} \cdot P_{s,i}, \quad i = 0,1,2,..,83, s = 1,2, \\ N_{s,85}^{t+1} = N_{s,84}^{t} \cdot P_{s,84} + N_{s,85}^{t} \cdot P_{s,85}, \quad B = 1/2 \cdot \sum_{j=15}^{49} (N_{2,j}^{t} + N_{2,j+1}^{t+1}) \cdot R_j, \\ N_{1,0}^{t+1} = 0.517 \cdot B \cdot P_1', \quad N_{2,0}^{t+1} = 0.483 \cdot B \cdot P_2'. \end{gathered} \tag{1}$$

$N_{s,i}^{t}$ is the number of males (s=1) or females (s=2) belonging to i^{th} age group (defined as [i,i+1) for i=0,1,..,84 and [i,∞) for i=85) in year t. R_i, i=15,16,..,49, are one-year specific fertility ratios and $P_{s,i}$, s=1,2, i=0,1,..,85 one-year specific survival ratios. P_s', s=1,2, are survival ratios for infant children. Constants 0.517 and 0.483 represent the ratios of the numbers of live-born boys and girls with respect to the total number of live-born children.

3 Basic programme structure and design

The programme consists of the following basic units (see figure 1):

- **Central procedure**, which computes demographic projections on the basis of model (1) from one-year input data (fertility ratios, survival ratios and population age distribution). The projection horizon is given by the user.
- **Data-base** containing one-year and five-year fertility ratios, survival ratios and population age distribution for several countries. We plan to develop and enlarge it including new data, to be able to serve researchers also as an easily available and valuable source of world demographic data. At the moment it contains data for 23 European countries.

It is possible to include also hypothetical data, which could serve for the demographic analysis of the type "what if...". Data can be used already in the base or it can be created and added new data to the data-base for our specific use. The data are stored

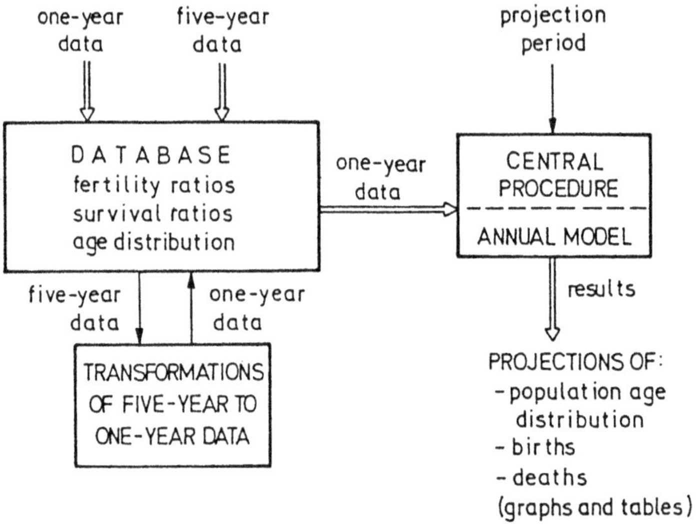

Figure 1: Program DEMOGRAPHER - flow chart

in separate files for each country and each country has its own file for fertility ratios, survival ratios and population age distribution. A small, user-friendly editor for entering, correcting and viewing data is added to the programme. A password protects the data from being accidentally erased or overwritten. Data-base allows a combination of different data of different countries for simulation purposes. For instance, Slovenia's age distribution, Austrians fertility ratios and Belgian's survival ratios can be combined in one projection.

- **Transformations of five-year to one-year data.** Often the data available in demographic publications are five- year and not one-year data. Since one-year data is needed as the input for the model, transformations have been provided for trying to give the best approximation of one-year data on the basis of five-year data and some other demographic rules and specifics. They are described by *Čepar et al. (1991)*.

Outputs and their graphic and tabular presentation. The following can be obtained through the programme for any year in the time interval chosen by the user: population age and sex distribution, total number of men and women, number of births per sex, number of deaths per sex, numbers of people in some age intervals, some ratios of these numbers, total fertility rate, etc. They can be given in a form of graph in high resolution or in tabular form. In figure 2 the way of presenting age distribution in graphic form is illustrated on the case of Slovenia. Time dependence and development of these quantities can also be shown in a form of graph.

System requirements. The software package Demographer requires PC compatible personal computer with:
- two 360 K or one 1.2 M floppy disk or hard disk (recommended),
- 640 K RAM (1 M or more recommended) - graphic card HERCULES, CGA, EGA or VGA (or compatible),
- operating system DOS 3.0 or higher.

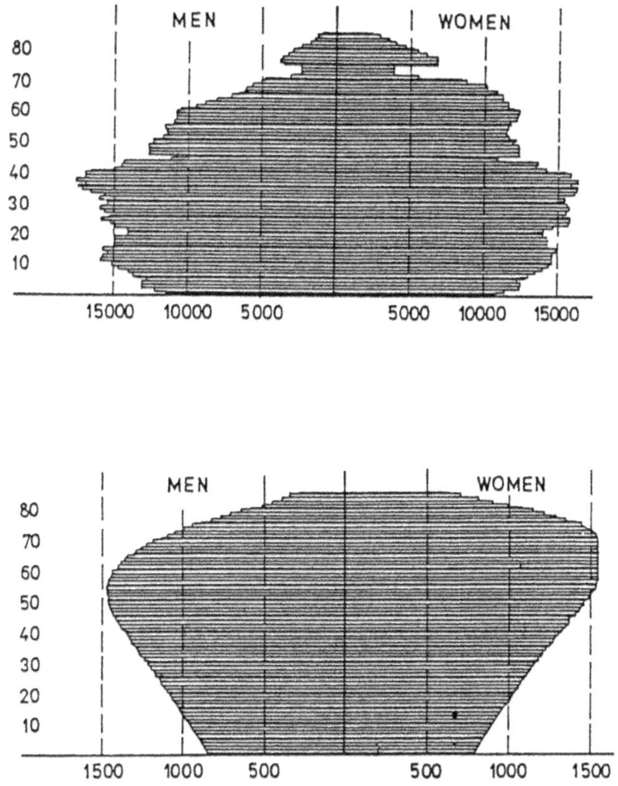

Figure 2: Population sex and age distribution for Slovenia 1990 (up) and its projection for the year 2190 on the basis of 1990 demographic data (down).

5 Conclusion

Programme DEMOGRAPHER could be of great help for everybody who works in the field of demographic analysis and planning. Its population projections can be used as reasonable approximations of future demographic processes, if relevant statistical data are used as input. We can use it also to simulate the demographic consequences of hypothetical changes in fertility and mortality. The results of these simulations can give us some guidelines suggesting the eventual choice or changes of demographic policy.

We intend to continue work on our programme, enlarge its data- base, supplement the model with the other methods and further develop it. We are willing to co-operate with other researchers dealing with similar problems. On request, we will make population projections for any country, state or community, provided input data for chosen population is given.

6 References

Čepar D., Gosar L., Uršič E. (1992), Natural growth population projections, Operations research '91, P. Gritzmann, R. Hettich, R. Horst, E. Sachs editors, Physica - Verlag, Heidelberg 1992, p.p. 305-308.

Natural Growth Population Models

Drago Čepar, Erika Uršič
Jožef Stefan Institute, University of Ljubljana
Jamova 39, 61111 Ljubljana, Slovenia

1 Introduction

Population projections by natural increase are studied. They forecast changes in population structure and size based on fertility, mortality and population age distribution, without considering migrations. In section 2, a well-known model of natural population growth based on one-year age-group data is described; in section 3, a simple, demonstrative linear difference equations model is introduced, the solution for which can be obtained analytically. With this simple model, the effects of different levels of fertility and mortality on long-term demographic processes are mathematically described and illustrated, which can be simulated by annual model.

2 Annual model for natural population growth

It is described by the following equations:

$$N_{s,i+1}^{t+1} = N_{s,i}^{t} \cdot P_{s,i}, \quad i = 0,1,2,..,83, s = 1,2,$$
$$N_{s,85}^{t+1} = N_{s,84}^{t} \cdot P_{s,84} + N_{s,85}^{t} \cdot P_{s,85}, \quad B = 1/2 \cdot \sum_{j=15}^{49} (N_{2,j}^{t} + N_{2,j+1}^{t+1}) \cdot R_j, \tag{1}$$
$$N_{1,0}^{t+1} = 0.517 \cdot B \cdot P_1', \quad N_{2,0}^{t+1} = 0.483 \cdot B \cdot P_2'.$$

$N_{s,i}^{t}$ is the number of males (s=1) or females (s=2) belonging to i^{th} age group (defined as [i,i+1) for i=0,1,..,84 and [i,∞) for i=85) in year t. R_i, i=15,16,..,49, are one-year specific fertility ratios and $P_{s,i}$, s=1,2, i=0,1,..,85 one-year specific survival ratios. P_s', s=1,2, are survival ratios for infant children. Constants 0.517 and 0.483 represent the ratios of the numbers of live-born boys and girls with respect to the total number of live-born children. For more about this model see in *Čepar D. et al. (1991)*.

3 Demonstrative model

We consider a hypotetical population consisting of male and female individuals. Their lives consist of three time periods: childhood, the fertility period of female individuals and old age. An individual can survive or die in each life period, but none can survive the last life period. The natural growth of this population is described by the following equations:

$$N_{1,1}^{t+1} = P_{1,0} \cdot N_{1,0}^{t}, \quad N_{2,1}^{t+1} = P_{2,0} \cdot N_{2,0}^{t}, \quad N_{1,2}^{t+1} = P_{1,1} \cdot N_{1,1}^{t}, \quad N_{2,2}^{t+1} = P_{2,1} \cdot N_{2,1}^{t},$$
$$N_{1,0}^{t+1} = \frac{1}{2} \cdot D_m \cdot P_1' \cdot R \cdot (N_{2,0}^{t} + N_{2,1}^{t}), \quad N_{2,0}^{t+1} = \frac{1}{2} \cdot D_f \cdot P_2' \cdot R \cdot (N_{2,0}^{t} + N_{2,1}^{t}). \tag{2}$$

where $N^t_{s,i}$, s=1,2, i=0,1,2, is the number of male or female individuals belonging to the ith life period in time t; $P_{s,i}$, s=1,2, i=0,1, are survival ratios for male and female individuals belonging to the ith life period. They indicate probability that male/female individuals, who belong to i^{th} life period, will survive the end of this life period. P'_s, s=1,2, are survival ratios for male and female infant children. Fertility rate R is the average number of children given birth to by one female during her life. Ratios of live-born males and females are denoted by D_m and D_f. These two constants tell us that among 100 live-born individuals there are $D_m \cdot 100$ males and $D_f \cdot 100$ females.

From the second and the sixth equations of (2) a difference equation of order two for the number of female individuals in their fertility life period $N^t_{2,1}$ is obtained:

$$N^t_{2,1} - \frac{1}{2} \cdot D_f \cdot R \cdot P'_2 \cdot N^{t-1}_{2,1} - \frac{1}{2} \cdot D_f \cdot R \cdot P'_2 \cdot P_{2,0} \cdot N^{t-2}_{2,1} = 0. \tag{3}$$

Its solution is:

$$N^t_{2,1} = A_1 \cdot G^t_1 + A_2 \cdot G^t_2, \tag{4}$$

where:

$$G_{1,2} = \frac{1}{4} \cdot (D_f \cdot R \cdot P'_2 \pm \sqrt{D^2_f \cdot R^2 \cdot P'^2_2 + 8 \cdot D_f \cdot R \cdot P'_2 \cdot P_{2,0}}), \tag{5}$$

$$A_1 = \frac{P_{2,0} \cdot N^0_{2,0} - N^0_{2,1} \cdot G_2}{G_1 - G_2}, \quad A_2 = \frac{N^0_{2,1} \cdot G_1 - P_{2,0} \cdot N^0_{2,0}}{G_1 - G_2}. \tag{6}$$

As D_f, R, P'_2 and $P_{2,0}$ are real and nonnegative, it follows from (5): G_1, $G_2 \in \mathcal{R}$; $G_1 \geq 0$, $G_2 \leq 0$; $| G_1 | \geq | G_2 |$. The value of $| G_1 |$ can be smaller or greater than 1, whereas $| G_2 | < 1$. The solution (4) of difference equation (3) is a linear combination of two exponential functions. The asymptotical behaviour (when $t \to \infty$) is determined by the first root G_1, which has greater absolute value than root G_2. The second root alternately contributes positive and negative values to solution's value, but as $| G_2 | < 1$ this contribution exponentially disappears with time. If $R = \frac{2}{D_f \cdot P'_2 \cdot (P_{2,0}+1)} = R_0$ then $G_1 = 1$, $G_2 = \frac{1-\sqrt{1+4 \cdot P_{2,0} \cdot (P_{2,0}+1)}}{2 \cdot (P_{2,0}+1)}$, and $\lim_{t\to\infty} N^t_{2,1} = A_1 = \frac{2 \cdot P_{2,0} \cdot (P_{2,0}+1) \cdot N^0_{2,0} - N^0_{2,1} \cdot (1-\sqrt{1+4 \cdot P_{2,0} \cdot (P_{2,0}+1)})}{2 \cdot P_{2,0}+1+\sqrt{1+4 \cdot P_{2,0} \cdot (P_{2,0}+1)}}$. If $R > R_0$, $N^t_{2,1}$ grows exponentially; when $R < R_0$, $\lim_{t\to\infty} N^t_{2,1} = 0$ (see figure 1).

The solutions for other $N^t_{s,i}$ can be obtained from solution (4), initial conditions $N^0_{1,0}$, $N^0_{1,0}$, $N^0_{1,1}$, $N^0_{1,2}$, $N^0_{2,0}$, $N^0_{2,1}$, $N^0_{2,2}$ and equations (2). The total population, say N^t, is given by $N^t = N^t_{1,0}+N^t_{1,1}+N^t_{1,2}+N^t_{2,0}+N^t_{2,1}+N^t_{2,2} = a \cdot N^{t+1}_{2,1}+b \cdot N^t_{2,1}+c \cdot N^{t-1}_{2,1}+d \cdot N^{t-2}_{2,1}+e \cdot N^{t-3}_{2,1}$ where: $a = 1/P_{2,0}$, $b = 1+0.5 \cdot D_m \cdot P'_1 \cdot R/P_{2,0}$, $c = P_{2,1} + 0.5 \cdot D_m \cdot P'_1 \cdot R \cdot (1 + P_{1,0}/P_{2,0})$, $d = 0.5 \cdot D_m \cdot P'_1 \cdot P_{1,0} \cdot R \cdot (1 + P_{1,1}/P_{2,0})$, $e = 0.5 \cdot D_m \cdot P'_1 \cdot P_{1,0} \cdot P_{1,1} \cdot R$. The asymptotical behaviour of function N^t as $t \to \infty$, is the same as the asymptotical behaviour of function $N^t_{2,1}$.

If $R = R_0$, model (2) will give stable, nonzero solutions. Which parameter in model (1) corresponds to R? It is total fertility rate given by $T_f = \sum_{i=15}^{49} R_i$. The value of T_f which would lead neither to population explosion nor implosion, is 2.11 for Slovenia, while its actual value was 1.4371 in 1990. Let us take $D_f = 0.483$ (ratio of live-born girls in Slovenia), $P'_2 = 0.9919$ (survival ratio for female infant children in Slovenia). To get $P_{2,0}$ for Slovenia, model (2) is mapped on model (1) in the following way: 0-19 years is childhood period, 20-39 years is fertility period, 40-59 years is old age. So $P_{2,0}$ = (number of women who will be 20-39 years old by projection of annual model) / (total number of women 0-19 years old in

Slovenia 1990) = 0.9916. From these values we get $R_0 = 2.10$, which is close to 2.11. From figure 2 we can see how the number of women in fertility period $N_{2,1}^t$, according to model (2), would fall in case total fertility rate remain unchanged, and how it would rise if Ireland's T_f is substituted for R. The behaviour of these solutions is very similar to the behaviour of respective solutions for model (1).

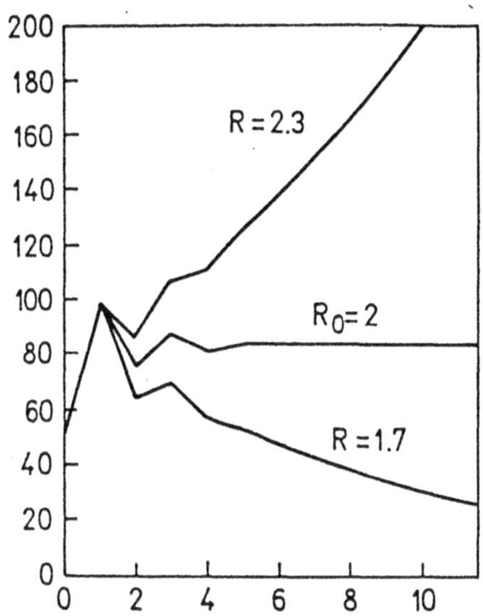

Figure 1: Solutions $N_{2,1}^t$ for $D_f = 0.5$, $P_2' = P_{2,0} = 1$ and $N_{2,0}^0 = 100$, $N_{2,1}^0 = 50$.

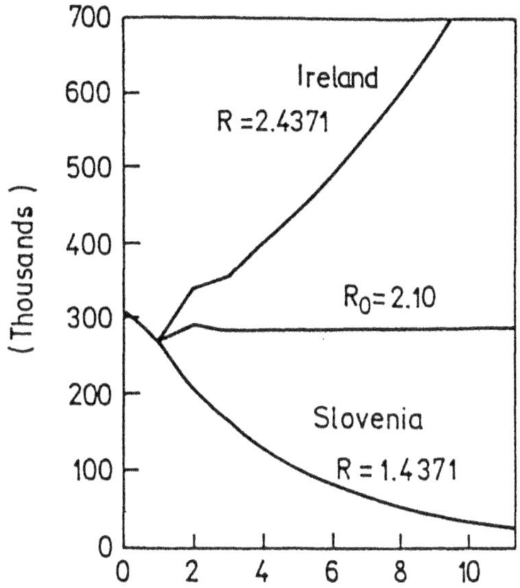

Figure 2: Solutions $N_{2,1}^t$ for $D_f = 0.483$, $P_2' = 0.9919$, $P_{2,0} = 0.9916$ and $N_{2,0}^0 = 272261$, $N_{2,1}^0 = 312756$.

4 Conclusion

Model (1) is elaborate and realistic, however, its solution cannot be expressed analytically. Model (2) is very simple and can be solved analytically. Its solutions demonstrate all the main features of long term behaviour of the solutions of model (1) and its parameters (especialy in the expression for R_0) have meanings evident also to nonprofessionals. Both can show some temporary periodic behaviour and both tend towards zero gravity or grow without limits as $t \to \infty$. With an appropriate mapping of one model on another analogy or correspondence between parameters of both models can be obtained. So model (2) can also be used for teaching purposes as an example of a very simple mathematical modelling of a demographic process.

5 References

Čepar D., Gosar L., Uršič E. (1992), Natural growth population projections, Operations research '91, P.Gritzmann, R.Hettich, R.Horst, E.Sachs editors, Physica-Verlag, Heidelberg 1992, p.p. 305-308.

Estimated Accuracy of Data and Intervals of Admissible Values for Parameters of Fitting Functions

Drago Čepar, Matija Marolt, Zoran Radalj, Marijan Ribarič
Jožef Stefan Institute, University of Ljubljana
Jamova 39, 61111 Ljubljana, Slovenia

1. *INTRODUCTION*

Suppose we know the function $f(x,\beta_1,...,\beta_J)$ representing a particular natural law, where $\beta_1,...,\beta_J$ are unknown free parameters to be determined by experiments. The selection of $f(x,\beta_1,...,\beta_J)$ depends on physical theory chosen to explain the natural phenomenon considered. Given a set of experimental observations (x_i,y_i) of this phenomenon and estimates of their accuracy ε_i, $i=1,...,N$, let our objective be the determination of intervals of admissible values of parameters $\beta_1,...,\beta_J$ that are consistent with the estimated accuracy of experimental data.

The traditional approach in fitting $f(x,\beta_1,...,\beta_J)$ to experimental data is based on the assumption that $\eta_i = f_i - y_i$ are realizations of random variables distributed normally with the same variance σ^2. Using the least squares (LS) method, the parameters β_j and their standard errors $SE(\beta_j)$, $j=1,...,J$, are estimated by minimizing the sum

$$\sum_{i=1}^{N}[y_i - f(x_i,\beta_1,...,\beta_J)]^2 \quad . \tag{1}$$

$SE(\beta_j)$ gives an estimate of the reliability of the value of parameter β_j that minimizes (1).

Our approach provides additional information about the accuracy of the minimizing values of parameters β_j. It is based on the estimates of maximal errors ε_i of experimental data y_i and does not require any statistical assumptions about η_i. The interval $[\beta_j^{(m)},\beta_j^{(M)}]$ of admissible values for individual parameter β_j is determined so that inequalities

$$y_i - \varepsilon_i \le f(x_i,\beta_1,...,\beta_J) \le y_i + \varepsilon_i \ , \qquad i=1,2,...,N \tag{2}$$

are satisfied for values of parameter β_j within this interval. We present an algorithm for determining this interval by changing the values of a particular j-th parameter β_j and adjusting the values of remaining parameters $\beta_1,\beta_2,...,\beta_{j-1},\beta_{j+1},...,\beta_J$ so that $f(x,\beta_1,...,\beta_J)$ satisfies inequalities (2). The method is described in Section 2. In Section 3, we illustrate the method by a case study.

2. *ALGORITHM FOR CALCULATING MAXIMAL INTERVALS OF ADMISSIBLE VALUES FOR PARAMETERS*

For parameter β_j, whose interval of admissible values we are interested in, we find an interval $[\beta_j^{(m)},\beta_j^{(M)}]$ of its values such that we can choose the values of remaining parameters $\beta_1,\beta_2,...,\beta_{j-1},\beta_{j+1},...,\beta_J$ so that inequalities (2) are satisfied. The main part of the algorithm for determining interval of admissible values for j-th parameter is described in Chart 1.

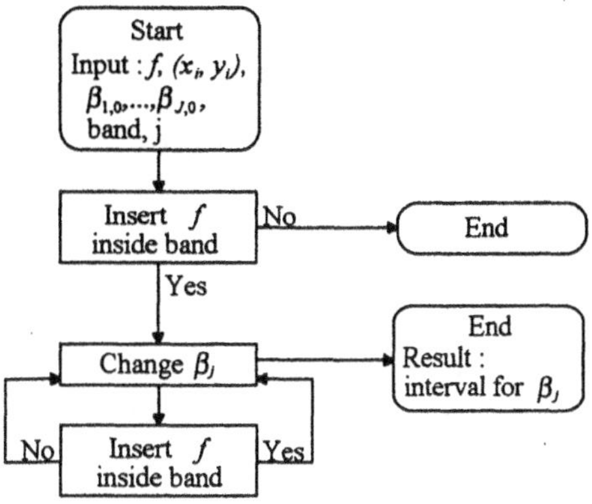

Input :

f - fit-function : $y = f(x, \beta_1, ..., \beta_J)$

(x_i, y_i) - experimental data

$(\beta_{1,0}, ..., \beta_{J,0})$ - initial values of fit-function parameters

band - upper $b_M(x)$ and lower $b_m(x)$ limits of the band are, e.g., straight lines joining endpoints of estimating intervals $[y_i - \varepsilon_i, y_i + \varepsilon_i]$

j - the index of parameter for which the interval of admissible values is to be calculated.

Result :

interval of admissible values for β_j

Chart 1: Flow chart of the algorithm for calculating interval of admissible values for parameter β_j.

<u>Procedures :</u>

Insert f inside band

With this procedure we calculate values of β_j that place all values of the fitting function $f(x, \beta_1, ..., \beta_J)$ inside band so that $b_m \le f \le b_M$. We start with (a) fitting the data using the Marquardt algorithm for nonlinear least squares (Box Jenkins 1970 p. 504). Then we (b) check if all function values are inside the band. If not, we (c) insert a new datum in the place where differences $(f - b_M(x))$ or $(b_m(x) - f)$ are maximal provided ordinates of data to be fitted differ more than some value given in advance. These steps (a-c) are repeated until no additional data can be inserted. If values of $f(x, \beta_1, ..., \beta_J)$ are still not inside the band after the preceding steps (a) to (c) have been performed, we (d) increase the power p in expression for calculating the sum of squares in Marquardt algorithm

$$ss = \sum_{i=1}^{N} \left(\frac{f(x_i, \beta_1, ..., \beta_J) - y_i}{\varepsilon_i} \right)^{2p} . \tag{3}$$

Steps (a) to (d) are repeated until :

(i) a set of parameter estimates β_j, for which $f(x, \beta_1, ..., \beta_J)$ is inside the band, is found (the procedure returns Yes).

(ii) the power in expression (3) is larger than a prescribed value (the procedure returns No).

Change β_j.

The procedure calculates the relative increment δ of parameter β_j that is used for the calculation of new values of β_j.

The procedure starts with two possible inputs :

(i) the function is inside the band (input = Yes). We increase preceding increment δ : $\delta = \delta * 2$ and calculate new value of parameter β_j : $\beta_j = \beta_j * (1 + \delta)$.

(ii) the function is outside the band (input = No). We decrease preceding increment δ : $\delta = \delta / 2$ and calculate new value of parameter β_j : $\beta_j = \beta_j * (1 - \delta)$.

3. *CASE STUDY*

We illustrate the performance of our method by applying it to the Richards model (Ratkowsky 1990) :

$$f(x,\beta_1,\beta_2,\beta_3,\beta_4)=\frac{\beta_1}{[1+\exp(\beta_2-\beta_3 x)]^{\beta_4}} \tag{4}$$

that is known to have very poor statistical properties in estimation, possessing very high nonlinearity. We have generated 40 values f_i for $x_i = 10,20,30,...,400$ with chosen values of parameters $\beta_1 = 1000$, $\beta_2 = 1$, $\beta_3 = 0.001$, $\beta_4 = 2$. We have simulated experimental data y_i : $y_i = f_i*(1+e_i/100)$, where e_i is an error uniformly distributed [−2,2]. Then we have analyzed the data assuming maximal inaccuracy $\varepsilon_i = 0.05*y_i$ by our method and by Marquardt LS algorithm. The results of analysis are given in Table 1.

Par.	LS Best Fit	$SE(\beta_j)$	$[\beta_j^{(m)},\beta_j^{(M)}]$ with $\varepsilon_i = 0.05*y_i$		$\frac{2*SE(\beta_j)}{\beta_j^{(M)}-\beta_j^{(m)}}$
β_1	1000.0	29391.350	957.9105	1041.391	704.15
β_2	0.99999998	35.73896	0.9722061	1.029306	1251.8
β_3	0.00100318	0.021419	0.0008572	0.0011438	149.37
β_4	1.99999998	62.15612	1.969650	2.032722	1970.96

Table 1 : Standard errors of parameters obtained by LS and our method on Richards model (4).

Results show that standard error of each parameter obtained by LS is very high and is of limited use. Our method gives estimates of parameter intervals that are about 1000 times better than LS standard error estimates.

4. *CONCLUSION*

Our method gives additional information about parameters of a function fitting experimental data that is independent of classical statistical assumptions. Without any statistical assumptions, it enables us to infer the maximal uncertainty of parameter estimates implied by the maximal uncertainty of experimental data. The case study shows that useful intervals of admissible values of parameters are obtained by our method in an example where classical statistical estimates give disastrous results (Ratkowsky 1990).

REFERENCES

Box G., Jenkins G. (1970) 'Time Series Analysis: Forecasting and Control', Holden-Day, San Francisco.

Čepar D., Radalj Z., Ribarič M., Vovk B.(1991) 'Determination of Admissible Values of parameters from the Estimated Accuracy of Data', Proceedings of the 16th Symposium on Operation Research, Trier, Anton Hain Verlag. (in print).

Ratkowsky David A. (1990) 'Handbook of nonlinear regression models', Marcel Dekker.

Identification of Multiple Outliers in Time Series

Thomas Flak, Wolfgang Schmid
Abteilung Stochastik, Universität Ulm
Helmholtzstraße 18, 7900 Ulm, Germany

1. Introduction

In order to find outliers in a data set, mostly consecutive procedures are applied. In literature it is distinguished between consecutive inward testing and consecutive outward testing (e.g. Barnett/Lewis (1984), Davies/Gather (1992)). Using an inward testing procedure it is additionally assumed that an upper bound s for the number of outliers is known.

While inward procedures are vulnerable to masking, outward procedures are largely immune to it, provided that the actual number of outliers does not exceed s (Simonoff (1991), Davies/Gather (1992)). In the context of outliers in time series, only inward procedures have been proposed (e.g. Abraham/Chuang(1989), Lee/Wei (1988), Tiao (1985)).

In this paper we consider the problem of detecting outlying observations in a contaminated autoregressive-moving average process. We introduce a consecutive outward testing procedure. By means of simulations we have compared our method with other ones. The results are very encouraging.

2. An Outward Testing Procedure

Let $\{ Y_t \}$ be an autoregressive-moving average process, i.e.

$$\Phi(B)\, Y_t = \Theta(B)\, \varepsilon_t \tag{2.1}$$

with $\Phi(z) := -\sum_{v=0}^{p} \alpha_v z^v$ and $\Theta(z) := \sum_{v=0}^{q} \beta_v z^v$,

where B denotes the backshift operator, $\alpha_0 := -1$, $\beta_0 := 1$ and $\{ \varepsilon_t \}$ is a white noise process. Furthermore we assume that $\{Y_t\}$ is stationary, causal and invertible.

We denote by $x_1, .., x_n$ a realization of the process $\{X_t\}$, which is connected with $\{Y_t\}$ as follows (δ_{tq} Kronecker delta)

$$-\sum_{v=0}^{p} \alpha_v \left(X_{t-v} - \sum_{i=1}^{s_1} a_{1i}\, \delta_{t-v,q_{1i}} \right) = \sum_{v=0}^{q} \beta_v \left(\varepsilon_{t-v} + \sum_{j=1}^{s_2} a_{2j}\, \delta_{t-v,q_{2j}} \right) . \tag{2.2}$$

a_{1v} is called a type I outlier (additive outlier) and $a_{2\mu}$ a type II outlier (innovation outlier), iff $a_{1\nu} \neq 0$ resp. $a_{2\mu} \neq 0$.

Here, s_1 and s_2 denote the number of type I resp. type II outliers. Our aim is to find the unknown positions of the outliers, namely $q_{1\nu}$ and $q_{2\mu}$. We assume that an upper bound s for the total number of model outliers is known.

Our procedure can be divided into the following steps:

a) **Model Selection**

Using the BIC order selection criterion as given in Brockwell/Davis (1991, p.304), we obtain estimators $\hat{p}$, $\hat{q}$, $\hat{\alpha}_1, \dots, \hat{\alpha}_{\hat{p}}$, $\hat{\beta}_1, \dots, \hat{\beta}_{\hat{q}}$ and $\hat{\sigma}^2$ of the parameters. Since outliers may occur, it is possible that the estimators are distorted. However, these estimators only serve as a starting-point in our procedure and will be improved in the following steps.
Another possibility is the use of robust estimators (Martin/Yohai (1985)).

b) **Determining the s most outlier suspicious positions**

Replacing the parameters in Φ and Θ by the above estimators we get $\hat{\Phi}$ and $\hat{\Theta}$ and the estimated residuals $\hat{\varepsilon}_t := \hat{\Theta}(B)^{-1}\hat{\Phi}(B)Y_t$.

First it is supposed that $s_1 = 1$, $s_2 = 0$ and that $q_{11} = t$ is known. Additionally, all parameters of $\{Y_t\}$ are assumed to be known. The likelihood-ratio method is used for testing $H: a_{11} = 0$ against $K: a_{11} \neq 0$. The same procedure is applied on $s_1 = 0$, $s_2 = 1$ and $q_{21} = t$. If the parameters p, q, $\alpha_1, \dots, \alpha_p$, $\beta_1, \dots, \beta_q$ and σ^2 are estimated as above, we obtain the test statistics (Tiao (1985))

$$\lambda_{AO,t} = -\frac{1}{\gamma\,\hat{\sigma}_n}\sum_{i=0}^{n-t}\hat{\Psi}_i\,\hat{\varepsilon}_{t+i} \qquad \text{and} \qquad \lambda_{IO,t} = \hat{\varepsilon}_t/\hat{\sigma}_n\,,$$

where $\gamma = (\sum_{i=0}^{\infty}\hat{\Psi}_i^2)^{1/2}$, $\hat{\Psi}_0 := -1$, $\Psi(z) = \Phi(z)/\Theta(z) = \sum_{i=0}^{\infty}\Psi_i z^i$ and $\hat{\Psi}_i$ is obtained by replacing the parameters in Ψ_i by the above estimators. Note that $\lambda_{AO,t}$ and $\lambda_{IO,t}$ are functions of the estimated residuals.

These considerations show that in the case of unknown positions the test statistic $\lambda := \max_{1 \le t \le n}\{|\lambda_{AO,t}|, |\lambda_{IO,t}|\}$ seems to be reasonable. If $\lambda = |\lambda_{AO,t_0}|$, a type I outlier is taken into account at position t_0, otherwise a type II outlier.

Next the estimated residuals are corrected. If we have concluded on a type II outlier, we set $\hat{\varepsilon}_{t_0} = 0$. In the case of a type I outlier all residuals $\hat{\varepsilon}_t$, $t \ge t_0$ are contaminated and these quantities are replaced by $\hat{\varepsilon}_t + \lambda_{AO,t_0}\hat{\sigma}_n\hat{\Psi}_{t-t_0}/\gamma$ for $t \ge t_0$.

Step b is repeated s times. The new estimated residuals are used for the next step. In each step we store the position and the type of the suspicious value.

c) **Intervention Analysis**

We consider (2.2), but now the positions and the types of the suspicious values are known. We choose the quantities obtained in step b. Thus an intervention problem is present. By means of the least squares or the maximum - likelihood method we estimate all model parameters.

Now it is possible to apply the results given in Schmid (1991). The extension to the case of an autoregressive - moving average process is obvious.
We are interested to decide whether at a certain (known) position an outlier is present or not. For this we calculate the test statistics for each suspicious position l_v, $v = 1, .., s$. Then we consider the corresponding order statistics $T_{1:s}, \dots, T_{s:s}$. If $T_{1:s} \leq c$ and $T_{1:s} = T_{\pi(l_1)}$, no outlier occurs at position $\pi(l_1)$. We repeat c) with $s-1$ instead of s. If $T_{1:s} > c$, we conclude that at all positions $l_1, \dots, l_s$ model outliers are present.

3. Simulation Study

It turns out to be difficult to compare various outlier identification procedures, since each method heavily depends on the choice of the critical value. We have chosen similar measures of performance as given by Burns (1980). By means of a simulation study we have compared our procedure with the methods proposed by Abraham/Chuang (1989), Lee/Wei (1988) and Tiao (1985). It has shown that our procedure is comparable with the best inward testing procedure, the method of Tiao. Our method shows advantages, if small type II outliers occur, while Tiao's procedure is better, if small type I outliers are present.

References

Abraham, B. and Chuang, A. (1989). Outlier detection and time series modeling. Technometrics, 31, p. 241 - 248.

Barnett, V. and Lewis, T. (1984). Outliers in Statistical Data. Wiley.

Brockwell, P.J. and Davis, R.A. (1991). Time Series. Springer - Verlag.

Burns, G.C. (1980). Procedures for the detection of outliers in weekly time series. ASAProBuEc, p. 560 - 563.

Davies, L. and Gather, U. (1992). The identification of multiple outliers. To appear in JASA.

Lee, J.H. and Wei, W.W.S. (1988). A robust procedure for detecting outliers in time series. ASAProBuEc, p. 522 - 526.

Martin, R.D. and Yohai, V.J. (1985). Robustness in time series and estimating ARMA - models. In: Handbook of Statistics, Vol. 5, Hannan, E.J., Krishnaiah, P.R. and Rao, M.M. , eds, Elsevier Science Publishers, p. 119 - 155.

Schmid, W. (1991). Classification of type I and II outliers. Methods of OR, 64.

Simonoff, J.S. (1991). General approaches to stepwise identification of unusual values in data analysis. In: Directions in Robust Statistics and Diagnostics, Stahel/Weisberg, eds, Springer - Verlag, p. 223 - 241.

Tiao, G.C. (1985). ARMA models, intervention problems and outlier detection in time series. In: Handbook of Statistics, Vol.5, Hannan, E.J., Krishnaiah, P.R. and Rao, M.M., eds, Elsevier Science Publishers, p. 85 - 118.

Semiparametric Approaches to Dimension Reduction

Wolfgang K. Härdle
FB Wirtschaftswissenschaften, Humboldt Universität zu Berlin
1086 Berlin, Germany
Berwin A. Turlach
C.O.R.E. and Institut de Statistique, Université Catholique de Louvain
1348 Louvain-la-Neuve, Belgium

Abstract

We give an overview on several semiparametric methods utilised to model high-dimensional data. Our approach is semiparametric in nature and is related to Generalised Linear Models. We focus on dynamic estimation techniques in this setting. In particular we discuss Generalized Additive Models (GAM), Alternating Conditional Expectations (ACE), Average Derivative Estimation (ADE), semiparametric weighted least squares (Single Index Models, SIM), Projection Pursuit Regression (PPR), and Sliced Inverse Regression (SIR). Their performance in practice and theory is compared.

1. Introduction and Motivation

Due to the increasing availability of computer power and graphical tools over the last decades non parametric estimation methods became more and more popular for the analysis of the relationship between a response variable $Y \in I\!R$ and its explanatory variable $X \in I\!R^d$. For the case $d = 1$ a rich basket of tools exists such as kernel estimators, nearest-neighbour estimators and spline estimators. A good access to these topics is given by the recent monographs of Eubank (1988), Härdle (1990), Müller (1988), Wahba (1990), and Hastie and Tibshirani (1990, Chapter 2 and 3). However, most of these techniques are very unappealing for $d > 1$ since they are based on the idea of local (weighted) averaging *(smoothing)*. Since in higher dimensions the observations X are sparsely distributed this process of local averaging results in a poor performance for reasonable sample sizes. This behaviour, also known as the *curse of dimensionality* (Huber, 1985), makes it necessary to search for methods and models which reduce the dimension of the smoothing problem — preferably to a one-dimensional problem which is the best-studied case. In this paper we describe some lines of thought and research to this goal.

This idea of dimension reduction is an old one and is build in parametric models such as

Generalized Linear Models (GLM). A GLM as defined by McCullagh and Nelder (1989) connects the mean μ of the response variable Y with the *linear predictor* $\eta = X^T\beta$ via a *link function* G_1,i.e., $G_1(\mu) = \eta$. The aim is to estimate β when the link function G_1 is fixed. From the point of view of dimension reduction this is equivalent to say that for given G_1 the projection β from $\mathbb{R}^d$ to $\mathbb{R}^1$ is searched such that η, the projected X variable, fits the (by G_1) transformed mean μ of the Y variable "best". Most of the ideas which we present here can be seen as generalizations of GLMs. Such a model can be generalized by nonparametric methods in two ways. Either the fixed form of the link function is abandoned, i.e., a flexible or parameter free form is allowed, or the linear form of the predictor is abandoned allowing for any unknown function of the explanatory variables.

Relaxing the form of the link function means to keep the linear predictor but to replace the link function by a non-parametric (preferably monotone) function. More generally several of these types of response models can be added, each using a different linear predictor and (non-parametric) link function. These models are known as Projection Pursuit Regression (PPR) models due to an algorithm developped by Friedman and Stuetzle (1981). If we take just one term, i.e., an unknown (inverse) link function operating on a linear combination of the explanatory variables, this is called a one term projection pursuit model, in econometrics also called a *Single Index Model* (SIM). This type of model will be discussed in Section 3.

Allowing for any functional form of influence for the predictor variables leads again into the dimensionality problems mentioned above. In order to avoid these problems Hastie and Tibshirani (1990) proposed to keep the link G_1 but to generalize the linear predictor by a sum of non-parametric univariate functions. This leads to so called *Generalized Additive Models* (GAM) which will be discussed in Section 4.

However, both of the above approaches make a priori assumptions on the structure of the model. Most generally, the hope that interesting features of high-dimensional data are retrievable from low-dimensional projections is expressed by saying that the conditional distribution of Y given X depends on X only through a p-dimensional variable $(X^T\beta_1, \ldots, X^T\beta_p)^T$. The hope is that p is much smaller than d. Here the model is $Y = g(X^T\beta_1, \ldots, X^T\beta_p, \varepsilon)$, where the β's are unknown vectors, ε is independent of X and g is an arbitrary unknown function on $\mathbb{R}^{p+1}$. In this model we of course have an identification problem. Without any assumptions on g it is impossible to identify the β's, we can only hope to identify the linear space which they span. Li (1991a) proposed a method called *Sliced Inverse Regression* (SIR) for estimating this linear space and some β's forming a base of this space. In his terminology which we will adopt here this space is called the effective dimension-reduction (e.d.r.) space and each vector of this space is called an e.d.r. direction. Once a set of e.d.r. directions is fixed Li (1991a) proposes to use standard smoothing techniques to smooth $(X^T\beta_1, \ldots, X^T\beta_p)^T$ against Y. We will discuss his approach in Section 5.

In Section 2 we will describe running examples which we will use to illustrate the different methods which we discuss. Section 6 finally shows how these methods can be implemented on a computer.

2. Nonparametric Approaches to Generalized Linear Models

We have argued that some dimension-reduction models can be seen as generalizations of GLMs were the assumptions on the link function are weakened or the linear form of the explanatory variables is abandoned. To fix ideas let $X \in \mathbb{R}^d$ denote the explanatory variable and $Y \in \mathbb{R}$ be the response variable. Here and in the following we use the term *link* where McCullagh and Nelder (1989) mean the inverse link,i.e., the mean μ of Y is connected with the predictor $\eta = X^T\beta$ via a link function G such that $\mu = G(\eta)$. Since in our examples this link is monotone there is no problem of confusion. As a running example we shall use the case of binary response models, i.e., $Y \in \{0, 1\}$. The GLM then reads as $P[Y = 1|X = x] = G(x^T\beta)$.

Single Index Models

Single Index Models keep the linear component but generalize the link. In our running example this reads as

$$P[Y = 1|X = x] = g\left(x^T\beta\right) \tag{2.1}$$

with g an unknown univariate "smooth" function. Note that here some standardization of the parameter β is asked for, since as such, (2.1) does not identify β but rather the direction of β. The aim here is to estimate β and the unknown link. For illustration of statistical and numerical procedures to be described later we would like to introduce

example 1:

$$\begin{aligned} &X \sim \mathcal{N}_2(0, I_2), \quad \beta = (1,1)^T \\ &g(\eta) = L(\eta) + \rho\varphi'(\eta), \quad L(\eta) = \exp(\eta)/[1+\exp(\eta)], \quad \varphi(\eta) = \frac{1}{\sqrt{2\pi}}\exp\left(-\frac{\eta^2}{2}\right) \\ &P[Y = 1|X = x] = g(x^T\beta) \end{aligned} \tag{2.2}$$

This model is almost a Logit model, only the skew deviation term $\rho\varphi'(\eta)$ makes it different from a GLM. For $\rho = 0$ it falls into the class of GLMs. For later illustrations we have set $\rho = 0.6$ and have generated $n = 200$ datapoints (x_i, y_i) according to (2.2). A graphical inspection of the data gives a taste of the nonparametric structure. Figure 1 shows a three dimensional scatterplot of the data. If we project the X variables in the 45° line we obtain Figure 2. This picture shows the projected data $x_i^T\beta$ against y_i together with the link $g(\eta)$. All the graphics and computations were done in the computing environment XploRe (1992).

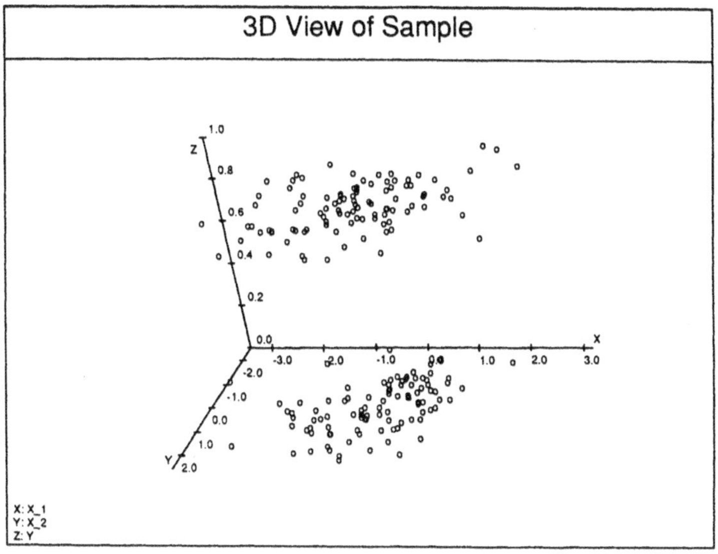

Figure 1: A three-dimensional scatterplot of the sample $\{(x_{1i}, x_{2i}, y_i)\}_{i=1}^{200}$ for example 1.

Generalized Additive Models

Generalized Additive Models keep the link but generalize the linear predictor to a sum of nonparametric functions. In our running example this reads as

$$P[Y = 1|X = x] = G\left(\alpha + \sum_{j=1}^{d} g_j(x_j)\right) \tag{2.3}$$

where x_j denotes the jth component of the vector $x = (x_1, \ldots, x_d)^T$ and the g_j are unknown univariate "smooth" functions. Again some standardization is necessary since the model as such does not identify the unknown $\{g_j\}_{j=1}^{d}$. The aim here is to estimate the nonparametric functions g_j. For illustrations of later techniques let us introduce

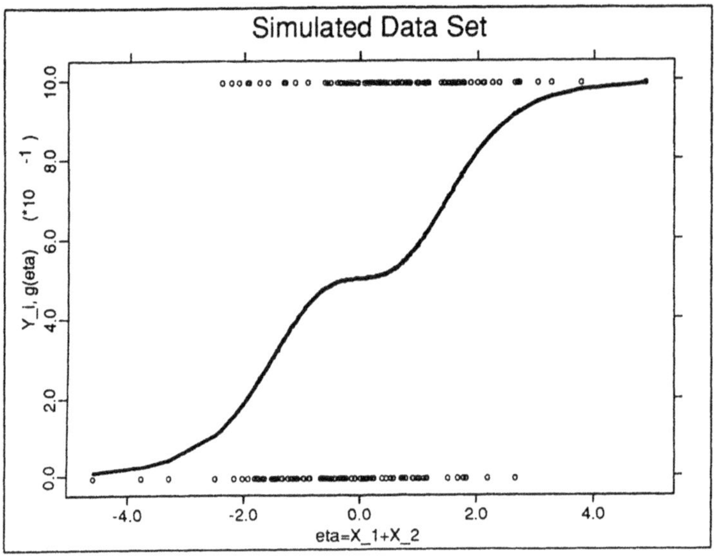

Figure 2: The observations y_i for example 1 plotted against $\eta = x^T\beta = x_{1i} + x_{2i}$. The link $g(\eta) = L(\eta) + 0.6\varphi'(\eta)$ is shown as the solid line.

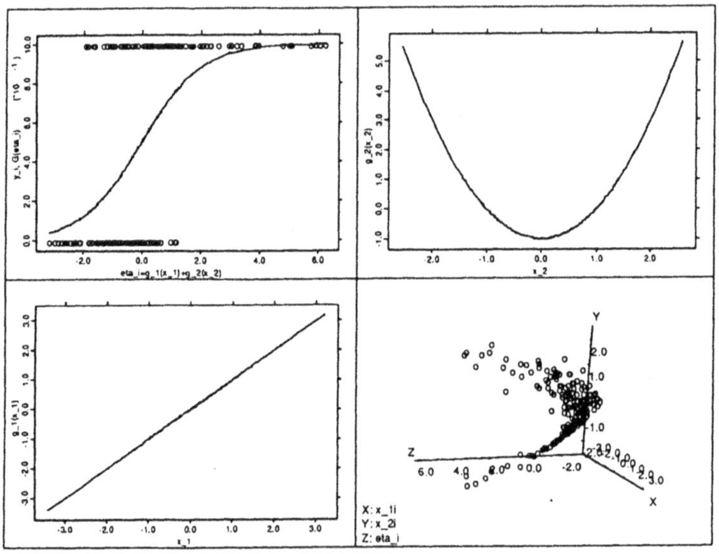

Figure 3: A four picture display with $\{(\eta_i, y_i)\}_{i=1}^{200}$ and $G(\eta_i)$ in the upper left. The nonparametric components are in the lower left and upper right. A rotated view of the surface $\{(x_{1i}, x_{2i}, \eta_i)\}_{i=1}^{200}$ is given in the lower right.

example 2:

$$
\begin{aligned}
&X \sim \mathcal{N}_2(0, I_2), \quad g_1(x_1) = x_1, \quad g_2(x_2) = (x_2)^2 - 1 \\
&G = L \\
&P[Y = 1|X = x] = G(g_1(x_1) + g_2(x_2))
\end{aligned}
\tag{2.4}
$$

This model is almost a Logit model, only the second predictor variable has a nonlinear influence on η. Figure 3 shows a four picture display with the data $\{(\eta_i, y_i)\}_{i=1}^{200}$ in the upper left corner together with the Logistic link. Note that the predictor is $\eta_i = g_1(x_{1i}) + g_2(x_{2i})$. The "non-parametric" components g_j are shown in the lower left und the upper right. An impression of the nonlinear components can be gained by rotating the three dimensional surface $\{(x_{1i}, x_{2i}, \eta_i)\}_{i=1}^{200}$. The rotated point cloud is shown in the lower right.

Sliced Inverse Regression

In our running example Sliced Inverse Regression estimates the effective dimension reduction directions $\beta_1, \ldots, \beta_p$ of the model

$$
P[Y = 1|X = x] = g(x^T\beta_1, \ldots, x^T\beta_p). \tag{2.5}
$$

where g is an arbitrary unknown function on $\mathbb{R}^p$. Note that SIR contains the above two models as special cases. To demonstrate this technique we will use a modified version of example 1 and example 3 defined below. Example 1 is modified by adding three additional components to X so that $X \sim \mathcal{N}_5(0, I_5)$. But these additional components will have no influence on Y.

example 3:

$$
\begin{aligned}
&X \sim \mathcal{N}_5(0, I_5), \quad g_1(x_1) = x_1, \quad g_2(x_2) = (x_2)^2 - 1 \\
&\varepsilon \sim \mathcal{N}_1(0, (0.6)^2) \\
&Y = g_1(x_1) + g_2(x_2) + \varepsilon
\end{aligned}
\tag{2.6}
$$

3. Single Index Models

Model (2.1) is called a single index model or a one term projection pursuit model. This terminology is due to Friedman and Stuetzle (1981) who considered the more general model:

$$P[Y=1|X=x]=\sum_{j=1}^{K} g_j(x^T\beta_j)$$

where the $\beta_j \in I\!R^d$ are unknown parameters and the g_j's are unknown smooth functions. In order to make the β_j's and the g_j's identifiable one has to impose restrictions on the scale, usually $\|\beta_j\|=1$, or $\beta_{j1}=1$.

Friedman and Stuetzle (1981) proposed to estimate K, β_j and g_j by the method of Projection Pursuit Regression (PPR) algorithm. This procedure estimates terms $g_j(x^T\beta_j)$ as long as the fraction of unexplained variance is below a user specified threshold. In each step that β_j is chosen which maximizes the fraction of unexplained variance given the previous terms (*projection pursuit*). The fitted model with $\hat{K}$ is

$$P[Y=1|X=x]=\sum_{j=1}^{\hat{K}} \hat{g}_j(x^T\hat{\beta}_j).$$

A drawback of this method is that it is not evident which value of K is to be chosen. Research has therefore focused on one term projection pursuit models. In this line Hall (1989) constructs a root-n consistent estimator of β. A different method is that of Härdle and Stoker (1989) also called ADE for Average Derivative Estimation. It is based on the following idea. Define $m(x)=g(x^T\beta)$ and observe that for the average derivative δ, as defined below, we have

$$\delta = E_X[m'(X)] = E_X[\frac{dg}{d(x^T\beta)}(X^T\beta)]\beta. \tag{3.1}$$

Thus δ determines β up to scale. Let $f(x)$ denote the density of X and l its vector of the negative log-derivatives (partial), $l=-\frac{\partial \log f}{\partial x}=-\frac{f'}{f}$ (l is also called *score vector*). Under assumptions on f this enables us to write

$$\delta = E[m'(X)] = E[lY] \tag{3.2}$$

and to estimate δ by $\hat{\delta}=n^{-1}\sum_{i=1}^{n}\hat{l}_h(x_i)y_i$. Here $\hat{l}_h$ is an estimator of l based on a kernel density smoother with bandwidth h. For an easy access to kernel density smoothing see the book by Silverman (1986). With root-n estimates for δ precise estimates for the link can be obtained. The convergence rate for g is one dimensional. Stoker (1991) proposed alternative estimators for δ based on first estimating the partial derivatives $m'(x)$ and then to average over the observations. A Monte Carlo comparison of these methods is presented in Stoker and Villas-Boas (1992).

The estimation of the score vector l via a kernel density estimator involves a number of intensive calculations, especially when we optimize over h. Therefore discretization or WARPing ideas should be used (Turlach, 1992). For our simulated example Figure 4 shows the result of this method. We calculated $\hat{\delta}$ and used the *Nadaraya-Watson* regression estimator to estimate $\hat{g}$. Note that the horizontal scale on this figure is different since (3.1) suggest that δ has different scale than β. In fact for ADE the scale of δ changes with g but it does not matter for the statistical interpretation of the link g that we are interested in.

The estimation of δ and its asymptotic covariance matrix $\hat{\Sigma}_\delta$ for example 1 was done with Program 1 in Section 6. Note that for this example we have $\delta = \binom{0.135}{0.135}$. The binning parameter d was chosen in such a way that maximal 20 bins were used in each coordinate, i.e., $d \approx \binom{0.33}{0.256}$. The estimate for the average derivative and the asymptotic covariance matrix was calculated using the three adjacent bins which equals a bandwidth $h \approx \binom{0.99}{0.78}$. As result we have

$$\hat{\delta} = \begin{pmatrix} 0.124 \\ 0.118 \end{pmatrix}, \qquad \hat{\Sigma}_\delta = \begin{pmatrix} 0.188 & 0.036 \\ 0.036 & 0.206 \end{pmatrix}.$$

These results allow us to test some hypothesis formally using a Wald statistic (see Stoker, 1992, pp. 53–54). In particular, to test the restriction $R\delta = r_0$, the Wald statistic

$$W = n(R\hat{\delta} - r_0)^T (R\hat{\Sigma}_\delta R^T)^{-1} (R\hat{\delta} - r_0)$$

is compared to a $\chi^2(\text{rank } R)$ critical value. Table 3.1 gives some examples for this technique.

Restriction	Value W	d.f.	$P[\chi^2(\text{d.f.}) > W]$
$\delta^1 = \delta^2 = 0$	25.25	2	0
$\delta^1 = \delta^2 = 0.135$	0.365	2	0.83
$\delta^1 = \delta^2$	0.027	1	0.869

Table 3.1: Wald Statistics for some restrictions on δ.

Turlach (1992) shows that the results of such tests depend on the chosen bandwidth h, i.e., in practice it remains the problem of selecting h. The theoretical optimal bandwidth is calculated in Härdle, Hart, Marron, and Tsybakov (1992). They found that for an optimal estimation of δ the bandwidth h should be of the rate $n^{-\alpha}$ (α depending on the dimension d and the "smoothness" of f and g) where this rate is typically different from the optimal rate for estimating f or g for example. Thus one has to work with two different bandwidths for estimating δ and g.

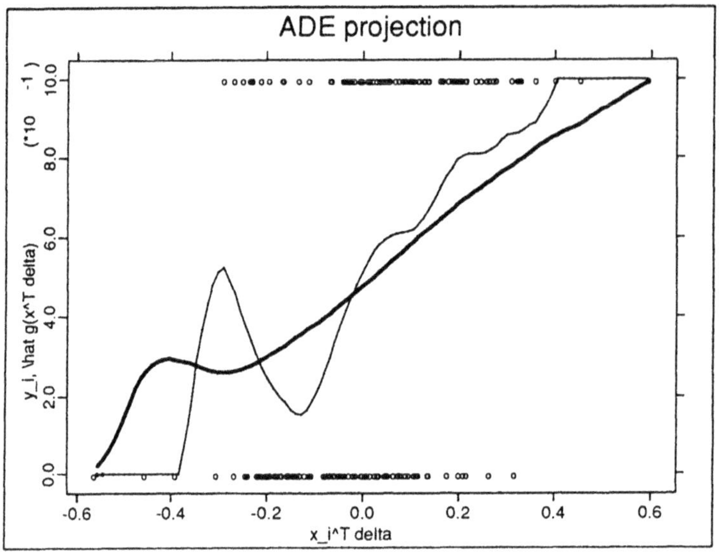

Figure 4: For the simulated data set of example 1 $x_i^T\hat{\delta}$ vs. y_i and two estimates of $\hat{g}(x_i^T\hat{\delta})$ are shown. The thick line shows the Nadaraya-Watson regression estimator for $\hat{g}$ with a bandwidth of $h = 0.3$, for the thin line $h = 0.1$ was chosen.

This unappealing feature is avoided by an approach due to Ichimura (1993). Let ε denote the error term inherent to the response variable. Observe that (β_0 denotes the true parameter):

(1) The variation in Y results from both the variation in $X^T\beta_0$ and the variation in ε.

(2) On the contour line $X^T\beta_0 = c$, where c is a given constant, the variability in Y results only from the variation in ε.

(3) Observation (2) does not necessarily hold on a contour line defined by $X^T\beta = c$ for $\beta \neq \beta_0$. Along this contour line, the value of $X^T\beta_0$ changes and therefore the variability in Y again results from the variation in both $X^T\beta_0$ and ε.

To identify β_0 Ichimura (1993) thus proposes to estimate

$$S(\beta) = E[\{Y - g(X^T\beta)\}^2] \tag{3.3}$$

since β_0 is the minimizer of (3.3). Using

$$\hat{S}(\beta, h) = n^{-1}\sum_{i=1}^{n}[y_i - \hat{g}_{-i,h}(x_i^T\beta)]^2,$$

where $\hat{g}_{-i,h}$ denotes a leave-one-out kernel smoother of Y on $X^T\beta$, as estimator for $S(\beta)$ and minimizing $\hat{S}(\beta, h)$ with respect to β and h Härdle, Hall and Ichimura (1992) showed that this yields a root-n consistent estimator of β_0 and an asymptotically optimal estimator of h_0, the bandwidth which should be used to calculate the kernel estimate of g.

A way of testing a GLM against this specific single index alternative has been given by Horowitz and Härdle (1992). They constructed a conditional moment test based on ideas of Bierens (1990) and Newey (1985). Another approach for such a test via Bootstrapping ideas was investigated by Rodríguez-Campos and Cao-Abad (1993) and Proença (1992).

4. Generalized Additive Models

For the Generalized Additive Model we have to estimate α and functions g_j in the model

$$P[Y=1|X=x] = G\left(\alpha + \sum_{j=1}^{d} g_j(x_j)\right).$$

This estimation is a highly iterative procedure. Estimation of α and $g_1, \ldots, g_d$ in the above model is accomplished by an algorithm for fitting a weighted additive model (Hastie and Tibshirani, 1990). This iterative fitting of a weighted additive model is known as *local scoring* since it generalizes the Fisher scoring procedure. Each estimation of a weighted additive model is done in an iterative process known as *backfitting*. In the backfitting step non-parametric estimates for $g_1, \ldots, g_d$ are calculated. The explicit algorithm of finding the nonparametric components is given by (see Hastie and Tibshirani 1987):

Local Scoring Algorithm

Initialization $\hat{g}_j^{(0)} \equiv 0$ for $j = 1, \ldots, d$, $\hat{\alpha}^{(0)} = \text{logit}(\bar{y})$.

Loop over outer iteration counter m

$\hat{\eta}^{(m)}(x_i) = \hat{\alpha}^{(m)} + \sum_{j=1}^{d} \hat{g}_j^{(m)}(x_{ji})$

$\hat{p}_i = \text{logit}^{-1}(\hat{\eta}^{(m)}(x_i))$

$z_i = \hat{\eta}^{(m)}(x_i) + (y_i - \hat{p}_i)/[\hat{p}_i(1-\hat{p}_i)]$

$w_i = \hat{p}_i(1-\hat{p}_i), \qquad i = 1, \ldots, n.$

Obtain $\hat{\alpha}^{(m+1)}, \hat{g}_j^{(m+1)}, j = 1, \ldots, d$ by applying the backfitting algorithm to z_i with explanatory variables x_i and observation weights w_i.

until the deviance $D(y, \hat{p}) = -2\sum_i [y_i \log(\hat{p}_i) + (1-y_i)\log(1-\hat{p}_i)]$ converges.

Backfitting Algorithm

Initialization $\hat{g}_j^{(0)} \equiv 0$ for $j = 1, \ldots, d$, $\hat{\alpha}^{(0)} = \bar{y}$.

Repeat for $j = 1, \ldots, d$ repeat such cycles:

$$r_i = y_i - \hat{\alpha} - \sum_{\substack{k=1\\k\neq j}}^{d} \hat{g}_k(x_{ki}) \quad i = 1, \ldots, n$$

$$\hat{g}_j(x_{ji}) = S(r|w, x_{ji}) \quad i = 1, \ldots, n$$

Until $RSS = \sum_{i=1}^{n} \left(y_i - \hat{\alpha} - \sum_{j=1}^{d} \hat{g}_j(x_{ji}) \right)^2$ converges.

Here $S(r|w, x_{ji})$ denotes the value of the function obtained by smoothing the scatterplot (x_j, r) with weights w at the point x_{ji}.

Since non-parametric estimation methods are used in the backfitting step some typical questions arise. We have again the question of how to choose the smoothing parameter in this non-parametric fit regardless whether splines, kernel estimators or others are used, see Buja, Hastie and Tibshirani (1989). Another question is how to incorporate the weights in the non-parametric smoothing step (see Hastie and Tibshirani 1990, pp. 72–74). Especially in binary models, as we discuss them here, these weights can cause numeric problems. If the estimated probability $\hat{p}_i = P[Y_i = 1|X = x_i]$ is very close to 0 or 1 the weight w_i for this observation in the backfitting step will be very small. Thus the adjusted dependent variable z_i may be very big resulting in a large partial residual within the backfitting algorithm. This can result in a bad fit which leads in the next step of the local scoring to the same problem.

Program 3 in Section 6 demonstrates how the Generalized Additive Model can be estimated in XploRe (1992). The result of this fitting is visualized in Figure 5. The backfitting algorithm provides estimates of the function g_j in the multiple additive regression model $E[Y|X = x] = \alpha + \sum_j g_j(x_j)$ with $E[g_j(X_j)] = 0$ for $j = 1, \ldots, d$. It is easily seen that in example 2 given by (2.4) we have $E[g_j(X_j)] = 0$, $j = 1, 2$. Thus for our example we would expect that α is estimated as 0. In fact the result is $\hat{\alpha} = 0.25$.

GAMs can be further generalized by relaxing the assumptions on the link function G. A general model would be in this case

$$\Psi(Y) = \sum_{i=1}^{d} g_i(X_i) + \varepsilon \tag{4.1}$$

where $\Psi, g_1, \ldots, g_d$ are arbitrary univariate functions and ε is independent from $X = (X_1, \ldots, X_d)^T$. For estimating model (4.1) Breiman and Friedman (1985) proposed the method of Alternating Conditional Expectations (ACE). Here $\Psi, g_1, \ldots, g_p$ are estimated by the minimizers of the fraction of variance not explained by a regression of $\Psi(Y)$ on $\sum_{i=1}^{d} g_i(X_i)$, i.e. the minimizers of

$$\frac{E\left[\{\Psi(Y) - \sum_{i=1}^{d} g_i(X_i)\}^2\right]}{E\left[\Psi(Y)^2\right]}.$$

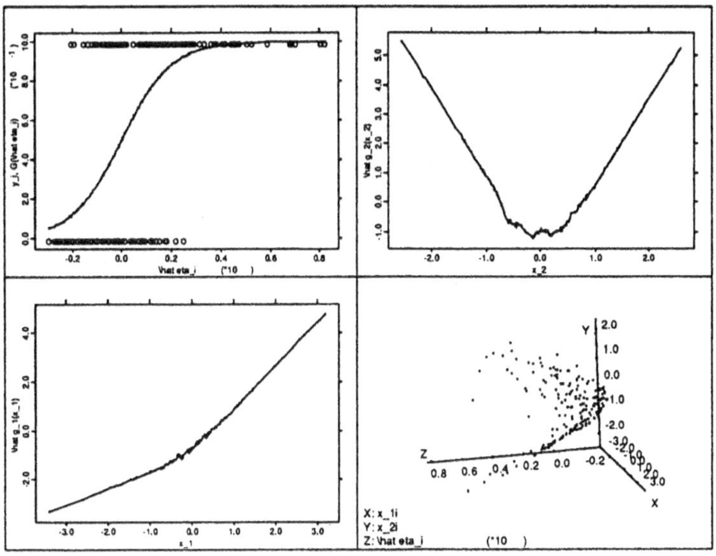

Figure 5: A four picture display with the results of the fitting procedure for the Generalized Additive Model. Legend is the same as for Figure 3 where η_i is replaced by $\hat{\eta}_i$.

Since

$$g_j(X_j) = E\left[\Psi(Y) - \sum_{i \neq j} g_i(X_i) \middle| X_j\right] \quad \text{and} \quad \Psi(Y) = E\left[\sum_{i=1}^{d} g_i(X_i) \middle| Y\right]$$

this can be done by iteratively estimating each of the above conditional expectation, using at each step the current estimates of the functions on the right hand side, until convergence is reached, i.e., estimating alternatively conditional expectations.

These estimates are chosen to optimize a correlation criterion. There are a number of properties of the ACE procedure that are somewhat misleading if one views ACE as a regression tool (see comments on Breiman and Friedman, 1985 and Hastie and Tibshirani, 1990, Chapter 7.2.6). To overcome these anomalies Tibshirani (1988) proposed a modification called AVAS (Additivity and Variance Stabilization). It differs from ACE by using an *asymptotic variance stabilizing transformation* instead of the estimate $\Psi(Y) = E\left[\sum_{i=1}^{d} g_i(X_i) \middle| Y\right]$. To our knowledge there is not much theoretical support for this technique until know and it is thus sill an open field of research. Especially global convergence of AVAS has not yet been established. There is also no consent which methods of inference should be applied for ACE and AVAS.

5. Sliced Inverse Regression

Sliced Inverse Regression (Li, 1991a) attempts to estimate the effective dimension-reduction (e.d.r.) directions $\beta_1, \ldots, \beta_p$ in the model

$$Y = g(X^T\beta_1, \ldots, X^T\beta_p, \varepsilon) \tag{5.1}$$

where the β's are unknown vectors, ε is independent of X and g is an arbitrary unknown function on $I\!R^{p+1}$. In our running example (5.1) reads as

$$P[Y = 1|X = x] = g(x^T\beta_1, \ldots, x^T\beta_p) \tag{5.2}$$

with g an arbitrary function on $I\!R^p$.

The idea to estimate the β's is to use inverse regression, i.e., to estimate $E[X|Y]$. Before we present the justification for this approach we have to introduce some further notation. Let Σ_X denote the covariance matrix of X and $Z = \Sigma_X^{-1/2}(X - E[X])$ the standardized version of X. With $\eta_i = \Sigma_X^{1/2}\beta_i$, $i = 1, \ldots, p$, Li (1991b) calls any vector in the linear space generated by the η's a standardized e.d.r. direction.

Observe now that the centered inverse regression curve $E[X|Y] - E[X]$, in general, describes a curve in $I\!R^d$. Li (1991a) showed that if for any $b \in I\!R^d$ we have that $E[b^T X|X^T\beta_1, \ldots, X^T\beta_p]$ is linear in $X^T\beta_1, \ldots, X^T\beta_p$ and (5.1) holds, the centered inverse regression curve is contained in the linear subspace spanned by $\Sigma_X\beta_i$, $i = 1, \ldots, p$. As a corrollary we have that the standardized inverse regression curve $E[Z|Y]$ is contained in the linear space generated by the standardized e.d.r. directions $\eta_1, \ldots, \eta_p$. Thus the covariance matrix $Cov[E[Z|Y]]$ is degenerate in any direction orthogonal to the η's. Therefore the eigenvectors η_i, $i = 1, \ldots, p$, associated with the largest p eigenvalues of $Cov[E[Z|Y]]$ are the standardized e.d.r. directions. So we have the following algorithm to estimate the e.d.r. directions

The Sliced Inverse Regression algorithm

I. Divide the range of Y into H slices

II. Within each slice compute the sample mean of X, denoted by $\bar{x}_h$, $h = 1, \ldots, H$

III. Compute the sample covariance matrix for X, $\hat{\Sigma}_X = \frac{1}{n-1}\sum_{i=1}^n (x_i - \bar{x})(x_i - \bar{x})^T$ and the weighted covariance matrix for the slice means, $\hat{\Sigma}_\eta = \sum_{i=1}^H \hat{p}_h(\bar{x}_h - \bar{x})(\bar{x}_h - \bar{x})^T$ where $\hat{p}_h$ is the proportion of cases that fall into the slice h, and $\bar{x}$ is the sample average of X.

IV. Conduct an eigenvalue decomposition of $\hat{\Sigma}_\eta$ with respect to $\hat{\Sigma}_X$. Order the eigenvectors $\beta_1, \ldots, \beta_d$ according to the descending order of the corresponding eigenvalues, $\hat{\lambda}_1 \geq \ldots \geq \hat{\lambda}_p$

Steps I and II produce a crude estimate of the inverse regression curve. Li (1991b) advocates the method of slicing due to its simplicity although more sophisticated nonparametric regression methods could be used. We want to study the performance of this algorithm on example 1 and example 3 introduced in Section 2. For example 1 we changed the explanatory variable X to have a $\mathcal{N}_5(0, I_5)$ distribution keeping the relationship between the first two components of X and Y as described in Section 2. Example 2 is not suitable for this method since it has two e.d.r. direction (the same as example 3). For estimating p e.d.f. directions the number H of slices has to be greater than p (see discussion of Li, 1991a). But in a binary response model one has in fact always $H = 2$. To our knowledge it is an open question whether this theory can be extended to binary (discrete) response models. The program for these calculations is listed in Section 6 and the results are given below for each example.

Example 1

In this example we have only one e.d.r. direction which is $\beta_1 = (1,1,0,0,0)^T$. Li (199a) gives (under additional assumptions) a result which allows to test for the significance of an e.d.r. direction β_i by the mean of the eigenvalues smaller than the eigenvalue associated with β_i. The eigenvalues estimated for this example are 0.152, 0, 0, 0, and 0. Thus we would interfere that there is only one e.d.r. direction. The estimate for this direction is

$$\hat{\beta}_1 = (0.7331,\ 0.6726,\ -0.0752,\ -0.0152,\ 0.0654)^T.$$

Note that as with the SIMs we can only estimate the e.d.r. direction, here $\hat{\beta}_1$ is standardized to have Euclidean norm 1. In this example the e.d.r. direction β_1 is recognized. If we change $\hat{\beta}_1$ to the same scale as δ, the Average Derivative Estimate, and do a regression of Y against $X^T\hat{\beta}_1$ we get a picture similar to Figure 4.

Example 3

In this example we have two e.d.r. directions, $\beta_1 = (1,0,0,0,0)^T$ and $\beta_2 = (0,1,0,0,0)^T$. However, the eigenvalues which are estimated in this examples are 0.4037, 0.0392, 0.0199, 0.0122, and 0.0076. Thus we would interfere again the existence of only one e.d.r. direction!. Even if we ask for estimates of two directions the result is

$$\hat{\beta}_1 = (0.9680,\ 0.1574,\ -0.0563,\ -0.1158,\ -0.1474)^T$$

and

$$\hat{\beta}_2 = (0.1810,\ 0.0903,\ 0.3044,\ 0.1951,\ 0.9101)^T.$$

Thus the first e.d.f. direction is fairly well identified whereas the second one is not at all identified. The problem is that in this example $E[X_2|Y] = 0$. Therefore the inverse regression curve is degenerated in the second e.d.r. direction and SIR fails to find it. A solution to this problem is to estimate higher orders too. If for example the conditional variance $Var[X_2|Y]$ varies with Y we could hope to identify this e.d.r. direction by exploring the variability of the conditional variance $Var[b^T X|Y]$. This approach is called SIR II by Li (1991b) and is a very promising development of research.

6. The implementation in XploRe

The above calculations have been performed in the language XploRe (1992). In this section we give some programs that are useful in solving the iterative procedure for Generalized Additive Models for example or for ADE. The Single Index Model for example 1 has been estimated using the ADE technique with the following program.

```
library(smoother)                           ;load the necessary libraries
library(addmod)
randomize(0)
x = normal(200 2)                           ;generate the explanatory variable
rho = 0.6
beta = #(1 1)
eta = x*beta                                ;eta, notation as in (2.2)
g = 1./(1+exp(-eta)) - rho * eta.*pdfn(eta);calculate g(eta)
u = uniform (200)
y = u.<g                                    ;generate the response variable
d = (max(x)-min(x))/20                      ;choosing a binning parameter
(xb yb) = bindata(x d 0 y)                  ;binning the data
(del dvar) = adeind(xb yb d 3)
    ;estimate the average derivative and the asymptotic covariance matrix
est = (x*del)~y                             ;calculate the projection
gh1 = regest(est 0.1)                       ;find estimates for g
gh2 = regest(est 0.3)
show(est gh1 gh2 s2d)                       ;show results (Picture 4)
```

Program 1: This program generates and estimates example 1

The commands of XploRe (1992) are similar to GAUSS but more fine tuned for smoothing and nonparametric methods in high dimensions. The Generalized Additive Model (GAM) of example 2 was created using the following code:

```
randomize(0)
x = normal(200 2)
g1 = x[,1]
g2 = x[,2].*x[,2]-1
eta = g1+g2
px = 1./(1+exp(-px))
u = uniform(200)
y = u.<px
createdisplay(pic3, 2 2, s2d s2d s2d d3d)
show(eta~y eta~px s2d1, x[,1]~g1 s2d2, x[,2]~g2 s2d3, x~eta d3d1)
```

Program 2: This program generates Picture 3

The estimation of the GAM was done by

```
proc(fx alpha devs)=lscore(x y)
  dim = cols(x)
  gx = matrix(rows(x) dim 0)            ;initialize g_j
  xs = 1                                ;used to store information
                                        ;to sort the covariates
  ybar = mean(y)
  alpha = ln(ybar/(1-ybar))             ;initialize alpha
  devs = 0
  loop = 1
  do
    eta = alpha + sumr(gx)
    p = 1./(1+exp(-eta))
    w = p.*(1-p)                        ;calculate the weights
    z = eta + (y-p)./w                  ;calculate the adjusted
                                        ;dependent variable
    (gx alpha xs)=backfit(x z xs w 0.4) ;the backfitting step
    dev = -2*sum(y.*ln(p)+(1-y).*ln(1-p));calculate the deviance
    devs = defs|dev
    chg = abs(devs[loop,1]-dev)/dev
    loop = loop+1
  until( (chg < 0.001) || (loop == 6) )
  devs = devs[2:loop,1]
endp
```

Program 3: This program implements the Local Scoring Algorithm

The following program calculated the SIR estimates for the two models used above and modified as described in Section 5.

```
library(xplore)                          ;load the necessary libraries
library(addmod)
randomize(0)
x = normal(200 5)                        ;generate the explanatory variable
```

```
rho = 0.6
beta = #(1 1 0 0 0)
eta = x*beta                                    ;eta, notation as in (2.2)
g = 1./(1+exp(-eta)) - rho * eta.*pdfn(eta);calculate g(eta)
y = (uniform(200).<g)                           ;generate the response variable
b_sim = sir1(x y 1 3)
randomize(0)
x = normal(200 5)                               ;generate the explanatory variable
g1 = x[,1]
g2 = x[,2].*x[,2]-1
eps = 0.6*normal(200)
y = g1+g2+eps
b_gam = sir1(x y 2 10)
```

Program 4: This program generates the two modified models and applies SIR

REFERENCES

Bierens, H.J. (1990), "A consistent conditional moment test of functional form," *Econometrica*, **58**, 1443–1458.

Breiman, L. and Friedman, J.H. (1985), "Estimating optimal transformations for multiple regression and correlation (with discussion)," *Journal of the American Statistical Association*, **80**, 580–619.

Buja, A., Hastie, T.J. and Tibshirani, R.J. (1989), "Linear smoothers and additive models (with discussion)," *The Annals of Statistics*, **17**, 453–555.

Eubank, R.L. (1988), *Smoothing Splines and Nonparametric Regression*, Marcel Dekker, New York and Basel.

Friedman, J.H. and Stuetzle, W. (1981), "Projection Pursuit Regression," *Journal of the American Statistical Association*, **76**, 817–823.

Härdle, W. (1990), *Applied Non-parametric Regression*, Econometric Society Monograps No. 19, Cambridge University Press.

Härdle, W., Hall, P. and Ichimura, H. (1992), "Optimal Smoothing in Single Index Models," *The Annals of Statistics*, to appear.

Härdle, W., Hart J., Marron J.S., and Tsybakov, A.B. (1992), "Bandwidth Choice for Average Derivative Estimation," *Journal of the American Statistical Association*, **87**, 218–226.

Härdle, W. and Stoker, T.M. (1989), "Investigating Smooth Multiple Regression by the Method of Average Derivatives," *Journal of the American Statistical Association*, **84**, 986–995.

Hall, P. (1989), "On Projection Pursuit Regression," *The Annals of Statistics*, **17**, 573–588

Hastie, T.J. and Tibshirani, R.J. (1987), "Non-parametric Logistic and Proportional Odds Regression," *Applied Statistics*, **36**, 260–276.

Hastie, T.J. and Tibshirani, R.J. (1990), *Generalized Additive Models*, Chapman and Hall, London.

Horowitz, J. and Härdle, W. (1992), "Testing a parametric model against a semiparametric alternative," *CentER Discussion Paper.*

Huber, P.J. (1985), "Projection Pursuit," *The Annals of Statistics*, **13**, 435–475.

Ichimura, H. (1993), "Semiparametric Least Squares (SLS) and Weighted SLS Estimation of Single-Index Models," *Journal of Econometrics*, special issue on "Nonparametric Approaches to Discrete Choice Models", ed. W. Härdle and C.F. Manski.

Li, K.C. (1991a) "Sliced Inverse Regression for Dimension Reduction (with discussion)," *Journal of the American Statistical Association*, **86**, 316–342.

Li, K.C. (1991b), Notes from the course MATH277–DATA ANALYSIS–Winter 1991, University of California, Los Angeles.

Müller, H.G. (1988), *Nonparametric Regression Analysis of Longitudinal Data*, Lecture Notes in Statistics 46, Springer, New York.

Newey, W.K. (1985), "Maximum likelihood specification testing and conditional moment test," *Econometrica*, **53**, 1047–1070.

McCullagh, P. and Nelder, J.A. (1989), *Generalized Linear Models, 2nd Edition*, Chapman and Hall, London.

Proença, I.M. (1992), *On the performance of a test against a semiparametric alternative*, manuscript in preparation.

Rodríguez-Campos, M.C. and Cao-Abad, R. (1993), "Nonparametric Bootstrap Confidence Intervals for Discrete Regression Functions," *Journal of Econometrics*, special issue on "Nonparametric Approaches to Discrete Choice Models", ed. W. Härdle and C.F. Manski.

Silverman, B.W. (1986), *Density Estimation for Statistical and Data Analysis*, Chapman and Hall, London.

Stoker, T.M. (1991), "Equivalence of Direct, Indirect and Slope Estimators of Average Derivatives," in *Nonparametric and Semiparametric Methods in Econometrics and Statistics*, Barnett, W.A., J.L. Powell and G.Tauchen, eds., Cambridge University Press.

Stoker, T.M. (1992), *Lectures on Semiparametrics Econometrics*, CORE Lecture Series, Louvain-la-Neuve.

Stoker, T.M. and Villas-Boas, J.M. (1992), "Monte Carlo Simulation of Average Derivative Estimators," *Discussion Paper*, Sloan School of Management, MIT.

Tibshirani, R.J. (1988), "Estimating optimal transformations for regression via additivity and variance stabilization," *Journal of the American Statistical Association*, **83**, 394–405.

Turlach, B. (1992), "On Discretization Methods for Average Derivative Estimation," *CORE Discussion Paper N° 9232.*

Wahba, G. (1990), *Spline Functions for Observational Data*, CBMS-NSF Regional Conference series, SIAM, Philadelphia.

XploRe (1992), XploRe 3.0 — a computing environment for e**X**ploratory **Re**gression and data analysis. Available from XploRe Systems, C.O.R.E., Université Catholique de Louvain, Belgium.

Maximum Likelihood Estimators in Non Linear Autoregressive Processes

Henkouche Meriem
Institut d'Informatique
USTO BP 1505 El M'naouar, ORAN, Algerie

Summary

This paper is concerned with some asymptotic properties of the maximum likelihood estimator of a multivariate parameter for a stable non linear autogressive process. Under suitable assumptions, the consistency, the asymptotic normality and the rate of convergence in distribution ($O(n^{-\frac{1}{2}})$) are settled. This rate is the same as in idd case.

Notations

Let $(X_n)_N$ be a non-linear autoregressive process defined by the following equations.

$$\begin{aligned} X_0 &= x_0, \dots, X_{-d+1} = x_{-d+1} \\ X_n &= f(X_{n-1}, X_{n-2}, \dots, X_{n-d}, \theta) + \epsilon_n \end{aligned} \tag{1}$$

Where $x_0, \dots, x_{-d+1}$ are real numbers, the parameter θ lies in the compact parametric set Θ included in R^d, $(\epsilon_n)_N$ is a sequence of unobserved real valued random variables on probability space (Ω, a, p). The random $(X_n)_N$ are observed.

Let us denote the d-dimensional random vector

$$\begin{aligned} Y_n &= {}^t(X_n, \dots, X_{n-d+1}) \\ Y_0 &= y_0 = (x_0, \dots, x_{-d+1}) \\ e &= {}^t(1, 0, \dots, 0) \text{ element of } R^d. \end{aligned}$$

Therefore

$$\begin{aligned} Y_n &= F(Y_{n-1}, \theta) + \epsilon_n e \\ Y_0 &= y_0 \end{aligned}$$

We denote by $P_{y,\theta}$ the distribution on R^N of the chain $(Y_n)_N$ with $Y_0 = y_0$.

The Results

THEOREM 1: Under assumptions the Markov chain $(Y_n)_{n\in N}$ is aperiodic, Harris recurrent and ergodic with an invariant measure of probability ν_θ equivalent to the Lebesgue measure $l^{\otimes d}$ of R^d. Moreover this invariant measure ν_θ has a finite moment of order δ.

THEOREM 2: Under certain assumptions the sequence of maximum likelihood estimators (MLE) $(\hat{\theta}_n)_N$:

(i) $(\hat{\theta}_n)_N$ is consistent
(ii) $\mathcal{L}_{y,\theta}\left(\sqrt{n}\|\hat{\theta}_n - \theta\|\right) \longrightarrow N(0, I_\theta^{-1})$
(iii) Large deviation inequality.

For all real positive numbers γ and any compact set in R^d, there exist two positive real constants A_1, A_2 such that

$$\sup_{\Theta \times K} P_{\theta,y}(\|\hat{\theta}_n - \theta\| > \gamma) \leq A_1 exp - A_2 \gamma^2 n$$

(iv) There exists a positive real number B such that
$\sup_{\Theta \times K} P_{\theta,y} \left(\sqrt{n} I_\theta^{+\frac{1}{2}} \|\hat{\theta}_n - \theta\| > B\sqrt{\log n}\right) = O\left(\frac{1}{\sqrt{n}}\right)$

(v) for any compact set K in R^d there exists a positive constant $C(K)$ such that for every convex set E in R^d
$\sup P_{\theta,y} \left(I_\theta^{\frac{1}{2}}(\hat{\theta}_n - \theta) \in E - \Phi(E)\right) \leq (C(K)/\sqrt{n})$

where Φ is the standard normal distribution on $R^{d'} N(0, I_{d'})$ and $I_{d'}$ is the identity operator on $R^{d'}$.

References

R.N. Bhattachrya and Ranga Rao (1976), *Normal approximation and Asymptotic expansion.* J. Wiley, New York.

P. Doukhan, M. Ghindès (1), (1980), *Etude du processus* $X_n = f(X_n - 1) + \epsilon_n$. Thèse de 3ème cycle. Université Paris Sud, Départ de Mathématiques, Orsay, France. (2) (1980), *Etude du processus* $X_n + 1 = f(X_n)\epsilon_n$. CRAS I T 290 serie A p 921-923.

I.A. Ibragimov et Khasminsky, *Asymptotic behaviour of statistical estimators in the smooth case (1981). Statistical estimation. Asymptotic Theory.* Springer-Verlag, New York.

M. Henkouche. *Thèse de doctorat.* Université Paul Sabatier. Laboratoire de statistique et probabilités. Toulouse, France.

T. Kato (1966), *Perturbation theory for linear operators.* Springer-Verlag, Berlin, Heidelberg.

X. Milhaud et A. Raugi (1989), *Etude de l'estimateur du maximum de vraisemblance dans le cas d'un processus autoregressif linéaire.* Annales de l'institut Poincarré (1989) $N^0 = 4$.

J. Pfanzagl (1971), *The Berry Essen Bound for minimum contrast estimate.* Metroka 17 p 82-90 2. On the normal approximation for estimates of vector parameters. Z. Warhr. Verw 25 p 171-198.

Bayes Sequential Estimation Procedures

Ryszard Magiera
Institute of Mathematics, Technical University of Wrocław
50–370 Wrocław, Poland

The Bayesian sequential estimation problem is considered for a family of continuous time stochastic processes whose likelihood functions have the exponential form

$\exp[\vartheta Z(t) + \Phi(\vartheta)S(t)]$,

where $Z(t)$ and $S(t)$ are real valued processes under observation, ϑ is a parameter with values in an open interval $\Theta \subset R$, and $\Phi(\vartheta)$ is a twice continuously differentiable real valued function with $-\Phi''(\vartheta) > 0$ for all $\vartheta \in \Theta$. It is assumed that $Z(0) = 0, S(0) = 0$ and $S(t)$, which may be nonrandom as well, is strictly increasing and continuous as a function of t and $S(t) \to \infty$ as $t \to \infty$.

Denote $\mu = -\Phi'(\vartheta)$ (the other parameterization of the model) and $V(\mu) = -\Phi''(\vartheta)$. For the family of processes considered the following relations $E_\mu Z(t) = \mu E_\mu S(t)$, $E_\mu[Z(t) - \mu S(t)]^2 = V(\mu)E_\mu S(t)$ hold. It is assumed that the function $V(\mu)$ has the quadratic form $V(\mu) = \eta_2\mu^2 + \eta_1\mu + \eta_0$, where η_2, η_1, η_0 are some constants. The problem is to estimate the parameter μ. An exponential family of conjugate prior distributions over μ is introduced. In addition to a quadratic error loss for the inaccuracy of the Bayes estimator of μ, it is assumed that the total loss involves a polynomial sampling cost.

METHODS

Consider the process $(r_t, \alpha_t), t \geq 0$, with $r_t = r + Z(t), \alpha_t = \alpha + S(t)$, where r, α are parameters of the family of priors. Sequential estimation procedures of the form (τ, d) are considered, where τ is a stopping time with respect to $\mathcal{F}_t = \sigma\{Z(s), S(s), s \leq t\}, t \geq 0$, and $d = d(r_\tau, \alpha_\tau)$ is an $\mathcal{F}_\tau$-measurable function. The weighted quadratic error loss $V^{-1}(\mu)(d-\mu)^2$ is used for the inaccuracy of the estimator d in estimating μ. The Bayes estimator of μ and the posterior expected loss, given $\mathcal{F}_\tau$, are r_τ/α_τ and $1/\alpha_\tau$, respectively. Thus, the Bayes estimation problem can be reduced to the following optimal stopping problem. The total loss (cost) of observing the process up to the moment τ is defined to be

$\mathcal{L}(r_\tau, \alpha_\tau) = 1/\alpha_\tau + c_1\alpha_\tau + w(r_\tau)$, where $w(r) = \sum_{k=1}^m c_{k+1}r^k$

and $c_1, c_2, \ldots, c_{m+1}$ are nonnegative constants. If the stopping time τ^* minimizes the expectation of the total loss $\mathcal{L}(r_\tau, \alpha_\tau)$ over all stopping times τ, then τ^* is called the Bayes sequential procedure or the *optimal stopping time*.

First, the solution is given in the case $S(t) \equiv t$, i.e., when the exponential family of processes reduces to processes with stationary independent increments. As the Bayes sequential procedures, the infinitesimal look ahead procedures are considered which are derived from the infinitesimal operator at $\mathcal{L}(r, \alpha)$ for the process $(r_t, \alpha_t), t \geq 0$. To determine the form of this operator, the properties related to higher order moments of both the conjugate priors and the process have been investigated.

The procedures can be shown to be optimal via Dynkin's identity if the infinitesimal operator changes sign at most once, a method analogous to that one which has been used by Ross (1971), Starr, Wardrop and Woodroofe (1976), and Shapiro and Wardrop (1980).

Next, the solution in the general model is presented by applying a random time transformation.

RESULTS

Theorem 1. *Let $c_1 > 0$ and $w(r) \equiv 0$. Then the stopping time*

$$\tau_\alpha^* = \inf\{t \geq 0 : S(t) \geq c_1^{-1/2} - \alpha\},$$

$\alpha > \eta_2$, is optimal.

In the case of the cost function with $m \geq 1$ the process $Z(t)$ is assumed to have nondecreasing sample functions.

Theorem 2. *Assume that $m = 1$. Let $c_1 \geq 0$ and $c_2 > 0$. Then the stopping time*

$$\tau_{r,\alpha}^* = \inf\left\{t \geq 0 : r + Z(t) + \eta_1 \geq \frac{\alpha + S(t) - 2\eta_2}{c_2}\left[\frac{1}{(\alpha + S(t))^2} - c_1\right]\right\}$$

with $r > 0$ and $\alpha > 4\eta_2$ is optimal.

In the case when $m \geq 2$ the Bayes sequential procedures are not obtainable explicitly for the whole family of processes under consideration. A general solution to the problem is intricate and requires a computer. If the exponential family of processes has the property $V(\mu) = \mu$, then the Bayes sequential procedures are obtainable explicitly for every $m = 1, 2, \ldots$

Theorem 3. *Suppose that the condition $V(\mu) = \mu$ holds. Let $c_1 \geq 0, \ldots, c_m \geq 0$ and $c_{m+1} > 0$. Then the stopping time*

$$\tau_{r,\alpha}^* = \inf\left\{t \geq 0 : [r + Z(t) + 1]\sum_{k=1}^{m} c_{k+1}[(r + Z(t) + 1)^k - (r + Z(t))^k] \geq \right.$$
$$\left. \geq \frac{1}{\alpha + S(t)} - c_1[\alpha + S(t)]\right\},$$

$r > 0, \alpha > 0$, is optimal.

Theorem 3 gives an explicit form of the Bayes sequential procedures for the polynomial cost function of any degree in $Z(t)$, and consequently for any function of the state component $Z(t)$ of the process, which can be approximated by a polynomial of respective degree with nonnegative coefficients.

SPECIAL MODELS

Let $X(t), t \geq 0$, be a counting process with intensity of the form

$\lambda(t) = \mu H(t), \mu > 0, t > 0,$

where $H(t)$ is a positive, predictable stochastic process. Under certain conditions the likelihood function is given by

$$\exp\left[\vartheta(X(t) - x_0) + \Phi(\vartheta)\int_0^t H(s)ds\right],$$

where $X(0) = x_0$, $\vartheta = \log\mu$ and $\Phi(\vartheta) = -\exp\vartheta$. In this case $V(\mu) = \mu$.

Examples of the model considered are the Poisson process where $H(t) \equiv 1$, the Weibull process where $H(t) = bt^{b-1}$ (b being a known value), the pure birth process where $H(t) = X(t-)$, and the logistic birth process where $H(t) = X(t-)[M - X(t-)]^+$ with M being a known constant.

According to Theorem 3, the Bayes sequential estimation procedure is $(\tau^*_{r,\alpha}, d(\tau^*_{r,\alpha}))$, where $\tau^*_{r,\alpha}$ is defined in the theorem for $Z(t) = X(t) - x_0$ and $S(t) = \int_0^t H(s)ds$, and

$$d(\tau^*_{r,\alpha}) = \frac{r + X(\tau^*_{r,\alpha}) - x_0}{\alpha + S(\tau^*_{r,\alpha})}.$$

In a special case, for the Poisson process and for $m = 1$, the Bayes sequential procedures have been obtained by Novic (1980), and Shapiro and Wardrop (1980).

References

Novic B (1980) Bayes sequential estimation of a Poisson rate: A discrete time approach. *Ann Statist* 8: 840-844.

Shapiro CP, Wardrop RL (1980) Dynkin's identity applied to Bayes sequential estimation of a Poisson process rate. *Ann Statist* 8: 171-182.

Starr N, Wardrop R, Woodroofe M (1976) Estimating a mean from delayed observations. *Z Wahrscheinlichkeitstheorie und Verw Gebiete* 35: 103-113.

Ross SM (1971) Infinitesimal look-ahead stopping rules. *Ann Math Statist* 42: 297-303.

Time-Series Forecasting by Pattern Imitation—further Development

Barbara Motnikar, Drago Čepar, Peter Žunko, Marijan Ribarič
'Jožef Stefan' Institute
Jamova 39, 61111 Ljubljana, Slovenia

INTRODUCTION

We are proposing certain improvements over a time–series forecasting method based on the imitation of similar patterns, presented by *Motnikar et al. (1992)*. Given a time–series $z_1, \ldots, z_n$, we defined its patterns $\vec{r} \equiv (z_{b(\vec{r})}, z_{b(\vec{r})+1}, \ldots, z_{b(\vec{r})+s-1})$ as vectors of s subsequent observations starting at index $b(\vec{r})$. According to a chosen similarity measure we sorted out patterns $\vec{r}_1, \ldots, \vec{r}_k$ that were sufficiently similar to the last pattern $\vec{p}$ in the time–series. Then we estimated the future observations by a linear combination of the observations that follow the k most similar patterns. In the method we also considered some details, e.g., the normalization of the patterns to enable proper comparison, the definition of a similarity measure, the determination of the pattern length s, the number k of chosen similar patterns and their weights.

THE PATTERN LENGTH

In the previous method, pattern length s was equal to the maximum lag of significant values of time–series partial autocorrelation function. The improved method, however, enables the analyst to choose the pattern length s so that

- it minimizes mean absolute error (MAE) or mean square error (MSE) of single–step forecasts on a chosen validation set, or
- it is equal to the mean distance between the neighbouring turning points.

There is a variant of the last criterion that varies pattern length according to the distance between the forecast origin and the preceding turning point: in such a case pattern $\vec{p}$ consists of the two observations just before the last turning point and all the succeeding observations up to the forecast origin. The method proposed allows user to choose s also by other criteria or utilize additional information about time–series.

THE CHOICE OF SIMILAR PATTERNS

To select similar patterns, we have developed a two–stage comparison algorithm based on chosen characteristic features, which are divided into the *eliminating* and *ordering* group. First we eliminate all patterns, where at least one of the eliminating characteristic features differs from those of pattern $\vec{p}$. For all the remaining patterns $\vec{r}$, we then calculate the distance $D(\vec{r},\vec{p}) \equiv \sum_f u_f \cdot D_f(\vec{r},\vec{p})$; D_f being similarity measures of the ordering characteristic features, and the weights u_f being determined by the user's judgement of the relative importance of the characteristic features for the given time–series.

Using distance $D(\vec{r},\vec{p})$, k similar patterns are selected by choosing all patterns $\vec{r}$, for which the distance $D(\vec{r},\vec{p})$ is shorter than the allowed upper value D_{max} (proper normalization of the similarity measures enables us to choose D_{max} *in percentage*).

FORECASTING

To forecast the observation that is l time–steps–ahead of the forecast origin n we use the following linear combination of the observations that follow the k chosen patterns:

$$\hat{z}_{n,k}(l) \equiv z_n + \sum_{j=1}^{k} w_j\left(z_{b(\vec{r}_j)+s-1+l} - z_{b(\vec{r}_j)+s-1}\right) . \tag{1}$$

To make more similar patterns have more impact on the forecasts, we use the weights $w_j = Const \cdot (D_{max} - D(\vec{p},\vec{r}_j)) \;/\; D_{max}$ for $j = 1,\ldots,k$, where $Const$ is determined by the requirement $\sum_{j=1}^{s} w_j = 1$.

AN EXAMPLE

We choose vector $\vec{t}(\vec{r})$ of signs in the differentiated pattern: $t_i(\vec{r}) \equiv sign(r_{i+1} - r_i)$, $i = 1,\ldots,s-1$, as the only *eliminating* characteristic feature; it eliminates patterns with the different number or different position of local extremes. Three *ordering* characteristic features and corresponding similarity measures are chosen as follows:

1) mean value $\bar{r} = \sum_{i=1}^{s} r_i/s$ and $D_1(\vec{r},\vec{p}) = |\bar{r} - \bar{p}| \;/\; (|\bar{p}| + \epsilon)$;

2) standard deviation $\sigma_r \equiv \sqrt{\sum_{i=1}^{s}(r_i - \bar{r})^2/s}$ and $D_2(\vec{r},\vec{p}) = |\sigma_r - \sigma_p| \;/\; (\sigma_p + \epsilon)$;

3) vector $\vec{o}(\vec{r})$ of orders: for $i = 1, \ldots, s$, $o_i(\vec{r}) \equiv j$, when r_i takes j-th place in the sorted vector of observations in $\vec{r}$ and $D_3(\vec{r}, \vec{p}) = \sum_{i=1}^{s} |o_i(\vec{r}) - o_i(\vec{p})|/s^2$;

in which an arbitrary small positive value ϵ is used to prevent division by zero.

To demonstrate the proposed method we use the time-series considered in *Weigend et al. (1990)*, where the 221 observations are sunspot numbers. We divide this time-series into the *training set* (determination of the optimal parameters), *validation set* (fit-quality-test) and *prediction set* (forecasting future observations). Disjunct training and validation sets are determined by the *leave-one-out* (LOO) test. The prediction set consists of the last 20 observations in the time-series (which are unknown as input data).

Results of the training set suggest the following parameters: $D_{max} = 0,25, s = 6, u_1 = 0,50, u_2 = 0,25, u_3 = 0,25$. Single-step forecasts on the validation set and multi-step forecasts on the prediction set are calculated by the proposed method, by ARMA(2,0) model (that is optimal according to *Box, Jenkins (1970)*) and by a simple model $\hat{z}_{t+1} = z_t$ (which is taken only to show the capability of other two methods). In Table 1, we compare the corresponding MAE and MSE. The results show that errors in the pattern imitation method proposed are $15 - 45\%$ smaller than those of the Box-Jenkins method.

method	Validation S.		Prediction S.	
or model	MAE	MSE	MAE	MSE
$\hat{z}_{t+1} = z_t$	0,0850	0,0120	0,1602	0,0602
ARMA(2,0)	0,0590	0,0061	0,1014	0,0170
patterns	0,0499	0,0046	0,0755	0,0093

Table 1: Forecast errors on the Sunspot numbers.

GENERALIZATION TO THE MULTI-INPUT SINGLE-OUTPUT CASE

When we are given a d-dimensional time-series of equal lengths, we define (i) a multidimensional pattern as d univariate patterns that end on the same time index in the corresponding univariate time-series (the lengths of univariate patterns may be different), and (ii) a generalized distance between multidimensional patterns as a weighted sum of univariate distances that correspond to univariate patterns. If the generalized distance between a given multidimensional pattern and the last multidimensional pattern in the time-series is lower than D_{max}, then we take the corresponding univariate pattern of the output time-series as a similar one. To forecast the future observations of the output time-series, we use the same formula (1) as in the univariate case.

CONCLUSION

The modifications proposed improve applicability of the method because: (a) new criteria and possibilities for determining the pattern length and characteristic features result in better quality of forecasts; (b) a most time-consuming part (determination of the number k of similar patterns) of the previous method is avoided; (c) generalization to the multidimensional case enables us to use additional information from the influential time-series; (d) algorithms used for standard fit-quality-tests facilitate adequate comparison with other methods.

In future, we intend to further develop the multi-input single-output and multi-input multi-output versions of the proposed method. Another important task is to combine the proposed method sequentially or simultaneously with other time-series forecasting methods so as to extract the advantages of the individual methods.

REFERENCES

Box G., Jenkins G. (1970), Time Series Analysis: Forecasting and Control, *Holden-Day, San Francisco.*

Motnikar B., Čepar D., Žunko P., Ribarič M., Vovk B. (1992), Time Series Forecasting by Imitation of Preceding Patterns, *16th Symposium on Operation Research, Trier, Sept. 1991; extended abstract, Operations Research '91, GMÖOR, p. 272 - 275, Physica-Verlag, Springer-Verlag Company.*

Weigend A., Huberman B., Rumelhart D. (1990), Predicting the Future: A Connectionist Approach, *International Journal of Neural Systems 1, p. 193 - 209, Stanford, California.*

Characterizations of the Existence of UMP Tests for Hypotheses Induced by Groups

D. Plachky
Institute for Mathematical Statistics, University of Münster
Einsteinstraße 62, 4400 Münster, Germany

Abstract

Let $(\Omega, \mathcal{A}, P_j)$, $j = 1,2$, denote probability spaces, G a group of $(\mathcal{A}, \mathcal{A})$-measurable mappings $g : \Omega \to \Omega$, and $\mathcal{P}_j$ the sets of probability distributions P_j^g, $g \in G$, $j = 1,2$. It is shown that the existence of an UMP level α-test for testing $\mathcal{P}_1$ against $\mathcal{P}_2$ for any $\alpha \in [0,1)$ is equivalent to one of the following conditions:

(i) The envelope power function β_α on the convex hull of $\mathcal{P}_2$ is equal to the constant value of β_α on $\mathcal{P}_2$ for any $\alpha \in [0,1)$, if $\mathcal{P}_1$ is dominated by some σ-finite measure.

(ii) Any optimal level α-test for testing $\{P_1|J\}$ against $\{P_2|J\}$, where J denotes the sub-σ-algebra of $\mathcal{A}$ consisting of all G-invariant sets, is an UMP level α test for testing $\mathcal{P}_1$ against $\mathcal{P}_2$ for any $\alpha \in [0,1)$, if G is a locally compact, σ-compact, (topologically) amenable group acting measurably on Ω and $\mathcal{P}_1$ is dominated by some σ-finite measure.

(iii) The P_1continuous part P_{2P_1} of P_2 is G-invariant, if G is a locally compact, σ-compact, (topologically) amenable group acting measurably on Ω and P_1 is G-invariant.

The starting point is a characterization of the existence of an UMP level α-test for testing $\mathcal{P}_1$ against $\mathcal{P}_2$, where $\mathcal{P}_j$, $j = 1,2$, are sets of probability distributions on a σ-algebra $\mathcal{A}$ of subsets of a set Ω, based on the notion of a most stringent level α-test, which might be of separate interest. A test $\varphi^* \in \Phi_\alpha(\mathcal{P}_1)$ is called most stringent level α $(0 \leq \alpha \leq 1)$ test for testing $\mathcal{P}_1$ against $\mathcal{P}_2$ if $\sup_{P \in \mathcal{P}_2}(\beta_\alpha(P) - E_P(\varphi^*)) = \inf_{\varphi \in \Phi_\alpha(\mathcal{P}_1)} \sup_{P_2 \in \mathcal{P}_2}(\beta_\alpha(P) - E_P(\varphi))$ is valid, where β_α denotes the envelope power function defined by $\beta_\alpha(P) = \sup_{\varphi \in \Phi_\alpha(\mathcal{P}_1)} E_P(\varphi)$, for any probability distribution P on $\mathcal{A}$ and where $\Phi_\alpha(\mathcal{P}_1)$ stands for the set of all level α-tests with respect to $\mathcal{P}_1$, i.e. $\Phi_\alpha(\mathcal{P}_1) = \{\varphi$ test: $E_P(\varphi) \leq \alpha$, $P \in \mathcal{P}_1\}$. It is well-known that a most stringent level α-test for testing $\mathcal{P}_1$ against $\mathcal{P}_2$ exists if $\mathcal{P}_1 \cup \mathcal{P}_2$ is dominated by a σ-finite measure μ on $\mathcal{A}$. A proof might be based on the weak compactness argument that for any sequence φ_n of tests there exists a subsequence φ_{n_k} and some test φ^* satisfying $\int \varphi_{n_k} f\, d\mu \to \int \varphi^* f\, d\mu$ for all $f \in \mathcal{L}_1(\Omega, \mathcal{A}, \mu)$. If one takes into consideration that a convex linear combination of φ_{n_k} converges strongly (i.e. with respect to the norm of $\mathcal{L}_1(\Omega, \mathcal{A}, \mu)$) to φ (cf. Dunford/Schwartz (1964), V.3.14, p. 422), one might only assume that $\mathcal{P}_1$ is dominated by a σ-finite measure in order to prove the existence of a most stringent level α-test for testing $\mathcal{P}_1$ against $\mathcal{P}_2$. The characterization of the existence of an UMP level α-test φ^* for testing $\mathcal{P}_1$ against $\mathcal{P}_2$, i.e. $E_P(\varphi^*) = \beta_\alpha(P)$, $P \in \mathcal{P}_2$, is valid, looks as follows:

Lemma. Let $\mathcal{P}_1$ be dominated by some σ-finite measure. Then there exists an UMP level α-test for testing $\mathcal{P}_1$ against $\mathcal{P}_2$ if and only if the envelope power function β_α is affine-linear on the convex hull of $\mathcal{P}_2$. In particular, any most stringent level α-test for testing $\mathcal{P}_1$ against $\mathcal{P}_2$ is an UMP level α-test, if there exists some UMP level α-test for testing $\mathcal{P}_1$ against $\mathcal{P}_2$.

Proof: Since $P \to \beta_\alpha(P) - E_P(\varphi)$, P probability distribution on $\mathcal{A}$, is convex for any test φ, one gets

$$\sup_{P \in \mathcal{P}_2} (\beta_\alpha(P) - E_P(\varphi)) = \sup_{P \in co(\mathcal{P}_2)} (\beta_\alpha(P) - E_P(\varphi)),$$

where $co(\mathcal{P}_2)$ denotes the convex hull of $\mathcal{P}_2$. Furthermore $\varphi \to \beta_\alpha(P) - E_P(\varphi)$, $\varphi \in \Phi_\alpha(\mathcal{P}_1)$, is convex, weakly continuous, and $\Phi_\alpha(\mathcal{P}_1)$ is weakly compact, since $\mathcal{P}_1$ is dominated by some σ-finite measure μ on $\mathcal{A}$, $P \to \beta_\alpha(P) - E_P(\varphi)$, $P \in co(\mathcal{P}_2)$, is concave, since $\beta_\alpha(P)$ is affine-linear. This allows to apply the minimax-theorem, which leads to

$$\inf_{\varphi \in \Phi_\alpha(\mathcal{P}_1)} \sup_{P \in co(\mathcal{P}_2)} (\beta_\alpha(P) - E_P(\varphi)) = \sup_{P \in co(\mathcal{P}_2)} \inf_{\varphi \in \Phi_\alpha(\mathcal{P}_1)} (\beta_\alpha(P) - E_P(\varphi)) = 0,$$

since by a weak compactness argument one gets for any $P \in \mathcal{P}_2$ a level α-test $\varphi_P \in \Phi_\alpha(\mathcal{P}_1)$ satisfying $E_P(\varphi_P) = \beta_\alpha(P)$. Therefore, $\sup_{P \in co(\mathcal{P}_2)}(\beta_\alpha(P) - E_P(\varphi^*)) = \sup_{P \in \mathcal{P}_2}(\beta_\alpha(P) - E_P(\varphi^*)) = 0$ holds true for any most stringent level α-test φ^* for testing $\mathcal{P}_1$ against $\mathcal{P}_2$, i.e. φ^* is an UMP level α-test for testing $\mathcal{P}_1$ against $\mathcal{P}_2$ if β_α is affine-linear on $co(\mathcal{P}_2)$, which is in particular valid, if there exists some UMP level α-test for testing $\mathcal{P}_1$ against $\mathcal{P}_2$. □

This lemma will now be applied to characterize the existence of an UMP level α-test for hypotheses $\mathcal{P}_j$, $j = 1, 2$, which are generated by a group G of $(\mathcal{A}, \mathcal{A})$-measurable transformations in the following sense: $\mathcal{P}_j = \{P_j^g : g \in G\}$, $j = 1, 2$, where P_j, $j = 1, 2$, are given probability distributions on $\mathcal{A}$. In this case the envelcpe power function β_α is constant on $\mathcal{P}_2$ because of

$$\beta_\alpha(P_2^g) = \sup_{\varphi \in \Phi_\alpha(\mathcal{P}_1)} E_{P_2^g}(\varphi) = \sup_{\varphi \in \Phi_\alpha(\mathcal{P}_1)} E_{P_2}(\varphi \circ g) = \beta_\alpha(P_2),\ g \in G,$$

since $\varphi \in \Phi_\alpha(\mathcal{P}_1)$ is here equivalent to $\varphi \circ g \in \Phi_\alpha(\mathcal{P}_1)$ for any fixed $g \in G$. Furthermore, the following notion of amenability of G will be important in the sequel: A locally compact and σ-compact group G is called (topologically) amenable if and only if there exists a right-invariant probability charge ν on the σ-algebra $\mathcal{B}_G$ of Borel subsets of G. This property of a locally compact and σ-compact group is equivalent to the existence of an asymptotically right-invariant sequence ν_n of probability measures on $\mathcal{B}_G$ (cf. Paterson (1988), p. 148). In particular, any subnet ν_{n_α} of the sequence ν_n, which converges set-wise to some probability charge ν yields some left-invariant probability charge ν on $\mathcal{B}_G$ (cf. Paterson (1988), p. 148). Finally a locally compact and σ-compact group G of $(\mathcal{A}, \mathcal{A})$-measurable transformations $g : \Omega \to \Omega$ acts measurably on Ω if and only if the mapping defined by $(\omega, g) \to g(\omega)$, $\omega \in \Omega$, $g \in G$, is $((\mathcal{A}, \mathcal{B}_G), \mathcal{A})$-measurable. Now everything is prepared to prove the following main result:

Theorem. Let $(\Omega, \mathcal{A}, P_j)$, $j = 1, 2$, denote probability measures, G a group of $(\mathcal{A}, \mathcal{A})$-measurable transformations, and $\mathcal{P}_j$ the set $\{P_j^g : g \in G\}$, $j = 1, 2$, of probability distributions on $\mathcal{A}$. Then the existence of some UMP leves α-test for testing $\mathcal{P}_1$ against $\mathcal{P}_2$ for all $\alpha \in [0, 1)$ is equivalent to one of the following conditions:

(i) The envelope power function β_α on the convex hull of $\mathcal{P}_2$ is equal to the constant value of β_α on $\mathcal{P}_2$ for any $\alpha \in [0, 1)$, if $\mathcal{P}_1$ is dominated by some σ-finite measure.

(ii) Any optimal level α-test for testing $\{P_1|J\}$ against $\{P_2|J\}$, where J denotes the sub-σ-algebra of $\mathcal{A}$ consisting of all G-invariant sets, is an UMP level α-test for testing $\mathcal{P}_1$ against $\mathcal{P}_2$ for any $\alpha \in [0, 1)$, if G is a locally compact, σ-compact, and (topologically) amenable group acting measurably on Ω and $\mathcal{P}_1$ is dominated by some σ-finite measure.

(iii) the P_1-continuous part P_{2P_1} of P_2 is G-invariant, if G is a locally compact, σ-compact, and (topologically) amenable group, which acts measurably on Ω, and P_1 is G-invariant.

Proof: Part (i) follows immediately from the lemma, if one takes into consideration that $\beta_\alpha(P_2^g) = \beta_\alpha(P_2)$, $g \in G$, $P_2 \in \mathcal{P}_2$, is valid. For the proof of (ii) one might start from the observation that the additional assumption on G implies the existence of some G-invariant most stringent level α-test for testing $\mathcal{P}_1$ against $\mathcal{P}_2$, which can be shown as follows: Let φ^* denote some most stringent level α-test for testing $\mathcal{P}_1$ against $\mathcal{P}_2$, which exists, since $\mathcal{P}_1$ is dominated by some σ-finite measure. Then ψ^* defined by $\psi^*(\omega) = \lim_\alpha \int \varphi^*(g(\omega))d\nu_{n_\alpha}(g)$, $\omega \in \Omega$, where ν_{n_α} is a subnet of some asymptotically right-invariant sequence ν_n of probability measures on $\mathcal{B}_G$ converging setwise to some right-invariant probabiliy charge ν on $\mathcal{B}_G$, is $\mathcal{A}$-measurable, since ν_{n_α} is a subnet of a sequence ν_n. Furthermore, Fubini's theorem and the theorem of dominated convergence for nets (cf. Dunford/Schwartz, III.3.7, p. 124) implies $E_P(\psi^*) = \lim_\alpha \int_G \int_\Omega \varphi^*(g(\omega))dP(\omega)d\nu_{n_\alpha}(g)$ for any probability distribution P on $\mathcal{A}$, from which $E_{P_2^g}(\psi^*) \geq \beta_\alpha(P_2^g) - \sup_{g\in G}(\beta_\alpha(P_2^g) - E_{P_2^g}(\varphi^*))$, $g \in G$, follows because of $E_{P_2^g}(\varphi^*) \geq \beta_\alpha(P_2^g) - \sup_{g\in G}(\beta_\alpha(P_2^g) - E_{P_2^g}(\varphi^*))$, $g \in G$, i.e. $\sup_{g\in G}(\beta_\alpha(P_2^g) - E_{P_2^g}(\psi^*)) \leq \sup_{g\in G}(\beta_\alpha(P_2^g) - E_{P_2^g}(\varphi^*))$ holds true. Finally, $E_{P_1^g}(\psi^*) \leq E_{P_1^g}(\varphi^*) \leq \alpha$, $g \in G$, implies that ψ^* is a most stringent level α-test for testing $\mathcal{P}_1$ against $\mathcal{P}_2$, which is G-invariant and, therefore, J-measurable. Hence ψ^* is according to the lemma an UMP level α-test for testing $\mathcal{P}_1$ against $\mathcal{P}_2$, if there exists some UMP level α-test for testing $\mathcal{P}_1$ against $\mathcal{P}_2$. In particular, ψ^* is an optimal level α-test for testing $\{P_1|J\}$ against $\{P_2|J\}$, since ψ^* is J-measurable and $\Phi_\alpha(\{P_1|J\}) \subset \Phi_\alpha(\mathcal{P}_1)$ is valid. Part (iii) follows from part (ii), if one takes into consideration that the likelihood ratio occuring in the Neyman-Pearson lemma for some optimal level α-test for testing $\{P_1\}$ against $\{P_2\}$ might be represented by $\frac{dP_{2P_1}}{dP_1}$. The special case $P_1 = P_1^g$, $g \in G$, i.e. $\mathcal{P}_1 = \{P_1\}$ together with the assumption that some UMP level α-test for testing $\{P_1\}$ against $\mathcal{P}_2$ exists for any $\alpha \in [0,1)$ implies that according to the Neyman-Pearson lemma and part (ii) the set $\{\frac{dP_{2P_1}}{dP_1} > k\}$ belongs for any $k \geq 0$ up to some P_1-zero set to J, i.e. $\frac{dP_{2P_1}}{dP_1}$ has an J-measurable version, and, therefore, P_{2P_1} is G-invariant. Conversely, G-invariance of P_{2P_1} leads to the existence of some J-measurable version of $\frac{dP_{2P_1}}{dP_1}$, which implies together with the lemma of Neyman-Pearson that any optimal level α-test for testing $\{P_1|J\}$ against $\{P_2|J\}$ is an UMP level α-test for testing $\{P_1\}$ against $\mathcal{P}_2$ for any $\alpha \in [0,1)$. □

The main result will be applied to the problem of testing uniformity according to the following

Example. Let Ω itself be a compact group G, where $\mathcal{A}$ stands for the Borel σ-algebra of G and μ for the normed Haar-measure of G. Then G acts naturally as a group $G^{(n)}$ on the n-fold Cartesian product $\Omega^{(n)}$ of Ω endowed with the n-fold direct product $\mathcal{A}^{(n)}$ of $\mathcal{A}$ according to $g^{(n)}(\omega_1,\ldots,\omega_n) = (g(\omega_1),\ldots,g(\omega_n))$, $(\omega_1,\ldots,\omega_n) \in \Omega^{(n)}, g^{(n)} \in G^{(n)}$, $g \in G$. Furthermore, let μ_n denote the n-fold direct product of μ and P_n the n-fold direct product of some probability measure P defined on $\mathcal{A}$, which is absolutely continuous with respect to μ. According to the theorem above there exists some UMP level α-test for testing $\{\mu_n\}$ against $\{P_n^{g_n} : g_n \in G^{(n)}\}$ for any $\alpha \in [0,1)$ if and only if P_n is $G^{(n)}$-invariant, which is equivalent to the property of P to be G-invariant, i.e. $P = \mu$. This illustrates that the efforts of testing uniformity by tests which are necessarily not UMP level α-test for all $\alpha \in [0,1)$ are justified (cf. Ajne (1968), Beran (1968), Ng (1976), Uthoff (1970), and Watson (1976)).

References

Ajne, B. (1968): A simple test for uniformity of a circular distribution. Biometrika 55: 343 - 354

Beran, R. J. W. (1968): Testing for uniformity on a compact homogeneous space. J. Appl. Prob. 5: 177 - 195

Dunford, N. and T. Schwartz (1964): Linear Operators, Part I. Interscience, New York

Ng, V. M. (1976): A note on the best test for discrimination between exponentiality and uniformity. Technometrics 18: 237 - 238

Paterson, A. L. (1988): Amenability. Mathematical Surveys and Monographs 29. Providence, Rhode Island

Uthoff, V. A. (1970): An optimum test property of two well-known statistics. J. Amer. Statist. Ass. 68: 1597 - 1600

Watson, G. S. (1976): Optimal invariant tests for uniformity. In: Studies in Probability and Statistics, ed. by E. J. Williams, New York

Statistical Scaling

Werner Pölz
Institut für Systemwissenschaften, Johannes-Kepler-Universität Linz
Altenbergerstraße 69, 4040 Linz-Auhof, Austria

A newly developed correlation coefficient for variables of different scaling levels will be discussed.

1) If we want to make data the subject of statistical analyses, we have to take the nature of the variables (nominal, ordinal, interval) into consideration, because the type of scale dictates the appropriate statistics (Pearson-Product-Moment correlation coefficient, rank correlation, χ^2).
This is not necessary for the correlation coefficient discussed below.
With this correlation coefficient it is possible to combine systems of nominal and/or ordinal and/or interval natures.

2) In several data analyses it may be necessary to express, for example, the ordinal character of a variable in the weights of its categories in a way that most of the ordinal information is put into these weights. Instead of "forced metrization" - that is the assignment of arbitrary numbers to the categories and their treatment as quantitative values - we get weights which contain the whole one-dimensional distribution of frequencies by means of "statistical scaling".

3) Apart from this, we can easily build up a system of discrete Legendre Polynomials on these weights obtained by "statistical scaling". With this system we can develop a stepwise approach to optimal scaling (correspondence analysis) for ordinal variables.

METHODS

Suppose that a scoring scale has n points (a variable X has n categories) with the corresponding relative frequencies $p_1, p_2, ..., p_n$.

We transform this variable to uniform distribution by "statistical scaling" (Pölz, 1988). Doing this the single categories get values which are restricted to lie between -1 and +1. It can be shown that the mean of these values for the categories is zero and that the variance only depends on the relative frequencies and is independent of the order of the categories.

We can proceed with an other variable - let us call it Y with m categories - in the same way. Having obtained the two-dimensional frequencies for X and Y, we can very easy calculate a correlation coefficient as a first approximation to the Pearson correlation coefficient.

Our coefficient has the great advantage as compared to the classic correlation coefficient that it is not restricted to interval data. Variables X and Y can also be of nominal and/or ordinal nature.

By simulations it can be shown that this correlation coefficient is never bigger but in the relevant areas ($|r| \geq 0{,}05$) just a little bit less than the Pearson coefficient.

By using bootstrapping, statements concerning the confidence intervals of the correlation coefficient can be made, but tests for these coefficients are in the stage of development.

The second advantage of "statistical scaling" is that these starting values are excellently suited for setting up a system of discrete Legendre polynomials:

Let us consider a contingency table with variable X as rows and variable Y as columns. The variables are transformed to uniform distribution by means of "statistical scaling". By means of orthogonal polynomials we carry out a spectral decomposition of the variables into constant, linear, quadratic, cubic etc. components. With theses results we build up a Burt Matrix (Greenacre, 1984 p. 164) which serves as a basic matrix for a correspondence analysis.

The first dimension of the correspondence analysis provides optimal weights for the categories of the variables of the rows and columns. "Optimal" in this case means that the correlation coefficient between the rows and columns is maximised for a given frequency distribution through the optimal weights. Theses results are in no way different from those we obtain by using the traditional methods of correspondence analysis (optimal scaling):

But, if one (or as well the other) variable is ordinally scaled, it may occur that the optimal weights do not reflect the given order.

In the matrices of the spectral decomposition we now cut the orthogonal polynomials of highest degree and thus reduce the amount of information contained in the variables until the weights calculated from the modified Burt matrix reflect the given order.

The traditional solutions to the problem of ordered constraints in the area of correspondence analysis are not satisfactory (Nishisato, Arri, Gifi), as the number of scale points (categories of variables) have to be reduced until the given relation of order in the weights is reached. Uniting categories, however, means a loss of information: The method presented here is intended to determine better weights for the individual categories without uniting categories. Instead of arbitrary values (e.g. 1, 2, 3, 4, 5) "optimal weights" will be assigned to each of the categories of the variables for further calculations.

REFERENCES

Gifi A. 1990 *Nonlinear Multivariate Analysis*. John Wiley & Sons, Chichester, New York, Brisbane, Toronto, Singapore.

Greenacre M. J. (1984) *Theory and applications of correspondence analysis*. Academic Press London.

Nishisato S. and Arri P. S. 1975 "Nonlinear programming approach to optimal scaling of partially ordered categories." *Psychometrika*, 40: 525 - 548.

Pölz W. (1988) *Ein dispositionsstatistisches Verfahren zur optimalen Informationsausschöpfung aus Datensystemen mit unterschiedlichem Ausprägungsniveau der Merkmale*. Peter Lang Verlag. Frankfurt.

Full-Information Best Choice Problems with Imperfect Observation

Zdzisław Porosiński
Institute of Mathematics, Technical University of Wrocław
Wybrzeże Wyspiańskiego 27, 50–370 Wrocław, Poland

The following full–information (FI) best choice problem (BCP) was studied by Gilbert and Mosteller (1966). A known number, N, of *iid rv*'s $X_1, X_2, \ldots, X_N$ from a known continuous distribution F are observed sequentially with the object of choosing the largest. After X_n is observed it must be chosen (and the observation is terminated) orrejected (and the observation is continued). Neither recall nor uncertainty of selection is allowed and one choice must be made.

The problem with imperfect observation was considered first by Enns (1975). In his model the number of observations is known and the only available information is whether observed *rv* is greater than, or less than some level specified by the observer (the exact value is not known). This model could describe e.g. situation when the measurement of the exact value of a sampled variable is very difficult or expensive. Another example could be taken from destructive testing where each sample is tested on whether it breaks or survives at some level of strength. This corresponds to the single level case of Gilbert and Mosteller (1966). Sakaguchi (1984) generalized Enns' model in five natural kinds of objectives and two types of strategies.

In this paper FI BCP with imperfect observation is considered when the number of observations N is allowed to be a *rv* with known distribution. Since N is unknown the observer faces an additional risk. If he rejects any observation, he may then discover it was the last one, in which case he receives nothing at all.

We shall consider the following five cases when the objective is to choose:

(A): the largest *rv* by accepting one *rv*;

(B): the largest or the second largest by accepting exactly once;

(C): the largest by accepting twice;

(D): both the largest and the second largest by accepting twice;

(E): the largest or the second largest by accepting twice.

The optimal strategy for each of these problems when N is geometric or uniform is obtained. In the uniform cases (A)–(E) simple asymptotically optimal strategies are found and asymptotic probabilities of winning are obtained. More details can be found in Porosiński (1991).

THE MODEL

Assume that $X_1, X_2, X_3, \ldots$ is a sequence of *iid rv*'s with a continuous distribution function F, defined on the probability space $(\Omega, \mathcal{F}, P)$ and the number of observations N is a *rv* independent of the sequence $(X_n)_{n=1}^{\infty}$ with a known distribution: $P(N = k) = p_k$ $(\sum_{k=0}^{\infty} p_k = 1)$.

The observer specifies a decision level L and is informed only whether the observed *rv* is greater or less than L. As long as the observation is less than or equal to L it is rejected and as soon as it is greater it is accepted. If the *rv* N is bounded, i.e. $P(N \le n) = 1$ and $p_n > 0$, then the observer slightly modifies his strategy. E.g. for Case (B), if no *rv*'s are accepted until $n-1$ then the last observation X_n is accepted (if it occurs) without respect to its value.

In each problem an event in which the objective is achieved is called a *win* and its probability is called the *probability of winning*. A strategy which maximizes the probability of winning is called *optimal*. Since F is known and continuous, without loss of generality it is assumed in the sequel that the observations have the uniform distribution on $[0,1]$.
It is not difficult to find probabilities of winning. E.g. in Case (B) if $1 \le s \le n$ then

$$P(stop\ at\ s\ \&\ win\ \mid N = n)$$

$$= P(X_k \le L, k \le s-1, X_s > L \text{ and at most one from } X_{s+1}, \ldots, X_n \text{ is greater than } X_s)$$

$$= L^{s-1} \int_L^1 \left(x^{n-s} + (n-s)x^{n-s-1}(1-x)\right) dx = L^{s-1}\left(1 - L^{n-s} - (n-s-1)\frac{1-L^{n-s+1}}{n-s+1}\right),$$

thus $P(win) = \sum_k p_k L^k \sum_{r=1}^{k} \left(2(L^{-r}-1)/r - L^{-1}(1-L)\right)$ $(+2p_n L^n/n$ if N is bounded$)$.

In the general case, when the distribution of N is not specified, it is impossible to check open forms of optimal strategies.

SPECIAL CASES

Theorem 1 *Let N be geometric with parameter p (i.e. $P(N = k) = pq^k, k = 0, 1, \ldots$).*

Case (A): *If $p < e^{-1}$ then the optimal decision level is $L^* = (1 - ep)/q$ and the probability of winning is $P(win) = e^{-1} \cong 0.36789$. If $p \ge e^{-1}$ then $L^* = 0$ and $P(win) = -p \ln p$.*

Case (B): *If $p < \alpha$, where $\alpha \cong 0.30171$ is a root of the equation $2x - 2\ln x - 3 = 0$ in $(0,1)$ then $L^* = (1 - \alpha^{-1}p)/q$ and $P(win) = \alpha(2-\alpha) \cong 0.51239$. If $p \ge \alpha$ then $L^* = 0$ and $P(win) = p(p - 1 - 2\ln p)$.*

Case (C): *The solution is identical with Case (B).*

Case (D): *If $p < \alpha$, where $\alpha \cong 0.28466$ is a root of the equation $2x \ln x - x + 1 = 0$ in $(0,1)$ then $L^* = (1 - \alpha^{-1}p)/q$ and $P(win) = \alpha(1-\alpha) \cong 0.20363$. If $p \ge \alpha$ then $L^* = 0$ and $P(win) = 2p(p \ln p - p + 1)$.*

Case (E): *If $p < \alpha$, where $\alpha \cong 0.23978$ is a root of the equation $8x - 4(x+1)\ln x - 9 = 0$ in $(0,1)$ then $L^* = (1 - \alpha^{-1}p)/q$ and $P(win) = \alpha(5\alpha - 5 - 2(\alpha+2)\ln\alpha) \cong 0.62244$. If $p \geq \alpha$ then $L^* = 0$ and $P(win) = p(5p - 2(p+2)\ln p - 5)$.*

Proof. E.g., in the case (B) we obtain

$$P(win) = \sum_{n=1}^{\infty} pq^n L^n \sum_{r=1}^{n} \left(2\frac{L^{-r}-1}{r} - \frac{1-L}{L}\right) = \frac{p}{1-qL}\left(\frac{p}{1-qL} - 2\ln\frac{p}{1-qL} - 1\right).$$

Let $p/(1-qL)$=x. Since $0 \leq L \leq 1$ we have $p \leq x \leq 1$. The function $f(x) = x(x - 2\ln x - 1)$ in $(0,1)$, connected with $P(win)$, has a unique local extremum (maximum) in $(0,1)$ at the point α for which the derivative $f'(x) = 2x - 2\ln x - 3$ is equal to zero. So, since $x \in [p,1]$, the function $f(x)$ attains its maximum at α if $p < \alpha$ or at p if $p \geq \alpha$. Thus $L^* = (1-\alpha^{-1}p)/q$ and $P(win) = f(\alpha) = \alpha(2-\alpha)$ if $p < \alpha$ or $L^* = 0$ and $P(win) = f(p)$ if $p \geq \alpha$. Theorem is proved for the problem (B). The proof for the remaining cases is analogous.

Now, let N be uniformly distributed on $\{1,\ldots,n\}$, i.e. $p_k = 1/n$ for $k = 1,\ldots,n$. In this case denote the probability of winning under the level L as $P(L,n)$, the optimal decision level as $L(n)$ and $P(L(n),n) = P(n)$. Taking into account formulae of $P(win)$ it is easy to get by changing of order of sums and after some simplifications that e.g. in Case (B)

$$P(L,n) = (1 + 2/n^2)L^n + (n(1-L))^{-1}\left(L^n - 1 + 2\sum_{r=1}^{n}(1-L^r)(1-L^{n-r+1})/r\right).$$

In each case as n grows large, $L(n)$ tends to 1 but in such a manner that it is approximately linear in $1/n$, i.e. $L(n) = 1 - \alpha/n + o(1/n)$ or in other words $n(1 - L(n)) \to \alpha$ or $L^n \to e^{-\alpha}$.

Using the above property in the formulae of $P(L,n)$ we find by passing to the limit that $P(n) \to P(\alpha)$, where e.g. in Case (B)

$$P(\alpha) = e^{-\alpha} - \frac{1-e^{-\alpha}}{\alpha} - 2\frac{I(-\alpha) + e^{-\alpha}I(\alpha)}{\alpha} \quad \text{and} \quad I(\alpha) = \int_0^\alpha x^{-1}(e^x - 1)dx.$$

¿From the necessary condition that the derivative of $P(\alpha)$ is zero we find the unique point α at which the maximum of the function $P(\alpha)$ is attained. E.g. in Case (B), α is a solution of the equation $1 - e^{-\alpha}(\alpha^2 + \alpha + 1) + 2(\alpha+1)e^{-\alpha}I(\alpha) + I(-\alpha) + 4(e^{-\alpha} - 1) = 0$.

Numerical results of α and the asymptotic probabilities of winning $P(\alpha)$ are as follows:

(A): $L(n) = 1 - 2.8397/n + 1.516/n^2$, $P(n) = 0.42632 + 0.561/n + 0.22/n^2$,
(B): $L(n) = 1 - 3.7900/n + 2.091/n^2$, $P(n) = 0.59531 + 0.789/n + 0.29/n^2$,
(C): $L(n) = 1 - 3.7900/n + 2.10/n^2$, $P(n) = 0.59531 + 0.789/n + 0.31/n^2$,
(D): $L(n) = 1 - 4.1255/n + 2.60/n^2$, $P(n) = 0.26140 + 0.422/n + 0.38/n^2$,
(E): $L(n) = 1 - 5.15283/n + 2.79/n^2$, $P(n) = 0.71427 + 0.930/n - 0.14/n^2$,

with the error less than 0.0001 for $n \geq 15$.

REMARKS

1. FI BCP's when the observation is perfect have been solved, as far as the author knows, only in Case (A) (Gilbert and Mosteller (1966)) and (C) (Tamaki (1980)) when the N is fixed, and in Case (A) (Porosiński (1987)) and (B) (Porosiński and Szajowski (1989) - only geometric N) when N is random.

2. In the geometric case it is interesting and quite unexpected that the probabilities of winning in all *natural* situations (i.e. when p is *small*) are constants independent of p.

3. In Case (A) and (C) for N geometric the optimal decision level does not depend on the number of preceding observations even if the class of admissible strategies is not bounded (Porosiński (1987), Porosiński and Szajowski(1989)). It seems that optimal strategies in the problems (B)–(E) when N is geometric ought to obey this principle. Then our results for (B)–(E) would also be optimal when the observation is perfect.

4. In Case (A) for the uniform N and perfect observation the probability of winning is estimated by Porosiński (1987) as 0.4352. It is surprising that the optimal strategy when the observation is imperfect has the probability of winning and its asymptotic value (0.4263) less only a bit, in spite of its very simple structure. It seems that also in the cases (B)–(E) when N is uniform our single level strategy may be only a little worse than the optimal strategy for perfect observation.

REFERENCES

Enns E.G. (1975) Selecting the maximum of a sequence with imperfect information. J. Amer. Stat. Assoc. **70**, 640–643.

Gilbert J.P., Mosteller F. (1966) Recognizing the maximum of a sequence. J. Amer. Stat. Assoc. **61**, 35–73.

Porosiński Z. (1987) The full-information best choice problem with a random number of observations. Stoch. Proc. Appl. **24**, 293–307.

Porosiński Z. (1991) Full-information best choice problems with imperfect observation and a random number of observations. Zastosow. Mat. **21**, 2, 179-192.

Porosiński Z., Szajowski K. (1989) On some selection problem. Proc. 14 IFIP Conf. Leipzig, 1989, Lect. Notes Control Inf. Sci. **143**, 679–687.

Sakaguchi M. (1984) Best choice problems with full information and imperfect observation. Math. Japonica **29**, 241–250.

Tamaki M. (1980) Optimal selection with two choices – full information case. Math. Japonica **25**, 359–368.

A Term Structure Model and Interest Rate Options

Klaus Sandmann, Dieter Sondermann
Statistische Abteilung, Universität Bonn
Adenauerallee 24–42, 5300 Bonn, Germany

Closely related to option contracts over stocks are interest rate options like caps and floors which offer the possibility of protection against unfavorable interest rate movements. The properties of interest rate options are similar to those of European call and put options over debt contracts. In principle we are looking for a protection against upward movements of the interest rate, called a cap contract and for protection against downward movements, which is known as a floor contract. The underlying security of these contracts is the interest rate (e.g. 3 months LIBOR). In general cap and floor contracts are defined by the following characteristics:

- the specification of the interest rate r; e.g. LIBOR
- the specification of an interest rate level L
- a set of comparing dates $\underline{T}$ = { 0=t< t<...<t } where the payoff is fixed (tenor of the contract); e.g. every 6 months in the following 3 years
- a set of payment dates; e.g. end of the period
- the specification of the vace value V.

The resulting payoff of a cap with level L and face value V at time $t_i \in \underline{T}$ can be calculated by

$V\cdot[r_{t_{i-1}} - L]^+ := V\cdot\max\{0, r_{t_{i-1}} - L\}$ For a floor the payoff at time $t_i \in \underline{T}$ can be similarly calculated by $V\cdot[L - r_{t_{i-1}}]^+$. Since the cash flow takes place at the end of the period it can be discounted to the beginning of the period. For the cap contract this yields to

$$V\cdot[1 - \frac{1+L}{1+r_{t_{i-1}}}]^+ = V\cdot(1+L)\cdot[\frac{1}{1+L} - \frac{1}{1+r_{t_{i-1}}}]^+$$

where r_t is the unknown interest rate. This can be reinterpreted as V time the payoff of a European put option with exercise price 1 and expiration date t_i where the underlying security is a zero coupon bond with maturity t_{i-1} and face value 1+L. Summing up for all payment dates we can characterize cap and floor contracts as portfolio of European debt options where the underlying securities are zero coupon bonds $B(0,t_i)$ with maturities $t_i \in \underline{T}$.

$$Cap[r, L, \underline{T}, V] = V\cdot\sum_{i=0}^{N-1} (1+L)\cdot put_E[B(0, t_{i+1}, \frac{1}{1+L}, t_i]$$

$$Floor[r, L, \underline{T}, V] = V\cdot\sum_{i=0}^{N-1} (1+L)\cdot call_E[B(0, t_{i+1}, \frac{1}{1+L}, t_i]$$

If we consider an interest rate swap (floating rate against fixed rate) then the relation between caps and floors is given by the cap-floor-parity

$$Cap[r, L, \underline{T}, V] = Floor[r, L, \underline{T}, V] + Swap[r, L, \underline{T}, V]$$

Obviously the swap contract has to be defined on the same interest rate process r with fixed rate equal to L and the payment frequency $\underline{T}$. The discussed relations between interest rate options, debt option, zero coupon bonds and interest rate swaps suggest the direct analysis of the term structure in one step.

The Term Structure Model

The model of the term structure is formulated in a discrete time framework. We assume that there are no transaction costs or taxes. Furthermore we assume that for any maturity $t_i \in \underline{T}$ the prices of the zero coupon bonds $B(0,t_i)$ are known at time 0. Equivalently we could assume these with respect to forward rates or coupon payments. The aim is to construct the process of the interest rate such that

- negative spot rates are excluded
- actual market information (t_0 bond prices) are supported
- the local expectation hypothesis for zero coupon bonds is satisfied (Alternatively we could incorporate the excess return per unit risk, which has to be independent of the maturity)

This leads to the following existence and uniqueness result

Theorem 1

Let $A = \{(n,j) \,/\, t_n \in \underline{T},\ j=0, \ldots, n\}$ the set of time and state tupels. If the prices of zero coupon bonds at time t_0 are strictly decreasing in the maturity, then for any volatility function of the spot rate $\sigma : A \to \mathbb{R}_{\geq 0}$, $\sigma(n,j) = Var[\log r_{t_{n+1}} \mid r_{t_{n,j}}]$

and any transition probability function $p : A \to]0, 1[$

there exists a unique non negative and path independent solution for the spotrate process $\{r_t\}_{t \in \underline{T}}$ defined by

$$r_{n,j} = r_{n,0} \cdot \prod_{i=0}^{n-1} \exp\left\{ \frac{\sigma(n-1,i)}{\sqrt{p(n-1,i) \cdot (1 - p(n-;1,i)}} \right\}$$

such that the local expectation hypothesis for the zero coupon bonds is satisfied.

The transition probability is not an observable market parameter. Therefore the influence should be discussed. The transition probability determines the limit model if the time increment goes to zero.

Theorem 2

Suppose σ is independent of the state and $\sigma^2(t_i)=h(t_i)\ \Delta t$ where h converges against an integrable and bounded function on $[0,t_N]$. Then for any constant transition probability function $p \in\ ]0,1[$ the logarithm of the spot rate process satisfies the Central Limit Theorem.

In this situation the spot rate process can be characterized by $dr = \mu(t)r\ dt + \sigma(t)r\ dW$ where $\mu(t)$ is given by the Local Expectation Hypothesis:

$$B(0,t,R) = E\left[\exp\left\{-\int_0^t r_s\, ds\right\} \mid r_0\right] \qquad \forall\ t \in [0, T]$$

Therefore the spot rate process becomes independent of the transition probability $p \in]0,1[$.

The Arbitrage Price of the Interest Rate Options

Using the binomial model of spot rate the arbitrage price of the interest rate options are given by

$$Cap\,[r,L,\underline{I},V] = V\cdot\sum_{i=0}^{N} E_p\left[\frac{[r_i - L]^+}{\prod_{j=0}^{N}(1+r_j)}\right]$$

$$Floor\,[r,L,\underline{I},V] = V\cdot\sum_{i=0}^{N} E_p\left[\frac{[L - r_i]^+}{\prod_{j=0}^{N}(1+r_j)}\right]$$

By construction the unique measure by which all discounted zero bond price processes are martingales is defined by p. Therefore the market is complete. Furthermore it is possible to contstruct self-financing portfolio strategies which duplicate the payoff of the interest rate option. These strategies are not unique because all available instruments (bonds, swaps etc.) can be used. But the initial price to implement one of these strategies is always equal and given by the arbitrage price.

For a constant transition probability $p \in]0,1[$ the arbitrage price and hedging strategies of interest rate options are in the limit independent of p.

Analysis of Dispersion Effects in Fractional Factorial Two-Level Designs

Steffen Uhlig
Institut für Statistik und Ökonometrie, Freie Universität Berlin
Garystraße 21, 1000 Berlin 33, Germany

Introduction and modeling

In factorial designs that are used in the development of new products or in other applications the response Y frequently has unequal variances depending on the factor levels. The response can be written as a function $Y = f(x)$, where $x = (t', Z')'$ entails all factors influencing Y. t denotes the treatment, i. e. the levels of the controllable factors (design factors), while Z denotes the levels of the (non-observable) random factors. It is assumed that all components of Z are stochastically independent. An additive parameterization of the dispersion function $\sigma_t^2 = \text{Var}[Y]$ by factorial effects of the design factors allows to explain these so-called dispersion effects as follows:

- If there are no interactions in $f(t, Z)$ involving more than two factors, then there are no dispersion effects involving more than two factors, too.
- If a dispersion effect exists which involves the design factors $t_{m_1}, \ldots, t_{m_n}$, then there is a random factor Z_m which is interacting with each of the design factors $t_{m_1}, \ldots, t_{m_n}$.

Therefore, the additive modeling makes it possible to interpret the dispersion effects as a result of interactions between design factors and random factors. Further, under quite reasonable assumptions, interaction effects of higher order in the dispersion function can be neglected. For example in fractional factorial two-level designs the dispersion function can be written as

$$\sigma_t^2 = \theta_0 + \sum_i \theta_i t_i + \sum_{i<j} \theta_{ij} t_i t_j + \quad \text{interaction terms of higher order.}$$

θ_i is $\neq 0$ if t_i is involved in interactions with random factors. θ_{ij} is $\neq 0$ if there is a random factor Z_m such that t_i and t_j both are interacting with Z_m.

The general model assumed in this paper is

$$Y \sim \text{N}(X\beta, \Sigma_\theta), \quad \Sigma_\theta = \text{diag}(u_1'\theta I_{n_1}, \ldots, u_r'\theta I_{n_r}),$$

where $n_1, \ldots, n_r \geq 1$, $\theta \in R^q$ is the dispersion vector to be estimated and $u_i \in R^q$ is a known vector depending on the design factors.

*Freie Universität Berlin, Institut für Statistik und Ökonometrie, D-1000 Berlin 33, Garystr. 21, Tel.: (030)8384777, Fax.: (030)8382129

Estimation of dispersion effects

For the estimation of the dispersion effects many methods based on least squares or on the likelihood principle are available. The REML estimator — which is the maximum likelihood estimator based on a maximum number of linearly independent error contrasts — is of special interest, since it compensates the loss of freedom associated with preliminary estimation of the location parameters. This is important especially for factorial designs which have many location effects. The REML estimator equals an iteratively reweighted least squares estimator which is adjusted for preliminary estimation of location parameters. Using this iteration process it can easily be calculated. During the iteration negative values for the variance estimations cannot be excluded, but the iteration process converges in the admissible area, if a simple correction is be used. Let $Y = (Y_1', \ldots, Y_r')'$ and $S = (s_1^2, \ldots, s_r^2)'$, where Y_i consists of n_i elements of Y and s_i^2 is the residual variance calculated from the submodel belonging to Y_i. Then the REML equations can be written as

$$U'V_\theta^{-2}(S - U\theta) + \frac{\partial}{\partial\theta}(Y'K_\theta Y + r(\theta)) = 0$$

where $U = (u_1, \ldots, u_r)'$ and $V_\theta = \operatorname{diag}(u_1'\theta/f_1, \ldots, u_r'\theta/f_r)$. $f_1, \ldots, f_r$ denote the degrees of freedom of the residual variances $s_1^2, \ldots, s_r^2$. K_θ is a symmetric matrix and $r(\theta)$ is a real-valued function of θ. It can be shown that $s_1^2, \ldots, s_r^2$ and $Y'K_\theta Y$ are stochastically independent. The first part of the equation, $U'V_\theta^{-2}(S - U\theta)$, can be interpreted as the least squares equation of S using the inner product matrix V_θ^{-2}. Since the latter is strongly depending on θ, the equation is highly nonlinear, causing some difficulties for small samples. An alternative to the REML estimator is the logarithm method based on the logarithmic residual variances (LRV), which minimizes $\sum_{i=1}^r (\ln s_i^2 - \mu_i(\theta))^2/V_i$, where $\mu_i(\theta) = \mathrm{E}_\theta[\ln s_i^2]$ and $V_i = \mathrm{Var}[\ln s_i^2]$. The LRV estimator does not depend on unknown weights — unlike the REML estimator.

Now consider a 2^{k-m}-design with J replications ($J \geq 1$) and two variance levels corresponding to the levels of one of the design factors:

$$\Sigma_\theta = \theta_1 I_N + \theta_2 \operatorname{diag}(-I_{N/2}, I_{N/2}), \quad N = J2^{k-m}. \tag{1}$$

The columns of the design matrix X are pairwise orthogonal and consist of $+1$'s and -1's. For this model the REML equations can be written as

$$\tilde{U}'\tilde{V}_\theta^{-2}(\tilde{S} - \tilde{U}\theta) = 0,$$

where

$$\tilde{U} = \begin{pmatrix} 1 & -1 \\ 1 & 1 \\ 1 & 0 \end{pmatrix}, \quad \tilde{V}_\theta = \operatorname{diag}\left((\theta_1 - \theta_2)^2/f, (\theta_1 + \theta_2)^2/f, \theta_1^2/(N - p - 2f)\right),$$

$N = \sum_{i=1}^r n_i$, $p = \operatorname{rank}(X)$ and $\tilde{S} = (s_1^2, s_2^2, s_3^2)'$. s_1^2 and s_2^2 are the residual variances for the submodels corresponding to the two variance levels and $s_3^2 = \frac{1}{N-p-2f}(Y'Y - Y'X(X'X)^{-1}Y - fs_1^2 - fs_2^2)$. s_1^2 and s_2^2 have the same number f, say, of degrees of freedom. $s_1^2/(\theta_1 - \theta_2)$, $s_2^2/(\theta_1 + \theta_2)$, s_3^2/θ_1 are stochastically independent χ^2-distributed random variables with f, f and $N - p - 2f$ degrees of freedom.

For this model a small simulation study has been performed with the REML estimator and the logarithm method based on s_1^2, s_2^2 and s_3^2. The results show that there are large deviations from the asymptotic distribution for both estimators. Generally, neither the REML nor the LRV estimator is superior. Concerning the MSE[$\hat{\sigma}_i^2$], the REML estimator seems to be better, whereas, concerning the MSE[$\ln \hat{\sigma}_i^2$], the LRV estimator performs better.

To get an impression of the two estimators in more complex dispersion models another simulation study has been performed using a 2^4-design with 4 replications. Here the dispersion model contains three main effects A, B and C and the design matrix X contains all $2^4 - 1$ factorial effects. Hence the REML as well as the LRV estimator depends on the residual variances $s_1^2, \ldots, s_8^2$ only. The results essentially confirm the facts found in the first study.

In general, the coefficient of variation of $\hat{\sigma_i}^2 = u_i'\hat{\theta}$, MSE[$\widehat{\sigma_i^2\theta}$]$/\sigma_i^2$ as well as the MSE of $\ln \hat{\sigma}_i^2$ seems to increase if $\sigma_i^2 / \sum_{j=1}^{r} \sigma_j^2$ is decreasing. That suggests that observations having small variances σ_i^2 contribute much to the estimation of large variances, but, vice versa, observations with large variances contribute not much to the estimation of small variances.

Identification of dispersion effects

Consider a fractional factorial two-level design with the covariance matrix (1). For testing the hypothesis $\mathrm{H}_0 : \theta_2 = 0$ Box and Meyer [1986] propose the test statistic $S(-)/S(+)$, where $S(-)$ and $S(+)$ are the sums of squared residuals on the two levels of the tested factorial effect. The residuals are calculated by a joined regression of both levels. Using the notation as in the section before, this test statistic can be written as

$$\frac{S(-)}{S(+)} = \frac{f s_1^2 + \frac{N-p-2f}{2} s_3^2}{f s_2^2 + \frac{N-p-2f}{2} s_3^2}.$$

s_3^2 is not depending on θ_2 and hence a test based on the statistic s_1^2/s_2^2 is intuitively more powerful than a test based on $S(-)/S(+)$. This has been confirmed by a simulation study. The statistic s_1^2/s_2^2 has the additional advantage that its distribution can be approximated by a F-distribution even if other dispersion effects exist. The degrees of freedom of this F-distribution can be estimated by a function based on unweighted residuals.

The test based on s_1^2/s_2^2 is powerful if there are only a few 'active' dispersion effects, but the power decreases with an increasing number of active dispersion effects. Therefore this test is recommended for small samples only, since for designs with many replications a likelihood ratio test can be used.

References

Box, G. E. P and Meyer, R. D. [1986], Dispersion effects from fractional designs, Technometrics 30, 1-17

Davidian, M. and Carroll, R. J. [1987], Variance function estimation. Journal of the American Statistical Association 82, 1079-1091

Ghosh, S. and Lagergren, E. S. [1990], Dispersion models and estimation of dispersion effects in replicated factorial experiments. Journal of statistical planning and inference 26, 253-262

Rao, C. R. [1979], MINQE theory and its relation to ML and MML estimation of variance components. Sankhya 41, 138-153

Section 9

Micro-Economics and Game Theory

Pure Spatial Competition among Firms with more than one Facility

Horst Behnke
Sozialökonomisches Seminar, Universität der Freien und Hansestadt Hamburg
Von-Melle-Park 5, 2000 Hamburg 13, Germany

Since Hotelling's (1929) famous paper about the competition between two firms on a linear market with equal amount of demand on every point of the line, (where its single Nash equilibrium is given in locating both firms at the midpoint of the line), the model of pure spatial competition has been extended and modificated in many different ways. The main contributions in context to this paper since Hotelling are the following two: Selten (1971) had given the necessary and sufficient conditions for Nash equilibria in the standard Hotelling model extended to n firms. Eaton and Lipsey (1975) had further extended the model to various amounts of demand on the line (beside other variations). In this paper the pure spatial competion model will be analysed for a given number of firms, which each have to locate a given (individual different) number of facilities on the linear market.

Assumptions and notations

The general assumptions and used notations of this model are:

- The market area is bounded line with a given quantity of demand on every of its points. The both boundaries of this line are set to 0 and 1.
- Each of M firms sells a costless produced homogeneous good at every of its N^j, $j=1,..,M$ facilities and ask for the same fob-price.
- The costs of transport from a facility location to another point of the line are a constant rate of the distance between them, so that demand is captured by the nearest facilty. (If two or more facilities are nearest to a point of the line, then every of these facilities would get an equal part of that point's demand).
- For a given constellation formed by L facility locations, P_l ,$l=1,..,L$ are the distances from the left boundary to the locations, where l runs in order from the left boundary to the right. $\forall l$, $l=1,..,L$ the number of facilities which are located at l is denoted by Z_l, and the demand captured by l is denoted by D_l. D_j^i, $j=1,..,M$; $i=1,..,N^j$, is that demand captured by firm j's facility i.

Each of the firms $j=1,..,M$ tries to maximize its sum of captured demand: $D_j := \sum_{i=1}^{N^j} D_j^i$.

This static model must be seen as a n–person constant sum game. Then, all possible combinations of locations for all facilities of a firm are building the set of an infinite number of pure strategies for that firm. (Modifications to sequential games are thinkable, but not subject of this paper.)

Conditions for Nash equilibria

A Nash equilibrium in pure strategies would be given, if no firm j=1,..,M could get a larger D_j by changing the locations of any possible part of its N^j facilities. If demand gets an equal amount at every point of the line, then the following eight conditions would be each necessary, and together sufficient, for a constellation of facilities locations to be a Nash equilibrium in pure strategies. (At which the first five are a new formulation of Selten's (1971) necessary and sufficient conditions for the model of n firms with each one facility.)

a) $Z_l \leq 2$, $\forall l=1,..,L$.

b) $Z_1 = Z_L = 2$.

c) $\forall l$, $l=2,..,L-1$ with $Z_l = 2$ must be fulfiled, that
$(P_l - P_{l-1})/2 = (P_{l+1} - P_l)/2 = P_1 = 1 - P_L$.

d) $\forall l$, $l=2,..,L$ must be satisfied that $P_l - P_{l-1} \leq 2 P_1$.

e) $\forall l$, $l=2,..,L-1$ with $Z_l = 1$ must be fulfiled, that
$(P_l - P_{l-1})/2 + (P_{l+1} - P_l)/2 \leq 2 P_1$.

f) $\forall l$, $l=1,..,L$ with $Z_l=2$ must be fulfiled, that the both facilities are facilities of different firms.

g) $\forall l$, $l=2,..,L-1$ with $Z_l=1$ must be fulfiled, that its facility's firm has no facility at P_{l-1} and no facility at P_{l+1}.

h) $\forall j=1,..,M$ must be fulfiled, that D_j^i is equal for all its facilities $i=1,..,N_j$.

If demand could be of a different amount at different points of the line, the following nine conditions are necessary and sufficient in the above sense. (Without changing the conditions substantially, amount of demand is represented by a integrable function f.)

A) $Z_l \leq 2$, $\forall\, l=1,..,L$.

B) $Z_1 = Z_L = 2$.

C) $\forall l$, $l=2,..,L-1$, with $Z_l = 2$ must be fulfiled, that

$$\int_{x=(P_l-P_{l-1})/2}^{P_l} f(x)\,dt = \int_{x=P_l}^{(P_{l+1}-P_l)/2} f(x)\,dt = \int_{x=P_L}^{1} f(x)\,dt = \int_{x=0}^{P_1} f(x)\,dt\ .$$

D) $\forall l$, $l=2,..,L-1$, with $Z_l = 1$ must be fulfiled, that

$$D_l = \max_{r\in(P_{l-1},P_{l+1})} \int_{x=P_{l-1}+(r-P_{l-1})/2}^{r+(P_{l+1}-r)/2} f(x)\,dt\ .$$

E) For every Interval $(a,b) \in \{[0;P_1],]P_1;P_2[,\ldots,]P_L;1]\}$ must be fulfiled, that

$$\max_{r\in(a,b)} \int_{x=a+(r-a)/2}^{r+(b-r)/2} f(x)\,dt \le \int_{x=0}^{P_1} f(x)\,dt .$$

F) $\forall l$, $l=1,..,L$ with $Z_l = 2$ must be fulfiled, that the both facilities are facilities of different firms.

G) $\forall l$, $l=2,..,L-1$ with $Z_l = 1$ must be fulfiled, that its facility's firm has no facility at P_{l-1} and no facility at P_{l+1}.

H) $\forall l$, $l=2,..,L-1$ with $Z_l = 1$ and the facility is one of firm j's must be fulfiled, that

$$\int_{x=P_{l-1}}^{P_{l-1}+(P_l-P_{l-1})/2} f(x)\,dt + \int_{x=P_l+(P_{l+1}-P_l)/2}^{P_{l+1}} f(x)\,dt \le \min_{i=1,..,N} D_j^i .$$

I) $\forall l$, $l=2,..,L-2$ with $Z_l = 1$ and $Z_{l+1} = 1$ the following must be fulfiled, that

If $D_l > D_{l+1}$, then $D_l - D_{l+1} \le \int_{x=P_l+(P_{l+2}-P_l)/2}^{P_{l+2}} f(x)\,dt$, and

if $D_{l+1} > D_l$, then $D_{l+1} - D_l \le \int_{x=P_{l-1}}^{P_{l-1}+(P_{l+1}-P_{l-1})/2} f(x)\,dt$.

A comparison of conditions and examples for Nash equilrian constellations shows, that every such constellation in the model with multi-facility firms is also a Nash equilibrium in the case where every facility is an own firm, but not ever vice versa.
An extension from the line to finite undirected graphs shows, that this proposition could not maintained. (For this the necessary and sufficient conditions for Nash equilibria for the one-firm–one-facility model are given in Behnke (1990). Based on these conditions, it is possible to construct many necessary conditions for the multi-facility model, but no set of them, what is sufficient.)

References:

Behnke, H. (1990): "Gleichgewicht im Wettbewerb durch Standortwahl auf Straßennetzen", Doctoral Dissertation at: Universität der Freien und Hansestadt Hamburg

Eaton, B.C. /Lipsey, R.G. (1975): "The Principle of Minimum Differentiation Reconsidered: Some New Developments in the Theory of Spatial Competition", Review of Economic Studies 42, 27–49

Hotelling, H. (1929): "Stability in Competition" , Economic Journal 39, 41–57

Selten, R. (1971): "Anwendungen der Spieltheorie auf die politische Wissenschaft", in: Maier, H./Ritter, K./Matz, U. (Ed.): Politik und Wissenschaft, München, 287–320.

CS-Continuity and Separability

Thomas Bradtke
Institut für Statistik und quantitative Ökonomik, Universität der Bundeswehr Hamburg
2000 Hamburg 70, Germany

1. Introduction

Let $x=(x_1,x_2,\dots,x_m) \in X \subseteq \mathbf{R}^m$, $y=(y_1,y_2,\dots,y_n) \in Y \subseteq \mathbf{R}^n$, Φ a real-valued function: $\Phi: X \times Y \to \mathbf{R}$. The **aggregation problem** is to check the existence of functions $f: X \to \mathbf{R}$, $F: f(X) \times Y \to \mathbf{R}$ s. t.:

(1.1) $\Phi(x,y) = F(f(x),y)$ for all $(x,y) \in X \times Y$.

The "classical" central concept for the construction of solution (1.1) is "separability" of Φ. As a new key-concept Mak [1988] suggested to consider instead of "separability" "similarity" for continuous functions:

(1.2) If conditioned on some $y°$ both x' and x'' belong to a connected subset of the boundary of a component of an isoquant (1.3), then conditioned on every y

$\Phi(x',y) = \Phi(x'',y)$; with

(1.3) $\{x | \Phi(x,y°) = \text{constant}\}$ = isoquant conditioned on $y°$, in general composed of components which are disjoint continua.

Pokropp [1986] considered the aggregation problem without assumptions on monotonicity or continuity. He used "local similarity" in a point:

(1.4) If $\Phi(x',y°) = \Phi(x'',y°)$ then $\Phi(x',y) = \Phi(x'',y)$ for all y.

We will extend a result of Färe and Primont [1981] on the distinction between "strict separability", as defined by Debreu [1959], Stigum [1967] and Gorman [1968] and "separability", as defined by Bliss [1975]. Also we will include the term of "similarity". Blackorby, Primont and Russell [1977] showed, that "separability" and "strict separability" are equivalent if one assumes that the function Φ is locally nonsatiated at **every** point in its domain with respect to the separable subset. Färe and Primont [1981] relaxed this to the weaker condition of possibly isolated local-nonsatiation.

All these reflections were given for continuous utility functions. Since analytic assumptions have hardly any economic background, we can discuss the properties quite formally. First we use any analytic assumptions. With the terms of "local-nonsatiation" and "componentwise semi-continuity" (cs-continuity) instead of the stronger term of continuity we are able to clarify the missing link between the different terms of "similarity" and "separability". This is given in the second part of this paper.

2. Assumptions and Definitions

The definition of non-strictly local separability is a generalization of "global" separability defined in Mak (1986) and of the "local" separability of Pokropp (1984).

(2.1) Definition: Let $y^\circ \in Y$. Φ is called **in y° strictly (non-strictly) locally separable** iff $\Phi(x',y^\circ) \leq (<) \Phi(x'',y^\circ)$ implies:

$$\Phi(x',y) \leq \Phi(x'',y) \quad \text{for all } x',x'' \in X, \text{ for all } y \in Y.$$

(2.2) Definition: Let $y^\circ \in Y$. Φ is called **in y° locally similar** iff $\Phi(x',y^\circ) = \Phi(x'',y^\circ)$ implies: $\Phi(x',y) = \Phi(x'',y)$ for all $x',x'' \in X$, for all $y \in Y$.

3. Separability, Strict Separability and Similarity

In the next lemmata without any use of analytic assumptions like continuity or differentiability we will give a map, how the different terms of separability and similarity are interrelated.

(3.1) Lemma: Φ is in y° strictly locally separable implies Φ is in y° locally similar.

Proof : Let $x',x'' \in X$ and $y^\circ \in Y$ with $\Phi(x',y^\circ) = \Phi(x'',y^\circ)$.
This implies the two inequalities: $\Phi(x',y^\circ) \leq \Phi(x'',y^\circ)$ and $\Phi(x'',y^\circ) \leq \Phi(x',y^\circ)$.
From the strict local separability we get:

$$\Phi(x',y) \leq \Phi(x'',y) \text{ and } \Phi(x'',y) \leq \Phi(x',y) \quad \text{for all } y \in Y,$$

but this means $\Phi(x',y^\circ) = \Phi(x'',y^\circ)$ for all $y \in Y$.

■

(3.2) Lemma: Φ is in y° strictly locally separable implies Φ is in y° non-strictly locally separable.

(3.3) Lemma: Φ is in y° non-strictly locally separable and locally similar implies Φ is in y° strictly locally separable.

To complete the picture we introduce some analytic assumptions like "local nonsatiation" and the new concept of "cs-continuity" (see Bradtke [1992]):

(3.4) Definition: Let $z^\circ \in X \times Y$ and $U_\delta(z^\circ) := \{ z \in X \times Y \mid |z-z^\circ| < \delta \}$ be the usual **δ-neighborhood** of a point z° in $X \times Y$. In the same way we define neighborhoods in X and Y.

Φ is called **locally nonsatiated with resp. to X** iff for every $(x^\circ,y^\circ) \in X \times Y$ and every δ-neighborhood $U_\delta(x^\circ)$ there exists a point

$$x^* \in U_\delta(x^\circ) \text{ with:} \qquad \Phi(x^*,y^\circ) > \Phi(x^\circ,y^\circ).$$

(3.5) Definition: Φ is called **componentwise semi-continuous with resp. to X (cs-continuous)** iff for all $x',x'' \in X$ and $y' \in Y$ with $\Phi(x',y') > \Phi(x'',y')$ there exists a δ-neighborhood $U_\delta(x'')$ of x'' with:

$$\Phi(x',y') > \Phi(x^*,y') \qquad \text{for every } x^* \in U_\delta(x'').$$

(3.6) Theorem: Let Φ be locally nonsatiated and cs-continuous with resp. to X. Φ is in y° non-strictly locally separable implies Φ is in y° strictly locally separable.

Proof : From (3.2) we know, that strict local separability in y° implies non-strict local separability in y°. So we only have to show the opposite way:
We assume that there exist x' and $x'' \in X$ for $y^\circ \in Y$ with:

$$\Phi(x',y^\circ) \le \Phi(x'',y^\circ) \qquad \text{(a)}$$

and

$$\Phi(x',y^*) > \Phi(x'',y^*) \qquad \text{(b)},$$

i. e. we assume, that Φ is non-strictly locally separable in y°. This will lead to a contradiction.

From (b) we know, since Φ is cs-continuous, that there exists a δ-neighborhood $U_\delta(x'')$ with:

$$\Phi(x',y^*) > \Phi(x^*,y^*) \qquad \text{for all } x^* \in U_\delta(x'') \qquad \text{(c)}.$$

For this δ-neighborhood $U_\delta(x'')$ there exists, since Φ is locally nonsatiated with resp. to X, a point $x^{**} \in U_\delta(x'')$ with:

$$\Phi(x',y^\circ) \le \Phi(x'',y^\circ) < \Phi(x^{**},y^\circ) \qquad \text{(d)},$$

Since Φ is non-strictly locally separable in y° we get:

$$\Phi(x',y) \le \Phi(x^{**},y) \text{ for all } y \in Y\text{,especially}$$

$$\Phi(x',y^*) \le \Phi(x^{**},y^*) \qquad (e).$$

Since x^{**} lies in $U_\delta(x'')$, we get with (c) :

$$\Phi(x',y^*) > \Phi(x^{**},y^*) \qquad (f).$$

(e) and (f) lead to a contradiction.. ■

(3.7) Lemma: Let Φ be locally nonsatiated and cs-continuous with resp. to X. Φ is in $y°$ non-strictly locally separable implies Φ is in $y°$ locally similar.

All techniques and details of proof can be found in Bradtke [1992].

4. References

Blackorby, Charles/ Primont, Daniel/ Russell, R.Robert [1977] Separability vs functional structure: A characterization of their differences, Journal of Economic Theory, 15, 1977, 135 - 144.

Bliss, C. J. [1975] Capital Theory and the Distribution of Income, North-Holland, Amsterdam, 1975.

Bradtke, Thomas [1992] Separabilität in Funktionen zur Darstellung ökonomischer Prozesse, Doctoral thesis, 1992.

Debreu, G. [1959] Topological methods in cardinal utility theory, in "Mathematical Methods in the Social Sciences" (K. Arrow, S. Karlin, and P. Suppes, Eds.), Stanford University Press, Palo Alto, 1959.

Färe, Rolf / Primont, Daniel [1981] Separability vs functional structure: A Further Result, Journal of Economic Theory, 25, 1981, 455 - 460.

Gorman, W. M. [1968] The structure of utility functions, Review of Economic Studies 35, 1968, 369 - 390.

Mak, King-tim [1986] On Separability: Functional Structure, Journal of Economic Theory, 40, 1986, 250 - 282.

Mak, King-tim [1988] Separability and the Existence of Aggregates, Measurement in Economics ed. by W. Eichhorn, Physica-Verlag Heidelberg, 1988, 649 - 670.

Pokropp, Fritz [1984] The Functional Equation of Aggregation with Weakly Monotonically Increasing Functions, Methods of Operations Research, 48, 1984, 63 - 81.

Pokropp, Fritz [1986] Existence of Aggregates without Monotonicity and Continuity Assumptions, Methods of Operations Research, 57, 1986, 289 - 296.

Stigum, B. P. [1967] On certain problems of aggregation, International Economic Review 8, 1967, 349 - 367.

A Shapley Value for Games with Restricted Coalitions

Jean Derks, Hans Peters
Department of Mathematics, University of Limburg
P.O. Box 616, 6200 MD Maastricht, Netherlands

1. Introduction A *transferable utility game* is a pair (N,v) where $N := \{1,2,\ldots,n\}$ $(n \geq 1)$ is the set of *players* and $v : 2^N \to I\!R$ is a map assigning to each *coalition* $S \subset N$ its *worth* $v(S)$, with $v(\emptyset) := 0$. By way of an example, consider the game $(\{1,2,3\},v)$ with $v(1) = 10$, $v(2) = v(3) = 0$, $v(12) = 20$, $v(13) = 30$, $v(23) = 0$, and $v(N) = 30$ (braces are omitted for simplicity). Here player 1 is the seller of an object who values this object at 10 dollars; 2 and 3 are buyers who value the object at 20 and 30 dollars, respectively. Assuming that the *grand coalition* N will be formed, the question arises how to divide the worth $v(N)$ among the players. A well-known answer to this question was provided by Shapley (1953), now known as the *Shapley value*. The Shapley value assigns the distribution $(21\frac{2}{3}, 1\frac{2}{3}, 6\frac{2}{3})$ to the game $(\{1,2,3\},v)$.

Next suppose (same example) that player 2 can veto the sale of the object. This gives rise to a new game $(\{1,2,3\},w)$ with $w(13) = 10$ and $w(S) = v(S)$ otherwise. The Shapley value assigns the distribution $(18\frac{1}{3}, 8\frac{1}{3}, 3\frac{1}{3})$ to the game $(\{1,2,3\},w)$: This new distribution reflects the additional power of player 2. Observe that the second game arises from the first one by adding constraints on formable coalitions. In the present paper these kinds of constraints are modelled by the concept of a *restriction*, which is defined to be a map $\rho : 2^N \to 2^N$ with the following three properties:

(R1) For all $S \in 2^N$, $\rho(S) \subset S$.

(R2) For all $S,T \in 2^N$, if $S \subset T$ then $\rho(S) \subset \rho(T)$.

(R3) For all $S \in 2^N$, $\rho(\rho(S)) = \rho(S)$.

With each restriction ρ we associate a *restricted Shapley value* φ^ρ by

$$\varphi_i^\rho(N,v) := \sum_{S:S\not\ni i} \frac{|S|!(n-|S|-1)!}{n!}[v(\rho(S\cup\{i\})) - v(\rho(S))]$$

for every $i \in N$. If ρ is the identity, then φ^ρ is the familiar Shapley value (Shapley, 1953; Roth, 1988), and we write φ instead of φ^ρ. Obviously, $\varphi^\rho(N,v) = \varphi(N, v\circ\rho)$ for every restriction ρ and every game (N,v). In the example above, $w = v\circ\rho$ where $\rho(\{1,3\}) = \{1\}$, $\rho(\{3\}) = \emptyset$, and $\rho(S) = S$ otherwise. Apparently, $\varphi(N,w) = \varphi(N,v\circ\rho) = \varphi^\rho(N,v)$, so the Shapley value of (N,w) is obtained by applying an appropriate restricted Shapley value to (N,v).

The present paper focuses on the study of such restricted Shapley values. Its main result is an axiomatic characterization of these values.

2. An axiomatization The axioms to be used in the announced characterization, are formulated for a so-called *value* $\psi : G^N \to \mathbb{R}^N$, where G^N denotes the class of all transferable utility games with player set N. A restriction ρ will not be exogenously given, but endogenously determined by the axioms.

Let S be a coalition. Call S *ψ-essential* if $S = \emptyset$ or for all $v, w \in G^N$ with $v(T) = w(T)$ for all $T \neq S$ we have: if $v(S) \neq w(S)$ then $\psi(v) \neq \psi(w)$. (Here, we write v instead of (N, v) if no confusion is likely to arise.) Call S *ψ-inessential* if $S \neq \emptyset$ and for all $v, w \in G^N$ with $v(T) = w(T)$ for all $T \neq S$ we have: $\psi(v) = \psi(w)$. A player $i \in N$ is a *veto player* in a game v if $v(S) = 0$ for every S with $S \not\ni i$.

Observe that the worth of a nonempty ψ-essential coalition always matters for the distribution $\psi(v)$, whereas the worth of a ψ-inessential coalition never matters. The empty set is defined to be ψ-essential just for convenience; it guarantees the existence of maximal ψ-essential coalitions, i.e., ψ-essential coalitions S such that no proper superset of S is ψ-essential.

The axioms are as follows, for a value ψ.

(A1) Every coalition S is ψ-essential or ψ-inessential.

(A2) If S and T are ψ-essential coalitions, then so is $S \cup T$.

(A3) For every $v \in G^N$, $\sum_{i \in N} \psi_i(v) = v(S)$ for some maximal ψ-essential coalition S.

(A4) For all $v, w \in G^N$ and $i \in N$, if for all S, T with T ψ-essential, $i \in T$ and S a maximal ψ-essential subcoalition of $T \backslash \{i\}$ we have $v(T) - v(S) \geq w(T) - w(S)$, then $\psi_i(v) \geq \psi_i(w)$.

(A5) For every $v \in G^N$ and $i, j \in N$, if i and j are veto players in v, then $\psi_i(v) = \psi_j(v)$.

Axiom A1 excludes the existence of a coalition whose worth is taken into account by ψ in one game but not in some other game. Axiom A2 states that if the worths of coalitions S and T always matter for the determination of ψ, then so should the worth of the union $S \cup T$. Axiom A3 is a generalization of the usual efficiency axiom. Similarly, axiom A4 generalizes the monotonicity axiom proposed by Young (1985). Axiom A5, finally, states that veto players in a game should be treated as equally powerful.

The paper demonstrates that these five axioms characterize the class of restricted Shapley values. The proof of this result is inspired by the characterization of the Shapley value by Young (1985).

THEOREM *Let ψ be a value satisfying A1–A5. Then there exists a unique restriction ρ such that $\psi = \varphi^\rho$. Conversely, every restricted Shapley value satisfies A1–A5.*

3. Related literature Our approach is related to several other ones in literature. Gilles *et al.* (1992) define a ***permission structure*** as a map $F : N \to 2^N$ with the property that if $j \in F(i)$ then $i \notin F(j)$ for all $i, j \in N$. $F(i)$ is interpreted as the subset of immediate "subordinates" or "followers" of player i. Let Ω_F^c denote the collection of those coalitions S with the property that if $i \in S$, then also every j with $i \in F(j)$ is in S, for every $i \in S$. Further, let Ω_F^d denote the collection of those coalitions S with the property that if $i \in S$, then at least one $j \in N$ with $i \in F(j)$ is in S (if such a j exists), for every $i \in S$ (see Gilles and Owen, 1991). It is easily established that both Ω_F^c ("c" for "conjunctive") and Ω_F^d ("d" for "disjunctive") can be derived as the images of appropriate restrictions. Also the variant of the Shapley value proposed by Gilles *et al.* (1992) coincides with our concept of a restricted Shapley value. Their Shapley value can be obtained axiomatically by strengthening the system A1–A5. For instance, by requiring instead of A2 that the collection of ψ-essential coalitions be a discerning lattice (see Derks and Gilles, 1992) the class of Shapley values corresponding to restrictions ρ with image equal to Ω_F^c for acyclic permission structures F would be obtained.

Faigle and Kern (1992) consider cooperative games under precedence constraints, which is equivalent to the conjunctive approach described above with acyclic permission structure. They define and axiomatize a Shapley value for such games, which does *not* coincide with our restricted Shapley value. For instance, their Shapley value does not have to be symmetric for the players of an essential coalition T (i.e., $T \in \Omega_F^c$) in the so-called unanimity game u_T, which assigns 1 to supersets of T and 0 to other coalitions, but instead may reflect the asymmetries inherent in the permission structure F.

Our approach can also be used to define a Shapley value for so-called multi-choice games, as introduced by Hsiao and Raghavan (1990). A multi-choice game is a refinement of a transferable utility game in the sense that each player i has a finite number of "activity levels" $a_0^i < a_1^i \ldots < a_m^i$. Level a_0^i is interpreted as "not present". A *coalition* is an n tuple of activity levels, one for each player, and each coalition is assigned a real number, its worth. One can regard each activity level of each player as a separate player and define a permission structure F by $F(a_j^i) := \{a_{j+1}^i\}$ for every i and every $0 \leq j < m$, $F(a_m^i) := \emptyset$ for every i. This F is acyclic and Ω_F^c contains exactly those "coalitions" which for each activity level of a member also contain all lower activity levels. Such a "coalition" for the extended player set is given the worth of the corresponding coalition in the multi-choice game, obtained by taking for each player his highest activity level occurring in the "coalition" within the extended player set. As before, Ω_F^c is the image of a restriction on the extended player set, to which a restricted Shapley value can be associated. Hsiao and Raghavan (1990) also propose a Shapley value for multi-choice games. Again, theirs is different from ours. Consider a unanimity game, which in this context is determined by a vector $\hat{a} \in A := \times_{i=1}^n \{a_0^i, \ldots, a_m^i\}$ such that a coalition $b \in A$ has worth 1 if $b \geq \hat{a}$, 0 otherwise. A Shapley value as proposed by Hsiao and Raghavan (1990) distributes the worth of the grand coalition (which equals 1) among the levels or "players" occurring in $\hat{a}$, and, in an equal fashion, to all n-tuples of higher levels. Our restricted Shapley value distributes 1 among the levels not exceeding those occurring in $\hat{a}$. In Hsiao and Raghavan's model (and interpretation) each player can only be present at one specific level. In our adaptation of their model (which is equivalent to the adaptation proposed by Faigle and Kern, 1992) the presence of a player at a certain level implies the presence of that player at all lower levels. This distinction largely accounts for the distinction between the respective

Shapley values. In fact, Hsiao and Raghavan's Shapley value may be transformed into our restricted Shapley value for this special context of multi-choice games. This requires an appropriate choice of weights for the Hsiao-Raghavan Shapley value.

Finally, the weighted ordered partitions on which Kalai and Samet (1987) and Nowak and Radzik (1991) base their weighted Shapley values *cannot* be obtained as the image of a restriction: monotonicity (R2) will be violated. Also the class of values recently characterized by Dragan (1992) does not contain our class of restricted Shapley values, since the latter in general do not satisfy the carrier axiom used by Dragan.

4. References

Derks, J.J.M., and Gilles, R.P. (1992): "Hierarchical organization structures and constraints in coalition formation", Working paper, Department of Economics, VPI & SU, Blacksburg.

Dragan, I. (1992): "Multiweighted Shapley values and random order values", Technical Report 286, Department of Mathematics, University of Texas at Arlington.

Faigle, U., and W. Kern (1992): "The Shapley value for cooperative games under precedence constraints", Memorandum 1025, Faculty of Applied Mathematics, University of Twente, The Netherlands.

Gilles, R.P., and G. Owen (1991): "Games with permission structures: the disjunctive approach", Working Paper, Department of Economics, VPI & SU, Blacksburg.

Gilles, R.P., G. Owen, and R. van den Brink (1992): "Games with permission structures: the conjunctive approach", *International Journal of Game Theory*, 20, 277–293.

Hsiao, C.-R., and T.E.S. Raghavan (1990): "Shapley value for multi-choice cooperative games", to appear in *Games and Economic Behavior*.

Kalai, E., and D. Samet (1987): "On weighted Shapley values", *International Journal of Game Theory*, 16, 205–222.

Nowak, A.S., and T. Radzik (1991): "Weighted values for n-person games", to appear in *International Journal of Game Theory*.

Roth, A.E. (ed.) (1988): *The Shapley value: essays in honor of Lloyd S. Shapley*. Cambridge University Press, Cambridge.

Shapley, L.S. (1953): "A value for n-person games". In: A.W. Tucker, H.W. Kuhn (eds.), *Contributions to the Theory of Games II*, 307–317, Princeton University Press, Princeton, NJ.

Young, H.P. (1985): "Monotonic solutions of cooperative games", *International Journal of Game Theory*, 14, 65–72.

Relationships between Bankruptcy Games and Minimum Cost Spanning Tree Games

Theo S.H. Driessen
Department of Applied Mathematics, University of Twente
P.O. Box 217, 7500 AE Enschede, Netherlands

The cost allocation problem of setting charges to the users in a given network is considered with the aid of minimum cost spanning trees in the network. In addition, the bankruptcy problem of dividing the estate of the bankrupt concern among the various creditors according to their claims is treated. The paper aims to establish that, under certain circumstances, the bankruptcy problem can be seen as a minimum cost spanning tree allocation problem. In the game theoretic setting, the paper provides the conditions on the estate and the claims which are sufficient and necessary for the representation of bankruptcy games as minimum cost spanning tree games.

Consider the situation in which one central source (the common supplier) provides institutions or individuals (the users) with certain goods or services. When once the installation costs of the various connections between two different users or a user and the common supplier are determined, they cooperate in the undertaking of a joint installation of a network of connections in order to supply all users. The least cost of undertaking such a joint venture can be achieved by the construction of a minimum cost spanning tree in the complete graph. Now the common supplier is confronted with the cost allocation problem of setting charges to the users. How to allocate the least total installation cost to the users?
The game theoretic approach to the cost allocation problem is based on the notion of a cooperative game in characteristic function form. Let $N = \{1,2,\dots,n\}$ be the set of users and denote the common supplier by 0. It is supposed that the complete graph with node set $N \cup \{0\}$ and undirected edge set $E(N) := \{(i,j) \mid i,j \in N \cup \{0\}, i \neq j\}$ is equipped with a nonnegative weight function $w : E(N) \longrightarrow \mathbb{R}_+$. The weight $w((i,j))$ is interpreted as the installation cost of the connection between the two nodes i and j, or equivalently, of the undirected edge (i,j). Let $\mathcal{P}(N)$ denote the power set of N. The network situation above can be modelled as a cooperative cost game

$\langle N,c\rangle$ whose characteristic cost function $c : \mathcal{P}(N) \longrightarrow \mathbb{R}$ is given by

$$c(S) := \sum_{e \in E_S} w(e) \qquad \text{for all} \quad S \subset N$$

where E_S represents the edge set of

any minimum cost spanning tree on node set $S \cup \{0\}$.

Thus, $c(S)$ equals the least total installation cost to connect merely the members of S with the common supplier, i.e., the cost of a minimum cost spanning tree on S together with the common supplier. The so-called minimum cost spanning tree (mcst) game $\langle N,c\rangle$ was introduced in Bird (1976) and studied in Granot and Huberman (1981) and Aarts and Driessen (1991, 1992).

With the given cost function c we associate the cost savings function v by means of $v(S) := \sum_{i \in S} c(\{i\}) - c(S)$ for any subset S of users. Here the expression $v(S)$ represents the cost savings that would result from cooperation between the members of S instead of acting alone. Evidently, there are no cost savings for individuals, i.e., $v(\{i\}) = 0$ for any user $i \in N$. In view of the cost savings function, one can say the cost allocation problem is similar to the division problem in terms of savings.

A peculiar example of the division problem is the bankruptcy problem. The data of the bankruptcy situation are given by the estate of the bankrupt concern and the claims of the various creditors. The problem is that the claims are mutually inconsistent in that the estate is insufficient to meet all of the claims. The bankruptcy problem can be formulated as a game theoretic division problem by modelling the bankruptcy situation as a cooperative savings game. Let $N = \{1,2,\ldots,n\}$ be the set of creditors and denote the estate of the bankrupt concern and the claims of the n creditors by $E, d_1, d_2, \ldots, d_n$ respectively. Without loss of generality, these n claims may be ordered so that $0 < d_1 \leq d_2 \leq \ldots \leq d_n$ and furthermore, the estate E satisfies $0 \leq E < \sum_{i \in N} d_i$ (otherwise, the bankruptcy problem would not exist). The bankruptcy situation above can be modelled as a cooperative savings game $\langle N,u\rangle$ whose characteristic savings function $u : \mathcal{P}(N) \longrightarrow \mathbb{R}$ is given by

$$u(S) := \max[0,\ E - \sum_{i \in N \setminus S} d_i] \qquad \text{for all} \quad S \subset N.$$

Thus, $u(S)$ equals either zero or what is left of the estate after each creditor outside S is paid his claim. The so-called bankruptcy game $\langle N,u\rangle$ was introduced in O'Neill (1982) and studied in Aumann and Maschler (1985). Throughout the remainder of the paper, we replace the bankruptcy game $\langle N,u\rangle$

by its zero-normalized version <N,v> which is defined by

$$v(S) := u(S) - \sum_{i \in S} u(\{i\}) \qquad \text{for all} \quad S \subset N.$$

The main goal is to state that, under certain conditions on the estate and the claims, the zero-normalized bankruptcy game can be interpreted as the cost savings game arising from a minimum cost spanning tree game. In other words, given the zero-normalized bankruptcy game <N,v>, we look for a mcst game <N,c> satisfying $v(S) = \sum_{i \in S} c(\{i\}) - c(S)$ for all $S \subset N$.

Theorem.
Let $D := \sum_{i \in N} d_i - E$ represent the part of the claims that cannot be met by the estate. The zero-normalized bankruptcy game <N,v> can be represented as the cost savings game arising from a mcst game with user set N if and only if one of the following two conditions is satisfied:

(i) $0 < D \le d_3$

(ii) There exists a unique $k \in \{3,4,\ldots,n-1\}$ such that

$$d_k < D \le d_{k+1} \qquad \text{and} \qquad \sum_{i=1}^{k} d_i \le D.$$

REFERENCES

H.F.M. Aarts and T.S.H. Driessen (1991), A survey on minimum cost spanning tree games. Working Paper No. 1003, Department of Applied Mathematics, University of Twente, Enschede, The Netherlands.

H.F.M. Aarts and T.S.H. Driessen (1992), On the core-invariance of minimum cost spanning tree games. Working paper, Department of Applied Mathematics, University of Twente, Enschede, The Netherlands.

R.J. Aumann and M. Maschler (1985), Game theoretic analysis of a bankruptcy problem from the Talmud, Journal Economic Theory 36, pp. 195-213.

C.G. Bird (1976), On cost allocation for a spanning tree: a game theoretic approach, Networks 6, pp. 335-350.

D. Granot and G. Huberman (1981), Minimum cost spanning tree games, Mathematical Programming 21, pp. 1-18.

B. O'Neill (1982), A problem of rights arbitration from the Talmud, Mathematical Social Sciences 2, pp. 345-371.

Controlled Communication Networks

V. Feltkamp, A. van den Nouweland
Dept. of Econometrics, Tilburg University
P.O. Box 90153, 5000 LE Tilburg, Netherlands

In a cooperative *TU* (Transferable Utility) game (N, v) as modelled by von Neumann & Morgenstern (1944), N is a finite set of players, and the characteristic function v assigns to each subgroup of players a real number which is to be interpreted as the maximal gains this coalition can secure by cooperating.

It is generally assumed that each subgroup of players can form and cooperate. However, this doesn't take into account communication restrictions that may cause deficiencies in cooperation in some coalitions. Myerson (1977) added communication graphs to model non-transitive communication restrictions. In such a graph the vertices are the players and an edge between two players represents the fact that these players can communicate directly. A survey on this subject is given in Borm, Van den Nouweland & Tijs (1991).

Here, we generalize communication situations by starting with an arbitrary graph and a reward function r. We assume that the players control the vertices and edges of the graph through *control games* and introduce three solution concepts for these networks, which we characterize axiomatically and we present a TU-game corresponding to a controlled communication network, and we show that all TU-games can be obtained as such a network game.

Consider a finite undirected graph (V, E) without loops or parallel edges. We assume that for each vertex $v \in V$ a *simple control game* (N, c_v) with *veto players* is given and, similarly, for each edge $e \in E$ a simple control game (N, c_e) with veto players is given. Here, a TU-game (N, c) is called *simple* if $c(S) \in \{0, 1\}$ for all $S \subseteq N$ and $c(N) = 1$. Moreover, a player $i \in N$ is called a *veto* player of the simple game (N, c), denoted by $i \in \text{veto}(c)$, if i can block a positive outcome, i.e. $c(S) = 0$ for all $S \in 2^{N\setminus\{i\}}\setminus\{\emptyset\}$. A coalition $S \subseteq N$ is allowed to use the vertex v if and only if $c_v(S) = 1$. The control games (N, c_e) for edges have a similar interpretation.

Furthermore, we assume that there is a real valued reward function r on subsets of vertices and edges, measuring the economic value of subnetworks. Because edges are to model communication channels, the reward of a network (W, F) should not depend on the edges not in $F(W) := \{\{v,w\} \in F \mid v \in W, w \in W\}$. Moreover, in a network (W,F), we denote W/F the partition of W in *communication components* : $C \subseteq W$ is a component of (W,F) if and only if $(C, F(C))$ is a maximal connected subgraph of $(W, F(W))$. We assume that the reward function is additive with respect to these components, i.e.

$$r(W,F) = \sum_{C \in W/F} r(C, F(C)) \qquad \forall W \subseteq V, \forall F \subseteq E.$$

For simplicity, we assume that r is *zero-normalized*, i.e. $r(\{v\}, \emptyset) = 0$ for all $v \in V$.

A *controlled communication network* is a 6-tuple $\langle N, V, E, \{c_v | v \in V\}, \{c_e | e \in E\}, r\rangle$ as described above. The set of all controlled communication networks with player set N is denoted CCN^N. Let $\mathcal{C} = \langle N, V, E, \{c_v \mid v \in V\}, \{c_e \mid e \in E\}, r\rangle$ be a controlled communication network. The *Myerson value* μ is defined by

$$\mu_i(\mathcal{C}) := \sum_{v \in V : i \in \text{veto}(c_v)} \frac{\Phi_v(V, r_E)}{|\,\text{veto}(c_v)|} \qquad \forall i \in N,$$

where the *vertex game* (V, r_E) is a game in which the vertices are the players, defined by $r_E(W) = r(W, E)$ for all $W \subseteq V$, and where Φ is the value introduced by Shapley (1953). The *position value* π is defined by

$$\pi_i(\mathcal{C}) := \sum_{e \in E : i \in \text{veto}(c_e)} \frac{\Phi_e(E, r_V)}{|\,\text{veto}(c_e)|} \qquad \forall i \in N,$$

where the *edge game* (E, r_V) is a game in which the edges are the players, defined by $r_V(F) = r(V, F)$ for all $F \subseteq E$. Finally the *mixed value* ρ is defined by

$$\rho_i(\mathcal{C}) := \sum_{j \in V \cup E : i \in \text{veto}(c_j)} \frac{\Phi_j(V \cup E, \tilde{r})}{|\,\text{veto}(c_j)|} \qquad \forall i \in N,$$

where the game $(V \cup E, \tilde{r})$ is defined by $\tilde{r}(J) = r(J \cap V, J \cap E)$ for all $J \subseteq V \cup E$.

Some common properties of solution concepts are :

• A solution concept on CCN^N is *efficient* if for each controlled communication network $\mathcal{C}$, the reward $r(V,E)$ is divided among the players.

• A solution concept on CCN^N is *additive* if it is additive with respect to the reward function (ceteris paribus).

• A solution concept on CCN^N has the *superfluous edge property* if the deletion of a superfluous edge does not influence the solution. Here, an edge $e \in E$ is *superfluous for*

$\mathcal{C}$ if $r(V,F) = r(V,F\backslash\{e\})$ for all $F \subseteq E$.

• A solution concept on CCN^N is *anonymous* if for all $\mathcal{C} \in CCN^N$ in which r only depends on the number of non-isolated vertices and edges, the solution is proportional to the veto power of the players over the non-isolated vertices and edges.

• A solution concept on CCN^N is *vertex anonymous* if for all $\mathcal{C} \in CCN^N$ in which r only depends on the number of non-isolated vertices, the solution is proportional to the veto power of the players over the non-isolated vertices.

• A solution concept on CCN^N is *edge anonymous* if for all $\mathcal{C} \in CCN^N$ in which r only depends on the number of edges the solution is proportional to the veto power of the players over the edges.

Theorem

(i) The mixed value ρ is the unique solution concept on CCN^N satisfying efficiency, additivity, the superfluous edge property and anonymity.

(ii) The Myerson value μ is the unique solution concept on CCN^N satisfying efficiency, additivity, the superfluous edge property and vertex anonymity.

(iii) The position value π is the unique solution concept on CCN^N satisfying efficiency, additivity, the superfluous edge property and edge anonymity.

References

• Borm, P., Nouweland, A. van den, and Tijs, S.H. (1991). "Cooperation and communication restrictions: a survey", in: 'Economic Behaviour in an Imperfect Environment', Gilles, R.P. and Ruys, P.H.M. (Eds.), North-Holland, Amsterdam. (To appear)

• Myerson, R.B. (1977). "Graphs and cooperation in games", Math. Oper. Res. 2, 225-229.

• Neumann, J. von and Morgenstern, O. (1944). "Theory of Games and Economic Behavior" (3rd edition, 1953), Princeton University Press, Princeton.

• Shapley, L.S. (1953). "A value for n-person games", in: Contributions to the Theory of Games, II (Eds. Tucker, A.W. and Kuhn, H.), Ann. Math. Studies 28, Princeton University Press, 307-317.

This research was sponsored by the Foundation for the Promotion of Research in Economic Sciences, which is part of the Dutch Organization for Scientific Research (NWO).

Reducing Sequencing Situations

Herbert Hamers, Peter Borm, Stef Tijs
Tilburg University,
P.O. Box 90153, 5000 LE Tilburg, Netherlands

Extended abstract

Curiel, Pederzoli and Tijs (1989) were the first to consider sequencing situations in a game theoretical context by letting each job correspond to an agent and to introduce corresponding cooperative sequencing games. These games were elaborated in Potters, Curiel, Rajendra Prasad, Tijs and Veltman (1990) and Hamers, Borm and Tijs (1992).

In this paper we define generalized sequencing situations, where it is assumed that some jobs need not correspond to an agent, and introduce corresponding generalized sequencing games. Further we introduce a reduction of a sequencing situation to a generalized sequencing situation with respect to a coalition S at an imputation x of the corresponding sequencing game.

Davis and Maschler (1965) defined the reduced game (S, c_S^x) to a coalition S at an imputation x of a cooperative cost game (N, c) by

$$c_S^x(T) = \begin{cases} 0 & \text{if } T = \emptyset \\ \min_{R \subset N \setminus S}(c(T \cup R) - \sum_{i \in R} x_i) & \text{if } T \subset S, T \neq S, T \neq \emptyset, \\ \sum_{i \in S} x_i & \text{if } T = S \end{cases} \tag{1}$$

In generalised one-machine sequencing situations each job has to be processed on one single machine. There exists a set of agents $N = \{1, ..., n\}$ such that each agent owns one job. The set of jobs is denoted by $J = \{1, ..., m\}$ where $n \leq m$. Each job is specified by its ready time $r_j \in [0, \infty)$, the earliest time the processing of a job can begin, and its processing time $p_i \in (0, \infty)$, the time a machine takes to handle the job. We assume that the costs $k_j : [r_j, \infty) \to [0, \infty)$ of a job j only depends on its completion time and is an increasing function. The costs of an agent equal the costs of his job. Furthermore, there is an initial order on the jobs before the processing of the machine starts. By a permutation σ of J we describe the position of a job in the queue. Specifically, $\sigma(j) = k$ means that job j is in position k. An injective mapping $\tau : N \to J$ assigns to each player a job. W.l.o.g. we assume that the intial order of jobs σ_0 is defined by $\sigma_0(j) = j$ for all $j \in J$ and the initial order of agents τ is such that for all $i_1 < i_2$ it holds that $\sigma_0 \circ \tau(i_1) < \sigma_0 \circ \tau(i_2)$. A generalized sequencing game is denoted by $(N, J, \sigma_0, \tau, (r_j, p_j, k_j)_{j \in J})$.

A sequencing situation is a generalized sequencing situation where each job corresponds to a player, i.e. $n = m$. For these sequencing situations Curiel et al. introduced cooperative sequencing games by letting:

$$c(S) = \min_{\pi \in \Pi_S} (\sum_{i \in S} k_i(C(i, \pi)) \quad \text{for all} \quad S \subset N \tag{2}$$

where Π_S is the set of admissible rearrangements of a coalition S and $C(\pi, i)$ the completion time of player i in the order π.

In the same way we introduce here a generalized sequencing game corresponding to a generalized sequencing situation $(N, J, \sigma_0, \tau, (r_j, p_j, k_j)_{j \in J})$. Therefore we define the set of dummy players $D := \{d_1, ..., d_{m-n}\}$ and the one to one mapping $\tau^* : N \cup D \to J$ defined by

$$\tau^*(j) = \tau(j) \quad \text{for all } j \in N, \quad \tau^*(d_1) = \min\{J \backslash \tau^*(N)\} \quad \text{and}$$

$$\tau^*(d_i) = \min\{J \backslash \tau^*(N) \cup \{\tau^*(d_1), ..., \tau^*(d_{i-1})\}\} \quad \text{for all} \quad i \in \{2, ..., m-n\}.$$

If we consider the dummy players as real players then we have transformed a generalised sequencing situation in a sequencing situation. Hence, we can define a sequencing game $(N \cup D, \bar{c})$ like in (2). However, we are only interested in minimizing the costs of the coalitions $S \subset N$. These coalitions can decrease their costs possibly more by making use of jobs that are related to a dummy player. This is reflected in the definition of a generalised sequencing game. Before introducing this game we need some definitions.

Let $S \subset N$. The coalition $S \subset N$ is *connected* with respect to τ^* if for all $i, j \in S$ and $k \in N$ such that $\tau^*(i) < \tau^*(k) < \tau^*(j)$ it holds that $k \in S$.

We define $\max S := \{j \in S \mid j \leq i \text{ for all } i \in S\}$ and $\min S := \{j \in S \mid j \geq i \text{ for all } i \in S\}$.

For convienence we introduce the mapping $\tau^{**} : N \cup D \cup \{0\} \cup \{n+1\} \to J$ defined by $\tau^{**}(i) = \tau^*(i)$ for all $i \in N \cup D$, $\tau^{**}(0) = 1$ and $\tau^{**}(n+1) = m$.

For connected S , the *hull* is defined by

$H(S) := \{a_j \mid \sigma^{**}(\min S - 1) \leq \sigma^{**}(a_j) \leq \sigma^{**}(\max S + 1)$.

For any arbitrary $T \subset N$, the set of components of T with respect to $\tau^*$is denoted by $T/_{\sigma^*}$.
The hull of T is then defined by $H(T) := \bigcup_{S \in T/_{\sigma^*}} H(S)$.

The generalised sequencing cost game (N, c^*) related to a generalized sequencing situation is

$$c^*(S) := \min_{E \subset H(S)} \bar{c}(S \cup E) \quad \text{for all} \quad S \subset N \tag{3}$$

In the following we describe the reduction of a sequencing situation to a generalized sequencing situation to a coalition S at an allocation x. Let $(N, J, \sigma_0, \tau, (r_j, p_j, k_j)_{j \in J})$ be a sequencing situation. Then the reduction to a coalition S results in a generalized sequencing situation by removing the players of $N \backslash S$ from their jobs. Furthermore, the new costfunction $\tilde{k}_i$ is defined by $\tilde{k}_i(t) = k_i(t) - x_i$ for all $i \in N \backslash S$ and $\tilde{k}_i(t) = k_i(t)$ for all $i \in S$. Hence, the reduction yields the generalized sequencing situation $(S, J, \sigma_0, \tau_{|S}, (r_j, p_j, \tilde{k}_j)_{j \in J})$.

We now have the following result

Theorem 1 *Let $(N, J, \sigma_0, \tau, (r_j, p_j, k_j)_{j \in J})$ be a sequencing situation and (N, c) the corresponding sequencing game. Let $(S, J, \sigma_0, \tau_{|S}, (r_j, p_j, \tilde{k}_j)_{j \in J})$ be the reduced generalized sequencing situation to S at x of $(N, J, \sigma_0, \tau_0, r, p, k)$ and (S, c^*) the corresponding generalized sequencing game.*

If $x \in C((N, c))$ then $c^*(T) = c_S^x(T)$ for all $T \subset S$

References:

CURIEL I., PEDERZOLI G. and TIJS S. (1989) Sequencing games, *European Journal of Operational Research* **40**, 344-351.

DAVIS M. AND MASCHLER M. (1965) The kernel of cooperative games, *Naval Research Logistics Research* **50**, 223-259.

HAMERS H., BORM P. and TIJS S.(1992) On the convexity of sequencing games, *Working paper Tilburg University: june 1992*

POTTERS J., CURIEL I., RAJENDRA PRASAD V., TIJS S. and VELTMAN B. (1990), Sequencing and cooperation, *Report 9031, Department of Mathematics Nijmegen.*

Coordination Failure and Endogenous Timing[1]

Sjaak Hurkens
CentER, KUB
P.O. Box 90153, 5000 LE Tilburg, Netherlands

In game theoretic modelling there are generally two problems. The first the problem of leadership. In most models it is assumed either that all players act simultaneously or that the players act in an exogenously given order. In reality it is often the case that it is not clear whether there is a leader, and if so, who is the leader. Therefore I endogenize the timing decision.

The second problem is one of coordination failure. Normal form games can have multiple equilibria. Even when there is a Nash equilibrium that Pareto dominates all other equilibria, coordination failure might occur.

These problems can be resolved by the introduction of endogenous timing, at least if the notion of persistent equilibrium (Kalai and Samet (1984)) is used.

Throughout this paper it is assumed that (S_1, S_2, u_1, u_2) is a two person normal form game, where S_i is the finite set of pure strategies of player i and $u_i : S_1 \times S_2 \to \mathbf{R}$ is the payoff function for player i. Let Σ_i be the set of mixed strategies of player i and let $\Sigma = \Sigma_1 \times \Sigma_2$. One extends u_i to Σ in a natural way. If $\sigma = (\sigma_1, \sigma_2) \in \Sigma$ and $\bar{\sigma}_i \in \Sigma_i$ then $\sigma|\bar{\sigma}_i$ denotes the strategy combination where i plays $\bar{\sigma}_i$ and $j \neq i$ plays σ_j. σ_i is a best reply against $\tau \in \Sigma$ if for all $\bar{\sigma}_i \in \Sigma_i$: $u_i(\tau|\sigma_i) \geq u_i(\tau|\bar{\sigma}_i)$. Moreover, we say that $\sigma = (\sigma_1, \sigma_2)$ is a best reply against τ if σ_1 and σ_2 are. Let BR(τ) denote the set of best replies to τ.

Definition 1 *(Kalai and Samet (1984))*
A retract is a cartesian product $R = R_1 \times R_2$ where $R_i \subset \Sigma_i$ is non-empty, convex and compact. A retract R is said to absorb $A \subset \Sigma$ if for all $\tau \in A$: $BR(\tau) \cap R \neq \emptyset$. That is, for every strategy combination in A there is a best reply in the retract. A retract

[1]This research was sponsored by the foundation for the Promotion of Research in Economic Sciences, which is part of the Netherlands Organization for Scientific Research (NWO).

is called a Nash retract if it absorbs itself. A retract is called absorbing if it absorbs a neighbourhood of the retract. An absorbing retract is called a persistent retract (PR) if it does not properly contain an absorbing retract. A Nash equilibrium that is contained in a persistent retract is called a persistent equilibrium (PE).

The following theorem summarizes the main results of Kalai and Samet (1984).

Theorem 1 *Every game has a persistent retract. Every persistent retract contains a proper Nash equilibrium. If (σ_1, σ_2) is in a persistent retract then σ_1 and σ_2 put no weight on dominated strategies. If no player has equivalent strategies among his undominated pure strategies then every persistent retract is of the form $co(\tilde{S}_1) \times co(\tilde{S}_2)$, where $\tilde{S}_i$ is a subset of the pure undominated strategies of player i. If no player has equivalent strategies among his undominated pure strategies then two distinct persistent retracts are disjoint.*

Let $\gamma = (S_1, S_2, u_1, u_2)$ be a two person normal form game. Throughout this paper we have $S_1 = \{a_1, \cdots, a_n\}$ and $S_2 = \{b_1, \cdots, b_m\}$. Furthermore we have that

Assumption 1 *For every pure strategy a_i (b_j) there is a unique best reply $b(a_i) \in S_2$ ($a(b_j) \in S_1$).*

For games that satisfy this assumption we will construct an associated game Γ. The only difference between Γ and γ is that in Γ each player is free to carry out his action in one of two periods. This implies that if one player acts in the first period and the other in the second period the latter can observe the action of the first player. Obviously, the second player will then play his best response. Then $\Gamma = (\Phi_1, \Phi_2, v_1, v_2)$ where $\Phi_1 = \{a_{11}, \ldots, a_{n1}, \tilde{a}_{12}, \cdots, \tilde{a}_{n2}\}$, $\Phi_2 = \{b_{11}, \ldots, b_{m1}, \tilde{b}_{12}, \cdots, \tilde{b}_{m2}\}$, $v_k(a_{i1}, b_{j1}) = v_k(\tilde{a}_{i2}, \tilde{b}_{j2}) = u_k(a_i, b_j)$, $v_k(a_{i1}, \tilde{b}_{j2}) = u_k(a_i, b(a_i))$, $v_k(\tilde{a}_{i2}, b_{j1}) = u_k(a(b_j), b_j)$

Here one should interpret strategy $\tilde{a}_{i2}$ as playing a_i in period 2 if the other player did not act in period 1 and playing $a(b_j)$ if the other player played b_j in period 1. (Similar for strategy $\tilde{b}_{j2}$.)

Let γ^i be the game derived from γ by letting player i be the leader and player $j \neq i$ be the follower. In γ^i player j observes player i's action.

Definition 2 *γ is an Anonymous Stackelberg game with outcome (a, b) if the following holds*

(1) γ^1 has a unique subgame perfect equilibrium (s, f)

(2) γ^2 has a unique subgame perfect equilibrium (t, g)

(3) $s = a = g(b)$ and $t = b = f(a)$

The main result of this paper is the following theorem.

Theorem 2 *Let γ be an Anonymous Stackelberg game with outcome (a_1, b_1). Then every persistent equilibrium of Γ yields player k $(k = 1, 2)$ a payoff of at least $u_k(a_1, b_1)$.*

Definition 3 *(Aumann and Sorin (1989))*

γ is a Common Interest game with outcome (a, b) if for $k = 1, 2$ and for all $(s, t) \neq (a, b)$ $u_k(a, b) > u_k(s, t)$.

Common Interest games are special cases of Anonymous Stackelberg games. Now we have the following reformulation of theorem 2 for Common Interest games.

Theorem 3 *Let γ be a Common Interest game with outcome (a_1, b_1). Then every persistent equilibrium of Γ yields player k $(k = 1, 2)$ a payoff of exactly $u_k(a_1, b_1)$.*

Thus far the problem of coordination failure has not been solved entirely, because there might be a multiplicity of persistent retracts and equilibria.

Theorem 4 *Let γ be a Common Interest game in which no player has equivalent strategies among his pure undominated strategies. Then Γ has a unique persistent retract.*

REFERENCES

Aumann R. and Sorin S. (1989). Cooperation and bounded recall. Games and economic behavior, 1, 5-39.

Kalai E. and Samet D. (1984). Persistent equilibria in strategic games. International journal of game theory, 13, 129-144.

A Decision Support System for Negotiations on Financing of the Public Divisible Good

Andrzej Jakubowski
Systems Research Institute, Polish Academy of Sciences
Newelska 6, 01-447 Warsaw, Poland

Computer-aided multistage negotiation procedure for collective decision making is presented. One main task of multi-person decision making is considered. This is connected with the choice of the quantity and financing of the public divisible good. It is assumed that the collective members differ in their opinions on the amount of this public good to be produced (or purchased) as well as on the share of total cost.

For instance, such a situation takes place when a decision on the purchase of a plot necessary for some joint venture (university, recreational center, repair shop etc) is to be made - or a joint construction (sewage treatment plant, water reservoir etc) is to be financed.

The collective decision making problem is defined as follows. There is a collective, whose members (referred to as participants, negotiators or individuals) intend to realize a joint venture (called throughout the public good) and conditions of it are to be established on the basis of collective agreement. In other words, a collective reaches an agreement, when the outcome of the decision process is some compromise solution with respect to individual preferences of its members.

It is assumed that participants have to contribute the private good (it is to be understood more generally, i.e. it can be measured not only in monetary units) for the provision of public one. To solve this problem the computerized multistage negotiation procedure is considered. The procedure makes it possible to reveal the preference of each participant for the public good and gives him a possibility to change his decisions - at a given step of negotiations - on the basis of information on the behaviour of others.

We assume that: (i) the quantity of the private good the participant is willing to pay for the public one (i.e. his bid) reveals his preference for it; (ii) each participant knows the utility of the public good to himself but does not know its utility to others; (iii) the participants behave competitively.

Taking into account that in general, the negotiation procedures used to solve these problems can be considered as realizations of noncooperative multistage games with non-zero sum of payments, different types of equilibrium for such games are discussed. The economical interpretation of these equilibrium conditions is given. The formalized approach is applied and some specific types of the collective members' utility functions are expressed in mathematical terms. Some special cases, in which the negotiators' objectives can be described in the form of the preference orderings only, are also taken into account.

So called Free-Rider (manipulation) problem is then analysed. It is related to false reporting - by some of the collective members - their preferences announced at the successive steps of negotiations; such a behaviour is aimed at misleading of other individuals. The examples, illustrating - the Free-Rider versus "fair" - behaviour of particular negotiators, are presented. Some procedures making it possible to prevent the Free-Rider behaviour are discussed.

It is generally believed that an application of the computer-aided negotiation supporting systems would be significantly advantageous for effective functioning of various democratic institutions, in which collective decisions are very often made. These systems can facilitate - usually very tedious - negotiations on the institution current activity, desired outcomes and future development. Some compromise solutions, taking into account - to maximal possible extent - the preferences of particular individuals - are necessary for practical implementation of such ideas as active participation, partnership, economic democracy, etc. From the above it immediately follows that the implementation of presented research would be helpful for the construction of democratic institutions and their analysis.

The results obtained extend those achieved by de Bruin (1991), Groves, Ledyard (1977), Jakubowski (1991), Jakubowski, Kulikowski,

Wagner (1987), Kulikowski, Jakubowski (1986), Marwell, Ames (1979), Smith (1977, 1979, 1980), Sweeny (1973) and others.

Keywords: Collective decision making, Public goods, Competitive behaviour, Conflict resolution, Negotiation procedure, Multistage game, Equilibrium conditions, Active participation.

References:

de Bruin G P (1991), Decision - Making on Public Goods. Het Spinhuis, Amsterdam.

Groves T, Ledyard J (1977), Optimal allocation of public goods - a solution to the Free-Rider problem. Econometrica 45: 783-809.

Jakubowski A (1991), Collective decision making problems and their interactive solution. Automatic Control in the Service of Mankind, Proc. of the 11-th IFAC World Congress, V. Utkin and U. Jaaksoo, Eds., Pergamon Press, Oxford, 6: 118-124.

Jakubowski A, Kulikowski R, Wagner D (1987), Allocation of research funds in competitive environment - a computerized negotiation system. Scientometrics, Elsevier, Amsterdam, 12: 179-196.

Kulikowski R, Jakubowski A (1986), Interactive systems for collective decision making. Systems analysis, Modelling and Simulation, 3: 13-28.

Marwell G, Ames R (1979), Experiments on the provision of public goods - resources, interests, group size and the Free-Rider problem. American J. of Sociology, 84: 1335-1360.

Smith V (1977), The principle of unanimity and voluntary consent in social choice. J. of Political Economy, 85: 1125-1139.

Smith V (1979), Incentive compatible experimental process for the provision of public goods. In: Research in Experimental Economics, V. Smith, Ed., Greenwich, Conn., JAI Press, 1: 59-169.

Smith V (1979), An experimental comparison of three public good decision mechanisms. Scandinavian J. of Economics, 3: 198-215.

Smith V (1980), Experiments with a decentralized mechanism for public good decisions. The American Economic Review, 70: 584-599.

Smith V (1980), Relevance of laboratory experiments to testing resource allocation theory. In: Evaluation of Econometric Models, J. Kmenta, Ed., Academic Press, 345-377.

Sweeny J (1973), Experimental investigation of the Free-Rider problem. Social Science Research, 2: 277-292.

The Consumer Budget Set: The Meaning of a Mathematical Transformation

Theo Junius, Klaas Nevels
Department of Econometrics, University of Groningen
P.O. Box 800, 9700 AV Groningen, Netherlands

1. INTRODUCTION

For the purpose of explaining first-order conditions El-Hodiri presents an example[1] in which a standard utility maximization problem is regarded as a mathematical transformation of a nonlinear programming problem defined on the semi-positive orthant in $\mathbb{R}^{n+1}$.
The mathematical model of El-Hodiri reads

$$(1) \quad \tilde{z}(p, M) = argmax\,[g_{p,M}(\tilde{z})\; s.t.\; \tilde{z} \geq 0, \tilde{z} \neq 0]$$

where $\tilde{z} = (z_0, z_1, \ldots, z_n) = (z_0, z)$, the (extended vector) $\tilde{z}$ is an $n+1$-vector of **transformation** variables, the relationship between a specific consumption plan, say $x \in \mathbb{R}^n$ and the related vector of transformation variables $\tilde{z}$ is given by a mapping $h_{p,M}$, i.e. $x = h_{p,M}(\tilde{z})$, $h : \mathbb{R}^{n+1} \rightarrow \mathbb{R}^n$. The objective function in terms of the transformation variables z_i, $i = 0, \ldots, n$ is given by $g_{p,M}(\tilde{z}) = u(h_{p,M}(\tilde{z}))$, where $u(x)$ is a utitlity function.

On the one hand, the advantage of El-Hodiri's procedure is that the first-order necessary conditions for a nonlinear programming problem over the nonnegative orthant in $\mathbb{R}^{n+1}$ are of a more handsome character compared with the first-order conditions for a nonlinear programming problem over a simplex. One can e.g. obtain first-order necessary conditions without using the Lagrange-function and without using the related Kuhn-Tucker conditions. Furthermore, it is interesting to note that the introduction of the mapping $h_{p,M}$ is an example from the field of **projective geometry**. On the other hand we are of opinion that, when applying his procedure to a standard utility maximization problem, El-Hodiri *(i)* insufficiently explains the mathematical background of his transformation method and *(ii)* gives no information concerning the economic interpretation of the transformation variables $z_i, i = 0, \ldots, n$, and *(iii)* makes number of serious analytical mistakes. The main purpose of this paper is to extend the analysis of El-Hodiri, such that the the two first objections are removed.

[1] M.A. El-Hodiri, Extrema of Smooth Functions: with Applications from Economic Theory, Springer-Verlag, 1991, chapter 1.

2. MATHEMATICAL PROPERTIES

Without further explanation El-Hodiri proposes[2] to consider the following concrete specification of the transformation function $h_{p,M}$:
Let $0 \neq \tilde{z} = (z_0, z) \geq 0$ be fixed. The mapping $x = h_{p,M}(\tilde{z})$ is given by

(2) $$x_i(\tilde{z}) = Mz_i/[z_o + \sum_{j=1}^{n} p_j z_j]$$

with $i = 1, \ldots, n$. Below we present the mathematical proporties of the transformation (2). In the next section we deal with the economic interpretation of the transformation magnitudes z.

We now list a number of mathematical properties which can be easily obtained from eq. (2).
THEOREM 1:
The transformation $x = T(\tilde{z})$ is **homogeneous of degree zero** with respect to $\tilde{z}$. Which implies that for any scalar $t \geq 0, x := T(t\tilde{z}) = T(\tilde{z})$.

THEOREM 2:
1. Let $z_0 = 0, z \gg 0$, then $px = pz = M$.
2. Let $z_0 = z_j = 0, z_i > 0, j \neq i$ then $x_j = 0, x_i = M/p_j$.
3. Let $z_0 \neq 0 \neq z_i, z_j = 0$, then $x_i = z_i M/[z_0 + p_i z_i] < M/p_i$, $p_j = 0$.
4. Let $z_0 \neq 0$, $z = 0$, then $x = 0$; hence if $z_i = 0$, for each $i \geq 1$, then the consumer does not consume any commodity.
5. Let $\tilde{z} \gg 0$, then $x \in$ interior of the budget set $\{x : px \leq m, x \, geq \, 0\}$.

From properties 1 and 2 one can deduce that any element x of the budget set is the unique image of some half-ray $\tilde{z}$ in the nonnegative orthant in $\mathbb{R}^{n+1}$.

3. ECONOMIC IMPLICATIONS

In the last section we observed that the transformation (2) has the property of homogeneity of degree 0. An implication of this property is that we can normalize the vector $\tilde{z}$. For that purpose we assume that the transformation vector $\tilde{z}$ is restricted to $\tilde{z} \in \tilde{Z}(p)$, where for given $p \gg 0, M > 0$ the set

(3) $$\tilde{Z}(p) = \{\tilde{z} \in \mathbb{R}^{n+1} : z_0 + \sum_{j=1}^{n} p_j z_j = 1, \; z_i \geq 0, i = 0, \ldots, n\}$$

I.e., for any $\tilde{z} \neq 0$ there exists a scalar $t > 0$ and a $\tilde{z}' \in \tilde{Z}$, such that (a) $\tilde{z} = t\tilde{z}'$ and (b) if $\tilde{z}$ is a solution of problem (1), then $\tilde{z}'$ is a solution of problem (1.

[2]See El-Hodiri, 1991, chapter 1, p. 20.

Observe *(i)* that $\tilde{Z}(p)$ is an n-dimensional simplex in $\mathbb{R}^{n+1}$ and *(ii)* that $\tilde{Z}(p)$ functionally depends on the price vector p. Eq. (3) will be the basis for an economic interpretation of the magnitudes z_i, $i = 1, \ldots, n$.

Let $(x(p, M), \tilde{z}(p, M))$ be an equilibrium of our consumer, i.e. and the vector $\tilde{z}(p, M)$ solves eq. (1). It is obvious that for $i = 1, \ldots, n$ we have $z_i(p, M) = x_i(p, M)/M$. I.e. for $i \neq 0$ the magnitude z_i can be interpreted as the purchase of commodity i per unit disposable liquidity[3].

Next, multiply each equation in (2) by p_i and sum over i. After rearranging we obtain $pz(p, M) = px(p, M)/M$. Hence $pz(p, M)$ meassures **the fraction of disposable income used for commodity purchases.** It is obvious to interprete each term $p_i z_i(p, M)$ as **the fraction of disposable income attributed to the purchase of commodity** i. Furthermore, we conclude that $z_0(p, M) = 1 - pz(p, M)$. So the magnitude $z_0(p, M)$ may be interpreted as **the fraction of disposable liquidity not used for commodity purchases.** Recall that if $z_0(p, M) = 0$ then $px(p, M) = M$. If $z_0(p, M) > 0$ then $x(p, M) < M$, the consumer is **satiated** at a consumption plan in the **interior** of the budget set $B(p, M)$. In contrast with the analysis of El-Hodiri, no smoothness conditions have been used.

4. FINAL REMARKS

As general conclusions we state the following. Firstly, from a mathematical point-of-view the transformation method is interesting, in particular its link with projective geometry. Secondly, from an economic point-of-view the transformation method of El-Hodiri is in our view only of minor importance, since El-Hodori's approach does not fit very well into the modern (dual) approach to microeconomics, which can be used so efficiently for e.g. the measurement of preferences and the derivation of comperative statics results[4].

[3]Let $v(p, M) = u(x(p, M))$ be differentiable, then the application of Roy's Identity yields $z_i(p, M) = -(\partial v/\partial p_i)/M(\partial v/\partial M)$.

[4]For an overview see L.G. Epstein, Generalized Duality and Integrabilty, Econometrica, 49 (3), 1981, 655-678.

Correlated Equilibria in Nonzero-Sum Stochastic Games

Andrzej S. Nowak
Institute of Mathematics, Technical University of Wrocław
Wybrzeże Wyspiańskiego 27, 50–370 Wrocław, Poland

Nonzero-sum stochastic games play an increasing role in studying various dynamic economic models. In most mentioned applications it is assumed that the state spaces of the games are uncountable. For a broad discussion on these topics we refer the reader to [2], [3] and their references. The aim of this presentation is to report some correlated and/or Nash equilibrium theorems for a large class of nonzero-sum stochastic games with a continuum of states contained in [11], [12], and [13].

The stochastic game model.

An N-person nonzero-sum stochastic game is defined by the following objects: S, X_k, r_k, q, where

(1) S is the state space for the game and is assumed to be a non-empty Borel subset of a complete separable metric space.

(2) X_k is a non-empty compact metric space of actions for player k. We put $X = X_1 \times \cdots \times X_N$.

(3) $r_k : S \times X \to R$ is a bounded Borel measurable payoff function for player k. It is assumed that $r_k(s, \cdot)$ is continuous on X, for every $s \in$ S.

(4) q is a Borel measurable transition probability from $S \times X$ to S, called the law of motion among states. If s is a state at some stage of the game and the players select an $x \in X$, then $q(\cdot \mid s, x)$ is the probability distribution of the next state of the game. We assume that the transition probability q has a density function, say z, with respect to some probability measure μ on S, satisfying the following L_1 continuity condition:

For any sequence of joint action tuples $x^n \to x^o$,

C: $\int_S \mid z(s,t,x^n) - z(s,t,x^o) \mid \mu(dt) \to 0$ as $n \to \infty$.

A strategy for player k is a sequence $\pi_k = (\pi_k^1, \pi_k^2, \ldots)$, in which π_k^n is the probability distribution on X_k , depending (in a Borel measurable way) on the entire history of the game up to its n-th stage. A stationary strategy for player k is a constant sequence $(f, f, \ldots)$ in which f is a Borel measurable transition probability f from S to X_k. Using such a strategy f, player k selects (on any stage of the game) an action in X_k according to the probability distribution $f(\cdot \mid s)$ if the game is in state $s \in S$, no matter what was the history leading to the state s. Thus, a stationary strategy $(f, f \ldots)$ for player k can be identified with the Borel measurable transition probability f from S to X_k. For each strategy profile $\pi = (\pi_1, \ldots, \pi_N)$ of the players, any initial state $s \in S$, and any stage n of the game, we write $r_k^n(\pi)(s)$ to denote the n-stage expected payoff to player k corresponding to π. The average payoff per unit time for player k is defined as

$$E_k(\pi)(s) = \limsup_{T\to\infty}[\sum_{n=1}^{T} r_k^n(\pi)(s)]/T,$$

and if β is a fixed real number in (0, 1), called the discount factor, then we can also consider the β-discounted expected payoff to player k defined as

$$E_k^\beta(\pi)(s) = \sum_{n=1}^{\infty} \beta^{n-1} r_k^n(\pi)(s).$$

Let $\pi^* = (\pi_1^*, \ldots, \pi_N^*)$ be a fixed strategy profile of the players. For any strategy π_k of player k, we write (π_{-k}^*, π_k) to denote the strategy profile obtained from π^* by replacing π_k^* by π_k .

A strategy profile $\pi^* = (\pi_1^*, \ldots, \pi_N^*)$ is called a Nash equilibrium for the average payoff stochastic game if no unilateral deviations from it are profitable, that is,

$$E_k(\pi^*)(s) \geq E_k(\pi_{-k}^*, \pi_k)(s),$$

for every player k, any his strategy π_k , and for all $s \in S$.

Of course, Nash equilibria are analogously defined for the β-discounted stochastic games.

It is still an open problem whether the β-discounted stochastic games with uncountable state space have stationary equilibrium solutions. A positive answer to this problem is known only for some special classes of games, where the transition probabilities are state independent [14], satisfy certain additional separability assumptions [7], or together with the payoff functions satisfy some other specific conditions (see [3] and the references therein). Whitt [15] and Nowak [10] proved the existence of stationary ϵ-equilibrium strategies in discounted stochastic games using some (different) approximations by games with countably many states. The assumptions on the model in [10] are as in (1) - (4) and **C** above plus some extra integrability condition for the transition probability density. Whitt [15] imposed some uniform continuity conditions on the payoffs and transition probabilities. Recently, Mertens and Parthasarathy [9] proved the existence of non-stationary Nash equilibria for discounted stochastic games with uncountable state space without any absolute continuity assumption concerning the law of motion q.

Correlated equilibria with public signals.

We now extend the sets of strategies available to the players in the sense that we allow them to correlate their choices in a natural way described below. The resulting solution (which we obtain for stochastic games) is a kind of extensive-form correlated equilibrium (see Forges [5]). Let $\{\xi_n : n \geq 1\}$ be a sequence of so-called signals, drawn independently from [0, 1] according to the uniform distribution. Suppose that at the beginning of each period n of the game the players are informed not only of the outcome of the preceding period and the current state s_n, but also of ξ_n. An extended strategy for player k is a sequence $(\pi_k^1, \pi_k^2, \ldots)$, in which π_k^n depends on the entire history of the game up to stage n and also on the random signals $\xi_1, \ldots, \xi_n$. An extended stationary strategy for player k is a transition probability f from $S \times [0,1]$ to X_k. If s_n , and ξ_n represent the state and the signal observed at the beginning of the n-th period of the game, then, using such a strategy f, player k selects an action in X_k according to the probability distribution $f(\cdot \mid s_n, \xi_n)$.A Nash equilibrium in extended strategies is also called a correlated equilibrium with public signals. The reason is that after the outcome of any period of the game, the players can coordinate their next choices by exploiting the next (known to all of them, i.e.,public) signal. The following result was proved by the author and Raghavan [13].

THEOREM 1: *Every nonzero-sum discounted stochastic game satisfying* (1) - (4) *and* **C** *has a stationary correlated equilibrium with public signals.*

A related result is reported by Duffie et al. in [2]. They use some stronger assumptions on the primitive data of the game, but showed that there exists a stationary correlated equilibrium which induces an ergodic process. To state our second result we need some additional assumptions on the transition probability q. For any stationary strategy profile f and $n \geq 1$, let $q^n(\cdot \mid s, f)$ denote the n-step transition probability determined by q and f.

GE(Geometric Ergodicity): There exist scalars $\alpha \in (0,1)$ and $\gamma > 0$ for which the following holds: For any stationary strategy profile f of the players, there exists a probability measure p_f on S such that

$$\| q^n(\cdot \mid s, f) - p_f(\cdot) \|_\nu \leq \gamma\alpha^n \text{ for each } n \geq 1.$$

Here $\| \cdot \|_\nu$ denotes the total variation norm in the space of probability measures on S.

It is well-known that **GE** follows from the following assumption: There exists a positive integer p, a constant $\vartheta > 0$, and a positive measure δ on S, such that $q^p(D \mid s, f) \geq \vartheta\delta(D)$, for every stationary strategy profile f, any $s \in S$, and for each Borel set $D \subseteq S$.

It is also well-known that **GE** is equivalent to the following condition: There exist a positive integer r and a positive number $\delta < 1$ such that

$$\| q^r(\cdot \mid s, f) - q^r(\cdot \mid t, f) \|_\nu \leq 2\delta,$$

for all $s, t \in S$, and for every stationary strategy profile f of the players. There are many other equivalent formulations of **GE** and also some natural and easier to verify conditions (known in the theory of Markov decision processes) which essentially reduce to **GE**. For a detailed discussion consult [1], [6], [8], [12], and their references.

For a proof of the following result see [12].

THEOREM 2: *Every nonzero-sum average payoff stochastic game satisfying* (1) - (4) *and* **GE** *has a stationary correlated equilibrium with public signals.*

In [12], we apply Theorem 2 to some special classes of nonzero-sum average payoff stochastic games (considered in [7] and [14] with the discounted payoff criterion) and prove that they have stationary Nash equilibria without public signals. An existence theorem contained in [3] is concerned with a different class of games. As shown by Federgruen [4], stationary equilibria without public signals also exist in stochastic games with countably many states. Of course, **GE** is also assumed in [4]. As far as 2-person zero-sum games are concerned, we can drop our assumption that $q \ll \mu$ and also **GE** can be essentially weakened. For a detailed exposition see [11].

REFERENCES

[1] CAVAZOS-CADENA. R. (1991). Recent Results on Conditions for the Existence of Average Optimal Stationary Policies. Annals of Operations Research 28, 3-28.

[2] DUFFIE, D., GEANAKOPLOS, J., MAS-COLELL, A., and McLENNAN, A.(1988). Stationary Markov Equilibria. Technical Report, Dept. Economics, Harvard University.

[3] DUTTA, P.K. and SUNDARAM, R. (1992). Markovian Equilibrium in a Class of Stochastic Games: Existence Theorems for Discounted and Undiscounted Models. Economic Theory 2.

[4] FEDERGRUEN, A.(1978). On N-Person Stochastic Games with Denumerable State Space. Adv. Appl. Probab. 10, 452-471.

[5] FORGES, F.(1986). An Approach to Communication Equilibria. Econometrica 54, 1375-1385.

[6] HERNANDEZ-LERMA, O., MONTES-DE-OCA, R., and CAVAZOS-CADENA, R. (1991). Recurrence Conditions for Markov Decision Processes with Borel State Space: a Survey. Ann. Oper. Res. 28, 29-46.

[7] HIMMELBERG, C.J., PARTHASARATHY, T., RAGHAVAN, T.E.S., VAN VLECK, F.S.(1976). Existence of p-Equilibrium and Optimal Stationary Strategies in Stochastic Games. Proc. Amer. Math. Soc. 60, 245-251.

[8] HORDIJK, A.(1977). Dynamic Programming and Markov Potential Theory. Math. Centre Tracts 51, Math. Centrum, Amsterdam.

[9] MERTENS, J.-F., and PARTHASARATHY, T.(1987). Equilibria for Discounted Stochastic Games. CORE Discussion Paper No. 8750, Universite Catholique de Louvain.

[10] NOWAK, A.S.(1985). Existence of Equilibrium Stationary Strategies in Discounted Noncooperative Stochastic Games with Uncountable State Space. J. Optim. Theory Appl. 45, 591-602.

[11] NOWAK, A.S. (1992). Zero-Sum Average Payoff Stochastic Games with General State Space. Games and Economic Behavior (forthcoming).

[12] NOWAK, A.S. (1992). Stationary Equilibria for Non-Zero-Sum Average Payoff Ergodic Stochastic Games with General State Space. Technical Report, Institute of Mathematics, Techn. University of Wroclaw.

[13] NOWAK, A.S. and RAGHAVAN, T.E.S.(1992). Existence of Stationary Correlated Equilibria with Symmetric Information for Discounted Stochastic Games. Math. Oper. Res. 17, 519-526.

[14] PARTHASARATHY, T. and SINHA, S.(1989). Existence of Stationary Equilibrium Strategies in Non-Zero-Sum Discounted Stochastic Games with Uncountable State Space and State Independent Transitions. Internat. J. Game Theory 18, 189-194.

[15] WHITT, W.(1980). Representation and Approximation of Noncooperative Sequential Games. SIAM J. Control Optim. 18, 33-48.

On the Core of a Set of Coalitions

Hans Reijnierse
Department of Mathematics, University of Nijmegen
6525 ED Nijmegen, Netherlands
Jean Derks
Dept. of Mathematics, Rijksuniversiteit Limburg
P.O. Box 616, 6200 MD Maastricht, Netherlands

EXTENDED ABSTRACT

1 Introduction.

A *restricted cooperative game* (N, Ω, v) is a triple consisting of a (finite) player set N, a collection Ω of subsets of N and a function $v : \Omega \backslash \{\phi\} \longrightarrow \mathbb{R}$. We assume that $N \in \Omega$. If Ω equals 2^N, we get a regular cooperative game. The interest in subcollections of the power set of N is inspired by the fact that in case of restricted communication possibilities the regular model of a cooperative game is not realistic.
The core of a restricted game is defined as:

$$\text{Core}(v, \Omega) = \{x \in \mathbb{R}^N : x(N) = v(N) \text{ and } x(S) \geq v(S) \text{ for all } S \in \Omega\}.$$

This core is, if non-empty, the algebraic sum of a cone and a compact polyhedral set (see Klee (1959), page 83). The cone equals $\{x \in \mathbb{R}^N | x(N) = 0 \text{ and } x(S) \geq 0 \text{ for all } S \in \Omega\}$. We can also describe it as the core of (v_0, Ω), where v_0 is the null-game ($v_0(S) = 0$ for all $S \in \Omega$). Therefore we call the cone $Core(\Omega)$.

We will describe the extremal rays of this set in the case that Ω is a lattice. Furthermore we will give two characterizations of collections Ω with core $\{0\}$.

2 Lattices.

A collection Ω is a *lattice* if $\phi, N \in \Omega$ and $S \cap T, S \cup T \in \Omega$ for each $S, T \in \Omega$. In this case we can find the extremal rays of Core(Ω) easily. Let us denote the indicator vector of a player i respectivily coalition S by e_i respectivily e_S. We will prove that the core of a lattice Ω is a cone generated by the vectors $e_j - e_i$, with $i \in N$ and player j chosen such that $j \in S$ for each $S \in \Omega$ with $i \in S$. These vectors can be interpretated as *side payments* between players which are not unfavourable for any coalition $S \in \Omega$. Let us denote the set of these players j by D_i^Ω, or, when no confusion can occur, by D_i:

$$D_i^\Omega = \bigcap \{S \in \Omega : i \in S\}.$$

Because $N \in \Omega$, all D_i are non empty, in fact $i \in D_i$ for all i.
Theorem 1: *Let $\Omega \subseteq 2^N$ be a lattice. The core of Ω equals the cone generated by the allocations $e_j - e_i$, with $i \in N$ and $j \in D_i$.*

Proof: Observe that for arbitrary collections Ω the allocations $e_j - e_i$, $i \in N$, $j \in D_i$, are contained in the core of Ω. Therefore,

$$\text{Cone}(\{e_j - e_i : i \in N,\ j \in D_i\}) \subseteq \text{Core}(\Omega).$$

Let us now prove the reverse inclusion. Let $x \neq 0$ be a core allocation of Ω. We choose player j such that $x_j > 0$. We are looking for a player i such that $x_i < 0$, $j \in D_i$, and an $\varepsilon > 0$ with $x' = x - \varepsilon(e_j - e_i) \in \text{Core}(\Omega)$. Notice that for any S with $x(S) = 0$ and $j \in S$, player i has to be in S, otherwise x' is not an element of Core(Ω). Thus, player i has to be chosen among the members of the set

$$E = \bigcap\{S \in \Omega : j \in S, x(S) = 0\}.$$

Since $N \in \Omega$ and $x(N) = 0$, this set is well defined. Furthermore, because Ω is a lattice it holds that $E \in \Omega$ and it is easy to check that $x(E) = 0$.
Of course, since $j \in E$, $x_j > 0$ and $x(E) = 0$, there is a player $i \in E$ with $x_i < 0$. Let

$$E' = \bigcup\{D_i : i \in E,\ x_i < 0\}.$$

Suppose for the moment that j is not a member of D_i for each player $i \in E'$. Both coalitions E' and $E \cap E'$ are members of Ω, so

$$0 < x_j \leq x(E \backslash E') = x(E) - x(E \cap E') = -x(E \cap E') \leq 0$$

implies a contradiction. We conclude that there is a player $i \in E$ with $x_i < 0$ and $j \in D_i$. Now we consider the allocation $x' = x - \varepsilon(e_j - e_i)$, with ε chosen as the minimum of x_j, $-x_i$ and $x(S)$ for coalitions $S \in \Omega$, $j \in S$, $i \notin S$. Player i has been chosen in such a way that for these coalitions S the sum $x(S)$ is positive. Therefore ε is positive. It can be checked that x' is a core allocation. First observe that for all $S \in \Omega$ it holds that $0 \leq x'(S) \leq x(S)$. Therefore it holds that the number of coalitions S in Ω with $x'(S) = 0$ is at least the number of coalitions S in Ω with $x(S) = 0$. also, the number of players with a zero coefficient in x' is at least the number of players with a zero coefficient in x. The choice of ε is such that one of the two numbers for x' is at least one smaller than the corresponding one of x. So, repeating the above procedure finitely many times, say with outcomes $x^0(= x), x^1, \ldots, x^m$ such that $x^{k+1} = x^k - \varepsilon_k(e_{j_k} - e_{i_k})$, with $j_k \in D_{i_k}$, we eventually terminate with the zero allocation $x^m = 0$. Then $x = \sum_{k=0}^{m-1} \varepsilon_k(e_{j_k} - e_{i_k})$, which is an element of Cone($\{e_j - e_i : i \in N,\ j \in D_i\}$). This proves

$$\text{Cone}(\{e_j - e_i : i \in N,\ j \in D_i\}) \supseteq \text{Core}(\Omega). \qquad \square$$

Theorem 1 gives us directly:
Corollary: *In the lattice case the core of* Ω *equals* $\{0\}$ *if and only if* Ω *equals* 2^N.

3 Balanced and complete collections.

In general there are of course more sets with core $\{0\}$. The first characterization for the general case uses two lemmas. To understand these lemmas we first have to consider two notions, well known in Cooperative Game Theory. The first one is *balancedness*. This notion was defined by Bondareva (1963) and Shapley (1967) to give a characterizion of the core of a cooperative game. A set of coalitions Ω is called balanced if there are reals $\lambda_S > 0$ ($S \in \Omega$) such that $\sum \lambda_S e_S = e_N$.

The second one is *completeness*. If a coalition is identified by its indicator vector it has exactly the same meaning as in Linear Algebra. First we define the *Span* of a set of coalitions:

$$\mathrm{Span}(\Omega) := \{R \subseteq N : e_R = \sum \lambda_S e_S \text{ for } \lambda_S \in \mathbb{R},\ S \in \Omega\}.$$

A set of coalitions Ω is called complete if $\mathrm{Span}(\Omega) = 2^N$.
Now we can give the two lemmas:
Lemma 1: *A collection Ω is balanced if and only if Core(Ω) is a linear subspace.*
Lemma 2: *A collection Ω is complete if and only if 0 is an extreme point of Core(Ω).*
Because a cone which is a linear subspace and which has an extreme point can only have one element, we have:
Theorem 2: *Core(Ω) $= \{0\}$ if and only if Ω is balanced and complete.*

Proof of the first lemma: Let $x \in \mathrm{Core}(\Omega)$. Let $\lambda_S > 0$ $(S \in \Omega)$ such that $\sum_S \lambda_S e_S = e_N$. Then $(T \in \Omega)$:

$$-x(T) = \langle -e_T, x\rangle = \frac{1}{\lambda_T}\langle -e_N + \sum_{S \neq T} \lambda_S e_S, x\rangle = \frac{1}{\lambda_T}\sum_{S\neq T} \lambda_S \langle e_S, x\rangle \geq 0$$

So for all $T \in \Omega$, $x \in \mathrm{Core}(\Omega)$ it holds that $x(T) = 0$. So $\mathrm{Core}(\Omega) = \{x \in \mathbb{R}^N | x(S) = 0$ for all $S \in \Omega\}$. This proves that a balanced set Ω has a linear subspace as its core.
Now suppose Core(Ω) is a linear subspace. The inequalities $x(N) \leq 0$ and $x(S) \geq 0$, $S \in \Omega$, therefore imply that $x(T) \leq 0$ for all $T \in \Omega$ (recall that $N \in \Omega$). According to the theorem of Farkas (cf. Weyl 1950, theorem 3) we may conclude that $-e_T$ is in the cone generated by the allocations e_S, $S \in \Omega$, and $-e_N$, say

$$-e_T = \sum_{S \in \Omega} \lambda_S^T e_S - \mu_T e_N, \tag{2}$$

where the coefficients in (2) are supposed to be non-negative. Adding these inequalities we obtain:

$$\sum_{T\in\Omega} \mu_T e_N = \sum_{T\in\Omega} e_T + \sum_{S,T\in\Omega} \lambda_S^T e_S,$$

This shows that Ω is balanced. □
Proof of the second lemma: Core(Ω) is a pointed cone if and only if for an $x \in \mathbb{R}^N$ with $x(S) = 0$ for all $S \in \Omega$ we must have $x = 0$. And this is equivalent to the assertion that Ω is a basis, i.e., Ω is complete. □

4 Exact collections.

Another characterization for such type of collections Ω can be obtained by examining under which conditions a coalition $R \subseteq N$ yields $\mathrm{Core}(\Omega) = \mathrm{Core}(\Omega \cup \{R\})$. Trivially we have $\mathrm{Core}(\Omega) \supseteq \mathrm{Core}(\Omega \cup \{R\})$. The reverse inclusion holds in case the inequality $\langle e_R, x\rangle \geq 0$ is implied by the inequalities $\langle e_S, x\rangle \geq 0$, with $S \in \Omega$, and $\langle -e_N, x\rangle \geq 0$ (note that $N \in \Omega$). Using again the lemma of Farkas (cf. Weyl 1950, Theorem 3) we may conclude that e_R is a non-negative weighted sum of the vectors e_S, $S \in \Omega$, and $-e_N$. Let us denote the set of coalitions with this property by $E(\Omega)$:

$$E(\Omega) = \{T \subseteq N :\ e_T = \sum_{S\in\Omega} \lambda_S e_S - \lambda_N e_N, \text{ with } \lambda_S \geq 0 \text{ for } S \in \Omega \text{ and } \lambda_N \in \mathbb{R}\}.$$

If $R \in E(\Omega)$ and $x \in \text{Core}(\Omega)$ then, for $e_R = \sum_{S\in\Omega} \lambda_S e_S - \lambda_N e_N$ with $\lambda_S \geq 0,\ S \in \Omega$ and $\lambda_N \in I\!R$ we have

$$\sum_{i\in R} x_i = \sum_{S\in\Omega} \lambda_S \sum_{i\in S} x_i - \lambda_N \sum_{i\in N} x_i \geq \sum_{S\in\Omega} \lambda_S.0 - \lambda_N.0 = 0.$$

Therefore,

$$\text{Core}(\Omega) = \text{Core}(\Omega \cup \{R\}) \text{ if and only if } R \in E(\Omega). \tag{1}$$

Using (1), an interpretation of $E(\Omega)$ is that it contains exactly those coalitions which do not shrink the core after adding to Ω. $E(\Omega)$ is the largest collection which has the same core as Ω. The largest game which has the same core as an ordinary cooperative game v is called the *exact cover* of v. Because of this similarity, $E(\Omega)$ is called the *exact cover* of Ω.

Theorem 3 *The core of a collection Ω of coalitions equals $\{0\}$ if and only if $E(\Omega) = 2^N$.*

Proof: Of course, $\Omega \subseteq E(\Omega)$. Furthermore, $E(\Omega) = E(\Omega \cup \{R\})$ for each $R \in E(\Omega)$, as easily can be checked. Therefore

$$\text{Core}(\Omega) = \text{Core}(\text{E}(\Omega)).$$

For collections with exact cover equal to 2^N we thus have core equal to $\{0\}$.
On the other hand, according to (1) we have, for $R \notin E(\Omega)$, $\text{Core}(\Omega \cup \{R\}) \subsetneq \text{Core}(\Omega)$. This proves that for collections Ω with $E(\Omega) \neq 2^N$ the core unequals $\{0\}$. □

5 Final comments.

The collection $E(\Omega)$ need not have the lattice property as the following example shows. Let $N = \{1,2,3,4\}$ and let $\Omega = \{\phi, \{1,2\}, \{3,4\}, \{1,4\}, \{2,3\}, N\}$. Then it can be easily checked that $\Omega = E(\Omega)$ and that $\text{Core}(\Omega) = \{(\lambda, -\lambda, \lambda, -\lambda) : \lambda \in I\!R\}$. This example also shows that in general $\text{Core}(\Omega)$ is larger than the cone generated by the side payments $e_j - e_i,\ j \in D_i$.

As already said in the introduction, the core of a restricted game (N, Ω, v) is, if non-empty, the algebraic sum of a compact polyhedral set and $\text{Core}(\Omega)$. So we can simply generalize (for instance) theorem 2:

If $\text{Core}(v, \Omega) \neq \phi$, it is compact if and only if $\Omega$is balanced and complete.

References.

Derks J.J.M., The Core of the restricted null game, Mimeo RL Maastricht, March 1992.

Weyl, H., The elementary theory of convex polyhedra, Contributions to the Theory of Games (Annals of Mathematic Studies No. 24), edited by H.W. Kuhn and A.W. Tucker, Princeton University Press, Princeton, pp. 3-18, 1950.

Klee, V., Some characterizations of convex polyhedra (Acta Mathematica, 102), edited by Almqvist & Wiksells Boktryckeri, Uppsala 1959.

Some Remarks on Simple Games and Matroids

Dieter Stumpe
Faculty of Mathematics, Technical University of Magdeburg
Postfach 4120, 3010 Magdeburg, Germany

Between simple games and matroids there are certain connections. Edmonds showed that the core of a supermodular game (it is a simple game) is a polymatroid. The combinatorial structure of a simple game is not known in general. However for a matroidal simple game we can use cetain combinatorial results.

Consider now the simple game $G =< N, v >$. In a simple game the worths of the coalitions are v(S)=0 or v(S)=1 for each coalition $S \in 2^N$.If v(S)=0 then S is a losing coalition,if v(S)=1 then S is a winning coalition. Therefore v determines a family F of subsets of N; F contains only the winning coalitions or F contains only the losing coalitions. For a given family F the system M=(N,F) is said to be an independent system if

(1) $\emptyset \in F$,

(2) $S_1 \in F$ and $S_2 \subseteq S_1 \Longrightarrow S_2 \in F$.

In an independent system M=(N,F) a subset $S_2 \subseteq S_1$ is said to be a maximal independent subset of S_1 if for each $x \in S_1 \setminus S_2$ holds $S_1 \cup \{x\} \notin F$.

A maximal indepedent subset of N is called also a basis of the independent system. A minimal dependent set $S \subseteq N$ is called a circuit.

An independent system (N,F) is called a matroid if in addition to (1) and (2) one of the many combinatorial equivalents of Steinitz basis exchange theorem for vector spaces holds,e.g. if $S_1, S_2 \in F$, $|S_1| = |S_2| + 1$ then exist a $x \in S_1 \setminus S_2$ such that $S_2 \cup \{x\} \in F$.

Let F be the family of each losing coalition then the independent system M=(N,F) is a matroid and the game $G =< N, v >$ is said to be a simple game with matroidal structure or shortly a matroidal game.

We know from the Combinatorial Optimization that an independent system M=(N,F) is a matroid if the greedy algorithm yields for any nonnegative weighting w_j of elements in N the optimal solution of

$$max(\sum_{j \in S} w_j | S \in F)$$

(Theorem of Edmonds).

The greedy algorithm works as follows:

(1)$S := \emptyset$,

(2) choose a $j \in N$ such that $w_j \geq w_i$ for each $i \in N$ and put
$S := S \cup \{j\}$,
$N := N \setminus \{j\}$,

(3) repeat as long as either $S \notin F$ or $N = \emptyset$.

It is obviously that the core of v

$$\text{core(v)}=\{x \in 2^N | \sum_{j \in N} x_j = v(N) \text{ and } \sum_{j \in S} x_j \geq v(S) \text{ for each } S \subseteq N\}$$

corresponds with the greedy algorithm for matroids,e.g. we can determine a core allocation by the greedy algorithm.

Example: Consider a weighted majority game. Let be
$w = (w_1, w_2, ..., w_n) \in R^N$ a vector with nonnegative components and
$w(S) = \sum_{j \in S} w_j$ for each $S \in F$.
We choose now a real number q (majority quota) such that

$\frac{1}{2}\sum_{i=1}^{n} w_i < q \leq \sum_{i=1}^{n} w_i,$

then $[q; w_1, w_2, ..., w_n]$ is a weighted majority game of $G =< N, v >$ if

$$v(S) = \begin{cases} 1 & \text{if} \quad w(S) \geq q \\ 0 & \text{if} \quad w(S) < q \end{cases}$$

holds.
We use now the greedy algorithm for the following problem: Let G=[16;5,6,8,5,7].
We begin at $S := \emptyset$.
We have $w_3 \geq w_i$ for each $i \in N$, therefore

$S := S \cup \{3\} = \{3\}$ and
$N := N \setminus \{3\} = \{1, 2, 4, 5, \} \Longrightarrow$

$S \in F$ and $N \neq \emptyset$, we repeat the procedure.
$w_5 \geq w_i$ for each $i \in N$,
$S := S \cup \{5\} = \{3, 5\}, N := N \setminus \{5\} = \{1, 2, 4\} \Longrightarrow$
$S \in F, N \neq \emptyset$, therefore we repeat the procedure.
$w_2 \geq w_i$ for each $i \in N$,
$S := S \cup \{2\} = \{2, 3, 5\}, N := N \setminus \{2\} = \{1, 4\}$.
$S \notin F$, e.g. $S = \{3, 5\}$ is a maximal independent subset or a basis of the independent system M=(N,F).In other words: all coalitions with three and more player are winning coalitions.

Consider now the simple games $G_1 =< N, v_1 >$ and $G_2 =< N, v_2 >$.
v_1 induces the set system $M_1 = (N, F_1)$ and v_2 induces the set system
$M_2 = (N, F_2)$.Let M_1 and M_2 be matroids (then F_1 and F_2 are the families of the losing coalitions). We are interested in the solution of a simple game
$G =< N, v >$ at which v induces the set system $M = (N, F_1 \cap F_2)$. The system is a matroid if the greedy algorithm yields an optimal solution of

$max\{\sum_{j \in S} w_j | S \in F_1 \cap F_2, w_j \geq 0\}$.

For the solution of this problem we use conceptions of the theory of graphs:

Consider the undirected bipartite graph $\Gamma = (U, V, K)$. A subset $K_1 \subset K$ of edges is said to be a matching if each node $u \in U$ and each node $v \in V$ is incident to at most one edge of K_1 . We shall construct a new matching K_2 such that $|K_2| = |K_1| + 1$.

We add an edge i to the set K_1 such that all edges of $K_1 \cup \{i\}$ are incident to exact one node $u \in U$ or $v \in V$. If $K_1 \cup \{i\}$ is a matching then the procedure is finished, else we take away a edge $j \in K_1$ such that $K_1 \cup \{i\} \setminus \{j\}$ is a matching.If there are nodes in the sets U and V for which incident edges don't exist then we construct an edge l to these nodes and $K_2 := K_1 \cup \{i\} \setminus \{j\} \cup \{l\}$ is a matching such that $|K_2| = |K_1| + 1$.

Analogously we proceed in the game $G =< N, v >$. For a given coalition $S_1 \in F_1 \cap F_2$ we construct qa coalition $S_2 \in F_1 \cap F_2$ such that $|S_1| > |S_2|$. We obtain succesively the maximal independent subset $S \in F_1 \cap F_2$.

We coose an $i \in N$ such that $S_1 \cup \{i\} \in F_1$. If $S_1 \cup \{i\} \in F_2$ then $S_2 = S_1 \cup \{i\}$. If $S_1 \cup \{i\} \notin F_2$ then the set $S_1 \cup \{i\}$ contains a circuit. We coose a $j \neq i$ in this circuit such that

$S_1 \cup \{i\} \setminus \{j\} \in F_1 \cap F_2$. Now we attempt to find a $l \in N$ such that $S_1 \cup \{i\} \setminus \{j\} \cup \{l\} \in F_1$ and $S_1 \cup \{l\} \notin F_1$. If $S_1 \cup \{i\} \setminus \{j\} \cup \{l\} \in F_2$ then we put $S_2 = S_1 \cup \{i\} \setminus \{j\} \cup \{l\}$, else $S_1 \cup \{i\} \setminus \{j\} \cup \{l\}$ is a circuit in M_2 and we go like above. That we will do so long up to an element k doesn't exist which produces an increase of the cardinality. The cardinality of a set $S \in F_1 \cap F_2$ is maximal with respect to all sets $I \in F_1 \cap F_2$, if and only if in this procedure an increase of the cardinality is not possible.

Simple games $G =< N, v >$ at which v induces the set system $M = (N, F_1 \cap F_2 \cap ... \cap F_r)$ can be reduced to a game $G =< N, v_3 >$ at which v_3 induces the set system $M = (N, F_1 \cap F_2 \cap F_3)$. However a polynomial- bounded algorithm does not exist for these problems.

References

[1] K. G. Ramamurthy and T. Partasaraty,Matroidal Games, International Journal of Game Theory, Vol. 15 , 1986.

[2] Sagonti,E., On the Strong Monotonicy of Power Indices, Internatinal Journal of Game Theory, Vol.21 , 1991.

[3] Edmonds,J., Submodular Functions, Matroids and Certain Polyhedra, in Guy(Ed.), Combinatorical Structures and there Applications, 1971.

[4] Aigner,M.,Kombinatorik 2, Berlin-Heidelberg-New York, 1976.

[5] Lawler,E.L.,Combinatorical Optimization.Networks and Matroids, New York 1976.

[6] Jeworrek,T. Zur Lösung von Optimierungsproblemen über den Durchschnitt von drei Matroiden,Dissertation A, TU Magdeburg 1988.

Risk Averse Utility Functions

Götz Uebe
Institut für Statistik und quantitative Ökonomik, Univ. Bundeswehr Hamburg
Holstenhofweg 85, 2000 Hamburg 70, Germany

1. Introduction

In a most recent paper Cox and Huang describe a class of strictly concave and differentiable utility functions by two asymptotic concepts: regular variation at infinity, asymptotic constancy of relative risk aversion, and a norm of loglinear closeness. By generalization and by direct analysis of the underlying second order nonlinear differential equation two constructive schemes for the generation of appropriate utility functions are outlined.

2. Asymptotic constancy of risk

Definition 1 (Regular variation at infinity)
A function y(x) is called to be regularly varying at infinity if ,

(R) $$\lim_{\lambda \to \infty} \frac{y(x\lambda)}{y(x)} = \lambda^h \quad \forall x \in [c,\infty),\ c \in \mathbf{R}.$$

Condition (R) of regular variation at infinity obviously is equivalent to asymptotic homo-geneity, and (plain) homogeneity implies trivially regular variation at infinity, see e.g. Eichhorn [1978] or Uebe [1976]. I. e. we look for classes of functions which converge into a specific target class of functions. The essential point is the existence of nonhomogeneous functions, which are nevertheless regularly varying at infinity.

Definition 2 (Asymptotic constancy of relative risk aversion)
A function y(x) is called to be of (asymptotic) constant relative risk aversion if

(A) $$\lim_{x \to \infty} \frac{-x\, y''(x)}{y'(x)} = b,\ b \in \mathbf{R}_{++}.$$

Condition (A) obviously is associated to the Arrow-Pratt risk function, provided y(x) is a utility (felicity) function:

$$r_a := -\frac{y''}{y'};\ r_a x =: r := -\frac{x\,y''}{y'}$$

r_a, r the coefficient of *absolute*, resp. *relative* risk aversion.

Definition 3 (Asymptotic closeness to loglinearity)
A function y(x) is called to be of Cox-Huang type, if the inverse function of the first derivative, i.e.

$$g(y) := y'(x)^{-1}$$

can be bounded as follows: There exist positive constants A_1, A_2, b, y* such that

$$\text{(L)} \qquad \left| g(y) - \frac{A_1}{y^{1/b}} \right| \le \frac{A_2}{y^{a}}, \forall y \le y^*, a \in [0, \frac{1}{b}).$$

Clearly all loglinear functions $y = \alpha x^{\beta} + \gamma$ satisfy this norm.

Theorem 1 (Cox-Huang, proposition p.497): (L) ⇒ (R).

As noted by Cox and Huang (p.498) (L) is only a sufficient condition for regular variation.
By explicit integration of the differential equation

$$\text{(D-CH)} \quad r(x) = \frac{-x\, y''(x)}{y'(x)} = b, \; b \in \mathbf{R}$$

their result can be sharpened, the target class of utility functions is given by theorem 2:

Theorem 2 (Constant risk aversion utility functions):
Condition (D-CH) ⇔ condition (C),
where (C) denotes the class of utility functions, which is given by definition 4.

Definition 4 (The solution class of differential equation (D))
A function y(x) is called to be of constant risk aversion (CRA) type ⇔ (C)
The functions y(x) of constant risk aversion are either of functional type

(i) $y(x) = \alpha x^{\beta} + \gamma$, or

(ii) $y(x) = \alpha \ln x + \gamma$ (α, β, γ real constants).

The proof of Theorem 2 follows from the solution of (D-CH):

$$y(x) = x^{[1-a \pm (a-1)]/2} [C_1 + \frac{C_2 x^{\pm(a-1)}}{\pm(a-1)} - \frac{C_1^{\pm(a-1)} C_2}{\pm(a-1)}], \; a := -b.$$

3. Generation of utility functions

A first generalization is given by the solution the following differential equation:

(D-M(a,b,c,d)) $(a + bx)\, y(x)'' + (c + dx)\, y'(x) = 0$, $a,b,c,d \in \mathbf{R}$, $r(x) = -\dfrac{(c + dx)\, x}{a + bx}$

$$y(x) = \exp\left(\frac{-dx}{2b} - \frac{z}{2} - \frac{(bc - ad)\log(a + bx)}{2b^2}\right)\left(\frac{a}{b} + x\right)^{\frac{B}{2}} C_1\, \mathcal{F}(\alpha, \beta, z) + C_2\, \mathcal{G}(\alpha, \beta, z),$$

where

$$A := \pm\frac{bc - ad}{2b^2} + \frac{1+B}{2},\ \alpha := A;\ B := \pm\frac{b^2 - bc + ad}{b^2},\ \beta := 1 + B;\ z := \pm\frac{d}{b}\left(\frac{a}{b} + x\right),$$

$\mathcal{F}$ and $\mathcal{G}$ are the integral representation of Kummer's equations, the confluent hypergeometric functions

$$\mathcal{F}(\alpha, \beta, z) = \frac{1}{\Gamma(\alpha)} \int_0^{\infty} \exp(-zt)\, t^{\alpha-1} (1 + t)^{\beta - \alpha - 1}\, dt$$

and

$$\mathcal{G}(\alpha, \beta, z) = \sum_{k=0}^{\infty} \frac{(\alpha)_k z^k}{(\beta)_k k!}$$

where the series (γ_k) is given by

$$\{\gamma\ \ \gamma(\gamma+1)\ \ \gamma(\gamma+1)(\gamma+2) \ldots \gamma(\gamma+1)(\gamma+2)(\gamma+3)\ldots(\gamma+k-1)\}\ (\gamma=\alpha,\beta).$$

The total class of functions nor the risk coefficient appear to be a promising approach, since in particular $\lim\limits_{x \to \infty} r(x)$ need not converge for all a, b, c, d.

However, *useful* subcases (among others) are

(D-M(0,1,c,0)) $\Leftrightarrow$ (D-CH), and

(D-M(a,b,c,0)) $\Leftrightarrow$ (D-L(a,b,c)).

where (D-L(a,b,c) is a generalization of Leland's differential equation

(D-L(a,b,1)) $(a + bx)\, y''(x) + y'(x) = 0$, $a,b \in \mathbf{R}$.

A second generalization is given by the following construction of monotonous risk functions:

Definition 5 (self adjoint form)

A nonlinear differential equation is of the self adjoint form, if:

(UV) $(f(x)y'(x))' = \hat{0} \Leftrightarrow f'(x)y'(x) + f(x)y''(x) = 0.$

The implications of (UV) can be summarized by theorem 3:

Theorem 3 (Self adjoint utility functions):

If utility function y(x) satisfies condition (UV), then the corresponding risk coefficient is given by condition (R)

(R) $r(x) := -\dfrac{x\, y''}{y'} = \dfrac{x\, f'}{f}.$

Theorem 3 is a most general construction rule for utility functions.

Two examples are: a very simple one of Kamke (p. 444) -a trend function-

$$xy''(x) + 2y'(x) = 0 \Leftrightarrow x^2 y''(x) + 2xy'(x) = 0 \Leftrightarrow (x^2 y'(x))' = 0$$

$$y(x) = C_1 + \frac{C_2}{x} = C_1 + C_2 x^{-1}$$

and a utility function of Huberman and Ross (p. 1346)

$$y(x) = \sqrt{x} \ln x, x>1.$$

Both function are *not* homogeneous, and yet the risk function converges to a constant. For illustration consider the second one, which Huberman and Ross could not explain:

$$y(x) = \sqrt{x} \ln x; y(x\lambda) = \sqrt{\lambda}[\sqrt{x} \ln x + \sqrt{x} \ln \lambda] = \lambda^{1/2} [y(x) + \sqrt{x} \ln \lambda]$$

One explanation is to construct an adjoint form, i.e. given y' and y" the differential equation (UV) which is solved for f(x):

$$f(x) = \frac{C_1 \sqrt{x}}{2 + \ln x}$$

i.e. $$r(x) := \frac{x f'}{f} = \frac{-\ln x}{2(2 + \ln x)}; \lim_{x \to \infty} r(x) \to \frac{1}{2}.$$

4. References

Cox, John C.; Huang, Chi-fu

[1992] A continuous - time portfolio turnpike theorem, Journal of Economic Dynamics and Control, 16, No. 3/4, 491-507

Eichhorn, Wolfgang

[1978] Functional Equations in Economics, Addison Wesley, London

Huberman, Gur; Ross Stephen

[1983] Portfolio turnpike theorems, risk aversion, and regularly varying utility functions, Econometrica 51, No. 5, 1345-1361

Kamke, Erich

[1983] Differentialgleichungen, Lösungsmethoden und Lösungen, B.G.Teubner, Stuttgart, 10. Auflage

Leland, Hayne E.

[1972] On turnpike portfolios, in Szegö, K.Shell (eds), Mathematical methods in investment and finance, North-Holland, Amsterdam, 24-33

Uebe, Götz; Fischer Joachim

[1976] Produktionstheorie, Springer, Heidelberg

Wolfram, Stephen

[1988] Mathematica, Addison Wesley, Redwood City

A Logic of Rational Play for Games of Perfect Information

Arnis Vilks
Institut für Statistik und Ökonometrie, Universität Hamburg
Von-Melle-Park 5, 2000 Hamburg 13, Germany

Following Bonanno (1991), we represent games by *propositions* (or *formulas* in the sense of propositional logic). Consider, for instance, the following game-tree:

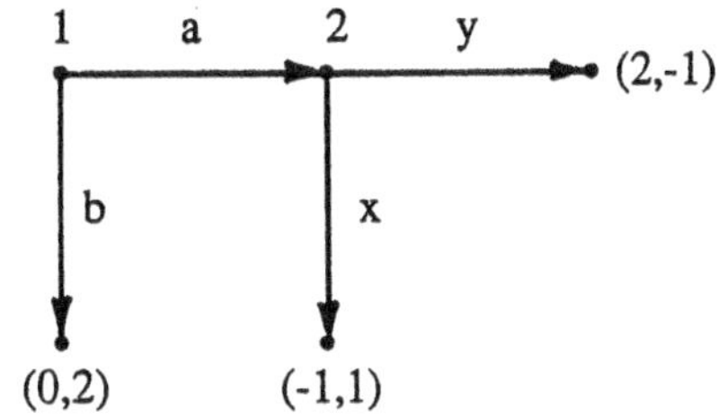

If one interprets the string of symbols "a_1" as the proposition "player 1 takes action a", "$\pi_i=\alpha$" as "player i's payoff is α", etc., the above game-tree can be represented by the the following proposition Γ_1:

$$(a_1 \vee b_1) \wedge \neg(a_1 \wedge b_1) \wedge (x_2 \vee y_2 \Leftrightarrow a_1) \wedge \neg(x_2 \wedge y_2)$$
$$\wedge\ (b_1 \Rightarrow \pi_1=0 \wedge \pi_2=2) \wedge (x_2 \Rightarrow \pi_1=-1 \wedge \pi_2=1) \wedge (y_2 \Rightarrow \pi_1=2 \wedge \pi_2=-1).$$

Only pure strategies are considered in this paper. Player 2 in Γ_1, for instance, has just two strategies that can be represented by the following two formulas:

$$x_2 \vee y_2 \Rightarrow x_2, \qquad x_2 \vee y_2 \Rightarrow y_2.$$

If games and strategies are represented this way, it is natural to formulate one's assumptions about the players' knowledge and rationality in the language of formal logic, and to investigate what can be formally deduced from the game-formula and the chosen assumptions.

In this paper we consider a particular set of assumptions that - to some extent - describe the reasoning process of "rational" players. We use a dynamic epistemic operator K^t and interpret the expression "$K^t(A)$" as the statement "after the t-th step of reasoning, it is known to a rational player that A." The operator K^t is applied only to *simple* formulas, i.e., to formulas made up from action-propositions (such as a_i), payoff-propositions (such as $\pi_i \leq \alpha$), and the connectives of propositional logic (such as $\wedge$, $\Rightarrow$, and $\neg$). (For details about formal logic cf. Bell and Machover (1977). Lenzen (1980) is a rather comprehensive survey of epistemic logic. Bacharach (1987) introduced epistemic logic into the analysis of games.)

With a given game-formula Γ we associate the following five *rules of inference* (where t may be any nonnegative integer.)

(R1t) If $\Gamma \Rightarrow A$ is a tautology, then $K^t(A)$.

After each step of analysis, all simple tautological implications of Γ are known. In particular, all simple tautologies are known.

(R2t) If $K^t(A)$ and $K^t(A \Rightarrow B)$, then $K^t(B)$.

The set of statements that are known after a given step of analysis is closed under modus ponens.

(R3t) If $K^t(A)$, then A.

Only what is true can be known.

(R4t) If $K^t(A)$, then $K^{t+1}(A)$.

Once a proposition is known, it will never be forgotten.

For any action a, we define H(a) to be the set of all actions $b \neq a$ such that the formula $\Gamma \wedge a \Rightarrow b$ is a tautology. We write a~b, if H(a)=H(b). As we consider only games of perfect information without trivial moves and without moves by nature, the condition a~b ensures that a and b are choices from the same decision node. With this notation, our last rule of inference can be stated as follows:

(R5t) If $K^t[(a_i \Rightarrow \pi_i \leq \alpha) \wedge (b_i \Rightarrow \pi_i \geq \beta)]$ with $\alpha < \beta$ and $b_i \sim a_i$, and not: $K^t(\neg b_i)$,
then $K^{t+1}(\neg a_i)$.

I.e., an action a_i that is known to be "strictly dominated" by some other action b_i form the same decision node, will be "eliminated" in the next step of reasoning, provided that b_i has not already been excluded.

A formula S that represents a strategy profile for a game represented by Γ is called *a solution of* Γ in the associated logic (R1t) to (R5t), iff S is deducible in this logic.

The paper proves the following

THEOREM. If Γ represents a game of perfect information (without trivial moves and without moves by nature) that has a unique subgame perfect equilibrium, represented by S, then S is a solution in the logic (R1t) to (R5t).

Moreover, any two solutions induce the same play. However, as strategies are construed as material implications, solutions may "prescribe" *any* choice for unreached information sets. It is argued that - if the knowledge assumptions are taken seriously - this is not less reasonable than the promise "if you walk through the wall, I will eat my hat." In fact, from a broader perspective it should be considered as rational *not* to waste one's time with day-dreaming and other forms of making plans for unlikely "contingencies".

REFERENCES

Bacharach, M. (1987). "A Theory of Rational Decision in Games." *Erkenntnis* 27: 17-55.

Bell, J., and M. Machover (1977). *A Course in Mathematical Logic*. Amsterdam: North-Holland.

Bonanno, G. (1991). "The Logic of Rational Play in Games of Perfect Information." *Economics and Philosophy* 7: 37-65.

Lenzen, W. (1980). *Glauben, Wissen und Wahrscheinlichkeit. Systeme der epistemischen Logik.* Wien: Springer.

Learning Effects in a Heterogeneous and Asymmetric Duopoly

Harald Wiese
Koblenz School of Corporate Management
Burgplatz 2, 5414 Vallendar, Germany

Learning effects (experience curve, progress curves) have long been a topic for management and industrial organization research. Learning effects make today's average costs depend negatively on past sales. Therefore a small "lead down the experience curve" provides a decisive advantage over rivals, as the management literature points out. Since small historical events can easily topple the market outcome to a monopoly of one of the firms, I suggest incorporating historical asymmetries between firms into the models in order to reflect this lead. In the literature, however, there are oligopoly models that are symmetric from the outset and generate symmetric equilibria (Fudenberg/Tirole 1983; Smiley/Ravid 1983; Ghemawat/ Spence 1985; Chu 1988). Would the equilibria in these models be drastically upset if small historical asymmetries were introduced?

These questions can only be answered within an asymmetric oligopoly model. A second modelling feature that seems important is the heterogeneity of products since it allows for situations where one firm has the historical advantage, but still does not monopolize the whole market due to market niches. Thus heterogeneity can be part of a defense strategy against an opponent's monopolizing behaviour. To the best of my knowledge of the literature, no oligopoly model for learning effects with endogenous pricing or quantity setting exists which solves for an equilibrium and allows for both historical asymmetry and heterogeneity of products. The aim of this paper is to study such a model in the context of a two-period duopoly based on price competition, with three different information structures imposed. The model is presented in section I, interesting results are summarized and interpreted in section II.

I The two-period learning effect duopoly model

Within each of the two periods, the two firms called x and y set prices p and q and have a demand of x respectively y, respectively. Prices and quantities are indexed with time, t, where t=0, 1, 2. Period 0 is called the historical period and quantities x_0 and y_0 enter the model as exogenous parameters. Demand functions are derived with the help of the Hotelling linear unit space, which allows to introduce a heterogeneity parameter, h (where h>0), into the analysis. This yields the following demand function for good x:

$$x_t = \begin{cases} 0 & \text{if } p_t > q_t + h \quad \text{(i)} \\ \dfrac{q_t - p_t + h}{2h} & \text{if } |p_t - q_t| \leq h \quad \text{(ii)} \\ 1 & \text{if } p_t < q_t - h \quad \text{(iii)} \end{cases} \qquad t=1,2$$

We get $x_t+y_t=1$, t=1, 2. Also, $x_0+y_0=1$ by assumption. Overall demand is thus independent of the price level.

Learning effects operate on average costs as follows. Basic average costs, k, are reduced linearly according to last period sales only. This may be interpreted as instant depreciation of the knowledge capital. The strength of the learning effect is measured by a parameter e (where e>0). It indicates how much average costs are reduced with every additional unit of past sales. Finally, a specificity parameter, s ($0 \leq s \leq 1$), determines whether the learning rests on a company's own sales only (s=1) or also (partly) on the sales of the other firm (s<1), as in the so-called Silicon Valley effect.

Thus, in each period t (t=1,2) average costs for firm x are given by

$$k-e(x_{t-1}+(1-s)y_{t-1})$$

and profits for firm x in period t, Π_t, are then

$$\Pi_t = [p_t-k+e(x_{t-1}+(1-s)y_{t-1})] \frac{q_t - p_t + h}{2h}$$

Cumulated profits for firm x, Π, are the sum of Π_1 and Π_2, disregarding discounting of second period profits. The profit function for firm y can be set up analogously, where the parameters k, e and s are the same for both firms.

The basic model is solved for equilibria of the games resulting from three different information structures, which I call "open loop" and "closed loop" and Stackelberg, the last of which is not covered here due to space restrictions. In the open loop equilibrium firms can condition their strategies only on the time parameter (and on the parameters of the model, including x_0), whereas in the closed loop equilibrium strategies can depend on the history of play until that date. The solution of these games, i.e. the respective Nash equilibria, involves rather straightforward but very tedious computations. Details can be obtained from the author.

II. Results

As it turns out, in the case of open and closed loop, the distribution of Nash equilibria depends only on two parameters, x_0 and λ. λ is defined as the ratio es/(2h). The less differentiated the products are, and the stronger and more specific the learning effect is, the easier it is to monopolize the market. The dependency of profits on h and on the effect product, namely e times s, support and strengthen Porter's hypothesis (1980), that firms should concentrate on either cost leadership or differentiation. The results are presented in two propositions.

Proposition 1:

For firm x, profits in an open loop equilibrium are

h	in case of e=0 or s=0	(i)
h-es/4	in case of x0=0.5 and λ<1.5	(ii)
2esx0-2h	in case of a monopoly and λ<2	(iii)

Case (i) addresses the usual non-effect duopoly where profits depend positively on heterogeneity. This positive dependency follows from the lessened rivalry. If we let h>0 tend to zero, we would get the familiar Bertrand-paradox, where even in a duopoly, firms cannot commit to prices above their average costs.

As with case (i), case (ii) also reflects a symmetric situation of the two firms. Here we note that profits are lower than in the non-effect case. The cost reduction possibility leads to a "price war". This price war reduces prices more than average costs are lowered through learning. Though we still have to keep the peculiarly inelastic demand in mind, the result points to the possibility that firms can actually suffer from an environment that allows fast learning, especially if they are not in a very strong position.

Proceeding from symmetric situations to monopoly situations, in case (iii) we get 2esx0-2h. This formula has an interesting interpretation. The monopolizing firm can conquer the market more easily when both the effect product and the historical sales are large and when the competing products are homogeneous. The more homogeneous products are, the easier it is to lure away customers from the rival's product, by undercutting the rival slightly.

Proposition 2:

When no firm enjoys an historical advantage ($x_0=y_0$), profits are

h-es/4	in the open loop equilibrium	(i)
h-es/3	in the closed loop equilibrium	(ii)

The open loop formula has been studied in proposition 1. Here, we are concerned with comparing the two results. Starting from an open loop equilibrium, we can see why profits are lower when firms think in terms of backward induction. Firm x considers lowering its first period price. A lower first period price will then lower the competitor's first period sales and hence increase y's second period average costs. Higher average costs will then lead to higher prices by firm y in the second period. This effect is welcomed by firm x which will indeed lower its first period price. Since both firms will proceed along these lines, profits for both will suffer.

References

Chu, Wan Wen (1988) The Effect of Learning on Market Structure, in: Southern Economic Journal, 55, 196-201.

Fudenberg, Drew/Tirole, Jean (1983) Learning by Doing and Market Performance, in: Bell Journal of Economics, 14, 522-530.

Ghemawat, Pankaj/Spence, A. Michael (1985) Learning Curve Spillovers and Market Performance, in: The Quarterly Journal of Economics, 100, Supplement, 839-852.

Porter, Michael (1980) Competitive Strategy, The Free Press, New York/London.

Smiley, Robert H./Ravid, S. Abraham (1983) The Importance of Being First: Learning, Price and Strategy, in: The Quarterly Journal of Economics, 353-362

Section 10

Macro-Economics and Applied Econometrics

Chaotic Behaviour in a Simple Macroeconomic Model

David Chappell
Sheffield University Management School
P.O. Box 598, Crookesmoor Building, Conduit Road, Sheffield S10 1FL, U.K.

A simple dynamic monetary model of a closed economy is proposed in which the Government uses money creation as a means of financing budget deficits. It is assumed that all money in the economy is Government fiat money which is costlessly produced and pays no interest and that real Government expenditure is a fixed proportion of real GNP.

The model is specified in discrete time and consists of four equations; a semi-logarithmic demand-for-money function, an expectations-augmented Phillip's curve, an equation relating Government expenditure to the real money supply and real GNP and a mechanism for the formation of expectations of the rate of inflation. Two versions of the model are considered: the first version assumes that expectations of the rate of inflation are formed adaptively; the second version assumes rational expectations which, in the deterministic setting of the model, is equivalent to perfect foresight. The particular functional forms adopted here have been widely employed in the literature. Chappell and Peel (1979) analyse a continuous-time version of the adaptive expectations variant of the model and a discussion of appropriate functional forms, together with several references, may be found therein. It could be argued that the discrete-time model has greater intuitive appeal. Typically, Governments plan their fiscal and monetary activities and announce their plans on a quarterly or annual basis. In this paper it is assumed that Government expenditure for the period commencing at time t is determined at time t and is at prices pertaining at time t.

Both versions of the model are non-linear and each implies that the inflation rate is generated by a non-linear iterative mapping. In the adaptive expectations version the inflation rate satisfies a two-dimensional iterative mapping whilst the rational expectations version implies a one-dimensional mapping. The models are simulated, using spread-sheets, for a range of plausible parameter values and initial conditions. It is shown that many types of dynamic behaviour are possible: these range from monotonic convergence to a stable point through cyclical convergence, limit cycles and deterministic chaos, to complete instability.

The spread-sheet is also used, in each case, to calculate the largest Lyapunov of the mapping, directly from the definition of the Lyapunov exponent. (See, for example, Wolf (1986)). Existence of a positive Lyapunov exponent is taken as evidence that deterministic chaos is possible. It would appear that deterministic chaos is much more likely under the rational expectations hypothesis. It can also be shown that, starting from a position of equilibrium, a reduction in the Government's share of GNP may well result in the economy entering a chaotic regime.

The rational expectations version of the model contains only two independent parameters. Again using the simulations, a diagram is constructed to depict combinations of parameter values which result in the different types of dynamic behaviour identified above. Each type of dynamic behaviour is associated with a particular region of the two-dimensional parameter space. A similar exercise is carried out for the adaptive expectations version of the model.

References

Wolf A (1986) Quantifying chaos with Lyapunov exponents. Chapter 13 of Holden A V (Ed) Chaos. Manchester University Press, Manchester.

Chappell D and Peel D A (1979). On the dynamic stability of monetary models when the money supply is endogenous. The Manchester School, 47: 349-358.

A Stochastic Model of Foreign Exchange Dynamics and an Exact Option Pricing Formula

Michael Tow Cheung, David W.K. Yeung
School of Economics, University of Hong Kong
Hong Kong, Hong Kong

When applying the theory of options to foreign exchange, the stochastic specification for the spot price of the currency underlying the option must be able to accommodate a fundamental result of the theory of international trade, that the spot price of a currency would converge over time to its purchasing power parity. Fluctuations in the exchange rate are anchored, so to speak, by its long period equilibrium value. In the existing literature on options, the stochastic process is generally assumed to be geometric Brownian motion, so that the exchange rate would display the characteristics of a random walk. To incorporate the non-random walk effects of purchasing power parity, we develop a two dimensional stochastic process to model exchange rate dynamics. After obtaining a closed form expression for the transition density function, we proceed to derive an exact formula to price options on the currency, which in particular is conditional upon its purchasing power parity.

A foreign currency's exchange rate, or spot price relative to the home currency, is $B(t)/H(t)$, where $B(t)$ and $H(t)$ are the accounting prices of the foreign and home currencies. In the options literature, a currency is regarded as a stock paying a continuous dividend equal to the interest rate. Therefore, we have $[d(B/H)/dt]/(B/H) = r_f - r$, where r_f and r are foreign and domestic rates of interest. An individual holding the foreign currency earns a net dividend of $r_f - r$. If a rate of change $Q(t)$ actually obtains in the spot price of the foreign currency, the individual would realise a premium rate of return $R(t) = Q(t) - (r_f - r)$. With a net dividend $r_f - r$ paid continuously, the growth equation of the currency's exchange rate is then:

$$dP(t) = R(t)P(t)dt, \tag{1}$$

where the initial spot price P_0 is given. To characterise the behavior of the premium rate of return $R(t)$, we identify the following factors. The first is the intrinsic value of the currency, as reflected in its purchasing power parity. If the current spot price of the currency is above (below) its purchasing power parity $\hat{p}$, its premium rate of return would decrease (increase). Second, if the current value of the premium rate of return is positive (negative), with competition it would tend to fall (rise). Finally there is a random factor, which following standard practice we assume to be represented by a Wiener process. We can then specify the dynamics of R(t) as:

$$dR(t) = \{-\alpha R(t) - \beta[\ln P(t) - \ln \hat{p}]\}dt + \sigma dZ(t), \qquad (2)$$

where $\{Z(t)\}$ is a standard Wiener process, α and $\sigma > 0$ are serial correlation and variance scaling parameters, $\beta > 0$ is an adjustment coefficient, and the initial value R_0 is given.

The dynamic behavior of the exchange rate and its rate of change over time is described by (1) and (2). Introducing the transformation $W(t) = \ln P(t) - \ln \hat{p}$, (1) and (2) become:

$$dW(t) = R(t)dt, \qquad (4)$$

$$dR(t) = -[\alpha R(t) + \beta W(t)]dt + \sigma dZ(t). \qquad (5)$$

(4) and (5) then yield the second order Langevin equation:

$$d^2W(t)/dt^2 + \alpha[dW(t)/dt] + \beta W(t) = \sigma A(t), \qquad (6)$$

where A(t) is a Gaussian white noise with a zero mean, covariance of $\delta\sigma^2(t - s)$, and $\delta(.)$ is Dirac's delta function.

Following Chandrasekhar (1943), for $\alpha_1 \equiv \surd(\alpha^2 - 4\beta)$ real and positive, W(t) has the transition density function:

$$\phi(W,t;W_0,R_0) = \surd[1/2\pi\sigma^2F(t)]\exp \frac{-1}{2\sigma^2F(t)}\Big[W - W_0\exp(-\frac{\alpha t}{2})$$

$$(\cosh\frac{\alpha_1 t}{2} + \frac{\alpha}{\alpha_1}\sinh\frac{\alpha_1 t}{2}) - \frac{2R_0}{\alpha_1}\exp(-\frac{\alpha t}{2})\sinh\frac{\alpha_1 t}{2}\Big]^2 , \qquad (7)$$

where $F(t) \equiv \frac{1}{2\alpha\beta} - \frac{\exp(-\alpha t)}{2\alpha\alpha_1^2\beta}\Big[2\alpha^2\sinh\frac{\alpha_1 t}{2} + \alpha\alpha_1\sinh(\alpha_1 t) + \alpha_1^2\Big]$,

and W_0 is the initial value for W(t). For α_1 imaginary or $\alpha_1 = 0$, $\cosh(\alpha_1 t/2)$, $[\sinh(\alpha_1 t/2)]/\alpha_1$ and $[\sinh(\alpha_1 t)]/\alpha_1$ in (7) are replaced by $\cos \gamma_1 t$, $(\sin \gamma_1 t)/2\gamma_1$, $(\sin 2\gamma_1 t)/2\gamma_1$, where $\gamma_1 \equiv \surd(\beta - \alpha^2/4)$ and 1, t/2, t respectively.

As Chandrasekhar (1943) noted, (6) characterises a harmonic oscillator, and the behavior of W(t) is that of the harmonically bound particle, which can be approximated by a white noise excitation around 0 as $t \to \infty$. In particular, $\lim E[W(t)] = 0$ as

$t \to \infty$. The time path of $E[W(t)]$ depends on which of the three possibilities for α_1 obtains. If α_1 is real and positive or 0, $E[W(t)]$ is damped over time towards 0. If α_1 is imaginary, $E[W(t)]$ would fluctuate towards 0 over time. In the present case where $W(t) = \ln P(t) - \ln \hat{p}$, the behavior of $E[W(t)]$ reflects the influence of the currency's purchasing power parity. Since $W(t)$ excites around 0, $P(t)$ would describe a typical sample path under attraction around $\hat{p}$, even in the limit. Fluctuations in the spot price of the currency are anchored by its purchasing power parity, as required by the theory of international trade. As information becomes complete in long period equilibrium so that in the limit probability densities collapse on their means, the market would value the currency at its purchasing power parity.

Since $W(t) = \ln P(t) - \ln \hat{p}$ is a 1:1 mapping, applying a standard variate transform to (7), we obtain the transition density function of the exchange rate $P(t)$ as:

$$\theta(P,t;P_0,R_0) = (1/P)\sqrt{[1/2\pi\sigma^2F(t)]}\, \exp \frac{-1}{2\sigma^2F(t)}\Big[\ln P - \{\ln \hat{p} + c\exp(-\frac{\alpha t}{2})(\cosh\frac{\alpha_1 t}{2} + \frac{\alpha}{\alpha_1}\sinh\frac{\alpha_1 t}{2}) + \frac{2R_0}{\alpha_1}\exp(-\frac{\alpha t}{2})\sinh\frac{\alpha_1 t}{2}\}\Big]^2, \quad (8)$$

where $c \equiv \ln P_0 - \ln \hat{p}$. The exchange rate $P(t)$ has a transition density function which depends on its purchasing power parity $\hat{p}$.

If we look forward from the present $t = 0$, at the expiry date $T > 0$ an European call option on the currency has the value:

$$C(T) = \int_Q^{\infty} (P - Q)\theta(P,T;P_0,R_0)dP, \quad (9)$$

where Q is the exercise price. Substituting (8) into (9) and discounting back to $t = 0$ using an appropriate (given) rate of interest ρ, we obtain the exact option pricing formula:

$$C^*(T,Q,\rho,\hat{p},P_0,R_0)$$
$$= \exp(-\rho T)\{k(T)P_0N([\ln P_0 + \ln k(T) - \ln Q + \sigma^2F(T)/2]/\sigma\sqrt{F(T)})$$
$$- QN([\ln P_0 + \ln k(T) - \ln Q - \sigma^2F(T)/2]/\sigma\sqrt{F(T)})\}, \quad (10)$$

where $N(.)$ is the standard normal distribution function and $k(T) = E[P(T)]/P_0$ is the number of times the currency is expected to rise in price to T. In particular, (10) captures the influence of the purchasing power parity on the value of the option.

Reference

Chandrasekhar, S. (1943). Stochastic Problems in Physics and Astronomy, *Review of Modern Physics*, 15, 1-89.

Transition of Socialist Economies and Redistribution of Wealth

Jože Andrej Čibej
Faculty of Economics, University of Ljubljana
Kardeljeva pl. 17 p.p. 103, 61000 Ljubljana, Slovenia

Slovenia is one of the former socialist countries which is nowadays in a state of intensive transition processes towards a strictly market - oriented economy. These changes, basically connected with privatization, induce different forms of redistribution-of-wealth processes, too.

Some aspects of such processes are generally to be noticed all over former socialist Middle- and East Europe, while others are very specific for Slovenia. One of such was (is) an abnormal indebtedness of the potential private entrepreneurs, which was mainly caused by inflational distortion of some loans for durable goods and,.specifically, apartments.

Different activities were initiated by the state (and even commercial banks) to help solving these problems. The main intention of the measures involved is to activate private funds, which were traditionally kept as "untouchable" reserves of foreign (German in the first place) currency and to induce a new development cycle, possibly accelerated with foreign help, too.

There still is discussion about advantages and pitfalls of two different financial models which are intended to be used on large - scale to change the structure of indebtedness. We will present both models to compare the social cost of both solutions offered and to estimate possible simultaneous effects of inflation which has not been defeated definitively (yet).

PROBLEM: Somebody borrowed G monetary units ($m.e.$) for n time periods, at $p_1\,\%$ per time period. A subvention can be obtained in two different ways:

a) authorities (whoever they are) enable him to pay interest at $q\,\%$ ($q < p$) instead of $p_1\,\%$ or

b) enable him that one part of the loan, $G \cdot k$ ($0 \leq k \leq 1$), is hired at a very low interest rate $p_2\,\%$($p_2 \ll q < p$).

To compare both "charity systems" we calculate annuities, since all other conditions are the same (first of all, the time horizons of the loans):

a) Instead of normal annuity

$$a_1 = \frac{G r_1^n (r_1 - 1)}{r_1^n - 1} = \frac{G(1 + \frac{p_1}{100})^n p_1}{100\,((1 + \frac{p_1}{100})^n - 1)} = \frac{G}{100} F_1$$

the following amount, corresponding to the reduced interest rate, is paid per time period:

$$a_1^* = \frac{G r_q^n (r_q - 1)}{r_q^n - 1} = \frac{G(1 + \frac{q}{100})^n q}{100\,((1 + \frac{q}{100})^n - 1)} = \frac{G}{100} F_q$$

meaning that the borrower's gain per period is

$$\Delta_1 = a_1 - a_1^* = \frac{G}{100}(F_1 - F_q)$$

b) For one part of the loan $(G \cdot k)$ symbolic interest (at $p_2\,\%$ per period) is being paid, and for the rest of it, the interest is charged at the normal interest rate $p_1\,\%$. Treating these two parts of the loan as separate loans, we have

$$a_{2(T)} = a_{2(s)} + a_{2(n)}$$

where $a_{2(s)}$ and $a_{2(n)}$ are given by

$$a_{2(s)} = \frac{Gk}{100} \cdot \frac{(1 + \frac{p_2}{100})^n p_2}{100\,((1 + \frac{p_2}{100})^n - 1)}$$

and

$$a_{2(n)} = \frac{G(1 - k)}{100} \cdot \frac{(1 + \frac{p_1}{100})^n p_1}{100\,((1 + \frac{p_1}{100})^n - 1)}$$

respectively. The total annuity is

$$a_{2(T)} = a_{2(s)} + a_{2(n)} = \frac{G}{100}\{k F_2 + (1 - k) F_1\}$$

and in these case the "subvention" is

$$\Delta_2 = a_1 - a_{2(T)} = \frac{G}{100} k (F_1 - F_2)$$

Since the subvention represents kind of social cost, it is interesting to calculate when $\Delta_1 = \Delta_2$. In Slovenian case the question would be, e.g., what is – at given interest rates - the equivalent value of parameter k, measuring the share of loans for which "symbolic" interest is paid.

$$\Delta_1 = \Delta_2 \Rightarrow k = \frac{F_1 - F_q}{F_1 - F_2}$$

The simplicity of this expression for k disappears as soon as we substitute corresponding expressions for F_1, F_2 in F_q.

Equal Rates of Return and/or Clearing of Factor Markets in Two-Sector OLG-Models with Heterogeneous Capital Goods

Karl Farmer
Department of Economics, University of Graz
Schubertstraße 6A, 8010 Graz, Austria

INTRODUCTION

This paper has its origins in a controversy between Filippi (1980) and Morishima (1980) in the recent history of macro-theoretic general equilibrium models. It concerns the compatibility of two short-run equilibrium conditions in general equilibrium models of capital accumulation and growth: the equality of the rates of return on heterogeneous capital goods and the clearing of the markets of capital services.

Morishima (1977) presented a short-period GE-model in chapter 7 of *Walras' Economics* where both conditions hold without contradiction. For the sake of easier reference to Morishima in Filippi's (1980) critique, the alleged equilibrium conditions are now reported (Morishima, 1977, Kap. 7, 109 - 113):

Denote the (imputed) prices of the services of capital goods with index 3 (4) by Q^3 (Q^4) and their production prices by P^3 (P^4). The arbitrage condition for capital goods in a deterministic world, where agents have static price expectations and capital goods completely depreciate during one period, and the conditions of factor market clearing are as follows:

$$Q^3/P^3 = Q^4/P^4 \qquad (10)$$

$$\sum_i N^{i\rho} = L \qquad (13)$$

$$\sum_i N^{ij} = K^j, \quad i = 1,\ldots,4; \; j = 3,4.$$

Here $N^{i,0}$, $N^{i,j}$, respectively, denote the demand for the services of labour and of the capital good j (= 3,4) in industry i
(= 1,...,4), while L, K^j denote the inelastic labour supply and the stock of the capital good j available for utilisation in the two industries, respectively.

Filippi (1980, p. 363, 4. "On 'Normal Rate of Return'") criticised this model because of (1) lacking behavioural foundations and (2) because of being contradictory in his review of *Walras' Economics*:

"... I *suspect* that it is <u>contradictory</u> to include in the same model Eq. (10) and the second and third of Eqs. (13). For, either the price of capital services is decided according to the rule given by Eq. (10) or it is determined according to the second and third of Eqs. (13). But, in general, the two rules will give different results: one rule is redundant. So, in general, one will not get full employment of capital services *and* an equal rate of return on capital goods, unless the stocks of capital goods bear some special relation to each other.

So my final opinion is that the inclusion of Eq. (10) in Morishima's model has no firm theoretical basis."

In his reply to Filippi's critique Morishima (1980) reinforces only his original position without further explanations. Thus, the question arises who is right.

METHOD AND RESULTS Of THE MODEL-THEORETIC ANALYSIS

The underlying paper tries to clarify somewhat the involved controversial topics of substantial and methodological nature. For this sake a simple overlapping-generations model with two heterogeneous capital goods and two production sectors is formulated, and intertemporal general equilibria with perfect foresight are defined.

Following similar procedures in the literature (Diamond, 1965, Hahn, 1966, Reichlin, 1986), the example of a Leontief production function in one, of a Cobb-Douglas production function in the other sector and of a log-linear inter-temporal utility function is further analysed. Existence and determinacy of a short-period equilibrium under static expectations (= static perfect foresight) of next period's (service) prices of capital goods and the existence of a unique long-period equilibrium are easily shown.

But experiments with a numerical specified version of a two-sector OLG-model with two heterogeneous capital goods on a PC show that the dynamics of temporary equilibria with static expectations of capital service prices is highly unstable in the sense that all short-run equilibrium paths originating not exactly in the stationary state diverge to not feasible states where only one commodity is produced while the other is not produced at all. This last fact implies a not feasible negative stock of one capital good because utility maximising consumption is always positive.

APPLICATIONS OF THE MODEL-ANALYTIC RESULTS ON THE FILIPPI-MORISHIMA CONTROVERSY

(1) In accordance with Morishima and in contrast to the critique of Filippi the equality of the rates of return on the capital goods and the clearing of their services' markets in the short run are not contradictory because a temporary equilibrium with static expectations of the prices of capital services exists and is determinate in the sense that there are not more endogenous variables than functionally independent equations. This result is explained by the fact that even in the short-run with historically given capital stocks, investment demands in newly produced capital goods may be perfectly flexible if the rates of return on the demanded quantities of newly produced capital goods are equal. In this Say's Law like situation the supply of new capital must be determined by the equilibrium conditions on factor markets and the arbitrage condition. In this way both

(10) and (13) are consistent despite not demand-adjusted capital stocks.

(2) What is true in the short-run does not necessarily hold in the medium-run. Despite static expectations of the relative prices of capital services a feasible intertemporal equilibrium dynamics may not exist. The computer experiments and the eigenvalues of the Jacobian of the four-dimensional difference equation system of the capital stock dynamics near the stationary state show that the discrete-time overlapping-generations equilibrium dynamics with static price expectations has much in common with the continuous-time equilibrium dynamics of heterogeneous capital goods models with non-static perfect foresight (Hahn, 1966).

The implication of this result for the Filippi-Morishima exchange is profound: Not the determinacy of the short-period equilibrium, but the existence and the stability of the intertemporal equilibrium dynamics of the Walras-Morishima model of capital accumulation and growth are its main problems. In other words: With respect to the existence and the stability of the equilibrium dynamics of the Morishima-model Filippi´s criticism is right while, on the other hand, Morishima´s insistence on the determinacy of his short-period equilibrium model is warranted, too.

REFERENCES

Diamond, P. A. (1965), National debt in a neoclassical growth model, American Economic Review 55, 1126 - 1150.

Filippi, F. (1980), Morishima´s interpretation of Keynes: Some comments and criticisms, Journal of Economics 40, 355 - 367.

Hahn, F. H. (1966), Equilibrium dynamics with heterogeneous capital goods, Quartely Journal of Economics 80, 633 - 645.

Morishima, M. (1977), Walras Economics, C. U. P., Cambridge.

Morishima, M. (1980), Towards Keynes: A Reply to Mr. Filippi, Journal of Economics 40, 369 - 373.

Reichlin, P. (1986), Equilibrium cycles in an overlapping-generations economy with production, Journal of Economic Theory 40, 89 - 102.

Purchasing Power Parity and Cointegration

Tilmann Gerhards
University of Karlsruhe and SGZ BANK AG
P.O. Box 6960, 7500 Karlsruhe 1, Germany

Introduction

Purchasing power parity (PPP) as a theory of exchange rate determination implies that exchange rate movements are determined by changes of the relative prices between two countries. Absolute purchasing power parity is based on the 'law of one price', i.e. the price of one good is the same in two different countries, when denominated in the same currency. Under a number of restrictive assumptions such as perfect competition and substitution on world markets, no transaction costs and aggregated price indices having the same construction and weights, the law of one price does not only hold for a single good but also for aggregated price indices:

$$e = P/P^* \tag{1}$$

Where P and P^* denote the price levels in the domestic respectively foreign country and exchange rate e is defined as the home currency price for one unit of foreign currency. As it is immediately clear there are several reasons for structural or transitory deviations from PPP. Price indices of two countries usually are not the same and nontraded goods are often included in the price indices but no arbitrage is applied to them. Changes of productivity between countries occur whereas prices and wages behave not perfectly flexible. While in the short run empirical studies of exchange rates indicate significant and persistent deviations from equilibrium levels, long-run evidence remains controversial. In this context the methodology of cointegration offers a useful possibility to test for long-run relationships, while allowing for short-run deviations from parity.

The Concept of Cointegration

In general, econometric and statistical theory is based on the assumption that the underlying data processes are stationary and ergodic. A time series x_t is defined as (weakly or covariance) stationary, if mean value and variance of the series are time invariant and if the covariance between x_t and x_{t-k}, $k \epsilon T$, depends on k and not on t. A stationary process is called I(0), denoting 'integrated of order zero'. If a series needs differencing d times to become stationary it is called integrated of order d. However, the majority of aggregated time series which are of interest in applied economics are obviously non-stationary (Nelson and Plosser [1982]). And a non-stationary series will have a time-varying mean or variance and the expected time until the process returns to an earlier value is infinite.

The serious problem which arises from attempting to analyse time series that are non-stationary is that the usual statistical properties do not hold. Ignoring the stationarity requirements and continuing to apply standard procedures to economic time series can lead to models where undoubtedly unrelated variables are included (Phillips [1985]). To overcome such problems of spurious correlations, suggestions of differencing and prefiltering data to render it stationary were proposed based on ideas of Box and Jenkins [1976]. One consequence of this procedure is that by analysing only the differences of economic time series all information about potential long-run relationships between the levels of economic variables is lost. As a means to deal with these implications error correction models (ECM) based on the concept of cointegrated series seem to offer an especially useful solution (Hendry [1986]).

In order to test for long-run equilibrium relationships between non-stationary time series, estimation techniques and tests are provided by the cointegration methodology, which was initially proposed by Granger [1983] and Engle and Granger [1987]. If each element of the vector x_t is integrated of order 1 (x_t~I(1)), then in general the linear combination $z_t = \alpha' x_t$ will also be I(1) (z_t~I(1)). However, the important exception to this rule is, where in the long run two or more series of the vector move closely together and, even though the series themselves are trended, the difference between them is constant. As a consequence there can be constraints on the vector that can be regarded as a long-run equilibrium relationship. Therefore the components of the vector x_t are said to be cointegrated, if the linear combination $z_t = \alpha' x_t$ is stationary, z_t~I(0). And vector α is called the cointegrating vector. Additionally the order of convergence of OLS estimators of this vector is $O(T^1)$ i.e. much faster than in the standard stationary case $O(T^{1/2})$ and the OLS estimates are consistent (Stock [1987]). Therefore standard modelling strategies seem applicable.

Testing a long-run relationship between two variables X_t, Y_t in the form of the cointegration regression: $X_t = a + bY_t + \epsilon_t$, the procedure usually takes two steps. In the first step X_t and Y_t are tested for integration of order one and in the second step the residuals ϵ_t are tested for I(0), which is equivalent to: X_t and Y_t are cointegrated. For this procedure the Dickey-Fuller- (DF) and the Augmented-Dickey-Fuller- (ADF) unit root tests are used (Dickey and Fuller [1979, 1981]).

An important result in connection with the cointegration framework implies that if a set of variables is cointegrated then there exists a valid error correction representation of the data. For a multivariate system with the backshift operator B, the general error correction model may be derived as

$$A(B)\ (1-B)x_t = -\gamma z_{t-1} + u_t \qquad (2)$$

where u_t is a stationary multivariate disturbance, $A(0)=I$, $A(1)$ has all elements finite and $z_t = \alpha' x_t$, where α is the cointegrating vector and $\gamma \neq 0$. These models combine equilibrium relationships of the long run, suggested by an economic theory, with the type of short-run dynamics introduced by time series theory and analysis, while avoiding the spurious regressions problem. Within such a dynamic model a proportion of the disequilibrium of one period is corrected in the next period.

Empirical Analysis

We examine nominal exchange rates and consumer price indices for the United States, Japan, Germany, United Kingdom, France and Switzerland for two data periods (Jan. 1973 - Dec. 1991 whereas the second period excludes the years after the breakdown of the Bretton-Woods-System and runs from Jan. 1977 - Dec. 1991). To investigate the importance of the grade of aggregation monthly, quarterly and biannual averages were used. All variables were converted into natural logarithms and tested for stationarity. Since all series appeared to be integrated of order one, the necessary preconditions for cointegration tests are given.

We test for purchasing power parity using the following cointegration equation:

$$e_{tij} = \alpha_0 + \alpha_1 p^i_t + \alpha_2 p^j_t + \epsilon_t \qquad (3)$$

where e_{tij} = nominal exchange rate in units of currency of country i for one unit of currency of country j.
p^i_t = prices in country i
ϵ_t = residual

And we expect α_1 having a positive and α_2 a negative sign. With the DF- and ADF-tests the residuals ϵ_t are tested under the null hypothesis of nonstationarity (ϵ_t~I(1)), and the alternative of ϵ_t stationary, i.e. that the three variables are cointegrated.

The results provide empirical support to long-run equilibrium tendencies. The exchange rates and prices between Germany, France, Switzerland and Japan are cointegrated and confirm the long-run validity of PPP. Often prices are approximately symmetrical but there is little evidence for proportionality of value one between nominal exchange rates and prices. Only in the case of Germany and France, which is probably due to the effects of the European Monetary System (EMS), changes in purchasing power parity are accompanied by proportional movements in the nominal exchange rate, thus the real exchange rate is stationary, confirming absolute purchasing power parity. While the long-run relationships should be the same whether using monthly, quarterly or (bi-)annual data, short-run movements and deviations might overlay the long-run properties, therefore making it more difficult to receive significant results. As a consequence averaging and aggregating data might help to detect long-run relationships. The results obtained are consistent with these considerations. While the values of the coefficients of the cointegration vector do not change with the grade of aggregation, the nullhypothesis of no cointegration can be rejected on the highest levels of significance, when using quarterly or biannual averages instead of monthly data.

Turning to the estimated quarterly error correction models the results concur with our cointegration analysis: significant long-run equilibrium constraints are part of the error correction representation. Adjustment effects due to purchasing power parity are detectable and explain part of the long-run behaviour of the exchange rates. Prices and price changes are also important for the determination of the short-run dynamics of the exchange rates. Considering, that we did not include other important variables, like interest rates, money or output, the estimated ECMs are quite impressive and pass a battery of diagnostic checks (Table 1). Additionally, applying error correction mechanisms structural changes in DM/FFR and DM/SFR exchange rates in 1979 due to effects of the start of the European Monetary System can be detected.

Table 1
Error Correction Model for Quarterly DM/FFR Rate[a]

Long-Run Relationship					
e_t =	-1.12	+ 1.17 p^G_t	− 1.06 p^D_t		
R^2=0.96	DW=0.25	DF=-2.06	ADF(4)=-3.53		
Error Correction Model					
Δe_t =	+ 0.38 Δe_{t-2} [3.85]	+ 0.50 Δe_{t-3} [5.41]			
	+ 0.41 Δp^G_{t-2} [1.41]	− 0.67 Δp^G_{t-3} [-2.22]			
	+ 0.89 Δp^F_{t-3} [2.75]	− 0.79 Δp^F_{t-4} [-2.56]	− 0.27 RES_{t-1} [-5.34]		
R^2=0.66	DW=1.98 SEE=0.009	Q(10)=10.278 [0.67]	LM(6)=6.65 [0.35]	BP(21)=20.25 [0.51]	
WH(15)=22.20 [0.10]	ARCH(1)=1.42 [0.23]		CHOW(5,38)=0.54 [0.74]		

[a] Exchange rates e_t and prices p^i_t, where i denote F=France and G=Germany are in natural logarithms. RES is the residual from the long-run equilibrium cointegration regression

$$e_t = \alpha_0 + \alpha_1 p^i_t + \alpha_2 p^j_t + RES_t.$$

Figures in brackets are t-values / marginal significance levels.
Estimation period is 2.Quarter 1979 to 4.Quarter 1991

On the other hand, considering exchange rates of the United States and the United Kingdom non-cointegration cannot be rejected on usual significance levels. In these cases no support for long-run PPP is provided. An important reason for deviations from PPP can be expected from productivity differentials (Balassa [1964]). Therfore using the bilateral exchange rates of the United States we applied the cointegration framework to test for productivity bias by including productivity indices into the cointegration regression (3). Indeed, the evidence that could be obtained indicates that for the DM/USD and the YEN/USD rates productivity changes are a major factor explaining deviations from purchasing power parity.

References

Balassa, Bela. 1964. The P-P-P Doctrine: A Reappraisal. Journal of Political Economy, 72, 584-596.

Box, G.E.P., Jenkins, G.M. 1976. Time Series Analysis: Forecasting and Control. San Francisco: Holden-Day.

Dickey, David A., Fuller, Wayne A. 1979. Distribution of the Estimators for Autoregressive Time Series With a Unit Root. Journal of the American Statistical Association, 74, 427-431.

Dickey, David A., Fuller, Wayne A. 1981. The Likelihood Ratio Statistics for Autoregressive Time Series With a Unit Root. Econometrica, 49, 1057-1072.

Engle, Robert F., Granger, C.W.J. 1987. Co-integration and Error Correction: Representation, Estimation, and Testing. Econometrica, 55, 2, 251-276.

Granger, C.W.J. 1983. Co-integrated Variables and Error-Correcting Models. UCSD Discussion Paper 83, 13.

Hendry, David F. 1986. Econometric Modelling with Cointegrated Variables: An Overview. Oxford Bulletin of Economics and Statistics, 48, 3, 201-212.

Nelson, C.R., Plosser, C. 1982. Trends and Random Walk in Macroeconomic Time Series: Some Evidence and Implications. Journal of Monetary Economics, 10, 139-162.

Phillips, P.C.B. 1985. Understanding Spurious Regressions in Econometrics. Cowles Foundation Discussion Paper, 757.

Stock, James H. 1987. Asymptotic Properties of Least Squares Estimaters of Cointegrating Vectors. Econometrica, 55, 5, 1035-1056.

On the Modelling of Economic Equilibria by Variational Inequalities

Joachim Gwinner
Institut für Angewandte Mathematik, Universität Erlangen-Nürnberg
8520 Erlangen, Germany

Let us consider a single commodity that is produced at n supply markets and consumed at m demand markets. There is a total supply g_i in each supply market i ($i = 1, \dots, n$). Likewise there is a total demand f_j in each demand market j ($j = 1, \dots, m$.) Since the markets are spatially separated, x_{ij} units of the commodity are transported from i to j. Introducing the excess supply s_i and the excess demand t_j we must have

$$g_i = \sum_{j=1}^{m} x_{ij} + s_i \,, \qquad i = 1, \dots, n \,; \tag{1}$$

$$f_j = \sum_{i=1}^{n} x_{ij} + t_j \,, \qquad j = 1, \dots, m. \tag{2}$$

Moreover the transportation from i to j gives rise to unit costs π_{ij}. Further we associate with each supply market i a supply price p_i and with each demand market j a demand price q_j. As in the recent model of Nagurney and Zhao (1990), we assume there is given a fixed minimum supply price $\underline{p}_i \geq 0$ for each supply market i and also a fixed maximum demand price $\overline{q}_j > 0$ for each demand market j. These bounds can be absent and the standard traffic network equilibrium model due to Dafermos (1980, 1990) results, where the markets are required to be cleared, i.e.

$$s_i = 0 \text{ for } i = 1, \dots, n \,; \qquad t_j = 0 \text{ for } j = 1, \dots, m$$

are required to hold. Since $s_i \geq 0$ and $t_j \geq 0$ are admitted, the model is also termed a disequilibrium model. In addition to the model of Nagurney and Zhao (1990) we also include upper bounds $\overline{x}_{ij} > 0$ for the transportation fluxes x_{ij}.

Assuming perfect equilibrium the economic market conditions take the following form

$$s_i > 0 \Rightarrow p_i = \underline{p}_i, \qquad p_i > \underline{p}_i \Rightarrow s_i = 0 \qquad i = 1, \dots, n; \tag{3}$$

$$t_j > 0 \Rightarrow q_j = \overline{q}_j, \qquad q_j < \overline{q}_j \Rightarrow t_j = 0 \qquad j = 1, \dots, m; \tag{4}$$

$$p_i + \pi_{ij} \begin{cases} \geq q_j & \text{if} \quad x_{ij} = 0 \\ = q_j & \text{if} \quad 0 < x_{ij} < \overline{x}_{ij} \\ \leq q_j & \text{if} \quad x_{ij} = \overline{x}_{ij} \end{cases} \qquad i = 1, \ldots, n; \;\; j = 1, \ldots, m. \tag{5}$$

The last condition (5) extends the well–known Samuelson (1952) equilibrium conditions in that $p_i + \pi_{ij} < q_j$ can occur because of the flux constraint $x_{ij} \leq \overline{x}_{ij}$. For notational simplicity we group the introduced quantities in vectors $f \in I\!R^m$, $g \in I\!R^n$, $p \in I\!R^n$, $q \in I\!R^m$, $x \in I\!R^{nm}$ and $\pi \in I\!R^{nm}$ omitting the indices i and j. As in the models of traffic equilibria and exchange price equilibria given by Dafermos (1980, 1990) we assume that we are given the functions

$$g = \breve{g}(p), \; f = \breve{f}(q), \; \pi = \breve{\pi}(x).$$

This is in contrast to the model of Nagurney and Zhao (1980) where the prices are assumed to depend on the total supply g, resp. the total demand f, what leads to a somewhat simpler structured complementarity problem. In our constrained economic market model the feasible set for the vectors $u = [p, q, x]$ is given by the product set

$$\mathcal{M} := \prod_{i=1}^{n} [\underline{p}_i, \infty) \times \prod_{j=1}^{m} [0, \overline{q}_j] \times \prod_{i=1}^{n} \prod_{j=1}^{m} [0, \overline{x}_{ij}].$$

In the first step of our analysis we characterize a market equilibrium $u = [p, q, x]$ introduced above as a solution to a variational inequality.

Proposition 1 *Suppose that for each $i = 1, \ldots, n;\; j = 1, \ldots, m$ there holds*

$$q_j = 0 \Rightarrow \breve{f}_j(q) \geq 0; \;\; x_{ij} > 0 \Rightarrow \breve{\pi}_{ij}(x) > 0. \tag{6}$$

Then $u = [p, q, x] \in \mathcal{M}$ satisfies the market equilibrium conditions (1)–(5), if and only if u is a solution to

$$\begin{aligned} &\sum_{i=1}^{n} (\breve{g}_i(p) - \sum_{j=1}^{m} x_{ij})(\tilde{p}_i - p_i) - \sum_{j=1}^{m} (\breve{f}_j(q) - \sum_{i=1}^{n} x_{ij})(\tilde{q}_j - q_j) \\ &+ \sum_{i=1}^{n} \sum_{j=1}^{m} (p_i + \breve{\pi}_{ij}(x) - q_j)(\tilde{x}_{ij} - x_{ij}) \geq 0, \quad \forall \tilde{u} = [\tilde{p}, \tilde{q}, \tilde{x}] \in \mathcal{M}. \end{aligned} \tag{7}$$

In the second step we investigate the variational inequality (7). Existence of solutions can be guaranteed under appropriate monotonicity conditions for the functions $\breve{g}_i, \breve{f}_j, \breve{\pi}_{ij}$. If in addition the model is linear as in the examples in the paper of Nagurney and Zhao (1980), that is the functions $\breve{g}_i, \breve{f}_j, \breve{\pi}_{ij}$ are affine–linear then we can prove a stability result which complements the sensitivity analysis given by Dafermos and Nagurney (1984).

We vary the bounds in the simple inequality constraints of the set $\mathcal{M}$ and introduce the convex closed sets

$$\mathcal{M}^{(\nu)} := \prod_{i=1}^{n}[\underline{p}_i^{(\nu)}, \infty) \times \prod_{j=1}^{m}[0, \overline{q}_j^{(\nu)}] \times \prod_{i=1}^{n}\prod_{j=1}^{m}[0, \overline{x}_{ij}^{(\nu)}],$$

where we suppose $\underline{p}_i^{(\nu)} \geq 0, \overline{q}_j^{(\nu)} > 0, \overline{x}_{ij}^{(\nu)} > 0$. Then based on the abstract approximation theorem by Gwinner (1991) we have the following result.

Proposition 2 *Suppose that the bounds $\underline{p}_i^{(\nu)}, \overline{q}_j^{(\nu)}, \overline{x}_{ij}^{(\nu)}$ converge to $\underline{p}_i, \overline{q}_j, \overline{x}_{ij}$ respectively for all $i = 1, \ldots, n$; $j = 1, \ldots, m$. If the solution u of (7) is unique, then the solutions $u^{(\nu)}$ of the perturbed problem converge to u.*

References

1. Dafermos S. (1980) *Traffic equilibrium and variational inequalities.* Transportation Sc. 14: 42–54.

2. Dafermos S. (1990) *Exchange price equilibria and variational inequalities.* Math. Programming 46: 391–402.

3. Dafermos S., Nagurney A. (1984) *Sensitivity analysis for the asymmetric network equilibrium problem.* Math. Programming 28: 174–184.

4. Gwinner J. (1991) *Discretization of semicoerive variational inequalities.* Aequationes Math. 42: 72–79.

5. Nagurney N., Zhao L. (1990) *Disequilibrium and variational inequalities.* J. Computational Appl. Math. 33: 181–198.

6. Samuelson P.A. (1952) *A spatial price equilibrium and linear programming.* Amer. Econom. Rev. 42: 283–303.

The Policy of the Deutsche Bundesbank: An Empirical Investigation

Matthias Hillmer
SGZ BANK
P.O. Box 6960, 7500 Karlsruhe 1, Germany

LATENT VARIABLES AND CAUSAL ANALYSIS OF TIME SERIES INNOVATIONS

In this study a new latent variables approach of causal modelling under rational expectations is used to evaluate some important aspects of monetary policy. Latent variables are hypothetical concepts or constructs such as permanent/transitory income, human capital, price level, business cycle, socioeconomic status, economic expectations or shadow economy, that cannot be observed directly, but in economic theory are supposed to influence the relationships among observed (manifest) variables. In order to estimate and test structural relations among latent variables, measurement models are necessary, relating the theoretical constructs to multiple indicators. The **LISREL**–approach (*Jöreskog* [1982]) is such a linear structural model with latent variables, combining econometric and psychometric data analysis traditions (simultaneous equation model, confirmatory factor analysis). As a result of the causal structure imposed by a substantive theory, specific parametrizations of the covariance matrix of the manifest variables arise and can be used to identify the unknown parameters of the model. The statistical method of covariance structure analysis has been developed to estimate and test those models by means of overidentifying covariance restrictions (statistical foundations cf. *Jöreskog* [1969, 1978], *Jöreskog/Goldberger* [1972], *Browne* [1974, 1982, 1984]). The confirmatory approach allows to test the adequacy of the conditions and therefore of the whole structural model (goodness of fit measure). Examinations of theoretically derived hypothesis about relationships among abstract constructs are emphasized (causal modelling). Models with latent variables are well–known in sociological and psychological empirical research (*Bentler* [1980, 1986]), but actually rarely used to deal with macroeconomic problems.

We introduce a modified procedure for causal modelling with time dependant variables, which especially takes care of the trend and dynamical properties of the data. In a first step, univariate **ARIMA**–filters transform each manifest time series under investigation into white noise innovations (individually prewhitening). The uncorrelated random shocks/ innovations driving the stochastic part of the time series are just the one–step ahead forecast errors under weak rational expectations. Therefore, residuals of such optimal linear

MMSE–forecasts are measures of the unanticipated parts of the variables, that cannot be predicted from their own past history. In the second step, cross–series dependencies are modelled with linear structural equations among the unexpected parts (= time series innovations) of the variables. Measurement models relate latent variables to suitable indicators and causal relationships are estimated and tested by restrictions of the covariance matrix of the estimated innovations. Therefore, the approach is in the tradition of macroeconomic modelling under rational expectations/efficient markets (*Muth* [1961], *Barro* [1977, 1978]). Only unexpected changes are supposed to have influence on the endogenous variables.

THEORY AND PRACTICE OF MONETARY POLICY

In this empirical study we consider unanticipated money growth as a latent variable, which is measured by several indicators like innovations of currency in circulation, sight and time deposits, savings or monetary capital formation. Confirmatory factor analysis of these components of the usual monetary aggregates allows to test the adequacy of a one–dimensional monetary factor to describe the relations among these variables. The policy of the Deutsche Bundesbank bases upon money supply targeting and regulation. Therefore, the crucial element is the existence of a single monetary aggregate, which can be controlled by the Bundesbank and is in sufficient connection with the final aims of monetary policy (suitability as an interim target and monetary indicator). The statutory function of the Deutsche Bundesbank is to guarantee monetary stability (§3 BBankG) and to support the economic policy of the government (§12 BBankG). Because of the independence from the government, the Bundesbank is theoretically in a position to control the process of creating money by fulfilling or limiting banks' funding requirements. However, the practical instruments of the Bundesbank (minimum reserve policy, refinancing policy, open–market operations) are only suitable to control money market rates and the liquidity in the banking system (money market control). Monetary policy has no direct influence on the real sector of the economy and on economic goals like price stability, economic growth, full employment or external equilibrium. By limiting the expansion of money supply and the annoucement of official monetary targets, the Bundesbank tries to influence price increase by pushing back inflationary pressures and anticipations. Two major problems arise with this policy of money supply regulation. First, stable, long–term relations between money supply and the final target–variables are necessary. Unfortunately, the only thing really known is that the transmission mechanism of monetary policy is long and variable. The second point is the existence of a stable money creation multiplier and stable money demand. In the short–run, the behaviour of banks and non–banks dominates money growth by their portfolio choices. In addition, the problem of a suitable monetary aggregate arises: there are many concepts in use but none is acceptable for all purposes. Under the conditions it can be asked whether monetary policy can be successful.

EMPIRICAL RESULTS: CAUSAL ANALYSIS OF MONETARY POLICY

We use seasonally adjusted quarterly data for West–Germany over the sample period of Q1/1980 – Q4/1989. All variables (with exception of interest rates and price rates) are transformed using nat. logarithm, so that first differences of the data can be interpreted as growth rates. Besides the monetary aggregates and indicators to model latent money supply we deal with a short– and long–term interest rate (rate for three–month funds, yield on public authority bonds), the rate of inflation (cost–of–living index) and several indicators of the economic situation (GNP, new orders to manufacturing, industrial production, employed persons, turnover in the producing sector and capacity utilization) in order to analyse a latent variable real economic activity. Besides, we include the discount, lombard and repurchase agreement (repos) rate to model the practical policy of the Bundesbank as a further latent variable.

The first step of our procedure consists of a careful investigation of the trend and dynamical properties of the variables (**Dickey/Fuller**–unit root tests) in order to get stationary time series and to fit **ARMA**–models to the variables (individually prewhitening). The causal analysis of the monetary policy of the Deutsche Bundesbank in the second step depends only on the time series innovations (unexpected parts) of the variables under economically rational expectations (*Feige/Pearce* [1976]). All advantages of an uncorrelated data–set like unbiased estimators and the absence of multicollinearity can be used to model complex constructs (latent variables) and measurement errors, and to test overidentifying restrictions in order to allow confirmatory examinations of theoretical model–structures.

The empirical results strongly support this approach. The hypothesis of a one–dimensional latent money variable is supported: the fluctuations in the five monetary indicators can be explained by a *single* factor, but the innovations of time deposits (and monetary capital formation) behave opposite to currency, sight and savings deposits – in contradiction to the usual additive monetary aggregate M3! The different interest sensitivities are clearly expressed. It turns out, that the money market rate has an important effect on monetary surprises ($R^2 = 0.53$!) with a time lag of one quarter. The influence of interest rates (liquidity–preference relation of money demand) is the outstanding factor for the determination of money growth. Can the Bundesbank control monetary supply also? We can show that the main effect of practical monetary policy also occurs after one quarter, but influences money growth only indirectly by money market control (causal analysis of Bundesbank–policy). Therefore, the reactions of banks and non–banks to actions of the monetary authorities are very important for the Bundesbank to be successful in controlling the expansion of money supply.

A second interesting result concerns the liquidity effect. The relationship between money growth and interest rates is a crucial element in the Keynesian theory of transmission mechanism of monetary policy. Theoretically, an exogenous increase in money supply should – at least in the short term – lower interest rates, before the income and price expectations effect reverses the initial decline. Using rational expectations/efficient markets–models, several empirical studies (*Mishkin* [1981, 1982], *Makin* [1983], *Reichenstein* [1987], *Grier* [1986], *Thornton* [1988]) recently failed to find any evidence for the hypothesis that the impact of unanticipated money on interest rates is negative (assumed reasons: policy anticipation effect and rational expectations of corrective actions of the monetary authorities; rapidly arised inflationary expecations). We can show that our latent measure of monetary innovations lowers significantly the long–term interest rate in the same period. The liquidity effect explains about 24% of the variation in the bond rate surprises. One can ask, whether this relationship is a spurious one, as money demand depends heavily on interest rates and the Bundesbank controls directly only the money market and not the money supply (is money really exogenous to the interest rate?). A causal analysis in this connection shows, that the correlation between monetary surprises and long–term interest rate cannot completely traced back to a third variable, Bundesbank–policy, there *are* hints for an independent liquidity effect.

Further insights in the mechanism of monetary transmission can be obtained by the examination of real effects of monetary policy. There are significant price–effects after three and 7–8 quarters of monetary policy actions. Again, the main effect is an indirect one by influencing monetary growth with a time lag of one quarter. An exogenous increase of the Bundesbank–rates by one standard deviation (= about 60 basispoints) lowers prices after two years by 15 points in the quarterly rate. Further, monetary stimulations are subject to positive effects on economic activity after 5–7 quarters (for example, effect on industrial production after 7 quarters: 75 basispoints). All these results explicitly account for money market control of the Bundesbank and interest sensitivity (endogenity) of money supply.

A final point in this investigation concerns the determinants of the behaviour of the Bundesbank. Negative/undesired growth of money supply, prices or economic activity are due to corrective actions of monetary policy (feedback between final goals and monetary policy). We show, that reactions to price movements occur very fast, but that the realizations of the official interim target monetary supply are more important (time lag: one year) than short run fluctuations of prices. Here, the credibility and reputation of the Bundesbank in achieving the announced monetary target plays an important role, just as the confidence in a stable, long–run relationship between money supply and inflation. Besides, there are surprisingly significant and relatively fast reactions to undesired developments in the real sector. Altogether, we can explain 60% of the autonomous changes of the Bundesbank-rates by lagged real and monetary variables.

REFERENCES

Barro, R.J. [1977], Unanticipated money growth and unemployment in the United States, American Economic Review, 67, Seite 101–115.

Barro, R.J. [1978], Unanticipated money, output, and the price level in the United States, Jornal of Political Economy, 86, Seite 549–580.

Bentler, P.M. [1980], Multivariate analysis with latent variables: causal modeling, Annual Review of Psychology, 31, Seite 419–456.

Bentler, P.M. [1986], Structural modeling and psychometrika: an historical perspective on growth and achievements, Psychometrika, 51, Seite 35–51.

Browne, M.W. [1974], Generalized least squares estimators in the analysis of covariance structures, South African Statistical Journal, 8, Seite 1–24.

Browne, M.W. [1982], Covariance structures, in: D.M. *Hawkins* (ed.), Topics in Applied Multivariate Analysis, London, Seite 72–141.

Browne, M.W. [1984], Asymptotic distribution free methods for the analysis of covvariance structures, British Journal of Mathematical and Statistical Psychology, 37, 62–83.

Feige, Edgar L. / *Pearce*, Douglas K. [1976], Economically rational expectations: are innovations in the rate of inflation independent of innovations in measures of monetary and fiscal policy?, Journal of Political Economy, 84, Seite 499–522.

Grier, K.B. [1986], A note on unanticipated money growth and interest rate surprises: Mishkin and Makin revisted, Journal of Finance, 41, Seite 981–985.

Jöreskog, K.G. [1969], A general approach to confirmatory maximum likelihood factor analysis, Psychometrika, 34, Seite 183–202.

Jöreskog, K.G. [1978], Structural analysis of covariance and correlation matrices, Psychometrika, 43, Seite 443–477.

Jöreskog, K.G. [1982], The LISREL approach to causal model-building in the social sciences, in: *Jöreskog/Wold* (eds), Systems under indirect Observation: Causality-Stucture-Predicton, Part I, Amsterdam, Seite 81–99.

Jöreskog, K.G. / *Goldberger*, A.S. [1972], Factor analysis by generalized least squares, Psychometrika, 37, Seite 243–260.

Makin, J.H. [1983], Real interest, money surprises, anticipated inflation and fiscal deficits, Review of Economics and Statistics, Seite 374–384.

Mishkin, F.S. [1981], Monetary Policy and long-term interest rates: an efficient markets approach, Journal of Monetary Economics, 7, Seite 29–55.

Mishkin, F.S. [1982], Monetary Policy and short-term interest rates: an efficient markets–rational expectations approach, Journal of Finance, 37, S. 63–72.

Muth, J.F. [1961], Rational expectations and the theory of price movements, Econometrika, 29, Seite 315–335.

Reichenstein, W. [1987], The impact of money on short-term interest rates, Economic Inquiry, 25, Seite 67–82.

Thornton, Daniel L. [1988], The effect of monetary policy on short–term interest rates, Federal Reserve Bank of St. Louis Review, Seite 53–72.

Population Dynamics for the Federal Republic

Günter Köpp
Institut für Statistik und quantitative Ökonomik
Universität der Bundeswehr Hamburg
Holstenhofweg 85, 2000 Hamburg 70, Germany

1. Introduction

For our research project on the long run prospects of social security we need a model to forecast the population of the Federal Republic. The most popular methods to project population distributions are the component and the cohort methods. In case of our database we use a component method, which is also used by the Federal Statistical Office. The technique of this projection method was developed by Bernadelli (1941), Lewis (1942) et. al.. Leslie at first showed it in a compact matrix form, so it is also called "Leslie-model". A short description of the projection technique is shown in section 2 and some results of forecasting are in section 3.

2. The Projection Technique

In this section there is a given population distribution by m+1 age groups, where the people of age 0-1 are in group 0, the people of age 1-2 are in group 1 and so on, all people who are older than m are in age group m. For every age group we have fertility and survivor rates.

2.1 A deterministic one-sex model

In this case the projection method for any population distribution without migration can be written in linear equations:

$$P_{x+1,t+1} = s_x P_{x,t} \qquad x = 0,1,...,m \quad (1)$$

$P_{x,t}$ number of people who live in age group x at time t

s_x probability that the people in age group x at time t are alive in age group x+1 at time t+1, $s_m = 0$

$$P_{0,t+1} = \sum_{x=0}^{m} f_x P_{x,t} \tag{2}$$

f_x fertility rate of age group x

The equations can be transformed in the following matrix-form:

$$P_{t+1} = M P_t \tag{3}$$

$P_t = \begin{pmatrix} P_{0,t} \\ P_{1,t} \\ \dots \\ P_{m,t} \end{pmatrix}$ population distribution vector at time t

$M = \begin{pmatrix} f_0 & f_1 & f_{m-1} & f_m \\ P_{0,t} & 0 & 0 & 0 \\ 0 & P_{1,t} & 0 & 0 \\ & & \dots & \\ 0 & 0 & P_{m-1,t} & 0 \end{pmatrix}$ matrix of the fertility and survivor rates, "Leslie-Matrix"

2.2 A deterministic two-sex model with migration

There are linear migrations in every age group at the time unit t to t+1 which have the same fertility and survivor rates as the population distribution.

$$P^w_{x+1,t+1} = s^w_x P^w_{x,t} + 1/2(1+s^w_x) W^w_{x,t} \qquad x = 0,1,\dots,m \tag{4}$$

$$P^w_{0,t+1} = \sum_{x=0}^{m} \left(f^w_x P^w_{x,t} + \tfrac{1}{2}\left(1 + f^w_x\right) W^w_{x,t} \right) \tag{5}$$

$P^w_{x,t}$ number of females who live in age group x at time t
s^w_x probability that females in age group x at time t are alive in age group x+1 at time t+1, $s^w_m = 0$
$W^w_{x,t}$ number of net female migration in age group x at the time unit t to t+1
f^w_x probability that a daughter was born by a female of age group x

$$P^m_{x+1,t+1} = s^m_x P^m_{x,t} + 1/2(1+s^m_x) W^m_{x,t} \qquad x = 0,1,\dots,m \tag{6}$$
$$P^m_{0,t+1} = q\, P^w_{0,t+1} \tag{7}$$

$P^m_{x,t}$ number of males who live in age group x at time t

s^m_x probability that males in age group x at time t are alive in age group x+1 at time t+1, $s^m_m = 0$

$W^m_{x,t}$ number of net male migration in age group x at the time unit t to t+1

q sexualproportion

The result of transforming the equations is also a nonnegative square matrix as described above in section 2.1.

3. Some Results of Forecasting

We make two projections of the German population in the Federal Republic. One without any migration and another with positive net migration. So the first one is a lower bound and the second a upper bound for the future population in the Federal Republic.

One part of the database is a projection of the census of 1987 up to 1992 for the "old" Federal Republic, the other part is data of the microcensus for the "old German democratic Republic". The database and the results of the two forecasts are shown in the table.

In the projection without migration we can see that the group of the old people grows until the other groups become smaller. We call this effect "greying". In the second projecting we see the same effect only more slowly.

	male	female	total	population total:
1992				
0 - 20	8103118	7690823	15793941	
20 - 60	21974936	21487094	43462030	75557291
60 -100	6141108	10160212	16301320	
2030 without migration				
0 - 20	5047719	4786171	9833890	
20 - 60	14224869	13787426	28012295	59979243
60 -100	9700354	12432504	22132858	
2030 with migration				
0-20	5532109	5245598	10777707	
20-60	15578552	15076476	30655028	64821508
60-100	10271263	13117510	23388773	

4. References

Keyfitz N.: On Future Population, in: Journal of the American Statistical Association, Vol. 67, 1972, 347-363.

Keyfitz N.: Applied Mathmetical Demography, 2. Edition, Springer-Verlag, New York, Berlin, Heidelberg, 1977.

Köpp G., Uebe G.: Eine Langzeitprognose für die deutsche Bevölkerung, Discussion Papers in Statistics and Quantitative Economics, No. 52, 1992.

Leslie P. H.: On the Use of Matrices in certain Population Mathematics, in: Biometrika, 33, 1945, 183-212.

Leslie P. H.: Some further Notes on the Use of Matrices in Population Mathematics, in: Biometrika, 36, 1948, 213-245.

Pflaumer P.: Methoden der Bevölkerungsvorausschätzung unter besonderer Berücksichtigung der Unsicherheit, Volkswirtschaftliche Schriften, Heft 377, Berlin, 1988.

Rogers A.: Introduction to Multiregional Mathematical Demography, John Wiley & Sons, New York, London, 1975.

Statistisches Bundesamt: Bevölkerung und Erwerbstätigkeit, Fachserie 1, Reihe 1, laufende Hefte.

Statistisches Bundesamt: Statistisches Jahrbuch für die Bundesrepublik Deutsch-land, jährliche Ausgabe.

Testing for a Long Run Relationship between Trend and Difference Stationary Series

Peter Kugler, Peter Schwendener
Abt. Ökonometrie, Universität Bern
Laupenstraße 2, 3008 Bern, Switzerland

The theory of cointegration and error correction models developed in the last couple of years by, among others, Engle and Granger (1987), as well as Johansen (1988) proved very useful for testing and estimating long-run relationships between difference stationary [I(1)] series. However, there is an increasing literature expressing the view that the autocorrelation of macroeconomic time series could be produced either by trend or difference stationary models [e.g. Christiano Eichenbaum (1990) and the evidence presented by Stock (1991)]. Of course, the idea of cointegration cannot be applied to trend stationary series, but there is the related idea of codependence suggested by Gourieroux and Peaucelle (1989) which is designed for testing a long run relationship between stationary series. This paper uses this approach in a VAR framework which can be applied to trend <u>and</u> difference stationary variables.

Consider the following VAR model for the vector of series X_t, including intercept and deterministic trend terms:

$$X_t = \mu + bt + A_1X_{t-1} + \ldots + A_kX_{t-k} + \varepsilon_t$$

We have the impulse response function

$$X_t = \delta + \gamma t + \sum_{\tau=0}^{\infty} \theta_\tau \varepsilon_{t-\tau} .$$

Now consider an equilibrium relationship $\beta' X_t$, which adjusts more quickly to shocks than the original series. Thid means that $\beta'\theta_{c+i} = 0$ (i = 0,1,...) holds for some c > 0 and $\theta_{c+i} \neq 0$ (i = 0,1...k). In addition, we assume that $\beta' X_t$ has no deterministic trend.

If the series are stationary, these restrictions hold for a relatively low value of c in order to make them codependent. For cointegrated I(1) series, they are approximately valid for a relatively large value of c, which depends on the adjustment speed.

These restrictions can be tested most conveniently by considering the regression

$$\beta'X_t = \beta'd + \beta'ct + \beta'\Gamma_1 X_{t-c} + \ldots + \beta'\Gamma_k X_{t-c-k+1} + \upsilon_t$$

which is obtained by repeated substitution of lagged X_t in the VAR equation and taking $\beta'X_t$. The error term υ_t is, therefore $\beta'(\varepsilon_t + \theta_1\varepsilon_{t-1} + \ldots + \theta_{c-1}\varepsilon_{t-c+1})$. If $\beta'X_t$ fully adjusts to shocks after c periods and if it has no deterministic trend, all p·k+1 coefficients (except the intercept) of this equation should be zero. This hypothesis can be conveniently tested by an OLS based Wald statistic correcting the covariance matrix for MA (c-1) error by an approach proposed by Levine (1983). According to the work of Park and Phillips (1989), the test should be asymptotically valid for I(1) series too, as the RHV's are cointegrated. In practical application, the test has to be repeatedly applied for reasonable values of c (see Kugler and Neusser, 1992). In addition, it should be mentioned that this test is easily extended to more than one equilibrium relationship.

The Monte Carlo experiments reported by Kugler and Schwendener (1991) as well as Kugler and Neusser (1992) indicate that the test works reasonably well for mean stationary series. The conjecture that it can also be applied to trend stationary series and cointegrated series is confirmed by the Monte Carlo results obtained in the framework of this paper.

REFERENCES

Christiano, L.C. and M. Eichenbaum (1990) Unit Roots in GNP: Do We Know and Do We Care?, Carnegie Rochester Conference Series on Public Policy 32 (1990), 7-62.

Engle, R.F. and C.W.J. Granger (1987) Cointegration and Error Correction: Representations, Estimation and Testing, Econometrica 55, 251-276.

Gourieroux, C. and I. Peaucelle (1989) Detecting a Long Run Relationship (With an application to the P.P.P. Hypothesis). CEPREMAP, working Paper N-8902.

Johansen, S. (1988) Statistical Analysis of Cointegration Vectors, Journal of Economic Dynamics and Control 12, 231-254.

Kugler, P. and K. Neusser (1992) International Real Interest Rate Equalization: A Multivariate Time Series Approach, under revision Journal of Applied Econometrics.

Kugler, P. and P. Schwendener (1991) Codependence in a VAR Framework, paper presented at the European Meeting of the Econometric Society, Cambridge, September 2-6, 1991.

Levine, D. (1983) A Remark on Serial Correlation in Maximum Likelihood, Journal of Econometrics 23, 337-342.

Park, J.Y. and P.C.B. Phillips (1989) Statistical Inference in Regression with Integrated Processes: Part 2. Econometric Theory 5, 95-131.

Stock, J.H. (1991) Confidence Intervals for the Largest Autoregressive Root in U.S. Macroeconomic Time Series, Journal of Monetary Economics 28, 435-459.

Deficit Financing Strategies and the Fiscal Multiplier

H. Molana
Department of Economics and Management, University of Dundee
Dundee, DD1 4HN, Scotland, U.K.

A significant proportion of the recent literature on various macroeconomic policy issues bases the analysis on models which possess precise microeconomic foundations. This is mainly motivated by the ability of such models to allow for the structure of preferences, technologies and market imperfections to be taken into account explicitly (see the reference list for a sample of studies within this category). These studies usually assume that the economy consists of three types of agents: households who consume, save and supply labour; firms which demand labour and supply a homogeneous consumption good; and a government which has real expenditure plans financed by taxation, borrowing and/or issuing money. The typical model assumes that the three agents described above engage in transactions in four markets: goods, labour, money and bonds (the last two issued by the government). The corresponding demand and supply equations are derived from some optimising behaviour and a general equilibrium model is constructed by setting demand equal to the corresponding supply and taking account of the relevant budget constraints which imply some adding up restrictions. The model is then solved to determine the endogenous variables in terms of the exogenous ones and the solution is used to obtain some policy implications regarding, for instance, the effect of a fiscal expansion. This paper looks at the structure of such general equilibrium models and argues that the effect of a fiscal expansion is sensitive to the way the model is set up. The point is illustrated by examining various ways of financing a fiscal expansion. It is shown that different deficit financing strategies can lead to a positive, neutral or even negative multiplier effect and that the size and sign of the fiscal multiplier is in fact sensitive to the specification of households' preferences. We maintain the following assumptions: *(i)* goods market is characterised by a monopolistic competition structure, *(ii)* the aggregate demand function is unit price elastic, *(iii)* labour market is perfectly competitive, *(iv)* production technology exhibits constant returns to scale, and *(v)* labour is the only input used in production. Our analysis is based on a simple structure which omits the financial sector, assumes that there is only one good in the economy which is consumed by both households and government, and does not use capital as a means of production. These are nevertheless common simplifying assumptions and, in fact, introducing product differentiation, capital and a financial sector only complicates the issue without changing the results.

Section 2 assumes that the representative household chooses the optimal levels of consumption, leisure and real money holding (C,L,M/P) to maximise utility $U(C,L,M/P) = C^{\alpha}L^{\beta}(M/P)^{\gamma}$, $\alpha+\beta+\gamma=1$, subject to the budget constraint, $PC+M=W(1-L)+\Pi+M^{o}-T$, where M^{o} denotes the initial money holdings, W is money wage rate, (we have normalised the time endowment such that maximum leisure is unity), Π is the profit income (firms are owned by households), and T is the tax paid to the government. Given the government budget constraint T=PG, the size and sign of the fiscal multiplier, dY/dG, depends on the choice of taxation as follows: a lump sum or a proportional profit income tax, $T=t\Pi$, implies $0<dY/dG<1$; a proportional total income tax, $T=t[W(1-L)+\Pi]$, yields dY/dG=0; and finally a proportional tax on labour income only, T=tW(1-L), leads to dY/dG<0.

Section 3 uses $C^{\alpha}[L^{1-1/s} + (M/P)^{1-1/s}]^{\beta/[1-1/s]}$ to characterise households' preferences and shows that *(i)* dY/dG>0 even all income is taxed proportionally, and *(ii)* this specification also alters the effect of market structure on the fiscal multiplier.

The above analysis corresponds to a long-run situation which omits dynamics and does not allow for the government to finance its deficit by borrowing. Section 4 looks at the implications of introducing simple dynamics due to assuming an overlapping generations structure. The representative household lives for two periods corresponding to 'young' and 'old'. A household is assumed to consume in both periods but work, pay tax and save only when young and retire and consume all the saving when old. Hence, we now choose (C,L,C_o) to maximise the life time utility

$$U(C,L,C_o) = C^{\alpha}[L^{1-1/s} + C_o^{1-1/s}]^{\beta/[1-1/s]}$$

where C and L denote consumption and leisure when young, $\alpha+\beta=1$, and s ($\neq 1$) is the elasticity of substitution between leisure when young and consumption when old, C_o (we have omitted money holdings for simplicity). We assume that the government issues bonds, denoted by B, which households can purchase at price q (=1/(1+r), r is the real interest rate) when young and redeem at unit price when old. Thus, at any period the demand for bonds by young households is given by $B=C_o$, and the government budget constraint is $T+qB=G+B_{-1}$ where we assume again that T is proportional to total income. Now, the long-run tax multiplier again turns out to be zero whereas a fiscal expansion financed by borrowing leads to the following long-run multiplier

$$\frac{dY}{dG}=\left(\frac{1}{1-C_y}\right)\left(\frac{1}{1-\delta}\right)$$

where $-1<\delta<1$, ($\delta=dB/dB_{-1}$) is the sufficient condition for stability and $0<C_y<1$, C_y is the marginal propensity to consume by young. Thus, now even $dY/dG>1$ is a possibility since $\delta>0$ is a likely outcome.

The above results demonstrate the importance of recognising and acknowledging the limitations of models which use microeconomic foundations to construct macroeconomic models that possess certain policy implications. The paper argues, using the simplest possible structures, that such models can be constructed so as to yield opposite and conflicting policy implications. For instance, under certain assumptions we derive a positive multiplier effect which increases as goods market deviates from perfect competition, and we show that, under equally plausible assumptions and slight modification of the microeconomic structure of the demand side, an opposite result can be achieved. Given that there is now a strong tendency to use such models, we wish to use the simple demonstrations in this paper to highlight the pitfalls which otherwise may remain unnoticed.

REFERENCES

Auerbach, A. J. and Kotlikoff, L. J. (1987) *Dynamic fiscal policy*, Cambridge University Press.

Blanchard, O. J. and Kiyotaki, N. (1987) 'Monopolistic competition and the effects of aggregate demand', *American Economic Review*, 77, 647-66.

Dixon, H. (1987) 'A simple model of imperfect competition with Walrasian features', *Oxford Economic Papers*, 39, 134-60.

Frenkel, J. A. and Razin, A. (1987) *Fiscal policies and the world economy*, MIT Press, Cambridge, Massachusetts.

Hart, O. (1982) 'A model of imperfect competition with Keynesian features' *Quarterly Journal of Economics*, 97, 109-38.

Mankiw, N. G. (1988) 'Imperfect competition and the Keynesian Cross' *Economics Letters*, 26, 7-13.

Molana, H. and Moutos, T. (1991) 'A note on taxation, imperfect competition and the balanced budget multiplier' *Oxford Economic Papers*, 43, 68-74.

Molana, H. and Moutos, T. (1992) 'Returns to scale, imperfect competition, and aggregate demand and trade policy effects in a two-country model' *Open Economies Review*, forthcoming.

Rankin, N. (1986) 'Debt policy under fixed and flexible prices', *Oxford Economic Papers*, 38, 481-500.

Startz, R. (1989) 'Monopolistic competition as a foundation for Keynesian macroeconomic models' *Quarterly Journal of Economics*, 104, 737-52.

The Disappearing Multiplier: A System Dynamics Approach to Macroeconomics

Günther Ossimitz
Institut für Mathematik, Universität Klagenfurt
Universitätsstraße 65, 9022 Klagenfurt, Austria

Macroeconomical models are usually described with equations or function graphs, which are more or less statical. In this paper I will sketch a dynamical approach to macroeconomics. This approach will have some remarkable features:

- I will use numerical modelling instead of algebraical or graphical reasoning;
- the modelling will on the level of elementary arithmetics;
- for experimentation a spreadsheet program will be used;
- the dynamical approach will reveal some new aspects of the theory of Keynes.

I will use the system-dynamics method, which originally has been developed by J. Forrester (1961) at MIT. In system dynamics modelling the time continuum is divided into intervals (steps) of equal length. This leads to a distinction between state-variables (which are related to points of time) and flow-variables, which are related to time-intervals. For a more detailed discussion of system dynamics see Ossimitz (1990).

THE THEORY OF KEYNES

As an example for dynamical modelling in macroeconomics I will show a dynamical model of the simplest case of the Keynesian equilibrium model: a closed economy containing just households and business firms, without foreign or government activies (Fig. 1).

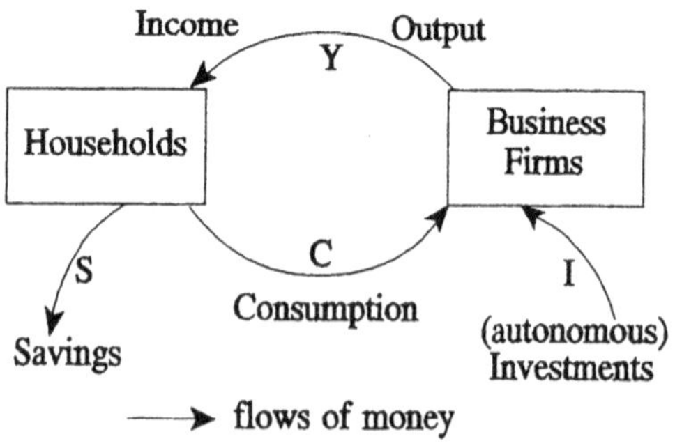

Fig. 1 Keynesian model

The traditional theory is based upon following assumptions:

- $Y \equiv C+S$ and $Y \equiv C+I$. No liquid money is being kept.
- The consumption of the households is proportional to the aggregate income: $C=c \cdot Y$; $c<1$: marginal propensity to spend.
- Investments I are independent from the other model variables (autonomous investments); actually I is (mostly) constant.
- Aggregate demand AD is the sum of consumption and planned investment: $AD = C+I = c \cdot Y+I$.

The traditional method answers two important questions:

* Which conditions describe the equilibrium state (i.e. AD=Y)?

* How does the equilibrium output Y_0 change, if the autonomous investment is changed by some amount ΔI?

The equilibrium state can be formulated in different ways: $Y_0 = AD$ or $Y_0 = C \cdot Y+I$ or $Y_0 = 1/(1-c) \cdot I$ or $S = I$ (since $S = (1-c) \cdot Y$). The factor $\alpha=1/(1-c)$, called the investment-multiplier, is also a key for answering the second question. If autonomous investment increases by one unit, the equilibrium output increases by an amount of $\alpha=1/(1-c)$. If $c=0.9$, the multiplier $\alpha=1/(1-0.9)=10$. This means that an additional investment of e.g. \$1.000,000 would lead to a increase in equilibrium output of \$10.000,000. This multiplier effect is the core of the Keynesian theory.

The multiplier can be derived in different ways, e.g. algebraical or geometrical. One argument is the following: An initial increase increase in autonomous spending of \$1 causes an increase of C by an amount of c; this again gives another increase to Y by c; (first turn in the Y-C-cycle in Fig. 1). The additional consumption of c raises output=income Y; this increases the consumption by another $c \cdot c=c^2$ (second round) etc. After an infinitesimal number of rounds around the Y-C cycle in Fig.1 the initial increase of \$1 will cause an increase of equilibrium output of $1+c+c^2+c^3+.. =1/(1-c)=\alpha$.

A DYNAMICAL VIEW OF THE KEYNES MODEL

This way to derive the multiplier raises two questions:

1) How long does it actually last until the new equilibrium is reached?
2) Has the additional investment to be invested only once or in every period in order to reach the new equilibrium?

We construct a simple dynamical model, which is based upon the assumptions given above plus one extra assumption:

- We suppose that the income of one month is consumed in the next month. This implies a time-step of one month.

Fig. 2 gives an example of a model in equilibrium with c=0.9 (⇒α=10); I=100 ⇒ Y_0=1000 and C_0=900, S_0=100. If autonomous spending is increased by ΔI=50, the multiplier α=10 predicts a raise of the equilibrium output by 500 from 1000 to 1500.

KEYNES1
Y_0: 1000 c: 0.90
I: 100 I: 50 **EVERY MONTH**

month	Y Y=C+I	C C=c*Y	S S=Y-C	I (aut)
0	1000	900	100	100
1	1000	900	100	150
2	1050	945	105	150
3	1095	985	110	150
4	1136	1022	114	150
5	1172	1055	117	150
6	1205	1084	120	150
7	1234	1111	123	150
8	1261	1135	126	150
9	1285	1156	128	150
10	1306	1176	131	150
11	1326	1193	133	150
12	1343	1209	134	150
:				
24	1456	1310	146	150
:				
36	1487	1339	149	150
:				
48	1496	1347	150	150

Fig. 2 Dynamical view of Keynesian theory

The model calculations show:

1) it lasts about 3 years until the new equilibrium is reached;
2) 50 extra units must be invested <u>every month</u> in order to achieve the new equilibrium of 1500.

The second finding makes the multiplier concept of the static model rather questionable. The dynamic model shows that it is by far not enough to make an additional investment only once. If only in one month 150 units were invested (and 100 units in all other months), the output Y would raise to 1050 in the next month, then 1045, then 1040.5 etc., until the original equilibrium of 1000 is reached again. Just the sum of values above 1000 (50+45+40.5+...) will sum up to 500; but will not be achieved in one single month.

REFERENCES:

Forrester J (1961): Industrial Dynamics. MIT Press. Cambridge, Mass

Ossimitz G (1990): Materialien zur Systemdynamik. Verlag Hölder-Pichler-Tempsky, Wien und B.G. Teubner, Stuttgart.

Chaotic Foreign Exchange Rates

Beate Reszat
HWWA-Institut für Wirtschaftsforschung
Neuer Jungfernstieg 21, 2000 Hamburg 36, Germany

Studies of chaotic exchange rates often concentrate on empirical aspects. They comb large numbers of data in search of traces of a strange attractor. In contrast, this paper tries to explain how exchange rates may become chaotic. Starting from an assumption about different groups of traders that goes beyond recent models of fundamentalists' and chartists' behaviour it emphasizes the need to model the foreign exchange market as a dissipative system and not, as usual, as a closed conservative one.

Dissipation ...

Chaos, in short, stands for two characteristics of a dynamic system: It never reaches a single point twice and its time path is highly sensitive to initial conditions and parameter values. From the natural sciences it is known that only dissipative systems can become chaotic. That are open systems which are exposed to some kind of friction. They lose "energy", i.e. the stuff that makes them run. But, being in a continuous exchange with their environment they permanently get new impulses that hinder them from coming to a standstill. Any approach claiming to explain chaotic exchange rates has to discuss what in the system presented would become dissipated and get lost.

In foreign exchange markets, information takes this role. Here, new information is regarded, not as in traditional models of exchange rates as a transitory shock, but as a permanent stream of impulses from the outside world that keeps the system running. However, with information being spread among, and becoming known to, more and more market participants, and with its being transformed to a respective set of price signals, this "energy" gets lost bearing no further incentive to trade. Then, without a permanent supply of fresh news from outside markets would dry up.

... and Stretching and Folding Effects

Information is not a homogeneous good. Actors in the markets differ and, accordingly, tend to use various kinds of information and a variety of methods to process it. To emphasize this aspect, a distinction is made, first between fundamentalists and chartists, and then between a short term and a longer term time horizon in forming expectations that is characteristic for the trading activities of different groups.

There are banks, nonbanks and central banks in the markets. A System Dynamics approach is chosen to shed light on the complex structures and interactions between them. Foreign exchange positions - the levels in the system - are supposed to be held for five reasons: By nonbanks in connection with international trade and portfolio investments or as outright positions for speculative purposes, by banks as a result of arbitrage activities, and by central banks as official reserves. With exemption of the last, all decisions related to these levels are determined by risk/return considerations into which exchange rate expectations enter as one argument.

Essentially, the foreign exchange market is an interbank market. Accordingly, each nonbank wanting to sell or buy foreign currency needs a bank. The bank, in turn, acts for the nonbank as a mere intermediary closing open positions due to nonbank activities at once. There is one peculiarity to be mentioned in this context, namely the possibility of revolving. Banks, as well as nonbanks doing outright transactions, that decide to keep an open position longer than originally intended have the possibility to prolong this position by a swap. This has two implications: On the one hand, it adds to the actors' flexibility. On the other hand, it makes the share of trades unrelated to "market fundamentals" greater than otherwise. And, since here both kind of activities are assumed to be based on chart analyses rather than fundamentals it puts an extra weight on these techniques further loosening the ties between exchange rate changes and so-called basic influences.

Information flows and resource flows in the system depend, among other things, on actors' targets and motives, their time horizon, market access and flexibility. Each decision they make affects the exchange rate, and each exchange rate change in turn enters the expectations of all actors once again. However, these "reaction cycles" differ in length and magnitude depending on the kind of information used, the way it is processed and the speed at which decisions are made. Those interacting cycles - that at times dampen one another's effects and at times reinforce each other's influence - exert typical "stretching and folding" effects that, besides dissipation, are the second crucial prerequisite for chaos to emerge.

In this scenario, no dramatic event or "shock" is needed for the exchange rate to start fluctuating. The simple monitoring and processing of per se "harmless" looking news - of regularly published data of income, price and current account statistics and the like - and of successive small price signals would, in their interplay, suffice to generate variability.

References

Allen, H. and M.P. Taylor. 1990. Charts, Noise and Fundamentals in the London Foreign Exchange Market. *Economic Journal* 400:49-59.

Mandelbrot, B. 1963. The Variation of Certain Speculative Prices. *Journal of Business* 36:394-419.

B. Reszat: Dissipation and Chaos in Foreign Exchange Markets, forthcoming, Utrecht 1992.

Disequilibrium Models and the Use of Business Survey Data

Peter Stalder
Konjunkturforschungsstelle, ETH Zürich
Mousson-Straße 15, 8092 Zürich, Switzerland

Considerable work has been done in recent years on constructing macro-econometric disequilibrium models. The characteristic feature of these models is that prices and wages are not assumed to clear markets instantaneously so that some agents (those on the "long" side of a market) may get rationed. Rationing in turn entails revisions of trade plans, causing so-called spill-over effects across markets. In an aggregate two-market setting, the economy can be located in four possible regimes, which are endogenously determined by the model. The regime of 'Keynesian unemployment' is characterized by excess supply for both labor and goods; it closely replicates the traditional IS-LM analysis with the corresponding policy implications. In the other regimes - 'classical unemployment', 'repressed inflation' and 'underconsumption' - the economy behaves differently and other policy measures are implied.

The problems of formulating, estimating and testing disequilibrium models have recently been discussed by Quandt (1988) and Laroque and Salanie (1989, 1992), among others. The purpose of this paper is to review the various possibilities of implementing such models econometrically and to present some empirical results for Switzerland.

Macro disequilibrium models may be distinguished into two broad groups, differing as to how the aggregation problem is tackled. In a first type of model, the minimum-condition is assumed to hold for the aggregates. This means, for instance, that the employment level of the economy (L) is given by the smaller of aggregate demand and supply of labor (LD, LS):

$$L = \min\left\{LD(x,\theta,\epsilon^d),\ LS(x,\theta,\epsilon^s)\right\} \quad (1a) \qquad L = \min\left\{LD(x,\theta),\ LS(x,\theta)\right\} + \epsilon \quad (1b)$$

If demand and supply are subject to additive disturbances and these are identical ($\epsilon^d = \epsilon^s = \epsilon$), which is a rather unnatural assumption though, (1a) simplifies to (1b). In both cases, the whole economy switches from one régime into another (stochastically or deterministically). In order for an aggregate economy to exhibit such 'discrete' behavior, all individual markets (defined in terms of qualification, location, industry etc.) would have to be in the same rationing situation in a given period. This is not a very appealing assumption. A second type of model therefore starts from the notion that aggregate markets consist of a multitude of 'micromarkets' on which demand/supply ratios may differ. The minimum condition is applied to these micromarkets. Under specific assumptions as to the micro-level distribution of demand and supply, total employment is obtained as a CES-function of aggregate demand and supply:

$$L = \left[LD(x,\theta,\epsilon^d)^{-\rho} + LS(x,\theta,\epsilon^s)^{-\rho}\right]^{-1/\rho} \tag{2a}$$

Again, if the aggregate error terms in LD and LS are identical (and multiplicative), (2a) may be recast as

$$L = \left[LD(x,\theta)^{-\rho} + LS(x,\theta)^{-\rho}\right]^{-1/\rho} \cdot \epsilon \ . \tag{2b}$$

In either case, there are no discrete switches from purely demand-determined to purely supply-determined situations but the transition between the regimes is gradual. Parameter ρ is inversely related to the dispersion of the demand/supply ratios in the population of micromarkets, i.e. it measures 'mismatch'. For small values of ρ, L falls substantially short of the minimum of LD and LS, except for large amounts of aggrègate excess demand or supply. For $\rho \to \infty$ (no mismatch), formulations (2) boil down to (1) - apart from the fact that we have assumed additive instead of multiplicative error terms in (1).

To allow for interactions between the markets for labor and goods, the above equations must be combined with similar equations for the goods market and spillover effects must be taken into account. This means that the trade offers in one market are affected by the imbalances between demand and supply in the other market. There are several ways of introducing such spillovers, but rather restrictive assumptions with respect to the micro level distribution of demand and supply are required to get tractable functional forms.

The main difficulty in estimating the parameter vector θ in the above equations arises from the latent character of demand and supply. If information on the ruling regime is absent and only aggregate transactions (L) are observed, estimation becomes quite tricky even for the simplest specifications. Assuming normality of ϵ^d and ϵ^s, (1a) can be estimated by FIML, but the likelihood function, obtained by "integrating out" the latent variables, turns out to be unbounded, i.e. it goes to infinity at some 'peculiar' points of the parameter space. In (1b) the likelihood function is not continuously differentiable. For the micromarket formulation (2a) no analytic expression for the likelihood is available. It is only (2b), which however relies on rather counterintuitive distributional assumptions, that lends itself to an easy NLS estimation.

In view of these difficulties, pseudo-ML methods (PML) have been proposed. In case of (1a), one computes $E(L|x,\theta)$ and $VAR(L|x,\theta)$ (where θ includes the unknown parameters of the distribution of ϵ^d and ϵ^s) and estimates the pseudo model $L = E(L|x,\theta) + \epsilon$ by ML, taking into account that the variance of ϵ is given by $VAR(L|x,\theta)$. Unfortunately, analytic expressions for the first and second moment of observed transactions do only exist for very simple disequilibrium models. However, it is almost always possible to compute numerical approximations via Monte-Carlo simulations. In case of (2a), for example, one may approximate the expectation and the variance of L, conditional on x and θ, by taking a sufficiently large number of random drawings from the (ϵ^d, ϵ^s)-distribution. The likelihood function is then based on these simulated moments (SPML). With the SPML method, one can even dispense with (2a) and carry out aggregation by simulating the micromarket disturbances as well - under more general distributional assumptions than those underlying (2a).

A more pragmatic route can be taken by exploiting the regime information provided by business survey data. Such data have a quite natural interpretation in a micromarkets framework. Indeed, the same assumptions yielding (2a) imply

$$L\cdot(1-\Pi_{ld>ls})^{-1/\rho} = LD(x,\theta,\epsilon^d) \qquad L\cdot \Pi_{ld>ls}^{-1/\rho} = LS(x,\theta,\epsilon^s)\,, \tag{3}$$

where $\Pi_{ld>ls}$ is the (endogenously determined) proportion of micromarkets in an excess demand regime. Measuring $\Pi_{ld>ls}$ by the proportion of firms reporting 'labor bottlenecks', the nonlinear two-equation system (3) can easily be estimated by FIML. Of course, this approach is also not without flaw. First, (3) again rests on rather specific assumptions as to the micro distribution of demand and supply, and connecting (3) with a goods market requires even more restrictive assumptions. Second, the business survey indicator is assumed to provide an exact measure of the regime proportion. Note that, due to the nonlinearity of (3), measurement errors in $\Pi_{ld>ls}$ are not captured adequately by ϵ^d and ϵ^s. But if one wants to estimate more than very simplistic models, there is probably no way around using survey indicators as regime classification information. However, in future research, one should try to relax the assumption that these indicators are exact.

A two market disequilibrium model (labor and goods) in the style of (3) has been estimated for Switzerland with quarterly data from 1967 to 1985, while data for the period 1986 to 1989 have been used to perform a post-sample test of parameter stability. The empirical results can be summarized as follows:

- The model indicates a growing micro-level dispersion of demand/supply ratios on the labor market: Structural unemployment, defined as unemployment in a situation where aggregate demand equals aggregate supply, increases from about 1% in 1967 to about 2% at the end of the estimation period. As far as cyclical developments are concerned, two broad subperiods are to be distinguished: In the late 1960s and the first half of the 1970s, the model shows varying amounts of excess demand for labor, reaching a maximum of sightly more that 5% in 1969/70. The picture changes with the recession of 1975; from that time on the model indicates mainly situations of excess supply (peak values of nearly 7% in the recessions of 1975 and 1982/83), interrupted in 1980 by a short interval with some excess demand.
- The short-run variations in employment are primarily due to fluctuations in labor demand. Labor supply in general tends in the same direction, but its movements are less pronounced and delayed, thus absorbing the swings in labor demand only partly. This gives rise to unemployment in recessions and rationing of labor demand in boom periods.
- The cyclical fluctuations in labor demand are mainly traced back to the Keynesian spillover effect, arising from 'insufficient demand' in the goods market. This spillover is strongest in the recessions of 1975 and 1982/83. Production capacities and associated 'notional labor demand' show much less cyclical variability, but the impacts of relative factor costs are significant.

- In boom periods like 1969/70, 1973, 1980 and 1985, effective output falls short of full capacity output, reflecting that firms were not able to fully realize labor demand. This 'repressed inflation'-spillover, amounting to a maximum output reduction of about 2.5% in 1969/70, is relatively small as compared to the above-mentioned Keynesian spillover in recession periods.

REFERENCES:

Büttler H.-J., G. Frei and B. Schips (1986), Estimation of Disequilibrium Models, Lecture Notes in Economics and Mathematical Systems (Springer-Verlag).

Laroque G. and B. Salanié (1992), Macroeconometric Disequilibrium Models, in: H. Pesaran and M. Wickens (eds.), Handbook of Applied Econometrics.

Quandt, R.E., 1988, The Econometrics of Disequilibrium (Basil Blackwell).

Stalder, P., 1991, Regime Transitions, Spillovers and Buffer Stocks - Analysing the Swiss Economy by Means of a Disequilibrium Model, Lecture Notes in Economics and Mathematical Systems (Springer-Verlag).

Increasing the Capital Income Tax Leads to Faster Growth

Harald Uhlig, Noriyuki Yanagawa
Department of Economics, Princeton University
Princeton, NJ 08544, U.S.A.

INTRODUCTION.

This paper shows that under rather mild conditions, higher capital income taxes lead to faster growth in an overlapping generations economy with endogenous growth. Government expenditures are financed with labor income taxes as well as capital income taxes. Since capital income accrues to the old, taxing it reliefs the tax burden on the young and leaves them with more income out of which to save. We argue that savings are sufficiently interest inelastic so that higher savings and therefore higher growth result. The basic argument is not seriously challenged by a grandfather clause for initial capital or by the old receiving some labor income as well. The reasoning is similar to Feldstein (1978), Auerbach (1979) and in particular Jones and Manuelli (1992), but in contrast to the conventional wisdom about the effect of capital income taxation as, say, in Lucas (1990).

THE MODEL.

Consider a two-period OLG with one consumption good per period and one representative agent born at each date $t = 0, 1, \ldots$. Agents have a homothetic utility function in consumption and thus consume a fraction $C(R)$ of their total life-time wealth, when young, given the interest factor R between the two periods of their life. They are endowed with λ units of time when young and $1 - \lambda$ units of time, when old, which they supply inelastically as labor.

Each period, the consumption good is produced by a competitive sector of firms according to the production function

$$y = k^{\rho} \left(n \frac{K}{\alpha} \right)^{1-\rho}, \qquad (1)$$

where k and n are the firm-specific capital and labor inputs, K denotes the aggregate capital stock and ρ, α are parameters (see e.g. Romer (1986) for a justification of this externality-extended production function). Aggregate production is thus $Y = aK$, where $a = \alpha^{\rho-1}$. Dividends per unit of capital are $d = \rho Y/K = \rho a$ and wages per efficiency unit α/K of time are $w = (1-\rho)\alpha^\rho$, independent of time. The aggregate resource constraint each period is $C + H + X = Y$, where H is government consumption and X is investment. The capital stock evolves according to $K_{t+1} = (1-\delta)K_t + X_t$, so that a unit of capital commands a price of $v = d + (1-\delta) = \rho a + 1 - \delta$.

Government consumes the fraction γ of output each period, which it can finance via a capital income tax τ_k on all of v (hence $R = (1-\tau_k)v$), a labor income tax $\tau_{L,t}$ or debt. We assume for simplicity that the debt-output ratio is constant at some $b \geq 0$ over time except the initial period. The budget constraint is achieved by adjusting $\tau_{L,t}$.

Solving the model leads to the equations

$$\tau_{L,t} = \frac{\gamma}{1-\rho} - \left(1 - \frac{R}{g_t}\right)\frac{b}{1-\rho} - \frac{\rho a + 1 - \delta}{(1-\rho)a}\tau_K,\; t \geq 1. \tag{2}$$

and

$$g_{t+1} = \frac{(1-C(R))\lambda - \dfrac{b}{(1-\tau_{L,t})(1-\rho)}}{C(R)\dfrac{1-\lambda}{R} + \dfrac{1}{a(1-\tau_{L,t})(1-\rho)}}, \tag{3}$$

where g_{t+1} is the growth rate from period t to t+1. These two equations can simply be simulated forward.

THE BENCHMARK CASE.

$b = 0$ and $\lambda = 1$ leads to

$$g = a(1-\rho)(1-\tau_L)S(R;1), \tag{4}$$

where $S(R;1)$ is the saving rate of the young, given that only the young earn income: $S(R;1) = 1 - C(R)$. The argument is now easy to see: a higher capital income tax leads to a lower labor income tax (see eqn. (2)) and thus to a lower growth rate, provided savings are not too interest elastic:

Proposition 1 *If the overall utility is characterized by a constant intertemporal elasticity of* *substitution of unity or lower, $\sigma \leq 1$, then a higher capital income tax rate will unambiguously result in a higher growth rate.*

Further calibration shows, that a higher growth rate results for the United States as long as $\sigma \leq 1.33$. Hall (1988) has measured $\hat{\sigma} \leq 0.2$.

OTHER OBJECTIONS.

A grandfather clause for capital in the hands of the initial old does not alter the result, provided the budget gap in the first period is financed through a higher labor income tax and not government debt, which is detrimental to growth. Furthermore, while allowing values for λ other than 1 is able to overturn the result, this will happen only in a rather slim parameter region or for parameters, at which savings of the young become negative.

CONCLUSIONS.

The result, that a higher capital income tax leads to faster growth is remarkably robust. Conventional wisdom needs to be rethought.

REFERENCES.

Auerbach, Alan J., 1979, The Optimal Taxation of Heterogeneous Capital, Quarterly Journal of Economics, Vol. 93, no. 4, 589-612.

Feldstein, Martin, 1978, The Welfare Costs of Capital Income Taxation, J. Political Economy, vol. 86, No. 2, S29 - S51.

Hall, Robert E., 1988, Intertemporal Substitution in Consumption, Journal of Political Economy, vol. 96, no. 2, 339-357.

Jones, Larry E., Rodolfo Manuelli and Peter Rossi, 1991, Optimal Taxation in Models of Endogenous Growth, draft, Northwestern University.

Lucas, Robert E., Jr., 1990, Supply-Side Economics: An Anlytical Review, Oxford Economic Papers 42, 293-316.

Romer, Paul M., 1986, Increasing Returns and Long-Run Growth, Journal of Political Economy, vol. 94, 1002-1037.

Section 11

Decision Theory, Utility and Risk

On Solving of a Multiobjective Nonlinear Programming Problem with General Parameters in the Objective Functions Using the Fuzzy Mathematical Programming

Elsaid Ammar
Abteilung Mathematik, Technische Universität Dresden
Mommsenstraße 13, 8027 Dresden, Germany

We study a convex multiobjective nonlinear programming (MOPNLP) problem with general parameters in the objective functions. We introduce the fuzzy problem using arbitrary transformation functions. Some fuzzy notions of this problem are given. The connection between the two problems is presented. $\vee$ and $\wedge$ denote the maximum and minimum.

Formulation of the problem

In this paper we shall study the following multiobjective parametric nonlinear programming problem :

(MOPNLP)

$$\operatorname*{Min}_{x} \; F(x,\lambda)$$

subject to

$$X = \{ x \in R^n : G(x) \leq 0\},$$

$$\Lambda = \{\lambda \in R^m : H(\lambda) \leq 0\},$$

where $F(x,\lambda)=(f_1(x,\lambda),\ldots,f_k(x,\lambda))^T$, $G(x)=(g_1(x),\ldots, g_r(x))^T$, $H(\lambda)=(h_1(\lambda),\ldots,h_s(\lambda))^T$, X, Λ are non-empty, closed, bounded, convex sets and F, G and H are convex continuous vector functions on R^{n+m}, R^n and R^m, respectively. Fundamental in regard to the problem PMONLP are the efficient solution and weak-efficient solution concepts.

Definition 1 (Efficient solution) A point x^* is called an efficient solution of the problem MOPNLP if and only if there is no $x \in X$ such that

$$f_i(x,\lambda^*) \le f_i(x^*,\lambda^*), \quad i=1,\ldots,k,$$

and $f_i(x,\lambda^*) < f_i(x^*,\lambda^*)$ for at least one $i \in \{1,\ldots,k\}$ and one λ^*. The parameter λ^* is called an optimal parameter corresponding to x^*.

Definition 2 (Weak-efficient) A point $x^* \in X$ is called a weak-efficient solution of the problem MOPNLP if and only if there is no $x \in X$ such that

$$f_i(x,\lambda^*) < f_i(x^*,\lambda^*), \quad \text{for each } i=1,\ldots,k,$$

for at least one λ^*. The parameter λ^* is called a weak-optimal parameter corresponding to x^*.

We will now introduce the use of the theory of fuzzy sets that will enable a decision-maker, by suitably strict monotone decreasing continuous transformation functions $\xi_{\lambda i} \longrightarrow [0,1]$, in order to describe which of the efficient vectors is prefered.

Fuzzy Problem

The general fuzzy optimization problem FMONLP to the problem MOPNLP may be defined in the following form :

$$\text{(FMONLP)} \qquad \max_{x \in X} \mu_{min}(x).$$

Where $\mu_{min}(x) = \bigwedge_i \mu_i(x)$, $\mu_i(x) = \bigwedge_{\lambda \in \Lambda} \phi_i(x,\lambda)$, $\text{supp}(\mu_{min}) \neq \emptyset$ and $\phi_i(x,\lambda) = \xi_{\lambda i}(f_i(x,\lambda))$ for each i.

Definition 4 (Fuzzy solution set) The fuzzy feasible solution set of the problem FMONLP for a specified $\varepsilon \in (0,1]$ is $\mu_{min} R^n \longrightarrow [0,1]$, defined as

$$\mu_{min}(x) = \bigwedge_i \bigwedge_{\lambda \in \Lambda} \phi_i(x,\lambda)$$

Definition 5 (Fuzzy solution) Let μ_{min} be a given fuzzy feasible solution set by arbitrary transformations, then x^* is called a fuzzy solution of the problem FMONLP with respect to μ_{min}, if

$$\mu_{min}(x^*) \geq \mu_{min}(x) \quad \text{for each } x \in X$$

Remark 1 The ordinary solution set of the problem FMONLP for a specified $\delta \in [0, \bigvee_x \mu_{min}(x))$, denoted by $M(\delta)$, is defined as

$$M(\delta) := \{x \in R^n : \mu_{min}(x) \geq m\} \text{ with } m = \bigvee_x \mu_{min}(x) - \delta,$$

and the ordinary optimal solution set of the problem FMONLP is $M(0)$.

Some results

Theorem 1 If x^* is a fuzzy solution of the problem FMONLP with respect to μ_{min} which is introduced by arbitrary transformations, then x^* is a weak-efficient solution of the problem MOPNLP.

Theorem 2 If the problem FMONLP has a unique fuzzy solution x^* with respect to μ_{min}, which is introduced by arbitrary transformations, then x^* is an efficient solution of the problem MOPNLP.

Theorem 3 Let $\lambda^* \in \Lambda$ be a weak-optimal parameter corresponding to x^*, and if x^* is a weak-efficient solution of the problem MOPNLP, then x^* is a fuzzy solution of the problem FMONLP with respect to μ_{min}, which is introduced by arbtirary transformations.

Lemma 1 Let $\lambda^* \in \Lambda$ is an optimal parameter corresponding to x^* and if x^* is an efficient solution of the problem MOPNLP, then x^* is a fuzzy solution of the problem FMONLP with respect to μ_{min} which is introduced by arbitrary transformation functions.

Theorem 4 If $F(x,\lambda)$ is a strictly quasiconvex vector function in x and λ^* is corresponding to x^*, then for each efficient solution x^* of the problem MOPNLP a fuzzy set μ_{min} exists, which is introduced by arbitrary transformations such that x^* is a unique solution of the problem FMONLP with respect to μ_{min}.

Literatur

Ammar E, Metz J (1992) On fuzzy convexity and parametric fuzzy optimization, Fuzzy sets and systems; Vol 49 No 2 pp 135-142.

Ammar E On solving of a multiobjective nonlinear programming problem with general parameters in the objective functions using the fuzzy mathematical programming. Fuzzy Sets and Systems; to appear.

Bellman E, Zadeh L A (1970) Decision-making in a fuzzy environment. Management of Science; 17 141-164

Buckley J J (1983) Fuzzy programming and pareto optimal set. Fuzzy sets and systems 10; 57-63

Feng Y (1983) A method using fuzzy mathematical programming to solve the vectormaximum problem. Fuzzy Sets and Systems 2; 131-136

Orlovski S A (1984) Multiobjective programming problems with fuzzy parameters, Control and Cybernetics; Vol 13 No 3. Shimiozu Kiyotaka (1976) Systems optimization theory, Korona, Tokyo.

Zimmermann H J (1978) Fuzzy programming and linear programming with several objective functions; Fuzzy Sets and Systems 1; 46-51.

Modeling Attitudes Towards Uncertainty and Risk Through the Use of Monotone Capacities

Alain Chateauneuf
UFR de Math. University Paris
90 Rue de Tolbiac, 75634 Paris Cedex 13, France

The aim of this lecture is to present a survey of some results related to Choquet Expected Utility -C.E.U.-Models, a promising class of models introduced separately by Quiggin (1982), Yaari (1987) and Schmeidler (1982,1989), which allow to separate attitudes towards uncertainty (or risk) from attitudes towards wealth while respecting the first order stochastic dominance axiom.

First assuming as Yaari that the decision maker displays a constant marginal utility of wealth, we introduce Schmeidler's and Yaari's models in a same unified framework as in Chateauneuf (1991).

We consider a decision maker faced with choices among acts X, the set V of such acts consisting of all bounded $\mathcal{a}$-measurable functions on S, where S is a set of states of nature and $\mathcal{a}$ a σ-algebra of events (i.e. of subsets of S). This decision maker -D.M.- is supposed to be under uncertainty, this means that no information on the occurrence of events is available to him. Let $\succsim$ be the preference relation on V of the agent. First, we state three axioms which are usual and natural requirements, whatever attitude towards uncertainty may be : (A.1) : $\succsim$ is a non-trivial weak order, (A.2) : continuity w.r.t. monotone uniform convergence, (A.3) : monotonicity. Such axioms characterize the existence for every act X of a certainty-equivalent I(X), monotone, monotonely continuous, which represents the preference relation $\succsim$.

Then we introduce the crucial axiom (A.4) of comonotonic independence both encountered in Schmeidler's and Yaari's models. Let us recall that X,Y $\in$ V are comonotonic if "they vary in the same sense" namely if $(X(s)-X(t))(Y(s)-Y(t)) \geq 0 \ \forall s,t \in S$. A recent result of CHATEAUNEUF, KAST, LAPIED (1992) shows that if $\mathcal{a}$ contains singletons {s}, s $\in$ S, X and Y are comonotonic iff $COV_P(X,Y) \geq 0 \ \forall P$ additive probability measure on $(S,\mathcal{a})$.

(A.4) : X,Y,Z $\in$ V, X,Z comonotonic, Y,Z comonotonic

$X \sim Y \Longrightarrow X + Z \sim Y + Z$

That comonotonic independence wants to allow for hedging effects is illustrated by simple examples.

Defining a normalized capacity v as a normalized monotone set function from $\mathcal{a}$ to [0,1], leads to Schmeidler's model : For a preference relation $\succsim$ on V satisfying axioms A.1, A.2, A.3, (i) and (ii) below are equivalent :

(i) $\succsim$ satisfies comonotonic independence A.4

(ii) There exists a unique normalized capacity v on $\mathcal{a}$ such that :

$$I(X) = \text{Choquet Integral} \int X\, dv \text{ where } \int X\, dv = \int_{-\infty}^{0} (v(X \geq t)-1)dt + \int_{0}^{+\infty} v(X \geq t)dt$$

The proof deduces from Schmeidler's representation theorem (1986), which states that Choquet integral functionals coincide with monotone, monotonely continuous, comonotonic additive functionals I on V ($I(X+Y) = I(X) + I(Y)$ $\forall X,Y$ comonotonic). Related results as Greco's representation theorem (1982) can be found in the self-contained textbook "Subadditive measure and Integral" of Denneberg (1992). Recent works of Gilboa and Schmeidler (1992) as "Additive representation of set functions " and "Canonical representation of set functions" also offer new stimulating developments.

Since comonotonic independence allows for hedging effects, uncertainty aversion of our D.M. can be modeled by substituting axiom A'.4 to A.4

(A'.4) : $X,Y \in V$ $X \sim Y$ Z comonotonic with Y

implies $X + Z \succsim Y + Z$

The previous Choquet integral representation $\int X\, dv$ remains valid but now v is convex, a nice property emphasizing the pessimistic inclinations of the D.M., since it is a well known result that when v is convex then $\int X\, dv = \min_{P \geq v} E_P(X)$ for any additive probability measure P on $\mathcal{a}$.

As recent applications of Schmeidler's model to economic topics let us mention Dow and Werlang's paper (1992) about the optimal choice of portfolio and Chateauneuf, Kast, Lapied's one (1992) about asset pricings. In this last work setting $I(X) = \int X\, dv$ with v concave and interpreting I(X) (resp. -I(-X)) as the selling price (resp. buying price) of an asset by a broker allows to explain positive profits since $I(X) \geq -I(-X)$.

Risk

Assume now that the decision maker is informed of the values of an objective additive probability P on $(S,\mathcal{a})$, satisfies axioms A.1 to A.4 plus the simple "first stochastic dominance axiom" A.5 : $A,B \in \mathcal{a}$, $P(A) \geq P(B) \longrightarrow A \succsim B$. Then we get Yaari's (1987) model : there exists a unique non-decreasing $f : [0,1] \longrightarrow [0,1]$ s.t. $f(0) = 0$, $f(1) = 1$ and

$$I(X) = \int_{-\infty}^{0} (f(P(X \geq t))-1)dt + \int_{0}^{+\infty} f(P(X \geq t))dt \ \forall X \in V.$$

Assume now P σ-additive and non-atomic, substitute axiom A'.2 of monotone convergence to A.2, and axiom A'.4 of uncertainty aversion to A.4, then f is convex and such a D.M. is risk averse in the sense that he respects second order stochastic dominance. Note that such a D.M. conveys pessimism since he relatively overvalues probabilities of low payments and relatively undervalues probabilities of high payments. Further results about stochastic dominance and non-additive probabilities can be found in Dyckerhoff and Mosler (1990) and Scarsini (1992).

As an application of Yaari's model let us mention Denneberg's (1990) paper about insurance premiums, where it is proved that reasonable premium principles lead to an insurance premium $I(X) = \int X \, df \circ P$ with f concave. Under risk a more general model than Yaari's one -and than expected utility- E.U.- one- is the E.U.R.D.P. model first initiated by Quiggin (1982), where the restriction of constant marginal utility of wealth is removed. Denoting u(x), the cardinal utility of wealth x, the E.U.R.D.P. models stipulates that $\forall X \in V$:

$$I(X) = \int_{-\infty}^{0} (f(P(u(X) \geq t))-1)dt + \int_{0}^{+\infty} f(P(u(X) \geq t)dt$$

with f defined as in the general Yaari's model.

It turns out that because of its flexibility, for the E.U.R.D.P. model some usual definitions of risk aversion are no longer equivalent as in E.U. theory. Thus Chew, Karni, Safra (1987) proved that risk aversion in the sense of second stochastic dominance is equivalent to f convex and u concave, but Chateauneuf and Cohen (1990) proved that even a decision maker with a convex u can be risk averse in the weaker sense of preferring $E_P(X)$ to X provided that u would be not too convex and that f(p) would be sufficiently below p for any $p \in [0,1]$.

We end this lecture in emphasizing the pioneer basic work of WAKKER (1989, 1991, 1992) in the axiomatization of E.U.R.D.P. theory, noting after several authors as Green and Jullien (1988) and Segal (1989) that the meaningful comonotonic sure-thing principle (named ordinal independence axiom, resp. irrelevance axiom by the previous authors) unfortunately fails to characterize the E.U.R.D.P. model.

Case-Based Decision Theory—An Outline

Itzhak Gilboa
J.J. Kellogg Graduate School of Northwestern University
Leverone Hall, Evanston Illinois 60208-2009, U.S.A.
David Schmeidler
Dept. Statistics, Tel-Aviv University
69978 Tel-Aviv, Israel

1. Introduction

The bulk of economic theory assumes "rational" agents interacting in an economic environment. The precise meaning of "rationality" varies from one model to another. It is almost always assumed that the decision maker is (at least implicitly) aware of all the options available to him/her, and is ("as-if") optimizing some utility function. In the presence of uncertainty "rationality" is typically assumed to also mean expected-utility maximization à la Savage (1954). That is, the economic agent is further assumed to entertain beliefs in the form of a probability measure, to maximize expected utility with respect to this measure, and often also to update the probability in the face of new information according to Bayes' rule. At times, "rationality" is stretched even further to imply that different economic agents would have the same beliefs ("priors") and that their choices would constitute and equilibrium of some sort.

Theoretically appealing as these assumptions may be, they have been found by many to be extreme idealizations which cannot be considered entirely realistic. Perhaps the best-known and most influential attack on the "rational agent" paradigm was Simon's (1957) notion of "bounded rationality" and the suggestion of March and Simon (1958) that rather than optimizing, people are merely "satisficing". According to this theory, a decision maker has an "aspiration level", and as long as his/her choices attain that level (say, of "utility"), he/she will not even attempt to further optimize the decision made.

While "bounded rationality" models have been studied quite extensively in economic and game theory, it appears that none of the theories suggested is general and simple enough to serve as a foundation for economic theory at large. Many of the models, which attempt to incorporate computation costs into the optimization problem, end up being even more computationally demanding than the original models they were supposed to refine. Moreover, to the best of our knowledge, there ist no formal model which captures the notion of "satisficing decisions".

In the context of decision under uncertainty, which, in one guise or other, is inherent to almost every economic interaction, little has been done towards a simpler model of decision, which will assume less "computational ability" and sophistication on the part of the decision maker. Indeed, the past decade has witnessed a wide variety of generalizations of expected-utility models, which were mostly designed to explain certain empirical evidence such as Allais' (1953) and Ellsberg's (1961) "paradoxes". Yet these models were almost invariably formulated in the same "language" as the corresponding expected utility ones; they assumed the same primitives (be it "probability" or "states", "lotteries" or "acts") and typically generalized the expected utility assumption, in a way that certainly did not simplify it.

In Gilboa-Schmeidler (1992) we propose a new theory of decision making, whether under uncertainty or not, which submits that a decision maker chooses an act which is "best" according to its past performance in similar decision problems. We dub it "Case-Based Decision Theory" (CBDT), a name which should bring to mind the theory of "Case-Based Reasoning" of Riesbeck and Schank (1989). They argue that the main reasoning technique people use, expecially in novel situations, is reasoning-by-analogy to previous cases, and they suggest some implementation of this idea to artificial intelligence systems.[1]

A full description of CBDT is certainly beyond the scope of this note. The reader is referred to Gilboa-Schmeidler (1992) for detailed exposition, axiomatizations, variants and theoretical discussions of CBDT, as well as for comparisons of it to expected utility theory for decision under uncertainty and some economic applications. Here we only provide a very sketchy outline of CBDT, which will hopefully convey its main ideas.

2. An Overview of the Model

The primitives of CBDT are:

P — a set of decision *problems*

A — a set of available *acts*

R — a set of possible *results* (or outcomes)

the set of *cases* is defined to be

$$C = P \times A \times R$$

That is, a "case" is a triple (p,a,r), where p is the problem encountered, a is the act chosen by the decision maker, and r is the result that was obtained in this case. We will assume that at any given point in time, a decision maker is equipped with some memory M, which is simply some subset of cases, and which will be interpreted as the set of problems the decision maker can remember.

CBDT postulates two main theoretical terms – "utility" and "similarity". As in the classical decision theory, the utility measures the desirability of the results, and is thus a function

$$u : R \longrightarrow \Re$$

The notion of "similarity" is new, and corresponds in many ways to that of "subjective probability" in expected utility theory. Similarity measures the extent to which one decision problem is similar to another; that is, it is a function

$$s : P \times P \longrightarrow [0,1]$$

Finally, we may describe the decision rule which is the heart of CBDT: Suppose that a decision maker, characterized by the utility u and the similarity s is faced a decision problem p, while his/her memory is $M \subseteq C$. Then every possible act $a \in A$ is evaluated by the functional

$$U(a) = \sum_{(q,a,r) \in M} s(p,q)u(r)$$

[1]While the term "case-based" is borrowed from Riesbeck and Schank, the basic idea is, of course, much older. Some of the more recent references in the economic literature would include Keynes (1921) and Selten (1978). However, Riesbeck and Schank appear to be the first to suggest case-based reasoning as the main reasoning technique people employ.

– and the decision maker will, according to CBDT, choose a maximizer of U.

A few comments are in order. First, notice that for two distinct acts $a, b \in A, U(a)$ and $U(b)$ are summations over *disjoint* sets of cases. Furthermore, for some acts this summation may be over an empty set, in which case its value is defined to be zero. This value is going to play a major role in the theory: one may think of it as the decision maker's "aspiration level". To be precise, this is the "default" (utility) value the decision maker seems to be attaching to an act that was never tried in the past (i.e., for which there are no cases in memory). If certain acts obtain higher U-value than zero, the decision maker is "satisficed", and will continue to choose from among them without trying new acts and *without trying to maximize u.* Once all the acts that were tried in the past turned out to be unsatisfactory — that is, to have negative U values — then the decision maker will choose a new act (assuming such exists), were the choice among these will be arbitrary.

One of the main features of CBDT is that is does not require the decision maker (DM) to "engage" in hypothetical reasoning: as opposed to expected utility theory, where the very definition of an "act" involves hypothetical statements such as "If state ω occurs then I get r", in CBDT all the DM is required to "know" is the history of cases which *actually happened* and the utility he/she *actually experienced.* (The terms "engage" and "know" above are within quotation marks since one may choose a purely behavioral interpretation of the theory, according to which the DM does not have to "know" or to reason about anything.)

Without details we mention here that the decision rule of CBDT, together with the theoretical terms "utility" and "similarity" may be axiomatically derived from preferences, in a way which parallels the axiomatic derivations of "utility" and "probability", combined with the expected utility formula, in models such as Savage's (1954). (See Gilboa-Schmeidler (1992) for one such axiom system, as well as additional discussions.)

The notion of a "case" will sometimes be interpreted in a broader fashion. For instance, a case in a decision maker's memory need not necessarily have been experienced by the same DM. It may well be a "story" told by someone else. Furthermore, it need not be a real case — it may be a hypothetical one, reflecting the DM's knowledge (or belief) about what would have occurred as a result of a possible choice.

Finally, let us briefly mention two variants of the basic CBDT model:

– *Averaged similarity* in which one uses a functional similar to U above, with the sole difference that for each act a, the similarity coefficients $s(p, q)$ are normalized to sum up to 1;

– *Act Similarity* according to which acts may also be similar to each other, and the evaluation of an act a depends not only on its own performance in the past, but also on that of similar acts. Thus, on top of the utility u and the problemsimilarity s_p functions, one assumes an act-similarity function s_A such that an act a is evaluated by

$$U'(a) = \sum_{(q,b,r)\in M} s_P(p,q)s_A(a,b)u(r)$$

In Gilboa-Schmeidler (1992) we axiomatize the first variant and discuss the conceptual difficulty with the axiomatization of the second.

References

Allais, M. (1953), *Le Comportement de l'Homme Rationel devant le Risque: Critique des Postulates at Axioms de l'Ecole Americaine*, Econometrica, 21, 503-546.

Ellsberg, D. (1961), *Risk, Ambiguity and the Savage Axioms*, Quarterly Journal of Economics, 75, 643-669.

Gilboa, I. and D. Schmeidler (1992), *Case-Based Decision Theory*, mimeo.

Keynes, J.M. (1921), *A Treatise on Probability*, London: MacMillan and Co.

March, J.G., and H.A. Simon (1958), *Organizations*, New York: Wiley.

Riesbeck, C.K., and R.C. Schank (1989), *Inside Case-Based Reasoning*, Lawrence Erlbaum Associates, Inc., Hillside, N.J.

Savage, L.J. (1954), *The Foundations of Statistics*, New York: Wiley.

Selten, R. (1978), *The Chain-Store Paradox*, Theory and Decision, 9, 127-159.

Simon, H.A. (1957), *Models of Man*, New York: Wiley.

An Interactive Decision Procedure with Multiple Attributes under Risk

Hartmut Holz, Karl Mosler
FB Wirtschafts- und Organisationswissenschaften, Universität der Bundeswehr
Postfach 70 08 22, 2000 Hamburg 70, Germany

Consider a finite set of alternatives under risk which have multiple attributes. MARPI is an interactive computer-based procedure to find an efficient choice in the sense of linear expected utility. The choice is based on incomplete information about the decision maker's preferences which is elicited and processed in a sequential way. The information includes qualitative properties of the multivariate utility function such as monotoneity, risk aversion, and separability. Further, in case of an additively separable utility function, bounds on the attribute weights are elicited, and preferences (not necessarily indifferences) between sure amounts and lotteries are asked from the decision maker. The lotteries are Bernoulli lotteries generated by MARPI using special strategies. At every stage of the procedure the efficient set of alternatives is determined with respect to the information elicited so far.

The procedure has been fully implemented on a PC. The paper exhibits the basic ideas of MARPI and some details of its implementation.

Objections against Multiple Attribute Utility Theory (MAUT), see Keeney and Raiffa (1976), have originated from descriptive decision analysis and from practical implementation problems. In descriptive decision analysis, there are the well known objections against the linear expected utility (LEU) paradigm arising from observed behaviour, like the Savage paradox and observed ambiguity aversion. As our goal is decision support, we adopt the prescriptive view and restrict ourselves to practical situations where some version of LEU axioms has been accepted by the decision maker. Further, if a more general model than LEU is assumed which allows, e.g., for ambiguity aversion, under decomposability of the utility function it may reduce to LEU. Dyckerhoff (1992) has proved this for the expected utility model with non-additive probabilities when the attributes satisfy the marginality condition.

Besides that, objections against MAUT come from the difficulties of implementing the procedure to real world situations. These are the main problems which often make it impossible to use the classical procedure:

(i) A decision analyst is needed to guide and to train the decision maker.

(ii) The procedure can be rather lengthy and expect too much of the decision maker's willingness and ability to respond. If the procedure is stopped before the utility function has been completely assessed the whole effort might be vain.

(iii) MAUT works only if the attributes show certain kinds of utility independence. But, information on this is difficult to assess.

(iv) The procedure urges the decision maker to reveal indifferences between sure amounts and lotteries. But, those responses are often biased and give rise to inconsistencies, see Hershey and Schoemaker (1985), von Nitzsch and Weber (1988).

The paper presents an interactive sequential procedure which avoids some of these problems. It is called *MARPI* for ***Multiattribute Analysis under Risk and Partial Information.*** Ad (i), a PC-based decision support system substitutes the decision analyst. The system is menue-driven; it elicites all necessary information from the decision maker in an automatic way. Ad (ii), MARPI can be stopped at any time. Then it gives the set of alternatives which is efficient with respect to the information elicited so far; i.e., this information is used to eliminate inferior alternatives. Ad (iii), before introducing a decomposition, MARPI assesses qualitative properties of the utility function – such as monotoneity, concavity, and others – and checks whether some alternative is stochastically dominated by another one with respect to all utility functions having this property. By this, inefficient alternatives are identified and eliminated. Ad (iv), in a second phase MARPI assumes an additive decomposition and faces the decision maker with binary choices between a sure amount and a Bernoulli lottery. (A Bernoulli lottery is a lottery with just two outcomes.) The decision maker is asked for a preferential decision only and *not* urged to find a certainty equivalent (CE) or probability equivalent (PE) to a given lottery. Thus, the biases connected with CE and PE methods do not occur.

In the literature, there are only a few publications on partial information and interactive assessment in MAUT under risk. Sarin (1977) introduces a sequential utility bounding procedure in an additive utility model, Weber (1987) gives a general framework for using partial information, and Mosler (1982, 1991) presents stochastic dominance rules to determine an efficient set. Interactive computer programs can be found in Keeney and Sicherman (1976), Kirkwood and van der Feltz (1986). For a comparison of computer programs, see Lotfi and Teich (1991).

To start with, consider a set $\mathcal{A}$ of decision alternatives. They are characterized by the levels of n relevant attributes, $n \geq 1$. For each alternative there is a finite number of possible outcome vectors x in R^n. Thus, an alternative is described by a random vector in n-space having finite support. We assume that the probability distributions of all alternatives are known (as either subjective or objective probabilities). I.e., we assume a situation of decision making under risk.

The procedure MARPI processes the set of alternatives in a sequential way. In each step, the decision maker is asked for some information on her preferences. MARPI uses the information elicited so far to eliminate inferior alternatives and presents the actual efficient set to the decision maker. The procedure stops when the decision maker wants it to stop or when the actual efficient set becomes a singleton.

Let $\mathcal{A}$ be a finite set of probability distribution functions in R^n. Let their joint support be finite, and let S be a rectangle containing it. We assume that the decision maker has a preference relation $\succeq$ on the set of lotteries on S and that she accepts some version of LEU axioms. Then, of two alternatives F and G in $\mathcal{A}$, F is not less preferred than G, $F \succeq G$, if

$$\int u(x)dF(x) \geq \int u(x)dG(x) \tag{1}$$

where u is the decision maker's n-variate utility function.

When the procedure starts, $\succeq$ and u are not known. Any set U of n-variate functions is called a *partial information* about u. If (1) holds for all $u \in U$ we say that F *dominates* G *with respect to* U, $F \succeq_U G$.

In each step t of the procedure a partial information $U(t)$ is assessed from the decision maker, $U(1) \supset U(2) \supset ...$, and an efficient set $\mathcal{A}(t)$ is computed containing all alternatives which are non-dominated with respect to $U(t)$,

$$\mathcal{A}(t) = \Big\{G \in \mathcal{A}(t-1) : \text{ there is no } F \in \mathcal{A}(t-1) \text{ with } F \neq G \text{ and } F \succeq_{U(t)} G\Big\},$$

where $\mathcal{A}(0) = \mathcal{A}$.

With MARPI, we distinguish two phases. In Phase One the partial information applies to general properties like monotoneity of the preference, global and pairwise risk aversion, and utility independence of attributes. If the marginality condition holds, i.e., the utility function has an additive decomposition, a second phase follows.

During Phase One, MARPI offers the following dominance checks with respect to the partial information mentioned.

- *strong FSD* w.r.t. increasing utility functions.
- *strong SSD* w.r.t. concave, convex, increasing concave, or increasing convex utility functions, respectively.
- *weak FSD* w.r.t. n-variate risk averse utility functions.
- *dual weak FSD* w.r.t. n-variate risk prone utility functions.
- *weak SSD* w.r.t. all utility functions, which are n-variate risk averse and risk averse in the attributes.
- *dual weak SSD* w.r.t. all utility functions, which are n-variate risk prone and risk prone in the attributes.

At the end of Phase One the decision maker is asked whether the marginality condition or an equivalent condition holds. If this is true, Phase Two is started in which further partial information is assessed and used to reduce the efficient set. In Phase Two the assessed information includes bounds on the attribute weights and revealed preference between given Bernoulli lotteries and sure amounts, which is used to compute bounds on the expected utility of the alternatives. This part builds on ideas of Sarin (1977), and uses special strategies by which the lotteries are generated.

MARPI is implemented on a personal computer. The program is written in Turbo Pascal 6.0 and can be run on a standard configuration of a PC IBM compatible with at least 640 Kbytes of RAM memory. The CPU-times are depending strongly on the given data. Because of the extensive mathematical computations a math coprocessor is recommended. For the solution of large problems with many attributes a 486 DX processor is necessary.

MARPI is designed as an interactive and event oriented program which uses window technique and provides mouse support. The conception of the program enables its usage by a user who has only little computer experience.

It is assumed that the users know the linear expected utility model and the basics of MAUT as exhibited in Keeney and Raiffa (1976). But it is not necessary that they are specialists in utility theory, because at every stage of the procedure a context sensitive information is provided.

The package consists of two modules:

- The first module, named "data", enables the user to input and edit multiattribute decision problems under risk. Moreover it is possible to save the data on and to load the data from disk. During input and edit the user is supported by consistency checks. So for example only valid probability distributions are accepted and in addition it is ensured that in each alternative no outcome occurs twice or more.
- The second module, named "session", controls the above interactive procedure of the identification of the efficient alternatives.

Some further developments of the package are in progress.

References

[1] Dyckerhoff, R. (1992). *Decomposition of multivariate utility functions in non-additive expected utility theory.* Paper presented to the 16th Symposium on Operations Research held at the University of Trier at September 9–11, 1991.

[2] Hershey, J.C. and Schoemaker, P.J.H. (1985). *Probability versus certainty equivalence methods in utility measurement, are they equivalent ?* Management Science **31**, p. 1213–1231.

[3] Keeney, R. and Raiffa, H. (1976). *Decisions with Multiple Objectives: Preferences and Value Tradeoffs.* Wiley, New York.

[4] Keeney, R. and Sicherman, A. (1976). *Assessing and analyzing preferences concerning multiple objectives: An interactive computer program.* Behavioral Science **21**, p. 173–182.

[5] Kirkwood, C.W. and van der Feltz, L.C. (1986). *Personal Computer Programs for Decision Analysis, Volume 1: User Manual.* Technical Report, Department of Decision and Information Systems, College of Business, Arizona State University.

[6] Lotfi, V. and Teich, J.E. (1991). *Multicriteria decision making using personal computers.* In: Korhonen, P., Lewandowski, A., and Wallenius, J. (eds.), *Multiple Criteria Decision Support,* Springer, Berlin.

[7] Mosler, K.C. (1982). *Entscheidungsregeln bei Risiko: Multivariate stochastische Dominanz.* Springer, Berlin.

[8] Mosler, K.C. (1991). *Multiattribute utility functions, partial information on coefficients, and efficient choice.* OR Spektrum **13**, p. 87–94.

[9] von Nitzsch, R. and Weber, M. (1988). *Utility function assessment on a microcomputer: an interactive procedure.* Annals of Operations Research **16**, p. 149–160.

[10] Sarin, R.K. (1977). *Interactive evaluation and bound procedure for selecting multiattribute alternatives.* In: Starr, M. and Zeleny, M. (eds.), *Multiple Criteria Decision Making,* North-Holland, New York, p. 211–224.

[11] Weber, M. (1987). *Decision making with incomplete information.* European J. of Operational Research **28**, p. 44–57.

An Insurance Contract for Financial Assets with Experience Rating

Werner Jammernegg
Institut für Informationsverarbeitung, Wirtschaftsuniversität Wien
Reithlegasse 16, 1190 Wien, Austria
Peter Kischka
Lehrstuhl für Wirtschafts- und Sozialstatistik, Friedr.-Schiller-Univ.
Fürstengraben 11, 6900 Jena, Germany

In traditional insurance situations contracts are based in general on experience rating. Usually it is assumed that the agent is insured during a given planning period. The problem then is to decide whether in some period a given loss should be claimed or not. The insurance premium depends on the individual claim history of the agent. Contrary, the insurance of financial assets is based on the performance of capital markets. It is known as portfolio insurance (cp. e. g. Schwartz (1986/87)).

In this paper we consider the insurance of financial assets with experience rating in the framework of a discrete-time dynamic decision model with finite planning horizon T. The model can be seen as the synthesis of traditional insurance with experience rating and portfolio insurance.

At the beginning of the planning period the agent owns a portfolio with value w. The return of the portfolio per period is described by a two-state distribution. The high return r (low return d) occurs with probability q (1-q). The agent's goal is to maximize the expected utility of wealth at the horizon T. We use the logarithmic utility function.

During the planning horizon the agent follows a constant proportion portfolio strategy, i. e. the composition of the portfolio is not changed. But at the beginning of the planning period the agent can buy a contract. This contract gives the possibility to insure against low portfolio returns.

Therefore the agent has to decide whether the contract should be bought. This ist done by comparing the expected utilities of terminal wealth. If no contract is bought, the expected utility can be computed directly by the return-generating process.

In the other case the agent can buy a contract at the price xw, $0 < x < 1$, at the beginning of the planning period. For example, xw can be thought of as transaction costs.

The contract offers the possibility to choose between three actions at each stage of the planning period. Action 1 means to buy insurance and to file a claim whereas action 2 means to buy insurance but to not file a claim. Action 3 says to suspend insurance.

The insurance guarantees that the portfolio return is at least s, $d < s \leq r$. The insurance premium per period is based on an experience rating scheme and is denoted by c(k,n). The number of periods where insurance is bought is given by k+n and n is the number of periods where a claim is filed. Experience rating implies that c(k,n) is decreasing in k and increasing in n.

The corresponding state transitions reflect the synthesis of the dynamics of the capital market and the individual preferences of the agent. The value of the premium c(k,n) is determined by the return history as well as the claim history.

We make the following assumption concerning the insurance premiums and the return probability:

$$\left[\frac{1 - c(k+1,n)}{1 - c(k,n+1)}\right]^q \geq \frac{1 - c(k,n)}{1 - c(k,n+1)}$$

With this assumption we are able to prove two structural properties of the optimal strategy in case a contract is bought:

- If it is optimal to suspend insurance in some period because the premium is too high, this action stays optimal up to the planning horizon ("stopping rule").
- It is not optimal to suspend insurance in a period if in the previous period it has been optimal to buy insurance and not to file a claim ("stay on insurance").

For the numerical analyses we choose the well-known expected value premium principle.
The numerical experiments show that the above assumption on c(k,n) is by no means necessary for the stopping rule to hold. Our experiences indicate that the strategy based on the stopping rule is an efficient heuristic.

In contrast to the results of related dynamic decision models (cp. e. g. Heyman and Sobel (1984)) the optimal decisions for a given period are not monotone with respect to the claim history.

Finally we analyse the basic decision whether the contract should be bought depending on the rate of transaction costs x. The numerical results show that this basic decision is very sensitive with respect to the experience rating scheme.

For a detailed analysis we refer to (Jammernegg/Kischka (1991)).

REFERENCES

Heyman D P and M J Sobel (1984) Stochastic Models in Operations Research. Volume II, McGraw-Hill. New York

Jammernegg W, Kischka P (1991) An Insurance contract for financial assets with experience rating. Working paper

Schwartz E S (1986/87) "Options and Portfolio Insurance". Finanzmarkt und Portfolio Management, 1: 9-17

Efficiency Improvement in Data Envelopment Analysis

Chiang Kao
Graduate School of Industrial Management, National Cheng Kung University
Tainan, Taiwan 70101, Republic of China

Data envelopment analysis (DEA) developed by Charnes, Cooper, and Rhodes (1978) is a methodology for measuring relative efficiencies within a group of decision making units (DMUs) which utilizes several inputs to produce a set of outputs. According to Banker, Charnes, and Cooper (1984), the DEA model can be formulated as:

$$\begin{aligned} \max.\ & h_0=\sum^{s}_{r=1} Y_{r0}u_r/(v_0+\sum^{m}_{i=1}X_{i0}v_i) \\ \text{s.t.}\ & \sum^{s}_{r=1} Y_{rj}u_r/(v_0+\sum^{m}_{i=1}X_{ij}v_i)\le 1,\ j=1,\ldots,n \\ & u_r,\ v_i\ge\varepsilon>0,\ v_0 \text{ unconstrained in sign} \end{aligned} \quad [1]$$

with a dual:

$$\begin{aligned} \min.\ & w_0-\varepsilon[\sum^{m}_{i=1}s_i^{+}+\sum^{s}_{r=1}s_r^{-}] \\ \text{s.t.}\ & \sum^{n}_{j=1}Y_{rj}\lambda_j-s_r^{-}=Y_{r0},\quad r=1,\ldots,s \\ & X_{i0}w_0-\sum^{n}_{j=1}X_{ij}\lambda_j-s_i^{+}=0,\quad i=1,\ldots,m \\ & w_0-\sum^{n}_{j=1}\lambda_j=0 \\ & \lambda_j,\ s_i^{+},\ s_r^{-}\ge 0 \end{aligned} \quad [2]$$

where X_{ij} and Y_{rj} are the known inputs and outputs of DMU j, index 0 indicates the particular DMU to be evaluated, and ε is a small non-Archimedean quantity (Charnes and Cooper 1984). The conditions for Pareto efficiency are $w_0^*=1$ and all slack variables (s_i^+ and s_r^-) equal zero. As shown in Charnes, Cooper, and Rhodes (1978), for an inefficient DMU, if Y_{r0} is increased by s_r^- and X_{i0} is reduced by s_i^+/w_0, then DMU 0 will be efficient. However, in reality, not all factors (inputs and outputs) can be adjusted at wish. In most cases adjustments are permitted only within certain ranges. There are also cases that some of the factors are fixed, varying their values is not possible. Suppose $h_0^*<1$ and DMU 0 is seeking for improvement. One way of taking the variability of each factor into consideration is to treat the factors as variables and restrict them to certain ranges. The solved set of values is then a *feasible* way for making improvement. The formulation is:

$$\begin{aligned}
\max.\ & g_0=\Sigma^{s}_{r=1}y_{r0}u_r/(v_0+\Sigma^{m}_{i=1}x_{i0}v_i) \\
\text{s.t.}\ & \Sigma^{s}_{r=1}Y_{rj}u_r/(v_0+\Sigma^{m}_{i=1}X_{ij}v_i)\leq 1,\quad j=1,\ldots,n \\
& \Sigma^{s}_{r=1}y_{r0}u_r/(v_0+\Sigma^{m}_{i=1}x_{i0}v_i)\leq 1, \\
& LX_{i0}\leq x_{i0}\leq UX_{i0},\quad LY_{r0}\leq y_{r0}\leq UY_{r0},\quad i=1,\ldots,m;\ r=1,\ldots,s \\
& u_r,\ v_i\geq \varepsilon>0,\ v_0 \text{ unconstrained in sign}
\end{aligned} \qquad [3]$$

It is possible that some lower bound LX (LY) coincides with upper bound UX (UY) indicating that the corresponding factor cannot be varied. Comparing [3] with [1], one extra constraint $\Sigma^{s}_{r=1}y_{r0}u_r/(v_0+\Sigma^{m}_{i=1}x_{i0}v_i)\leq 1$ is included in addition to the bounds. Since that in the original evaluation we had $h_0{}^*<1$, DMU 0 did not lie on the production frontier, the ratio constraint of DMU 0 in [3] can actually be deleted. Hence the total number of ratio constraints is still n.

Model [3] is intrinsically linear. The nonlinear terms $y_{r0}u_r$ and $x_{i0}v_i$ can be linearized by substituting by new variables p_r and q_i, respectively, and replacing $LX_{i0}\leq x_{i0}\leq UX_{i0}$ and $LY_{r0}\leq y_{r0}\leq UY_{r0}$ with $LX_{i0}v_i\leq q_i\leq UX_{i0}v_i$ and $LY_{r0}u_r\leq p_r\leq UY_{r0}u_r$ correspondingly. In solving [3], if $g_0{}^*<1$, then within the range that every factor is allowed to vary, it is impossible for DMU 0 to achieve Pareto efficiency. On the other hand, if $g_0{}^*=1$, then adjusting inputs and outputs according to the values of $x_{i0}{}^*$ and $y_{r0}{}^*$ will bring DMU 0 to Pareto efficiency. Obviously, there are enormous ways for making improvement. By adjusting the bounds in [3] properly, an ideal way will hopefully be derived.

A set of data from Kao and Yang (1991, 1992) in measuring the efficiency of forest management of seventeen forests is adopted. The inputs are budget, labor, area, and initial stocking; and the outputs are main product, average stocking, and recreation. In the original evaluation, Forest Exploitation Bureau had an efficiency score of 0.9749. To find a strategy for making improvement, model [3] is applied. With the measurements of area and initial stocking being fixed and other factors restricted to certain reasonable ranges, a feasible way of achieving Pareto efficiency is solved.

REFERENCES

Banker, R. D., Charnes, A., and Cooper, W. W. (1984) Some models for estimating technical and scale efficiencies in data envelopment analysis. *Management Science* 30:1078-1092.

Charnes, A. and Cooper, W. W. (1984) The non-Archimedean CCR ratio for efficiency analysis: A rejoinder to Boyd and Färe. *European J. Operational Research* 15:333-334.

Charnes, A., Cooper, W. W., and Rhodes, E. (1978) Measuring the efficiency of decision making units. *European J. Operational Research* 2:429-444.

Kao, C. and Yang, Y. C. (1991) Measuring the efficiency of forest management. *Forest Science* 37:1239-1252.

Kao, C. and Yang, Y. C. (1992) Reorganization of forest districts via efficiency measurement. *European J. Operational Research* (in press).

Separation in Insurance

Isaac Meilijson
School of Mathematical Sciences, Tel-Aviv University
69978 Tel-Aviv, Israel

This talk reports on joint work of the speaker with Michael Landsberger, University of Haifa. The details are covered in their two articles "Principal-Agent relations with adverse selection and limited liability constraints" and "Monopolistic and competitive markets with private information".

Consider a risk-neutral insurer and a population with two types of risk-averse agents. Agents of type i constitute a fraction γ_i of the population, have a concave utility function U_i and hold random wealth Y_i with distribution G_i agreed upon by the agent and the insurer. Let $c_i = U_i^{-1}(E(U(Y_i))$ be the certainty equivalent of the random wealth Y_i for type i and assume that $c_1 > c_2$.

If the insurer could identify each agent and offer each a separate contract, the insurer could arbitrarily approximate the "first-best" solution with expected income $\sum_i \gamma_i(E(Y_i) - c_i)$. An extensive literature has been devoted since 1976 (Rothschild and Stiglitz, Equilibrium in competitive insurance markets, *Quart.J.of Econ.* 38, 629-649) to the case where the insurer knows the "distribution" of the agents (their utilities and risk, the probabilities γ_i) but does not know the type of individual agents. All of these studies have been restricted to the case where G_1 and G_2 are supported by two points and differ only in the probabilities assigned to these points. Suppose Y has values y_j, $1 \le j \le n$, with probabilities p_j and q_j for types 1 and 2 respectively. The insurer offers a contract which pays α_j and another which pays β_j if $Y = y_j$. For example, the contract $\alpha_j = c - y_j$ corresponds to full insurance which replaces the uninsured position by the deterministic insured position c, whereas $\alpha_j = \max(c - y_j, d)$ corresponds to a stop-loss insurance contract. The pair of contracts must satisfy incentive compatibility

$$\sum U_1(y_j + \alpha_j)p_j \ge \sum U_1(y_j + \beta_j)p_j$$

$$\sum U_2(y_j + \beta_j)q_j \ge \sum U_2(y_j + \alpha_j)q_j$$

and individual rationality

$$\sum U_1(y_j + \alpha_j)p_j \ge \sum U_1(y_j)p_j$$

$$\sum U_2(y_j + \beta_j)q_j \ge \sum U_2(y_j)q_j \; .$$

With these constraints, the pair of contracts should maximize expected income

$$\gamma_1[E(Y_1) - \sum \alpha_j p_j] + \gamma_2[E(Y_2) - \sum \beta_j q_j] \; .$$

The optimum may involve one contract only, in which case it is either full insurance that only the 2-types buy, $\alpha_j = c_2 - y_j$, giving the insurer expected income $\gamma_2[\sum y_j q_j - c_2]$, or full insurance that all agents buy, $\alpha_j = c_1 - y_j$, giving the insurer $\gamma_1 \sum y_j p_j + \gamma_2 \sum y_j q_j - c_1$. It is clear that any viable alternative involves a pair of contracts of which at least one is partial insurance. Can the insurer do better by separation? How much better? To see that separation may be optimal and that there is no bound on how close can separation get the insurer to the ideal first best solution, suppose $p_1 > 0$, $p_2 = 0$, $q_1 = 0$ and $q_2 > 0$. If the insurer offers full insurance at level c_1 plus a severe punishment if $Y = y_2$ and also full insurance at level c_2 plus a severe punishment if $Y = y_1$, the insurer will achieve first best income. Motivated by this pathology, we henceforth assume that G_1 and G_2 are mutually absolutely continuous, and deal with three special cases: (i) Monopolistic insurer, $G_1 = G_2$ and U_2 is Arrow-Pratt more risk averse than U_1. (ii) Monopolistic insurer, $U_1 = U_2$ and (iii) Insurer under full competition, search for an equilibrium pair of contracts when $U_1 = U_2$. In all of these models we prove that at least one of the two contracts provides full insurance, identify the buyer of full insurance and characterize the nature of the partially insured position when it exists.

Case (i): Same distribution G, U_2 more risk averse than U_1.
If $U_2(x)/U_1(x) \to \infty$ as $x \to -\infty$ then the insurer may get arbitrarily close to first best performance by offering a two-valued insured position with a very probable top value slightly above c_1 and bottom value low enough to borderline discourage the 2-types. Under limited liability constraints (interval bound on the insured position) we prove that whenever there is separation, the optimal partial insurance contract yields a two-valued insured position. We first prove it to be at most three-valued by rephrasing the problem as Linear Programming with three linear constraints and then reduce the number of atoms to two by convexity arguments.
If U_2''/U_1'' is nonincreasing then, regardless of G, the bottom atom is as low as permitted to be (as Hell in the two-valued contract offered to the type-1 agent Faust to scare off the rest of Mankind). If U_2''/U_1'' is nondecreasing then the top atom is always as high as permitted to be (as the Heavenly Bliss offered to the ascetic in compensation for her/his bottom atom, or life of deprivation, very unattractive to the rest of Mankind which opt for a more secure, deterministic life).
If G is supported by more than two points, there will always be separation.
The reader should notice that no event with positive probability smaller than $\min p_j$ could be produced by a nonrandomized contract. Hence, randomized contracts may be a necessity of optimization. Some of our results seem at variance with the literature, but earlier work ruled out randomization.

Cases (ii) and (iii) are analyzed by Kuhn-Tucker methods. Randomization should never be used because all agents have the same attitude to risk. The dimension of the insured position is the number of different likelihood ratio values p_j/q_j. Even for arbitrarily related distributions G_1 and G_2, the assessment of the partially insured position by the agent buying it, dominates by the very strong Monotone Likelihood Ratio order its assessment by the agent declining it in favor of full insurance. Under regular smoothness assumptions on the utility function, there is always an equilibrium pair of contracts (case (iii)), i.e., a pair of contracts which simultaneously maximizes the expected utility of each agent, under incentive compatibility, individual rationality and two additional constraints modeling the requirement that the insurer shouldn't have negative expected income on any of the two single deals.

Collective Decisions on Euclidian Spaces

Wouter Peremans, Hans Peters, Hans v.d. Stel, Ton Storcken*
Department of Mathematics, Eindhoven University of Technology
P.O. Box 513, 5600 MB Eindhoven, Netherlands

Social Choice problems are considered where each individual i from a finite set of individuals N := {1, 2, 3, ..., n} reports a point p(i) in an m-dimensional Euclidean space $E := \mathbb{R}^m$. For example these points could represent an individual proposal for a location of a public facility. A solution φ assigns a compromise point to each combination of reported points. Hence, φ is a function from E^N to E.

Here we study solutions which are strategy-proof and impose no further condition. In for instance Border and Jordan (1983), Moulin (1980), Kim and Roush (1984), Barbera and Peleg (1990) and Peters, v.d. Stel and Storcken (1991) is dealt with these solution. The main difference with our approach here is that we only impose strategy-proofness with respect to the class of quadratic and separable preferences where the other authors impose additional conditions such as unanimity, continuity, surjectivity

---

*) We gratefully acknowledge the support by the Co-operation Centre of Tilburg and Eindhoven University.

and coordinatewise Pareto-optimality. Furthermore, the strategy-proofness conditions are not always considered with respect to the class of preferences discussed here. The solutions discussed in these papers are continuous and separable, i.e. coordinatewise determinable. Strategy-proofness with respect to quadratic separable preferences allows for solutions which are neither separable nor continuous. It is shown how these properties are induced by additional conditions such as mentioned before.

Let the tth coordinate of a point x in E be denoted by x_t. Let $V \subset E$ then $V_t := \{x_t \mid x \in V\}$ is the set of tth coordinates of elements of V. Furhermore, let $\overline{V}_t := V_t \cup \{\inf(V_t), \sup\{V_t)\}$.

A relation R on E is *separable and quadratic*, if there is a point $x \in E$ and there are positive weights $\alpha_1, \alpha_2, \ldots, \alpha_m > 0$ such that for all $y, z \in E$

$$\langle y, z\rangle \in R \Leftrightarrow \sum_{t=1}^{m} \alpha_t \mid x_t - y_t \mid^2 \leq \sum_{t=1}^{m} \alpha_t \mid x_t - z_t \mid^2.$$

In this case x is the *best* point of R.

Let $\varphi : E^N \rightarrow E$ be a solution. The solution φ is *strategy-proof*, if for every separable and quadratic preference R, every individual $i \in N$, and all combinations of reported points $p, q \in E^N$ with $p(i)$ is the best point of R and $p(j) = q(j)$ for all $j \in N - \{i\}$, it holds that $\langle\varphi(p), \varphi(q)\rangle \in R$. If φ is strategy-proof, then for each individual it is optimal to report the best element of this (true) preference.

A map $\delta : 2^N \rightarrow (\mathbb{R} \cup \{-\infty, \infty\})^m$ is an *assignment of disagreements*, if, for all coordinates $t = 1, 2, \ldots, m$ and all $S \subset T \subset N$, $\delta(\emptyset)_t > -\infty$, $\delta(N)_t < \infty$ and $\delta(S)_t \geq \delta(T)_t$. Given an assignment of disagreements δ and a profile $p \in A^N$, we define, for every coordinate $t = 1, 2, \ldots, m$: $\varphi_\delta(p)_t := \min_{S \subset N}\{\max_{i \in S}\{p(i)_t \vee \delta(S)_t\}\}$. The solution φ_δ is called the *coordinatewise vetosolution* (with respect to δ). See Border and Jordan (1983) and Peters, v.d. Stel and Storcken (1991).

In Peremans, Peters, v.d. Stel and Storcken (1992) the following theorems are derived:

Theorem 1 Let $\varphi : E^N \to E$ be a solution. Then (i) and (ii) are equivalent.

(i) φ is strategy-proof.

(ii) The range $\varphi(E^N)$ of φ is closed and $\varphi(E^N) = \varphi(E^N)_1 \times \varphi(E^N)_2 \times \ldots \times \varphi(E^N)_m$ and there exists an assignment δ of disagreements such that for all coordinates $t = 1, 2, \ldots, m$

a) for all $y \in \varphi(E^N)_t$ and all $p \in E^N$
$| \varphi_\delta(p)_t - \varphi(p)_t | \le | \varphi_\delta(p)_t - y |$.

b) for all $i \in N$ and all $p, q \in E^N$ with for all $j \in N - \{i\}$ $p(j) = q(j)$, if either $p(i)_t > \varphi_\delta(p)_t = \varphi_\delta(q)_t > \varphi(p)_t$ or $p(i)_t < \varphi_\delta(p)_t = \varphi_\delta(q)_t < \varphi(p)_t$, then $\varphi(p)_t = \varphi(q)_t$.

Let φ be a strategy-proof solution. If $\varphi(E^N)$ is not connected, then it follows that φ is not continuous. So there are strategy-proof solutions which are not continuous. There are also strategy-proof solutions which are not separable.

Theorem 2 Let $\varphi : E^N \to E$ be a strategy-proof solution. Then (1), (2) and (3) are equivalent and (4) and (5) are equivalent.

(1) φ is *coordinatewise Pareto-optimal*, i.e. for all coordinates $t = 1, 2, \ldots, m$ and all $p \in E^N$
$\min_{i \in N} p(i)_t \le \varphi(p)_t \le \max_{i \in N} p(i)_t$.

(2) φ is *unanimous*, i.e. for all $x \in E$ and all $p \in E^N$ such that $p(1) = p(2) = \ldots = p(n) = x$ $\varphi(p) = x$.

(3) There is an assignment of disagreements δ with for all coordinates t $\delta(N)_t = -\infty$ and $\delta(\emptyset)_t = \infty$ such that $\varphi = \varphi_\delta$.

(4) $\varphi(E^N)$ is convex.

(5) φ is continuous.

References

Barbera S. and B. Peleg (1990) Strategy-Proof Voting schemes with Continuous Preferences. Social Choice and Welfare 7: 31-38.

Border K.C. and J.S. Jordan (1983) Straightforward Elections, Unanimity and Phantom Voters. Review of Economic Studies 50: 153-170.

Kim K.H. and F.W. Roush (1984) Nonmanipulability in Two Dimensions. Mathematical Social Sciences 8: 29-43.

Moulin H. (1980) On Strategy-Proofness and Single Peakedness Public Choice 35: 437-455.

Peremans W., H. Peters, H. v.d. Stel and T. Storcken (1992) Strategy-Proof Collective Decisions on Eudicean Spaces, Report, Tilburg, The Netherlands (forthcomming).

Peters H., H. v.d. Stel and T. Storcken (1991) On Uncompromisingness and Strategy-Proofness, Report M 91-15, Maastricht, The Netherlands.

The Analytic Hierarchy Process (AHP): Basics and Software

Karl Weber
Department of Business Administration, University of Gießen
Licher Straße 74, 6300 Gießen, Germany

The Analytic Hierarchy Process (AHP) is one of the most outstanding multicriteria decision making approaches. It employs a method of multiple-paired comparison of attributes to rank order alternative solutions to a uniobjective problem. The attributes themselves are decomposed into levels. The top level contains only one element which reflects the overall objective of the system. The lower levels usually contain a larger number of elements which are thought to the independent of the elements at the same level. But these elements directly relate to, or influence, elements at the level immediately below them.

The evaluation of alternative solutions to a given problem has to be based on the aggregate of the hierarchically ordered results of the subordinate evaluations. This evaluation process consists of several basic steps. The formulation of a problem as a hierarchy represents the first step of the AHP approach.

The next step leads to the determination of the relative weights of the elements at each level of the hierarchy. For this, a method of multiple paired comparisons based on a standardized evaluation scheme (1 = equally important; 3 = slightly more important; 5 = much more important; 7 = very much more important; 9 = absolutely more important) is used.

The results of the pairwise comparison of n elements can be summarized in a (n,n) evaluation matrix whereby small errors in judgement are acceptable.

In a further step the largest eigenvalue of the evaluation matrix has to be determined. If no errors in judgement exist, the relation $Aw = nw$ or $(A - nI)w = 0$ holds; the evaluation matrix A is multiplied on the right by the vector of n evaluation weights w. This is a system of homogeneous linear equations which has a nontrivial solution if the determinant $(A - nI)$ vanishes, thus indicating that n is an eigenvalue of A. Furthermore, A has unit rank; every row of the matrix A is a constant multiple of the first row. This means that all the eigenvalues of A except one are zero. The sum of the eigenvalues of such a matrix is equal to its trace and in this case $tr(A) = n$.

Small errors in judgement lead to small perturbations of the coefficients of the matrix A and its eigenvalues as well. The basic relation for the eigenvalue problem now becomes $A'w' = \lambda_{max} w'$ where λ_{max} is the largest eigenvalue of the matrix A'.

It can easily be seen that $\lambda_{max} \geq n$. The difference λ_{max} - n can therefore be used as an index of departure from consistency. If the average deviation $(\lambda_{max} - n)/(n-1)$ exceeds a predetermined value (e.g. 0.1) the aforementioned evaluation procedure has to be repeated to improve consistency. In more advanced versions of the AHP approach an even more stringent consistency ratio has to be used; details can be found in the basic AHP literature. The aforementioned evaluation process has to be repeated for all levels of the hierarchy.

The next step leads to a combination of the priority weights of the various hierarchies in order to determine the overall priority weight of an alternative.

These composite weights are the final measure of importance for each alternative considered in the AHP evaluation process. The alternative with the highest total priority weight has therefore to be selected for decision making.

The calculations to be made for AHP studies will usually prove to be fairly complex and they will call for the use of special software packages. The most valuable programs are AutoMan, Criterium 1.1, Expert Choice, Newtech Expert Choice and Priorities. In addition some simple evaluation programs have been made available in various research papers. The use of AutoMan, Criterium 1.1 and/or Expert Choice is strongly recommended for practical AHP studies. The range of applications includes research (e.g. design specifications of a product), analysis (e.g. analysis of decision under varying environmental scenarios), planning (e.g. prioritizing marketing objectives), and evaluating (e.g. evaluating vendors and suppliers.).

Newtech Expert Choice is a special decision support system for the adoption of new technology. The program is based on a predetermined set of over 100 attributes that are arranged in a fixed four level hierarchical structure. The use of the program is, therefore, restricted to a special set of investment decisions.

Literature

Saaty, Thomas L. (1990). Multicriteria Decision Making. The Analytic Hierarchy Process. 2nd ed., Pittsburgh: RWS Publications.

Saaty, Thomas L. and Vargas, Luis G. (1991). Prediction, Projection and Forecasting. Applications of the Analytic Hierarchy Process in Economics, Finance, Politics, Games, and Sports. Boston: Kluwer.

Schneeweiß, Christoph (1991). Planung. 1. Systematische und entscheidungstheoretische Grundlagen. Berlin: Springer.

Weber, Karl (1992). Multikriterielle Entscheidungen. München: Oldenbourg.

Zimmermann, Hans-Jürgen und Gutsche, Lothar (1991). Multi-Criteria Analyse. Einführung in die Theorie der Entscheidungen bei Mehrfachzielsetzungen. Berlin: Springer.

Section 12

Banking, Finance and Insurance

ALLFIWIB: Distributed Knowledge Based Systems for Customer Support in Financial Services[1]

Hans Ulrich Buhl, Hans-Jürgen König, Andreas Will
Fachbereich Wirtschaftswissenschaften, Universität Gießen
Licher Straße 60, 6300 Gießen, Germany

1 Economic Foundation

In the markets for financial services we observe the trend to offer each customer individual, tailored solutions to his special financial problems. An optimal solution with respect to the customer's goal, often is a combination of different financial products. There are two main problems in finding such an optimal *mix of financial products*. First, the historically grown branches of financial services like banking and insurance lead to the geographical and functional *distribution* of data and knowledge among organizations, experts, and information systems. The customer consultant often lacks the competence of combining this distributed knowledge while working on problem solving. Considering this, the goal of ALLFIWIB is to develop knowledge based system prototypes working together to solve complex customer problems by combining knowledge from different domains in the area of financial services [1]. Second, in many cases good mixed solutions - even for simple goals like maximizing the present value of cash flows after taxes - are not yet known. ALLFIWIB claims not only to model usual supply processes, but to design 'surprising' solutions by applying new knowledge about good product combinations [2], [12]. This still needs more research. An example illustrates, what we mean by good mixed solutions:

Example: An entrepreneur plans to finance an office building with minimal constant monthly payments. Based on the specific parameters and because of German tax reasons a lease with single payment in $t = 0$ is optimal [3]. It is best to finance this single payment by a loan without any interest and discharge payments up to period $t = n$ [2]. To cover the one-time payment at the end of the contract in $t = n$, the entrepreneur signs a constant premium life policy. Altogether, the solution meets the requirement of constant payments with minimal after tax cash-flow. It consists of a combination of three products: leasing, loan and life insurance.

---

[1]ALLFIWIB, a joint project with the University of Marburg, is funded by the Deutsche Forschungsgemeinschaft (DFG) within its program "Distributed Computer Systems in Business Administration".

Having started with the knowledge domain of leasing and continuing with the domains of loan and life insurance, we are developing good solutions for pure cash-flow-criteria first. In a second step, we plan to extend our research to other domains and multi-value goals.

2 Distributed Problem Solving

For the discussion of problem solving [10], in all knowledge domains mentioned above and others like investment funds, the problem solving systems are called *agents*. Obviously, cooperation among the agents is necessary. We distinguish between two forms of cooperation: collaboration and competition. Two or more agents *collaborate implicitly* or *explicitly*, if they supply partial solutions to a global solution. Implicit collaboration means that an agent, who is not able to solve a problem on his own, only supplies a partial solution. As a consequence, he creates a subproblem to be solved by other agents. Explicit collaboration is triggered by meta-knowledge (i. e. knowledge overlapping several domains) about good combinations of financial products. Two or more agents *compete*, if they elaborate alternative solutions to the same problem. The same holds true for competing coalitions of agents.

We can now briefly discuss the process of problem solving. Starting with the (formalized) problem of the customer either meta-knowledge decomposes the problem into subproblems to be solved by several explicitly collaborating agents, or an agent tries to solve the problem on his own. If the meta-knowledge proposes various decompositions or different agents try to solve the problem on their own, then competing solutions are going to be elaborated. An agent's contribution to a solution will be compared with the (sub-)problem he had to solve in order to decide if this part of the solution is complete (A complete solution is either a global solution or the partial solution demanded by a decomposition). If not, we have a subproblem to be treated in the same way as the starting problem. All parts of a solution have to be collected, synthesized and evaluated. Competing solutions have to be compared and ranked. Finally, a number of "best" solutions in the ranking will be proposed to the customer.

Approaches for distributed problem solving range from architectures with a central supervisor monitoring the agents and controlling them to architectures with groups of agents without any (explicit) coordination. Two outstanding architectures follow the contract-net- and the blackboard-paradigm. The contract-net-approach [11] proposes a decentral coordination by bidding and contracting tasks directly among the agents: Here the agents must have at least knowledge about communication and possibly about other domains. In contrast, an agent in the blackboard approach does not know anything about other domains. The *blackboard* [5] is a central data-structure to store the problem, subproblems, partial and global solutions. The agents can read and write on the blackboard, but do not communicate directly with each other. A scheduler manages at least the concurrent operations on the blackboard; in addition it can interfere in the process of problem-solving by applying meta-knowledge. In ALLFIWIB we chose the blackboard-architecture as the best approach for distributed problem solving in the application domain [9].

3 The Architecture

While working on the solution, the agents use knowledge and facts. Because facts about economic reality have to be updated frequently and for reasons of integrity and efficient retrieval, facts are stored in database systems [4], [7]. Normally, individual locations of a geographically dispersed financial services company possess historically grown data bases. In addition, for economic reasons it is advantageous to prefer storing local data in their respective locations. To ensure an integrated and well-founded financial services support at the interface to the customer, the agents need online access both to local and remote data. For reasons of integrating historically grown data bases in a distributed environment [8] and to provide an economically advantageous allocation of data among the locations, we propose the flexible relational *Multi-Database-Server-Architecture* (MDBSA) [6], [7] based on the client-server-principle for database support of the agents. In ALLFIWIB, we implemented the MDBSA by using the OS/2 2.0 Extended Services Database Manager (Server).

In contrast to a distributed database system, no global scheme exists in MDBSA. In ALLFIWIB, each agent works on an individually customized virtual scheme, similar to a view over different databases on different machines. It provides a partial scheme-integration of data on different database-servers. A SQL-Query against the virtual scheme of an agent needs to be transformed into a set of SQL-Queries against databases on the database servers. The resulting relations then have to be semantically integrated to obtain the result of the original SQL-Query. These virtual schemes are currently implemented in Giessen.

The same as for data applies for files and processes (like agent- and blackboard-/scheduler-processes). For this reason, ALLFIWIB supports a *Multi-File-Server-Architecture* based on the OS/2 LAN-Services. A homogeneous IPC/RPC-Architecture allows processes to communicate at runtime and to run remote database access by using pipes and semaphores. The IPC/RPC-Architecture allows processes on different machines in the network to communicate. In ALLFIWIB, both LANs in Giessen and Marburg will be linked via WAN on TCP/IP. These features seem to be a quite realistic mapping of the geographic topology of a financial services company.

Altogether, we call the architecture described a *Multi-Server-Architecture* (MSA). It provides a great deal of flexibility in designing a distributed system. Aspects of computer science and business administration are combined to design a system providing the required functionality with approximately minimal costs. Theoretical work is currently be done to show "good" and feasible solutions for this data-, file- and process-allocation-problem in a MSA.

4 References

[1] Buhl, H. U.: Verteilte wissensbasierte Systeme für die Allfinanz-Kundenberatung; in: Spremann, K. / Zur, E. (eds.): Controlling, Wiesbaden 1992, 733 - 762

[2] Buhl, H. U.: Optimale Kreditfinanzierung im Allfinanz-Kontext; Disc.paper WI 29-1992, Professur für BWL, Wirtschaftsinformatik, Universität Giessen

[3] Buhl, H. U. / Erhard, N.: Steuerlich linearisiertes Leasing: Kalkulation und Steuerparadoxon; in: Zeitschrift für Betriebswirtschaft, 61, 12, 1991, 1355 - 1375

[4] Date, C. J.: Database Systems; Vol. I, Addison Wesley, Reading, 1990

[5] Hayes-Roth, B.: A Blackboard Architecture for Control; in: Artificial Intelligence, Vol. 26 (1985), 251 - 321

[6] König, H.-J.: A Multi-Database-Server-Architecture to Support Cooperating Knowledge Based Systems; in: Cellary, W. / Vossen, G. (eds.): Topics in Object-Oriented and Heterogeneous Database Systems; Report No. 9204, Giessen 1992

[7] König, H.-J.: Eine Multi-Datenbank-Server-Architektur zur Unterstützung kooperierender finanzwirtschaftlicher Problemlösungsagenten; Disc.paper WI 25-1992, Professur für BWL, Wirtschaftsinformatik, Universität Giessen

[8] Mullender, S. (ed.): Distributed Systems; Addison Wesley, Reading, 1989

[9] Roemer, M. / Sandbiller, K. / Will, A.: Ein Modell zur verteilten Problemlösung im Allfinanz-Bereich: Anforderungen, Eigenschaften, Auswahl; Disc.paper WI 27-1992, Professur für BWL, Wirtschaftsinformatik, Universität Giessen

[10] Sandbiller, K. / Weinhardt, Ch. / Will, A.: Cooperating Agents Solving Financial Problems: A Scenario; Disc.paper WI 26-1992, Professur für BWL, Wirtschaftsinformatik, Universität Giessen

[11] Smith, R. G.: The Contract Net Protocol: High-Level Communication and Control in a Distributed Problem Solver; in: IEEE Transactions on Computers, Vol. 29(12): 1104-1113, 1980

[12] Will, A. / Buhl, H. U. / Weinhardt, Ch.: Immobilienleasing und Steuern im Allfinanz-Kontext; Disc.paper WI 18-1992, Professur für BWL, Wirtschaftsinformatik, Universität Giessen

On the Use of Geometric Brownian Motion in Financial Analysis

Michael Tow Cheung, David Yeung, Alfred Lai
School of Economics, University of Hong Kong
Hong Kong, Hong Kong

Though geometric Brownian motion (GBM) is an essential tool in finance, a closed form solution for its transition density function has yet to be obtained. In option pricing, though Black and Scholes assumed GBM stock price dynamics, they transformed the problem to allow an option to be evaluated without the stock price's transition density. This paper presents a closed form solution of Kolmogorov's backward equation for GBM. As an application, the option price equation is derived directly.

In the general equilibrium theory of options, it is assumed the expected rate of return on each stock is equal to the risk-free rate of interest. We point out there is a divergence between the moments and sample path behavior of GBM stock price processes. A stock with an exponentially increasing expected value and a positive rate of return may have a typical sample path which approaches 0 asymptoptically a.s., so that a serious problem arises in the interpretation of equilibrium in asset markets. We suggest that by introducing risk adjustment in the equilibrium condition, this problem can be overcome.

The GBM stochastic process $X(t)$, $t \geq 0$ can be described by:

$$dX(t) = \alpha X(t)dt + \sigma X(t)dZ(t), \tag{1}$$

where $Z(t)$ is a standard Wiener process, $\alpha X(t)$ and $\sigma^2 X(t)^2$ the drift and diffusion coefficients. Given the initial condition $X_0 > 0$, let $X^*(t;X_0)$ denote the solution to the stochastic differential equation (1). For any $t > 0$, its transition density function $\phi(t,X,X_0)$ satisfies the Kolmogorov backward equation:

$$\partial\phi/\partial t = (\alpha X_0)\partial\phi/\partial X_0 + (\sigma^2 X_0^2/2)\partial^2\phi/\partial X_0. \tag{2}$$

To obtain a closed form solution to (2), let us write $x(t) = \log X(t)$. By Ito's lemma, (1) may then be written:

$$dx(t) = (\alpha - \sigma^2/2)dt + \sigma dZ(t). \tag{3}$$

Given the initial condition $x_0 = \log X_0$, for $t > 0$ the transition density function $\psi(t,x,x_0)$ of the solution process $x^*(t;x_0)$ to (3) satisfies the Kolmogorov backward equation:

$$\partial\psi/\partial t = (\alpha - \sigma^2/2)\partial\psi/\partial x_0 + (\sigma^2/2)\partial^2\psi/\partial x_0^2. \quad (4)$$

Lemma: The transition density which satisfies (4) has the form:

$$\psi(t,x,x_0) = (1/\sigma\sqrt{2\pi t})\exp\left[- \{x - [x_0 + (\alpha - \sigma^2/2)t]\}^2/2\sigma^2 t\right]. \quad (5)$$

Proof: The transition density function of the standard Brownian motion Y(t) is the Gauss kernel:

$$\theta(t,Y,Y_0) = (1/\sqrt{2\pi t})\exp[- (Y - Y_0)^2/2t]. \quad (6)$$

As may be verified by straightforward substitution, it is possible to express the function $\psi(t,x,x_0)$ in (4) in the form of a Gauss kernel, by replacing the arguments (t,Y,Y_0) of the function $\theta(t,Y,Y_0)$ by $(\sigma^2 t,x,x_0 + (\alpha - \sigma^2/2)t)$. That is:

$$\psi(t,x,x_0) = \theta(\sigma^2 t,x,x_0 + (\alpha - \sigma^2/2)t). \quad (7)$$

It must be shown that (7) (and therefore (5)) satisfies (4). Differentiating (7) with respect to x_0 and t:

$\partial\psi/\partial t = \sigma^2\theta_1 + (\alpha - \sigma^2/2)\theta_3$, $\partial\psi/\partial x_0 = \theta_3$, $\partial^2\psi/\partial x_0^2 = \theta_{33}$, so that:

$$(\alpha - \sigma^2/2)\partial\psi/\partial x_0 + (\sigma^2/2)\partial^2\psi/\partial x_0^2 = (\alpha - \sigma^2/2)\theta_3 + (1/2)\sigma^2\theta_{33}. \quad (8)$$

From (6), $\theta_1 = \theta_{33}/2$. Substituting into (8):

$$(\alpha - \sigma^2/2)\partial\psi/\partial x_0 + (\sigma^2/2)\partial^2\psi/\partial x_0^2 = (\alpha - \sigma^2/2)\theta_3 + \sigma^2\theta_1. \quad (9)$$

It is seen that the RHS of (9) is $\partial\psi/\partial t$. Therefore,

$$\partial\psi/\partial t = (\alpha - \sigma^2/2)\partial\psi/\partial x_0 + (1/2)\sigma^2\partial\psi/\partial x_0^2 , \quad (10)$$

so that (7) or (5) indeed satisfies (4).

For $t > 0$, $x(t) = \log X(t)$ is a 1:1 onto mapping of X(t) to x(t). Applying a standard variate transform to (5), we have:

Theorem: The transition density function of the stochastic process $X^*(t,X_0)$ is $\Phi(t,X,X_0) =$

$$(1/X\sigma\sqrt{2\pi t})\exp\left[- \{\log X - [\log X_0 + (\alpha - \sigma^2/2)t]\}^2/2\sigma^2 t\right]. \quad (11)$$

(11) yields the transition density function for GBM, and it is the closed form solution to the Kolmogorov backward equation (2). We readily observe that X(t) is lognormally distributed with mean $\exp(\log X_0 + \alpha t)$ and variance $\exp[2(\log X_0 + \alpha t)][\exp(\sigma^2 t) - 1]$.

Suppose the price of a common stock S(t) follows GBM, so that from (1), $dS(t) = \alpha S(t)dt + \sigma S(t)dZ(t)$. The transition density (11) may be used to derive the Black-Scholes valuation equation for an European option on this stock. At the expiry date t (t= 0 is the present), the option has the value:

$$C(t) = \int_K^\infty (S - K)\Phi(t,S,S_0)dS, \quad (12)$$

where S_0 is the current stock price, and K the option exercise price. Substituting the transition density $\Phi(t,S,S_0)$ from (11), discounting back t periods with the given rate of interest r and using the general equilibrium condition $\alpha = r$, (12) becomes:

$$C(t,S_0,K,r,\sigma^2) = S_0N([\log(S_0/K) + (r + \sigma /2)t]/(\sigma/\sqrt{t})) - \exp(-rt)KN([\log(S_0/K) + (r - \sigma^2/2)t]/(\sigma\sqrt{t})). \quad (13)$$

A problem of interpretation arises with the general equilibrium condition $\alpha = r$. As Kozin (1972) has shown, the sample path and moments behavior of a GBM process may differ. In the present case, if $0 < \alpha < \sigma^2/2$, the expected stock price is in the limit infinite, and yet the individual who holds it long enough would be "almost certainly ruined", in the sense that the price (sample points) would drop to 0 a.s. (Samuelson 1965). The existence of Kozin's divergence poses a serious problem, for the options general equilibrium condition does not exclude "almost certain ruin" stocks. To resolve the problem, consider an equilibrium in which risk adjusted expected rates of return are equalised: $\alpha = r + \gamma\sigma^2$, $\gamma > 0$. If the value of γ produced by asset markets equilibrium is γ^*, the stock price S(t) and s(t) = log S(t) would develop according to the dynamical equations:

$$dS(t) = (r + \gamma^*\sigma^2)S(t)dt + \sigma S(t)dZ(t), \text{ or} \quad (14)$$

$$ds(t) = [r - [(1/2) - \gamma^*]\sigma^2]dt + \sigma dZ(t). \quad (15)$$

Since rational investors would behave to exclude the possibility of "almost certain ruin", $\gamma^* \geq 1/2 - r/\sigma^2$. If $\gamma^* > 1/2$, the prices (sample points) of a stock with a higher σ are dispersed around a higher growth curve, each of which lies above the growth curve of the risk-free asset. If $\gamma^* = 1/2$, the growth curves of all stocks are same as that of the risk-free asset. If $1/2 - r/\sigma^2 < \gamma^* < 1/2$, prices of a stock with a higher σ are dispersed around a lower growth curve, each of which lies below the growth curve of the risk-free asset. However, none of these sample paths would decay.

References

Black, F. & M. Scholes (1973). The Pricing of Options and Corporate Liabilities, *J. Pol. Econ.*, 81, 637-654.

Kozin, F. (1972). Stability of the Linear Stochastic System, in R. Curtain ed., *Stability of Stochastic Dynamical Systems*, New York: Springer Verlag.

Samuelson, P. A. (1965). Rational Theory of Warrant Pricing, *Industrial Management Rev.*, 6, 13-31.

Modelling of Catastrophic Events in Insurance and Finance

Paul Embrechts
Department of Mathematics, ETH-Zürich
8092 Zürich, Switzerland

1. Introduction

In every branch of insurance a significant increase in the number of catastrophies and their financial impact is observed. In its series of publications SIGMA on catastrophic events, the Swiss Reinsurance Company gives a systematic review of the evolution of such claims. Its definition of catastrophic event is expressed in number of death (20 or more) or in terms of insured claims. For the latter to be catastrophic one uses lower limits of 10.4 million US$ in shipping, 20.8 in aviation and 26.0 for other branches. Some examples for 1990 are 4.6 billion US$ for winterstorm Daria and 3.2 billion US$ for winterstorm Vivian hitting Europe. In summary for 1990 one has that the insured claims (catastrophics and large claims) reached worldwide a record sum of 17 billion US$. First estimates on hurricane Andrew which recently hit the south-east coast of the USA are for a total loss of at least 20 billion US$ with possible insured claims in the order of 7 billion US$. Whether one looks at summary data across different insurance branches or stratisfies with respect to specific branches (looking at the number of such events or their financial amount) one notices an explosive increase beginning in the mid eighties. For instance, over the period 1970-1990, the number of nature-catastrophies fluctuated around 40 till 1985 (with only a slight increase) before increasing to more than 100 by 1990. Though statistical modelling is still a key factor in the global discussion relating to catastrophic events, one cannot however fail to express ones unease about the present evolution. The latter is nicely expressed in Brauner (1992): "Aller Schönrednerei von einer sicherer gewordenen Welt zum Trotz spricht die Statistik eine andere Sprache: Zahl und Ausmass der Katastrophen nehmen weltweit ständig und immer schneller zu. Bei näherem Hinschauen wird deutlich, dass dies weder Zufall noch Schicksal ist: Nicht die Natur, sondern der Mensch verursacht die meisten Katastrophen, sei es, indem er die Kontrolle über seine eigenen Systeme verliert, in natürliche Systeme eingreift oder indem die vom Menschen geschaffenen Systeme immer verletzlicher werden, zum Beispiel gegenüber Erdbeben und Überschwemmungen. Um den bedrohlichen Katastrophenboom zu stoppen, bedarf es eines anderen Vorgehens als bisher: nicht experimentieren, sondern mögliche Gefahren vorausschauend erkennen". One aspect of the badly needed dialogue between the various experts in the field will undoubtedly have to focus on the training of insurance mathematicians in techniques apt at modelling large claim phenomena. My talk aims at making a step in that direction.

2. The stochastic modelling of large claims

As expressed by Albrecht (1984), a pragmatic point of view leads to a definition of large claims as those claims exceeding some fixed amount. So what is an adequate dividing line between ordinary and large claims? Hence, what are the distribution-models for each category (ordinary versus large)? Given one or more dividing line(s), what is the probability of an excess claim (closely related; what is the expected number of excess claims?) and what is the mean excess amount? For these questions, precise mathematical models can of course be worked out and their statistical goodness-of-fit tested. In our work for instance, the following class of distributions has proved to be useful in modelling heavy tails. Suppose $X_1, \ldots, X_n$ (≥ 0) are i.i.d. random variable (claims) with distribution function F. Denote by $S_n = \sum_{k=1}^{n} X_k$ and $M_n = \max(X_1, \ldots, X_n)$.

Definition *F is* subexponential ($F \in \mathcal{S}$) *whenever*

$$\lim_{x \to \infty} \left(1 - F^{(2)}(x)\right) \Big/ \left(1 - F(x)\right) = 2 \,,$$

$F^{(2)}$ stands for the second convolution of F. □

One easily shows that $F \in \mathcal{S}$ if and only if for all $n \geq 2$, $P\{S_n > x\} \sim P\{M_n > x\}$ as $x \to \infty$. ($f(x) \sim g(x)$ for $x \to \infty$ if $\lim_{x \to \infty} f(x)/g(x) = 1$). From a statistical modelling point of view, this class $\mathcal{S}$ gives exactly the dividing line between short-tailed and long-tailed distributions. For instance elements of $\mathcal{S}$ are: Pareto type distributions, Lognormal, Loggamma, Weibull (τ) with $\tau < 1$. Distributions not belonging to $\mathcal{S}$ are: Bounded support distributions, Exponential, Gamma, Truncated Normal, Weibull (τ) with $\tau \geq 1$.

The usefulness of $\mathcal{S}$ in insurance mathematics can for instance be seen in the classical risk model where under a 'light-tail condition' an exponential estimate of the (ultimate) probability of ruin $\psi(u)$ with initial capital $u \to \infty$ is obtained

$$\psi(u) \sim c_1 \, e^{-\nu u} \,, \quad u \to \infty \,.$$

If one denotes $F_1(x) = (1/\mu) \int_0^x (1 - F(t)) \, dt$ where $\mu = E(X_1)$ assumed to be finite, then in Embrechts and Veraverbeke (1982), the following result is proved:

$$F_1 \in \mathcal{S} \Rightarrow \psi(u) \sim c_2 \int_u^\infty (1 - F(t)) \, dt \,.$$

Various generalisations of the above result exist, see for instance Embrechts and Villasenõr (1988), Beirlant and Teugels (1992) and the references therein.

3. From theory towards practice

As already indicated in the introduction a full solution of the modelling of catastrophic events will entail a broad discussion between practitioners and researchers. One example where a 'practical rule of thumb' on large claims is motivated via mathematical theory is to be found in Aebi, Embrechts and Mikosch (1992). In the latter paper the following large claim index $D_F(\alpha)$ is defined

$$D_F(\alpha) = \frac{1}{\mu} \int_\alpha^1 F^{-1}(t)\, dt\,, \quad 0 \le \alpha \le 1\,.$$

$D_F(\alpha)$ indicates to what extend the $100(1-\alpha)\%$ largest claims in a claim portfolio contribute to the overall portfolio claim amount. Using this measure one can for instance show that for a Pareto claim size distribution with parameter $p = 1.4$ (hence $E(X_1) < \infty$, Var $(X_1) = \infty$) 20% of the claims contribute 80% of the total claim amount. If $p = 1.01$, then 0.1% yields more than 90%! In the above paper, the 'dangerousness' of various claim size models is discussed.

References

Aebi, M., P. Embrechts and T. Mikosch (1992). A large claim index, *Mitteilungen der Schweizerischen Vereinigung für Versicherungsmathematiker*, 1992, Heft 2, to appear.

Albrecht, P. (1984). *Summary Report on Large Claims*, in: Proceedings of the 4 Countries ASTIN-Symposium, Akersloot, September 1984, ASTIN Groep Nederland, pp. 153-164.

Beirlant, J. and J.L. Teugels (1992). Modelling large claims in non-life insurance, *Insurance Mathematics and Economics* **11**, 17-29.

Brauner, C. (1992). *Verursacher ist in den meisten Fällen der Mensch.* Weltwoche.

Embrechts, P. and N. Veraverbeke (1982). Estimates of the probability of ruin with special emphasis on the possibility of large claims. *Insurance Mathematics and Economics* **1**, 55-72.

Embrechts, P. and J.A. Villaseñor (1988). Ruin estimates for large claims. *Insurance Mathematics and Economics* **7**, 269-274.

Life Insurance Solvency Assessment Using Stochastic Simulation Techniques

Mary Hardy
Department of Actuarial Mathematics and Statistics, Heriot-Watt University
Edinburgh EH14 4AS, United Kingdom

While most UK life insurance companies employ asset/liability models to project their emerging cash flows, few employ stochastic simulation methods. The preferred approach is to project the business deterministically, using sensitivity tests to assess any insolvency risk. This method has been notably advocated by Brender(1988) in his work on a solvency standard for the Canadian industry. But with many insurers being forced to slim their reserves in order to remain competitive, is this deterministic, generally rather ad hoc approach adequate? In contrast with Brender's conclusions, the Faculty of Actuaries Solvency Working Party (1986) recommended strongly that insurers should, once techniques were suitably developed, be required to demonstrate to the supervisory authorities that their estimated probability of ruin is acceptably low, using stochastic simulation. In this paper a model office is used to demonstrate the difference in the quality of information available from a set of stochastic simulations compared with a traditional deterministic approach.

The model office used is a mature, ongoing office which sells 25-year with-profit endowment assurances and 25-year non-profit term assurances to lives aged 30. Bonus is awarded, according to the usual UK method, in the form of guaranteed reversionary bonus during the term of the policy, plus a non-guaranteed terminal bonus on a claim by death or maturity. The terminal bonus is assessed such that participating policyholders receive, on average, 95% of their asset share on maturity, unless the guaranteed liabilities exceed this, in which case the terminal bonus will be 0%. It is assumed that the office's investments are held in UK gilts and UK equities.

The model office employs dynamic investment and bonus strategies. New business is assumed to continue at past levels of growth for 5 years, after which the total business of the office is run off as a closed fund.

Six versions of the model office are considered:
(i) A base office; (ii) A high equity version; (iii) A low equity version; (iv) A high reversionary bonus version; (v) A high payout office; (vi) An office with higher equity exposure, higher reversionary bonus, lower premiums and higher asset share payout than the base office.

All of these offices are assumed to start the projection period with the same assets and liabilities. The initial ratio of assets to liabilities (A/L) for all the offices is 1.87.

Under deterministic projection using best estimate assumptions, all six versions of the office appear to remain quite comfortably healthy, with A/L ratios level or increasing in each year of the projection. The weaker offices, after 5 years, appear to be the high reversionary bonus office and the high payout/equity/reversionary bonus office ((vi) above), with the other 4 offices having very similar A/L ratios.

Sensitivity tests for adverse mortality, lapse, growth, claim amounts and expenses experience, derived largely from Brender(1988), indicate that these offices are not particularly vulnerable in these areas. Brender's suggested interest scenarios were not used, as they do not reflect UK investment variability. The sensitivity tests of investment experience used, chosen to reflect the kind of test in use by UK offices, are (i) a gradual reduction in both equity and gilt yields, such that the rate of interest earned by the base office falls from around 9% to around 4% over 10 years, and (ii) a sudden fall in equity prices in the first projection year, followed by a 50% recovery in prices in year 2 and a full recovery in year 3. Dividends and gilts are assumed unaffected. The first test gives a very similar ordering of the offices to the best estimate test. The second shows the low equity office to be much healthier after 1 year than the other 5. After 5 years the offices are all quite close, and after 10 years the high equity office is projected to be the healthiest. In neither of these tests does any office's A/L ratio fall below 1.2, nor does the ratio of assets to liabilities + statutory margins fall below 1.0.

In the stochastic simulation of these offices the investment model developed by Wilkie(1986) was used for investment scenarios (including inflation rates), and claim amounts were simulated as Pareto distributed random variables. All other elements of the simulation were treated deterministically. The equity and gilt yields used in the deterministic runs were consistent with the mean yields emerging from the stochastic simulation. Each office's cash flows were projected for 25 years using the same investment simulations, so that the results are directly comparable. The number of simulations for each office was 1,000. The simplest test of solvency is the proportion of simulations in which the A/L ratio fell below 1.0, and for the 6 offices these were:

Office	Insolvent simulations %
(i) Base office	7.1
(ii)High equity office	13.6
(iii)Low equity office	0.1
(iv) High reversionary bonus office	15.0
(v) High payout office	10.8
(vi) High equity/payout/reversionary bonus, low premium office	20.7

The spread of results here is very much greater than indicated by the deterministic tests, and the ordering is much more intuitively satisfactory. In addition stochastic simulation gives information on the distribution of the projected cash flows and asset/liability ratios, and on the timing of potential solvency problems. Despite the simplicity of the model, these results provide evidence that simple sensitivity testing gives little useful information about the true solvency position of a life insurer, and may be positively misleading.

REFERENCES

Brender A (1988) Testing the solvency of life insurers. Proceedings of the 2nd International Conference on Insurance Solvency.

Wilkie A D (1986) A stochastic investment model for actuarial use. Transactions of the Faculty of Actuaries 39:341-373.

Faculty of Actuaries Solvency Working Party (1986) The solvency of life insurance companies. Transactions of the Faculty of Actuaries 39:251-317.

Optimal Stop-Loss Limits under Non-Expected Utility Preferences

Werner Hürlimann
Allgemeine Mathematatik, Winterthur-Leben
Römerstraße 17, 8401 Winterthur, Switzerland

The question of the selection of optimal retentions for insurance contracts is an old problem which has been discussed by almost all prominent actuaries, e.g. Borch, Bühlmann, DeFinetti, Straub and many others. Most of the solutions are based on expected utility preference theory. Recently the work by Denneberg(1985/1990) has shown that non-expected utility preferences may lead to desirable functional premium calculation principles. It is the purpose of this note to illustrate the impact of this approach on the retention problem. Only a specific case study is presented and no attempt to obtain more general results was made so far. We assume the reader is familiar with Denneberg(1990).

Given is a random variable X representing a potential loss to be insured. Let $F(x)$ be the probability distribution associated to X and assume that the corresponding density is $f(x)=F'(x)$. To fix ideas suppose the insured (index 1) and the insurer (index 2) conclude an insurance arrangement with payoff functions $X_2=(X-d)_+$ and $X_1=X-(X-d)_+$, where d is the deductible or stop-loss limit of the considered contract. Both parties agree on $F(x)$. The problem is to select an optimal value of d given $F(x)$ as well as the insured's attitude to risk and the insurer's premium rates. Let $\gamma_i(x)$, $i=1,2$, be quantile preference functions, that is distribution functions on the unit interval $[0,1]$. Consider the distorted probability functions $F_i(x)=(\gamma_i \circ F)(x)$, $i=1,2$, and assume the first derivatives $f_i(x)=F_i'(x)=\gamma_i'(F(x))\cdot f(x)$ exist. Suppose that $F_1(x)$ models the insured's attitude to risk and that $F_2(x)$ is used to set stop-loss premiums using the functional premium principle $\pi=\pi(d)=H[X_2]=\int(x-d)_+dF_2(x)$. By known wealth W the insured's non-expected utility is given by

$$U=U(d)=\int_{-\infty}^{d}(W-\pi-x)dF_1(x)+(W-\pi-d)(1-F_1(d)). \tag{1}$$

Assume the insured's goal is to maximize non-expected utility. Then the optimal deductible d^* is solution of the optimization problem

$$U(d^*)=\max_{d}\{\,U(d)\,\} \tag{2}$$

The following simple result is already quite general and allows intuitive interpretations as shown later on.

Theorem. Assume that $d>0$ satisfies the following condition :

$$F_1(d)=F_2(d) \quad \text{and} \quad f_1(d)<f_2(d). \tag{3}$$

Then d maximizes the non-expected utility of the insured and defines an optimal stop-loss contract.

Proof. Using Leibnitz' rule for the derivative of an integral one gets

(4)
$$\partial U/\partial d = (W - \pi - d)\cdot f_1(d) - \int_{-\infty}^{d} (\partial\pi/\partial d)\cdot dF_1(x) - (\partial\pi/\partial d+1)\cdot(1 - F_1(d)) - (W - \pi - d)\cdot f_1(d)$$
$$= -\{\ \partial\pi/\partial d + (1 - F_1(d))\ \}.$$

Since $\partial\pi/\partial d = -(1 - F_2(d))$, it follows that

(5)
$$\partial U/\partial d = F_1(d) - F_2(d) \quad\text{and}\quad \partial^2 U/\partial d^2 = f_1(d) - f_2(d),$$

and the result is shown by elementary calculus.

Remark. If both quantile preference functions $F_i(x)$ are equal (a case which is excluded by (3)), then one gets $U(d)=W-E[X]$ and no deductible is preferred. In this situation note that a criterion of maximum expected utility leads sometimes to a unique optimal deductible. For example assume exponential utility functions $u_i'(x)=(1-e^{-kx})/k$ with equal Pratt-Arrow coefficient of risk aversion $k > 0$ for both insured and insurer. Then a rational insurer sets premium rates according to the exponential premium principle $H[X]=\ln\{\ \exp(kX)\ \}/k$ for any insurable risk X. As shown by Boyle and Mao(1983), if risk X is normally distributed with mean μ and variance σ^2, then the unique optimal deductible under the expected utility criterion is equal to the premium for complete insurance, namely $d=\mu+\frac{1}{2}k\sigma^2$.

Let us interpret our result in terms of the non-additive probability measures $\mu_i=\gamma_i\circ F$, $i=1,2$. If both the insured and the insurer associate the same measure to the event $\{X \le d\}$, that is

(6)
$$\mu_1\{X \le d\}=\mu_2\{X \le d\},\ \text{but}\ \ \mu_1\{X=d\} < \mu_2\{X=d\},$$

then d is an optimal stop-loss limit. To obtain effective values of d apply the following recipe :

(i) find a zero x_0 of $\varphi(x) = \gamma_1(F(x)) - \gamma_2(F(x))$,

(ii) verify that $\varphi'(x_0) = \{\ \gamma_1'(F(x_0)) - \gamma_2'(F(x_0)\ \}\cdot f(x_0) < 0.$

Then the x_0-quantile $d=F^{\leftarrow}(x_0)=\inf\{\ x : F(x) \ge x_0\ \}$ is an optimal stop-loss limit.
Let us conclude with an illustration

Example. Assume that the insurer sets premium rates according to the absolute deviation principle implied by the quantile preference function (see Denneberg(1985))

$$\gamma_2(x) = \begin{cases} (1 - \rho_2)\cdot x, & x \le \frac{1}{2} \\ 1 - (1+\rho_2)\cdot(1-x), & x \ge \frac{1}{2} \end{cases}$$

On the other side assume that $\gamma_1(x)=x + \frac{1}{2}\rho_1 x(x-1)$, $0 \le \rho_1 \le 2$. The corresponding premium functional is called Gini principle (see Denneberg(1990)). Applying the recipe following our theorem, one shows immediately that d is an optimal stop-loss limit provided the following condition is fulfilled :

(7) $$0 < \tfrac{1}{4}\rho_1 < \rho_2 = \tfrac{1}{2}F(d)\cdot\rho_1 < \tfrac{1}{2}\rho_1 \le 1.$$

The ratio ρ_2/ρ_1, which we call "relative distortion factor", is a relative measure of the attitude to risk of both parties in the insurance agreement. It plays the role of the well-known measures of risk aversion used in expected utility theory. Let us compare the result (7) with the special exact solution obtained by Boyle and Mao(1983) mentioned in the above remark. Assume that $F(x)$ is normally distributed with mean μ and variance σ^2. Then the exponential premium for complete insurance $d=\mu+\frac{1}{2}k\sigma^2$ from expected utility theory is an optimal stop-loss limit under non-expected utility preferences provided the relative distortion factor satisfies

(8) $$\rho_2 = \tfrac{1}{2}N(\tfrac{1}{2}k\sigma)\cdot\rho_1,$$

where $N(x)$ is the cumulative distribution function of the standard normal variate. In the special result by Boyle and Mao(1983), one needs that the coefficients of risk aversion in the exponential utility functions of both insurer and insured are equal, while in non-expected utility theory one needs solely that the ratio ρ_2/ρ_1 be constant. With Casti(1989) one can only hope that these "alternate realities" may be better understood in the future.

References.

Boyle, P., Mao, J. (1983). An exact solution for the optimal stop-loss limit. Journal of Risk and Insurance, 719-26.

Casti, J.L. (1989). Alternate realities : mathematical models of nature and man. John Wiley and Sons, Inc.

Denneberg, D. (1985). Valuation of first moment risk for decision purposes in Finance and Insurance. In H. Göppel, R. Henn (ed.) 3. Tagung Geld, Banken und Versicherungen, Karlsruhe 12-15.12.1984. Verlag Versicherungswirtschaft, Karlsruhe, 855-69.

Denneberg, D. (1990). Premium calculation : why standard deviation should be replaced by absolute deviation. ASTIN Bulletin 20, no. 2, 181-90.

Forecasting Volatility and Option Pricing with GARCH Models

Jürgen Kähler
Zentrum für Europäische Wirtschaftsforschung (ZEW)
Kaiserring 14–16, P.O. Box 10 34 43, 6800 Mannheim 1, Germany

In this paper I will explore the applicability of GARCH (generalized *a*uto*r*egressive *c*onditional *h*eteroskedasticity) models to the modelling of volatility in financial markets. More specifically, I will examine the forecasting performance of GARCH models for the volatility of foreign exchange rates and study the implications of these models for option pricing.

The GARCH model (p,q), introduced by Bollerslev (1986), may be written as:

$$x_t = u_t \sqrt{h_t}, \tag{1}$$

$$h_t = a_0 + a_1 x_{t-1}^2 + \ldots + a_p x_{t-p}^2 + b_1 h_{t-1} + \ldots + b_q h_{t-q} \tag{2}$$

where x_t is the data series, u_t is Gaussian white noise with unit variance and h_t is the variance conditional on information available at time $t-1$.

The data to be analysed are daily and weekly exchange rates of the U.S.dollar against the German mark, the British pound, the Swiss franc, and the Japanese yen from July 1st, 1974 to December 31st, 1987.The exchange-rate dynamics are analysed in the form of $x_t = 100(e_t - e_{t-1})$ where e_t is the logarithm of the exchange rate.

Modelling Stochastic Volatility

Estimates of the GARCH(1,1) model are shown in Table 1 and standard errors are given in brackets. In most cases, a_1 is close to 0.1 and b_1 is close to 0.9. Since the mean lag of conditional variance effects is given by $(1-b_1)^{-1}$, the high value of b_1 implies that there is strong persistence in variances. There are also several series for which $a_1 + b_1 > 1$. This indicates violation of second-order stationarity of the estimated GARCH processes.

Table 1 also reports results from a likelihood-ratio (LR) test for the GARCH(1,1) model against the H_0 of a simple normal distribution. The LR test rejects Gaussian white noise very strongly against the GARCH(1,1) model for all series. According to the model, the "residuals" $\hat{u}_t = x_t / \hat{h}_t^{1/2}$ should have a standard normal distribution. Table 1 reports both the kurtosis of the data x_t and of the residuals. The H_0 of mesokurtosis can be rejected for all series of residuals. Even more surprisingly, leptokurtosis increases substantially in $\hat{u}_t$ as compared with x_t for both yen

Table 1
Estimates of the GARCH(1,1) model

		mark	pound	franc	yen
day	a_0	0.656 (0.128)	0.675 (0.109)	0.856 (0.179)	0.766 (0.120)
	a_1	0.169 (0.015)	0.135 (0.013)	0.143 (0.013)	0.190 (0.021)
	b_1	0.833 (0.013)	0.864 (0.011)	0.857 (0.012)	0.820 (0.017)
	LR	970.3 ***	908.5 ***	1015.1 ***	901.6 ***
	$\beta_2(x_t)$	8.3 ***	8.4 ***	8.9 ***	8.0 ***
	$\beta_2(\hat{u}_t)$	4.8 ***	10.6 ***	6.3 ***	17.4 ***
	$Q(x_t^2)$	355.2 ***	507.3 ***	516.0 ***	432.2 ***
	$Q(\hat{u}_t^2)$	22.9 *	8.4	54.1 ***	3.2
week	a_0	1.71 (1.34)	4.16 (1.68)	1.83 (1.22)	0.52 (0.38)
	a_1	0.095 (0.027)	0.114 (0.029)	0.095 (0.017)	0.076 (0.013)
	b_1	0.906 (0.027)	0.878 (0.025)	0.907 (0.016)	0.932 (0.011)
	LR	111.4 ***	103.0 ***	119.3 ***	133.8 ***
	$\beta_2(x_t)$	5.8 ***	7.4 ***	5.0 ***	7.0 ***
	$\beta_2(\hat{u}_t)$	4.3 ***	7.0 ***	4.3 ***	9.8 ***
	$Q(x_t^2)$	61.5 ***	123.9 ***	98.2 **	52.8 ***
	$Q(\hat{u}_t^2)$	29.6 **	8.0	11.7	4.4

Significance levels: * 10 percent, ** 5 percent, *** 1 percent.

series and the daily pound series. This points to a weakness of this model which might be due to a wrong distributional assumption about u_t or other misspecifications. Table 1 also reports the Ljung-Box statistic Q for squared residuals at lag 15. As compared with the same statistics for x_t, there is a dramatic drop in Q for the residuals of the GARCH(1,1) model. Only for the daily franc series is the Q of the residuals significant at the 1 percent level. One may, therefore, conclude from the Ljung-Box test that the GARCH(1,1) model captures the empirical volatility dynamics well.

Forecasting Volatility

In order to gain more insight into the applicability of the GARCH model and into its structural stability, I report results from some forecasting experiments. Benchmarks for the forecasting performance of the GARCH models are models which estimate volatility as the variance from past data and which extrapolate this variance into the future periods. I estimated the models on a "rolling basis". For the daily data, the GARCH model was first estimated for the observations from $t = 1$ to $T = 1000$. Forecasts were made for the next 20 days and the forecasts were compared with x_{T+i}^2 for i=1,...,20. In the next step, 100 observations were added, parameters were re-estimated and forecasts were again compared with observations. In this way, parameters and forecasts were computed 23 times for each daily series. A similar procedure was applied to weekly data. The forecasts of the GARCH model and the constant-variance model are compared with respect to mean errors and root mean square errors (RMSE). The results are summarized in Tables 2 and 3. Note that the mean errors and RMSE's are averaged over all forecast horizons for i=1,...,20.

Table 2
Comparison of models by forecasting variances: mean errors

		mark	pound	franc	yen
day	GARCH $\sigma^2(t)$	0.116 -0.217	0.165 -0.184	0.464 -0.005	0.144 -0.269
week	GARCH $\sigma^2(t)$	0.077 -1.193	2.571 -1.060	0.985 -0.605	0.188 -0.765

Table 3
Comparison of models by forecasting variances: RMSE

		mark	pound	franc	yen
day	GARCH $\sigma^2(t)$	1.32 1.20	1.16 1.02	2.16 1.27	1.35 1.20
week	GARCH $\sigma^2(t)$	5.09 4.75	7.63 4.95	6.08 5.60	3.87 3.66

As regards bias of the forecasts, the results are mixed. For daily data, the GARCH model achieves in 3 cases a smaller mean error in absolute value than the constant-variance model, but for weekly data it is not clear which forecast function is better. The most remarkable result, however, is that the constant-variance forecasts are clearly better than GARCH forecasts in terms of precision. For all daily and weekly series, the constant-variance models perform better than the GARCH models according to the RMSE criterion, sometimes quite substantially so. Statistically, this result is related to the fact, that there seems to be a unit root in the variance of the data.

Implications for Option Pricing

Recently, Duan (1991) established conditions under which the GARCH model is compatible with the risk-neutral valuation principle and examined whether the GARCH model can explain some systematic price biases of the option pricing model of Black and Scholes (1973). In the spirit of Duan's approach, I have examined the effects of a GARCH specification on the pricing of foreign-currency options. The pricing formula for foreign-currency options is equivalent to the Black-Scholes formula with the foreign interest rate substituted for the constant devidend yield (see Biger and Hull (1983)). I have compared GARCH option prices with options prices from the Black-Scholes model and from the jump-diffusion process introduced by Merton (1976).

Prices of call options are obtained from the mean of $\max(S_t - B, 0)$, where S_t is the spot rate and B is the exercise price. Since closed form solutions for GARCH option prices are not available, option prices are computed by Monte-Carlo simulations with 10 000 repetitions of the sample path. In order to reduce the impact of sample variation on the comparison of option prices from different models, option prices for the Black-Scholes model and the jump-diffusion model are also computed by Monte-Carlo simulation.

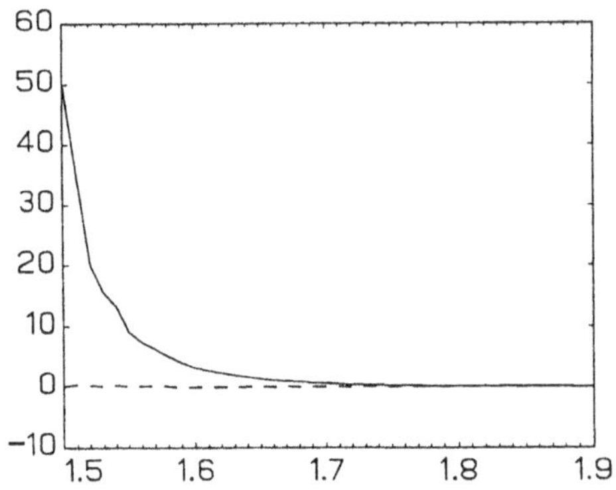

Figure 1a
Differences to Black-Scholes prices:
spot rate effect

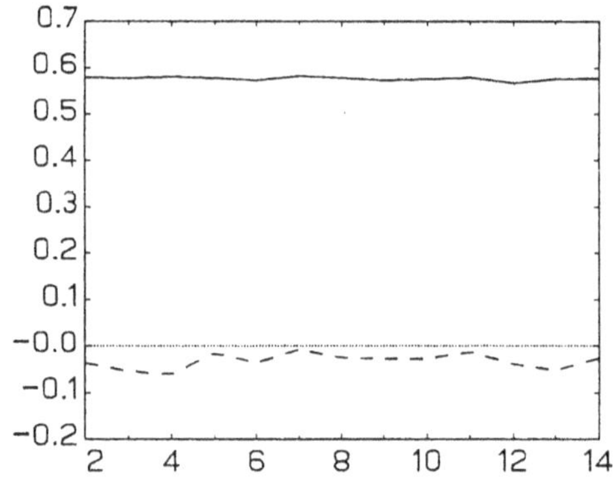

Figure 1b
Differences to Black-Scholes prices:
maturity effect

Figure 1a shows percentage differences between GARCH option prices and Black-Scholes prices as a function of the spot rate in a solid line and differences between jump-diffusion option prices and Black-Scholes prices in a dashed line. The simulations are based on estimates of the models for the weekly pound series. It is further assumed that the option expires in 10 weeks and that the exercise price is 1.70. It is apparent from Figure 1a that differences between GARCH option prices and Black-Scholes prices are very substantial for out-of-the money options. For instance, at a current spot rate of 1.50 GARCH option prices are higher than Black-Scholes prices by a factor of 50. In comparison, differences between jump-diffusion option prices and Black-Scholes prices are negligible for all values of the current spot rate.

Figure 1b displays the maturity effect on option prices for at-the-money options. Quite surprisingly, GARCH option prices are roughly 60 percent higher than Black-Scholes option prices for all maturities between 1 week and 15 weeks (solid line). Again, option prices derived from the jump-diffusion process do not differ substantially from Black-Scholes prices if maturity is varied (dashed line). Most of these differences may be attributed to sample variation.

Conclusions

GARCH models are capable of capturing the heteroskedasticity and leptokurtosis of financial time series. But this application to exchange-rate dynamics has shown that the model may still be misspecified because there is significant leptokurtosis in the residuals and the condition for second-order stationarity is often violated. Furthermore, it is surprising that the GARCH model is outperformed by a constant-variance model in the precision of forecasting volatility. On the other hand, estimates of the GARCH model imply very substantial price effects on out-of-the-money options. Those strong price effects have not been found before with alternative models of the return process or of the volatility process.

References

Biger, N. and J. Hull (1983): "The Valuation of Currency Options", *Financial Management*, **12**, 24-28.

Black, F. and M. Scholes (1973): "The Pricing of Options and Corporate Liabilities", *Journal of Political Economy*, **81**, 637-654.

Bollerslev, T. (1986): "Generalized Autoregressive Conditional Heteroskedasticity", *Journal of Econometrics*, **31**, 307-327.

Duan, J.-C. (1991): "The GARCH Option Pricing Model", McGill University, Faculty of Management, mimeo.

Merton, R.C. (1976): "Option Pricing When Underlying Stock Returns are Discontinuous", *Journal of Financial Economics*, **3**, 125-144.

Risk Management in Banks—A Stochastic Approach

Ulla-Christiane Kopp
Institut für Unternehmensforschung (OR), Hochschule St. Gallen
Bodanstraße 6, 9000 St. Gallen, Switzerland

1 Introduction

The following paper is divided into four main parts. The first part contains a brief overview of the one stage programming model already introduced in [3] and [4] and an overall description of the decision situation investigated. In part two the two stage stochastic programming model is presented and its structure is compared with that of the one stage model. Part three summarizes the results obtained with the models mentioned above. The paper concludes with remarks about the practical value of such models.

2 The one stage model

The most important business risks for banks are interest rate risk, exchange rate risk, and default risk.[1] Due to the interdependences between those risks it is essential to consider them in the same context. It is equally important to include hedging decisions in the decision process because sequential decisions on original deals (balance sheet deals) and hedges (off-balance sheet deals) lead to suboptimality.

Recently some decision models to manage the business risks have been published (e.g. [1], [2], [5]) but usually they only consider a single risk category and sometimes they do not include different kinds of off-balance sheet deals.

The main features of the one stage model described here are:

- its capability of dealing with the different risks mentioned above at the same time and
- the simultaneous decisions on balance and off-balance sheet deals.

The basic idea of the one stage model is to assume worst-case scenarios for the further development (rising/falling) of the most important market parameters considered here - interest rates, exchange rates and default probabilities. With those assumptions the possible losses (either for falling or rising parameters) in each risk category are calculated and limited to a given amount - the so called "capital to cover all risks".

The aim of the model is to find a strategy to maximize the bank's result for a given, deterministic scenario. The bank's result is calculated by subtracting costs for the supply of capital to cover all risks and transaction costs of hedges from the net interest income of the bank.

---

[1] Such operational risks as e.g. robbery, fraud, or breakdown of the computer centre are not considered here.

The shortcomings of the one stage model are:

- Expectations about the future development of market parameters (e.g. it is more likely for the interest rates to rise than to fall) cannot be considered.
- The static point of view prevents the analysis of the consequences of today's decisions in the future.

Therefore it seems to be appropriate to develop a two stage model with the same basic ideas but with the possibility to cope with the problems mentioned above.

3 The two stage model

The restriction structure of the first stage of the two stage model corresponds exactly to that of the one stage model. The restrictions are: balance sheet restrictions, interest rate risk restrictions, currency risk restrictions, default risk restrictions and the limitation of the total risk to the capital to cover all risks. (For more details see [3] and [4].)
In the second period the market parameters (interest rates and exchange rates) can attain two possible values with given probabilities. For them again worst-cases assumptions are formulated to describe their further development. Those assumptions are required for the restrictions in the second stage. Therefore we get eight possible states in the second period and for each state we have to fulfill the corresponding restrictions as in the one stage model. The decisions in the second stage depend on the state. Therefore the two stage model consists structurally of nine (8+1) one stage models.[1]
The objective function of the two stage model is different from that of the one stage model. The aim still is to maximize the bank's result, but in the two stage model it is calculated as:

the deterministic interest rate result of the first period
plus the discounted expected value of the interest rate result of the second period
minus the transaction costs of the off-balance sheet deals in the first period
minus the cost of capital to cover the risks in the first period
minus the expected value of the discounted cost of capital to cover the risks in the second period.

The expected interest rate result of the second period is obtained by summarizing all products of the interest rate result attained with a certain scenario and the probability of that scenario. The same holds for the expected cost of capital to cover all risks.
Off-balance sheet deals are not considered in the second period because of the big additional programming effort and the further enlargement of the problem.[2]

---

1 For the two stage problem that leads to the solution of a linear program with about 8000 columns and 13000 rows. The corresponding one stage problem consists of about 2500 columns and 3000 rows.

2 The neglection of off-balance sheet deals is one reason among others that the two stage model is not nine times as big as the one stage model (c.f. previous footnote).

4 Comparison of the results

Of course, the results of the two models can directly be compared for decisions in the first period only. Here the questions of main interest are:

- How do expectations about the future development of market parameters influence decisions in the first period?
- Are the results obtained with the two stage model better than those of the one stage model?

Expectations about the development of market parameters do in fact influence the decisions in the first period. In the example examined the decisions on off-balance sheet deals reacted more sensitively to changing scenarios than the decisions concerning the balance sheet deals.

In principle, results obtained with multi stage models are better than those obtained with single stage models because they take into account expectations concerning the future development of parameters. Here the results of the second period depend on the scenario, i.e. for each of the eight possible scenarios there are different optimal decisions. It seems difficult to see the practical value of that huge amount of information concerning the second period.

5 Conclusions

It is very encouraging to see that such large models can actually be solved on personal computers. Of course there arises an enormous computational effort - one run takes about 3 hours on a 386 PC.

The practical value of the two stage model is difficult to assess because of the amount of computational time required and the difficult interpretation of the results. With improved solvers and faster computers, however, its better results will be a point in favour of the more sophisticated two stage model.

6 References

[1] W. Bessler, G. G. Booth; Controlling interest rate risk in commercial banks; conference paper; Fifth Symposium on Money, Banking, and Insurance; 1990

[2] G. G. Booth, W. Bessler; Goal programming models for managing interest rate risk; OMEGA - the international Journal of Management Science; 1989

[3] U.-C. Kopp; Risk Management in Banks; to appear in: Proceedings of the 15th Symposium on Operations Research; (1992)

[4] U.-C. Kopp; Quantitatives Risikomanagement in Banken - Ein Entscheidungsmodell zum Management der Geschäftsrisiken; Dissertation Hochschule St. Gallen; 1992

[5] H. Meyer zu Selhausen; Ermittlung robuster Strategien für die Steuerung des Zinsrisikos einer Universalbank; Zeitschrift für Bankrecht und Bankwirtschaft; 1991

Testing Filter-Rule Profits in the Foreign Exchange Market

Walter Naggl
Hypo-Bank
Arabellastraße 12, 8000 München 81, Germany

The change in the exchange rate can be decomposed into four components: (1) the interest rate differential between the two currencies involved, (2) the risk premium, (3) the systematic error-of-forecast of the exchange rate, and (4) a random forecast error. The systematic components generate trends in a series. Trends due to systematic errors-of-expectations imply market inefficiency, whereas trends due to the other two systematic components of the change in the exchange rate do not.

Older investigations of filter returns evaluate filter-returns by comparison with a "buy-and-hold" strategy as proposed by Fama (1970). This comparison is based on Fama's model of non-negative returns expected by the market. In the case of data adjusted for interest-rate differentials this expected return equals the risk premium. Since the risk-premium is unobservable, filter-returns in excess of buy-and-hold are open to interpretation as being either due to a risk premium or evidence of market inefficiency. Furthermore, comparison with buy-and-hold leaves open the possibility, that excess returns are a result of chance. More recent investigations such as Sweeney (1986) explicitly test for excess filter profits. These tests are carried out under the assumption that the expected return of filter-rules equals the trend in a data series which is generated by a random walk with trend. This assumption is incorrect however, as has already been shown by Alexander (1964).

The present investigation tests for the existence of excess filter returns by generating a distribution of filter returns from randomized samples of daily Deutsche Mark-Dollar exchange rate data with a Monte Carlo simulation. This is done by cumulation of exchange rate changes which are selected randomly from the observed time series of the exchange rate, where the latter is adjusted for interest rate differentials. Adjustment insures, that filter returns are net of the interest differential influence. Constant trends in the adjusted non-differenced data are not eliminated. Filter profits are calculated from each of these randomly generated time-series. Repeating this process 1000 times results in a distribution of filter-returns under efficiency and under the assumption of a constant risk premium. It is the distribution under efficiency since preservation of the constant trend in the data allows for the influence of a constant risk premium on profits. Any other dependencies in the adjusted data which would show up in excess filter profits have been eliminated by the randomization procedure.

EMPIRICAL RESULTS

Filter rules are applied to daily data of the Deutsche Mark-Dollar exchange rate ranging from January 2nd 1980 to December 30th 1988. Expected exchange rate changes due to the interest rate differential were elimated by adjusting daily changes in the raw exchange rate series by the 62nd fraction of the difference in three-month interest rates. Profits from the application of the filter rule are calculated by applying the percentage gain or loss from each trade to the capital existing before that trade was carried out. Total profits for the whole of a data series thus reflect the relative profit or loss if the existing capital is always fully utilized. Next to total filter profits I calculate annualized profits. Transaction costs are measured by the difference between bid and ask.

The following tests of the filter rule were based on the principle of forming hypotheses before looking at the data. This means that instead of applying a wide range of possible filters and then choosing the best one, results from previous investigations were taken as a guide in choosing the filters. These have shown that filters in the range betwenn 1% and 2% gave the best results. Therefore, a 1%, 1.5%, and 2% filter were alternatively chosen in the present investigaton.

Table 1 shows filter profits made by applying the above filter rules in the case of a rising Dollar. This rule is applied when speculators calculating in Deutsche Mark try to increase their portfolio value by temporarily holding Dollars. When the filter rule indicates a rising Dollar, Deutsche Mark are exchanged for Dollars until the filter rule gives a sell signal. After that the speculator holds Deutsche Mark again until there is another buy signal.

TABLE 1: PROFITS FROM FILTER RULES, APPLYING THE RULES TO A RISING DOLLAR

FILTER RATE	1%	1.5%	2%
FILTER PROFIT			
1 TOTAL	60.2	103.8	88.3
2 AFTER TRANSACTIONS COSTS	28.6	79.4	71.2
3 2, ANNUALIZED	5.4	12.9	11.6
NUMBER OF CYCLES	151	89	66
FILTER IN USE, DAYS	1199	1209	1234

For comparison: The profit from buying and holding Dollars for the period investigated was 47.8% due to a rise of the adjusted exchange rate data from DM 1.715 to DM 2.535.

Every filter rate investigated results in a profit in excess of buy-and-hold. This implies that filter rules can successfully forecast short-run swings in the Dollar, at least on average.

Filter rule profits were tested for significance by Monte Carlo simulation methods as described above. Tests were carried out both for the case where the filter rule is applied in speculation against a rising Dollar as well as in speculation against a falling Dollar. Results are given in Table 2:

TABLE 2: FILTER PROFITS, 95% PERCENTILE AND MEDIAN OF SIMULATED DISTRIBUTIONS OF FILTER PROFITS

SPECULATION AGAINST A RISING DOLLAR

FILTER RATE	1%	1.5%	2%
FILTER PROFIT	28.6	79.4	71.2
95% PERCENTILE	57.5	69.8	80.4
MEDIAN	-10.5	2.0	8.2

SPECULATION AGAINST A FALLING DOLLAR

FILTER RATE	1%	1.5%	2%
FILTER PROFIT	-10.7	23.6	17.7
95% PERCENTILE	-14.6	-2.1	5.3
MEDIAN	-40.9	-32.9	-28.3

Note: the filter profits for the case of a rising Dollar and the 1% and 2% rule which are insignificant at the 5% level correspond to p-values of 0.15 and 0.07.

The null hypothesis that there are no dependencies in the data which lead to extraordinary filter profits can be rejected in four out of six cases. Even when rejection is not possible we at least get low p-values. The above tests have been constructed such that rejection implies market inefficiency if we are willing to make the assumption of a constant risk premium.

REFERENCES

Alexander S (1964) Price Movements in Speculative Markets: Trends or Random Walks, No. 2. Industrial Management Review 5: 25-46.

Fama, E F (1970) Efficient Capital Markets: A Review of Theory and Empirical Work. The Journal of Finance 25: 383-420.

Sweeney R J (1986) Beating the Foreign Exchange Market. The Journal of Finance 41: 163-82.

Bank Branch Computerisation: A Feasible Approach

Sharad M. Padwal
National Institute of Bank Management
NIBM Post Office/Pune 411048, Kondhwe Khurd, India

In Indian banking 30 top business centres in the country account for about 51 per cent of the total banking business. About 2500 branches out of total approximately 70000 bank branches are estimated to have a work load of 750 vouchers or more per day. These branches are situated in 30 top business centres referred above. It is proposed by the management of the banks to computerise all these branches over the next about five years. Computerisation at the branch level can be through one of the following alternatives:

- Selected branches can be linked to mini/super mini computers with the required number of on-line terminals.
- Branches may have PCs under LAN with the mini computer as the server.
- On-line terminals hooked on to one central system for that bank.

The paper uses the data simulated on the basis of observations, and data collected from 30 branches of four Indian banks. For estimation of the hardware requirement, the following features were considered:

- Disk space
- Number of terminals
- Printers
- Tape drives
- Floppy drives
- Main memory
- CPU
- TPS rating
- Other add-ons

For estimation of application software features such as: portability, modality, parameterisation, integration, common user interface, distribution of work load at service counters, context and field level help features, audit controls, fall back and recovery provisions, data transferability, network interfacing, access level controls alongwith security and control features were considered. These estimations were done for all three alternatives listed above.

Bank managements have to take decisions regarding branch computerisation under various constraints with a view to maximise the benefits of computerisation in the long run. A given set of branches can be categorised as follows:

- Commercial
- Industrial
- Residential
- Mixed pattern

A given branch can be computerised in one of the following ways, using:

- Advance ledger posting machines
- Local area network
- Mini computers
- Total branch computerisation approach

Thus, one can form a matrix of cost benefit for a given category of branches with a given approach.

A two-way table can now be developed using linear programming framework. The components of the table would include a number of branches of each category which should be computerised under each alternative. A linear programming formulation of the problem can thus be stated as below:

Objective function:

Maximise total effectiveness of computerisation.

Subject to:

1. Budgetary constraint, and
2. Minimum number of branches to be computerised under each category of branches.

Instalment Credits in a Model of Vertically Differentiated Consumer Durables

Udo Schmidt-Mohr
Theoretische Volkswirtschaftslehre, Universität des Saarlandes
Gebäude 31, Im Stadtwald, 6600 Saarbrücken, Germany

In markets for consumer durables, suppliers often provide 'pay as you use' services to their customers. These services include credit and leasing offers. At the same time, consumer credits are also offered independently by banks with no links to suppliers of durables.

This paper argues that price–competing suppliers of consumer durables have an incentive to offer credits (henceforth: instalment credit) to their customers even if a perfectly competitive market for consumer credits exists. Furthermore, the model presented predicts that consumer credits offered by suppliers of durables and competitive banks do co–exist in equilibrium not merely by chance. Rather, co–existence is implied by profit maximizing behavior on the part of suppliers in the product market and banks. Finally, the impact of credits offered by durable good oligopolists upon prices, profits and market shares in the product market is analyzed.

Products offered in the market for consumer durables are assumed to be vertically differentiated. In additon, using the type of model developed by SHAKED & SUTTON [1982]/[1983], willingness to pay for quality improvements is assumed to increase monotonically with lifetime wealth of consumers. Considering borrowing and lending in a framework with agents of a life of two periods, the terms of consumer credit contracts have an impact on consumers' willingness to pay for an improved quality of a durable, because net disposable lifetime wealth is affected by those terms. Therefore, suppliers of durables can influence consumers' incremental willingness to pay for their product by offering credits to customers.

Since suppliers of durables compete with banks in the credit market, they must offer more favorable credit terms than banks to increase their customers' willingness to pay. Given the assumption of competition among banks, this can only be accomplished by incurring losses on credits, which must be recouped by an increase in sales price to render this operation profitable. It is shown that profitable price discrimination via tying sales of consumer durables and consumer credits is possible. Two mechanisms are presented.

First, if preferences over credits vary across consumers (due to a positive correlation between current and expected future wealth, for example), self-selection of customers by their choice of credit can be induced. In this case, tying sales and credits is profitable for the following reason. By choosing credit terms such that only some subset of customers (those with low willingness to pay for one's product) prefer a supplier's credit offer to a bank credit, the supplier can limit losses on credits but nevertheless increase price without reducing demand.

Second, if current wealth of consumers is low compared to prices of durables, liquidity constraints faced by consumers come into play in the sense that borrowing a sufficient amount of future wealth becomes a necessary condition for purchase of a durable. In this situation, credit terms can be chosen by a supplier such that liquidity constraints faced by some subset of his customers become binding if they choose the credit offered by him. Those customers have to borrow from banks although they would prefer the credit offered by a supplier. Sorting customers by the liquidity constraint mechanism renders the tying of sales and credits profitable even if preferences over credits of all consumers are the same.

Summarizing, if a) different consumers prefer different credits and/or b) liquidity constraints must be considered, the supply of instalment credits will be observed in equilibrium. Whatever combination of a)/b) is assumed to hold, however, in equilibrium bank credits are never fully crowded out by instalment credits.

Comparing equilibrium prices, profits and market shares in a duopolistic product market to the benchmark case, where by assumption only banks offer consumer credits, the following is shown: If a) is assumed to hold but not b), then price competition among firms becomes more intense if supply of instalment credits is introduced. As a consequence, prices, profits and market share of the low quality supplier decline. Furthermore, it can happen that this supplier is pushed out of the market.

By contrast, if b) holds but not a), then price competition is less intense than in the benchmark case. Therefore, equilibrium prices and profits of both firms increase. Furthermore, the low quality supplier commands a higher market share than in the benchmark case.

Unfortunately, explicit solutions could not be derived if a) and b) are assumed to hold. With regard to the market share of the low quality supplier, however, it is argued that it is likely to decrease, at least if the low quality supplier covers a small portion of the overall market in the benchmark case.

REFERENCES

GALE, D. & HELLWIG, M.[1985], "Incentive-Compatible Debt Contracts: The One-Period Problem," *Review of Economic Studies*, 52, 647 - 663.

SCHMIDT–MOHR, U. [1992], *Informationsökonomische Theorien der Bankunternehmung und des Bankverhaltens*, Ph.D. dissertation, Universität des Saarlandes.

SHAKED, A. & SUTTON, J. [1982], "Relaxing Price Competition Through Product Differentiation," *The Review of Economic Studies*, 49(1), 3 - 13.

SHAKED, A. & SUTTON, J. [1983], "Natural Oligopolies," *Econometrica*, 51(5), 1469 - 1483.

SHAKED, A. & SUTTON, J. [1987], "Product Differentiation and Industrial Structure," *The Journal of Industrial Economics*, 36(2), 131 - 146.

The Pricing of Insurance Contracts by Financial Models and Rationality

Winfried Schott
Seminar für Bank- u. Versicherungsbetriebslehre, Universität Hamburg
Von-Melle-Park 5, 2000 Hamburg 13, Germany

Introduction

Actuarial risk can be appropriately described as the probability distribution of the costs for the potential claims, and it is a fundamental problem of actuarial science to evaluate a suitable risk premium when the risk shall be insured. As a first way to get a solution for this problem, there is a large number of real-valued functions of the set of probability distributions, the so-called **premium principles**. But there are two reasons why this way cannot be regarded as a solution for the problem of pricing insurance contracts:

The first reason is that none of the premium principles can simultaneously fulfil some desirable properties, and many investigations have been made to answer the question which properties are fulfilled by which premium principles (see Heilmann 1988). So there is still the problem to decide which premium principle should be reasonably used. The second reason, which is more important, is that premium principles neglect market effects so that they might not have any empirical relevance.

Market assumptions are constitutionally integrated in **financial models** which have been developed to get fair market rates of return from risky investments. As the underwriting business is a risky investment financial models have been adapted to price insurance contracts. This is therefore a second way to get a solution for the problem of finding an appropriate risk premium. We investigate how financial models are suitable for pricing insurance contracts, and a central topic will be the question whether these models lead to rational decisions which means whether they are generally compatible with the expected utility maximization criterion.

Aspects of the evaluation of actuarial risk using financial models

The most frequently used financial models are the **Capital Asset Pricing Model** (CAPM), the **Option Pricing Model** (OPM) and the **Arbitrage Pricing Model** (APM) which only use special parameters of the probability distribution for risk ordering. The OPM and the standard CAPM only use the expectation value μ and the standard deviation σ. This does not seem to be very sensible for pricing actuarial risks, for their monetary results are negatively skewed while normal financial risks are positively skewed and a preference for positive skewness can be assumed. Though skewness can be integrated in the CAPM (see Kraus/Litzenberger 1976) the evaluation of risk on the basis of probability moments does in general not lead to reasonable decisions. The consideration of a finite number of moments corresponds with unvalid polynomial utility functions. And if even a whole market with a finite number of participants with more valid non-polynomial utility functions (for example exponential or logarithmic utility functions) is considered paradoxa can be constructed that every rational decision maker is minimizing μ, maximizing σ, minimizing the skewness etc. (see Brockett/Kahane 1992). Even a decision which is based on ***all*** moments of a probability distribution may be unrational. The log-normal distribution and a log-normal distribution which is modified by a sinus function are an example of two different distributions with the same moments - and therefore the same central moments -, but these two distributions can have different expected utilities.

Remembering that in the APM there is a finite number of risk parameters which are not specified it is investigated whether insurance contracts can appropriately be priced by financial models if other risk parameters than moments are taken into account. The answer can be given with the help of a theorem of Schneeweiß (see Schneeweiß 1966): A rational decision criterion depending on a finite number of risk parameters must be the maximization of a linear combination of parameters which are expected values of the images of the random variables, evaluated by arbitrary real functions. As there are no further properties for the probability parameters only the investigation of the rationality of decisions which are based on parameters with empirical relevance is a sensible research. The only family of relevant parameters besides the probability moments are parameters of the probability distribution which depend on the realization of a minimal result, like ruin probabilities or expected losses. But modifying the already presented example it can be shown that probability distributions completely have the same risk parameters, but different expected utility values.

Another fundamental assumption of financial models is that the market is arbitrage free. This assumption also has undesirable consequences for insurance business as there is no natural place for insurance companies in such a model and different risk aversion and collective risk compensation cannot be sufficiently modelled. As an arbitrage free market is only compatible with restrictive stochastic assumptions (see Brockett/Witt 1991) which in general are not realistic for actuarial risks, and by further arguments, it is our opinion that a realistic market model for pricing insurance contracts should be better based on a non-efficient capital market, using the rationality axioms of the Bernoulli Principle.

References

Albrecht,P.: Kapitalmarkttheoretische Fundierung der Versicherung?; in: Zeitschrift für die gesamte Versicherungswissenschaft 80/3-4 (1991), p.499-530.

Brockett,P.L./Kahane,Y.: Risk, Return, Skewness and Preference; in: Management Science 38/6 (1992), p.851-866.

Brockett,P.L./Witt,R.C.: Relevant Distributions for Insurance Prices in an Arbitrage Free Equilibrium; in: The Journal of Risk and Insurance 58/1 (1991), p.13-29.

Cummins,J.D.: Asset Pricing Models and Insurance Ratemaking; in: The Astin Bulletin 20/2 (1990), p.125-166.

Feller,W.: An Introduction to Probability Theory and Its Applications, volume II; Wiley & Sons, New York/London/Sydney 1971.

Gänssler,P./Stute,W.: Wahrscheinlichkeitstheorie; Springer-Verlag, Berlin/Heidelberg/New York 1977.

Heilmann,W.-R.: Fundamentals of Risk Theory; Verlag Versicherungswirtschaft, Karlsruhe 1988.

Ingersoll, J.E.: Theory of Financial Decision Making; Rowman & Littlefield, Totowa (New Jersey) 1987.

Kraus,A./Litzenberger,R.H.: Skewness Preference and the Valuation of Risk Assets; in: The Journal of Finance 31/4 (1976), p.1085-1100.

Schneeweiß,H.: Entscheidungskriterien bei Risiko; Springer-Verlag, Berlin/Heidelberg/New York 1966.

Financial Engineering—A Knowledge Based Buy/Lease Decision Support System

Christof Weinhardt
Fachbereich Wirtschaftswissenschaften, Universität Gießen
Licher Straße 60, 6300 Gießen, Germany

I Introduction

The expanding leasing market - for movables as well as for real estates - , the continuously changing legal and fiscal regulations concerning leasing contracts and the growing awareness of the customers regarding their financial problems emphasize the need for a decision support system to find the optimum financial product for individual problems in this domain. By using default data for the lessor's side, many of the already existing systems take only the lessee's point of view into account. Theoretical work in the field of finance showed, however, that for example cooperation of both contract parties can lead to more profitable solutions for lessors **and** lessees.

Hence, any independent financial consultant faces the task to simultaneously consider, measure and evaluate the complex fiscal implications arising from a wide variety of alternative leasing contracts not only from the lessee's but also from the lessor's and the coalition's point of view. Therefore, he has to consider the different economic environments of both contract parties. How to integrate data and its implications which affect the decision of lessor and lessee, is the main subject in this paper.

II The System Requirements

In cooperation with IBM Germany a buy/lease decision support system, called **F**inancial **E**ngineering **S**ystem (FES)[1], is being developed at the University of Giessen. FES should work without any restriction to certain types of leasing contracts but with regard to the theoretical results concerning the current german taxation system and the individual decision criteria of the contract parties. Within a consultation, this should allow FES to acquire a set of innovative financial *recommendations* and offer it to the user. He should

[1]This work is funded in part by IBM Germany and in part by Deutsche Forschungsgemeinschaft within the ALLFIWIB project under the program "Distributed Information Systems in Business Administration", a joint venture of the universities of Gießen and Marburg.

then be able to select the preferred offers and to pass them to a *financial analysis* through FES to get finally hard facts for his decision making.

III The concept

There is a wide variety of leasing contracts treated in a number of decrees of the German Treasury (more than 300 different contract pattern). German law, however, allows free designing of any contract, including leasing contracts (even if they do not fit the pattern mentioned previously). It is the task of the Treasury to decide upon fiscal implications in individual cases, especially upon the right to include the leasing object to the set of depreciable assets of the lesser or lessee. This decision, the integration of the views of the contract parties, the design of the payment stream and many other details affect the search for the "optimum" alternative out of the large set of contract pattern in a given consultation.

Due to the complexity of the problem and of the acquisition of the relevant data (for a comprehensive approach) a knowledge based approach seems appropriate for generating first (still incomplete) recommendations, say contract pattern. Those recommendations preferred and selected by the contract parties subsequently can be evaluated by a financial analysis tool (which is already conventionally realized). For FES we developed the concept illustrated in figure 1.

Even for a KBS it would be too complex to generate the huge set of concievable contracts and then *selecting* the "best" feasible alternative. Another approach is propsed: the *configuration* of contracts, which adequately reflects the objectives of both contract parties. Figure 2 shows the basic configuration idea.

A contract is characterized through a combination of the data (e.g. name, address) of the contract parties and a number of components defining a specific contract pattern (e.g. type of leasing rates, period of lease). Each component can be represented through different instances. It is the first goal of the FES inference process to "fire" scores to this different instances according to the decision criteria of the contract parties inquired through the dialog module of the system along the inference process.

The scores calculated according to the inputs of the dialog must be aggregated first to the specific scorings of the instances (called horizontal aggregation, realized by an extended uncertainty approach, see [2]). They then represent the base for the total scoring: The

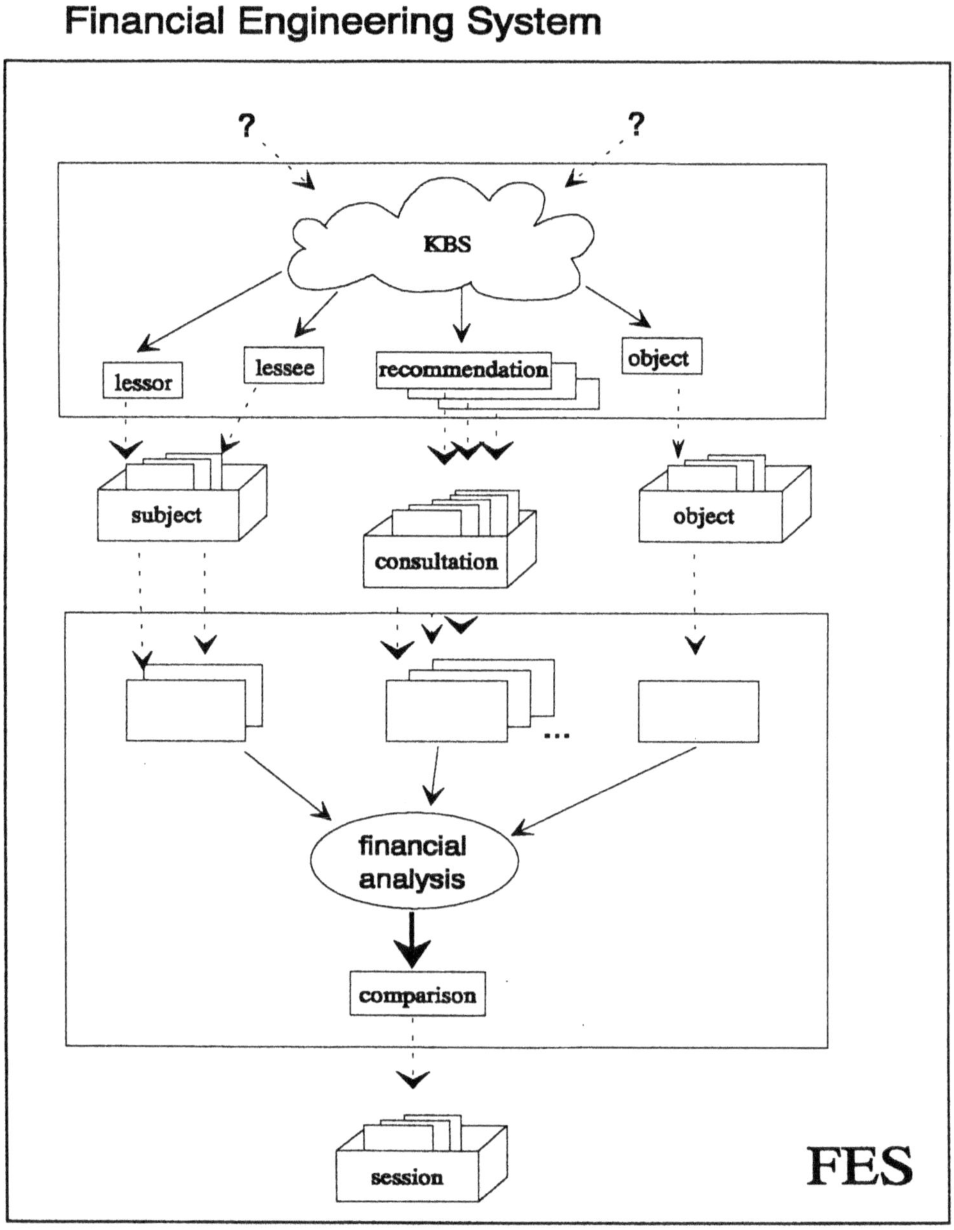

Figure 1: FES concept

vertical aggregation of these specific scoring values yields the total scoring and ranking of the contracts recommended by FES. Out of the set of recommended contracts the user can pass his preferred alternatives to the financial analysis, which is based on the net present value of the after tax cash flows of the project, in order to obtain a palpable criterion for his decision.

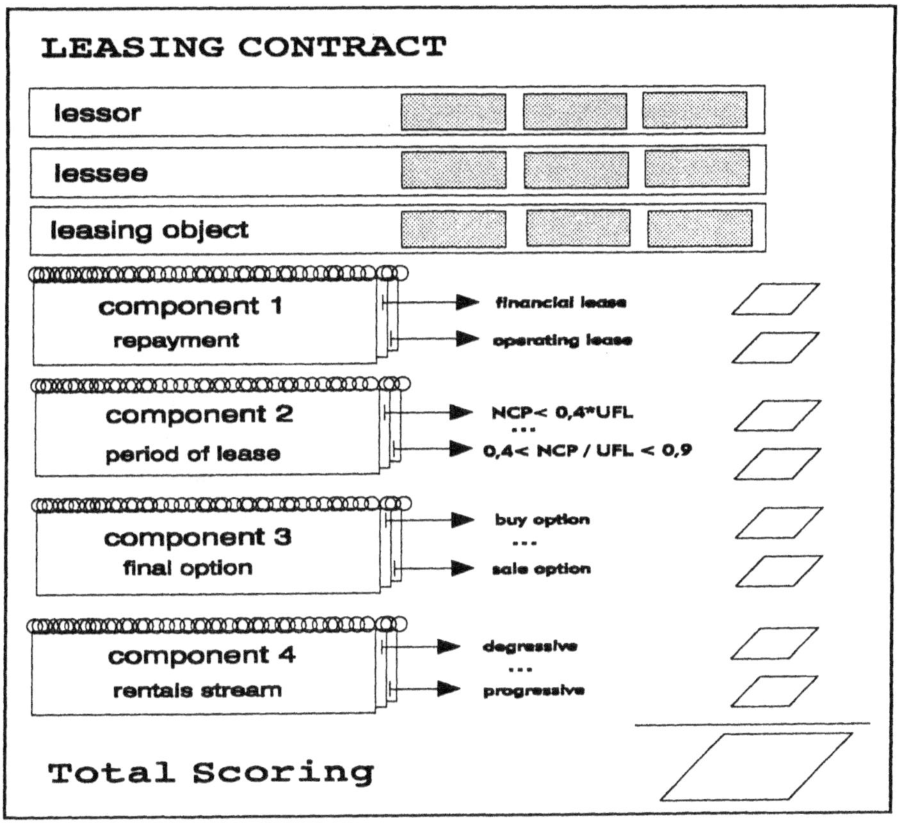

Figure 2: Configuration of Buy/Leasing Contracts

IV Outlook

Since different methods are applied in the two main modules of FES, namley the knowledge based configuration (using heuristics) in the first and the (conventionally and exactly implemented) financial analysis in the second part, the resulting rankings of these two modules are not necessarily identical. Hence, it is a very interesting question, whether it is possible to adjust these results by a learning process of the knowledge based tool. This will be a topic of further research.

References:

[1] Buhl, H.U. and C. Weinhardt[1992]: Financial Engineering System FES - Ein wissensbasierter Ansatz .zur Finanzierungsberatung, in Heilmann, W.R. et al. (eds.): Geld, Banken und Versicherungen, 1990/II, Verlag für Versicherungswirtschaft, Karlsruhe 1992

[2] Buhl, H.U. and C. Weinhardt[1992]: EAG: Ein Verfahren zur Gewißheitsverarbeitung in Wissensbasierten Systemen, in Informationstechnik ít:, 5,1992

The Distribution for Continuous Multiple Life Functions

Martine Van Wouwe, Sabine Lorimier
Department of Mathematics & Computer Science, University of Antwerp, UIA
Prinsstraat 13, 2000 Antwerpen, Belgium

Introduction.

Only recently the actuarial literature on life contingencies introduced the use of probability theory. In particular, Bowers, Gerber, Wolthuis and others have shown that probability theory in life insurances is of extended importance in the construction of measures for the actual risk of the insurer. In an article Wolthuis proved that the pure premium for the endowment insurance on one life can be less than the sum of the pure premiums of the composing elements, by considering a risk measure through probability theory.

These tools were brought together by De Pril [2] in a general and systematic treatment of the distributions of actuarial functions on one life.

Our aim is to extend the stochastic to actuarial functions in the two-life case, leaving the further generalization to the multiple life case as a trivial one. Only continuous actuarial functions will be considered. Also for several lifes the notion of risk measure is important and could be relevant for the pure premium for some important stochastics. Therefore an explicit expression for the probability density function of the endowment on several lifes, the whole life on several lifes , the annuities and the reversionary annuities will be presented.

2. Continuous description of multiple life contingencies

Let T_x and T_y be two continuous nonnegative random variables, respectively representing the future lifetime of a life-aged-x and a life-aged-y. In reality the individuals covered by a joint-life insurance have some association, implying that T_x and T_y are not independent. However, the dependence of these random variables is difficult to quantify. Consequently we will assume that T_x and T_y are independent random variables.

Furthermore, we consider the continuous nonnegative random variables T_{xy} and $T_{\overline{xy}}$, which are given by :

$$T_{xy} = \min(T_x, T_y)$$
$$T_{\overline{xy}} = \max(T_x, T_y)$$

The present value at policy issue of all the benefits to be paid by the insurer over the maximum random future lifetime $T_{\overline{xy}}$ of the two insured, is called the benefit function. The benefit function of a continuous life insurance on two lifes ages x and y at policy issue, can be presented by an appropriate function S of T_x, T_y, T_{xy} and/or $T_{\overline{xy}}$. The distribution function F_S and the probability density function f_S of this function S can be found from the distribution of the random variable (T_x, T_y). These characteristics are summarized in the *Tables 1 to 7* for a few continuous actuarial functions. All formulae are developed for a benefit equal to a unit amount and the following notations are used :

i : constant annual rate of interest, $i > 0$;

$\delta = ln(1+i)$: force of interest

$\overline{a}_{n\rceil} = (1-e^{-\delta n})/\delta$: present value of a continuous n-year temporary annuity-certain

The results for life insurances payable at the moment of death can be found in *Tables 1 to 3*. The formulae in Table 1 are normal extensions of the results of a life insurance on a single life, summarized by De Pril [2].

Table 4 contains endowment insurances, with death benefits payable at the moment of death. These results also match with those of a single-life endowment insurance.

Tables 5 and 6 summarize the formulae for continuous life annuities. The results obtained in Table 5 are again normal extensions of the single-life annuities.

The last table contains reversionary annuities, which are payable during the existence of a first status, but only after the failure of a second status.

References.

[1] Bowers, N. L., Gerber, H. U., Hickman, J. C., Jones, D. A., Nesbitt, C. J., (1986), *Actuarial Mathematics*. The Society of Actuaries, Itasca, Illinois.

[2] De Pril, N. (1989), *The Distribution of Actuarial Functions*, Mitteilungen der Schweizerische Vereinigung der Versicherungsmathematiker, p. 173-183.

[3] Wolthuis, H., Van Hoek, I., (1986), *Stochastic Models for Life Contingencies*. Insurance : Mathematics and Economics 5, p. 217-254.

	S		$F_S(s)$		$f_S(s)$	
$\mathbf{A}_{xyn\rceil}$	$e^{-\delta T_{xy}}$	$0 \leq T_{xy} < n$	${}_np_{xy}$	$0 \leq s \leq e^{-\delta n}$	${}_np_{xy}$	$s = 0$
	0	$T_{xy} \geq n$	${}_\tau p_{xy}$	$e^{-\delta n} < s < 1$	${}_\tau p_{xy}\mu_{x+\tau,y+\tau}/\delta s$	$e^{-\delta n} < s \leq 1$
			1	$s \geq 1$	0	elsewhere
$\mathbf{A}_{\overline{xy}n\rceil}$	$e^{-\delta T_{\overline{xy}}}$	$T_x, T_y \geq 0, T_{\overline{xy}} < n$	${}_np_{\overline{xy}}$	$0 \leq s \leq e^{-\delta n}$	${}_np_{\overline{xy}}$	$s = 0$
	0	$T_{\overline{xy}} \geq n$	${}_\tau p_{\overline{xy}}$	$e^{-\delta n} < s < 1$	$\dfrac{{}_\tau p_x(1 -{}_\tau p_y)\mu_{x+\tau} +{}_\tau p_y(1 -{}_\tau p_x)\mu_{y+\tau}}{\delta_s}$	$e^{-\delta n} < s \leq 1$
			1	$s \geq 1$	0	elsewhere
$\mathbf{A}_{\overset{1}{xy}}$	$e^{-\delta T_x}$	$0 \leq T_x < T_y$	$\int_0^\infty {}_tp_{xy}\mu_{y+t}dt$	$s = 0$	$\int_0^\infty {}_tp_{xy}\mu_{y+t}dt$	$s = 0$
	0	$T_x \geq T_y \geq 0$	$1 -{}_\tau q_{\overset{1}{xy}}$	$0 < s < 1$	${}_\tau p_{xy}\mu_{x+\tau}/\delta s$	$0 < s \leq 1$
			1	$s \geq 1$	0	elsewhere
$\mathbf{A}_{\overset{2}{xy}}$	$e^{-\delta T_y}$	$0 \leq T_x < T_y$	$\int_0^\infty {}_tp_{xy}\mu_{y+t}dt$	$s = 0$	$\int_0^\infty {}_tp_{xy}\mu_{y+t}dt$	$s = 0$
	0	$T_x \geq T_y \geq 0$	$1 -{}_\tau q_{\overset{2}{xy}}$	$0 < s < 1$	$(1 -{}_\tau p_x){}_\tau p_y\mu_{y+\tau}/\delta s$	$0 < s < 1$
			1	$s \geq 1$	0	elsewhere
$\mathbf{a}_{xyn\rceil}$	$\overline{a}_{T_{xy}\rceil}$	$0 \leq T_{xy} < n$	$1 -{}_\alpha p_{\overline{xy}}$	$0 < s < \overline{a}_{n\rceil}$	$\dfrac{{}_\alpha p_x(1 -{}_\alpha p_y)\mu_{x+\alpha} +{}_\alpha p_y(1 -{}_\alpha p_x)\mu_{y+\alpha}}{1 - \delta_s}$	$0 \leq s < \overline{a}_{n\rceil}$
	$\overline{a}_{n\rceil}$	$T_{xy} \geq n$	1	$s \geq \overline{a}_{n\rceil}$	${}_np_{\overline{xy}}$	$s = \overline{a}_{n\rceil}$
					0	elsewhere
$\mathbf{a}_{\overline{xy}n\rceil}$	$\overline{a}_{T_{\overline{xy}}\rceil}$	$T_x, T_y \geq 0, T_{\overline{xy}} < n$	$1 -{}_\alpha p_{xy}$	$0 < s < \overline{a}_{n\rceil}$	${}_\alpha p_{xy}\mu_{x+\alpha,y+\alpha}/(1 - \delta s)$	$0 \leq s < \overline{a}_{n\rceil}$
	$\overline{a}_{n\rceil}$	$T_{\overline{xy}} \geq n$	1	$s \geq \overline{a}_{n\rceil}$	${}_np_{xy}$	$s = \overline{a}_{n\rceil}$
					0	elsewhere

Table : Life Insurance

$\tau = \tau(s) = \frac{1}{\delta}\ln s \qquad \alpha = \alpha(s) = -\frac{1}{\delta}\ln(1 - \delta s) \qquad \beta = \beta(s) = -\frac{1}{\delta}\ln(e^{-\delta m} - \delta s)$

Author Index

Altmann, A. 165
Ammar, E. 505
Androutsopoulos, D. 245
Arakelian, T.A. 168
Artenjak, J. 303
Avenhaus, R. 3
Bac, F.Q. 132
Baier, D. 295
Barbatu, G. 306
Barle, J. 171
Bastic, M. 310
Baszczyńska, A. 333, 336
Behnke, H. 399
Belling-Seib, K. 249
Bilski, T. 99
Błażewicz, J. 102
Bockmayr, A. 252
Bodlaender, H.L. 105
Böhm, W. 63
Bogataj, L 217
Borm, P. 416
Bradtke, T. 402
Brandt, A. 67
Brauer, U. 109
Brauer, W. 109
Brimkov, V.E. 112
Brinkmann, K. 114
Buhl, H.U. 537
Cao, B. 118
Cegielski, A. 173
Čepar, D. 339, 343, 346, 375
Chappell, D. 453
Chateauneuf, A. 509
Cheung, M. 455, 541
Chichernea, V. 255
Čibej, J.A. 458
Conrad, K. 6
Domański, C. 333, 336
Damij, T. 259
Dempe, S. 177
Derks, J. 406, 432
Drexl, A. 313
Driessen, T.S.H. 410
Embrechts, P. 544
Farkas, Z.M. 55
Farmer, K. 460
Feltkamp, V. 413
Ferreira, U.R. 121
Fischer, A. 179
Flak, T. 349
Flåm, S.D. 220
Florkiewicz, B. 182
Folmer, H. 10
Gadjiev, A. 86
Gaul, W. 295
Geiselhart, W. 223
Gerhards, T. 464
Gernert, D. 262
Gilboa, I. 512
Gladys, S. 316
Gözlü, S. 320
Grad, J. 171
Grauer, M. 39
Groscurth, H.-M. 42
Grundt, A. 70
Günther, O. 13
Gwinner, J. 185, 469
Habinc, R. 339
Härdle, W. 352
Hantelmann, F. 265
Hamacher, H.W. 124
Hamers, H. 416
Hardy, M. 547
Hartl, R.F. 226
Hebbel, H. 17
Henkouche, M. 370
Hillmer, M. 472
Holz, H. 516
Hu, T.C. 128
Hürlimann, W. 550
Hurkens, S. 419
Ionescu, V. 306
Izhutkin, V.S. 188
Jafar-Shaghaghi, F. 270
Jakubowski, A. 422
Jammernegg, W. 520
Jansen, K. 105
Jansson, C. 190
Jasinski, S. 322
Joas, G. 193
Jongen, H.T. 196
Juhnke, F. 197

Junginger, W. 326
Junius, T. 425
Kähler, J. 553
Kamps, U. 74
Kao, C. 523
Karkazis, J. 20
Kassay, G. 201
Kindorf, J. 45
Kischka, P. 520
Knobloch, H.W. 230
Knüppel, O. 190
König, H.-J. 537
Köpp, G. 477
de Koning, W.L. 237
Kopp, U.-C. 558
Kor, A. 326
Küfer, K. 203
Kugler, P. 481
Kulej, M. 182
Lai, A. 541
Lain, J.L. 63
Lamberts, J. 13
Lang, R. 130
Lempio, F. 235
Ligeza, A. 274
Loan, D.T. 132
Lorimier, S. 576
Lucca, H. 78
Magiera, R. 372
Malarski, M. 316, 322
Marius, C.E. 306
Marolt, M. 346
Matulka, J. 278
Mayer-Föll, R. 23
Meilijson, I. 526
Milius, T. 130
Mohanty, S.G. 63
Molana, H. 484
Mosler, K. 516
Motnikar, B. 375
v. Mouche, P. 10
Mucha, H.-J. 27
Müller, W. 281
Naggl, W. 561
Neumayer, P. 135
Nevels, K. 425
van den Nouweland, A. 413
Novak, E. 207
Nowak, A.S. 428
Oder, C. 32
Ossimitz, G. 488
Padwal, S.M. 564
Peremans, W. 528
Peters, H. 406, 528
Pethig, R. 36
Petropavlovskii, M.V. 188
Plachky, D. 379
Pölz, W. 384
Porosiński, Z. 387
Radalj, Z. 346
Reijnierse, H. 432
Rentz, O. 32
Reszat, B. 491
Reuter, A. 42
Ribarič, M. 346, 375
Rinderle, K. 118
Różański, R. 82
Ruhe, G. 124
Sandmann, K. 391
Satzger, G. 285
Schaible, S. 58
Schiermeyer, I. 138
Schmeidler, D. 512
Schmid, W. 349
Schmidbauer, H. 86
Schmidt-Mohr, U. 566
Schott, W. 569
Schreiber, D. 39
Schweiker, A. 42
Schwendener, P. 481
Seredynski, F. 139
Skorupski, J. 316, 322
Skulimowski, A.M.J. 211
Snyder, C.A. 289
Sondermann, D. 391
Spera, C. 142
Spirakis, P. 245
Stalder, P. 494
Stehling, F. 45
v.d. Stel, H. 528
von Stengel, B. 145
Stoer, M. 149
Storcken, T. 528
Stumpe, D. 436
Szajowski, K. 82, 237
Tijs, S. 416
Tüshaus, U. 223, 292
Turlach, B.A. 352

Uebe, G. 439
Ugolini, M. 142
Uhlig, H. 499
Uhlig, S. 394
Uršič, E. 339, 343
Vilks, A. 443
Walkowiak, R. 102
Wartenberg, F. 295
Weber, K. 532
van Wee, G.J.M. 152
Weinhardt, C. 572
Weishaupt, J. 90
Wentges, P. 155
Wiese, H. 446
Will, A. 537
Wirth, A. 285
Wolffram, J. 159
van Wouwe, M. 576
Wysotzki, F. 281
Yeung, D. 455, 541
Yanagawa, N. 499
Yushkevich, A.A. 94
Zadnik Stirn, L. 49
Založnik, R. 339
Žunko, P. 375
Zhang, W.-B. 242